CHARLES THE SECOND

Charles the Second
King of England, Scotland, and Ireland

RONALD HUTTON

CLARENDON PRESS   OXFORD
1989

Oxford University Press, Walton Street, Oxford OX2 6DP

Oxford New York Toronto
Delhi Bombay Calcutta Madras Karachi
Petaling Jaya Singapore Hong Kong Tokyo
Nairobi Dar es Salaam Cape Town
Melbourne Auckland

and associated companies in
Berlin Ibadan

Oxford is a trade mark of Oxford University Press

Published in the United States
by Oxford University Press, New York

© *Ronald Hutton 1989*

British Library Cataloguing in Publication Data
Hutton, Ronald
Charles the Second: King of England, Scotland and
Ireland.
1. England. Charles II, King of England
I. Title
942.06 ́6 ́0924
ISBN 0-19-822911-9

Library of Congress Cataloging in Publication Data
Hutton, Ronald.
Charles the Second, King of England, Scotland, and Ireland /
Ronald Hutton.
p.   cm.
Bibliography: p.
Includes index.
1. Charles II, King of England, 1630–1685.   2. Great Britain—
Kings and rulers—Biography.   3. Great Britain—History—Charles
II. 1660–1685.   I. Title.   II. Title: Charles II, king of England,
Scotland, and Ireland.
DA446.H93 1989   941.06 ́6 ́092—dc20   [B]   89-34059 CIP
ISBN 0-19-822911-9

FOR

NATALIE GREENLY

a descendant of Charles by Lucy Walter

and

PETER GREENHOUSE

who reproduces all of this king's virtues
with none of his vices

Preface

I DECIDED to write this book because, in the course of working upon its predecessor, I became intrigued by the personality of Charles II. I found him a more complex and less appealing character than I had expected from his reputation. In the euphoria of completing *The Restoration*, I believed that I had the energy to take such an important figure, with a relatively long and crowded public life, as the subject of my first foray into the art of biography. Friends cast doubt upon the wisdom of devoting a significant chunk of my own life to a person with whom I was not in love. Now that five years have elapsed, it seems that we were all correct. The book is finished, but it has been a harder and more complicated project than I had expected.

One of the factors which caused me to embark upon it was the often-repeated remark, in universities, that there was no 'proper biography' of the King. What this meant was that there was none which attempted the sort of questions of interest to professional historians. It ignored the fact that Charles had already been the subject of two of the most magnificent 'popular' biographies ever written, by a master and mistress of the arts of narrative and portrayal, Sir Arthur Bryant and Lady Antonia Fraser. Nobody who has known them can forget the unrolling cadences of Sir Arthur's sentences, in which the word 'England' recurs like the name of God in a mantra. Until the moment of his death, a few years ago, he possessed the trick of leading eye and mind easily from one page to another so that thousands of words can pass and leave the reader ready for more. In turn, he lent encouragement to Lady Antonia in her own work, which has the distinction of being hitherto the only book about Charles which deals in some detail with his entire life, from cradle till grave. To this she brought a number of sources hitherto neglected or unknown by historians, and a formidable common sense. Time and again, approaching issues upon which a great deal of romantic silliness had been expended in the past, I found that Lady Antonia had cut a plain and convincing way through them. Furthermore, she also dealt with most of the questions about the King which the general public would want to have answered, such as what he built, what his pastimes were, how many mistresses he had, what he had to do with the King Charles's spaniel and with Newmarket, and what caused his death.

I had, at least, the consolation of the original premiss, that he was a figure comparatively unstudied by academics. But this in turn received some qualification. In 1987 Professor J. R. Jones, one of the most respected living historians, published his *Charles II: Royal Politician*. In the event, this book stimulated my work rather than rendered it unnecessary, for it concentrated upon certain aspects of the reign and provided a large number of exciting new contentions with which I was enticed to take issue. More of moment to my own work was that, a year after commencing it, I discovered that another biography of Charles had been put under contract, by Dr John Miller. Now, Dr Miller is such an able colleague that, had I known that such a development would occur, I might not have embarked myself upon the same subject. As things turned out, we were working upon different sorts of books and some discussions clarified the distinctions. He proposes to concentrate upon the reign after 1660 and the regime rather than the man. He is limiting his study to England and proposes to deal very fully with foreign policy. I was happy, in turn, to cover the entire life, to keep the King fairly firmly at the centre of events, and to include Scotland and Ireland. This last fits into an admirable recent trend towards the writing of 'British' history, but seemed to me, from my first research into the Secret Treaty of Dover, to provide the best means of examining royal policies and attitudes. When Dr Miller's book takes its place alongside mine, then perhaps some significant progress will have been made in our knowledge of the man and the reign.

To avoid the experience of researching solidly for years and then writing solidly for more years, I worked upon the book a chapter at a time. I tended to write each one while conducting the research for the next, or when travelling for work or pleasure. As a result, they were produced, with pen and paper, in a multiplicity of odd situations, including trains, ferries, planes, airports, stations, hotels, parks, and the homes of friends. Only thus could I keep the work moving at the pace which I required, and allow me to concentrate upon each segment of my subject's life as an entity. The liabilities of this method, for style and overall coherence, may or may not be obvious in the result.

Some other features of the book may require explanation. One is my habit of employing the term 'British' as shorthand for 'Irish, Scottish, and English' (and Welsh, Cornish, etc.). Some Irish readers may be understandably irritated by this, but (apart from the fact that I really do believe in a British family of peoples) no other name appeared to exist for the purpose. Slightly more eccentric was my decision to present all personal names in the form native to their country of origin, for the sake of consistency. Thus 'Philip IV' of Spain remained 'Felipe IV', and 'Frederick-William' stayed as 'Friedrich-Wilhelm'. The biggest problem with this method is that the familiar 'William of Orange' features as 'Wilhelm', which does serve, as I had wished, to emphasize his identity as a patriotic Dutchman but may give some readers pause. I did not employ the Gaelic form of the name of the Irish hero Owen Roe O'Neill, because he himself signed it in the English manner used here. I was not, of course, utterly consistent, because place-names such as Vienna, Rome, and Tuscany remain Anglicized. But to speak of 'Wien, Roma, Toscana', would, I felt, seem odd enough to be counter-productive. Finally upon this subject of national identities, I must warn that this book is not intended to be a history of Restoration Scotland and Ireland. Although it ought to make contributions to that history, it follows the preoccupations of a monarch who regarded himself as King of England, Scotland, and Ireland, very firmly in that order.

Readers may notice a shift in my treatment of fellow historians during the course of the book. In the earlier chapters, this remains very much as it was during *The Restoration*, of avoiding debates with scholars in the text and so indulging my personal dislike of academic infighting. After the publication of that book it became obvious that in this respect I had miscalculated, and appeared to undervalue the work of predecessors by not taking issue with it. Thus, in the later chapters of *Charles the Second* I have increasingly proceeded by reference to the views of others, in both text and footnote. If I have over-compensated, then I am sorry for this in turn. Stylistically, the work is of a piece with my former books, in that quotations are modernized in their spelling and the dates are all given in old style but the year is assumed to begin on 1 January.

Last, I would like to say how delighted I was to discover how great an interest this monarch and his age still command among so many people. A series of receptions by Historical Associations, Workers' Educational Associations, and schools, and conversations when travelling, drove home that impression. Three memories, however, stand out. The elderly lady in Devon who, having heard me speak upon Charles, told me privately that I had defamed a great man and added in an intense whisper that she hoped that I had 'no influence upon the young'. The official guide at Dublin Castle who informed her audience that Charles had forty-two acknowledged mistresses, and went on to say darkly that she would spare her innocent listeners the details (a neat vengeance upon this king for his attitude towards her country). And the Irishman at Drogheda, who, upon a brief drinking acquaintance, dragged me across the town when I actually wanted to get to Dublin, in order to show me the head of St Oliver Plunket. Those things are most glorious in life which lead to laughter and adventure, and as this book has done as much for me I am grateful to it. The rest is yours.

R.E.H.

Acknowledgements

⟨∿⟩

ANY book of this length and density of research is made possible for its author only because of the assistance given by many others. One enormous category of such contributions consists of permission to consult documents held in private hands, and here, for me, the family of Clifford of Chudleigh have led all the rest. The late Baron and the Baroness Dowager, and the present Baron and Baroness, have accorded me a consistent kindness, generosity, and sympathy which could not be surpassed. The result was a wonderful set of archival adventures culminating in the greatest sale of state papers in the history of the world. J. H. Prideaux-Brune and his family, of Prideaux Place, also accorded me a personal interest and hospitality which made my visits to Padstow some of my life's treasured memories. I must also thank Victor Montagu, Esq., and the Honourable John Montagu, for a courtesy and an entertainment which made my time at Mapperton delightful. More formal, but still heartfelt, thanks are due to Her Majesty the Queen, to His Grace the Duke of Devonshire and the Trustees of the Chatsworth Settlement, to the Most Honourable the Marquis of Bath, to J. Maxwell-Stuart, Esq., and to the Trustees of the Chiddingstone Castle Estate. In most of these cases, the personal assistance and kindness was provided by archivists, to whom I am also profoundly grateful. Similar thanks are due to most of the staff of the various more public record repositories in which I worked. Of all these, the heaviest burden fell upon that splendid team Vera, Clare, and Helen of the Upper Reading Room of the Bodleian Library.

Another sort of assistance, equally invaluable, was given by bodies which provided funding for the travels in four nations required to carry out the research. Most was granted by the British Academy, and the shortfall made up by the University of Bristol. Without this assistance this book would not so much have been impaired as impossible.

Finally, a group of individuals provided help of a more diverse nature. Lady Antonia Fraser (now Lady Antonia Pinter), my predecessor as a biographer of Charles, gave not only the stimulus of discussion but two key documents, a rare publication and a photocopy, thereby saving me much labour. Julia Buckroyd, the world authority upon the Restoration Scottish Kirk, not only debated ideas avidly but recommended sources for further research. I have repaid her by arguing with her own work at a dozen niggling points, and hope that readers will realize, from my constant reference to it, how much it dominates the field, and how splendid her achievement is. Her latest publication, a life of Archbishop Sharp, appeared just too late to be used by me for this book. Colin Jones, of Exeter University, sent me copies of letters in the Vatican Archive. David Haytor, of the History of Parliament Trust, and Robert Latham, of Magdalene College, Cambridge, both put me on to the trail of important material. Irena Grugulis acted as my guide along the route of Charles's escape through the Midlands in 1651. To list those who have contributed to my thoughts by challenge and debate would be virtually to provide a roll-call of living historians in the field. Other areas of study may be monarchies (some despotisms), but the scholars of the Stuart period remain truly a Republic of Letters.

Contents

ᔕᔕᔕ

Illustrations

❧

I

Boyhood

IN seeking to trace the development of a person who lived three hundred years ago, the historian has a fundamental handicap: the seventeenth century lacked the interest of the present age in child psychology, and generally failed to record those incidents which this discipline regards as important. So it was with the child who was born in St James's Palace upon 29 May 1630, christened Charles, and later styled Prince of Great Britain, though generally known by the more traditional title of Prince of Wales. Contemporary comments upon his boyhood may be divided instead into three broad categories: those concerned with the external trappings of an heir to the throne in the age of baroque monarchy; those upon his physical and mental characteristics; and those preoccupied with his relation to political affairs.

The first sort commenced with his birth. It was noted by many observers that a bright star appeared over London at noon upon that day, portending good fortune. There was less agreement over the significance of a solar eclipse which followed.[1] More prosaically, the nurses attending the birth predicted that he would be generous because he appeared with open hands.[2] Observers of the christening, in the Chapel Royal, remembered that the whole party wore white satin with crimson embroidery, that six barons carried the canopy over the baby, that the corporation of London gave the King a gold cup worth £1,000, and that the absent godmother, the Queen Mother of France, sent marvellous diamonds.[3]

A few of the State Papers relate to the administration of this royal childhood. It has been fashionable of late to note that the parents, Charles I and Henrietta Maria, were one of history's most happily married crowned couples, and to conclude from this that young Charles had a stable and loving background. The point has been overstressed, for both father and mother lived most of their time away from their children. From the beginning, the nursery was a large establishment, presided over by the Countess of Dorset and including eight people appointed merely to rock the cradle. It moved within a few months from St James's to Greenwich Palace, and then, in 1633, far up-river to Richmond Palace, where it settled for over seven years. Before Charles's third birthday, the annual wardrobe expenses of himself and his infant sister totalled £3,000.[4] The nature as well as the richness of the dress was important. When the boy was five, his father commissioned a portrait of his eldest children to be presented to the Duchess of Savoy. The result displeased the King, for it represented its subjects in infant clothes and thereby threatened to give the court of Turin the impression that the English royal family were effete.[5] In later life, Charles regarded his father with affection and respect but nothing more, and found his mother an embarrassment. It is significant that his most enduring love for a figure from his childhood was reserved for one of his nurses, Christabel, Lady Wyndham.[6]

By steps, the Prince began to take his part in court ritual. When five years old he first helped to receive distinguished foreign guests at White-hall. At six, he presided over a masque, clad in blue and crimson taffeta 'after the Roman fashion', as Prince Britomart. Just before his eighth birthday, he became a Knight of the Garter amid the full pageantry of robes, plumes, and heralds.[7]

Commentators upon his personal attributes agreed that he was an unusually large and healthy child.[8] In an age in which a quarter of all children died before the age of ten, and three of Charles's own siblings were among them, he reached maturity having suffered only a gastric infection, a fever, and a broken arm.[9] Nobody, however, called him handsome, and his mother described him as downright ugly and marred, in addition, by a swarthy complexion.[10] His great height, robust constitution, and dark, full-fleshed face were to remain his three principal physical characteristics throughout life. His personality did, however, develop markedly after infancy. In his first years he was disturbingly passive and introverted, but efforts were made to ensure him lively company[11] and achieved remarkable success.

Just before his eighth birthday, he was removed from the care of nurses and given a governor, William Cavendish, Earl of Newcastle. Newcastle was selected by the King himself, for his personal qualities and his dissociation from political faction,[12] and has generally been regarded as the greatest individual influence upon Charles's character. This may in part be a trick of evidence, in that there survives a paper of advice written by him for the Prince, and four letters sent to him from his pupil,[13] and thus we simply know more about their relationship than any other of Charles's childhood. Nevertheless, Newcastle did have a greater power to make an impression upon the boy, over a longer period and with less distraction, than anybody else. His instructions are, depending upon one's view, either admirably practical or appallingly philistine. They warned against learning or piety for their own sake, urging his charge to learn languages only for utility, to confine his studies to subjects of obvious importance to a monarch, such as the art of warfare, to show respect for religion only to set an example to the masses, to cultivate dignity, ceremony, and civility, to speak well of all and to reprimand criticism of others. He added that he thought the Prince an ideal subject as Charles was no bookworm and seemed just sufficiently religious. The letters written by his charge show an education proceeding very much according to these lines. They speak of daily riding lessons (the Earl was a famous horseman) and thank his governor for a copy of a play and for a gift which was clearly some elaborate ornament. In later life some of Charles's traits were those recommended by Newcastle: his dilettante attitude to culture, his indifference to the spiritual content of religion, and his good manners. Nevertheless, his sense of ceremony was rather more superficial than his mentor had intended, and in one respect, his pleasure in having his servants mocked behind their backs, he rejected the advice totally. As a man he treated his old governor with formal gratitude but never sought his support or counsel.

The strongest characteristics which emerge from records of Charles's later childhood are vitality, independence, and assertiveness. One of his letters to Newcastle contained a warning against taking medicine. This attitude, quite rational in view of the dubious nature of contemporary medicaments, occasioned a minor family crisis, for his mother wrote to him reproving his obstinacy.[14] In his ninth or tenth year his father showed him one of the magnificently bound and gilded books produced by the Ferrar family. The Prince immediately asked for it, whereupon the King commissioned the Ferrars to make another specially for his son. John Ferrar presented it, and was rewarded with Charles's passionate delight. When the Prince was eleven, and riding with the King, the latter saw a hare sitting in a nearby field. The monarch's reaction was to reach for a gun, and to shoot at and wound the animal so that it dragged itself off screaming. The Prince jumped from his horse, waded a couple of ditches, killed the hare and returned laughing at the adventure. Neither pity nor bloodlust inspired this behaviour: the conventions of sport demanded an end to the business and Charles was admired for the agility with which he provided it.[15]

At this stage as later, however, his personality was to signify far less to most of his contemporaries than his office. Even before his birth he had been caught up in the struggle that was to condition his life until its last moments, the confessional divide between Protestant and Roman Catholic Europe. The marriage between Charles I and Henrietta Maria had been the product of two very different wishes, that of the English for French help in a war against Spain, and that of the French to further the cause of the Catholic faith and to prevent Anglo-Spanish *rapprochement*. Such was the urgency, and weakness, of the English conduct of the negotiations that the first objective was not built into the marital treaty but the second was. In the public articles Charles I promised to allow his bride a retinue of priests and freedom to worship as a Catholic, while their children were to be baptized in that religion and reared by their mother until they were aged twelve. In a secret article he promised to permit private worship to the English followers of Rome.[16] For both nations the result was a failure. Not only did France give no help against Spain but was soon itself at war with England. Under these circumstances, Charles's government saw no need to keep its side of the bargain. The penal laws against Catholics remained in force, and the baby Prince was baptized by the Anglican Bishop of London and entrusted to a nursery run by a Protestant noblewoman. The King and Queen Mother of France were indeed made godparents, but in protest at the breach of the treaty the former declined to send a representative and the latter refused to attend.[17]

If Henrietta Maria disappointed the English in their first hope of her, to help put a dent in the crown of Spain, she initially failed them in their second one, that she would secure the Stuart dynasty. Her first child, a son, died soon after birth. This family tragedy inspired some quiet glee among radical Protestants in London, for if Charles I remained childless then the heiress was his sister Elizabeth, former Queen of Bohemia and present heroine of Protestant Europe. Thus the arrival of a healthy Prince of Wales provoked much public thanksgiving and some private lamentation.[18] During the following fourteen years, five more children survived infancy, christened Mary, James, Elizabeth, Henry, and Henriette-Anne. The royal succession was therefore entirely established, and a good supply of potential marriage alliances added to the counters of English diplomacy. Nevertheless, the memory of the broken treaty still rankled. When Charles was aged four or five, his mother took him to mass with her and promised a papal agent to educate her sons in the faith of Rome. The process was halted by the King's orders, and nobody discerned any effect upon the boy. Catholic attempts to convert the Earl of Newcastle broke upon the barrier of his indifference to religion.[19] Yet fear of the influence of a Catholic Queen upon the court in general and the Prince in particular remained strong in both capital and provinces.[20]

Charles's part in national affairs, and anxiety regarding it, both increased as his first decade of life ended and the system of government presided over by his father began to collapse. By 1640 the King was facing a rebellion against his religious policy in Scotland and considerable discontent with his whole style of government in England. The Spanish offered him assistance, coupled with the marriage of the Prince to a Spanish or Austrian princess.[21] This project, and the King's power, foundered as he was defeated by the Scots and forced to call a Parliament which articulated his English subjects' grievances. A general breakdown of order commenced in the country, and Charles was recalled to his father's side at Whitehall Palace after rioting broke out near Richmond.[22] The new Parliament proceeded to imprison or to drive into exile the ministers who had advised the King during the 1630s, and to condemn to death the most formidable, the Earl of Strafford. Charles I, distraught, sent the Prince to the House of Lords with a plea for pardon or postponement of execution. The Lords refused upon the grounds that to do this would expose the whole royal family to 'evident danger', a reference to the London mob calling for Strafford's blood.[23] The affair afflicted the King for the rest of his life, though its impression upon his son is less discernible. A few days after Strafford's head fell, in May 1641, Newcastle resigned his governorship and retired into the country. He had been on the fringe of a bungled plot to enable the King to resist Parliament's will by force, and found it wise to withdraw from the public eye.[24]

The royal family played its part in efforts by the King during the first half of 1641 to appease public opinion. To please Protestant sentiment, he married his eldest daughter, Mary, to the young Prince of Orange, the first citizen of the Calvinist Dutch republic. Newcastle was replaced as governor to the Prince by William Seymour, Marquis of Hertford, an aristocrat distantly related to the royal line, personally associated with opponents of government policies during the 1630s, and yet not implicated in the death of Strafford. Whether he had any influence upon Charles is dubious, for he was aged, distracted by participation in the House of Lords, and (according to one who respected him) bookish and lazy.[25] His appointment was certainly only partially successful in allaying the fears of many MPs. In August 1641 it was proposed in the Commons that two other peers be appointed joint governors with the Marquis. In November, after the revelation (and exaggeration) of another plot by courtiers to resist Parliament by force, the House instructed Hertford not to permit Charles to visit his mother. In January 1642 it ordered the Marquis to attend and watch the boy constantly, being agitated by fears that Charles was to be sent abroad into the hands of Catholics.[26] In February came the decisive struggle. The King sent Henrietta Maria overseas, to put her beyond danger and to permit her to raise men and munitions for him. He ordered Charles, left at Hampton Court Palace with Hertford, to meet him at Greenwich. The Commons countermanded this instruction and sent to the King asking him to withdraw it. The Marquis, putting his responsibility to his monarch above that to the MPs, moved Charles as ordered, whereupon both Houses sent a commission to Greenwich to seize the boy. In the nick of time his father arrived, took custody of the Prince and sent the commissioners back frustrated.[27] With the Queen in the Netherlands and his heir at his side, the King was now able to move to York and conduct a series of increasingly embittered exchanges with his opponents at Westminster, from which were to spring the Great Civil War.

Thus the Prince's ceremonial role enlarged from one associated with a court to include one appropriate to a military campaign, and he played it superbly. He was made honorary captain of the King's first troop of horse guards. As this moved into the field in July, its members presented him with a richly embroidered tent and a white horse trapped in gold-studded velvet. Clad in gilt armour, he mounted the steed at once, and paced it to delighted applause.[28] In September he was sent to encourage the King's supporters in South Wales, appealing to their racial nationalism by virtue of his own title. He addressed a large gathering of gentry from the region most charmingly, and closed his speech with a toast to the 'ancient Britons'. The audience, captivated, pledged their loyalty and made many financial donations.[29] For the next two years he accompanied his father, either in his headquarters at Oxford or marching with the field army. Hertford was absent for much of that period leading an army of his own. It is a sign of how much the importance of the post of governor had declined as the Prince grew that the Marquis was not replaced until early 1644. The new governor was another aged nobleman with a remote connection to the royal house, Thomas Howard, Earl of Berkshire. His sole surviving letter from this period proves him to have possessed considerable courage, gallantry, and devotion to the royalist cause, and he was apparently widely respected. Whether he had great intelligence may be doubted, and he certainly made no discernible impression upon his charge.[30]

Only one letter written by Charles himself seems to survive from the early years of the war,[31] being an enthusiastic acknowledgement of the gift of a pair of horses. Three anecdotes are recorded, however, which give some insight into his development. One relates to the first great battle, at Edgehill in October 1642, where one flank of the royal army was turned. The King, deciding to rally his centre in person, ordered a troop of horse to escort the Prince and his brother James far to the rear. *En route*, this party was sighted by a larger group of enemy cavalry, and only the caution of the latter prevented Charles from suffering the fate he had narrowly evaded in February, and becoming a valuable political hostage. He almost ensured this disaster himself, by cocking a pistol and preparing to charge the parliamentarians, but was dissuaded, mercifully for his cause, by a royalist soldier. The threatening cavalry drew off, the princes' convoy made its retreat from the field, and the battle continued to its bloody and indecisive close.[32]

Both other stories are set at Oxford. One concerns a captured parliamentarian officer brought into the city, who passed Charles in the street. The Prince asked the guards where they were taking the man, and heard that he was to be questioned by the King. Charles replied that he should be hanged immediately before his father had a chance to pardon him. The other tale is of how, at sermon-time in St Mary's, Charles I caught his son laughing at some ladies sitting opposite. The royal reaction to this breach both of reverence and decorum was to bring his staff down upon Charles's head.[33]

In a sense, all that these vignettes portray is a normal high-spirited boy, not burdened with any precocious common sense, tolerance, and dignity. But, to a disturbing extent, the man is there. Many times would Charles II take quite needless physical risks. His way with helpless opponents would be as brutal, and his interest in women and indifference to sermons remained constant.

In Charles's century, most boys were apprenticed or deputed to work by the age of fourteen and, at his elevated level, he was no exception. In May 1644 the Privy Council at Oxford debated sending him to take nominal command of royalist operations in the West Country. When the proposal created great opposition among the Counsellors, and the Prince himself proved hostile, it was shelved.[34] During the following winter the project was revived, and executed in March 1645. Charles was to make his headquarters at Bristol, advised by Lord Hopton, one of the best royalist generals and acting governor of the city; his own governor Berkshire; two superannuated soldiers, Lord Capel and the Earl of Brentford; and two of the King's most trusted civilian advisers, the Master of the Rolls, Lord Culpeper, and the Chancellor of the Exchequer, Sir Edward Hyde. Of these, almost certainly the youngest and certainly the most intellectually formidable was Hyde, a plump, fair, ruddy-faced man of thirty-six. Thus the Prince was made the figure-head of a relatively talented, experienced, and prestigious Council, with responsibility for co-ordinating and improving all aspects of the royalist war effort in Cornwall, Devon, Dorset, and Somerset. The corporation of Bristol, with some insight into the pressures of committee work, lodged them all in a large house with a pile of coal and four hogsheads of wine in the cellar.[35]

How and why this development occurred is difficult to determine.

Perhaps the reasons were as simple as those given in the only source, Hyde's recollections:[36] that the King himself resolved upon giving his son an independent command, both to further his education and to provide a separate focus for English royalism if he himself was captured. The West was the obvious area for this, being the most important regional zone of responsibility left to the royalists. It was also obvious that, both to guide the boy and to give his authority weight, his Council would have to be composed of important men. Nevertheless, the political implications of the initiative were profound, and disturbed Hyde so much that, by his own admission he was most unwilling to go with the Prince. Two other dignitaries, appointed to the Council, objected so strenuously that they were excused the service. It represented an exile from the effective source of power, the King's person. The two ministers thus removed, Culpeper and Hyde, were the ablest spokesmen of that body of royalist opinion which had favoured the conclusion of a negotiated peace, preserving the reforms of 1640–1, as the happiest end to the war. Their transfer to the West marked another stage in a long and uneven erosion of the strength of this group, to the profit of career soldiers and ultra-royalist courtiers.[37] Hence the change may indeed have represented a personal whim of Charles I, which reacted upon the patterns of royalist politics. Or, as even that most visionary of monarchs never took a decision without counsel, it may have been the product of intrigues which have left no trace in the records.[38]

The four western counties had been the scene of major campaigns in every year of the war. They contained parliamentarian garrisons at Poole, Weymouth, Lyme, Plymouth, and Taunton, the last three of which were blockaded with varying success by local royalists. The latter had lost most of their original leaders through death or retirement, and had been divided by bitter quarrels. The King's soldiers in the region were under three separate commanders. Two were based in Devon, being the Governor of Exeter, Sir John Berkeley, and Sir Richard Grenville, who supervised the Plymouth blockade. The third was George Goring, leading a detachment of the royal field army which had been ordered by the King to clear the West of parliamentarian field troops. In addition, there were a number of units from former royalist armies scattered among the villages, menacing nobody except the inhabitants, who had to feed and equip them. The region was currently undergoing its latest parliamentarian invasion, by an army under Sir William Waller which was moving through Dorset. The task thus set before Charles's Council was considerable. If its members could manage it, then they could turn the West into a local power-base to compensate for their distance from court. If they failed, then the presence of rivals closer to the King could ensure their ruin, whatever the final issue of the war.

In the emergency of Waller's invasion, the key to royalist strategy was Goring, a lean, saturnine soldier of long experience, ravaged by pain from an old ankle wound and the drinking-bouts with which it was associated, but still a splendidly dashing commander. As a field officer with the King's army, it was not altogether clear that he was subordinate to the Prince's Council, while he himself had been empowered by Charles I to command Berkeley and Grenville. The obvious way to avoid a clash was for him and the Council to co-operate as a team, and so, by a rapid exchange of letters, they did. The Council endorsed his orders to the two local generals to bring up their troops, and rushed munitions and reinforcements to him. In a brilliant brief campaign at the end of March, Goring chased Waller from the region.[39] The next step in securing it was immediately undertaken: the siege of the landlocked parliamentarian garrison at Taunton, using the available foot soldiers for the task while the horse fended off relief columns.[40]

By now, internal problems were appearing. The Council wielded authority by virtue of its members' commission from the King, not because of their innate prestige. Apart from Berkshire, whose opinions were disregarded by his colleagues,[41] they were all peers of very recent creation or (in Hyde's case) a commoner. None could claim the status of a western magnate. Yet they summoned, questioned, imprisoned, or ordered the local gentry about with a freedom shown by no previous royalist leaders.[42] Soon some of the Somerset royalists cordially hated them, while making a better relationship with Goring.[43] In this situation Goring was really not the man for the Counsellors to offend, but offend him they did. In early April they had all agreed that he would pursue the retreating Waller, reinforced by Grenville. When Grenville very reluctantly marched as far as Taunton and refused to go further (perhaps fearing that his western soldiers would desert), the Council changed its mind. Goring, preparing for pursuit, was ordered to besiege Taunton instead. This snub was compounded when for unknown reasons the Council chose to protect a disobedient officer whom Goring wanted punished. At the same time he was warned from court that stories that he had been behaving badly were reaching the King and encouraging his rivals. Not surprisingly, he sank into a sullen rage.[44] Yet while thus making enemies, the Council was effectively extending its powers. In late April it persuaded Grenville to accept command of a new western field army to be formed before Taunton, resigning Devon and Cornwall entirely to Berkeley. The problem of Goring was removed when the King recalled him and his cavalry to the royal army, and at a meeting of gentry from all over the region a programme of recruiting for the new force was agreed upon. With Waller routed and Taunton under attack, all prospects now bid fair.[45]

In all this activity, despite Hyde's later insistence that he was encouraged to join the debates,[46] Charles himself seems to have been only a rubber stamp for his Council's decisions. Indeed, what rankled most with both Goring and Grenville was that measures imposed with his authority were clearly the will of Hyde and Culpeper.[47] Only one initiative can be credited to the Prince in person at this time, which was to show passionate affection for his old nurse, Lady Wyndham, who was married to one of the Somerset royalists. This natural response had dire political repercussions, for she distracted his attention from business, mocked the Council to him without reproof, and tried to win offices for her friends. The Counsellors were obliged to separate them swiftly.[48] Again, the episode was a portent: many times in the future female company would remove Charles's attention from business, while one of his enduring vices would be his enjoyment of criticism of his advisers.

In mid-May a hail of troubles hit the Council that made Lady Wyndham seem a very trivial irritation. First, plague broke out in Bristol, causing the Counsellors to remove their base, and Charles, westward to Barnstaple. Then Taunton was relieved. Hopton and Berkeley had at last broken into the town and were burning it, before bombarding the remaining enemy soldiers in the castle. A small parliamentarian force took them by such complete surprise that they fled in ignorance of its numbers, leaving the town to be reprovisioned and its defences rebuilt. Next Goring reappeared, with his cavalry and also with powers from the King giving him control of the western royalist army, without responsibility to Prince and Council. This was the result of a decision made within the royalist High Command, to divide the royal field army for the new campaigning season. Part was to be sent to reinforce the West while most carried the war into parliamentarian territory, and Goring had reluctantly agreed to lead the former if he were given authority to spare him the slights and confusions of the spring. The worst nightmare of Hyde and his colleagues had occurred: their distance from the royal person had weakened their influence with him. Their response, through the Prince, was to write to the King with such indignation that, after much hesitation, Charles I agreed to place Goring beneath their authority once more.[49]

Meanwhile, the Council had alienated the other outstanding royalist soldier in the region, Grenville. Sir Richard was an officer as experienced as Goring, equally capable and more ruthless. His men felt fierce loyalty to him, and when he was incapacitated for weeks by a wound received before Taunton, they deserted in droves rather than serve under another. Their confidence in him was based largely upon his determination to keep them paid, which necessitated in turn his continual harrying of the civilian officers of Devon and Cornwall. Quite naturally, many of the latter loathed him. What came as a surprise to Grenville was that the Prince's Council, anxious to establish its role as an arbitrating force, listened sympathetically to their complaints. It also failed to support him against Berkeley, who was competing for the same resources. He was further discountenanced when, having agreed to surrender his command in Devon in order to lead the western field army, he was displaced in his new position by Goring. Accepting the post of Goring's subordinate, he found himself ordered to supervise the blockade of Lyme, a military backwater quite unsuitable for an officer of his calibre. When he was denied even the troops designated for this task, he resigned. He then tried to recover some of his old standing in Devon, employing his civilian office of High Sheriff of the county. When Berkeley and the local commissioners complained of him to the Council, he was summoned before the Prince, given a lashing rebuke, and assigned the dreary task of catching deserters. Admirers of Charles, misled by Hyde's account, have made much of this scene, portraying a gallant royal youth subduing a selfish and brutal soldier by force of personality. In reality, it was part of a long process of shabby treatment of an able officer by political leaders to whom he had temporarily become an embarrassment.[1]

Throughout June, Goring prosecuted the renewed siege of Taunton. The Council's recapture of supreme military power left him managing troops over many of whom he had no formal authority, in a county full of royalist garrisons which he could not control. The governor of Taunton had declared that he would eat his boots before surrendering. The royalist army was unpaid, and had to compete with the garrisons for supplies. Country people, weary of having to sustain soldiers who could almost never give cash for what they consumed, were forming associations to regulate or resist further demands. Charles received a deputation from one of these, and expressed sympathy but could only urge them to pay more to the soldiers. He then ordered Goring to suppress their meetings, but the general felt too weak to do so and tried to pacify them instead. In such miserable fashion the royalist war effort ran on into early July, when the main parliamentarian field army, the New Model, entered the West. Having destroyed the royal army at Naseby, it was ordered to eliminate Goring's. Grossly outnumbered, he could only fight a defensive action in the hope of reinforcement. At Langport his rearguard was caught and destroyed, and the rest of his force fled demoralized into Devon.[51]

There he and the Prince's Council were granted a respite of two months, for the New Model Army felt unwilling to advance further west while leaving powerful royalist fortresses in its rear. It accordingly settled down to reduce Bridgwater, Sherborne Castle, and Bristol. Having a train of siege guns, and regular supplies of pay and recruits from the east, it managed to carry out this work without serious debilitation. At the same time the western royalist army fell to bits. Its infantry, having endured an unsuccessful siege and a humiliating rout, made for home. Only money could have kept them, and there was almost none available. In the emergency, the leaders temporarily sank their differences. Goring and Grenville produced a scheme to rebuild a field force by combining existing field and garrison troops with new levies and apprehended deserters, and the Council gave approval. In late August Charles moved to Exeter, to preside over councils of war and provide a focus for the reconstituted force. A month later, he passed on to Launceston, to rally the militia of Cornwall with his hereditary authority as their duke, and send them to reinforce the new army.

It was all in vain. Grenville, gone into Cornwall to catch deserters, was not only unable to produce them but found himself having to suppress a rising against royalist rule, born of sheer war-weariness. Goring, waiting at Exeter, watched his existing troops eating up the area's supplies, and grew alarmed, impatient, and unwell. Some officers defied him, causing him to beg the Prince for formal powers as Lieutenant-General, and to arouse the suspicions of the Council again that he was trying to break free of their control. The continuing success of the New Model Army, as it captured the outlying fortresses, further reduced the morale of local gentry, and in early October that army at last marched into Devon. Goring raided its quarters, but found that the Exeter area was now incapable of maintaining the number of soldiers needed to launch a full-scale attack. He sent the remnants of his army into west Devon and, having informed the Council that he was going abroad to recover his health, he set sail for France. His instinct told him that the situation was hopeless.[52]

It was, but the end was postponed three months by the caution of the parliamentarian commanders and the onset of late autumn weather, turning roads into mires and soldiers into invalids. While the New Model Army settled around Exeter, the Prince and his Council made desperate attempts to combine their remaining soldiers and the Cornish militia into a relief force. Charles, primed by his advisers, addressed meeting after meeting but achieved no more success than Goring had done. The horse soldiers would only obey Goring's cavalry commander Lord Wentworth, while the foot would only follow Grenville. Wentworth was an ineffectual leader and his troopers were scattered in a surprise attack just as the formation of the new army seemed possible. The Cornishmen broke and fled to their homes when the rout of the horse was reported. By mid-January the remaining royalist leaders and their soldiers were all gathered in Cornwall. Grenville, demoralized by their quarrelling, advised the Prince to appoint one of his Council as unequivocal overall commander. Charles and his Counsellors did so, choosing the best general in their number, Hopton, and giving Wentworth charge of the horse and Grenville the foot, under his orders. Grenville, his nerves and body both worn out, considered that he would have most of the work while Hopton had most of the honour, and declined to serve. The Council's own temper, badly frayed, now snapped and it threw Grenville into prison. In mid-February Hopton led the remnant of the royalist army of the West into Devon, and was overwhelmed by the New Model at Torrington. The enemy poured into Cornwall, and rumours reached the Prince, Hyde, and Culpeper, sheltering in the powerful coastal castle of Pendennis, of a plot among some of the gentry to hand Charles over to Parliament and so win its favour. Since the New Model Army first entered Devon, Hyde and Culpeper had kept a frigate ready in case of disaster. On 4 March they went aboard this from Pendennis with Charles and many followers, and set sail for the Scilly Isles where they hoped to find security long enough to make further plans.[53] The Prince of Wales thus left the English mainland for the first time and was never to return, for, when Charles next trod his native soil four years later it was as King.

The royalist leaders in the West had been neither fools nor sinners, but men caught in an impossible predicament. The region had been subject for three years to the ravages and the demands of war. Parliament dominated the seas and the south-east of the country so that the principal trade routes were cut and the creation of new wealth difficult. Three of the four western counties contained enemy garrisons and the area was subject to repeated invasion, so that it had to be filled with royalist fortresses and field troops which consumed the resources needed for the recruitment of fresh strength. At the time that the Prince and the Council arrived, it was possible to hold the region against subsidiary armies but not to mount any offensive operations from it. The royalists there were doomed as soon as Parliament could bring against them the principal thrust of its effort, fuelled by the riches of all south and east England, an area always richer and larger and currently less ravaged, able to trade with relative freedom, and relatively unburdened by soldiers. The folly of the King, in exposing his main army to disaster at Naseby, made this possible.

It may be doubted if Charles I's decision to send his son to the West either contributed to or postponed defeat. On the one hand, the energy of his Council in regulating the flow of recruits and munitions was an asset to their cause. On the other, its need to assert its power over local royalists and military commanders increased bitterness within its party. The great benefit of the King's policy in giving the Prince this position was that in the event it enabled the latter to escape abroad and represent an alternative source of royalist strength. Upon this the political history of the next generation was to turn, but as Charles sailed from Cornwall this fact had not yet been realized. The effect of the whole experience upon the youth's personality is difficult to assess. Certainly the formal deference to him as nominal controller of the region, and the increasing frequency with which he wielded this authority over individuals and gatherings must have developed his self-consciousness and self-confidence as a ruler. Yet it is impossible to say whether he was at this time ever more than a cipher for his advisers, and, with the passage of time, for two of them in particular. The achievement of his own voice and views was to be the next stage in his progress.

The Exiled Prince of Wales

⟨⤜⟩

THERE can be few more delicious places in Britain than the Isles of Scilly in spring, where a silver-threaded sea rolls on to beaches of pure white sand and the rocks and scrub inland are full of migrating songbirds. On the other hand, there can also be days when a wet gale blows off the Atlantic and renders an existence upon the Isles wretched: and this latter experience befell Charles and his companions. So powerful was the sou'wester that no ship could approach from the mainland for five weeks, and having sent to France and Ireland for food and soldiers, the Prince's company settled down to wait upon events. The busiest was probably Hyde, who had commenced work upon a great history of the Civil War designed to vindicate himself, his friends, and his monarch at the expense of Goring, Grenville, Parliament, and the truth. The least happy were probably some courtiers who were put up in a shack hung with drying fish and woke up to find the spring tide in bed with them.[1]

When the wind dropped, on 10 April, there arrived not only Hopton, having supervised the surrender of the western army, but a trumpeter with an invitation from Parliament for the Prince's own capitulation. The next day, to prove the point, Charles found his island surrounded by a parliamentarian fleet. The amazing personal luck which was to attend him most of his life now intervened, for a storm rose and drove the enemy away. Virtually all his Council were now agreed that it was imperative to leave for a stronger and more remote royalist sanctuary, and the obvious one accessible from the Scillies was Jersey. On the 16th the group of refugees re-embarked, and arrived off their new destination the following evening. Charles enjoyed this voyage immensely, being permitted to steer his ship for two hours at a stretch.[2]

Jersey was in every way a more desirable residence, being better fortified, better supplied, firmly governed for the King by Sir George Carteret, and close to the French coast in case of disaster. Its principal stronghold, Elizabeth Castle, made an imposing base for the Prince and his Council, while their followers were quartered in comfortable town houses. It is larger than any of the Scilly Isles and even more beautiful, with a dramatic rocky coast lined with woods and enclosing fragrant heaths. Even here the war was not remote, for Parliament controlled most of neighbouring Guernsey and its ships prowled offshore. Charles had replied to its summons in the Scillies with a polite disingenuous letter stating that he would be pleased to negotiate from Jersey, whereupon both Houses ordered an attack upon the island. But the reduction of the King's mainland fortresses consumed all the parliamentarian strength, and the proposed expedition never sailed.[3]

It was a diplomatic, and not a military, problem which was to force Charles's departure. During the previous year, the King had given instructions providing for the event of his son's being forced to flee the West Country, but like so many of the directions of Charles I these were mutually contradictory. Sometimes he had ordered the Prince to make for France and there obey his mother in all matters but religion. In other letters he had instructed him to proceed to Denmark, or to where he wished.[4] No sooner had he left Cornwall than the Queen began a campaign to fetch him to her side.[5] For two years Henrietta Maria had been the guest of her parental family, who had made over to her the palace of St Germain-en-Laye, a relatively comfortable arcaded pentagon of brick and grey stone, set in a royal forest near Paris. From there she had conducted continual intrigues with the Catholic powers to obtain aid for her husband, and with his defeat looming and the prospect of a peace treaty imminent, wanted the heir apparent by her side to strengthen her own position.[6] This wish certainly coincided, for the moment, with those of the King. At the end of April, to avoid capture by Parliament, Charles I left Oxford and joined the army of Parliament's Scottish allies. This was the consequence of an informal promise from them that they would provide at worst protection and at best military assistance, obtained through the mediation of the French envoy. With France thus playing a crucial part in his affairs, it suited the King well enough that his son should reside there, and from March onward he assumed that this was what Charles would do. In letters to his wife he expressed satisfaction in this development.[7]

The French had their own reasons for desiring Charles's presence. For the past three years their monarch had been a child, Louis XIV, and the regency held by his mother Anne. She in turn was advised by an Italian cardinal, Jules Mazarin, famed for his rich blue clothes, his magnificent entertainments, his perfumed pet monkey, his permanent smile, his gentle manner, and his ruthless and calculating brain. For the past ten years France had been locked in a bloody and debilitating war with Spain, necessitating simultaneous military operations upon every frontier, heavy taxation, and an increase in the power and personnel of central government which provoked growing resentment. On the whole, the French had been winning, but the Spanish showed no sign of capitulation, and Anne and Mazarin were incapable of taking on the English as well. On the other hand, they had the strongest motive for diplomatic interventions which would either win English gratitude or leave the English so bitterly divided as to present no threat. To act as the hosts of the Prince of Wales as well as the Queen would strengthen their position as arbiters.[8]

An additional factor entered the situation upon 27 April,[9] when a ship full of Irish soldiers dropped anchor below Elizabeth Castle and disgorged a man with rounded features, a blond beard, and a mop of curly fair hair. This was George, Lord Digby, recently Charles I's most influential adviser and one of the most destructive individuals of his age. If it is the skill of an impressionist painter to reduce solid objects to particles of light and form, so it was the art of Digby to take the components of complex and delicate political situations and create from them scenarios of compelling (and fallacious) simplicity and plausibility. Had he only written a history of his times with the skill with which he misled its rulers, he would long have been regarded as a wronged hero. Having persuaded Charles I to lose his field army in the suicidal attack at Naseby and then to dismiss his best general, he had led the remaining royalist cavalry to destruction and escaped to intervene in the affairs of Ireland. This realm had for over four years been disputed by the forces of the King, Parliament, and the rebel Roman Catholic Confederacy. The last were the most powerful, but their Supreme Council recognized that when the English became capable of concentrating their power against them once more, they would probably be overwhelmed. Accordingly, they resolved to exploit the waning fortunes of Charles I by granting him military aid in exchange for the satisfaction of their religious and national grievances. On arrival, Digby leant his ready tongue to persuading them into accepting concessions more limited than those originally demanded, and on 28 March they signed a treaty with the King's representative in Ireland, the Lord-Lieutenant, James Butler, Marquis of Ormonde.[10] As soon as Charles's Council wrote from the Scillies, appealing for soldiers, Digby realized that the refugee Prince would be the perfect figure-head for a joint Protestant and Catholic expeditionary force. He set out with the reinforcements, intending to compel the Council to agree to this move if arguments did not suffice. Instead, he only caught up with his quarry at Jersey, where the garrison was more than a match for his Irish and the Counsellors were certainly not disposed to concur with his proposition. Digby accordingly dumped his men in the hands of

Carteret and crossed to France, to persuade the Queen into supporting the venture.[11]

The Council was initially united in the opinion that Charles should go nowhere for the time being. Its members considered the situation in Ireland was not yet stabilized, while they feared the effect upon public opinion if the heir to the throne moved to Catholic France: this was just the step which Parliament had striven so hard to prevent in early 1642. Furthermore, they felt that the French ought to guarantee substantial aid to his cause before he joined them.[12] They had, nevertheless, a personal reason for their advice: that once Charles joined either his mother or the Irish, their influence over him, and thus their political standing, would be greatly weakened.[13] Accordingly, they resisted the Queen's entreaties and agreed that Capel and Culpeper should attend her in person to argue their case.[14] By now, Digby and Mazarin were at Amiens making a deal. Having failed to win anybody for the scheme to ship Charles to Dublin, Digby agreed to support the arguments to get him to France, in exchange for a large sum of French money for the Irish royalists. The lord and the cardinal also resolved to send a French envoy to promote a scheme in England. The Scottish government had gone to war in Parliament's favour in order to establish presbyterian church government in England, as the best means to securing its existence in their own land. According to the plan of Digby and Mazarin, if the King made this concession himself then he would both win the Scots and divide the parliamentarians, who were already quarrelling over the future of the Church. A new civil war would ensue between Charles I's recent enemies, at the end of which the French, Irish, and royalists would join forces to mop up and to restore the King. In its tortuous duplicity, the project well represented the natures of the two men.[15]

Meanwhile, the subject of all this controversy was enjoying a summer holiday. His stint at the wheel of a frigate had engendered a love of sailing, and in Jersey he had a pinnace made for him which he steered around the bay. On land he had the more restrictive but not onerous work of representing royalty to the islanders, reviewing the militia, inspecting fortifications, holding levees for the gentry, and creating two knights and a baronet. The train of a seventeenth-century Prince of Wales, forced into hasty and penurious exile, consisted of about 300 persons, including shoemakers, tailors, and laundresses. Every day Charles dined off gold and silver, his attendants kneeling to present successive dishes for his choice. A local observer noted that his personal friends were two unimportant young gentlemen, one the son of his beloved Lady Wyndham. As always, he played his formal part well and the people of Jersey were charmed.[16]

This idyll ended upon Midsummer Day. Word had reached France that the Scots, far from declaring for the King, had set guards upon him. Culpeper believed that with his monarch a prisoner it was necessary to unite Queen and Prince, and so his voice was now added to those calling for this move.[17] In mid-June, Henrietta Maria lost patience and sent a deputation to fetch Charles which included Digby, Culpeper, and some of her courtiers, of whom the most important was Henry, Lord Jermyn, her secretary. A furious debate ensued at Elizabeth Castle. In a sense, it was the latest round in an old struggle, for Charles's Counsellors had always conceived the royalist cause as best served by winning English public opinion, while Digby, Jermyn, and the Queen had as long been associated with attempted *coups d'état* and intrigues for foreign aid. The Prince took the simple way out of the predicament and decided that he had to obey the commands of both parents. Hyde, Hopton, and Berkshire all declared their authority superseded and, despite the entreaties of Jermyn and Culpeper, refused to accompany Charles. He was conducted to the ship between Jermyn and Digby, and within a few days he arrived at St Germain.[18]

He was to be based there for nearly two years, paralysed by the failure of royalist diplomacy. The scheme of Mazarin and Digby had depended entirely upon Charles I granting presbyterian church government in England. This, despite the appeals of his wife, Jermyn, and Culpeper, he utterly refused to do upon both political and moral grounds.[19] After almost ten months of argument the Scots lost patience, handed him over to Parliament, and went home. He had long before entrusted the direction of Irish affairs to Queen and Prince, but here too catastrophe occurred. Ormonde's treaty was denounced by many of the Confederate Catholics as having made too many concessions, and repudiated. Far from receiving aid from them, the Lord-Lieutenant was soon under attack by their forces. In June 1647 he decided that his first loyalty was to Protestantism, and surrendered Dublin unconditionally to Parliament.[20] Under these circumstances it would have been madness for the French to take up the royalist cause, and despite the pleas of Henrietta Maria and some Catholic clerics,[21] the Queen Regent and Mazarin returned their whole attention to fighting Spain. All that Charles I and his followers could do now was to sit still and hope for a change of fortune.

Even so, it is doubtful that the Prince made the wrong decision in going to St Germain. There was some muttering in the House of Commons at the move,[22] but thereafter, as shall be seen, Charles became an ever more attractive potential leader for the disaffected in Britain. Upon his birthday in 1647 his emblem of ostrich feathers was worn by many in

London.[23] It is possible that, after finishing off the English royalists, the parliamentarians would have attacked Jersey had he still been there. The French never gave his presence on their soil any official recognition, and this undoubtedly accorded with their natural interest in avoiding giving offence to a victorious Parliament. On the other hand, the Venetian ambassador to France believed that the Prince also desired it, as it gave him greater freedom of movement,[24] and it does seem to have been mutually convenient. Certainly, nobody except the disgruntled Hyde ever maintained that Charles was shabbily treated. Very soon after his arrival an 'accidental' meeting was arranged between him and the French royal family in the Forest of Fontainebleau. After introductions had been made, the Prince was invited to the nearby palace to be entertained. He was given the exceptional honours of sitting and walking at the right hand of the boy king, of occupying a chair of the same size, of replacing his hat in the royal presence, and of being admitted to the select *petit lever*. Thereafter he appeared regularly at the balls, assemblies, hunts, and theatrical productions enjoyed by this court.[25] To support him, the French augmented his mother's pension by a quarter. This was no fortune, and the whole was badly paid, but the Queen Regent's finances were overstrained by war.[26] It was at any rate probably more than he would have got in Jersey, where in his short stay he ran up a large number of debts which he left behind him unpaid.[27]

The King's direction that no attempts be made to convert the Prince to Roman Catholicism were honoured, despite the initial irritation that they caused the devout Queen Regent.[28] Charles had already brought three Anglican chaplains from Jersey,[29] and one of them, his tutor John Earle, apparently spent an hour a day with him.[30] Within two months the King reinforced them by sending a Dr Stewart to be dean of his son's chapel,[31] but all this effort was perhaps superfluous as Charles showed no sign of deep interest in any religion. Henrietta Maria's principal interference in his affairs consisted of attempting to wed him, not to her Church but to an individual woman, the richest heiress in Europe.

She was Louis XIV's first cousin, Anne Marie Louise d'Orléans, Duchesse de Montpensier, to whom would be given the apt nickname 'La Grande Mademoiselle'. For half a century her magnificent person would stride through French history, pausing before every mirror, not from lack of confidence but simply to admire the result. What the glass showed was a tall, blonde, blue-eyed, heavy-featured, robust, and high-coloured woman, generally clad in a gorgeously jewelled costume of red, white, and black. Her personality was, like her exterior, striking to the point of overpowering: determined, courageous, never hampered by modesty or self-doubt, and only occasionally capable of perception. At this date she was nineteen years of age.[32] Her huge fortune made it virtually inevitable that, as the royalist cause grew increasingly impecunious, she should be viewed as a prospective match for the Prince, and rumours of one had been circulating since 1643.[33] To Henrietta Maria, 'Mademoiselle' possessed the additional virtues of being French and being a Catholic, and in the winter of 1646–7 she went to great pains to convince this princess of her son's love for her, while setting Charles to accompany 'Mademoiselle' at every court entertainment.[34] The marriage would probably have been a political mistake, for the bride's nationality and religion would have been as unwelcome to the British as they appeared assets to the Queen, and the news of the wooing caused disquiet amongst both royalists and parliamentarians.[35] But in any case the project was impossible. The Queen Regent did not want such an inheritance to leave France, 'Mademoiselle' herself considered only the Holy Roman Emperor to be worthy of her, and Charles, whatever his sense of the political implications, clearly found his prospective wife forbidding. Thus, while he partnered her as assiduously as his mother wished, he addressed not a single word to her upon the grounds that he knew no French, though, as 'Mademoiselle' noted with irritation, he appeared to understand it perfectly.[36]

Whether this dumb-show was the product of guile or sheer fright is difficult to determine, as the French court found him generally taciturn. He was no more forthcoming with the eight-year-old Louis XIV, and the two boys promenaded and exchanged bows together in almost total silence, like clockwork figurines.[37] Nevertheless, Charles pleased and impressed the courtiers with the same qualities which had gratified the Channel Islanders: exquisite manners, apparent sweetness of nature, and dexterity in the princely recreations of dancing and riding.[38] His opinion of the French may be surmised from the fact that, ever after, he followed their fashions. By contrast, he showed no particular affection for Jersey in later life. The atmosphere of St Germain seems to have consisted of gloom relieved by Henrietta Maria's tirades and bouts of toothache,[39] but the frequent marvellous entertainments of royal France must have made the Prince's stay there infinitely preferable to two years upon Jersey.

Another advantage of St Germain was that it was the biggest single rendezvous point for royalist exiles. The most important of these was Charles's cousin Rupert, one of the children of Elizabeth of Bohemia upon whom Puritans had fixed so much hope in the 1620s. Having served Charles I as a superb general and as a destructive and disastrous politician, Prince Rupert arrived at St Germain soon after the Prince. The Queen, whom he had offended with many others at Oxford, at first treated him

coldly, but the French Queen Regent was delighted to use such an able soldier, insisted upon a welcome for him, and gave him command of all the
English in her service.⁴⁰ Lesser commanders preceded and followed him,
including Charles's old governor Newcastle. One unfortunate consequence
of so many reunions was that some of the defeated generals, embittered
by old quarrels, fell upon each other like ill-trained dogs. Rupert started
the process by greeting Digby, who surfaced once more from the Irish
imbroglio, with a challenge to a duel. News of this was leaked to the
Queen, who arrested both of them at their rendezvous in the Forest of
St Germain and forced a reconciliation in front of herself and Charles. At
the same time Digby almost duelled with Jermyn, and he did end up doing
so with another former royalist commander, Henry, Lord Wilmot, whose
credit he had ruined with the King before dealing in the same manner with
Rupert. Digby's sword was quite as able as his tongue, and he defeated his
opponent with a stab in the hand. Finally, Rupert jumped on yet another
disgraced officer, Lord Percy, in the course of a hunt, and ran him through
the side after a swift fight. With these ritual blood-lettings, harmony was
established.⁴¹

During the first half of 1648, the prospect of action for all of them
grew increasingly more real, and the Prince was at the centre of every plan.
Many Scots had come slowly to suspect that the King's predilection for
episcopacy posed less of a threat to the establishment of presbyterianism
in England than the desire of many parliamentarians to tolerate independent Protestant churches. By the summer of 1647 both the great political
factions in Scotland, that led by the Hamilton brothers and that which
looked to the Marquis of Argyll, had sent secretly to Charles offering
to put him at the head of an army of invasion if he consented to their
religious programme. A number of former parliamentarians in England
agreed with them.⁴² In December, the King virtually committed his wife
and son to serious negotiation with the Scots by signing an Engagement
with their dominant party (led by the Duke of Hamilton) in his prison
in the Isle of Wight. By this, he conceded presbyterianism in England for
just three years in exchange for a Scottish army to restore him to his 'just
rights'. A clause in the agreement provided that the Prince would go to
Scotland if guaranteed 'safety, freedom and honour' there.⁴³

Simultaneously, the position in Ireland improved. In February 1648
Ormonde arrived at St Germain. The fair-haired, pale-skinned Marquis,
'James the White', was an able and chivalrous general, a vulpine diplomat,
and an unshakeable servant of the twin causes of the King and the episcopal Protestant Church. He had a gift for inspiring respect, and it is a sign
of Henrietta Maria's growing political maturity that she kept him in favour

even after his surrender of Dublin.[44] By the time of his arrival in France, the Confederate Catholics who favoured conciliation were again in power, and Lord Inchiquin, an important supporter of Parliament, was growing as disillusioned with the results of its victory as many in Scotland and England. Both sets of men contacted Ormonde, asking for his leadership, and he was rapidly followed to St Germain by agents from the Confederacy, asking for a treaty with the royalists and inviting the Prince to Ireland to lead a combined army.[45]

Experience had taught the Queen caution. The French envoy in Scotland fired off a series of letters warning her that the Scots only wanted custody of Charles as a useful ploy in forcing concessions from the English.[46] The Irish Catholics had proved unreliable before. Yet developments continued favourably. In April Inchiquin declared for the King, and on 13 May Henrietta Maria told the agents of the Catholics, to their delight, that she was sending Ormonde back to Ireland to make a treaty with them.[47] In March, despite the opposition of Argyll's party and most of the ministers of the Kirk, Hamilton rallied a majority of the Scottish Parliament behind the Engagement.[48] On 1 May they wrote a formal invitation to Charles,[49] and thereafter set about raising an army to invade England. In the latter country, also, the royalist cause was renascent. The fortunes of war had left three of the King's children, James, Duke of York, Elizabeth, and Henry, Duke of Gloucester, in Parliament's hands, warded at St James's Palace (the youngest, Henriette-Anne, being with the Queen). On the evening of 20 April, James elected to be the subject of a game of hide-and-seek, and then slipped into the nearby park to meet a man in a wig with black patches on his face. This character was Colonel Bampfield, a royalist officer who had plotted the episode with the boy on the King's instructions. He dressed the Duke as a girl, and had them both rowed down the Thames to where a Dutch pinnace was waiting. By the end of the month James had joined his sister Mary and her husband the Prince of Orange at The Hague. In the event of Charles's demise, the royalists now had another prince at liberty to take his place.[50] In the course of May, royalist risings broke out in Wales, the far north, Kent, and Essex, and at the end of the month the principal parliamentarian war fleet, stationed off Kent, declared for the King. Its familiar commander, William Batten, had been replaced and had taken vengeance by fomenting this mutiny among his former charges.[51] For the first time, the royalist party had control of the English seas, and Charles had a safe means of transport wherever he willed.

To those around him, his will seemed obvious: to get to Scotland and lead its army as swiftly as possible. His mother and some of their advisers were inclined to be less precipitate,[52] but at the end of May everybody agreed that he must move to Holland, a convenient springboard for any theatre of war and especially for Scotland if its masters agreed to suitable terms. On 13 June he and Henrietta Maria dispatched these, requiring that no further concessions be demanded of Charles than those in the Engagement; that he could take with him any companions he chose and take any advisers once in Scotland; and that he continue to observe Anglican worship. To soften the impact of such terms, the Queen paid for some arms and ammunition to be shipped from Holland to the Scots.[53] Charles left St Germain on 29 June, having taken farewell of his French hosts, and sailed from Calais on 6 July. With him went Rupert, Culpeper, Wilmot, Hopton, Brentford, and most of the royalist military men who had collected in France.[54] Digby stayed at Paris, apparently because the Queen and Jermyn had taken the measure of him during the previous winter and decided that the Prince was better spared his advice.[55] On the King's own instructions, summons were sent to all the Privy Counsellors living privately in exile, including Hyde in Jersey, to join the Prince and thus to afford him the greatest possible breadth of counsel.[56]

By 12 July Charles was at The Hague, dining with James, Mary, and the Prince of Orange [57] and attempting to resolve two difficulties. A few days before, the fleet which had declared for the King had arrived in the Dutch harbour of Helvoetsluys, to pick up supplies and offer its services to the titular royalist Lord High Admiral, Charles's brother. Colonel Bampfield, the man who had smuggled young James out of London, had immediately used his influence with the boy to gratify himself and his friends. He persuaded James to commission as his Vice-Admiral (and effective commander) Lord Willoughby of Parham, a former parliamentarian who had defected after some intrigues with Bampfield and had no experience of naval war. The rash colonel was attempting to launch the fleet into a strike against the English coast, without waiting for the Prince, when the latter arrived. Charles dealt briskly and firmly with the situation, dropping Bampfield quietly from employment but confirming Lord Willoughby in his new honour. Thus the first intervention of James in his brother's political affairs had resulted in embarrassment, establishing a pattern which was to last till the end of Charles's reign.[58]

The other problem concerned the seamen themselves. They had just betrayed one master, upon an impulse, and there was an unpleasant possibility that if the royalist cause suffered a reverse, then they would buy back Parliament's favour by delivering either Charles or James to it. Yet for the Prince to refuse to embark with them would be a considerable insult, and deprive him of a very valuable instrument. On the afternoon of

12 July James was sent down to Helvoetsluys to test their mood. The result was encouraging, for he was received with rapturous joy and the crews all agreed to subscribe on oath to restore the king to his full and just rights and to obey Charles and James.[59] Rather than let the ships lie idle in port, it was resolved that Charles himself would lead them against the English coast while awaiting an answer from the Scots. To provide some security for the royalist cause against the threat of his death or capture, his brother was left at The Hague. The Prince of Orange supplied the fleet and it set sail on about 22 July.[60]

If the momentum of his public actions since leaving St Germain suggests that Charles was a high-spirited youth making up for two years of virtual inactivity, his private life may have fallen into the same pattern. It is very likely that during his first brief stay at The Hague the future Charles II lost his virginity, to a young woman calling herself Mrs Barlow and actually named Lucy Walter. Nobody was ever to claim the distinction of having been his mistress before this time, and it is doubtful that under the wardship of his Counsellors in the West Country and in Jersey, and of the Queen at St Germain, anybody could have been. In the West he had responded affectionately to his former nurse and surrogate mother, while in Paris the only female with whom the gossip-hungry court linked his name was the Duchesse de Châtillon. He was to return to wooing her later (as will be shown), but at this stage his attitude was more of an adolescent 'crush' and the sophisticated French read nothing carnal into it.[61] For a while in more recent times it was thought that he had fathered a son while in Jersey, but the letters upon which this claim is based are now generally dismissed as forgeries.[62] It does seem, therefore, as though Charles's sudden accession to political and military power in 1648 was matched by a breakthrough of a more intimate kind.

On the other hand, it must also be said that the early history of his liaison with Lucy is very obscure.[63] It is assumed that it commenced in July 1648 because their son, the future Duke of Monmouth, was said to have been born in April 1649, but then our only source for Monmouth's birthdate is a pamphlet of 1683, which is inaccurate in some other respects.[64] No records dating from 1648–9 mention Lucy's association with Charles and only two accounts survive of how they met, by his brother James and by Hyde, both of whom had sound political reasons for disparaging Lucy in order to discredit her son. The former insisted that she was hired as a mistress by the parliamentarian Algernon Sidney, but instead took up that position with his brother Robert, who was Chamberlain to the Prince's sister Mary. Through Robert, therefore, the couple met and became lovers. Hyde stated briefly that she came to The

Hague when Charles first arrived there, intending to seduce him for her own profit, and that a Groom of his Bedchamber made the introduction. Of Lucy's previous history, it is known definitely that she came from a family of Pembrokeshire gentry, but that not only were they relatively impoverished but her parents had separated with noisy mutual accusations of infidelity. Her custody had been granted to her father, but she preferred to live with her mother in London. There she vanishes from the records, to reappear in Holland as Charles's mistress. She must have been about his age.

All this is slight enough stuff, and James's account of her relationship with Algernon Sidney accords neither with the latter's known movements nor his known character. He certainly had motives for slandering Sidney as well as Lucy. But the rival assertion in the historical debate over this momentous affair, that she secretly married Charles and that Monmouth was therefore legitimate, is not so much dubious as fantastic. Thirty years after his birth, when it was pressingly necessary for Monmouth's adherents to prove the existence of this marriage, all that they could turn up was a set of rumours among obscure people that such a wedding had taken place early in the relationship. They named two different clergymen as the reputed conductors of the ceremony, but neither individual was in Holland at the time. Modern suggestions that Lucy and Charles could have met and married in Pembrokeshire or Exeter during the Civil War founder upon the fact that there is no evidence that she was in either place at the time, while he never visited the former and passed swiftly through the latter in the course of a military emergency. The alternative conclusion open to those who favour the idea of a wedding, that in his hectic ten days in July Charles met a commoner and immediately married her, seems insanity.

Thus it may be concluded that the matter, at bottom, must remain a mystery. On balance, however, likelihood lies with the idea that Lucy Walter was introduced to Charles at The Hague by a courtier in July 1648 and became his mistress after virtually no courtship. This argues for some experience, and design, on her part. To prove otherwise was necessary to some in the seventeenth century to find an alternative heir to the throne. To others in the early twentieth century it seemed distasteful that a person (and particularly a woman) from a disturbed and impecunious background should strive for wealth and status by seducing one who could confer both. Politics and prudery have combined to produce 'defences' of Lucy's reputation. The present age may not find either impulse necessary.

If such an interpretation is correct, then it must have seemed to the Prince of Wales, in these summer weeks, as though fortune was raining blessings upon him. This sensation would have slowly vanished in the course of the next month. The fleet made first for Great Yarmouth, which, if the citizens could be persuaded to declare for the King, could anchor a fresh royalist rising covering East Anglia. On arrival off the port, the Prince and his advisers found many of the inhabitants sympathetic but the whole place held by soldiers. Before leaving Holland they had decided upon a public statement of their aims: to ensure the performance of the Engagement with the Scots; to restore the King to his rights; to maintain the freedom and privileges of Parliament; to abolish the taxes and disband the army associated with the regime at Westminster; and to obtain a general Act of Indemnity. A paper embodying these studiously moderate and popular proposals was now sent to the corporation of Yarmouth, but it dared do no more than deliver provisions.[65] The ships now sailed to the coast of Kent, where they could lie for a while giving support to the royalist garrisons holding Deal and Sandown castles and capturing merchantmen bound for London. Parliament retained control of a squadron in the Thames under its supreme naval commander, the Earl of Warwick, and another at Portsmouth. But neither was strong enough to challenge the Prince's fleet alone, and sailors in both expressed reluctance to fight their former comrades. Batten, who had fomented the original mutiny, defected to the Prince in person with another warship. He was welcomed with a knighthood and the post of Rear-Admiral, to bolster the landlubber Willoughby.[66]

If the royalist fleet was invulnerable, however, it presented the curious spectacle of being simultaneously impotent. It was said that Rupert urged an attempt to rescue the King from his prison in the Isle of Wight, while Batten wished to sail to the Firth of Forth to conclude negotiations with the Scots, the sailors urged an attack upon Warwick in the Thames, and some courtiers advised that the ships relieve Colchester, where a royalist army was under siege.[67] In fact, the King, Warwick, and Colchester were all equally inaccessible as Parliament held forts covering the seaward approaches to all. The Scots could be expected to contact Charles in any case. So, after much debate, the fleet remained off Kent. It captured some ships, but produced in the process the new problem that such depredations would alienate the sympathy of Londoners from the royalist cause. Charles accordingly wrote to the City's corporation and its largest trading company, insisting that his men had only seized shipping to raise money and offering to release every prize for a lump sum of £20,000. As an exercise in public relations it was partly successful: the City fathers petitioned Parliament to commence talks with the King, and although they dared not reply formally to the Prince, they did supply some cash secretly for the restoration of the vessels.[68] It did, however, have the effect of displeasing the seamen, who believed that the money represented a fraction of their prizes' worth. Morale aboard the fleet sank still lower on 10 August, when a party landed to relieve Deal and Sandown Castles was beaten back with heavy losses.[69]

On that day, at least, some diplomatic progress began. It was marked by the arrival of a Scottish nobleman, the Earl of Lauderdale. The terms insisted upon by Queen and Prince for the latter's coming to Scotland had shocked the governing party in that country. Already faced by a powerful minority group which regarded the Engagement as a betrayal of the presbyterian cause, they feared that further concessions would provoke a repudiation of the whole agreement of the sort suffered by Ormonde's treaty in Ireland in 1646. Lauderdale, probably the most forceful and cunning of the 'Engagers', had been particularly upset and volunteered to go in person to the Prince to argue their case. His colleagues had swiftly empowered him to do so.[70]

The Earl accomplished his task with ease, because Charles was so desperate to get to the head of an army that all Lauderdale had to do to secure concessions was to get the youth on his own. The Duke of Hamilton had already led an army into England and was moving south, and there was a danger that he would end the war before the Prince joined him. Thus Charles signed a pledge not to bring with him either Digby or a set of Scottish royalists, and gave a verbal promise not to be accompanied by Rupert or his brother, because the 'Engagers' would not work alongside these old enemies. His Counsellors had equipped him with a set of compromise formulae upon the religious question, but under Lauderdale's direction he crossed them all out and signed an agreement to worship according to the presbyterian rite while with Hamilton's army. Culpeper, Willoughby, Percy, and Wilmot all encouraged this step, but Hopton and others were horrified. It was a surrender which Charles's father would have refused to make even at the price of liberty.[71]

The Prince was now anxious to get back to Holland, where he would take shipping for Scotland and leave his battlefleet to be supplied. There was less and less point in keeping it off Kent: as August wore on Colchester and Deal Castle surrendered and the sailors were running out of food and drink. There was even a rumour that all was not well with Hamilton.[72] On the 26th a council aboard Charles's ship decided to sail for Helvoetsluys. Immediately the sailors' smouldering sense of grievance exploded, in a volley of demands that the Prince should not abandon them for the Scots. There was talk of throwing Lauderdale and Culpeper overboard. To the relief and delight of his Counsellors, Charles rose to the occasion, faced the mutineers boldly and explained the need for provisions. Swayed by him, the seamen hoisted sail and the ships moved north. Off the Thames, however, the sailors of the vessel containing Culpeper and Hopton suddenly began steering for the river. An ugly situation was only averted by the arrival of a ketch carrying the news that the Earl of Warwick was at last coming downstream with his fleet. The royalist sailors demanded to fight it, even on half rations, and there was nothing to be done but to agree. On the 29th they sighted Warwick. For the first time in history, two sections of the Royal Navy were preparing to attack each other.

Aboard the Prince's ship, Sir William Batten paced up and down, sweating with tension. Rupert was 'swearing bloodily' and snarling to Charles that he thought Batten would betray them and that he would shoot Sir William as soon as anything went wrong. As the stomachs of these veterans taughtened, Charles himself, the innocent of war, was literally dancing with joy. When Batten begged him to retire below to relative safety, he refused, waving a pistol and declaring that he would kill Warwick himself. This was the kind of childish bravado which had nearly led to disaster at Edgehill, but here it was precisely in place for the sailors were enraptured. Batten and his officers quietly decided between themselves to carry him down bodily when battle commenced. In fact, Warwick was luring the royalists into a trap. The six parliamentarian ships at Portsmouth had sailed for the Thames, where the Prince and Warwick were now evenly matched, having eleven warships each. The Earl's intention was to keep close to his enemies but to delay battle until the Portsmouth squadron arrived, catching the royalist fleet between two hostile forces, outnumbered and confined in an estuary. Again, fortune saved Charles. After two days of manœuvring, his ships began to run out of victuals completely, and a return to Holland was imperative. It commenced in the nick of time, for on the evening after setting sail the lights of the Portsmouth vessels were sighted. Rupert and some seamen wanted to attack them but Batten decided against this. He was probably correct, for night fighting was virtually beyond the capacity of seventeenth-century navies and Warwick was close behind. However, the royalist fleet reached Helvoetsluys on 4 September with yet another reason for anger and recrimination.[73]

Once there, almost every plan collapsed. First came definite news that Hamilton's army had been utterly destroyed in Lancashire by Parliament's best general, Oliver Cromwell. Lauderdale still urged Charles to come to Scotland, seeking to provide his party with the asset of the Prince's presence. This time most of the Counsellors, and Charles, rejected the invitation as it seemed obvious that Scotland itself was no longer secure.[74] Nor was it. The malcontents who had regarded the Engagement as a betrayal seized power during September with Cromwell's aid.[75] In October they formally notified Charles that the invitation to Scotland to lead an army was withdrawn.[76] On 19 September Warwick arrived off Helvoetsluys with eighteen ships and only the interposition of a Dutch fleet, instructed to maintain the peace of the harbour, prevented him from destroying the royalist vessels. Instead the Earl settled down to wait until the latter set sail, rendering them utterly immobile.[77]

The Prince himself had once more become the guest of the Prince and Princess of Orange, the latter his devoted sibling and the former an impetuous and bellicose man of twenty-two, determined to restore the Stuarts to power.[78] Nor was Charles short of advisers: indeed, these had multiplied with his problems. On his return to The Hague he was greeted by the familiar portly person of Hyde and by his father's Lord Treasurer, old Baron Cottington. The two of them had been captured and robbed on the way to Holland by privateers, and so their reunion with him delayed till this point. The effect of defeat upon Counsellors who already resented each other was to leave them so divided and embittered that they disgusted the agent appointed by the Prince of Orange to deal with them. The worst quarrel was between Rupert and Culpeper, who were only prevented from duelling by an order from Charles. Culpeper then had his nose punched in the street by one of Rupert's friends, whom Charles promptly exiled from court.[79] Shortly after, the Prince himself caught smallpox, and for weeks was too ill to be spoken to.[80]

The behaviour of the royalist sailors was as bad as that of their superiors, and with even more excuse. Frustrated, trapped, and underpaid as they were, it is a tribute to their integrity that only some of them disavowed their new allegiance and defected to Warwick. Willoughby was quite incapable of winning their respect, and they were now so disenchanted with their former hero Batten that he dared not go aboard the ships.[81] Two men very obviously wanted to succeed Willoughby as Vice-Admiral. One was Jermyn, who apparently preferred the prospect of naval warfare to the physical comfort and nervous strain of attending Henrietta Maria: historians have been too prone to dismiss this man as a parasitic courtier. The other was Prince Rupert, who having been Charles I's Captain-General, now wanted the greatest military command remaining open to a royalist.[82] As Rupert was on the spot, he was the only person for the job and entered upon it soon after Warwick appeared. He lacked experience of naval command (no less than Willoughby and Jermyn) and familiarity with the sailors, but compensated for both with sheer determination. First he had the ships' rigging removed to stop deserters from taking any vessels with them, and then he quelled a mutiny by picking up a ringleader bodily and suspending him over the side until he reconsidered his opinions.[83] On 9 November, the Dutch squadron at Helvoetsluys put out to sea, making for winter quarters on the instructions of its government, which feared it would be damaged if it remained at its station longer. Immediately, Warwick pounced upon the royalist ships and received or compelled the surrender of four of them. The remainder were saved by Rupert, who drew them into the inner harbour, raised forts of turves at its mouth, and placed cannon in them. When the Dutch government protested at this action, he replied that he would defend his fleet until the Dutch did so for him. Stalemate was resumed, but the prince was winning the respect of his crews.[84] In this long struggle he had received little help from his royal cousins. Charles was sick, and although he had ordered his brother to join Rupert and encourage the men, James refused to go. Distressed by the removal of Bampfield and the installation of the former governor of Exeter, Berkeley, as his governor, he was sulking at Rotterdam.[85] Most of the administrative support for the fleet was undertaken by Hyde, Hopton, and Culpeper, who laboured to borrow money from the Dutch and from English merchants and used it to provide pay, food, and drink.[86]

On 21 November, shut out of the inner harbour by Rupert and fearing the onset of winter, Warwick's fleet at last sailed for home.[87] The royalist ships could now sally out to capture English merchantmen, and brought in two. The proceeds of these vessels and cargoes were put towards the expenses of fitting out the whole fleet for a major expedition. Even while lying idle for three months, the seamen had got through 311 tuns of beer alone. To lay up victuals and repair the ships on top of meeting the regular bill for maintenance was a burden that the profits of the prizes and further borrowing by Charles's Counsellors could not bear. In the end it was met only by pawning the cannon of one ship and the jewels of Rupert's mother.[88] The privateering raids themselves hastened the need for departure. The Prince of Orange was merely the first citizen of a republic of federated provinces governed by a States-General. The majority of deputies who sat in this shared none of his enthusiasm for the Stuart cause, especially as it seemed increasingly likely to involve them in war with a victorious Parliament. The depredations of Rupert's ships promised to precipitate such a crisis, and Orange warned Charles privately to send them swiftly to sea.[89]

Their destination had seemed obvious since September. Although a few former parliamentarians like Willoughby still urged an alliance with the Scots, most of Charles's advisers told him to send the fleet to assist Ormonde.[90] In Ireland alone the royalist hopes of the spring had not been dashed. Before leaving France, the Prince had gratified Inchiquin by appointing him Lord President of Munster, and empowered Ormonde to make an alliance with the Confederate Catholics. The Lord-Lieutenant was delayed in France till the end of September by lack of money for his voyage and for sweetening Inchiquin's soldiers. But Mazarin, pursuing his policy of keeping the British divided and weak, finally supplied it.[91] When Ormonde returned to his native land, he found that his friends among the Confederate Catholics had overcome those of their colleagues who opposed negotiations and joined forces with Inchiquin. There was now no barrier to an effective military alliance between them and the royalists, and on 17 January 1649 the General Assembly of the Confederacy ratified one.[92] Since November, Ormonde had prepared harbours to receive the fleet, and four days after the ratification Rupert set sail for Ireland with the remaining seven warships. Charles had formally commissioned him Vice-Admiral and given the other commands to royalist officers of long service.[93] On the 22nd Ormonde wrote to Charles inviting him to come in person to lead the newly allied forces.[94]

During the autumn, the Prince had intended to move to Jersey, a convenient point of departure for most destinations and for Ireland in particular. The Prince of Orange, however, prevailed upon him to remain his guest at The Hague. It was James who left instead, in January for St Germain. Henrietta Maria desired to have one son by her and Orange was incapable of supporting them both, although he provided the money for James's journey. Nevertheless, the States-General had to intervene to prevent the lad's creditors from seizing his goods.[95] By now the appalling significance of the events in England had begun to dawn upon the exiled cavaliers. On 28 November, Charles I wrote to his son enclosing copies of all the papers he had exchanged with Parliament's commissioners since September. He apologized for the concessions he had made in them, which had consisted of permitting presbyterian church government in England and surrendering control of military power and political appointments to Parliament—but all only for a limited period. It was a disingenuous letter, clearly composed with the risk of interception and publication in mind, for he recommended to the Prince the way of peace and forgiveness which the King himself had never been inclined to follow.[96] Ironically, neither the apology nor the recommendation were relevant, for in December the parliamentarian army purged Parliament itself of all MPs, the majority, who felt that the royal concessions were acceptable. The remnant empowered a tribunal to try the King for his life. When news of this reached The Hague, it roused the Prince and his Counsellors to a furious diplomatic effort, Charles signing letters to the purged Parliament and its army directing them to desist, and to the heads of western European states begging them to intercede.[97] On 13 January he attended the Dutch States-General with some of his advisers and referred them to the King's resident at The Hague, who made an appeal for aid. The next day, the Dutch agreed to send an extraordinary ambassador to London.[98]

After this, nothing was heard from England until 4 February, when a newspaper arrived, containing the story that Charles I had been beheaded. There are two versions extant of how the information was conveyed to his son, perhaps compatible.[99] In one, he was told in a crowded room. In the other, he was approached by one of his chaplains, Dr Goffe, who after some hesitation addressed him as 'Your Majesty'. Both accounts agree upon Charles's reaction: he burst into tears. Well he might. The whole weight of ideals, loyalties, responsibilities, and dilemmas which had confounded and killed his father had just crashed on to his eighteen-year-old shoulders.

A King in Search of a Realm, 1649–1650

CHARLES I had died for two principles: that of a monarchy ruling with as little control by subjects as possible, and that of an episcopalian Church directed by such a monarchy. Years before his execution, it had become obvious that his political survival would depend upon his willingness to compromise those beliefs, if only temporarily. His offers in November 1648 represented the furthest that he would go in this regard, and their inadequacy, in the prevailing situation, killed him. The second Charles was therefore placed in a most unpleasant dilemma. His achievement of power in any of his titular kingdoms would depend upon an alliance with a party previously opposed to the royalists. Yet to buy this assistance with major ideological concessions would be a betrayal both of his father and of his natural and accustomed supporters. Two ways out of the problem were possible: to obtain allies upon terms which most royalists felt permissible, or to make promises to gain aid and then to betray them when he had achieved power. In the first two years of his reign, the new King was to attempt each solution in turn.

At his accession, Charles II appointed as his Privy Council those members of his father's who were present in Holland: Brentford, Hopton, Hyde, Culpeper, Cottington, and the Lord Keeper, Sir Richard Lane. The only addition he made was his own secretary, Robert Long, who henceforth fulfilled that service for the Council. Most of these men opposed any significant surrender of wartime royalist principles, but Culpeper had expressed support for compromise, and it was generally believed that the King was vulnerable to influence by people at his court, and his mother's, who held no formal conciliar rank.[1] Nor did his advisers find him very malleable: he had a habit of agreeing emphatically with private criticism of individuals, only to honour their persons and views in public.[2] In this situation the major force behind policy-making was the external pressure of events and the options that they presented.

All Charles's Counsellors agreed that his bargaining position would be strengthened if he were afforded aid by a foreign power. In an age when most European states were monarchies, it was a reasonable expectation that the unprecedented act of formal regicide would produce widespread revulsion and general sympathy for the exiled heir. Accordingly, in the first half of 1649 Charles's circle launched a great diplomatic effort. The permanent agents lodged by Charles I in the Dutch republic, the Spanish Netherlands, and France all had their credentials renewed. Missions were sent out to Spain, Portugal, the Italian and German states, the Vatican, Denmark, Sweden, Poland, Courland, and Russia. To staff these the Privy Council itself was stripped of some of its leading figures, Brentford being made ambassador to Sweden, Culpeper to Russia, and Cottington and Hyde to Spain. Of these the most reluctant was Hyde, whose assistance was requested by his friend Cottington and who departed from court with all his old fears of the consequences of absence revived. The most successful was Culpeper, who kissed the hem of the Tsar's robe, presented his requests to a committee of nobles whose titles took two hours to repeat, and was loaned 20,000 roubles in corn and furs. Small but significant achievements were made by Brentford, who obtained a secret supply of arms from the Queen of Sweden, and the envoy to the Portuguese, who offered their harbours to royalist warships. But in general, all that foreign states provided were successive assurances of goodwill. None would recognize the new English Commonwealth, but none were prepared to attack it. This was a poor return for such an expenditure of energy, made with very meagre financial resources. The royalist diplomats were usually forced to support the cost of their own missions on promise of repayment by Charles, which could only be provided for about half the missions. They accordingly subsisted from one expedient to another. Hyde and Cottington got as far as Brussels by borrowing from the Prince of Orange, and then had to negotiate another loan from the Duke of Lorraine to pay their way to Madrid.[3] The cumulative import of this diplomacy was that Charles would depend almost totally upon groups within the British Isles for such support as he could obtain.

It was equally clear that nothing was to be expected from England and Wales, where the King's supporters were thoroughly cowed. The regicide had been followed by the formal abolition of the monarchy and the House of Lords and the decapitation of three royalist nobles. Two of these were Hamilton and Charles's former Counsellor, Lord Capel. The great hope sprang from the treaty signed by Ormonde in Ireland, news of which arrived in March together with his invitation to Charles, carried by a former royalist general, Lord Byron. Charles himself, the majority of his Council and court, and the Queen (now, properly, the Queen Mother) all immediately agreed that the King should accept the invitation.[4] During the next few months, in which he made his preparations to leave, Charles was extremely careful to work with and through Ormonde when dealing with Irish affairs. All commissions that he issued to Irish leaders, and all instructions which he gave agents sent to that realm, were submitted to the Lord-Lieutenant first for his approval. Thus he avoided the complex secret diplomacy with which Charles I had confused Irish affairs.[5] The most delicate and important negotiation concerned the Roman Catholics of Ulster, the most fiercely independent of all the groups contending in the island. They possessed a good army and a formidable leader, Owen Roe O'Neill, who had played a considerable part in the failure of Ormonde's treaty in 1646 and now, in opposition to the majority of Irish Catholics, rejected the new alliance. With Ormonde's consent, Charles sent Owen Roe private promises of the title of earl and the rank of general for himself and of indemnity and liberty of conscience for his people.[6] The latter concessions were two that Charles I had never made in such unequivocal terms and they were successful. Before the end of the year O'Neill and Ormonde were allies. Two factors delayed the King's departure for his westernmost realm: sheer lack of money and a brief negotiation with the Scots.

Since the wars of 1638–40, in which the Covenanter party had destroyed episcopacy and most royal power in Scotland, supreme authority in Scottish secular affairs had rested in a Parliament. It consisted of three estates, the nobles and the representatives of the gentry and of the towns, and elected a Committee of Estates to wield executive authority. This numbered anything from 27 to 140, and continued to sit between parliamentary sessions. Power over religious questions was vested in a General Assembly of ministers and elders elected by the local presbyteries of the Kirk. This in turn elected a Commission of between 73 and 163 ministers and elders to supervise the Kirk's public affairs between assemblies. By early 1649, neither body was more than partially representative of the political nation, for both the royalists of the earlier 1640s and the Engagers of 1648 were excluded from public office. The process had removed most of the noble estate, opening power to men from other ranks of society who would normally never have wielded it. The greatest individual in the land was still the greatest magnate, the red-haired, squint-eyed, long-faced Archibald Campbell, Marquis of Argyll, who to the exiled royalists appeared virtual dictator of the land. This impression was illusory. Argyll had clung to power throughout every change of the decade because he combined a natural aptitude for politics with good fortune. His profound personal piety and conviction of the virtue of the Covenanter cause made him a formidable individual. But his pre-eminence was utterly dependent upon the support of the majority in the current Parliament, the Kirk party which represented the aims of the Covenanting movement in their most uncompromising form. These were embodied in two documents: the National Covenant of 1638 and the Solemn League and Covenant of 1643. The former had demanded the purification of the Kirk, and precipitated the destruction of episcopacy. The latter had been the basis of the Scottish alliance with the English Parliament in the Great Civil War. It provided for the preservation of the Crown but also the reformation of the Church of England (in a manner generally agreed to include removal of bishops) and the punishment of royalists.

On 5 February 1649 the Scottish Parliament declared Charles II the lawful successor to his father. The regicide had offended the two fundamental impulses of the Covenanting movement: the religious, by breaching the Covenant of 1643, and the patriotic, by killing a King of Scots without reference to the views of the Scottish nation. An alliance with Charles also had obvious practical advantages for the Kirk party, for it would give legal confirmation to their regime, which was detested by most of the traditional leaders of the nation. Argyll in particular desired one, from an unquantifiable mixture of concern for his own position, that of his party, and that of his noble estate which had declined so markedly in prestige together with the monarchy. Like Charles, however, they had to beware of making concessions which would betray their own cause. And unlike Charles they were negotiating from a position of relative strength. Hence they qualified their proclamation of him by insisting that before he was admitted to power he must take both Covenants, agree to establish presbyterianism in both his other realms, dismiss the exiled Scottish royalists at his court, and leave behind him any persons to whom the Kirk party might take exception. In mid-March both Parliament and the General Assembly sent commissioners to Charles bearing these terms.[7] Argyll sent an agent ahead to avow his personal loyalty and urge the King to make the alliance.[8]

Both the defeated Scottish parties were represented at The Hague. The two surviving leaders of the Engagers had fled there: William, the new Duke of Hamilton, and Lauderdale. They made a contrast in looks and personality, the former handsome, swarthy, uneasy in debate, and conciliatory by temperament, the latter coarse-featured, red of hair and complexion, swift-tempered, forceful, devoted to the cause of the Covenants, and an unforgiving enemy. Soon after them arrived the greatest of all Scottish royalists, the grey-eyed, chestnut-haired, aquiline-featured James Graham, Marquis of Montrose. In a set of dazzling campaigns in 1644–5 he had recovered Scotland for Charles I, and although subsequently defeated he had only abandoned the country upon that monarch's orders, during the latter's attempt to ally with the Covenanters in 1646. Montrose had a personal weakness, of over-confidence, and a more considerable political one. He had been the most distinguished of the first Covenanters, only to join the King against his former friends. He saw himself as utterly consistent, adhering to the ideal of a strong Crown joined with a presbyterian Kirk. To the Scottish royalists he was a self-seeking adventurer, and few would co-operate with him. To the Covenanters he was a despicable traitor, who had led Catholic and Irish soldiers to plunder Protestant Scottish territory. In 1648, when King and Prince were allying with the Engagers, Montrose was an embarrassment and forced to skulk neglected on the Continent. Now he turned up uninvited at the new King's court to offer his advice.[9]

On 27 March the Scottish commissioners were received and presented their terms. They found Charles as charming and mild-mannered as all who met him, but he and all his advisers considered their proposals unacceptable. Lauderdale and the Prince of Orange (like most of the Dutch, a presbyterian) urged the King to take the Covenants, yet even they disliked the other demands. Nor did King and Council find the Engagers much more appealing. On being begged by Charles and his mother to work with Montrose, they not merely refused but walked out of the royal presence when the Marquis entered it.[10] In these circumstances the King and his confidants were increasingly inclined to favour the great Graham and to accept his proposal that Charles take command in Ireland while Montrose invaded Scotland. At best he might reconquer the country, and at worst he could force the Kirk party into concessions. The Marquis had just, with amazing luck, managed to borrow nearly £10,000 from the Lord Chamberlain of Denmark, who was on a mission to The Hague and (mistakenly) believed that his master sufficiently favoured the royalist cause to approve the loan. This provided the resources for an invasion force.[11] Montrose was becoming extremely convenient to Charles.

Royal policy evolved accordingly. In March Charles had already renewed the Graham's commission as Captain-General and Lieutenant-Governor of Scotland. In April he instructed a German mercenary to raise soldiers for the Marquis and empowered Montrose to treat with foreign princes to obtain materials of war. In late May he formally rejected the terms offered by the Scottish government. Before doing so he took the advice of his Council and of Lauderdale, Hamilton, and Montrose, but it was the last who most influenced the form of the reply which the King made to the commissioners. Its essential point was that Charles would grant the Scots the government they wished but rejected their right to impose any form on other nations. On 29 May he formally notified the

Dutch States-General of his decision and applied to them for money for his journey to Ireland.[12]

Relations between Charles and the Dutch had in fact been deteriorating for months. Despite tremendous pressure by the Prince of Orange, the States-General had recognized him as King of Scots but not as ruler of the English. Its members generally approved of his dealing with the Covenanters but not of his alliance with the Catholic Irish. From March he had made informal requests to them to assist his journey to Ireland, and his public application received an equally negative response. In early May the new English Commonwealth had sent an agent to The Hague, selected because he possessed Dutch citizenship. He was more distinguished, however, for having served as prosecuting attorney in the regicide court, and on arrival he was stabbed to death in his lodgings by a group of Montrose's friends. Charles was careful to avoid giving approval of the outrage, and the States-General as delicately avoided blaming him for it. But it did draw his attention to the frequent brawling of the wilder royalist exiles. The Prince of Orange began to warn his brother-in-law that his departure might be necessary to forestall expulsion.[13] The Prince's now much depleted fortune was employed to pay off Charles's debts and cover his travel expenses,[14] and in late June the King at last set off.

As the Commonwealth's fleets dominated the Channel, it had been resolved that Charles must cross the Spanish Netherlands and France to La Rochelle, and sail from there to Munster.[15] The Spanish government had been making frantic efforts to avoid receiving his ambassadors lest this offend England's new rulers, but when he arrived in Flanders the local authorities behaved gracefully. The corporation of Antwerp entertained him for two days, and at Brussels he was given a royal salute of guns and lodged in the royal palace. The governor of the territory, Archduke Leopold, presented him with a magnificent coach and received him, though nothing resulted from the meeting.[16]

On his arrival in France, he found affairs even less propitious for his cause than before. The struggle with Spain continued, and under its strain the country was sliding fitfully but inevitably into civil war. Despite this, when Charles neared Compiègne he was met by the Queen Regent and young king once more, given royal honours at a feast, and offered St Germain for his residence as long as he wished. For once, his famous courtesy failed him. On his way to the town he chattered in fluent French to the prim Louis about the hunting in Holland, and at dinner he tucked into beef and mutton and ignored the great delicacy on offer, of ortolans. When the Queen Regent tried to question him about his political plans, he immediately pleaded ignorance of her language, and employed the same transparent excuse to avoid conversation with Mademoiselle. Partly because of their own troubles, and partly because of distaste, the French royal family paid him little attention after he left them for St Germain on 12 July. This certainly saved both sides some embarrassment, for Henrietta Maria immediately renewed her campaign to wed him to Mademoiselle. The unwilling couple were forced to suffer each other's company only once more in this year, on Mademoiselle's sole visit to St Germain to pay her respects. Charles made compliments but no suit, and the most encouraging thing that he said was that 'whatever attachment he might have formed as a bachelor would cease' the moment that he got married.[17]

This is one of the few references to Lucy Walter's continuing role as Charles's mistress in 1649. All are retrospective, indicating the remarkable discretion with which the affair was managed. In later years Prince Rupert's sister Sophia remembered how the King strolled with her on the promenade at The Hague and told her that she was prettier than Lucy (though she believed that his purpose was to solicit money from her for a friend). Long after, also, the diarist John Evelyn recalled how he travelled in Lord Wilmot's coach to St Germain with Lucy in August 1649 and found her 'a brown, beautiful, bold but insipid creature' (the insipidity presumably referring to her conversation). Put together, these remarks suggest that she provoked neither great loyalty nor great affection in him. When he left the Continent in 1650 he committed their baby son to Henrietta Maria, who placed him in turn with one of her maids.[18]

As in 1646, Charles found his stay at St Germain longer than anticipated, and this time the reason lay with Ormonde. Even as his monarch entered France, the Lord-Lieutenant heard that the English Commonwealth was sending Cromwell to Ireland with an army. He immediately wrote to Charles advising him to delay his arrival until Dublin had been captured or the power of Cromwell's force assessed. In August the King heard that Ormonde's attack on Dublin had been repulsed, and sent to him stressing his continued desire to join him and asking for full details of the situation. After this nothing more was heard from the Marquis until October.[19]

Enforced idleness, and the union of the King's court with his mother's, could only exacerbate tension among the exiled royalists. Traditionally, they have been divided into three factions: the 'Old Royalists', who included Hyde and Hopton and opposed the concession of principles or the employment of foreign forces to bolster their cause; the 'Louvre group' led by the Queen Mother, Jermyn, and Percy, who urged both these courses; and the 'Swordsmen', friends of Prince Rupert who opposed

whichever of the above two groups appeared to possess more influence.[20]
This picture is fundamentally true, but during this period it requires some
important qualifications. First, the 'Old Royalists' have left most of the
surviving evidence, and the 'Louvre group' may not have been as coherent,
unprincipled, and unscrupulous as it appears in the letters and memoirs
of its enemies. Second, there were cross-currents between the factions.
Berkeley was now a contented member of Henrietta Maria's court but
a personal friend of Hyde and Hopton. Another resident in the 'Louvre'
circle, Christopher, Lord Hatton, detested its leaders and was allied to
Hyde. Long, Charles's secretary who had just been made a Privy Counsellor,
was regarded as a client of Jermyn. Hyde and the Queen Mother disliked
each other, but she sometimes sought his assistance and advice.

Third, the ideological divide at this time really consisted of a difference
in attitude to the Scottish Covenanters and their natural allies in England,
those former parliamentarians who detested independent churches and
republicanism, and were generally known as 'the Presbyterians'. Hyde and
his friends were prepared to negotiate for aid from the Spanish, approved
of Ormonde's concessions to the Irish Catholics, and supported an offer
of relief for English Catholics in exchange for help from the Pope. Hyde
even suggested making an alliance with English radicals too extreme to
be acceptable to the Commonwealth, by promising them reforms which
would never in reality be carried out. What they could not bear was
the prospect of partnership with the very people whom they had fought
through the Great Civil War, based upon the betrayal of the very principles for which they had fought. By contrast, the Queen Mother and her
favourites believed that the Covenanters and 'Presbyterians' would make
the most effective possible allies. The one among them who worked most
powerfully for such an agreement, Percy, was the brother of a leading
'Presbyterian' and had been disgraced by Charles I in 1645 for urging him
to compromise with Parliament. Henrietta Maria, however, certainly never
intended that alliance to be bought with a major surrender of principle.
Thus to describe the 'Old Royalists' as the party of fidelity, rectitude, and
consistency, and the 'Louvre group' as self-seeking adventurers (as is often
done) is to adopt partisan, and ahistorical, terms.[21]

The new King's treatment of this muddle of people and attitudes was
certain to inflame tension: on arrival at St Germain he announced that he
would appoint no more Privy Counsellors and no officers of state until
settled in Ireland. This excluded from formal power those of the dead
monarch's advisers who had not been at The Hague at the time of the regicide. Among those thus left in the cold were the two Secretaries of State
last chosen by Charles I, the mercurial Digby and Sir Edward Nicholas, an

industrious, reliable, and unimaginative man closely allied to Hyde's group. The office of Secretary was potentially vital in exile, as a nerve-centre for conspiracy and diplomacy, and the Queen Mother made efforts to have Digby reappointed while the 'Old Royalists' did the same for Nicholas. When Charles did favour a candidate, his political vision turned out to have barely risen above the nursery, for the man was Edmund Wyndham, who possessed no other qualification than to be married to the King's beloved old nanny. The notion aroused general derision and (according to Hyde) Cottington asked Charles before the court if he would give an old falconer the post of chaplain, by the same logic. Charles and Wyndham were embarrassed, the courtiers delighted, and the project died.[22] The King subsequently told Nicholas to expect the office, but it was Long who continued to draft and receive official correspondence.[23] If Hyde can be trusted, Charles's most influential adviser at this time was one of his Gentlemen of the Bedchamber, Tom Elliot, of whom nothing is known but that he was young, ambitious, and Wyndham's son-in-law. He was correspondingly unpopular, and within a few months the King seems to have understood this too, for Elliot was sent on a mission to Portugal.[24]

In late September, Charles moved to Jersey as he had planned to do a year before. The approach of winter made an attack by Parliament upon the island unlikely and Carteret had proclaimed Charles as King there without qualifications. It was an obvious haven in which to review options. Even so, the Prince of Orange had to provide the frigates to transfer the exiled court from the mainland, and Charles only just evaded capture by an English fleet during the crossing. The islanders gave him a rapturous welcome, and for a while he was able to enjoy the life of a magnate upon his country estates, going shooting daily with his dogs and staying in the homes of gentry. The latter found him a tall, graceful figure, still clad in purple mourning, with exquisite manners and a sedate expression. They had more to thank him for than his courtesies, because he increased their right to customary rents, thus (in the manner of baroque kingship) identifying his cause with their economic interests. His sojourn was nevertheless a rather uncomfortable holiday. For one thing, his hunting expeditions were ended after a couple of months by rumours of republican sympathies among some islanders, which caused him to ride abroad rarely, and with guards.[25] For another, he was desperately short of money. The Jersey Parliament voted him £633, but he was soon having to sell Crown land in the island, to write begging letters to royalists in England, to dismiss some household servants, and to retain the loyalities of others only by giving them written promises of posts as soon as he had means to support them.

After four months he had no riding clothes fit to appear in before a foreign court.[26]

Nevertheless, even with such limited resources, Charles proceeded to distribute patronage in the manner expected of a king. He had made Jermyn Governor of Jersey, with Carteret as his Lieutenant, in effective control. Now he gave Percy the government of Guernsey, where the royalists held one castle, thus gratifying both the Queen Mother's principal favourites. He created three new Knights of the Garter: Ormonde, Rupert's brother Edward, and George Villiers, Duke of Buckingham. Only the first of these was for political services, Prince Edward being of the blood royal and Buckingham the greatest non-royal peer of the realm. He and his brother had been accorded the unusual honour of being reared in the royal nursery at Richmond, alongside Charles and his siblings, had appeared at St Germain in 1647, and had fought in the royalist risings of 1648, when his brother was killed. His destiny was to be twined with that of his royal playmate, but there is no evidence from these early years of any great attachment between them. Nor did anybody in the 1640s have any presage of the political, literary, and erotic achievements which were to give Buckingham fame. All observers saw was a perfect young aristocrat, tall, handsome, and dressed exquisitely in black mourning for Charles I.[27] To Hopton, Jermyn, Culpeper, Berkeley, Carteret, and others Charles signed away land in the North American colonies, which were at this date still firmly loyal to the monarchy.[28] All these were rather hollow rewards, but they must have done something to mollify followers irritated by his freezing of political posts. No evidence survives upon whose advice, if anybody's, he made them.

Until the end of the year Charles remained eager to get to Ireland, but with each month the royalist cause there declined. Cromwell, with an army more cohesive, better paid, and with better artillery than anything the Irish could muster, conquered most of Leinster. The seaports of Munster declared for the Commonwealth, and Rupert's fleet was forced to flee to the Mediterranean and subsist by privateering. Just after O'Neill allied himself with the royalists he died, leaving no capable successor. In October Charles sent Henry Seymour, one of his Grooms of the Bedchamber, to assess the situation. In December this man reported that it was hopeless. Ormonde himself wrote that the loss of the entire kingdom could only be prevented if a diversion were created in Great Britain.[29] Charles had sent agents and commissions from Jersey to royalists in North Wales and the West Country, to provide bridgeheads for an invasion from Ireland. In the West an organization of conspirators had been formed, but was incapable of rising without external aid.[30] By the end of 1649 it was obvious, as Ormonde himself told Nicholas,[31] that this could only come from Scotland.

Even while journeying towards Ireland and sponsoring Montrose, Charles had never entirely severed relations with the Covenanters. After the failure of the talks at The Hague he had sent private letters to Argyll and other Scottish leaders, probably expressing a willingness to accept less rigorous terms from them. In early August Argyll suddenly proposed to the Scottish Parliament that a fresh approach be made to the King, choosing a moment when some of the most obdurate Covenanters were absent. His ploy was partially successful, in that it was agreed to send an address, but offering only the terms Charles had rejected at The Hague. To deliver them it chose a noted lawyer, George Wynrame of Libberton. So little did any Scots expect a favourable response that Wynrame was only accredited in September, set out only in October, and arrived in Jersey only on 6 December. With him came representatives of the English 'Presbyterians', to assure Charles that if he joined the Covenanters then they themselves would rise for him in great force.[32] Charles's freezing of appointments had now made the Privy Council unworkable, because as Hyde, Culpeper, and Cottington were absent on their missions and Brentford had retired to Holland to rest, only Hopton and Long were available. To obtain a proper debate of policy, the King had to call Nicholas to the Council at last and enlarge it informally by inviting Wentworth, Wilmot, Percy, Byron, and other royalist lords to be present. An acrimonious discussion ensued for weeks, which Charles chaired with notable patience and where Wynrame argued the Covenanters' case with all his professional skill. What tipped the balance was Seymour's report on Ireland. In January the Council voted unanimously to invite the Covenanters to negotiate at Breda, a Dutch town dominated by the Prince of Orange, on 15 March.[33]

Charles's strategy henceforth was to persuade the Covenanters to support him in return for less extensive concessions. He wrote to Argyll and to the English 'Presbyterians', asking them to employ their influence to this end. He asked Hamilton to attend the talks and to reason with the delegates, and made him a Knight of the Garter. Montrose was still in Scandinavia, preparing his invasion force with the aid of the Danish money and Swedish arms obtained in the summer. The King instructed him to proceed exactly as planned, to weaken the Covenanters' bargaining position, and bestowed the Garter upon him also. To prepare a bridgehead for a Scottish invasion of England, the same honour was given to the two greatest royalist nobles of the North, the old royal tutor, Newcastle, and James Stanley, Earl of Derby, who was still holding the Isle of Man. With it came directions to command risings in the region.[34] Within twenty months three out of the four new Knights would be dead, together with about 10,000 Scots and English, because of the events thus set in train.

The Kirk party was determined not to co-operate with Charles's strategy. The Committee of Estates divided over whether to treat with him at all, and although Argyll and the majority decided for this, its opponents included some formidable figures. One was John Kennedy, Earl of Cassilis, another Sir Archibald Johnston of Wariston, who from the beginning had embodied the most inspiring and disturbing aspects of his cause. He coupled the brain of a brilliant and unscrupulous lawyer with the emotions of a man who conversed daily with God and then followed His instructions, without fear or mercy. The commissioners sent by the Scottish Parliament to Breda were divided equally between men opposed to any compromise, such as Cassilis, and those who were prepared for one, such as Wynrame. The Kirk's representatives were almost all noted for their rigid beliefs. The terms which these men carried were no gentler than before: Charles was required to recall Montrose, confirm all the acts of Scottish Parliaments since 1641 (including those against royalists and Engagers), sign the Covenants and declare that they applied to all his kingdoms, leave behind him all persons whom the Kirk party distrusted, disown Ormonde's treaty with the Irish Confederacy, and agree to persecute Catholics in all three realms.[35]

The King and his court left Jersey on 13 February, spent three weeks in discussions with the Queen Mother at Beauvais and arrived at Breda on 16 March together with the commissioners.[36] Throughout the ensuing talks Charles made his preference for episcopacy clear, danced all night to the disgust of the Scottish ministers, and continued to use the Anglican rite. But his conviction of the need for a treaty was shown by his attitude to his advisers: he rapidly disregarded Hopton and Nicholas, who opposed any concessions, and showed favour to those who urged them. He appointed three, Hamilton, Buckingham, and Newcastle, to the Privy Council, and listened to others, such as Lauderdale, with respect. He also behaved with formal courtesy towards the commissioners as a group and turned his now practised charm upon them as individuals. Wynrame was led by this to conclude that such a pleasant young man would be convinced of the merits of the Covenanting cause if only he could be removed from the malign influence of his advisers by being brought to Scotland. The way was thus paved towards an agreement based upon false expectations and mutual bad faith. On 17 April Charles agreed to declare his approval of the Covenants and to observe them when he came to the Scots; to confirm the Acts of Parliament; to execute existing laws against Catholics; and to recognize the supreme authority of Kirk and Parliament in their respective spheres. He also signed a separate promise to annul Ormonde's treaty in Scotland if its Parliament insisted, and gave this into the secret custody of Cassilis. In return, the commissioners of the Scottish Parliament promised him full sovereign powers once in their country, permission for the Engagers to reside there (though not to wield power), and consideration by Parliament of his wish to have royalists re-employed by the government. The rules of the commissioners stated that their decisions were determined by vote, and that their president only voted if the result was a tie. As the president was Cassilis, this procedure gave the 'moderates' an advantage, and on 29 April Parliament's commission declared that Charles's concessions were adequate and formally invited him to Scotland.[37]

The 'Old Royalists', Nicholas, Hopton, Hyde, and Cottington were all horrified by the treaty, but so were Rupert's friends and Henrietta Maria. So, indeed, were the commissioners of the Kirk, who observed that it fell far short of what the Scottish parliament had required.[38] The King himself saw it as a temporary and distasteful measure necessary to secure himself an army for the invasion of England. He immediately dispatched messengers to warn the English royalists and 'Presbyterians' to be ready to rise when this occurred. He promised Catholics in England 'liberty of conscience' in return for assistance to this rebellion, flatly contradicting the agreement just made. To Ormonde he sent an invitation to continue his alliance with the Catholics and to send representatives to the Scottish Parliament to argue its merits.[39] He also told the Scottish royalists that he would work hard to improve their position.

His toughest problem was Montrose. The Marquis had gathered a few hundred mercenaries in the Orkneys in the winter, and during the course of the Breda talks a rumour arrived that he had landed this force on the Scottish mainland. On 3 May Charles instructed a trusted Scottish agent, Sir William Fleming, to tell Montrose to disband his men and leave the country, in accordance with the new treaty. He was to be informed that he had invaded too late and with too small a force to afford the assistance which the King had expected of him, but would nevertheless be given a pension and re-employed as soon as possible. To the Scottish Parliament, Fleming was to deliver a request, dated upon the 8th, for co-operation with Montrose's withdrawal, and a copy of a formal order to the Graham to lay down arms. On the 9th Charles changed his mind and told Sir William that the Marquis must keep his force in arms if it had grown powerful, or if the Scottish Parliament rejected the treaty. On the 12th he reverted to the decision that Montrose had to disband even if he were a power in Scotland.[40]

In fact, everybody had overestimated Montrose. The Marquis had indeed landed on the Scottish mainland in early April. Three weeks later, he allowed his small army to be surprised and destroyed by an even smaller body of Covenanters. He was captured, brought to Edinburgh, and hanged on 21 May, in great haste to permit Charles no opportunity to intervene upon his behalf. For three hours his richly dressed corpse swung from a gibbet thirty feet high. Then he was cut down, his head removed and stuck upon the Tolbooth and his limbs hacked off for display in four major Scottish cities.[41] The news reached Charles within ten days, and shocked him. He wrote a letter of condolence to the dead man's heir, promising him favour for his father's sake.[42] Politically, Montrose's failure was a blow to the King, for it increased the confidence of the Kirk party, and its bitterness against royalists. Personally, it probably made little impact upon him. The great Graham had never been an intimate of his, but represented instead a momentarily impressive and persuasive servant who had not made good his promises. On being brought before Parliament he had not hesitated to defend himself by quoting Charles's express command to invade Scotland,[43] which, however true, was bound to increase distrust between King and Covenanters at this vital time. Far from assisting his new monarch's cause, he had left it worse off than before. His dreadful end provokes pity in the historian as it did in Charles, but Montrose assuredly brought it on himself.

A more serious blow was now to descend on the King. On the day upon which Montrose was brought to Edinburgh, the Scottish Parliament considered and rejected the Treaty of Breda, and issued instructions to its commissioners to insist upon the terms with which they had originally been equipped. The Commission of the Kirk vehemently agreed with this reaction.[44] At Breda the representatives of both bodies were growing increasingly uncomfortable. Those of the Kirk asked Charles to sign the Covenants and to abandon the Anglican rite at Whitsun, and were ignored. Those of Parliament reminded him that he was expected to leave behind all persons against whom their masters might take exception.[45] Instead, he was preparing to take to Scotland every follower who accepted the necessity of the treaty, including Hamilton, Lauderdale, Buckingham, Brentford, Wentworth, Long, and several other noted English and Scottish royalists. They all moved north through Holland to Terhey, where the invaluable Prince of Orange had prepared three warships to transport them to Scotland. There on 2 June, as embarkation was in progress, the commissioners received their new instructions. The 'moderates' among them persuaded the rest to conceal these until the King was under sail, making his refusal of the full terms much more difficult. As the little fleet anchored off Heligoland to await a favourable wind, Charles had the fresh demands sprung upon him. His fury was patent to all, but after ten days of argument and some time alone with the eloquent Wynrame, he agreed to sign the Covenants and to disavow Ormonde's treaty, though he still insisted upon informing Ormonde before he did so. The arguments employed to achieve this end were never recorded, but it is plain that having come this far, the King could not turn back without suffering intense humiliation.

On Midsummer's Eve, 23 June, the ships anchored off Garmouth in the Moray Firth. With the Scottish coast visible the King could not postpone signature of the Covenants any further, and proposed to do so with a qualification that the laws of England took precedence over them. The commissioners not merely rejected this but added a paragraph to the Solemn League and Covenant pledging the monarch to assent to future Acts of Parliament embodying the ideals of the text. Charles's anger was even more intense but equally unavailing, and he eventually signed. The commissioners of Parliament were now able to send an express to that body, informing it joyously that it had a Covenanted King. Those of the Kirk sent to their parent Commission that Charles had granted all its desires 'in the outward part', save that he brought bad companions.[46]

The words 'outward part' contained the essence of the tragedy. What the Kirk party had wanted was that their King would undergo a conversion to their cause, recognizing its godliness. At Breda, and during the voyage, one of the Kirk's delegates had repeatedly urged Charles not to sign the Covenants unless he genuinely believed in their contents.[47] Charles had never dissembled any such belief and indeed had repeatedly refused subscription, as a betrayal of his true cause. The commissioners of the Scottish Parliament had effectively tricked him into agreeing to it, by accidents of circumstance rather than design. Therein lay the hollowness of their achievement, and the canker at the heart of the new alliance: it had been based upon a gigantic lie which neither party had intended to produce.

The King of Scots, 1650–1651

I N the fortnight after his landing, as he progressed south slowly to Falkland Place, Charles knew briefly and wonderfully what it was like to rule a nation. On receipt of the news that a Covenanted King was on their soil, Parliament and the Commission of the Kirk sent deputations to congratulate and welcome him. They commenced preparations for his coronation, voted him funds, and ordered the raising of horse guards for him. The people of Edinburgh rang bells and lit bonfires, and the women selling cabbages in its markets sacrificed the stools upon which they sat to feed these blazes. The local nobility attended him through Angus and Fife. At Kinnaird House the old Earl of Southesk made him drink a gobletful of wine with one leg crocked over a door-bolt, according to local custom. Ministers, schoolmasters, and city fathers made speeches in his honour, and at Dundee he was presented with the keys of the town, modelled in silver. If he felt any qualms upon being lodged at Aberdeen opposite the gate upon which one of the Montrose's arms was fixed, these are not recorded. His landing itself provided another illustration of his constant personal luck, for it was discovered that he had arrived off Garmouth just after an English fleet, hunting the Moray Firth for him, had sailed away.[1] His determination to forget the humiliation of the voyage and to employ the strength of Scotland for his own purposes is revealed in his first political action ashore. This was to send an agent to Argyll, to promise him reward if he worked to increase royal power and obtained permission for all the followers who had sailed with the King to remain at court.[2]

Inevitably, so unsuitable an alliance had to turn sour, and the joy of the Kirk party was qualified almost from the beginning by news of the reluctance with which the King had signed the Covenants and of his train of political undesirables. The leaders of the Kirk itself agreed to prevent publication of the former information in order to give their monarch a chance to prove himself. But the suspicion now aroused amongst them was not so easily suppressed. Parliament and the General Assembly of the Kirk reacted to his followers immediately by banishing virtually all of them, despite the fact that Argyll spoke on their behalf as Charles wished. A

week later, after Wynrame had applied his arts, Parliament relented only
very slightly, allowing Buckingham (who had been too young to fight in
the Great Civil War) to remain at court and Wilmot and Long (who had
especially favoured the alliance) to stay in Scotland.[3] On receiving these
votes, Hamilton, Brentford, and Lauderdale retired to their homes but
did not leave the country, while all the others stubbornly accompanied
the King to Falkland. From there Charles himself argued their case.
To the General Assembly he merely expressed regret while promising
eventual compliance with the votes. His reply to Parliament was clearly
more spirited. John Campbell, Earl of Loudoun, the Lord Chancellor and
a friend of Argyll, carefully amended it before delivery to the Committee
of Estates (Parliament having gone into recess), to avoid provoking anger.
A month after his arrival, most of Charles's royalist companions were still
with him.[4] What was at stake was not merely that the new King of the
Chosen People was surrounded by companions from his ungodly past. It
was also that the members of the King's court and Household controlled,
by their position, the flow of advice to him and favour from him for all
except the most powerful. One detailed example of this survives from
the period: the experience of Anne Murray, a young gentlewoman who
had assisted Bampfield in the escape of the Duke of York. In mid-1650
she came to Scotland on family business and desired an audience with
Charles. She got into his presence with the aid of family friends, assisted
by the Groom of the Bedchamber who had been sent to Ormonde, Henry
Seymour. But she received no more than a smile from the King, and a
word with a Gentleman of the Bedchamber, another English royalist,
was needed to secure a proper conversation, where Charles thanked her
graciously for her services. Shortly after, Seymour obtained her a royal gift
of fifty gold pieces.[5]

   The Scottish leaders had currently far more than Charles's Household to
worry about. Their alliance with him to fulfil the Covenant was effectively
a declaration of war upon the English Commonwealth. Ironically, it is
doubtful whether the Kirk party saw it in this way. As said, Charles's
principal motive in dealing with them was to invade England, but they
most wanted to use the King's authority to consolidate their power in
Scotland. On his journey to Falkland one of the commissioners of the
Kirk asked him to declare that he was content to await a call from the
English people. Charles replied angrily that he had a duty to avenge his
father.[6] The English government took his view of the situation and decided
to forestall invasion with a pre-emptive strike. As Charles moved north
from Breda, Oliver Cromwell was recalled from Ireland, and as he arrived
in Scotland the great General reached the border with over 16,000 men.[7]

As he did so, the Scottish Parliament rushed through acts to levy over 10,000 immediately and a further 16,000 to reinforce them. Despite the obvious necessity of the measure, some of the most extreme Covenanters still voted against it, having never supported the policy of allying with the son of their principal former enemy, to fight old friends who had placed them in power.[8]

The coming struggle was forbidding in practical as well as moral terms. The Scottish Covenanters were terrible enemies. In England they had almost certainly prevented a royalist victory in the Great Civil War, in Ireland they had massacred the inhabitants of captured towns, and in their own land they had executed prisoners *en masse* after battles. Yet Cromwell's army was liable to be of better quality than theirs. Most of his units had been in existence for years, while most of theirs were newly formed, and though men in them may have had experience of war, it would have been discontinuous. Although the supreme military command in Scotland was vested in the Earl of Leven, who had been the Covenanters' leading soldier from the beginning, he was now too old to take the field. Effective control of the army devolved upon his Lieutenant-General and younger brother, David Leslie, a capable officer who had fought alongside Cromwell against Prince Rupert in the Great Civil War. Leslie accordingly had no illusions about the prowess of Oliver and his men, and adapted his tactics accordingly. Across the approaches to Edinburgh he dug formidable fortifications and concentrated his swelling army to hold these. Behind them he withdrew all the field troops and all the available food supplies from south-eastern Scotland and garrisoned its castles. He thus intended to halt the English before an impassable barrier, in a desert full of hostile fortresses, until they had no option other than retreat. These preparations were barely complete when, on 22 July, Cromwell commenced his march on Edinburgh. A week later his army faced Leslie's, now 17,000 strong, across the Scottish trenches.[9]

By then Leslie's soldiers had become counters in the increasingly tense exchanges between Charles and the leaders of the Kirk party. The King had, after all, come to Scotland to get control of an army, and on landing he had assured Leslie of his favour and of his intention to join the troops in person.[10] On arrival at Falkland he sent Argyll to the Committee of Estates, which was itself now with the army, to repeat this desire. It was precisely what Leslie and the Committee did not want, until Charles had proved his devotion to the Covenanting cause and could be trusted to employ military power for this end alone. The Committee accordingly politely informed him on 17 July that he should postpone his arrival at the camp until they believed the moment correct. Nor, until Argyll intervened, did they make any effort to raise the horse guards promised to their monarch.[11] Charles was further angered when, on 27 July, a declaration was issued in his name offering the English the terms which their Parliament had offered Charles I, and which had been rejected, in 1646–7. It was stipulated that these would be amended by a free English Parliament, so this was not a very restrictive promise, but it had been published without the King's orders.[12]

For his part, Charles persisted in interfering in military affairs even while he failed to dismiss his royalist courtiers. He relayed advice to the Committee on how to conduct the war, and in blatant disregard of its wishes he joined the army uninvited just as Cromwell appeared before Edinburgh. It had been entirely natural for the Committee to try to keep him in political quarantine in Fife until he had proved the sincerity of his 'conversion', preached at by a team of four ministers to assist the process. It was equally natural for Charles to resent the fact that the regal powers he had been promised were still withheld, and to find that constant sermons, even relieved by hawking expeditions, made idleness less endurable. What the more rigid Covenanters found particularly disturbing was that the King had been encouraged to arrive at the camp by the Earl of Eglinton, a reliable Kirk party noble whom the Committee had made commander of the royal guards. The party was already showing signs of fissuring.

The result was unfortunate for everybody. Charles was cheered lustily by the common soldiers, another illustration of the instinctive attachment of the Scots to monarchy. Numbers of Engagers and royalists hastened to the camp to salute him. He was able to watch as, during the next three days, Cromwell probed Leslie's defences without success and retired to receive seaborne supplies. But then he received a blunt request from the Committee of Estates to depart, backed by the threat that the Kirk would abandon him if he did not. Most of the Committee felt, correctly, that he was trying to wrest control of the army from them. The more pious, such as the terrible Johnston of Wariston, believed that the soldiers were according a living being the honour due only to their God, and inviting divine retribution. With bad grace, Charles departed for Dunfermline.[13]

The General Assembly of the Kirk, like Parliament, had gone into recess, leaving the usual commission of ministers and elders to supervise its affairs. The reluctance of the King to purge his Household, his defiant arrival at the camp and the scenes that had resulted, combined to provoke this body to fury. On 5 August it demanded the removal of all suspect persons from the court and army, called upon the Committee of Estates and the generals to admit their negligence in this work, and offered a new declaration to the King. It was designed to test his commitment to their cause to the limit, for he was expected to attest his devotion to the Covenants; his grief at his father's misdemeanours, his mother's idolatry and his own previous errors; his readiness to grant the English the terms Charles I had rejected in 1646 plus a pardon for all but leading royalists'; and his rejection of Ormonde's treaty with the Irish. The Committee of Estates, embarrassed by the attack upon itself, decided that the Kirk party had to close ranks and informed Charles that it endorsed the Commission's demands, save that the declaration would not be published.

The concessions now required of the King represented the loss of the last vestiges of the compromise he had tried so desperately to win from the Covenanters. At first he refused to make them. Argyll, foreseeing disaster, begged him to change his mind on the grounds that once Cromwell was defeated and England conquered, the King would be able to renegotiate the terms of settlement. Charles then agreed to everything except the condemnation of his parents. This reply divided the army officers, the Committee of Estates, and the Commission of the Kirk. With difficulty, Johnston persuaded both Commission and Committee to insist that the King subscribe the whole document, and to refuse to support him any further if he did not. All that Charles had laboured, and suffered, for appeared in danger of being lost. On Argyll's advice, he softened the declaration slightly by testifying to his respect for his parents, and then signed it. He retired immediately to Perth, even further from the army, and permitted the removal from his court of the men banished by the Scottish Parliament. So the crisis passed, the war continued, and the Kirk party was reunited. Upon the insistence of the Commission, the declaration was published and proclamation made of a day of national repentance for the King's sins and Scotland's.[14]

Charles was now reduced to an extremity of humiliation and wretchedness. On 3 September he wrote to Nicholas in Holland,[15] asking for the Prince of Orange to send a boat to lie off the nearest coast. It seems that he was considering giving up the whole venture and fleeing to the Continent. In this smuggled letter he railed against the 'villany' of the Kirk party and commented that it had been of benefit 'for nothing could have confirmed me more to the Church of England than their hypocrisy'. But hypocrites were precisely what the leaders of that party were not. Men like Johnston and the more rigid of the ministers genuinely believed that to deviate from the letter of the Covenants was to damn their own souls and to expose their nation to the wrath of an insulted deity. Their tragedy was that the Covenants contradicted themselves, prescribing loyalty to a monarchy which rejected the other ideals of the texts. Had Charles been made in their mould he would have refused absolutely the tests they set him, and remained to them a King only in name, exiled and unfit to be welcomed to Scotland. Had he been an utter opportunist he would have feigned enthusiasm for the Covenants and been admitted easily to power. Instead, he had signed every document required while making it plain that he detested the contents. The resulting situation was a mockery of both the royalist and Covenanting causes, and the misery of the King was reflected by the torture in the hearts of his new allies.

Prophecy was clearly not numbered among Charles's gifts, for on the very day upon which he penned these bitter words an event occurred which was to change everything. Leslie's tactics had succeeded remarkably. Throughout August Cromwell had tried in vain to break through the Scottish defences, testing them at every point and then trying to outflank them. Each time Leslie's troops had shadowed his, placed so that the ground favoured the defence, and the English had run out of provisions and retired to the coast to collect some. Hunger, exposure, and fatigue spread illness among Cromwell's men, so that by the end of the month they were reduced to 11,000. In the same period the Scottish army had swelled to 23,000. Following the complaints of the Commission some 3,000 men, including 80 officers, had been purged from it as politically suspect, but the arrival of fresh recruits had more than compensated for the loss in numbers.[16] At the opening of September, urged on by the Committee of Estates, Leslie judged that the time had come for battle. Cromwell had retreated to Dunbar to pick up more supplies, and thither the Scottish army advanced, and trapped him. Leslie was now in the position of a person holding a poisonous snake by the neck, who must alter the grip for one perilous moment to deal a lethal blow. On the 2nd the Scots left the high ground and camped before the enemy positions, to launch their attack the next day. Instead it was Cromwell who struck, at sunrise, catching the Covenanter army by surprise in difficult terrain and rolling it up from one end. It was destroyed, losing 14,000 killed and captured and all its artillery. Among those mortally wounded was Wynrame of Libberton, whose supple talents had done so much to bring about this war.[17]

Four days later Cromwell marched into Edinburgh, and two weeks after his army faced Stirling. Here he was halted by Leslie, who had concentrated his remaining men there behind new trenches, covered by the guns of the castle. Cautious as ever, Oliver retired to the capital, to commence the reduction of the south-eastern castles.[18] The Scots were thus left in peace awhile to rebuild their forces, but this work required policies as well as materials. Charles was swift to propose one. His personal reaction to the news of Dunbar is not recorded: it could not have been wholly pleasurable, as the defeat removed any prospect of his restoration in England in the near future. On the other hand, he clearly believed that the blow to the confidence of the Kirk party might permit the realization of that aim of reuniting all factions beneath his rule with which he had come to Scotland. He wrote to the Commission of the Kirk, the local synod of the Kirk (in Fife), and the Committee of Estates, inviting them to involve him in military decisions and proposing that an army be reformed by employing Engagers who confessed their fault.[19] This was one obvious course to take, as a force the size and quality of that destroyed at Dunbar could not be replaced from the Kirk party's followers alone: the loss of experienced soldiers had been too great. Indeed, historians have agreed that the defeat was due at least in part to the policy of purging, which removed too many good officers. Argyll himself may have endorsed this notion, for he carried the King's letter to the Committee.

A different view was taken by Johnston of Wariston and a group of young ministers and army colonels who had grown up during the Covenanting wars and imbibed to an extreme degree the beliefs that had inspired them. In the Kirk these men were led by James Guthrie, Minister at Stirling, and Patrick Gillespie of Glasgow. In the army their chief figures were Gilbert Ker and Archibald Strachan. To them, defeat could only be a sign of divine anger, and as the Covenanting cause had hitherto been victorious, Dunbar could only be a judgement upon its alliance with an ungodly King. Immediately after the disaster the Guthrie–Gillespie group drafted a declaration of a national fast, setting forth this reasoning and calling for repentance. To such people, salvation lay in a small but godly army and utter lack of compromise with royalists, Engagers, or Charles. Strachan, a brewer's son, had overcome Montrose with a few horse troops, and it was this model of the righteous few pitted against the godless multitude which he and his friends sought.

Faced with these conflicting proposals, the leaders of the Kirk party, now gathered at Stirling, strove desperately for unity. The synod of Fife and some of the Commission and Committee felt that the employment of Engagers would be sensible, but, rather than alienate the Guthrie–Gillespie group, the Commission resolved that such a step was untimely and published the declaration of a fast which that group had proposed. The Commission instructed Charles himself to repent his sins anew and replace every member of his Household with Covenanters of impeccable record. Spurred on by the ministers' invectives, the Committee ordered the banishment of his remaining royalist courtiers.[20] Johnston, Ker, and Strachan opposed not merely the admission of Engagers to the army but the continuation of Leslie as its commander, though he was popular with the soldiers and had been officially exonerated from blame after Dunbar. The problem was resolved by Gillespie, who brought to Stirling a proposal for a separate new army based upon Clydesdale, where the extreme Covenanters had always been most numerous, and commanded by Ker. The Committee rushed through an act empowering this Western Association, and Ker and Strachan departed to it. The enhanced role that Charles had requested in military planning turned out to consist mostly of signing commissions for this new force and orders for levies to fill up Leslie's army. When a deputation came from the Committee to inform him of developments, he was treated to another harangue from Johnston upon the evil deeds of his family.[21]

In attempting to preserve its own unity, the Kirk party almost lost the King. Its suspicion of his royalist courtiers had been correct, although, as in the case of its suspicion of Charles himself, this served in itself to drive them into hostility. The physician whom the King had brought with him was a Scot, Fraser. In the course of September this man began to suggest to his royal master that the Kirk party was now so weak and so lukewarm in its attachment to the King that the time had come to abandon it. The obvious alternative allies were the Engagers and royalists, with whom Fraser was in secret contact. Charles was by now growing desperate. On 24 September he gave Argyll a written promise to make him a duke, a Knight of the Garter, and a Gentleman of the Bedchamber whenever that man chose.[22] Such a mountain of honour has usually been taken by historians as a demonstration of the great Campbell's power over the King, exacted from him to satisfy Argyll's ambitions. It is more likely that the promise was made by Charles of his own volition, to encourage the Marquis to plead his case. Argyll's wretched lot, ever since his King had arrived, had been to plod between monarch and Committee, carrying Charles's requests and then the Committee's refusals and directions. On this occasion the pattern was sustained: the King's frenzied appeals to keep his followers met with an outright negative. At this, Fraser's plan was adopted. Charles had made direct contact with Hamilton and other leading Engagers, but his main hopes lay with a group in the hinterland of Aberdeen, a region accessible from Perth and always notably royalist. It was led by a former Engager general, John Middleton, and the greatest Scottish royalist magnate, Lewis Gordon, Marquis of Huntly. By the end of the month Charles had arranged with these men that he would ride to join them on 3 October, while they rose in this support, his guards mutinied and a party of Highlanders seized Perth. It was a dangerous enough plan from the beginning: the King turned it into a fiasco.

On the evening of the 2nd, he allowed himself to be talked out of the project by Wilmot and Buckingham, who convinced him that it could only be destructive. Fraser and others were sent to tell the north-eastern nobles to cancel the rising. The next day Charles received the refusal of the Committee of Estates to reprieve any of the courtiers it had exiled, and flew into rage and panic. He dispatched orders to the royalists to resurrect the plan immediately, and rode for the appointed rendezvous in the Glen of Clova with Seymour and his three Grooms of the Stable. There he found, not the expected thousands, but seventy clansmen, for he had moved faster than his messengers and the chiefs were not ready. The Committee of Estates, however, was. It is impossible to say who betrayed the plan to it, for Charles had discussed his intentions so freely with his court that far too many people knew. As soon as word reached Stirling of his flight, the Committee sent after him Robert Montgomery, second son to the Earl of Eglinton and an excellent cavalry commander, with 6,000 horse and a gently worded invitation to him to return. Montgomery reached Clova on the 4th, just as dawn was touching the great dun mountains. He found Charles lying on an old mattress, still in his thin riding suit, inside a stinking cabin, exhausted and terrified. The King yielded to the young officer's promises of safety and honour (and the silent argument of the waiting horsemen) and returned to meet the Committee at Perth. His reception was less unpleasant than he must have feared, for the leaders of the Kirk party realized that by driving him to desperation they had almost lost their principal claim to be the legitimate government of Scotland. Clearly a bargain was struck, for from then on Charles attended every meeting of the Committee—or rather it attended him, in his Privy Chamber. He was thus at last admitted to the formation of national policy. In return he deftly threw overboard his erstwhile allies, accusing Fraser of misleading him and ordering the nobles to lay down arms. Having thus bungled his way through the whole episode, which became known as 'the Start', he had accidentally emerged with profit.[23]

Two problems resulted. Certainly Fraser obediently left Scotland, and so did Seymour, Long, and other courtiers implicated in the affair. But Huntly and his allies refused to surrender without an absolute guarantee of indemnity: having been made fools by Charles they had no intention of being made martyrs. When the Committee sent a cavalry force against them, they destroyed it, and on 22 October the King was in the absurd position of signing an order to Leslie to employ the troops at Stirling to suppress men who had risen upon his orders. His government now had enemies to front and rear.[24] The second difficulty resulting from 'the Start' was that it convinced the extreme Covenanters that the King was not worth fighting for. The Western Association had raised 3,500 horse, a mobile force of good quality but not large enough to take on Cromwell unless joined with Leslie's soldiers. Immediately after 'the Start', the Committee ordered it to do just that, but it moved off in the opposite direction, to Dumfries where Johnston, Guthrie, and Gillespie joined it for a great discussion of Charles's perfidy. On 17 October the leaders of the Association signed a document which was to be known as 'the Western Remonstrance'. It renounced the King's cause as ungodly and declared that, although Cromwell had to be expelled from Scotland, the Covenanters had no right to intervene in the affairs of the English Commonwealth. Armed with this, Johnston and the two ministers returned to Stirling.[25]

The leaders of the Kirk party were thus suddenly left in control of nothing more than the waist of Scotland. It had become essential for them to make concessions to somebody, and to repudiate the King, with royalists in arms to the north, would be fatal. An unqualified pardon was immediately offered to Huntly and his colleagues, and Charles persuaded them to trust it in a long private interview with one of them, Lord Ogilvy, in a summer house on a lake at Perth.[26] Both the Committee and Commission tried to deal with the Remonstrance by ignoring it in the hope that it would not be pressed. This was to misjudge the temper of the extreme Covenanters, who proceeded to remind each body of their case. In later November the Committee lost patience and, led by Argyll, the majority of it declared the Remonstrance 'scandalous' and 'injurious', though it offered to forget the matter if it rested there. The Commission voted that the Remonstrants spoke much truth, excommunicated the leaders of the recent royalist uprising, and proclaimed another day of national repentance for the sins of the Stewarts (including 'the Start'). But it condemned the Remonstrance as divisive. With these judgements the Kirk party at last fissured. Johnston and his friends withdrew from the Committee and Guthrie's faction from the Commission.[27] Strachan resigned from the army: soon after, he joined Cromwell. The Scottish Parliament reassembled at Perth on 26 November and, disgusted with the inactivity of the Western Association, ordered its forces to reunite permanently with Leslie's. This provoked Ker into trying to salvage his name and independent command by achieving a rapid victory, and on 1 December he attacked what he took to be an English outpost at Hamilton. By bad luck and atrocious scouting he had actually chosen Cromwell's main cavalry force under the best English cavalry commander, John Lambert. Ker was taken prisoner, his right arm hanging by a strip, and his army was shattered. Thus, even as the most rigid Covenanters withdrew from the centres of power, their military importance was removed.[28] Their predicament after the Treaty of Breda was summed up in a line confided by Johnston to his diary. He thought it 'hard to fight in a business where God's quarrel is just but man's unjust'.[29]

As the year 1650 waned, Charles must have felt quiet glee to watch the political and military suicide of the Scots most opposed to his interest. Moreover, the tragicomedy at Hamilton had an indirect consequence even closer to his immediate interest. It delivered the south-west of Scotland to the English, who garrisoned Ayr to consolidate their hold on the region.[30] The third of the country south of the Forth, the rolling pastures and rich dales of Tweed, Teviot, Clyde, and the Lothians and the rain-soaked mountains of Galloway, had always supplied the Covenanters' strength. In the areas to the north they had been in a minority. As these alone still remained under Scottish control, it was now a practical impossibility to recruit another field army without employing Engagers and royalists. The withdrawal of the extreme Covenanters from Committee and Commission removed the main impediment to this course. When Parliament reassembled, the military situation ensured that the southern and western regions which had supplied the more uncompromising members were markedly underrepresented. The inevitable sequence of events followed. After a week Argyll moved that the Commission be asked whether repentant former enemies could be employed in the new army, and this was resolved. On 14 December that depleted body issued 'the Public Resolutions', returning an affirmative answer. Parliament immediately ordered the raising of twenty-five new regiments and, to the impotent fury of the Commission, among the colonels commissioned to lead them were not only Engagers but royalists who had risen in October and had shown no remorse for their past at all. The orders for the banishment of the English royalist nobles who had come over with the King, and were still living quietly in Scotland, were cancelled. Charles attended every meeting of both Parliament and the Committee, and naturally encouraged the change of policy with all his might.[31]

His increasingly active role in government was given ceremonial confirmation on New Year's Day 1651, when his coronation at last took place. In accordance with ancient Scottish custom it was held at Scone, where a platform six feet high was created in the little church to bear a throne. The rituals were placed firmly within the context of the Covenanting cause. Anointing was abandoned as superstitious. The sermon was delivered by the Moderator of the Assembly of the Kirk and devoted to the importance of the Covenants and the misdeeds of the King's ancestors. When the royal procession entered the church, Argyll bore the crown, Eglinton the gilt spurs, and another Kirk party noble, Lord Rothes, the sword of state. It was Loudoun who offered Charles the crown and

Argyll who placed this symbol of Scottish majesty, heavy with pearls, on his monarch's head. Before this crucial moment Charles had to subscribe the Covenants once more and declare them sacred. But the occasion was more than just a show of factional strength. Argyll acted as of right, being the realm's greatest subject, Loudoun as Chancellor, and Eglinton and Rothes had hereditary claims to their parts. The King was conducted from his chamber for the ceremony by the Earl Marischal, a royalist disabled from political office but called in to perform a family duty. What impressed all observers about Charles was the zeal with which he declared his faith in the Covenants. Probably a natural love of theatre prompted him to act his part properly. Perhaps also, now that events were running against the Kirk party, he could perform a masquerade with them and relish it, knowing that he had increasingly less need to take them seriously.[32]

Charles's own ideal remained that with which he had come to Scotland: to reunite all parties under his rule. During the first half of 1651 he more or less achieved it, the process that had commenced with 'the Public Resolutions' being pushed further and further by military necessity. Before going into recess for the coronation, Parliament confirmed the nobles of the Kirk party in power, appointing them to a new Committee of Estates and reaffirming the 'Acts of Classes' which excluded Engagers and royalists from political office. The prime objective of Argyll and his friends was that learned as a result of 'the Start', to keep Charles well-disposed to them. As a result, in the early months of the new year they permitted his English royalist friends, such as Wentworth, to resume their places and offices at court. Their most ambitious attempt to tie the King to their fortunes was to propose a match between him and Argyll's daughter. This Charles disposed of with perfect ease, by insisting that he must obtain the permission of Henrietta Maria, who as nimbly replied that the marriage had first to be approved by the English.[33] His political skill was increasing with confidence. What troubled the Kirk party nobles above all was the sight of large numbers of their old enemies striving to qualify themselves for military service by expressing repentance to the Kirk. This was no pleasant process, involving in every case a measure of grovelling, and at worst having to apologize for one's sins in the middle of a crowded church, clad in sackcloth. But men who have wielded power will do much to resume it. Middleton and Ogilvy duly donned the sackcloth, and Hamilton wrote a letter to the Commission so abject that Charles was shocked. By mid-March most of the leading Engagers and several royalists, including Huntly, had taken the test of apologizing to a local presbytery and been pardoned.[34]

Charles spent February taking his first active part in military affairs, inspecting the garrisons along the Forth and then riding to Aberdeen to encourage the levies in the royalist north-east. Already his court represented an enforced reconciliation of the old Covenanting party, for he took with him not just Argyll and Eglinton but Hamilton and Lauderdale. The Committee of Estates, which the previous summer had pushed Charles away from the field army, now begged him to visit Leslie's men and encourage them.[35] Instead, he returned to Perth for the reconvention of Parliament in mid-March and, to the consternation of the Kirk party, moved that repentant Engagers and royalists be admitted to the Committee itself. Despite the direct opposition of Cassilis, Parliament approved the point in principle and referred it to the Commission of the Kirk. The Commission tried to head it off by proposing that the repentant be eligible to sit, not in the Committee but on a special Commission to supervise military affairs: their strength was to be harnessed for the war, but politically they had to remain subservient. Immediately, Parliament set up such a body, and named to it not merely the leading Kirk party men, and Engagers and royalists who had done penance, but several men who had shown no repentance. The rules of the Scottish legislature permitted the sovereign to join debates, and it was Charles who urged on this course, and pushed it through against the vocal opposition of Argyll, Loudoun, Cassilis, Eglinton, and their entire faction. Four days after, he was offered, and accepted, the title of Commander-in-Chief of the armed forces, and voted to ask the Kirk to approve the repeal of the 'Acts of Classes'. Understandably, Argyll and his friends bewailed the ingratitude of their monarch as Parliament again adjourned.[36]

In fact there were two reasons why their complaints lacked justification. First, Charles was only following a policy which he had clearly favoured from the beginning. Second, he did not intend to turn them out of power, but to force them to compete with others for his favour and attention. This now happened. By May the court was divided (as Scotland had been in 1647–8) between the factions of Argyll and Hamilton, and to their irritation Charles held aloof from both. If he was close to any group it was to the English royalists present, though the greatest of these, Buckingham, became a nuisance by attaching himself to Argyll: an early warning both of his capacity for political adventuring and of his genuine and enduring taste for radical Protestants of all hues.[37] To keep the two factions satisfied, the army was made top-heavy with general officers. Leslie retained the post of Lieutenant-General under the King and Montgomery and two existing generals kept theirs, but Middleton and two more associates of Hamilton were given generals' rank.[38] The finishing steps to the process were taken in the summer. In late May Parliament reassembled and wrung a ruling

out of the Commission of the Kirk that royalists and Engagers could hold
political office, if they declared that they would uphold the prevailing
Kirk government and forswore any revenge for old injuries. Parliament
then repealed the 'Acts of Classes' and chose a Committee of Estates
on which Argyll, Hamilton, and Huntly headed many representatives of
their respective groups. After a decade the Scottish political nation had,
superficially, reunited. In July the General Assembly of the Kirk met,
and according to traditional practice Charles appointed a commissioner to
chair it. He chose Alexander Lindsay, Lord Balcarres, an ambitious noble
who had strongly supported his efforts in Parliament to readmit royalists
and engagers to power. Urged on by this man and (again) dominated
by representatives from the royalist north-east, the Assembly deprived
Guthrie, Gillespie, and another obdurate Covenanter of their livings. The
Kirk itself, conscience of the Covenanting cause, was becoming amenable
to Charles's authority.[39] In the confused and difficult circumstances of
September he had made a hash of politics, but once the tide was running
in his favour he managed affairs with some dexterity. There was one catch:
at the very moment that the General Assembly passed its resolutions, he
was on the point of losing his kingdom.

   The irony of Charles's political success was that it was a consequence
of the military success of the English Commonwealth: he was more and
more an effective monarch in less and less of Scotland. Yet this was the
very thing he was not content to be. In January, one of his new Scottish
courtiers begged him to treat with the English on the basis of resigning
his claim to their country. Charles replied that he would have the man
hanged upon the same gibbet as Cromwell, and arrested him. When a
royalist noble asked the King at least to open talks, Charles cut him dead.
For him as for the Commonwealth this was war to the death.[40] And now
Cromwell was seeking the kill. By the end of the winter his army had
completed the long, dreary work of battering the south-eastern fortresses
into surrender and planting garrisons in the south-west. Most of the sieges
had been conducted, ferociously, by a new protégé of Oliver's, a former
royalist officer, George Monck. Reinforced from England, Cromwell was
ready to attack the north as the campaigning season opened. To oppose
him, the Scots had by May gathered over 18,000 men along the Forth.[41]
Getting them there had been very difficult, because of the bitterness still
existing between the different parties now employed in the army. Lairds
opposed the levies made by agents of nobles and conscripts refused to
serve under the colonels they were given. Money was so scarce that it
was virtually impossible to pay the soldiers and the private fortunes of the
Commission for the Army had to be employed even to feed them.[42] But

at least they arrived, and Charles was delighted to set eyes on Highlanders, in force, for the first time. The Covenanters had disposed of such troops, but kept them at home to watch their royalist neighbours. Now the King heard eighty pipers perform in succession before their clansmen and chose the best, who instantly composed a new piece in his honour. Enraptured, Charles exclaimed that these regiments were the flower of his forces: unfortunately, rather a lot of Lowland officers overheard the remark.[43]

It was clearly madness to engage Cromwell with a force of uneven quality and internal animosities and weak in cavalry. So Charles and his generals reverted to Leslie's tactics of the previous summer. Most of the army was placed behind strong earthworks at Stirling and the rest put into garrisons on the north shore of the Firth of Forth, to hold the waist of Scotland. Charles took up residence in the main camp, regularly inspecting the guards himself, on foot. As the warm weather came, Cromwell began to probe the Scottish defences, having his ships bombard Kircaldy in May and marching past Stirling in June to ravage the Glasgow area. In mid-July he faced the defences of Stirling again and then, with the whole attention of the Scots concentrated upon him, he found the opening he wanted. On the 17th, a party of his men, left at Edinburgh, was shipped over the Firth of Forth and made a bridgehead on a strip of unguarded coast. Instantly, Cromwell sped John Lambert with a strong force to join them, while Charles and his officers sent a body of their own men to the scene. At Inverkeithing on the 20th Lambert overwhelmed the Scottish detachment, mortally wounding its leader and killing or capturing most of his men. the victorious soldiers lacerated the prisoners with their swords, to put 'Cromwell's mark' on them. The way into Fife was now open. Even as the General Assembly of the Kirk was deposing Guthrie and Gillespie, Cromwell's main army crossed on Lambert's heels, swept its enemies from the Forth coast, and made for Perth. On 2 August the city surrendered.[44]

Cromwell had now effectively won the war in Scotland. At Perth he was between the Scottish army and its sources of food and recruits: it had either to fight, against odds, or disintegrate. Inverkeithing had cost it about 4,000 men, and now thousands more deserted in face of an apparently hopeless situation. Charles and his generals had in fact only one hope left, and that a very desperate one: to make for England, at high speed, with all their remaining soldiers. During the winter, Charles had continued preparations for a rising there to support an invasion, sending messengers to Derby in the Isle of Man and blank commissions to Nicholas to be filled in and forwarded to conspirators in the West Country. In early 1651 more English royalists had joined Charles, and in May he formed them into a horse regiment under Buckingham, who held the highest social rank among them. There was talk of sending this unit into England to spark off the rising while Cromwell was held before Stirling, but on the latter's advice the Commonwealth placed a cavalry force on the Border to prevent this.[45] Now, with these horsemen the only body of troops between Charles and his principal realm, it would be possible for the royal army to sweep them aside. There, if fortune willed, the royalists and 'Presbyterians' would rise *en masse* to reinforce the King. Cromwell would follow, too late, and be caught between Charles and the army which the Scots, the pressure removed from them, would raise in his rear. Argyll, Loudoun, and Cassilis, hearing this plan, recognized it as virtual lunacy and swiftly retired to their homes. Balcarres and some royalists and Engagers were left to recruit in the Highlands. All the other leaders went with the King and his remaining men, numbering about 12,000,[46] who marched for Carlisle while Cromwell was negotiating the surrender of Perth.[47]

By the standards of the age, Charles's army moved at lightning speed. In six days it crossed the Border and he called upon the English to join him, promising a Church reformed according to the Solemn League and Covenant, a free Parliament, and indemnity to all except regicides. Before his soldiers he was proclaimed King of England and received an acclamation of trumpets and shots. In ten days more he had reached the Mersey, having been cheered through the towns on his march. At Warrington Bridge he found a small enemy force under Lambert, which withdrew after a token show of resistance, permitting Charles to claim a victory and to issue another summons of support. The King and Hamilton now wanted to make for London, but every other leader present agreed that the soldiers would soon need rest. It was reasonably resolved to give it to them in a strong place in the traditional royalist recruiting grounds of western England. Charles therefore moved on due south. Behind him he left the Earl of Derby, who had just landed from Man, to raise men in Lancashire. On 22 August the Scots limped into Worcester, which appeared in every way the haven they required. Its western side was protected by the rivers Severn and Teme, its others by the remains of Civil War fortifications, easily repaired. It lay in the centre of a rich county, with easy access to Wales, the Marches, and the West Country where many royalists lived. Carlisle, Chester, and Shrewsbury had all contained hostile garrisons, but Worcester was unguarded. As Charles entered, the mayor proudly carried the city's sword before him, and then proclaimed him King at the cross, seconded by the sheriff.[48]

The mayor and sheriff were not formerly royalists, and their action in welcoming their sovereign was almost certainly to save their city from the sack which would inevitably follow resistance. As it was, Worcestershire paid heavily for the honour of his company. In the succeeding week supplies of arms, clothes, and food were brought in from the county, and probably no more than promise of payment was given for them. Charles had hanged two or three plunderers on his march to stop private looting, with success, but official requisitions were another matter. The corporation of Worcester itself had to pay the expenses of the royal Household and the wages of its officers. Labourers were drafted to repair the fortifications, and the suburbs were burned. Local royalist gentry were summoned to form a committee to administer the county, and if they did not appear then cavalry were sent to fetch them. This work was due to be crowned by a huge muster of local men on Pitchcroft Meadow on the 26th, but only some of the leading royalist gentry appeared, with 200 followers. Instead, two days later Cromwell arrived to the east of the city, with 28,000 men. Simultaneously, Lambert seized the bridge over the Severn to the south, at Upton, and defeated a party sent to regain it. This coup gave the republicans access to both sides of the great river. A short while after Derby came in, to report that his force in Lancashire had been destroyed. The royal army was now trapped and outnumbered, with no prospect of aid.[49]

What had gone wrong? Three things in the main. First, as the Commonwealth's press tirelessly pointed out, Charles had entered England not in triumph but with the remnant of a defeated army pursued by the victors. He could offer recruits neither money nor a reasonable prospect of winning. Second, thanks to the heavy taxes which contributed to its general unpopularity, the Commonwealth could simultaneously carry on the Irish war, invade Scotland, and retain enough regiments to watch the English. When Charles moved south, Cromwell could leave Monck with 6,000 field troops to finish off the Scots and still follow the King with a bigger army. Large numbers of militiamen were raised to reinforce these regulars, because the men had a good expectation of both pay and loot. Altogether, the Commonwealth had about 50,000 men under arms, enough to overwhelm Charles while guarding all other parts of the country.[50] Derby got 1,200 recruits together in Lancashire in a week only to be broken by a few hundred regular cavalry with superior equipment and training.[51] Third, the Commonwealth had captured two key royalist agents who had revealed the plans made for the risings. As a result, most of the leaders had been arrested before the invasion.[52] In brief, suicidal loyalty was required to assist Charles, and the majority of the men who possessed this quality were not available.

On the morning of 3 September Cromwell felt strong enough to attack Worcester from both sides. He had moved a strong detachment over

Upton Bridge which now arrived at the Teme. This he reinforced by throwing bridges of boats across both Severn and Teme outside Worcester, so that the consolidated party could outnumber the Scots holding the western suburb of Powick. This manœuvre was observed by Charles and his chief supporters, gathered on the cathedral tower, and they made the most intelligent response. The King rode immediately to Powick, where the attack was developing, to encourage the soldiers there under Montgomery to resist. Then he dashed back into the city, gathered all his remaining men and led them against the army Cromwell had left upon the eastern side, in the hope that it had been weakened enough to become vulnerable. All who fought with him that day remembered the faultless courage and confidence which Charles displayed: the man who could play his expected part to perfection at a coronation, in a royal court, or in a manor house in Jersey now brought this talent to the role of warlord. With Buckingham and Hamilton he sallied from the Sudbury Gate at the head of the first horse regiments and Cromwell's men gave ground before their charge.

Courage was not enough. The royalists were attacking uphill, into ground divided by hedgerows and held by an enemy still more numerous than themselves. Not only did the republicans outnumber them absolutely, but the Sudbury Gate could only emit them a few at a time and their vanguard consisted of cavalry pitted against musketeers. When Cromwell counter-attacked, the royal troopers were driven back and most of the officers had their horses shot under them. A huge slug smashed Hamilton's shin, another ball hit Middleton. The rout swept the King himself back to the Sudbury Gate, where he had to climb over an upturned ammunition wagon to get through. Behind him the triumphant enemy swarmed into the fort controlling the eastern defences, slaughtered the garrison, and began to storm Worcester, yelling 'The Lord of Hosts.' Over in Powick, the attackers had also broken through and Montgomery, wounded, was falling back with his remaining soldiers. Street by street the battle progressed, the combatants clambering over the corpses of men and horses. In the centre of the pandemonium Charles and his available commanders resolved that all was lost. Lord Wentworth's father, the aged Earl of Cleveland, led a desperate charge to hold the enemy while the King, Buckingham, Derby, Leslie, and parties of Scottish horse rode away through the one gate still open, to the north. Behind them the killing went on till midnight. The looting of the city had already begun.[53]

The battle of Worcester resulted in the death or capture of virtually the entire royal army. Hamilton, Lauderdale, Rothes, Cleveland, and Montgomery were all taken in the city, Derby, Leslie, and Middleton in flight outside it. Hamilton died of gangrene after a few days, Derby was beheaded and Leslie, Lauderdale, and Middleton committed to indefinite imprisonment. The only royalist leaders to get clean away were Buckingham, Wilmot, and, of course, Charles himself. The story of his escape has been told in detail in most previous accounts of his life, and a complete (and very spritely) book has been devoted to it.[54] What all these portrayals have in common is that they are relatively uncritical narratives, putting the various sources end to end. It may be useful here to see what a critical analysis reveals.

Very briefly, the undoubted course of events was as follows. On Derby's suggestion, Charles sought refuge with the Penderells, a family of Roman Catholic tenant farmers, at Whiteladies in Shropshire. These disguised him as a labourer, hid him in a wood and then a farm, and tried to get him into Wales. Walking to Madeley on the Severn, they found militia holding all the bridges. Charles was concealed in the barn of another Catholic and then walked back to Boscobel, home of the Catholic landlord of the Penderells. Here he was hidden successively in the house, a nearby oak tree, and the garden. On 7 September he rode to Moseley Hall, Staffordshire, and the care of Thomas Whitgreave, another Catholic gentleman. On the 10th he set out again in the guise of a tenant farmer's son, attending Jane Lane, sister of a Staffordshire royalist colonel, who had a pass to visit a friend at Abbots Leigh near Bristol. He stayed there at the manor, unknown to the owners but recognized by the butler. On the latter's advice, he and Jane rode across Somerset on the 16th to Trent Hall and the protection of a former royalist colonel, Francis Wyndham, brother-in-law of Charles's beloved Christabel. An attempt to sail to safety from Dorset failed, and the county's ports were full of soldiers bound for the long-delayed attack on Jersey. It was therefore resolved to find a ship on the coast of Hampshire or Sussex, and a set of royalists, John Coventry, Colonel Robert Phelips, Dr Humphrey Henchman, and Colonel Thomas Gunter, set to work on this task. Gunter succeeded in it, and on 14 October Charles sailed from Shoreham, landing at Fécamp, Normandy, two days later.

What emerges most powerfully from the agreed details of this story, even more than from the rest of Charles's life, is his incredible good luck. Thanks to Derby, he was delivered into the hands of the persecuted Roman Catholic community, the only people in the area of the battle who had the practice in concealment to save him. Even so, the republic's soldiers searched not only the houses but the woods and fields in this district, and fortune alone decided that only once did their descents coincide with Charles's presence: at Moseley, where Whitgreave persuaded them to leave without rummaging through the house. He was constantly recognized by former royalist soldiers, sailors, or courtiers. Apart from the butler at Abbots Leigh, such individuals included a vagrant on the road in Dorset, an ostler at Bridport, a gentlewoman in Wiltshire, an innkeeper at Brighton, and the master of the ship on which he crossed the channel. Yet, despite a £1,000 reward set on his head, he was never betrayed. On the failure of his attempt to get into Wales, he was able to remake contact with Wilmot and thereafter they concerted plans. This corpulent lord was in many ways a liability, for he refused either to disguise himself or to go on foot and appeared in public places recklessly. But his web of contacts, based on his career as Charles I's principal cavalry commander, continually assisted his monarch's progress. In Dorset, the royal party aroused the suspicions of a stable-hand, who informed a republican officer. Only its decision to change road on the spur of the moment, quite unaware of the danger, saved him from arrest. They subsequently got lost, but were rescued because the innkeeper of the village into which they blundered turned out to be a staunch royalist and concealed them overnight. Finally, soldiers arrived to search Shoreham only hours after Charles and Wilmot had left it for France.

In other matters the sources are less consistent. The King's own account, written down by an attentive courtier thirty years later, makes Charles appear virtually a genius. On the walk to Madeley, he is always soothing and managing his guide, Richard Penderell. At Abbots Leigh he hits upon the notion of the journey to Trent, and devises a marvellous ploy to release Jane Lane, this theoretical employer, to make this journey. When confronted with parties of enemy cavalry at Stratford-upon-Avon and Bridport, he insists on riding boldly through them. He has the idea of contacting Colonel Phelips, through whom the vital Colonel Gunter is found. He insists on keeping the master of the ship busy till the hour of departure to keep him from betraying them, and improvises a convincing story to quiet the suspicions of the crew. Throughout, he is a consummate actor, chatting to a smith in Warwickshire, the servants at Abbots Leigh, and the ostler at Bridport and convincing them all of his assumed role.

The reminiscences of those who assisted his escape contain none of these incidents, and those concerning Richard Penderell are directly contradicted. It is possible that some would have been known only to Charles, and a few are made believable by his behaviour in similar circumstances. Colonel Gunter noted that the King acted a part marvellously when introduced to the household of the colonel's sister as a puritanical parliamentarian. He also records that on facing guards posted at Bamber, Charles insisted on going nonchalantly through them as he himself claimed to have done elsewhere. Charles's companions at Bridport remembered him chatting to soldiers in a yard as they passed through, though not to an ostler. The discrepancy in the narratives, however, does mean that one should not accept all of the King's stories unquestioningly, as has been done. What the observers were unanimous about was his courtesy and courage during the escape. In every house which sheltered him he treated his protectors and their families with faultless grace and consideration. Throughout, he never once complained or lost his nerve (which Wilmot certainly did), acquiesced perfectly in everything required of him, and remained resolutely cheerful. Aside from the risk of near-certain death which it carried, assisting him was clearly a pleasure for all concerned.

One alleged incident should be subjected to particular scrutiny, because of religious and political implications. It is set at Moseley Hall and occurs in a pamphlet taken from the testimonies of Whitgreave and his chaplain, Father John Hudleston, published in 1688 as part of James II's campaign for Catholic emancipation. In this, Charles asked how Catholics lived, looked respectfully at the little altar in the chapel, and said that 'he had an altar, crucifix and silver candlesticks of his own, till my Lord of Holland broke them'. The King then read a defence of the Catholic faith, confessed it unanswerable, and asked to take a catechism with him. He then promised that if he were restored Catholics would have freedom of worship. Moseley is today the only one of Charles's hiding-places to survive more or less intact, and the visitor is treated to a radio-play about the King's stay in which this exchange is repeated. It also features in most accounts of his escape. Yet there are grounds to doubt it. Moseley made so little impression upon Charles's own memory that, alone of his hosts, he could not remember Whitgreave's name. More significant, a manuscript memoir by Whitgreave himself survives, probably one of the two upon which the pamphlet was based. This records Charles's visit to the chapel and has him only say that it was 'decent'. He also mentions that the King picked a catechism out of several books and called it 'pretty'. Both judgements may signify aesthetic appreciation rather than theological, and the latter echoes his childhood joy in the Ferrars' gorgeous volumes. Whitgreave does record that his monarch guaranteed to work for freedom of worship for Catholics after his restoration. This offer should hardly be doubted, for he had already made it to obtain support in 1650. But, given the evidence, the enthusiastic comments recorded in the pamphlet seem like embellishment on the part of the author or of Hudleston, whom we shall meet again later.

His brief reign as a resident King of Scots made a permanent and negative impact on Charles. During all the long years after his restoration, he never returned to Scotland nor expressed any private affection for its people. The devotion with which many had followed him and the delight he had taken in the Highlanders could clearly not counterbalance the unforgivable fact that they had failed him. They remained tools from start to finish, and provoked the greater contempt for having broken in the use.

A King in Search of Quarters, 1651–1656

❦

THE European scene to which Charles returned in October 1651 was even less favourable to his cause than that which he had left seventeen months before. France appeared to be in the process of disintegration, for upon the earlier disturbances by peasants and Parisians had been imposed a quarrel between the Queen Regent and the nearest princes of the blood, produced by the latters' jealousy of Mazarin and desire for control of the government. When Charles reached Paris, he was welcomed not by the King and his mother, but by Gaston, Duke of Orléans, uncle to Louis and father of 'Mademoiselle'. Louis, now thirteen and formally a reigning monarch, was in the provinces with his mother, Mazarin, and an army, facing an alliance between Orléans, the other rebel princes, several nobles, and the Parliament of Paris. The other great west European power, Spain, had recognized the Commonwealth in the hope of gaining its aid against France. Charles's greatest continental ally, the Prince of Orange, had died suddenly of smallpox a year before. He left his titles to an infant son, named Wilhelm after his father. This blow to his party had been compounded by a needless struggle over the guardianship of the baby, between his widow, Charles's sister Mary, and his mother, the Dowager Princess. To compound their folly, both women bid for the support of the great traditional rivals of the House of Orange, the city oligarchs of Holland. The latter seized the opportunity to become the dominant power in the whole republic, with a vested interest in keeping the Orangist party subservient and hence in ignoring the claims of the related House of Stuart. Charles had no alternative to moving in with his own mother, in the Louvre, in the hope that France's troubles would at worst postpone the question of his deportation.

The period immediately after his escape from the British Isles saw the total end of active royalism there. Conspiracy by his supporters in England disappeared completely and in the autumn of 1651 republican naval expeditions reduced the Isle of Man, the castle on Guernsey, and (at last) Charles's former refuge of Jersey. After the royal army and Cromwell's left Scotland, George Monck made short work of resistance there. By the end of the year only four fortresses held out for the King, and the last of these surrendered in May 1652. In Ireland, the diversion of the Commonwealth's resources by the Scottish war had prolonged, but not averted, the process of defeat. Continued loss of territory had shaken the alliance between the Catholic Confederacy and Ormonde, and at the end of 1650 the Marquis and Inchiquin had retired to Paris, leaving a Catholic Lord Deputy behind. In early 1652 Charles wrote to the Irish leaders to express support and encouragement. He also tried to obtain aid for them from the Catholic Duke of Lorraine, an exiled ruler like himself but one equipped with wealth and a mercenary army, employed by Spain. All was in vain. The Duke was swiftly disgusted by the quarrels of the Irish, and in any case it was too late. By the summer of 1652 resistance to the Commonwealth was confined to guerrilla bands, and the last of these surrendered in April 1653. For good measure, in early 1652 the Commonwealth secured the allegiance of the English American colonies. Charles was now the effective ruler of absolutely nowhere.[1]

On his arrival at Paris, he told a highly imaginative and fictitious account of his escape, which enabled him both to protect those who had actually helped him and to magnify his own daring and intelligence. Some details of the real story did emerge, such as his hiding in a tree and his considerable debt to the Catholics. Much of his conversation, however, was devoted to railing against the Scots and the English 'Presbyterians'. To 'Mademoiselle' he complained about the lack of violin music and female company in Scotland. To others, he accused the Scots of mistreating him in their own country and showing cowardice at Worcester, and the 'Presbyterians' of having betrayed their promise of support. On arriving at the Louvre he returned, immediately and permanently, to use of the Anglican rite.[2]

This revulsion also showed in his choice of Counsellors and friends. Even while still in Scotland as a Covenanted King, he had shown his renewed trust of Anglican royalists. In March, from Perth, he had sent a commission to his brother James and Ormonde, Inchiquin, Nicholas, and Hyde, all persons suspect to the Covenanters, empowering them to conduct his affairs abroad.[3] Now this shift of opinion was absolute. Of the 'Old Royalist' group, Brentford was dead and Cottington and Hopton dying, but Ormonde was already at Paris and received into Charles's high favour, and Hyde and Nicholas were summoned thither by the King's private invitation. Nicholas, ill and convinced of the hatred of Henrietta Maria, stayed at The Hague, but Hyde hurried up with such alacrity that he lost his own health on the winter journey. Charles also took the 'Louvre' set into his confidence, partly because they also had opposed the Treaty of

Breda and partly because, since he was living in the Louvre himself, he could hardly do otherwise. His hostility was reserved for those who had favoured an alliance with the Scots. Wilmot was absolved from this for his part in the King's escape, and Dr Fraser was pardoned for the supposed excellence of his medicine. But Robert Long, Culpeper, Newcastle, and Buckingham were not forgiven. Long compounded his offence, for having received a disingenuous letter forbidding him to attend the court until it had found a long-term residence, he ignored it and arrived at Paris. As he had failed to take a hint, he had now to be destroyed. Wilmot obligingly provided a former parliamentarian officer, who accused Long of having sent intelligence to the enemy in the West in 1646. Charles himself agreed privately that the charge was ridiculous, but it served as a lever. Examination of the case was handed over to the wretched man's enemies Hyde and Ormonde, and Long was duly deprived of his post of secretary and disgraced. Hyde enjoyed the affair, little realizing that he was participating in a dress rehearsal for his own ruin.[4]

What Charles emphatically did not do now was to grant his entire trust to the 'Old Royalists'. Instead, he balanced them against the 'Louvre' set, forming a policy-making committee upon which Hyde, Ormonde, and Inchiquin sat with Jermyn, Wilmot, and Lord Goring's old father the Earl of Norwich. Hyde carried out the duties of a Secretary of State without the title, but they gave him no monopoly of advice. Instead, Charles employed the tactic that came naturally to him, of agreeing with individuals in private and giving them an impression of absolute favour while doing just the same with their rivals. The Queen Mother and Jermyn were shaken when they proposed that Culpeper be made ambassador to the Netherlands, only to find that it was already arranged to send Hyde and Ormonde to undertake that work. Hyde was equally disturbed to find that a brilliant young royalist, William Coventry, had been sent on a fund-raising expedition to England without Hyde's even being told about it. He was even more upset when Percy, of the 'Louvre' faction, was made Lord Chamberlain, and William Crofts, a wild young courtier associated with that group, was made a Gentleman of the Bedchamber. Charles had assured him that he would grant neither appointment. As a result, observers reached utterly opposed conclusions to the question of who actually managed the King, and relations between his advisers grew increasingly embittered. The latter all worked hard, the policy committee sitting almost daily, all day. But most of what was formally debated concerned trivia, while important decisions were taken by Charles after his private consultations.[5] The King was saving himself the unpleasantness of argument, at the price of confusion and demoralization among his Counsellors and the threat of loss of coherence in his policies.

The circle of royal advisers was widened in the course of 1652 and 1653. In the former year Digby reappeared in Paris and, finding himself still disliked by the Queen, somehow managed to befriend Ormonde and to persuade Hyde that their former differences had all been misunderstandings. Whether his formidable charm was also turned directly upon Charles, or whether the 'Old Royalists' talked the King into giving him favour, it is clear that within a few months he was once again an important figure at court. In January 1653 he was made a Knight of the Garter and in April, having succeeded his father as Earl of Bristol, he was called to the Privy Council.[6] During that same spring, another important figure reappeared, as Rupert docked at Nantes with the last of the royalist warships which he had led towards Ireland in 1649. In the intervening years he had been chased around the Mediterranean and Atlantic by the Commonwealth's fleet, losing his favourite brother, his best friend, his health, and all of his vessels except this one. The whole court expressed sympathy for his sufferings and joy at his return, both factions hoping that they might enlist his support or that he might arbitrate between them. Charles gave him the great honorific office of Master of the Horse, while a client of his, a lawyer called Sir Edward Herbert, was made Keeper of the Seals and a Privy Counsellor. This did indeed create a third faction amongst the exiles, but far from bringing a greater amity to policy-making it worsened the existing tensions. Rupert and Herbert were both choleric personalities, and had soon alienated all their fellow Counsellors.[7]

One of the principal problems discussed by the policy-making committee was money. On arrival at the Louvre, Charles was thrown on to his mother's meagre resources, most derived from the small and badly paid pension awarded to her by the French. Although Henrietta Maria introduced such economies as having her two sons and daughter eat simple meals with her at the same table, the King still had to borrow heavily. Royalist diplomacy was virtually halted by the lack of money to pay even a courier. Charles's advisers generally had to live in cheap lodgings and to walk the streets as they could not afford carriages. Hyde could not pay for warm clothes or a fire in winter and was sometimes too cold to hold a pen. He ate one meal a day, bought and shared between five or six companions. In May 1652, after many missions by Jermyn, the French government agreed to pay Charles £450 per month. In their circumstances this was remarkably generous, but the grant was of course irregularly paid, less than half the amount due arriving in the first six months. Furthermore, these first instalments were needed to discharge his debts, including those which he had run up to his own mother. Nor were the problems of his courtiers relieved.[8]

In this predicament, one obvious way of finding money was to marry it, and both the royal brothers immediately attempted this course. In the first months of 1652 James bid for the hands of two heiresses, the daughters of the Dukes of Lorraine and of Longueville, and was refused by both as offering no political advantages. He thereupon removed himself from the family budget by joining the French royal army, with the tacit but not official permission of his brother who was trying to keep out of France's internal problems. The life of a soldier perfectly suited James's simple, courageous and passionate nature, and when he recalled his time in France in old age all he could remember were battles and sieges. Having been a moody and irritable youth at the Louvre, desperate to escape his mother's authority, he became for the next four years the most contented of the Stuarts. For Charles there was clearly only one obvious match, and so, with the reluctant agreements of his Counsellors he set himself at last upon a determined wooing of La Grande Mademoiselle. At first this showed some promise. Anne Marie Louise was impressed by the splendid bearing which he had acquired, and amused by the story of the oak tree. His genuine enthusiasm for dancing to violins, his calculated flattery (even in still imperfect French), and his willingness to defer to her opinions all added to his attractions. In the winter of 1651–2 they held assemblies every evening for the youth of Paris, at which Charles must have forgotten many of the horrors of the autumn. But she had no intention of marrying him, being perfectly aware that he was after her fortune, and finding other faults with him. For one thing, he was adamantly against joining her Roman Catholic faith, saying that he would do anything for her 'but sacrifice his conscience and salvation'. For another, he made the error of stressing love and social pleasures to her instead of projecting political and military ambitions. 'Mademoiselle' was looking for a hero, and sensed that in Charles, at least at this time, the fire had gone out. When he pressed the match she asked him to curtail his visits, and henceforth he treated her with petulant resentment.[9]

Another potential source of income lay in contributions by royalists in England. It was not a very promising one, for these people were themselves impoverished by war and punitive fines, and on learning that Charles was the guest of the French many believed him to be living in more comfort than they were.[10] Nevertheless, it was worth trying, and in the years 1652–5 agents were sent on rounds to make collections. The accounts survive of two: Henry Seymour, who raised £2,300, and James Halsall, who delivered £1,370, in both cases gathered from quite obscure individuals. Given the King's extreme need, these were significant sums, and in Halsall's case they were employed as a fund to co-ordinate conspiracy in England. Some of the exiles also came to their monarch's aid, such as Percy who, having retained the rents of his English estates, was able to lend Charles a timely £1,500 in November 1653.[11]

In addition, English people who felt no affection for the King found themselves unwillingly contributing to his upkeep through the activity of privateer captains commissioned by him. The greatest of these was Rupert himself, and when he made his return from his terrible voyage he did bring three prizes with him. But these proved totally useless to Charles, for his cousin presented him not with the proceeds but with a set of accounts. These demonstrated that over the years Rupert himself had laid out so much upon his fleet that the value of the captured vessels represented only a third of this sum, leaving the King still owing him the balance.[12] The Prince, however, was merely the most illustrious of many English, French, Dutch, and Flemish seafarers, who obtained a dubious right to plunder British shipping on registering themselves with Charles's officers. All they had to do in return was to hand over a fifth of their proceeds to Charles and another fifth to James, giving a bond upon registration for their performance of this duty. In August 1652, somebody at court tried to make a list of the captains thus employed, and gave up after naming fifteen, with an embarrassed note that there were many more but nobody could identify them. Courtiers with a little money to spare, such as Ormonde, invested in these raiding voyages. Trusted royalists were placed in key ports to supervise the sale of the proceeds and to take the royal share, such as Sir Richard Browne at Brest, Luke Whittington at Dunkirk, the Bishop of Derry in the Zealand harbours, and Colonel Wyndham, Charles's former choice as Secretary of State, in the most important base, of Boulogne. Not merely the King himself but his accredited representatives like Sir Henry De Vic at Brussels had authority to issue such commissions. The expeditions certainly benefited the captains and crews, for in one week in Flanders a pair of prizes realized £1,500 and £2,000 respectively. How much profit they brought the King is less easy to say, for it is clear that he did not always receive his percentage, and that the quantity which did come in was tiny in proportion to his needs. The clearest statement of this was made by Wyndham, who observed that over two years he had received £24 from the proceeds of privateering while Charles had sent him warrants for payments totalling £3,300. He had pocketed the £24 himself in part-repayment of £70 which he had lent the King. Charles was furious with him for this information, and the spell of the Wyndhams was broken for ever.[13] Certainly, it must be concluded that the raids were far more a scourge to English shipping than an asset to the royalists, and that the French pension, however erratic, was Charles's principal means of subsistence at Paris.

What effect, then, did enforced idleness and poverty have upon Charles? The great Gardiner supplied an answer without fear or footnote when speaking of events in 1653—'Since his return from Worcester Charles had been living a disreputable life in Paris, consoling himself in low debauchery for the kingdoms he had lost.'[14] It is a slur which has had considerable resilience, reappearing regularly and never directly challenged, but lacks substance. Accounts of the King's leisure pursuits in these years depict him playing billiards, swimming, and attending the occasional court masque. A republican spy active in Paris in September 1653 described to his employers that Inchiquin, Fraser, and other courtiers drank hard during conversation but that Charles himself was an admirable young man. In private, things were slightly less decorous. At some time in the early 1650s Charles slipped into bed with Elizabeth Killigrew, the wife of an Anglo-Irish gentleman. This affair only became apparent almost twenty years later, when its result surfaced in the form of a daughter named Charlotte Fitzroy. In Paris he may have slept with Lord Byron's widow Eleanor, to whom he gave a pension at the Restoration.[15] Still, during his French years he had no settled mistress, and it was apparently in this period that he made his decisive break with Lucy Walter. Our evidence is a terse statement by Hyde that she 'lived afterwards for some years in the King's sight, and at last lost His Majesty's favour'. She may also have been the subject of another passage in Hyde's memoirs, recounting a mysterious episode in which Henrietta Maria employed him to remove 'a young lady out of the Louvre, who had procured a lodging there without her Majesty's consent' and who showed her little respect. Hyde indeed persuaded Charles to move this woman out.[16] As Sir Edward always avoided naming his sovereign's mistresses, and indeed only mentioned them at all when absolutely necessary, this unfortunate lady might well have been Lucy. Her parting from Charles was almost certainly due to the fact that, now or while he was in Scotland, she gave birth to a daughter whom he refused to recognize as his own. The girl was later adopted by Theobald, Viscount Taaffe, a jolly and bellicose Catholic Irish exile who had attached himself to the court, and was later considered Lucy's lover.[17] He may have fathered her second child. Hereafter Charles's name was only linked in France with one other woman, the dazzling, dark-haired Isabelle-Angélique de Montmorency, Duchesse de Châtillon. He definitely paid court to her, having already been smitten by her in 1648, and may have been her lover, but then falling in love with La Châtillon was a custom of the age. Among her suitors in these years were also two of the rebel French princes, William Crofts, and Lord Digby, while the barely pubescent Louis XIV was smitten by her. A different sort of woman would have taken a quiet pride in such admiration. Isabelle-Angélique's response was to appear in society blazing with diamonds and boasting of the number and rank of her admirers.[18] Virtually all of Charles's real passions would be for women who possessed the attractions which Evelyn had noted in Lucy—beauty and boldness.

Nevertheless, it is true that Hyde could complain privately to Nicholas that the King's reputation was sinking because of his love of pleasure, but by this he signified not debauchery but attention to anything but work: his remark was followed by a description of a bathing party.[19] Charles did not lack energy for dramatic activity, as his brief dynamic career as King of Scots in 1651 had shown. But he hated paperwork, and admitted himself that he loathed writing letters above all: the one means by which exiled monarchs could project themselves to scattered followers. The demoralization of defeat had doubtless something to do with this fault, but it had already been noted in him in 1649 and was fully shared by his sister Mary. Clearly the nursery at Richmond had been an indulgent place. The problem meant that Hyde generally had a nightmarish task getting his monarch down to business, and there was a genuine danger that it would seriously weaken the royalist cause.[20] But the myth that Charles wallowed in vice or in luxury in exile while his supporters starved should now be discarded.

Despite lethargy at its head, indigence, and military impotence, the exiled royal government remained remarkably active. When it was quartered at St Germain in July 1652, Hyde could write to Browne that 'between the English and the Dutch letters, and the particular businesses from this place, there is no day passes without a messenger to Paris'. All that it could do was try to exploit every development, and the first of these occurred in the month before Hyde wrote, when the English Commonwealth went to war with the Dutch. Formally, it was a dispute over trade, but the English ambassadors were undoubtedly embittered by the strength of Orangist and pro-Stuart demonstrations in the United Netherlands. Charles, doubtless with the advice of his Counsellors, approached the situation with skill and delicacy. He did all that he could to reunite the Orange party by mediating between his sister and her mother-in-law. Hyde cultivated the Dutch ambassador in Paris, Wilhelm Boreel, while the King asked Mary to give this man's son a job. Charles systematically ignored advice from some exiled 'Presbyterians' to stir up mobs in the towns of Holland, and refused to make any concessions to the 'Presbyterian' interest unless certain profit was to be gained. His diplomacy was initially hampered by the fact that his current resident at The Hague, Sir William Macdowell, was, in Hyde's words, 'a codhead'. But having planned to send Hyde himself and Ormonde, he realized that he had a good agent on the spot, in Nicholas who was still living in the Dutch capital. When the States-General had ignored him for three months after the opening of hostilities, he offered the Dutch Guernsey in exchange for espousing his cause. After four more months and a Dutch defeat, he proposed to the States-General that he would join its fleet and persuade English sailors to defect. He and his advisers were clearly not men to let patriotism mar their business.

All this effort achieved was an agreement by the Dutch to provide facilities for Charles's privateers. The States of Holland believed that an alliance with him would restore the Orangists to influence and make peace with the Commonwealth far more difficult without yielding any real military benefit. The only development that might have made the Stuarts attractive partners was if France had offered to join the coalition, and France was too weak to do any such thing. As a result, though the insistence of the Commonwealth upon hard terms caused the war to drag on all through 1653, it was increasingly obvious that Charles could play no part in it.[21]

This was especially galling because the same year saw the reappearance of royalist activity in both Scotland and England which would have benefited considerably from foreign aid. It was spontaneous and took the King by surprise. His interest in Scotland had been stirred momentarily only five months after his arrival in France, when John Middleton escaped from the prison where he had been kept since Worcester and came to Paris. This tall, black-haired, red-faced, hook-nosed soldier had the gift of inspiring trust in all about him. He had already impressed Charles and now became the ally of Ormonde and Hyde, so that henceforth he was regarded as the King's principal Scottish commander. Also present was an aged Scottish royalist, James Livingstone, Viscount Newburgh, who had preferred exile to surrender and now functioned as the resident adviser upon his country's affairs. He received messages from other Scots and channelled them to Charles and his Counsellors. An agent was sent immediately to a group of Highland chiefs to enquire whether resistance in their mountains might be feasible.[22] When the Anglo-Dutch war broke out, it was decided immediately to send Middleton to the Netherlands to obtain supplies for a Scottish rebellion. Charles wrote to the Moderator of the General Assembly to urge the Kirk to remain faithful to him. He then commissioned Middleton as his Lieutenant-General in Scotland and dispatched him to The Hague. There he stuck, for the States of Holland were not disposed to involve themselves with royalism even in this indirect fashion.[23]

Suddenly, in November 1652, a messenger appeared from the chiefs to whom the King had written in the spring, asking for arms, ammunition, commissions, and the presence of Middleton as their leader. The Commonwealth's campaigns of 1651–2 had brought about the formal submission of the Highlanders without establishing an effective military presence among them. When, in 1652, initial attempts were made to disarm and patrol the region, certain chiefs grew irritated. A restless and ambitious lord, Angus Macdonald of Glengarry, began to agitate for a full-scale rising, and it was his group which now approached Charles. The exiled government was thus faced with the problem of co-ordinating a movement far away and concerning which it knew little. Taking these problems into account, it acted with caution and sagacity, submitting every document to Middleton and taking his opinion upon it. In this manner, a commission was drawn up to constitute Macdonald and his associates a Council of War. Charles and his advisers took three months to ensure that the names inserted were correct and the instructions practical, using information as it arrived. The major piece of this was an offer of services from a lowland royalist noble, the Earl of Glencairn. It was a tempting proposal, for Glencairn was brave and reliable, and promised a means of uniting Highlanders and Lowlanders in an enlarged rising. On the other hand, he might be unacceptable to the chiefs as an outsider. The problem produced long debates at Paris, from which emerged a remarkably sensitive compromise solution. Glencairn was instructed to meet Macdonald and his allies. If they invited him to lead them, he was to produce a royal letter inviting them to choose a general and recommending Glencairn. If they were united in declining his leadership, he was not to press it. If they were at odds with each other, he was to produce a royal commission as acting commander and take charge. In any event, Middleton was to take the supreme command as soon as he arrived. All these documents were sent to the Earl, and Lord Wentworth dispatched to Denmark to solicit aid. In this fashion Charles hoped that Middleton might repeat Montrose's invasion, with success, as unlike Montrose he was landing to support an existing army.[24]

For the rest of 1653, Charles's government struggled to follow up this policy amid all the constraints of poverty and international indifference. The Danes were no more inclined to provoke the Commonwealth by assisting its enemies than the Dutch, and Wentworth was forced to return for lack of money. Middleton proved quite incapable of raising even a small army without funds. Thus all the King could do was to encourage the existing leaders in arms and to appeal to others to join them. Middleton's frustration was increased by news that, with the Commonwealth's army in Scotland thinned because of the Dutch war, the rebellion was growing rapidly. Glencairn had been accepted as acting leader without trouble. It was also increasingly obvious that, although Charles had initially addressed the rebels in the language of a Covenanted King, they were mostly Civil War royalists, reinforced by a few young nobles. Most Covenanters held aloof and Argyll, too prominent to afford the comfort of neutralism, actively helped the Commonwealth. Nevertheless, the exiled government instructed Middleton to issue a declaration of aims as general and nebulous as possible in order to attract the widest support. He was also to tell Macdonald that he would be made an earl, but at some future date to prevent jealousy. In January 1654, all else having failed, Mary agreed to use the remnant of the Orange fortune to secure a loan for the invasion. A month after, Middleton landed in his native land, a year later than planned and equipped only with eighty soldiers and a small quantity of munitions.[25]

In dealing with the Dutch and the Scots, Charles's methods of doing business had produced no ill effects, because the elimination of the 'Presbyterian' interest from policy-making produced relative unity of counsel and the vetting of Scottish dispatches by Middleton removed remaining inconsistencies. It was otherwise with co-ordination of English royalist conspiracy. During 1653 there were signs of a revival of plotting amongst the King's adherents in England, fuelled by bitterness because the Commonwealth, rather than conciliate them, kept them outside the political system.[26] In November, some of them wrote to Nicholas proposing that a council be formed in England to supervise activity. He replied that they should propose their own members for this body, and that the King would empower them. He then wrote to Hyde asking him to secure Charles's compliance, and also to ensure that only the three of them and Ormonde knew of the existence of such a council, to ensure maximum protection for its activities.[27] By January 1654 it was in process of formation, and named the 'Sealed Knot'. The membership was complete by May, when Charles promised to inform it of all plots and authorized it to co-opt assistance, appoint commanders, and treat with anybody except regicides. The leaders numbered six, all younger sons of peers or gentry and all based in the Midlands or East Anglia.[28] From the beginning there was something absurd about the notion that this circle, based in one region of the country and associated with one faction at court, could control all English royalist activity.

The initiative immediately produced problems, centred upon Rupert's group at Paris whose contacts with English activists were at least as strong as those of Hyde and his friends. Herbert soon learned something of the

'Sealed Knot' and tried to dissuade people from joining it, and his circle commenced a separate intrigue. The key man in it was Charles, Lord Gerard, a burly and belligerent military man who had been made a Gentleman of the Bedchamber in 1649, had opposed the Treaty of Breda, and had been commissioned as captain of the royal guard in May 1652.[29] Once a client of Rupert's, he was always his friend. In February 1654 Rupert introduced a Major Henshaw to Charles, who proposed the assassination of Cromwell. The King approved the idea, but then received information that Henshaw was a double agent and disowned him. A few weeks later, Lord Gerard's young cousin John arrived in Paris, lodged with Gerard, and enthusiastically propounded a similar plan. The King met the two of them after supper, with three royalist agents with whom they were associated, heard the scheme, and ordered that it be delayed until he gave specific instructions. Whether these were given or not, a number of people knew that John Gerard left Paris in April, ready to put the scheme into action. He carried with him a proclamation in Charles's name, promising a reward of £500 a year for life to anybody who killed Cromwell and a royal pardon to all who assisted the ensuing rising. Almost certainly the King did not authorize this, for as Gardiner pointed out long ago its style and its failure to exclude regicides from pardon were at variance with every genuine royal declaration of the exile.[30] Unfortunately for the reckless John, Cromwell had spies in Paris and probably among his English associates. On arrival he was arrested, and beheaded with an accomplice. Three other friends of his were transported to the colonies, and many prominent royalists, including members of the 'Sealed Knot', put in custody.[31] The affair severely embarrassed Charles, who berated Lord Gerard furiously for letting his name be used and events set in train without permission. He also informed his courtiers, and the 'Sealed Knot', that he had never authorized the Gerards' plan.[32] This may well have been sincere. But his habit of pursuing parallel lines of policy, with separate Counsellors, had now reaped a first harvest of confusion and distrust.

One other hope remaining to the exiled King during his Paris years was that France itself, in which he sheltered, would lend him a degree of support when its civil wars ended. While it was most unlikely to attack the Commonwealth, if it could afford him a comfortable and honourable sanctuary then its prestige and its position opposite the English coast would weigh heavily in his favour. Accordingly, he tried from the beginning to ingratiate himself with the French court. In April 1652 he attempted to mediate between Louis XIV, at St Germain, and Orléans, at Paris, but the talks collapsed because Louis would not dismiss Mazarin. This venture at least ensured that the French were grateful enough to pay Charles his pension. As the campaigning season opened, the adventurer Duke of Lorraine brought his formidable mercenary army to join the rebels, and Charles commenced talks to persuade him to retire. 'Mademoiselle', loyal to her father, severed relations with the Stuarts and took the field herself, proving to be the greatest female commander since Joan of Arc. Henrietta Maria made the comparison herself, adding wryly that like that heroine she had driven out the English.[33] In June, Lorraine's soldiers appeared before Paris and the royal army drew up to face him. Rather to his surprise, Charles received a personal request from Louis to visit the Duke and to conclude a deal which the French and Lorrainers had secretly been making. He went with Wilmot and Jermyn, and found the Duke talking to envoys from Mazarin and Louis's general, including his own brother James. Charles begged the latter to assist him in winning generous terms from the French, only to be told, with infuriating priggishness, that James's first loyalty was now to his employers. Mercifully, the Duke decided that battle was not worth while, signed an ageement with Mazarin's man, and withdrew, plundering the countryside. Charles viewed the royal army and then returned to Paris and the fury of Orléans, 'Mademoiselle', and the populace, who blamed him for the loss of a vital ally. After this neither the King nor his followers dared to leave the Louvre.

They trembled there as the rebel field army, led by the Prince de Condé, arrived before Paris. Finding himself outnumbered by Louis's forces, Condé withdrew into the city, covered by the guns of the Bastille which 'Mademoiselle' turned upon the royal troopers. Now the defeated rebel army was added to the mob outside the walls of the Louvre, and the English royalists were in serious danger. When the leaders of the city refused to withdraw their formal allegiance from Louis, a mixture of soldiers and citizens killed about thirty of them and burned the town hall. To prevent a further tragedy, the nobles present agreed to allow the evacuation of the Stuart court to St Germain. Charles, Henrietta Maria, and their followers left the city in driving rain on 8 July, receiving a frigid farewell from Orléans and 'Mademoiselle' at the gate. It was perhaps the most humiliating moment of the exile.[34]

After this, the situation improved once more. The rebels left Paris under Condé and joined the Spanish army operating on the northern frontier. Charles was received warmly by Louis and his mother and then entertained luxuriously by Mazarin. When the French King re-entered his capital in October the Stuarts returned with him. Charles must have gained some unpleasant satisfaction from the banishment of 'Mademoiselle' to the provinces: thus she passed out of his life.[35] Thereafter, and all through 1653, the pattern of 1647 was repeated. Charles was treated courteously but otherwise ignored as combat was rejoined with Spain. In fact the 'juggling Cardinal', as Nicholas called Mazarin,[36] had been carrying on secret negotiations with the English Commonwealth since February 1652, in the hope of winning its alliance against the Spanish. In December 1652 the French recognized the regicide republic, though officially only to discuss the return of captured shipping. Charles was presumably allowed to remain at the Louvre because if the Commonwealth joined Spain he might be used to foment rebellion in England. Only English hesitation over a treaty with either monarchy prevented either his employment or his expulsion. In December 1653 the same army which had established the Commonwealth destroyed it and elevated Cromwell himself as Lord Protector. At once serious negotiations were undertaken to end the Anglo-Dutch war, and were completed in April 1654. By the provisions of the peace treaty, the States-General agreed not to shelter the Protectorate's enemies, closing the Netherlands as a refuge for Charles and his supporters. According to a secret arrangement made with Cromwell, the States of Holland formally excluded the Prince of Orange from any office under the States-General. In the same month a treaty of friendship was signed between the Protectorate and Sweden. Negotiations swiftly followed to the same purpose in Portugal and Denmark, while a commercial pact was made with France. It was now plain that the western European states were turning their backs upon Charles's cause one by one, and that he would at last have to quit France voluntarily if he was to do so with dignity. To encourage his decision, Mazarin arranged for £2,750 of the arrears of his pension to be paid at once,[37] and promised to continue its payment even after he had crossed the border.

Ever since his arrival in France, Charles had kept an alternative refuge in mind: Germany, which since 1648 had been at peace and which contained a multitude of princes and cities loosely owing allegiance to the Holy Roman Emperor at Vienna. Sympathy for an exiled monarch would be strong in at least some of these states, and their number made it likely that he could move to another each time his welcome waned in one. An excellent opportunity to canvass support was offered by the assembly in 1652 of the Imperial Diet at Ratisbon, to which most of the states sent representatives to acknowledge the son of the reigning Emperor, Ferdinand III, as heir to the imperial crown. Unfortunately, as with the Dutch, initial overtures were hampered by the deficiencies of Charles's agent. In this case he was an English Catholic called John Taylor, and whereas Macdowell had merely been incompetent, Taylor devoted his mission to getting jobs for his friends. By the end of the year Charles had resolved to send one of his own Counsellors and chose Wilmot. It was financially impossible for him to arrive at Ratisbon with any pomp, but at Wilmot's own suggestion the King improved his status by raising him to the rank of Earl of Rochester, the first English peerage he had bestowed.[38] Hyde held up the creation through sheer jealousy, but it was made on 11 December and the new Earl set out. He was instructed to obtain for Charles a declaration of support, money, and a residence, and secretly advised to promise the Catholic representatives the suspension of the laws against their co-religionists in England. Charles added that he would repeal these if possible, but this was 'as much grace and favour as I can show them'. The King wrote to Protestant princes and, somewhat to Hyde's disquiet, he hailed Lutherans and Calvinists impartially as fellow believers. Charles also penned appeals couched in more general terms to all the more important states. At Ratisbon the Stuart cause was viewed with considerable sympathy, not based upon geography or religion but personality: its strongest advocates were the Catholic Elector-Archbishop of Mainz and the Calvinist Elector of Brandenburg. Wilmot's (or Rochester's) boozy good humour proved extremely effective in nurturing this sentiment. Although the Diet resolved against armed assistance to Charles, at the end of 1653 it voted to supply him with £45,000, apportioned between its members, to which the Emperor added the promise of a further £23,000 from his own treasury. At last the exiled government appeared to have adequate funds, and in April 1654 the King arranged to meet his sister at the German resort of Spa just after midsummer.[39]

His removal permitted a considerable pruning of his advisers. In the course of 1653 two of those already in disgrace, Long and Wyndham, formed a conspiracy to destroy Hyde. Their ally was Sir Richard Grenville, the royalist general who had been treated so shabbily in 1645–6. It was Grenville who drove on the attack, basing it upon a rumour that Hyde had made a secret journey to London to confer with Cromwell. This was a silly story, but the injustice to be done was not more considerable than that which had been accorded to these three men. The difference was, of course, that they had been expendable to Charles whereas Sir Edward, at this time, was not. Gerard, Herbert, Berkeley, and Fraser supported the charge, and Henrietta Maria herself took an interest in it, so that Charles, much against his inclination, was obliged to have it debated in the Privy Council, swollen by favoured courtiers. Ormonde, Taaffe, Jermyn, Percy, and the Duke of York all took Hyde's part and Rupert held aloof, many of these men acting more from reluctance to irritate the King than affection for the accused. The charge failed, and Grenville was formally banned from the court.[40] The whole affair exacerbated Charles's growing distaste for Herbert and Gerard, which in turn reflected upon their patron Rupert.

In any case the King had a separate quarrel with his cousin. The arrears of the French pension turned out to suffice merely to pay off Charles's debts in Paris. To furnish his removal expenses, he ordered the sale of the single warship which Rupert had brought back. The ship itself proved rotten, and valueless, but its cannon were bought by the French government. Rupert promptly demanded the proceeds towards the repayment of the money Charles still owed him. Charles offered to give him half, and when the Prince still insisted upon the whole, he exploded with rage and ordered Rupert to be silent. The breach thus created remained open. John Gerard's doomed mission may have represented a last attempt by Rupert's friends to prove their value to Charles. If so, its results had the opposite effect. Rupert himself resigned his office of Master of the Horse a month before his cousin left Paris. He went to Germany to seek a separate fortune, claiming that Charles was ruled by Ormonde and Hyde. Gerard followed him. Herbert learned that the King was leaving him in Paris, and quit his own post of Lord Keeper. With Long and Grenville he was consigned to the backwaters of exile, as political debris. Fundamentally, the relationship of all three with their monarch was doomed by character. He concealed behind a gentle, easy-going exterior and a hatred of argument a determination to get his own way. They were all aggressive, self-confident men whose reaction to refusal or absence of attention was to repeat their views with greater violence. The breach had to occur.[41] In this manner one of the three principal groups of Privy Counsellors was removed. The second, Henrietta Maria's, had by definition to be shed, because she was remaining as always with her family in France. But its influence was weakened in addition by a quarrel, derived from her growing impatience with Charles's habit of conducting some business in secret from her. When she remonstrated with him, he simply told her that he preferred his way. The gap between them increased when she begged him to forgive Rupert, Herbert, and Gerard.[42] Thus, by process of elimination, he took to Germany a government reduced almost completely to Hyde and his friends.

Charles and his court left Paris on 3 July 1654. Most of the problem of money for the journey was that monarchs had to travel in style if they were to be taken seriously: thus he brought with him half a ton of baggage and a set of trumpeters.[43] At Peronne he was saluted by the French field army containing his brother, and the governors of towns in the Spanish Netherlands gave him royal honours and entertainments although the Archduke ignored him. After a week he reached Spa, and found Mary awaiting him. The royal siblings, reunited in a place associated with healing and pleasure after years of constriction and defeat, commenced a joyous summer holiday. Their joint court spent the days drinking spring water and hunting in the nearby hills and the evenings singing, dancing, and drinking Rhenish wine. Charles was generally admired as a splendid, and tireless, dancer. The idyll was interrupted by an outbreak of smallpox in the town, and on 11 August the royalists moved to the neighbouring spa of Aachen. There the merry-making was resumed, interspersed with bathing in the sulphurous springs and more hunting, with hawks or greyhounds. The corporation accorded the Stuarts modest but adequate honours, firing four cannon to salute them and presenting them with wildfowl, poultry, and wine. The cathedral clergy laid on an exquisite choral concert for them, and showed them the relics of Charlemagne. Mary politely kissed the emperor's skull and the reliquary containing his hand-bones, while Charles preferred to kiss his sword and then could not resist measuring it. In September Mary began to think of her return home and Charles of finding winter quarters other than Aachen: the smell of sulphur was becoming unbearable. It was resolved to try the great nearby city of Cologne, and thither they went on the 29th. The local potentate was the Elector-Archbishop, but this individual was a peculiar recluse who kept to his castle a few miles up the Rhine, studying alchemy and collecting jewels. The citizens therefore conducted their own affairs, and were noted for dedicated Catholicism. Yet they greeted Charles as a welcome novelty, with cheers from the crowd and volleys from the civic guard. He, Mary, and their retinues were all lodged in a lovely mansion owned by a Protestant widow, and the religious orders competed to entertain them to meals, music, and comedies. The cathedral clergy surpassed those of Aachen by opening the central shrine of their gigantic church to reveal the bones of the Three Wise Men. The parties continued until 19 October, when brother and sister went to Düsseldorf, and a last enormous reception at the court of Philippe-Wilhelm, Pfalz-Graf von Neuburg, a Westphalian potentate who felt exceptional sympathy for the exiled monarch. They then sailed down the Rhine, saluted with cannon by the passing towns, to the Dutch border at Xanten. There they parted, and Charles returned sadly to Cologne on the 26th.[44] It was to be his base for one and a half years.

Condemned by some commentators, both at the time[45] and since, this spree has added to Charles's reputation for fecklessness. But as he himself told his aunt, the Queen of Bohemia,[46] there was nothing else to do. During 1653 he had repeatedly assured Middleton and the Scottish rebels that he would enter their country in person as soon as they had won some victories. Hyde reassured Nicholas that the King had absolutely no intention of going back to Scotland unless it was safe to do so, but this contingency was certainly considered. On leaving Paris

Charles had empowered his brother James to conduct his English affairs for him if he went to his northern realm.[47] At Spa he received his first news from Middleton, a letter written in May which announced victories and invited the King to come over. At this, serious efforts commenced to find money and shipping for the journey, although in private Charles was most reluctant to risk himself in Scotland again.[48] Not only are his feelings understandable but they were justified, for Middleton had been hopelessly over-sanguine. In April 1654 Cromwell had sent George Monck to resume command in Scotland, with fresh supplies of men and money. That summer he entered the Highlands and chased the royalist leaders around until they were exhausted, demoralized, and deserted by all but a handful of clansmen.[49] On 10 September one of Middleton's officers brought news of this deteriorating situation to Aachen, and Charles was profoundly distressed to receive it. He wrote immediately to the General and Glencairn to encourage them, and sent these letters with an agent instructed to return with a judgement on the remaining chances of the rising. His government also struggled to find military supplies for the Scots, and sent further messengers to them when the first failed to report sufficiently swiftly.[50] As his master thus struggled with problems of distance and ignorance, Middleton slowly despaired. By midwinter the rebellion was clearly collapsing, and in April 1655 he sailed back to the Continent after giving his few remaining adherents permission to surrender.[51]

Nor, amid the revelry, did the King neglect the English royalists. On the way to Spa he was met by a representative of the 'Sealed Knot', complaining of the chaos caused by the 'Gerard Plot'. This man returned to England equipped with a royal letter urging the 'Knot' to continue its efforts. But the same agent also carried a set of proposals from a different group of conspirators, asking Charles to authorize planning for a rising to be launched as rapidly as possible.[52] These men, whom the exiled court referred to simply as 'the new council', were a scattered set of impoverished royalist gentry, altogether less impressive in rank and experience than the 'Knot'. At first Charles gave them no encouragement but in August his attitude began to shift. Then he received a warning from the 'Knot' that it considered any further plotting unwise, and enthusiastic proposals from 'the new council' for a rebellion in collusion with 'Presbyterians' and discontented Cromwellian officers.[53] In September, having received the news from Scotland, the King threw his support wholeheartedly behind the new activists, instructing them to get to work immediately and asking Lord Willoughby and other 'Presbyterians' to assist them. He commissioned Rochester to lead the prospective rising.[54]

Nor can an accusation of financial irresponsibility be made to stick. The summer holiday was Mary's treat, for she paid for their lodgings and meals and Charles only had to provide his servants' salaries. Taaffe hired the fiddlers for the dances. The King's original intention was to live off his French pension and to use the German money to support royalist rebellions.[55] The problem that developed was that neither was properly paid. Although the sum voted by the Diet began to trickle in as soon as Charles reached Spa, only £3,600 had arrived by the end of the year. More followed later, but slowly, and much was never paid.[56] The grandiloquent gesture made by the Emperor proved to be no more than that, for Ferdinand's war-ruined treasury could not pay his own household,[57] and nothing whatsoever was sent by him to Charles. The French pension was as irregular as ever, Jermyn intercepted some of it to reimburse himself for money spent in the royal service, and only a total of £1,900 (out of £15,000 due) reached Cologne in all the King's time there.[58] This income meant that for the first year in Germany, despite occasional panics, he could pay the salaries of his Privy Council and Household, afford a full if simple diet for all, and meet the considerable bills for postage and parchment run up in the effort to direct royalist activity in Britain and diplomatic activity in Europe. The money was managed very ably by Stephen Fox, a young client of Hyde.[59] Agents coaxed donations from individual well-wishers in England and Europe, and most of these sums seem to have been used to pay for the journeys of conspirators.[60] That so much German money came in was due largely to the efforts of Rochester, who was sent on a tour of princely capitals in late 1654, and of Richard Belling, a former Irish Confederate Catholic leader whom Hyde thought a 'jewel'.[61] By June 1655 the Privy Council had been forced to order retrenchments in the Household,[62] and by the end of that year penury was producing constant anxiety. When Charles ordered a sable muff from Paris, his agent there begged him to choose a less expensive, if less prestigious, fur. An order for new liveries for his servants failed for lack of credit. The King had got rid of his hounds, only for an idiot English royalist to send him another pack. It was calculated that it would cost almost as much to send them back as to keep them a while, so they were accepted.[63] By March 1656, Charles was £3,200 in debt.[64]

It is therefore unsurprising that the King's life in the Cologne years was somewhat austere. He walked on the city walls, hunted hares, played cribbage, and swam in the Rhine, a boat following in case of accidents. He occasionally applauded a particularly good sermon by a chaplain. He bought some spaniels and a little harpsichord, and took regular Italian lessons, although the books which he ordered in that language were fashionable light reading rather than great works. He took care over his dress but did not keep a coach, and enjoyed trading gossip about the marital affairs of acquaintances. He followed the details of political affairs as well, receiving newspapers and asking for a map of Arras to understand the course of the relief of that city by the French in mid-1654.[65] His single undoubted extravagance came in September 1655 when Mary reappeared and they both went to the great fair at Frankfurt. Hyde complained that the visit served no useful purpose to counterbalance its expense, but Charles insisted that he needed some holiday. Brother and sister certainly had a wonderful time there, and neither friend nor critic afterwards claimed that the money consumed was considerable. Hyde wrote to a friend that if rumour were true then some of the occurrences there were 'fitter for discourse than letters', but he seems to have been referring to a political embarrassment. Notable among the princes who had defaulted on their contributions was the Elector Palatine, elder brother to Rupert and cousin to Charles, and somebody upon whose behalf the Stuarts had once made great efforts. He attended the fair also, and it is not surprising that afterwards each party complained of being snubbed by the other.[66] If this is a true portrait of the King's life during this period, it is understandable that in October 1655 he confessed himself hardly able to bear the prospect of a second winter at Cologne.[67]

Certainly he was less troubled (or diverted) by quarrels among his advisers. His formal Privy Council now consisted of Ormonde, Rochester, Hyde, Lord Wentworth, Norwich, and Culpeper and Nicholas who had at last arrived from Holland. Wentworth's promotion was the reward which this hard-drinking but intelligent cavalry leader received for his fruitless mission to Denmark. The Catholic Irish were represented at court by Taaffe and the Scots by Viscount Newburgh and by Lord Balcarres, the noble who had been so useful to Charles in 1651 and who fled Scotland to join him in April 1654. There was still no unanimity of affection or opinion, for Rochester, Culpeper, and Balcarres allied to revive the old argument of 1649–50, for making an alliance with the 'Presbyterians' and the Covenanters. When one of Charles's (Anglican) chaplains preached against the notion of forcing terms upon a King, Balcarres, true to his Kirk party background, stormed out.[68] Yet these divisions were relatively muted. For one thing, shortage of resources meant that Privy Counsellors and important courtiers were often sent on missions in person, removing them for lengthy periods. For another, neither 'Presbyterians' nor royalists were in a position to deliver anything to the King immediately, so discussions of their respective merits as allies had an academic air. Furthermore, the failure of the attack on Hyde in late 1653 had made any serious

infighting among the royal advisers seem pointless. Sir Edward himself
was more than ever before the King's key Counsellor. The position of
his group was strengthened at Spa when Nicholas was at last restored
to his old post of Secretary of State, while Hyde continued to draft all
important policy documents. When Middleton returned from Scotland
in mid-1655 he became his fast friend and (to the horror of Balcarres)
adopted the Anglican communion. By February 1656, Nicholas could tell
a friend that if he wanted a place at court then only Hyde could get him
one. This situation did not make for perfect ease because of the plump
knight's personality. The Earl of Norwich, who held aloof from factional
squabbles, observed that Sir Edward was honest and had good principles
but his conceit and arrogance, and his obvious ambition, made him hard
to work with. If he had any real friends they were Ormonde and Nicholas,
of whom he always spoke warmly, but even Nicholas found him irritating
and thoughtless at times. The Secretary was not part of the informal 'inner
ring' of Counsellors who were especially trusted by Charles, whereas Hyde
definitely was. Nicholas's feelings were not improved by Sir Edward's habit
of introducing to these private discussions lesser royalists of whom he
currently thought highly but who had no formal conciliar rank.[69] Charles
himself coped with Hyde by taking the rise out of him. At a masque at the
French court the Queen Mother of France had asked who the fat man with
Ormonde was. Charles, realizing that she meant Sir Edward, answered
loudly that he was 'the naughty man who did all the mischief, and set
him against his mother', and hugely enjoyed the general embarrassment.
In a letter to Ormonde, the King spoke lightly of Hyde's grumbles. In
one to Hyde himself, Charles directed him to run upon his 'gouty feet' to
the King, and added that he wished Sir Edward were 'besh––t' (the two
polite dashes are Charles's own) for not giving him a manual of Spanish
court ceremonial. Nor did he tell his principal minister everything: knowing that Hyde would oppose the trip to Frankfurt, he left him to discover
from others that the decision to go had been taken.[70]

The great issue which rocked the exiled government in late 1654
concerned the King's second brother, Henry, Duke of Gloucester. This
unfortunate boy, aged fourteen at this time, had spent the years since
the Great Civil War in the custody of Parliament and then of the
Commonwealth. He had bid farewell to his father just before the latter's
execution, had seen his frail sister Elizabeth expire of illness the next year,
and had at last been released and sent into exile as a measure of mercy at
the beginning of 1653. He had joined the court at the Louvre, where a
flood of affection and admiration after so much misery rapidly made him
insufferable.[71] Despite this, Henrietta Maria begged to retain him when

Charles left for Germany, so that at least one son should be with her. The King consented to this with grave misgivings, having first secured her promise that she would not put pressure upon Henry to become a Roman Catholic, and instructed the youth himself to avoid this course above all. His doubts were justified, for in October she suddenly sacked Henry's Protestant tutor and sent him into an abbey for indoctrination in her faith. Henrietta was not generally a bigot: she accepted that it would be impolitic for Charles himself to follow this course, and her chief attendants, Jermyn, Percy, and Hatton, were all Protestant. All of them, her son James, and Henry himself, were aghast at her action now. But she was adamant, having decided that only such a course would ensure political and financial aid for the Stuarts from her Church. From the rigour with which she clung to her course, and with which she denied (against plain truth) that she was putting pressure upon Henry, it seems as if failure and poverty had temporarily unhinged her. Letters sped to Charles from the tutor, Henry, and Henrietta Maria about the affair, and his reaction was immediate. He replied to Henry that such a step would harm his cause and dishonour their father, and that if his brother took it he would never see him again. He made the latter threat also to their mother, and sent Ormonde to fetch the boy away to their sister Mary. Henrietta Maria was absolutely furious, but after five months she was writing to the King again as before.[72]

This story has been told many times, either as a family drama or as an example of Charles's capacity for decisive action. It may be more interesting now to set it in the context of his relations with the Catholic world as a whole. The exiled government always accepted that the King's conversion to Catholicism would make him unacceptable to the great majority of the English. Yet circumstances ensured that he spent most of the exile in Catholic countries. As a result he had to walk a political tightrope, but on the whole he made very slight concessions to the adherents of Rome. On escaping from England he wrote to the Pope offering to tolerate English Catholicism if papal aid contributed to his restoration. His Holiness made Charles's conversion the condition for negotiations, and the matter was dropped. In December 1652 Catholics complained that not a single Privy Counsellor favoured them. No more was done to improve relations between them and Charles until September 1654, when an agent was sent to their representatives in England.[73] It was in this setting that the battle over Henry occurred, and the King's response caused great offence in the Catholic world. The Venetian ambassador at Paris wrote that 'the House of Stuart, after having been expelled from the Kingdoms of this world, will now submit to banishment from the Kingdoms of Heaven'. There were dangerous mutterings in devout Cologne. Charles and his advisers tried, unsuccessfully, to hush the matter up, and Henry was removed to Holland, not brought to court, for this reason.[74] Great efforts were made to cultivate the principal Catholic resident in Cologne, the papal nuncio. This cleric wrote a letter to Rome about them,[75] upon which Gardiner based a claim that Charles made an offer of secret conversion in return for money.

This is not really what the letter says. The nuncio told how the King came up to him in a monastery garden and promised him toleration for Catholics in England if he were restored. The nuncio was then visited by Taaffe and an Irish Jesuit, Peter Talbot, who repeated the offer, and Talbot hinted that Charles himself might convert. Disbelieving this, the great ecclesiastic cited the intervention over Henry, for which the two Irishmen pleaded force of necessity, only for the nuncio to declare himself unconvinced. Talbot had been briefed by Hyde just before the interview, and wrote to him just after it, stating simply that the affair of Henry had blasted any hope of help from Rome.[76] He made no mention of an offer by Charles, and (as we shall soon see) was a man quite capable of outrunning the truth of a situation while negotiating. Shortly after, the Pfalz-Graf Philippe-Wilhelm, who was a devoted Catholic himself and now firm friends with the King, offered to intercede with the Pope. The terms which Charles offered to Rome, and which were drafted by Hyde and Ormonde, consisted, as ever, of the repeal of the penal laws in exchange for money and soldiers. As ever, they were not sufficient.[77] When Belling asked the King privately to consider his conversion, Charles replied that although he hoped to tolerate Catholics, neither political expediency *nor* his conscience would permit his acceptance of the Roman faith. This is his clearest personal statement upon the matter preserved from the exile.[78] Nor did anybody record any admiring comments made by him upon the cathedrals or rituals which he saw. Immediately after his death a number of people who knew him well asserted that during the 1650s Charles II became a Catholic in his private, though not his outward, beliefs. As Lady Antonia Fraser has already stated, not a scrap of evidence to support this idea survives from the decade itself.

Once reassured that his mother's action had not cost him his residence, the King turned most of his attention to the approaching rising in England. The complications resulting from the creation of the 'Sealed Knot' were growing more intense. A month after Charles had thrown his weight behind the 'new council', an agent arrived from the 'Knot' to receive his commands. With that glibness which confused his ministers, Charles replied that he had only dealt with the new men while the 'Knot' seemed dormant, that he still regarded the 'Knot' as the controlling authority of English royalism, and that he only wished it to co-opt more members. By the end of 1654 the 'new council' was expressing contempt for the 'Sealed Knot's' caution and proceeding with its plans, while the 'Knot' dismissed the 'new council's' ideas as illusions. It was a situation as difficult as that which had preceded the 'Start', and the King bungled it as badly, this time with the connivance of his advisers. At the end of January 1655 he authorized the 'council' to proceed, and dispatched Rochester to command the rising. When this was done, a messenger arrived from the 'Sealed Knot' to announce that most of the 'council's' leaders had been arrested, that Cromwell's government was obviously prepared for trouble, and that the rising had to be called off. Charles neither did this nor gave the 'Knot' a positive order to suport the 'council': instead, he sent an agent to London empowered only to view the situation and to mediate between the different groups. He then wrote desperately to some disaffected republicans asking for their aid, but as usual offering no concessions or incentives.[79] At the end of February he went secretly to Zealand as had been arranged, to lie hidden at the house of a Dutch Orangist and to be ready to reach England as soon as the rebellion gained ground. Ormonde, Hyde, Taaffe, and Wentworth did the same.

Disaster inevitably followed. When the moment for the rebellion came, in early March, the 'Presbyterians', disenchanted republicans, 'Sealed Knot', and most royalists all did nothing. A few scattered royalist bands did rise, but only one of these remained in arms once gathered and this was chased across two counties and finally surrendered to a single horse troop. The Protector's government made a great number of arrests, and eventually 38 men were convicted of treason and 12 executed. Rochester had to escape from England all over again, and, with daring and incredible luck, he did so.[80] Charles and his advisers lingered in Zealand, amid freezing winds and snowfalls, until news of the failure arrived and they slipped back ignominiously to Cologne. By now their presence was generally known, and the Dutch States-General wrote a peremptory letter to Mary demanding her brother's removal if he were indeed on their soil.[81] The consequences of the affair were uniformly unfortunate. Royalist activism in England lost some of its leaders and most of its morale. The States-General, offended by Charles's incursion into their territory, prepared to expel his brother Henry. He had to be brought, at last, to Cologne although Mary still paid for his upkeep.[82] The King's foray to the Netherlands also consumed much of his precious stock of money.[83] For all these woes, as Professor Underdown has pointed out, Charles must bear a large part of the responsibility. His policy widened divisions between his supporters in

England, and caused the more reckless to launch themselves into action without being either restrained or supported by the rest. Of course, the King and Hyde laid all the blame upon the royalists,[84] and followed the tragedy by appealing to them both in England and Scotland to prepare for a fresh attempt.[85]

If conspiracy engrossed the court in early 1655, then espionage produced its most dramatic concerns at the end of the year. Just before the rebellion, Cromwell's spy system pulled off its greatest success. During the second half of Charles's stay at Paris and the first months of Cologne, the Protectorate had kept agents in those cities who reported courtiers' gossip: Rochester, with his taste for a chat over a drink, had provided much of this. But then it had bought the services of a handsome, elegant, plausible young Catholic royalist, Henry Manning, who was able to find a place at court himself by February 1655. From there he sent regular dispatches to London, based upon his proximity to the King and his advisers, and received money and instructions in return. In late November royalist agents at Antwerp intercepted this flow of information. Manning was made drunk, so that courtiers could steal his keys and search his boxes while he slept. There they found all the evidence required. Manning was interrogated fiercely by Culpeper and Nicholas, and condemned to death by a 'council of war'. The Elector of Cologne did not consider this tribunal to possess legal authority upon his territory, so Philippe-Wilhelm kindly offered his own as a killing-ground. Begging for mercy, the young man was taken there ten days after his arrest, and executed.[86]

The Manning affair has, understandably, been generally considered to illustrate the excellence of the Cromwellian espionage system, and the vulnerability of the exiled Stuarts to it. Indeed, there were risible aspects to royalist security. Few agents came and went without being recognized by loquacious courtiers and then reported by the Protectorate's resident observers. Any important letters between the King's followers were sent in code and sometimes in white ink which showed up under heat, but occasionally ciphers were not known to recipients or the ink remained illegible. Hyde's handwriting was a formidable obstacle in itself: Middleton could not read it, and many a historian will sympathize with him.[87] The exiled government was so poor and inspired such little fear that its agents were few and it could suborn nobody in power in England. But it was not entirely ineffectual. Its messengers regularly slipped across the Channel despite all attempts to catch them at the ports, and several important royalists broke prison once arrested: both facts call the efficiency of Cromwellian security into question. Charles's web of contacts was sensitive enough to trap Manning himself. On the other side of the picture, it may be asked how much good Manning did his employers. He took up his position too late to play more than a marginal part in exposing the rising of March 1655. Thereafter, in his attempts to justify his pay, he portrayed an urgency and a menace in royalist planning which it actually lacked.[88] Cromwell's government was thereby encouraged in measures of sustained repression which made the reconciliation of English royalists, and thus the settlement of the country, even more remote. It might have been better all round had the Protectorate kept its money, and Manning his life.

The last months of Charles's stay in Cologne were taken up with two secret diplomatic missions, a major one to the Crown of Spain and a minor one to Lucy Walter. Lucy's movements during the period 1653–5 are as obscure as most of her story. In August 1654 she was said to be at Liège, *en route* to Charles, and the news caused consternation among the royalists at Paris who, for moral or personal reasons, by now thoroughly disliked her. In October she was rumoured to be involved with Taaffe. By January 1655 she was in Cologne, on a visit with the young son whom she had borne to Charles; her purpose was almost certainly financial, and on the 11th the King signed a warrant for a pension to her of £415 a year. This was to be paid at Antwerp, to keep her far from the court.[89] In May 1655 his sister Mary wrote Charles two letters, both referring to his 'wife'. In the first, the Princess commented that the 'wife' was wondering whether to send a letter or not. In the second, she wrote that this woman sent only her 'duty' to Charles, and was not, like him, constant but 'thinks of another husband'. Lucy's apologists have taken these to prove the existence of her marriage to the King. Her detractors have replied that a prim royal lady such as Mary would never have associated with her brother's mistress, that she could hardly refer to his constancy save in jest, and that therefore 'wife' was just a nickname for a sweetheart in Mary's entourage. Neither position is very strong. The Princess of Orange enjoyed revelry and had tolerated the constant infidelity of her own husband, so she need not have been too strict to receive Lucy. If the latter was living with Charles in 1649 when he was Mary's guest, she ought to have known her, and Lucy was certainly established at The Hague when the Princess wrote these letters. On 21 May Charles asked Taaffe to tell her that he would send money when he had any, but begged her to live in some place less public than the Dutch capital because of the harm she was doing his reputation. The evidence outlined above indicates that he was probably carrying on a celibate existence at this time. Mary's tone when referring to the 'wife' is absolutely cool and neutral. Upon the other side of the debate, it must be stressed that 'wife' was sometimes employed as a polite sobriquet for mistress.[90] If Lucy was the subject of these comments, then the impression of tension in them and the anxiety in Charles's letter were both justified. By January 1656 Charles had to employ an agent to deal with his former lover.

The man was Daniel O'Neill, a cousin of the great Owen Roe and a very rare example of a Gaelic Irishman who had made a successful career at the English court. He had carried out many missions for Charles I in the Great Civil War, and had reappeared in Paris in 1653. There he had impressed himself so much upon both Charles and Hyde that the former had made him a Gentleman of the Bedchamber and the latter had drawn him into the 'inner ring' and nicknamed him 'Infallible Subtle'. He was equally useful upon a diplomatic errand or mediating between Hyde and a landlady.[91] He had been the man sent to make contact with the royalist conspirators before the rebellion of 1655. Having escaped the imbroglio with characteristic agility, he found himself upon a less perilous if more sordid errand. This was, apparently, to investigate rumours that Lucy's behaviour was indeed bringing Charles's name into disrepute, and to determine whether it would be wise (for political or compassionate reasons) to get custody of their son. His reports provide the clearest insight which we possess into the nature of the woman who was the first recognized mistress of Charles II.[92] She had commenced an affair with a married man, Thomas Howard, Mary Stuart's Gentleman of the Horse, which was creating such scandal at The Hague that the Orange party leaders wanted her run out of town. She was also being blackmailed by her maid, who threatened to spread the story of her connection with Howard even further and to accuse her of provoking two abortions upon herself. O'Neill could not establish the truth of the last story, though Lucy had certainly suffered a miscarriage. Lucy herself proposed to him that she murder the maid by running a needle into her brain while she slept, through the opening of her ear to leave no trace of the crime. O'Neill quashed this ingenious plan, and bought off the woman instead. Lucy reminded him of Charles's promise to send money. He begged the King not to do so except upon strict conditions, for, whereas he himself had once importuned Charles on her behalf, he now realized that she would spend it all immediately and demand more. He also advised him to get young James away from her if he recognized the boy as his son.

This negotiation was not resolved when the King left Cologne, to conclude the far more protracted and important talks with the Spanish. His state of suspended political animation since his return to the Continent had been due primarily to the failure of the English republicans to intervene in the Franco-Spanish war. Representatives of both crowns had bid repeatedly for the support of the Commonwealth and then of Cromwell, producing much hard bargaining but no decision. At last, in late 1654, the

Protector and his Council chose a course: to avoid a French alliance but to attack Spain at sea and in its West Indian possessions. An expedition was launched, and seized Jamaica. As soon as the news broke in Europe, in the summer of 1655 the exiled Stuart government wrote to King Felipe IV of Spain urging him to take up Charles's cause. Philippe-Wilhelm was also employed as an intermediary.[93] Nothing came of these initial approaches, for the Spanish were as reluctant to get involved in all-out war with England, and to prejudice their chances of making peace by adopting the Stuarts, as the Dutch had been. But Cromwell's refusal to relinquish Jamaica and his hope of further conquests made a complete breach between him and Spain inevitable. In October 1655 diplomatic relations were severed, and Mazarin promptly took advantage of the rupture to sign an Anglo-French treaty of friendship. Most of the clauses were intended to foster trade, but there was one which the Stuarts had long been dreading: the French, while insisting upon sheltering Henrietta Maria as a Daughter of France, agreed never again to receive Charles, his brothers, and the principal royalist leaders within their borders. With the Dutch trying to seal their territory against him, the only hope that the King now possessed of gaining a base on the Channel coast lay with Spain.

By the winter of 1655–6, several royalists were urging Charles to force the issue by going in person, uninvited, to Brussels to confront the Archduke and offer a treaty. The most vociferous among them was the Irish Jesuit, Peter Talbot, who was now in the Netherlands and claimed to have the confidence of the Spanish. He attempted to serve both his King and his faith by telling Charles that the alliance would be a certainty if only he would declare his conversion to Catholicism in secret. Charles and his Counsellors were careful to ignore this advice. They correctly doubted the wisdom and the influence of Talbot, whom Hyde came to consider a menace deserving to be locked up. They also realized that the dignity and love of ceremony of the Spanish would only be offended if their prospective ally rushed impetuously into their territory. Instead, on 26 October, Charles instructed his accredited agent at Brussels, Sir Henry De Vic, to open negotiations. De Vic had been serving the Stuarts in this joyless and impecunious post since the Great Civil War, and on this occasion the pattern of his career remained unchanged: the Archduke and his advisers spoke well of Charles but offered nothing. Ormonde, that pattern of aristocratic dignity, was sent to reinforce Sir Henry at the end of the year, and reported that the Spaniards in Flanders would do nothing without express permission from Madrid. The royalists had been reluctant to apply to Felipe himself because of the time and expense involved, but now a messenger was prepared for the journey. Instead, His Most Catholic

Majesty moved first. Cromwell was preparing a powerful fleet for the spring, and in January Felipe gave the Archduke formal leave to treat with Charles. The ministers in the Spanish Netherlands insisted, however, that the Stuart King came to negotiate privately, leaving his Counsellors behind. They wished to avoid any open commitment to him until suitable terms had been agreed, and they seem to have expected him to be more inclined to make concessions without the support of his advisers.[94]

Here they were wrong, for Charles had changed since the days when Lauderdale dealt with him off the Kent coast. He did come to Brussels incognito at the opening of March, bringing with him only a few servants and Rochester, whose sociable ways had proved so useful at Ratisbon. Ormonde had impressed the Spanish as much as expected, and remained to assist with the talks. Soon after the King's arrival in the capital of the Spanish Netherlands, his presence became known and crowds gathered outside his lodgings. So he emerged, left the city and made a circuit of the walls to baffle any spies following him, and then settled at a royal hunting lodge in the village of Vilvorde. In fact Cromwell's agents rapidly located him there, but this did nothing to disturb the talks. The Archduke's chief ministers came to Vilvorde repeatedly, and were as impressed by Charles as most who met him. In less than three weeks they were framing a treaty, and upon 2 and 3 April its articles were signed. These were remarkably practical and restrained. The Spanish promised to lend Charles 6,000 soldiers, whom they would pay, as soon as the royalists secured an English port at which to land them. This force was intended to provide the nucleus for a great rebellion against the Protectorate which would replace the King on his throne. If this succeeded, he promised three rewards to Spain. First, he would return Jamaica, and also the islands of Antigua and Montserrat which the English had occupied since the last Spanish treaty in 1630. He would also prevent any further encroachment by his subjects upon the Spanish American possessions. Second, he would lend Spain twelve warships to help recover Portugal, which had been ruled by Felipe until it seceded in 1640. Third, and in a secret article, he agreed to suspend the penal laws against English Catholics and to try to repeal them.[95]

Thus both parties appeared to have made a good bargain. Felipe IV hoped to have found a means of ending Cromwell's attack at one blow. Charles, for relatively minor concessions, had obtained a promise of the body of foreign troops which the rising of 1655 had proved to be essential if the Stuarts were to fight their way home. Five years' wandering in the political wilderness had ended, but the Promised Land had yet to be regained.

The Pensioner of Spain, 1656–1660

IN 1656 the Spanish monarchy was arguably the greatest power in the world. Its possessions in the Netherlands, Italy, and the Americas gave its king the largest revenue of any ruler of the age, and a capacity to wage war in several theatres at once without allies. The liabilities associated with such advantages were the fear, envy, and greed which they provoked in other states and the ambitions which they aroused in Spanish governments. As a result, during the previous century the empire's resources had been repeatedly overstrained by warfare. In 1652 Spanish troops had driven their enemies simultaneously from Italy, Flanders, and Catalonia, only for their government to go bankrupt. By the time that Charles II took up residence in it, the monarchy had been continuously at war for thirty-six years, generally with at least two other powers at once. In 1656 its current enemies were France, England, and Portugal, and it was fighting in the Netherlands, Italy, Catalonia, Estremadura, and the West Indies. It had agreed to provide support for three separate notable exiles: the Duke of Lorraine, the Prince de Condé, and Charles himself. By October in this year King Felipe IV was in such penury that he feasted upon meat that was full of flies and stank. This was the ally upon whom the exiled Stuarts had fixed such hopes.[1] The story of their partnership has hitherto been told in detail only from Charles's point of view, whether by his biographers or by historians concerned with related subjects, such as Professor Underdown in his definitive study of royalist conspiracy. Accordingly, the Spaniards have been portrayed as having behaved towards their royal guest with dilatoriness, neglect, incompetence, and even deceit. The purpose of this chapter is to argue that such a viewpoint is fallacious, and to offer a more balanced picture.

The fundamental problem of the alliance was that, like Charles's treaty with the Covenanters, it was based upon conflicting interests and expectations. Charles wanted to be accorded public royal honours, a residence in the Spanish Netherlands, and a pension. He desired the seaports of Flanders to be opened to all ships which recognized his authority, to provide bases for royalist privateers and transportation for an invasion force. He wished

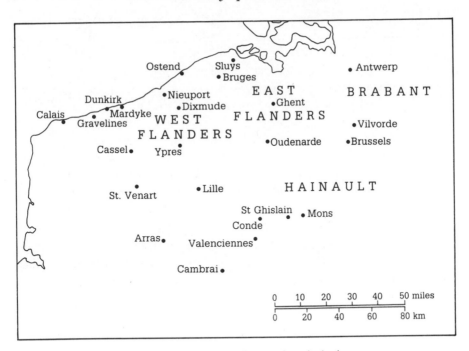

Map to illustrate Charles II's stay in the Spanish Netherlands, 1656–60

to be permitted to gather his own army of exiled royalists on the Flemish coast, maintained by Spain until the moment came when it took part in the invasion. This development would enhance his prestige in Europe and Britain, provide subsistence for his followers, and reduce his dependence upon foreign arms to reconquer his realms. Finally, he wanted the Spanish to make the attempt upon England an immediate priority, and to carry it out, if necessary, in advance of a royalist uprising. All this considerably exceeded the terms of the alliance. By contrast, the government in Madrid expected Charles to retire to Cologne and there set about organizing the rebellion in England and instructing his adherents in the service of France to defect to that of Spain. If the English royalists did seize and hold a port, then King Felipe was prepared to honour his word and to support an invasion. He and his governors were most unwilling to allow any ship claiming Charles's authority to sail into their own ports because of the security risk that this involved. They did not even want his couriers to pass through them, as Cromwellian spies could so easily claim to be in this service. Furthermore, the Spanish realized that to maintain a royalist army in Flanders would consume resources needed to support their own soldiers there. With the troops of Lorraine and Condé already weighing down their payroll in the Netherlands, they had no wish for any more.

Behind all, lay a determination not to embroil Spain too clearly with the exiled Stuarts lest such an involvement hamper the restoration of peace with England: the same consideration that had motivated the Dutch during their war with the Commonwealth.[2] What made the clash of the opposed attitudes particularly stark was that in their desperation, and arrogance, the exiled royalists pressed their claims as though all had been guaranteed by the treaty.

The men caught in the middle of this conflict were Felipe's principal ministers in the Netherlands. Charles's arrival there coincided with a reshuffle of the Spanish high command. The mediocre Leopold-Wilhelm was retired with thanks and replaced as governor of the province by Felipe's favourite illegitimate son, Juan-José. This small, lively, and ambitious young man had already won great applause by his campaigns in Catalonia. The direct command of the army in the region was given to Alonso, Marquis de Caracena, who had been a successful leader in Italy. Both men were joined, and advised, by Don Alonso de Cardeñas, the former ambassador to England and a notably shrewd, dour, and strong-minded diplomat.

The battle of wills between this formidable trio and Charles was joined as soon as they all had gathered in Brussels in May 1656. In the course of that first summer the Stuart King gained his right to reside in the Spanish Netherlands by the simple tactic of refusing to move. He was forced, however, to settle his court at Bruges, a city of considerable beauty and historic importance but by the seventeenth century an economic, political, and administrative backwater. He also obtained the promise of a pension of 3,000 *écus* per month, in view of his obvious inability to support himself, and the first instalment was paid in August. But this could do nothing to repay Charles's debts, and his Household had to be left at Cologne as security for them. It was only released in the autumn when Philippe-Wilhelm managed to gather more of the money voted by the Imperial Diet. Neither of the Stuart King's other immediate wishes, public recognition and the opening of ports to royalist ships, were granted.[3]

Most of the direct argument was conducted between the royalists and Cardeñas, for Juan-José and Caracena were occupied with the latest round in the Franco-Spanish War. During the summer of 1656 both monarchies were intent upon the same strategy, of conducting serious peace talks while trying to win a major victory upon the frontiers of the Netherlands to force concessions. The French had the larger army, and in June this laid siege to the very important Spanish frontier fortress of Valenciennes. Juan-José entrenched his soldiers nearby until they had been reinforced by German mercenaries and his enemies had grown careless.

Then he shattered the French in a sudden attack and having thus made himself master of the field he spent the rest of the campaigning season reducing a French-held town, Condé. This spectacular opening to his career in the north combined with two other developments to make a decisive shift in the Franco-Spanish war. At the end of the summer Cromwell's ships destroyed one of the two annual silver fleets from the Americas upon which much of King Felipe's war finance depended. Almost simultaneously, the negotiations between France and Spain collapsed. The reaction of the Madrid government to these events was to decide that, with Juan-José fighting so well in the Netherlands and the resources of the monarchy reduced, it was wisest to concentrate during 1657 upon knocking out Portugal. This effort promised the best results for the smallest outlay, while Juan-José was relied upon to hold the northern territories against attack. Mazarin, considering the year's developments in turn, decided reluctantly that France stood no chance of making headway against Spain without direct help from England. On 8 November he signed an agreement whereby English units would join the French army for an all-out invasion of Flanders. Thus the portion of the Spanish monarchy upon which Charles's fortunes depended was being relegated to a sideshow in Felipe's strategy, just as it faced a considerable new threat.

Even as Juan-José carried out his first triumphant campaign, Charles was commencing the formation of his own army. The most obvious step in this was to recall from French service the royalists who remained in it, and the greatest of these was his own brother James. Although the Anglo-French treaty of 1655 had stipulated the expulsion of this prince from French soil, both governments had connived in his actual continuation there. If Charles was allying with Spain, James represented a focus for royalist sentiment in France which would split the King's party. He was, moreover, growing into a capable general devoted to the French army. Nevertheless, when Charles ordered his presence at Bruges he swallowed his distress and arrived in September with over a hundred men.[4] The second most important of the newcomers from France was George Digby, Earl of Bristol. His interference in French politics had reproduced the pattern of his career in every country, of initial striking success followed by catastrophe. Having made a mortal enemy of Mazarin, he was only too happy now to decamp to the new arena in the Netherlands. His talents there were sorely needed. Hyde's ingrained contempt for most foreigners extended to a refusal to learn their languages, while his fiery temperament was ill-matched to the dignified Spanish habit of indicating disagreement by silence. Acting as Charles's chief negotiator with the ministers at Brussels in the summer of 1656, he achieved a hostile mutual incomprehension.[5] Bristol, by contrast, spoke fluent French and Spanish and was fitted by nature to the arts of flattery and insinuation. On arrival he discovered that Juan-José's chief interests were scholarly disputation, astrology, and his own glory. He got an audience with the prince and discoursed brilliantly upon texts and planetary influences. Soon he was asked to draw up Juan-José's own horoscope and found the prediction of a crown in it. In this manner Charles acquired a very able and highly favoured agent at the governor's side.[6]

In August Charles felt confident enough to summon all royalists to join him in arms. Those gathered into the most numerous and compact existing units, and in whom the Spaniards had most interest, were the Irish regiments serving France. The most prominent commander among them was Inchiquin, who had preferred to remain when Charles left for Germany, and was rewarded for his past services with the dignity of an earldom.[7] When Condé surrendered, Juan-José himself requested Ormonde to approach the Irishmen in the garrison, led by Lord Muskerry, the chief of the MacCarthys. Their nominal Lord-Lieutenant gave them the King's invitation to join him with as many of their compatriots as possible. In the event, Inchiquin stayed at Paris but Muskerry and hundreds of the Irish came over. They were joined in Flanders by English and Scottish royalists arriving from all directions. Charles's army numbered 400 by the end of August, 1,140 in mid-November, and 2,500 by the first days of March. In early December it was formed into regiments: one of English, commanded by Rochester, one of Scots under the nominal command of Middleton and the effective charge of Newburgh, and three of Irish. Ormonde, and Charles's brothers James and Henry were the Colonels of these, and Richard Grace, Cormac MacCarthy, and Taaffe led them in the field. James was made Lieutenant-General of the whole force.

Its growth presented a nightmare to the Spaniards. The quartering of the Army of Flanders through each winter was a precise and complex business. The regiments were spread carefully across the Spanish Netherlands, after negotiation with the estates of each duchy and county, to ensure that the resources of no area were pressed until the inhabitants became desperate. In the winter of 1656–7, Caracena had to reckon with Charles's body of British soldiers in Flanders, entirely dependent upon Spanish pay and expanding weekly with no guarantee of their final number. Repeatedly, he was obliged to redraw his plans for the distribution of units and to disband some Spanish regiments for lack of room. Charles and Hyde treated any delay in this process as the result of incompetence or mendacity, and only the patient mediation of Bristol prevented a serious quarrel. The behaviour as well as the numbers of Charles's men gave the Spaniards reasons for alarm. The difficulty of quartering and paying their swelling number forced them to exist in overcrowded, penurious conditions in which disease and disorder repeatedly broke out. A captain in Ormonde's regiment threatened to plunder a town unless its people gave his soldiers money. The dress of the Highland recruits caused the Flemish to regard them as barbarians, and when a church was robbed of its plate the royalists were blamed. Rochester annoyed the ministers at Brussels further by attempting the old soldier's trick of exaggerating the number of his men and pocketing the surplus pay. There was also a problem regarding the command of the royalists, for the Madrid government made it plain that they must be incorporated into the Army of Flanders and not left in Spanish pay but under foreign control. In February 1657 an acceptable compromise was reached whereby Charles accepted one of Juan-José's officers, Jean Ferdinand de Marsin, Comte de Graville, as his Lieutenant-General. His brother preserved a shadowy authority as Commander-in-Chief, and Marsin agreed to join his own brigade to the British for an invasion of England. Charles set out to charm the Walloon, and had soon turned him into an enthusiastic adherent.[8] From this muddle of political bargaining and personal squalor would descend the oldest surviving regiment in the British army, the Grenadier Guards.

As his military resources developed, so did Charles's plans for the invasion of Great Britain. The first area designated a target was the Scottish Highlands. In September 1656 Middleton was sent to Danzig, to enlist Scottish soldiers serving there with the Swedish army and to pay them from loans provided by their countrymen trading in the Baltic. He proposed to land in northern Scotland with this small army and to rekindle the rebellion which had collapsed in 1655. This would fulfil an obvious diversionary function, of forcing Cromwell to send more soldiers to Scotland and so reduce his power in south-eastern England where Charles's army could most easily land. But in October Charles spoke to Juan-José of concentrating the whole effort against Scotland, and taking his soldiers there in person. The prince was sceptical about the readiness of the Scots to rise, and in this he was correct. Middleton collected men at Danzig but had to disband them for lack of money. A royalist agent went 'up and down the hills in a plaid' talking to Highland chiefs, but found them cowed after the defeats of 1654–5. Thus the Scottish venture foundered completely.[9] The scheme in which Cardeñas was most interested was the limited and practicable one of assassinating Cromwell. A former radical leader, Colonel Edward Sexby, had arrived in the Spanish Netherlands offering to master-mind such an operation, and had been recommended enthusiastically to the government by the egregious Father Talbot. Charles and his advisers disliked Sexby both for his background and for the manner in which he had ingratiated himself with their hosts. The King received him without insisting that he bend the knee (which action offended the Colonel's egalitarian principles) and wrote to encourage his associates in England to rise. But he refused either to lend him aid or to involve him in the invasion project, and the plot against the Protector went ahead independently of the Stuart court. Bristol expressed the hope that Talbot would go to England in person, and get martyred.[10] Instead it was Sexby who died in the Tower in 1657, after the failure of his plan and his arrest.

Thus, to keep his part of the treaty and provide a port at which the invasion force could disembark, Charles was left dependent upon the royalists in England. The objective truth about these was that they were now almost completely passive. A scatter of adventurers, devoid of social standing and unity, corresponded with the exiled court and attempted to prepare risings. A few sets of more reputable cavaliers, including the 'Sealed Knot', kept up their contacts with the King. But in the winter of 1656–7 there was no real chance of launching a rebellion even on the scale of the fiasco of 1655.[11] For Charles to admit this to the Spanish would destroy most of his credit with them. Hence a game of bluff commenced, in which the exiled royalists behaved as though their adherents across the North Sea were ready and eager to co-operate. How far wishful thinking and the reports of irresponsible conspirators had deceived the King is difficult to say, but he certainly could not have felt the complete assurance which he showed to his allies. It is very likely that he and his advisers hoped that serious preparations for invasion would themselves stimulate royalist activity. In October 1656 they began to press for men, money, and shipping, whereupon the Spaniards naturally requested details of the preparations for the rising in England. In November, Juan-José allocated funds for the enterprise. The King immediately informed him that the rising was to take place before Christmas, and pressed him to supply the royalist army in Flanders with arms, ammunition, and pay. As described, coping with Charles's soldiers strained Spanish resources and energies to the full, and they consumed money which would, among other purposes, have been used to pay his pension. By January 1657 he was in as much financial trouble as he had ever been before, and by March his servants' wages were eighteen months in arrears. This added to the irritation felt by him and by Hyde with their hosts, without making them any more sensitive to the Spaniards' problems.[12]

The ministers at Brussels responded to Charles's talk of a December rebellion by promising all necessary aid for one. Instead, when December came, he was asking for more time in which to mobilize the rebels. None the less, the following February he did not hesitate to accuse his allies of having ruined the opportunity by inadequate support. When they offered him soldiers for an immediate attempt he rejected them as too few and advised the postponement of the venture till the next winter. He followed this with a request that, none the less, he received the money for it immediately. By now the Spanish were in no condition to provide funds to anybody, for they were themselves waiting desperately for remittances from Madrid. Rather than admit this candidly to the royalists, they chose for a time to spin out the talks: thus a double deception entered the situation. On 30 March, driven desperate by his mounting debts, Charles himself came to Brussels informally. He soon made himself personally attractive to Juan-José, and they attended balls, watched comedies, and played tennis together. But the campaigning season was now so close that any invasion was out of the question anyway. When money did arrive from Spain it was, given King Felipe's preoccupation with Portugal, inadequate even to Juan-José's needs in the Netherlands. On 17 April Charles issued a memoir to the prince blaming him firmly for the failure to conquer England that winter, and proposing that the project be carried into the following November. To this last plan, all agreed.[13]

Despite these exchanges, Juan-José had reason for warm feelings towards his British guests at this time. One of the most troublesome of the French outposts had been St Ghislain, to the south of Brussels, which was held mainly by Irish soldiers. In early 1657, Ormonde, his secretary George Lane, and Bristol, embarked between them upon secret negotiations to win over these men. Three times during the English Civil War Bristol had tried to reduce garrisons by treachery, and at last this tactic succeeded. When Juan-José appeared before St Ghislain in March, the suborned Irishmen surrendered the outworks, and the fortress fell. The Spanish were delighted, Bristol was made Colonel of a new regiment formed from the defectors, and Lane got a knighthood.[14] This success was sorely needed to keep Spanish morale high. Even as it occurred, Cromwell and Mazarin finalized arrangements for the coming campaign. Their combined army in the Netherlands numbered 35,000, to meet which Juan-José could only muster 15,000. Charles's British army, fluctuating between 2,000 and 4,000 men, was therefore a significant addition to Spanish strength, even if it consumed money which might have been employed to hire other soldiers. It tended to be paid and quartered worse than the main Army of Flanders, partly because as the latest addition it was accorded the lowest priority, and partly because its officers failed to keep Caracena accurately informed of their numbers and needs. Its size remained unstable because its condition resulted in constant desertion, made good at times by the arrival of more royalist volunteers. In June 1657, both Charles's brothers and all of the military men at his court led it into the field.[15]

The campaign began late because Juan-José was too weak to take the offensive and the French and Cromwellians took time to unite their forces. The Spanish prince ably prepared a defence, filling the Flemish seaports with infantry and stationing a flying army behind them to harry besiegers. When the French tried to capture Cambrai by a surprise attack in May, the Prince de Condé relieved it in a lightning counter-stroke. The French generalissimo now decided that, despite the treaty with the Protectorate, an attack upon Flanders was hopeless. He led the combined army to the opposite end of the frontier and besieged a town in Luxembourg. When this fell in late July, he turned upon St Venant, which covered the south-eastern approach to Flanders. This surrendered on 16 August, and only now, pushed by the anger of Cromwell, did the allied army move on to Flemish soil. On 9 September it reduced the fort of Mardyke, near Dunkirk, and handed it over to the Protectorate. With autumn at hand, and Juan-José's army dispersed into the main strongholds of Flanders, the French retired. During these operations the Spanish could not do more than mount two diversionary operations, which were bungled, and indulge in a lot of wearisome countermarching. Pay soon failed and food became meagre in both armies, and desertion and illness troubled both. It is a tribute to the loyalty of Charles's force that none seem to have defected from it to the Cromwellians. Scores of the Protector's soldiers did go over to the King, but finding the conditions no better in his service many of these joined the stream of royalists escaping from the war.[16]

At the opening of the campaign, Juan-José had asked Charles to retire to Bruges, and from there to co-ordinate preparations for the rebellion in England which would make the invasion in November possible.[17] He stayed at Brussels instead, but did pursue this work with alternate hope and frustration. One Francis Roper had been sent to Vienna in the winter to solicit money for the invasion force from the Emperor Ferdinand, but the imperial treasury was as overstrained as ever.[18] In April Charles had sent Lord Muskerry to Spain itself to gather the Irish serving there and to lead an expedition against their homeland. This was hoped to produce the effects formerly expected of Middleton's project for Scotland, but Felipe needed the soldiers for the Portuguese war, and the plan was scrapped.[19] Communication with England was hampered by the naval blockade which Cromwell had now imposed upon Flanders, so that couriers had to reach Charles through Calais or Zealand. There was a constant danger that they would be suborned by the Protectorate, and at this time one of the principal royalist messengers to Scotland, and a notable English royalist officer, were disgraced because of the suspicion that they had become double agents. The King's natural disinclination to concert plans with his mother or brothers was increased by the fear (in his mother's case correct) that some of their associates had turned traitor.[20] In England one of the 'Sealed Knot', Sir Richard Willis, was now almost certainly in Cromwell's pay. The 'Knot's' security was further damaged when on Charles's instructions it commenced talks with a radical republican leader: he professed himself a convert but was another double agent. It was a mercy to the royalists that the 'Knot's' ingrained caution made it even less active in 1657 than before. Instead, new activists bombarded Charles with pleas to appoint them as leaders of the next conspiracy. The most highly born was John Mordaunt, brother of the Earl of Peterborough. In his youth, courage, and unflinching optimism, Mordaunt typified the latest generation of plotters—wild spirits who served the King as much for the adventure as from ideological conviction. His scattered associates consisted of a few gentry, some merchants, and handfuls of commoners.[21] They were not the material of which a viable rebellion was made, but they were better than nothing, and in July Charles told the Spanish that all was ready for the winter.[22]

By then, his overriding preoccupation was not with conspiracy but with money. Juan-José's own desperate shortage of funds, and the military emergency which he faced, meant that most of the pension promised to Charles could not be paid. Ormonde spoke the plain truth when he told Hyde in June that the Spanish preferred 'the setting forth the least ammunition wagon' to the personal needs of their royal guest. They could not afford to have other priorities, but the royalists left at Brussels and Bruges, led by Charles himself, Hyde, and Nicholas, made no attempt to consider this. The King ranted at his 'scurvy usage' and told Hyde that he was inclined to follow his advice and swear at Juan-José. Sir Edward's reaction was to fear that his monarch disliked expostulation too much to be capable of it when the moment came. By July the principal Household officers were pawning their belongings. Ormonde thought that he had found a solution, by persuading Juan-José to sell an office to a Brussels financier, with the understanding that Charles would get a share of the price. In October, however, the two parties were still haggling over what the price should be.[23] From July onward, the King resolved that he could secure both an enhanced income and an enhanced importance by joining the army on campaign. This was absolutely refused by Juan-José, upon the grounds that to receive Charles in appropriate state would require funds that he did not possess. Doubtless this was true, but doubtless also the prince was more concerned to obey his sovereign's orders to keep the English monarch firmly in the background. The situation of July 1650 was repeated, but this time Charles had learned a little more patience.[24] He waited until the campaign was well over, on 1 October, before joining the Spanish High Command at Dunkirk. He inspected the remnant of the royalist army, 1,200 men, and designated the English regiment his own Guards, to encourage desertion to it from the Cromwellian garrison at Mardyke. On the 22nd he accompanied a raid by the Army of Flanders upon the fort, in which its outworks were demolished. The expedition came under cannon fire from the citadel, and Ormonde had his horse killed beneath him as he and Charles reined in their mounts to watch the action. Hyde wrote the inevitable letter to his monarch begging him not to take such risks: clearly the horror of Worcester had not diminished the King's physical courage.[25]

Juan-José was pleased enough to see his royal guest, for by this stage he was anxious to confer with him. As soon as the winter passed, the Anglo-French attack upon Flanders would be renewed. The previous spring, Cromwell's navy had destroyed a second of the fleets which brought silver from the Americas to Spain. Without this money, Felipe's offensive against Portugal had collapsed, and a Portuguese invasion of Spain itself was expected. In the same summer of 1657, the Spanish had been defeated in Lombardy. The Spanish Netherlands were thus in grave danger, and had no prospect of reinforcement. In this situation, Charles's assurance that the English royalists were ready to rise offered a wonderful hope, of knocking England out of the war before spring. As his enemies closed in upon Mardyke, Juan-José sent the King a message that plans for the rebellion and invasion were to be enacted as soon as the campaign in Flanders ended. He promised full military and financial support. On 26 September James, Bristol, and Caracena decided to launch the invasion force from Ostend as soon as money arrived from Spain. In October royalists and Spaniards sent agents to Dutch ports to buy ships. As a mark of his enhanced value Charles received the full arrears of his pension, from the sale of the office to the financier which was now concluded. To equip himself for the expedition, he asked his sister to pawn her jewels, and the long-suffering Mary complied. The 'enterprise of England' was fixed for the beginning of December.[26]

It had, of course, a fundamental flaw: that the prospective royalist rising existed only in the imagination of a few individuals. In midwinter, when the event was due and Cromwell's ships had lifted their blockade for fear of storms, nothing was ready in England. Growing suspicious, Juan-José insisted that Ormonde himself cross to London to galvanize the royalists.

The Marquis had to consent, and took O'Neill back with him to lend his knowledge and cunning to the work. They spent over a month having an absolutely dreadful time, pursued relentlessly around the capital by Cromwell's spies and soldiers. Ormonde had disguised himself in a wig, which unfortunately changed colour when rained upon. In early February he escaped to the Continent, convinced that a rebellion was impossible unless the Spanish landed first.[27] Charles and Hyde now resorted to the game of bluff played the previous winter. Throughout February and early March they spoke confidently of the forthcoming invasion and of royalist preparations in England. They attempted to persuade Juan-José to launch the expedition without awaiting a rising, and assured him that Great Yarmouth would be betrayed to it as a landing place. Exiled royalists, let alone the Spaniards, found this project incredible. Even had the prince been prepared to send his soldiers into such danger, they could not now get out of Ostend. Cromwell's fleet had reimposed the blockade, and captured most of the handful of ships hired from the Dutch to provide transports. The campaigning season was approaching. In late March the whole scheme was cancelled and O'Neill recalled, leaving Juan-José disgusted and the King, as before, trying to blame him. Nicholas informed the royalist ambassador in Madrid that the Spaniards had 'grossly failed in all their undertaking to send the King into England'. There was a tragic postscript to the affair. Between March and May Cromwell arrested most of the people involved in the plotting in London. Mordaunt's life was saved by a casting vote, but five of his associates were executed.[28]

Thus, as in 1657, Charles's principal contribution to the Spanish war effort in 1658 consisted of his little army. Since October it had been quartered in Flanders, and suffered terribly. The local climate was normally damp and this winter exceptionally severe. The Spaniards continued to place the royalists last in order of priority for pay and clothing. The Cromwellian soldiers at Mardyke fared as badly, and some defected to the King only to find that, as in the summer, they had gained nothing by the change. Many of the men fell sick, and so did Henry of Gloucester, Taaffe, and Rochester. In Rochester's case the misfortune was mortal, for he died in March and was buried beside that other royalist general, Lord Hopton. So, worn out by war, perished the man who had been Charles's companion in the wanderings after Worcester. Command of the Guards was given to Wentworth. By spring even this most prestigious regiment lacked shoes and was close to starvation. Its men deserted daily and their officers were extorting money from the burghers of Dixmude to preserve the remainder. When it was gathered into the Army of Flanders in late May it was short of wagons, clothes, and arms.[29]

Worse was ahead for the royalist soldiers. The prelude to the campaign had gone well for the Spaniards, who obtained the betrayal of another border fortress and defeated a French seaborne attack on Ostend. But now Juan-José made a fatal mistake. His intelligence service informed him that the main enemy thrust would be into Hainault, so he reinforced Cambrai and neighbouring towns. As a result, he was taken by surprise in mid-May when the Anglo-French field army pushed into Flanders again. Its first victims were the men of Henry of Gloucester's regiment, who were caught in their quarters at Cassel and annihilated. Immediately after, it besieged Dunkirk and was reinforced until it numbered 28,000. To match it, Juan-José could muster only 16,000 but, nevertheless, he advanced to the relief of this vital seaport. On 4 June the Army of Flanders was overwhelmed on the sandhills to the east, in the so-called Battle of the Dunes. Those of it who stood their ground most bravely suffered worst, and among the 5,000 killed or captured were the majority of the Spanish veterans, Charles's Guards, and the regiments of James and of Bristol. Mercifully for them, the royalists almost all became captives of Lorrainer mercenaries who were willing to ransom them: a sergeant who fell into the hands of the Cromwellian soldiers was hanged as a traitor. James retired with the remainder into Nieuport, and other portions of the shattered Spanish army reinforced Bruges, Ostend, and Ypres. Dunkirk surrendered ten days later and was handed over to Cromwell. The Anglo-French force, invincible in the field, spent the rest of the summer reducing Dixmude, Gravelines, Oudenarde, and Ypres, so that by the end of the campaign it held most of West Flanders. Victory did not give its members regular pay and provisions, and some of the English in it still deserted to the royalists who had, as ever, no money with which to welcome them. But, whatever the discontents of its members, there was certainly no underestimating the achievements of the Anglo-French army. In August many German princes formed a League of the Rhine with France to prevent Spain from reinforcing Juan-José. If the fighting were renewed in 1659, the whole of the Spanish Netherlands seemed doomed. Charles and King Felipe had each backed a loser.[30]

At the opening of this campaign, as at that of the last two, Charles himself had been dumped at the rear to await its conclusion. As before, the irritation of underemployment was compounded by penury. He repeatedly applied to the Spaniards for money or an expedient to raise it, but as before his hosts were more appalled by the prospect of a starving army. Cardeñas, the principal minister left at Brussels, was responsible for fending off his importunities, and Charles soon named this man 'Don Devil'. One additional reason for the neglect of his needs was the belief of the Spanish that he was being supplied by his adherents in England and abroad. This was true, and the sums given could be significant: the following March one agent handed over £960. But this source of income was infrequent, unreliable, and quite insufficient to contain the mounting level of debts. As the summer of 1658 opened, Charles and his brother Henry had to pawn their jewelled badges symbolizing the Order of the Garter.[31] When the news of the Battle of the Dunes reached Brussels, the King retired precipitately towards the Dutch border. This was partly to avoid being trapped in the city if the victorious enemy attacked it, but principally to start strengthening his links with other states as his Spanish alliance appeared to be failing. At first it was projected that he would enter Germany to attend the coronation of the new Holy Roman Emperor, Ferdinand's son Leopold, and lobby for support. But this plan was dropped in favour of the easier and more practicable one of developing his alliance with the Dutch Orange party. During the late summer he made his base in the elegant little town of Hoogstraten, just within the Spanish side of the frontier. From there he, Hyde, Ormonde, and O'Neill commenced a series of secret forays into Dutch territory, to improve relations with that section of the Orangists, led by the Dowager Princess, who were opposed to his sister Mary. Between, he rested at Hoogstraten, flying his hawks at the partridges in the surrounding cornfields.[32] He was there in early September when an express reached him from James, soon seconded by one from Mary. The event which royalists had been trying to contrive for years had been accomplished by providence: Oliver Cromwell was dead.[33]

The great Protector had been succeeded by his almost unknown son Richard, and many of the exiles shared Hyde's belief that this 'young coxcomb' would fail to establish himself. They expected that the Protectorate, which they had tried for years to push over, would now collapse of itself, and made diplomatic efforts to prepare for this event. Charles and James met Juan-José immediately at Brussels, and told him to expect great opportunities in England. The King then sped to Holland and Friesland to meet leaders of the Orange party, and to ask for the hand of the Dowager Princess's third daughter Henrietta Catherine: thus he hoped to tie the Orangists permanently to his cause. The results of all these hopes and efforts was a disappointment as crushing as any before. The Protectorate's ambassador at The Hague, George Downing, complained of Charles's presence in Dutch territory to the States-General, and he had to scuttle out of it once more. England, far from being in chaos, proved to be, in the opinion of one royalist agent, more peaceful than ever before. Richard Cromwell was being accepted with enthusiasm by precisely those conservative interests in the country which might have been expected to support a Stuart restoration. The royalist ambassador at Madrid reported that King Felipe wanted to know why Charles's predictions had been so badly mistaken. Henrietta Catherine was soon betrothed to a Dutch cousin.[34]

Thus the exiled court had to adapt, yet again, to long-term scheming. Its new interest in English affairs did not abate, and henceforth it observed weekly developments, through its agents, in a fashion unknown earlier in the exile. In October Charles raised the project of invasion once more with Juan-José, but provoked no interest. His man at Madrid informed him that Felipe had instructed his son to assist the Stuarts only in the case of a rising in England. Yet Cromwell's death had raised Charles's reputation perceptibly in Europe, and in December, after two months of surviving on money borrowed from other exiles, he received a moderate sum from the Spanish. With this he was able to fit himself out in winter clothes.[35] In any case, the European scene itself was altering. King Felipe had been decisively defeated in the Netherlands, and had only just repelled the Portuguese counter-thrust into Spain. France's alliance with the Protectorate gave 'Red Cape' (as royalist agents termed Mazarin)[36] a better insight into Richard Cromwell's government than either Felipe or Charles possessed. His ambassador informed him that Richard was seriously distrusted by his army and that the Spanish war had brought the Protectorate to the verge of bankruptcy. In any case, the capture of Dunkirk had yielded the Cromwellians their principal objective in the Netherlands. France itself had come close to breaking under the strain of that last glorious campaign: there had been disturbances in its provinces during the summer. The way was open for a Franco-Spanish treaty, and in November Felipe offered Louis XIV the hand of his daughter Maria-Therese as the basis of one. Talks were immediately opened.

The prospect of an end to the great war between the Catholic monarchies held out the promise of joint aid by them to Charles's cause. He and his advisers also recognized that this would be the more likely the weaker the Protectorate became, and in the winter of 1658–9 they made great efforts to destabilize it. At James's insistence, Middleton, Ormonde, and Bristol surrendered formal control of their regiments to officers who would reside permanently with their men and care for them. To encourage the Irish, who formed the majority, Lord Muskerry was created Earl of Clancarty. In this manner it was hoped that the morale of the depleted royalist army would be restored in readiness for action.[37] In December Richard Cromwell called a Parliament, and the exiled government urged the English royalists to attend and to disrupt it. At the end of February the irrepressible Mordaunt arrived in Brussels, and returned to England rewarded with the title of Viscount. He also carried powers to set up a 'Great Trust' of conspirators to absorb and replace the 'Sealed Knot', representing the long-awaited alliance between royalists and 'Presbyterian' leaders to restore the monarchy.[38] Charles settled down to await developments at Brussels, which was at last established as his permanent base. King, court, and Household operated together out of a town house rented from a Walloon noble.[39]

Initially, the results were disappointing. Richard Cromwell's Parliament, though quarrelsome, showed an increasingly obvious loyalty to the Protectorate and this was fostered by some of the very 'Presbyterians' upon whom Mordaunt was counting. Then, in late April, everything altered. The army forced the dissolution of the Parliament, abolished the Protectorate, and restored the original Parliament which had been created at Pride's Purge, had abolished the monarchy, and had proclaimed the Commonwealth. This was widely expected to produce a reform programme more radical than anything the Protectors had countenanced. Mordaunt's obscure talks now made rapid progress, and on 24 June he reappeared in Brussels to announce that the 'Trust' was ready to rise. For Charles, the situation was the reverse of that in 1656–8. He had a rebellion prepared, but no foreign aid available. The six royalist regiments had all been re-established, but no shipping was obtainable for them and it is unlikely that they contained much more than 1,000 men in total.[40] The Spanish were not interested. Juan-José had been recalled to Spain in disgrace that spring and replaced by Caracena. The Anglo-Spanish war was suspended because of the troubles in England, and the Franco-Spanish conflict had been formally halted by a truce. Preparations were being made for Mazarin to meet Felipe's chief minister, Don Luis de Haro, on the Bidassoa river in Navarre to negotiate a treaty. With no fighting in the Netherlands, Felipe had reduced still further the funds sent there from Spain, and Charles's pension was now unpaid for months at a time. The board-wages of his servants were almost two years in arrear. When Mordaunt arrived, the King was planning to journey to the Bidassoa to draw attention to himself. Instead, he resolved that he and James would slip across to England separately as soon as the rebellion had established itself.[41]

From now on, events moved fast but in confusion. In mid-July, just as Charles was preparing to set out, he heard that the 'Sealed Knot' had declined to co-operate and that the rising was postponed. A few days later he learned that the 'Trust' had decided to rise anyway, on 1 August, but he received no details of the location or leaders of the proposed outbreaks.[42] It was now time for him and his advisers to consider what terms they would offer adherents. Hyde had drafted such a declaration as part of the abortive invasion project of 1656–8. It contained the promise made in 1651, of pardon to any old enemies who supported the rising except regicides. Now, however, there was no talk of the Covenant or a reformed Church: instead the exiles ducked the whole question of a settlement by referring it to a freely elected Parliament. After Cromwell's death the exiled government drew up a simple offer of indemnity to all regicides. On 19 July 1659 Sir Edward drafted yet another declaration. It repeated the offer of pardon, but was more explicit upon the religious question, promising toleration for all peaceful people who dissented from the national Church. The exiles were now considering bidding for the goodwill of precisely those groups, the independent churches, who had been the mainstay of the republican cause. The proclamation was not published, but Charles enacted the same policy informally instead. He directed the English royalists to assure former opponents that he guaranteed the 'known laws', free and frequent Parliaments, the disbandment of all armies, and indemnity (save for regicides) as well as this religious liberty.[43] On 6 August, expecting the rising to have won ground, he and James left Brussels at dawn. They took few followers and different routes, James to Boulogne and Charles to Calais.[44]

Once at the sea-coast, they heard that the rebellion was indeed under way, but on the wrong side of England. Just as in 1655, small groups of royalists had gathered in several places, only to disperse or to be routed. But Mordaunt's alliance with the 'Presbyterians' had actually borne fruit, and an important group of the latter led by Sir George Booth had taken possession of Cheshire, Lancashire, and North Wales. The King accordingly left his brother at Boulogne to receive dispatches, while he himself headed for Brest to find a ship for Chester, and Booth. Ormonde was sent to Paris to discuss the possibility of French aid for the rising with Henrietta Maria. He was unsuccessful, and late in his return to the King, but this eventuality saved the royal party. It waited for him at St Malo instead of proceeding directly to Brest. Had it done so, and found a vessel at once, Charles would have landed in Cheshire just in time to fall into the hands of the victorious republican army which destroyed Booth's force at Winnington Bridge on 19 August. Instead, the news of the absolute defeat of the rebellion reached him on the Breton coast, and left him both disappointed and safe.[45]

This time he was not going to slink back to base ignominiously as in 1655. Instead, he resurrected his original plan to attend the Franco-Spanish conference, and turned south. With him were only Bristol, as interpreter, O'Neill, to hunt accommodation and carry messages, and Ormonde, the nearest thing his court possessed to a grandee. The royalist ambassador at

Madrid had repeatedly assured Charles that de Haro would be delighted to receive him. By contrast, reports represented Mazarin's attitude as varying from indifference to actual hostility. There was a danger that if the Stuart King passed near the French court on his way to the frontier, he would be turned back or even arrested. Accordingly, his party reached La Rochelle in mid-September, with the plan that Charles would sail direct to Spanish Navarre while Ormonde went to cultivate Mazarin. Instead the weather turned so stormy that the voyage proved impossible, while O'Neill reported a rumour that the conference was already over. The King resolved to proceed to Madrid to see King Felipe, and entered Spain around the eastern end of the Pyrenees to avoid the Cardinal returning from the western end. He was at Saragossa on 5 October when he heard that the great meeting was still in progress. Now he swung north-west again, and at last reached de Haro's headquarters in the Spanish frontier town of Fuenterrabia upon the 18th. Despite these mishaps, the journey was clearly quite a merry one. Bristol and O'Neill were sparkling company, cracking jokes and writing French love poetry, while Charles himself found everything in Spain agreeable except the choking dust of Aragon. It was his first real holiday since Frankfurt in 1655.[46]

On 28 October, de Haro and Mazarin signed the Peace of the Pyrenees. Spain gave Louis XIV the hand of Felipe's eldest daughter, Maria-Therese, though she was to bring with her no claim to Spanish land if her dowry were punctually paid. France pardoned Condé and the other rebels. Spain ceded Arras, Gravelines, a few other Netherlands border towns, and a province of Catalonia. France returned most of the Flemish areas conquered in 1658. It seemed like a durable agreement, and Charles's great hope in it was that both monarchies would now combine to restore him. Don Luis certainly gave him support in this notion. The great Spanish minister, even more deceptively diffident and gentle than the Cardinal, met his Stuart guest outside Fuenterrabia. Despite wind and rain, he got out of his carriage to kneel and kiss the king's hand. Thereafter Charles received royal honours, and reciprocated by exerting all his now famous charm. De Haro made a genuine proposal to Mazarin of joint action to invade England and Jermyn arrived from the Queen Mother to increase pressure on the Cardinal. Mazarin, however, was not a man easy to press, for he fended off the entreaties by sending Charles his traditional expressions of goodwill while suggesting that action might be concerted later. These deceived the royalists so little that Charles resolved that any personal interview with 'Red Cape' was pointless. Instead, he left Fuenterrabia on 7 November and passed quietly and privately north through France. To avoid entering Paris, and risking notice by the French court, he met his

mother at a country house at St Colombe, outside the city. After a fortnight with her, he went on to Brussels and was reunited with his brothers
and ministers upon 16 December. He broadcast stories of the success of
his mission, reporting 'very fair promises' from Spain and 'hopes' from
France. More practically, he brought with him a sum of money from de
Haro sufficient to pay all his servants something and to cover a few of the
Household's bills.[47]

His expedition had thus been thoroughly worthwhile, in both personal
and political terms, and this run of well-being was to continue with a
dramatic and decisive turn in fortunes. Before recounting this, it may be
profitable to make a general survey of the political and moral climate of
his court during the years of the Spanish alliance. In most respects, this
represented a continuity, and natural development, of that at Cologne.
The ascendancy of Hyde over other ministers remained obvious. An Irish
soldier described him as 'the great oracle' at court in March 1658. He
continued to undertake much of the government's administrative work,
and it is a mark of their relative importance that Nicholas was left at
Bruges during the first two years while Sir Edward accompanied the King
to Brussels and Hoogstraten. Ormonde, Charles's other principal servant,
was Hyde's firm friend and happy to leave to him the paperwork which Sir
Edward loved and the Marquis found a chore.[48] It might have seemed that
the reappearance of Bristol would provide a challenge to Hyde's position,
especially after the Earl's brilliant success with the Spanish in 1656, Charles
restored him at last to the office of senior Secretary of State which he had
held until the regicide. But the King's distrust of the volatile George Digby
was not so easily removed, and he was confined to negotiations with Juan-
José and Caracena. For his own part, he settled down to work easily enough
with Hyde and Ormonde. Our only vignette of the governing team at
work was recorded by James. In this, Bristol made a proposal to Charles,
whose response was to call him together with James and Hyde to discuss
it. Significantly, the place appointed for the discussion was Sir Edward's
private chamber.[49] Almost by accident, Charles had recreated much of
his father's administration of the mid-1640s, with Nicholas and Bristol
as Secretaries, Hyde as a frequent adviser, and Ormonde as an important
executive agent. The impression is reinforced by the reappointment of
Charles I's Secretary at War, Sir Edward Walker, to administer the new
royalist army.[50]

As before, one major reason for the dominance of the 'Old Royalists'
was the lack of any effective rivals. The influence of the 'Louvre' circle
remained diminished by distance, and was further weakened by the death
of Lord Percy in March 1659.[51] The embryo 'opposition' group noticeable

at Cologne dispersed. Rochester, as said, died. On leaving Germany Charles at last lost patience with Dr Fraser and dismissed him. Culpeper chose to move to Holland instead of Spanish territory and to work for understanding between the King and the Dutch,[52] though for unknown reasons he made his way to Fuenterrabia to assist Charles there. Balcarres destroyed his own career. Observing the increasing disregard of his monarch for the Covenanter cause, he determined to reverse this process. His initiative, commenced after the King had gone ahead to Flanders, was to incite his friends in Scotland to insist upon a royal declaration to uphold the Covenant and to appoint somebody other than Middleton to command future rebellions. He thus followed Long in discovering how ruthless Charles could be with servants who attempted to coerce him. When he heard of these instructions in March 1657, the King banished Balcarres from court and treated him as a traitor.[53]

Likewise, any lingering possibility that Bristol would come to equal Hyde as an adviser was removed in January 1659, when the Earl committed political suicide. He did so by making a personal conversion to Catholicism, the reasons for which are lost. For lack of any obvious practical advantage, one must assume that it was a genuine alteration of belief. A number of prominent royalists of formerly strong Protestant faith, such as Inchiquin, were convinced by Rome during the exile. Bristol's flamboyant, over-active, and rather unstable personality may have been more suited to such dramatic alterations than most. Whatever the cause, the result was that Charles immediately deprived him of his office of Secretary, as part of the consistent policy of distancing the King from Popery. The possibility that the Earl might ingratiate himself further with the Spaniards in compensation was removed by a typical piece of carelessness. He let slip to friends a plan by Juan-José to draw off more Irish soldiers from French service during the truce which prevailed pending the peace conference. The news leaked to the French, the Brussels High Command was furious, and James deprived Bristol of his regiment. Thus when the Earl accompanied Charles to Spain in the autumn, this was simply because his linguistic skills made him indispensable. At Fuenterrabia, O'Neill persuaded the King to jettison him, because Mazarin's detestation of him made him a liability in the attempt to combine French and Spanish behind Charles. Bristol went alone, miserably, to Madrid as his sovereign returned north.[54] In view of this it is ironic that a rumour spread in England that the King himself had attended mass and taken communion while at Fuenterrabia. His companions and followers were most indignant to hear about this and indeed there is no evidence for its truth. In the gloom of mid-1658, Charles had made another secret attempt to gain help from the

Pope, through the mediation of an exiled French cardinal. However, he got Hyde to draft his terms, and these consisted only of the suspension of the penal laws if Catholics produced a Stuart restoration, followed by a request to a Parliament for their repeal.[55] As before in the decade, his attitude towards Rome was one of extreme caution.

Momentarily, it seemed as if the reappearance of James would create a second powerful faction in the court. He brought with him from France his own followers, of whom the most notable was the former royalist soldier Sir John Berkeley. Berkeley and Hyde had been friends until the exile, but were estranged by a typical piece of self-righteousness upon the part of Sir Edward. Berkeley had become engaged to marry another of Hyde's circle, but Hyde, believing that the match would be unfortunate for both, persuaded her to break it. Sir John had never forgiven him, and had encouraged the attack upon Sir Edward in 1653. When he arrived at Bruges, Hyde and Bristol combined to ruin Berkeley before he could pose a threat to them. They had an ally in the Prince's entourage, a clever, burly young man called Sir Henry Bennet. Bennet carried a scar across his nose from a parliamentarian sabre, covered with a black plaster, which symbolized his devoted service to the royalist cause since the Great Civil War. Charles had found him a lively companion, at home in the world of high fashion and gossip which the King found entertaining. He had foisted him upon his brother in the post of secretary to maintain an agent near James. Now Hyde, Bristol, and Bennet cooked up between them the inevitable charge that Berkeley had been in contact with the enemy. Charles was easily persuaded, and soon after James's arrival he ordered his brother to dismiss Sir John and his associates. James's reaction astonished everybody: in January 1657 he simply stormed out of the Spanish Netherlands, taking his friends with him. Charles and his advisers realized that the Prince was a vital magnet for the British soldiers whom they were trying to lure from French service. His loss would be a serious blow, and his royal brother had to capitulate in order to induce him to return. Berkeley and his other old companions stayed with him and it was Bennet who was removed, packed off to Spain with the compensation of the important post of ambassador. All parties learned from the episode. Sir John took care to remain aloof from court politics, and the King and his ministers were courteous to him in turn.[56]

James's flight was the most dramatic and short-lived of a series of new tensions within the royal family. Charles chose to interpret his position at its head as giving him the powers over it of a monarch governing subjects. His brother's reaction to this attitude was the first sign of its dangers. It was even less wise to apply it to his sister, who could claim to be a political power in her own right and upon whose funds he had repeatedly drawn. Yet Charles failed to recognize this fact. Mary was at Bruges during the quarrel between her brothers, and gently took James's part. As a result she was treated (in her words) like a plague-sufferer, and Bristol was openly rude to her. The following spring she received Balcarres after his disgrace, made his wife her lady-in-waiting and fended off Charles's furious objections by asserting her right to choose her own court. Part of this action may have been founded upon personal bonds, and part upon her position as a Princess of Orange, a natural ally of Scottish Calvinists. The wrangle dragged on into 1658, though he still asked for, and she still provided, financial help. Then came a more serious quarrel. Mary fell a little in love with Jermyn's nephew, Henry. On learning of the attachment, Charles censoriously intervened, informing his sister that she was risking her reputation and insisting upon the removal of the young man. Mary obeyed, but felt that her brother had himself created a scandal by drawing such dramatic attention to an innocent flirtation: she apparently managed not to remind him of Lucy Walter. By May 1659 she was telling her courtiers that she wanted nothing more to do with Charles.[57]

During this same period, the King's relations with his mother remained delicate. He made no pretence of consulting her opinions, and she responded, like Mary, by favouring Balcarres. Charles deliberately neglected to inform her of important decisions which he knew she would contest, a typically short-sighted policy as her anger, when she inevitably heard about them, was the more intense.[58] It seems that their meeting at St Colombe in November 1659 did much to reduce ill feeling, and it certainly yielded Charles a new happiness in the rediscovery of his youngest sister, Henriette-Anne, 'Minette'. She was now fifteen and disturbingly frail, with a crooked shoulder, bright chestnut hair, brilliant blue eyes, perfect teeth, a marvellous rosy complexion, and her royal brother's powerful charm. His new affection for her is revealed in the series of letters to her which he now commenced, which were to become increasingly involved with international politics. At the beginning, however, they contained an almost delirious affection, a doting solicitude, and a deliberate lapse from dignity, which suggest that she represented to him both a substitute for Mary and another escape from the burdens of office.[59]

All these developments served to reinforce the dominance of the exiled court by Hyde and his friends but, as before, Charles ensured that this was never absolute. In December 1657 the abandoned Lord Keeper, Herbert, died at Paris. The King used this event as the occasion to revive the great office of Lord Chancellor and to bestow it upon Hyde as recognition of his political importance and of the burden of administration which he carried. Yet the promotion of Sir Edward was associated with the creation of three barons, each chosen from a set other than his own. One was Berkeley, to complete the reconciliation of the royal brothers. Another was Sir Marmaduke Langdale, a notable Yorkshire royalist who was intended to play a leading part in the projected rebellion. He was yet another of the King's followers to have converted to Catholicism in exile. The third was William Crofts, Captain of Henrietta Maria's guards and the member of the Louvre group whom Charles found most companionable. At the same time old Norwich, who still remained apart from any faction, was made Captain of the Yeoman of the Guard.[60] Nor were the 'Old Royalists' completely successful in getting their friends into jobs. As part of the round of promotions detailed above, Nicholas's eldest son John was made Clerk of the Signet, and Ormonde's secretary Lane, already knighted for his part in reducing St Ghislain, became both Clerk of Wards and Liveries, and Clerk to the Irish Parliament. But the problems involved with offices are illustrated by the case of Hyde's friend Richard Fanshaw, a devoted royalist and talented linguist who had already served Charles as his Secretary at War in 1645–6. In June 1659 Hyde thought that he had obtained Fanshaw the lesser post of Secretary for the Latin Tongue and the greater one of Master of Requests. Six months later he discovered that the King had already promised the Mastership to a man whom Charles himself agreed to be totally unworthy, and so it was concluded simply to leave it vacant. By now Sir Edward was angling for a still better office for his friend, that of Secretary of State, vacated by Bristol. All that the King would promise was that he would confer it if Fanshaw paid him £2,000 within six months, although he did not exclude the possibility of appointing him in any case. No wonder that at one point Hyde's patience snapped, and he wrote to his monarch begging for 'one day's clear and frank declaring your purposes'.[61]

What was the moral tone of the court in Flanders? Reports by outsiders are remarkably inconsistent. On the one hand, a Cromwellian spy could describe Charles's entourage as full of drunkenness, fornication, and adultery. On the other, a radical Protestant visionary who crossed from England to harangue the King noted that religious services were held twice daily in the royal presence, with the chaplains choosing different psalms and prayers for each.[62] Both views can be substantiated. Not only did Charles attend divine worship regularly as the role of a seventeenth-century monarch required, but he set aside every Friday for fasting and prayer in memory of his father.[63] At the same time, the court at Bruges and Brussels was disorderly as it had not been before. The military men around

Charles had always been prone to violence: at Cologne, Wentworth and another officer had belaboured each other drunkenly with fists in the chamber next to the King's. Rochester and Newburgh had to be kept from duelling.[64] In Flanders, however, the excitement and frustrations of active military service produced an epidemic of quarrels. In one week in February 1658, duels were prevented between two officers over a gambling debt, and between two others over a jest, while one actually occurred and ended in injury. Newburgh and Taaffe were usually in the thick of the trouble. In 1658 the Scot fought and wounded an English officer, and was almost stabbed to death by one of his own captains. The following year, he crossed swords with another Englishman. In 1657 Taaffe tried to pick a fight with Bristol and was attacked with a club by a French quartermaster. The next year, he killed a Scottish officer in a multiple sword fight involving three matched couples. It had been over seven sovereigns wagered upon a tennis match and then unpaid. The details of the squabble between Newburgh and the Englishman in 1659 reveal the sheer puerility of which the exiled royalists were capable. Both arrived drunk to watch the King and James play tennis. The English officer pulled Newburgh's hair and then hid behind another man. The Scotsman insulted him volubly, whereupon the Englishman went off to fetch a club. He returned to find Newburgh relieving himself in a nearby lane and beat him. As they were falling to sword-play, Henry of Gloucester appeared and parted them. This ridiculous squabble divided the court, the Scots and Irish (from Ormonde downwards) supporting Newburgh, and the English (from the King's brothers downwards) excusing their own compatriots.

Charles's reaction to these clashes was to ignore them as far as possible, till August 1658 when the homicide by Taaffe and the wounding of Newburgh occurred in the same three weeks as the death of another Scottish captain in a duel. Then the King formally decreed that all duellists would be henceforth banished from his court, and made Taaffe the first example. Its force was somewhat undermined by his action in writing privately to the Irishman to assure him of his continued favour, a gesture which Taaffe promptly abused by showing the letter gleefully to many other exiles. The King understood the Irishman well enough not to risk any important political or military appointment in his hands, but his contribution to Charles's pleasures was such that he was not dispensable for long. Still, the decree had now been made, and when Newburgh and the Englishman had their brawl the following spring, the King confined them both until they made a reconciliation in his presence. Thereafter the incidence of violence at court seems to have declined.[65]

If his followers gave more concern in Flanders than before, so did

Charles himself. All the leading 'Old Royalists' agonized over him. Nicholas commented that the King's lack of dignity with commoners was losing him the respect of the Spaniards. Ormonde wrote to Charles asking him to mend his ways, shaking him profoundly and delighting Hyde, who felt that it justified his own 'preaching'. To Sir Edward himself, the Marquis confided the fear that Charles's 'immoderate delight in empty, effeminate and vulgar conversations' would 'become an irresistable part of his nature'.[66] A variety of evidence survives for the traits that disturbed these great royalists. The King was as careless of administrative detail as ever. When confusion arose over the execution of some orders which he had sent to a regiment, it was found that he could not remember having sent them at all. Certainly, also, he enjoyed idling away hours in 'effeminate' company. Parlour games with ladies feature in his letters to Taaffe. On his return from St Colombe he brought back a friend of Minette's, a young Frenchwoman called Janton, who taught him French songs and whom he called 'the best girl in the world'. His Household accounts testify to the verve with which he pursued pleasure. They include payments for the hire of tennis courts and the purchase of a pet monkey, to a mountebank who brought a camel to court, to French comedians and a travelling harper, and of a small sum lost at cards. His letters to Bennet furnish evidence of his passion for fashionable clothes and for fiddlers. Yet not all his leisure pursuits were mere recreation. He took regular Spanish lessons from mid-1658, though there is no evidence that the results were impressive.[67] The most to show for all those hours of Italian at Cologne is a sentence in that language written to Taaffe, which is both scurrilous and scatological.[68]

Charles's letters to Taaffe display most clearly the traits which disturbed Ormonde. About half of those still in existence are concerned with romantic manœuvres in early 1657, involving the wooing of a young woman at Brussels known as 'the infanta'. After a lot of trouble with her family, she moved to a residence of her own to compose relations with a suitor. The convoluted and disguised language of the correspondence leaves it unclear whether the 'infanta' was the same woman as an unnamed dear female friend of Charles, resident at Brussels and concerned in the affair. Likewise, one cannot tell whether the 'infanta's' suitor was Charles himself or a companion of his known as 'Don Lauren'. The context being so uncertain, it is also impossible to say whether Taaffe, who acted as the initial intermediary between the King and the lady or ladies, was being a loyal friend or a royal pimp. The negotiations with the 'infanta's' family were clearly undignified at points, and on one occasion Charles or 'Don Lauren' received a painful jab with a knee from behind. It is easy to see why the Spanish grandees of the city might have been unimpressed. It is also apparent that this intrigue consumed just as much of the King's energy as the contemporary project to invade England.[69]

There is a chance that the mysterious business may refer to the beginning of Charles's second sustained sexual partnership, with Catherine Pegge, the beautiful daughter of a Derbyshire gentleman. There are no certain contemporary records of their affair, and retrospective comments are very few. It is known only that it took place in Flanders in 1657–8, and produced a son and a daughter. The former was named Charles Fitz Charles, nicknamed 'Don Carlos', and appeared in London about fourteen years later, when his father acknowledged him. The girl, Catherine, either died young or became a nun at Dunkirk. Catherine Pegge married an Essex baronet in 1668.[70] There is no evidence that Charles ever regarded her as more than a physical convenience, unless she was the 'infanta' and/or 'friend' pursued so eagerly through the Taaffe letters. There survives among them also, however, a letter from Taaffe to his monarch in May 1656, congratulating him upon his new lady friend at Bruges, so there was obviously more than one woman in Charles's life during the Flanders period. None of his followers ever took exception to Catherine or regarded her as a problem. She seems to have been one of the most compliant and downtrodden of Charles's womenfolk.

One may perhaps forgive the royalists for being grateful to her, because Lucy Walter was now fulfilling their worst fears.[71] As soon as the King moved to the Spanish Netherlands, she visited him with her lover Thomas Howard and her equally impecunious brother. Charles saw their son again and somehow Lucy obtained enough money to purchase a pearl necklace valued at £1,500. She, her two companions, and her children, set out for England in June 1656 to collect money left to her by her mother. Lucy told the others that she would have a coach lined with velvet. All were promptly arrested by Cromwell's government. Upon her was found Charles's warrant for a pension, which was given full publicity in the Protectorate's official press. Cromwell then deported her.[72] Back in Holland during the winter of 1656–7 she and Howard quarrelled and parted. He had entrusted her with certain papers relating to his activities as a royalist conspirator, which she now sold. Some ended up in the hands of Cromwell's ambassador at The Hague. In August 1657 Howard went to Brussels on business, saying some understandably nasty things about Lucy. She trailed him and persuaded a cousin to murder him in the street with a stiletto. Howard emerged from the attack wounded, and Lucy, having thus drawn attention to her presence in this spectacular way, threw herself upon Charles's charity.[73] He lodged her with the family of Sir Arthur Slingsby, an exiled royalist who had a house at Brussels and whom the King fortified against the experience with a baronetcy. There she began to talk of publishing Charles's letters to her if he did not send her more money. By November he had determined to get their son out of her hands. This he ordered Slingsby to do, but Lucy foiled them by running screaming into the street and rousing a mob to come to her aid. Cardeñas was embarrassed and furious, and wrote stiffly to the King. Whether Lucy's protestations of maternal love were genuine, or whether she realized that the child represented her principal hold over Charles, is debatable. Certainly she was a dreadful mother. A royalist agent noted that although the boy was very pretty, clever, and eager to learn, she had taught him neither to read nor to count beyond twenty. By January 1658 she was beginning to recognize defeat, and in March Charles at last got custody of young James.[74] He was sent to Paris to be brought up by the recently ennobled Lord Crofts. Lucy remained at Brussels quarrelling with the royalists, but in about November she died suddenly. Later tradition had it that she did so at Paris (perhaps in pursuit of her son), and that she was decently buried by a Scottish royalist.[75] Her child was to prove, with spectacular force, the old assertion that the wages of sin are death.

This, then, was the pattern of Charles II's life during his alliance with Spain. It was to culminate, with the whole exile, in the events of the winter of 1659–60. During his absence at Fuenterrabia, the victorious republican army fell out with its 'purged' Parliament, and expelled it once again. This action was opposed by the scourge of Scottish royalism, George Monck, who declared for the evicted MPs. Monck had long been known as a man of relatively conservative views, and had been royalist in the Great Civil War, though he later developed a personal loyalty to the Cromwells. When the Protectorate fell, it seemed as if he might reconsider his allegiances, and Charles wrote to him appealing to him to employ his army in Scotland to support the rebellion of August 1659. He refused to receive the letter and set about keeping the Scots quiet, though he was reported to have no great enthusiasm for the revived Commonwealth. Yet he had now emerged as the defender of the 'purged' Parliament. As Charles returned to Brussels, Monck was encamped at Coldstream on the Tweed, facing an England falling into increasing division and disorder.[76] These developments had filled the defeated royalists with new hope, but none of them could propose a likely way of exploiting them. During the fortnight after the King's reappearance in the Netherlands the army in England threw off its generals and restored the 'purged' Parliament, which promptly invited Monck's army to London to protect it. Nicholas must have echoed the feelings of many royalists when he felt that a great opportunity for a rising had been wasted.[77]

During January 1660, therefore, royal policy reverted to the attempt to launch an invasion of England, this time as a joint Franco-Spanish effort. It rapidly became obvious that the project was even more stillborn than previous schemes. Neither power wanted to carry the greater weight of the effort, and so put itself at a disadvantage to the other. An England in chaos was no menace to either, and so there was no pressing need to tamper with it. France wanted time to recuperate, and Spain to finish off Portugal. Thus Mazarin made no preparations. Felipe rewarded James for his services in the field by making him High Admiral of Spain. This was a post with no obvious active duties which represented merely a way of keeping him on the Spanish payroll. Charles wrote to English royalists, yet again, to prepare a rising to concert with the invasion. But the 'Sealed Knot' was now in ruins, wrecked by the revelation of Willis's treachery, while Mordaunt's prestige had been damaged by the failure of 1659. Lingering hopes that Monck might come over were dispelled by the uncompromising speeches of loyalty to the 'purged' Parliament which the General made on his march to London. In keeping with Spain's relative disinterest in Charles's affairs, he received no money from the time of his return to Brussels.[78]

Then, in mid-February, at dusk, Ormonde brought an exhausted young man called Bayley to Hyde's lodgings. In keeping with Sir Edward's importance, these were now directly beneath the royal bedchamber so that Charles could visit daily to discuss business. The King was called down now, for Bayley, anxious for reward, had dashed across the Channel to deliver fantastic news. Monck had suddenly turned upon the 'purged' Parliament and endorsed the cry of the Londoners for a new Parliament to be called. In Hyde's words, this report 'turned their heads',[79] and better was to come. A week later, the general reversed Pride's Purge, inviting back to the Commons the Members excluded in 1648. These sat till mid-March and then dissolved the whole Parliament to make way for a new one to settle the constitution. A royal restoration was now a real possibility, though almost certainly upon terms which would limit the King's powers. Accordingly, the whole direction of Charles's strategy altered. Instead of concentrating upon royalist rebels, the exiled government began to probe gently toward the people now actually in power, trying to make secret contact, and a deal, with each.

The greatest of these, naturally, was George Monck, whose army controlled the land and had to underwrite any settlement. The existing evidence suggests that far from having any long-term plan to restore

Charles, the General's policy had evolved steadily in response to circumstance. By mid-March of 1660 he was ready to contemplate the possibility
of a restoration, and to employ a ready-made avenue of approach to the
King. He had been joined in London by a kinsman, William Morice, who
had been one of the MPs excluded by Pride's Purge. The two men had
a royalist cousin of some distinction, Sir John Grenville, nephew of the
unfortunate Sir Richard. He had governed the Scilly Isles for Charles II
in 1648–50 and had kept close contact with the exiled court since. Like
the 'Sealed Knot' he had steered clear of uprisings, but the qualities of
caution and discretion which made him a lukewarm conspirator were
perfectly suited to a negotiator. In early March he undertook to deliver
an appeal from Charles to Monck. Soon after the Parliament dissolved,
Morice arranged an interview, and once alone with the General Sir John
delivered a letter from the King and his own commission to treat, together
with spectacular verbal promises of high office. Monck replied that he had
always intended to restore Charles, and a few days later, very courteously,
he offered his own terms. They were exclusively concerned with the needs
of his soldiers: indemnity, arrears of pay, confirmation of titles to former
Church and Crown lands, and a degree of religious toleration. He added
that it would improve the King's reputation if he abandoned his alliance
with Spain, because of that state's associations with Popery, despotism,
and the recent war with England. All these messages were only verbal,
as Monck would commit nothing to paper, and Grenville carried them in
his head to Brussels.[80]

Charles and his ministers must by now have been giving thought to
the terms that they themselves might offer. In September, while he was
journeying south, his ministers had issued a proclamation presumably
agreed before he left and intended to rally support in the wake of Booth's
defeat. It elaborated the proposals drafted in July, offering pardon to all
but seven regicides, abolition of most taxation, the repurchase of the
Crown lands, a free Parliament, and regular successors to it. Just before
Grenville brought Monck's message, they seem to have been considering
the reference of any settlement to the Parliament to be convened in April.
This was upon the thoroughly reasonable and cynical grounds that, as it
was not called by a King, the terms it made could be renegotiated with a
more regular, and tractable, successor. The only reservation was to exclude
the regicides from pardon. Then Sir John arrived and, having spent years
projecting a restoration involving the defeat and destruction of the English
republic's army, the King found himself negotiating with that army. He
discussed with Hyde, Nicholas, and Ormonde whether a means could
be found to circumvent Monck's terms, by which they were no more

willing to be bound than others. The solution was to incorporate these in their original plan, by referring the specific problems of indemnity, lands, and arrears to the forthcoming Parliament. In one clause only, devised by Hyde, was this rule made ambiguous: religious toleration was immediately promised to all peaceful Christians in order to soothe the separate churches which had supported the Commonwealth. Parliament was invited to confirm this ruling after 'mature deliberation'. Monck's advice to move residence was also debated. It was initially considered best to move to France, for fear that either the Dutch or the Spanish would force an inclusion of their interests in any peace treaty between Charles and his subjects. In the end the destination chosen was Breda, so conveniently close to the border between the Spanish and Dutch Netherlands and dominated by the House of Orange. Just as in 1650, so ten years later, it was an ideal place from which to bargain. It had the added advantage of enabling Charles to disguise his flight under cover of a visit to his sister Mary. Grenville was at Brussels by 27 March, and within a few days the King and his three advisers had made the journey north. On 4 April his offer to the English was signed, copied five times, and enclosed in separate letters to Lords, Commons, Army, Fleet, and City. It was to become known as the Declaration of Breda, often wrongly attributed to Hyde, but in reality a joint effort of the King and his three advisers. With these bundles was wrapped a commission for Monck as Commander-in-Chief and (as Fanshaw had not produced his £2,000) an invitation to choose a Secretary of State. Grenville was given a written promise of an earldom, a court office, and a large sum of money if Charles was restored, and on the 8th he sailed quietly for England.[81]

After Monck, the most important individual to be won was the commander of the fleet, Edward Montagu. Like the General, he had been a favourite of Cromwell's, but unlike him had an impeccably parliamentarian past. Nevertheless he made an easier catch. In early April, when he was on shipboard, he received an agent from Charles carrying a letter requesting support. This he acknowledged in writing, with protestations of loyalty, and so, while making no public avowal, linked himself to the King's cause. There was little doubt of the allegiance of the Council of State appointed by Parliament before its dissolution. It was dominated by 'Presbyterians' who had striven to preserve the monarchy in 1648. Their surviving leaders in England were the Earls of Northumberland, Manchester, and Clare, William Pierrepoint, John Crew, Denzil Holles, and Sir Harbottle Grimston. The problem with this group was that, although monarchists, they also believed in the imposition of strict limits upon royal power of a sort unpalatable to royalists. The exiled government was more directly interested in Arthur Annesley, another Civil War parliamentarian who had been removed at Pride's Purge. Relatively young and patently clever, this Anglo-Irishman had emerged as the most respected of the new Council. The King wrote to him as early as the end of February, and in mid-April he deftly won royal favour by sending Charles reports of the consultations of his fellow councillors. In addition, the King wrote dozens of other letters to former parliamentarians and republicans whose support was thought attainable. He also began to receive approaches of a new sort, from former enemies who were offering their services unsolicited. One of these was from Charles Howard, a member of an important Border family, who had been an ardent supporter of Parliament and of the Protectorate and was now in high favour with Monck. Another was from Sir Charles Coote, one of the group currently in control of Ireland. Charles warmly accepted all such offers, but Coote's was exceptionally important as it gave the King a hold on his western realm. He promised the knight high office and the title of earl, and sent him commissions to command an Irish army. The most amusing of these approaches was possibly from George Downing, who as the Protectorate's and the Commonwealth's ambassador to the United Netherlands had repeatedly intervened to have the King and his followers expelled from Dutch soil. Charles's move to Breda made this man's services worth having, and they were accepted.[82]

The most ironic feature of the new situation was that the King's traditional adherents now threatened to become his greatest liability. Nothing would be more certain to deflect the people controlling Britain from his restoration than the boasts which some royalists were making of the vengeance which they would exact when he returned. Accordingly, he wrote to groups of both English and Scottish royalists in April, urging them to make positive gestures of reconciliation.[83] Likewise, he replied to the growing number of petitions for offices by deferring a decision upon almost all until his return to England. At the same time he attempted to safeguard the position of his most loyal followers in exile. He advertised the fact that Hyde would enjoy the same favour after a restoration. He knighted Fanshaw as some compensation for the loss of the post of Secretary. To delight the 'Louvre' group, he raised Jermyn to the honour of Earl of St Albans. O'Neill was promised the Keepership of St James's Palace, a lesser agent who had given long service was made master of a hospital near his home, and another made surveyor of the Port of London. In the excitement of these April days at Breda, the King's quarrel with his sister was forgotten.[84]

The event which swelled the stream of applications and offers to Charles was the election of the new Parliament, to be known as the

Convention. From quite early in the hustings it was obvious that the republicans would be resoundingly defeated and that many actual royalists were being elected, contrary to the prevailing law. The Convention met upon 25 April, and six days later Sir John Grenville delivered the King's letters. Unanimously, both Houses voted the restoration of the monarchy. News of this reached Breda by several messengers on the 8th, followed by a loyal address from Monck's army. Charles, realizing to whom he owed most, took care to reply immediately to the General, promising to undertake all that he had asked for his men. Breda was now filling up with royalists and couriers from England, and the States-General had formally invited Charles to be their guest. So he determined to meet Parliament's commissioners at The Hague.[85] When the deputation from the Dutch government arrived at Breda he insisted that they kept their hats on and told them that he loved their country for the good of his own. Too late, the Princess Dowager of Orange offered him the hand of her remaining daughter, Marie, and was politely refused. The citizens of Breda lent him a magnificent yacht, and on 14 May he sailed to Delft with his sister, brothers, and ministers. There the next day he was greeted by a convoy of 73 coaches, which escorted him to the Dutch capital where he had inherited his crowns.

His week at The Hague was part rhapsodic celebration and part political manœuvring. There was a state banquet in his honour, a night of fireworks and salutes by cannon, and round after round of sycophantic speeches by the Dutch leaders, foreign ambassadors, and British deputations. Charles had to exercise great care in his replies to these, with the entire Restoration Settlement yet to be made by the Convention. The Spanish were understandably surprised and irritated that, having been their guest for over four years, he had slipped away to the Dutch as soon as his restoration seemed likely. To mollify them, he spent more time with their ambassador then any other, sent his profound gratitude to de Haro, and promised Caracena that one of his first projects upon landing in England would be an alliance with Spain. He reminded the representatives of the City of London that he was himself born a Londoner, and knighted the lot. He was equally charming to the Convention's delegates who came to invite him home. The most distinguished of them was Lord Fairfax, who had, as Parliament's Commander-in-Chief, chased Charles out of Cornwall in 1646. The King took care to spend time with him alone, seeking his opinions. Downing's pardon was crowned with a knighthood. At Breda Charles had already met the representative of the Kirk, a relatively young minister called James Sharp. Not merely did the King express the expected affection for Scotland and its clergy, but he delighted

Sharp by remembering all the principal churchmen. At The Hague a set of England's leading presbyterian clergy appeared, and Charles was as courteous, solicitous, and non-committal to them. And, with the timeless gesture of a politician canvassing support, he took care to kiss Admiral Montagu's baby son.

During the whole of his stay, an English fleet had been lying off nearby Schevelingen. On 23 May, flanked by his brothers, the King rode between files of Dutch soldiers to that harbour. Over 100,000 people crowded its quays. His party was rowed out to the flagship, where the muscular figure of Montagu waited to welcome him. At 3 p.m. Mary and her young son Wilhelm went ashore, and the fleet weighed anchor for Kent.[86] It was completely unclear, not merely whether Charles would make a good king, but over what secular and religious governments he would preside. The general rejoicing was so unrestrained because it had purely negative sources: the end of the republic, and the end of exile.

The Year of Restoration, 1660–1661

UPON arrival in London, Charles settled down at the greatest of all English royal palaces, Whitehall. There he remained almost continuously for two years, and during every winter thereafter. He was to die in it. It has been likened by the historian Kevin Sharpe to 'an unwieldy, chaotic and decaying hotel'.[1] Some rooms housed government departments such as the Treasury and those of the Secretaries of State, while most of the hundreds of others were apportioned amongst important courtiers. Charles initially intended to rebuild the entire place, but when financial constraints made this impossible he contented himself with restructuring his own apartments three times over in twenty years. This redevelopment, and the lack of any plans of any of his suites, make it impossible to describe the layout of the rooms concerned. That this is so is very frustrating, for so many of the key events of the reign were to be set there. Meetings of the Privy Council and formal receptions of ambassadors were held slightly further north in the palace, in the Council Chamber and Banqueting Hall respectively. But most meetings and consultations took place in the set of rooms beside the Thames, the Presence Chamber, Withdrawing Room, Privy Chamber, and Bedchamber. Around these was a network of corridors and stairs which enabled Charles and his visitors to move with relative secrecy. The Bedchamber was formally the most private of these 'Privy Apartments', being restricted to its staff, to princes and important councillors, and to people invited by the King, but during the day it seems to have been often as crowded and noisy as the others. Often Charles would withdraw to a small chamber leading off it, the Cabinet or Closet, where he kept paintings and statuettes. Among these *objets d'art* he received reports from state servants and held private consultations. But there were other small rooms in the suite, with multiple locks to which only the King and his Page of the Backstairs (an entirely passive and apolitical servant) had keys. These likewise were used for secret discussions.[2] Thus the architecture of the palace was admirably suited to Charles's style of kingship, at once very open and very devious. His habit of strolling through the great warren of rooms, or in the garden planted in a courtyard, or in St James's Park beyond, made access to him very easy. A post in the Bedchamber or Privy Chamber, crucial to politicians wishing to tender advice to previous monarchs, was of only limited advantage in this reign. Yet much policy was to be made in corners or behind locked doors, in conversations between the King and selected persons, usually ministers but sometimes other courtiers, agents, or ambassadors.

As yet, however, this was in the future. During his first two months as effective king of three nations Charles spent much of his time simply receiving congratulations from foreign envoys, county and municipal delegations, and individual nobles. His evenings were spent supping with his brothers as the guests of successive aristocrats. Playing a part in this manner was precisely the activity at which Charles excelled, and all who commented upon the King's behaviour at these functions praised his charm and stamina. Indeed, he added to his burdens by his insistence upon performing the ancient ceremony of touching victims of scrofula. Legitimate monarchs, it was believed, had the power to heal this malady. Charles had already employed the ritual while in exile,[3] and now he revived it at Whitehall on a grand scale, running his hand over two hundred diseased heads at one sitting alone. It was a pointed reminder that royalty owed its titles to more than parliamentary declarations: it also endeared the King to the populace. This last sentiment was compounded by his willingness to take all his meals in public. His athletic recreations impressed observers almost as much as the responsible attitude which he took to kingship and his patience, courtesy, and good humour. One example of the latter was recorded. When a group of nobles arrived to compliment him, he told them that he was prepared to forgive anybody in the country except his horse, which had thrown him that morning. By the end of the summer, the favourable reaction which he had provoked was unmistakable: the English nation, like so many smaller groups before, had surrendered to Charles's winning manner.[4]

Alongside this crucial exercise in public relations went the equally important work of forming the new royal administration. The Convention Parliament had left this task entirely to him. The Parliament itself was divided between the two wartime parties and neutral or new men. The expected step for Charles to take was to appoint a Privy Council which represented the differing groups, and so he did. It contained his brothers and his seven Counsellors surviving from the exile, of whom one, Culpeper, died just after his return to England: it was tragic that he did not live to enjoy the fruits of the Restoration. To these were added three more of the exiles, six royalists who had remained at home during the Interregnum, four former supporters of Cromwell (including Monck and Montagu), and eight men who had been wartime parliamentarians but opposed subsequent regimes (including Annesley and Morice).[5] Likewise the great ministerial and Household offices were divided between eight royalists, five of their old enemies, and Heneage Finch, a newcomer to politics who had made a great impression in the current House of Commons. Hyde and Nicholas retained their old posts, while Morice became the second Secretary of State on Monck's nomination. Monck was made Captain-General of the armed forces and Master of Horse. A 'Presbyterian', Lord Robartes, became Lord Privy Seal. Ormonde was made Lord Steward, with another 'Presbyterian' noble, the Earl of Northumberland, as Lord High Constable. A former parliamentarian general, the Earl of Manchester, became Lord Chamberlain to balance a former royalist colonel, the Earl of Lindsey, as Lord Great Chamberlain. Montagu was made Master of the Wardrobe, and also Vice-Admiral of the navy under James. The financial offices were at first put into commission, but after ten months one of Charles I's wartime Counsellors, the aged Earl of Southampton, was made Lord Treasurer. The subordinate post of Chancellor of the Exchequer was offered to a wartime parliamentarian, but on his refusal it passed to Sir Anthony Ashley Cooper. This minute, brilliant, and unnerving man was a renegade royalist who had supported the Commonwealth, only to turn against Cromwell and finally to emerge as a leading supporter of Monck. It is typical of the age that his record and his talents probably counted for less in his appointment than the fact that he was Southampton's son-in-law.[6]

The lesser posts of central government were less completely in the King's gift. In deference to the principle of legitimacy upon which he based his monarchy, he had to recognize the claims of those who had obtained these offices, or the reversion of them, under his father. To displace them was a cumbersome and provocative business. Thus, when Charles wanted to make Sir William Compton, of the 'Sealed Knot', Master of the Ordnance, he had first to suspend the existing Master and then to grant Compton the rights to administer the post and to inherit it. The same procedure was employed to free at least five other important positions for Charles's nominees, but in most cases the legal claimants were simply reinstated if they brought a suit. The administration that actually emerged resulted from a network of private deals. Thus Montagu obtained the important naval office of Clerk of the Acts for his young relative and client Samuel Pepys. To enjoy it, however, Pepys had first to satisfy the previous occupant, now an aged man, by arranging to pay him a percentage of the salary. He then pressed to get his patent sealed, in case Montagu lost royal favour, and immediately considered selling it to another man for a lump sum.[7]

All told, the new English government symbolized the reunion of the nation and mixed social prestige with natural ability. In contrast with his behaviour during exile, Charles led it energetically and began to meet even Hyde's standards of industry.[8] He soon formed an inner ring of Counsellors to discuss the most important matters, termed the Committee for Foreign Affairs and consisting of Hyde, Ormonde, Nicholas, Monck, Southampton, and Morice.[9] Of these, Hyde soon emerged as by far the most important and confirmed the special relationship which he had established with Charles in Europe. His office as Chancellor gave him enormous influence, for he could expedite or delay the sealing of all pardons and patents. It also carried with it the job of Speaker of the House of Lords. The King and he exchanged notes at Council meetings in which he took the tone of a strict but kindly uncle. Charles advised petitioners to apply to him rather than to other ministers, and they did, in thousands. By early July, the representative of the Scottish Kirk, Sharp, could describe Sir Edward as the 'prime minister' and 'this great man'.[10]

In Scotland Charles continued the policy of reunification which he had adopted when resident there. During June most of the important Scottish nobles and gentry 'ran up' to London, and on the 18th the King asked them to advise him upon the form of an interim government. The next day, after acrimonious debate, they decided that it would be simplest to restore the Committee of Estates of 1651. To this Charles assented, and two weeks later he began to fill the great offices. Middleton, who had emerged from the exile as the King's favourite Scot, was given the highest honour, of Royal Commissioner to Parliament. Glencairn was rewarded for his efforts in 1654–5 with the post of Lord Chancellor. The Earl of Crawford-Lindsay was allowed to retain the office of Lord Treasurer, which Charles I had given him, in return for his support of the Engagement and his nine years' imprisonment by the English republicans. The 'Kirk party' was represented by Cassilis, as Justice-General, and by Rothes, as Lord President of the Council, while its now very aged military man, Leven, was made governor of Edinburgh Castle. The most sensitive job was that of Secretary of State, which involved residing near the King's person and enjoying unique opportunities for the exertion of covert influence. To fill it, both Hyde and Middleton recommended Newburgh, but Charles appointed Lauderdale. Since his capture after Worcester, this Earl had been incarcerated in successive English fortresses, with no dampening effect upon either his spirit or his wits. Released just before the Restoration, he had crossed at once to Breda. Uncouth, boisterous, shaggy, ugly, and cunning as always, he won the grudging goodwill of Hyde and remade with the King the rapport which had been so potent off the coast of Kent in 1648. He returned to Britain with the influential office of a Gentleman of the Bedchamber and obtained the friendship of the existing Secretary of State, the Earl of Lothian. Success duly followed, and Newburgh instead was appointed to the honorific duties of Captain of the Scottish Life Guard. The legal posts of Advocate and Clerk Register were filled by the same mixture of patronage and bargaining which had dealt with lesser English appointments. Both the successful men, Sir John Fletcher and Sir Archibald Primrose, had cultivated Middleton, though Fletcher had collaborated with the Cromwellians and Primrose had been a royalist and Engager. Primrose confirmed his chances by buying out the former Clerk Register.

At the end of this process none of the factions of the 1640s had been disgraced or ignored. Although dropped from the government, the 'Kirk party' leaders Loudon and Lothian were compensated with a large pension for the former and the post of Director of Chancellery for the second son of the latter. Nevertheless, it was obvious to most at court that Charles had no affection for the 'Kirk party' which had tried to control him in 1650, and its surviving members lacked influence. There was also a dearth of wartime royalists in the new administration. Instead, power had been lodged firmly in the hands of moderate Covenanters who had supported the Engagement and whose personalities had recommended them to Charles since. It was not so much a reconciliation as a reliance upon the old middle ground. It was also an illustration of the King's determination to choose his own servants. The case of Lauderdale's appointment mirrors this well. Hyde suspected that the red-haired Earl was also behind Crawford-Lindsay's survival as Treasurer. He was both amused and disturbed to learn that Charles simultaneously promised Middleton, without Lauderdale's knowledge, that he would rapidly replace Crawford-Lindsay with Middleton himself. The King's ingrained habit of coping with conflicts by stealth and circumvention had not been diminished by his restoration.[11]

In Ireland, by contrast, Charles merely confirmed in power the group of men whom he found holding it. These were an alliance of wartime parliamentarians and supporters of Cromwell who had deposed the republican leaders at the end of 1659. Sitting as a national Convention at Dublin, they had endorsed the return of the monarchy with joy and sent commissioners to congratulate the King. Two men stood out from all others in the kingdom: Sir Charles Coote, who dominated the north, and Roger Boyle, Lord Broghil, who led the south. Coote, moody, irascible, and bloodthirsty, had already secured royal goodwill by his overture to

Charles in March, as described. Broghil was in a more vulnerable position, for he was not only a renegade royalist but had been one of Cromwell's principal advisers and favourites. Moreover, Coote was anxious to turn the King against him. He may have made his own secret approaches to the exiled court,[12] but certainly he arrived in London in June in doubt concerning his future. He traded upon his greatest asset, his amiable, witty, and seductive personality. Applied to Hyde, this soon earned him the latter's support and an introduction to his monarch. Charles found himself so charmed that he asked Broghil to write a play for performance in London. To this the lord readily agreed, and so his career survived. The King's willingness to leave the current leaders in charge of Ireland was primarily a sign of his lack of interest in his western kingdom. On his arrival at London he proclaimed that the Catholic rebels of the 1640s were still to be regarded as traitors, so pleasing Protestants in all three kingdoms and disowning his alliance with the Confederacy in 1649. Next he made Monck himself Lord-Lieutenant, to the delight of men like Broghil who had worked with the General under the Protectorate. Ormonde was diverted to English politics by being put in charge of the Household and given a seat in the Westminster Parliament as Earl of Brecknock. On 25 July Charles named the former parliamentarian Lord Robartes as Monck's Lord Deputy, to take control in Dublin and commence the settlement of the kingdom. Coote and Broghil were confirmed as regional masters by being appointed Presidents of Connacht and Munster respectively. A committee of the English Privy Council which consisted mostly of 'Presbyterians', was set up to advise upon Irish affairs.[13]

What held up settlement was the choice of Robartes, convenient in his politics but disastrous in his personality. By the end of the summer his morose and arrogant manner had made him equally unacceptable to Monck and to the Irish commissioners, and he was relieved of his Irish office before ever setting out. The absence of an established government in Dublin led to growing disorder, and growing complaints from Coote. In October Charles just handed over the job to the men on the spot. He gave the office of Lord Chancellor to the aged and respected Sir Maurice Eustace, a Protestant who had been Speaker of the Irish Parliament in 1634. Then he vested authority, under Monck, in Eustace, Coote, and Broghil, as joint Lords Justices. The last two swallowed their mutual hatred and settled down to work. Broghil's brother Richard, Earl of Cork, became Lord Treasurer and got a voice at Westminster as Baron Clifford. The 'Presbyterian' Annesley was made Vice-Treasurer. As some belated balance of interests, Ormonde and O'Neill, from London, were allowed to place their clients in the judicial offices. To Hyde's resentment, his opinions were not asked. Finally, on 19 December, the King named an Irish Privy Council dominated by former supporters of the Long Parliament and Protectorate.[14]

By this time the remodelling of both central and local government in England was more or less complete. The navy was run from day to day by a board similar to the Commonwealth's commission, consisting of Montagu and two former Cromwellians and Berkeley and another royalist. In the course of the summer the King restored the two surviving royalist judges and reappointed four from the Commonwealth and eight from the Protectorate. Charles I had tried to appoint judges during his own pleasure, while the Long Parliament had wanted them to enjoy the more independent tenure 'during good behaviour'. To reinforce his association with legality and tradition, Charles II reverted to the Tudor pattern of employing both formulae, using one for some courts and the other for the rest. Simultaneously Charles put the militia of each English county, and of Wales, under the leading local magnate, according to custom, irrespective of his Civil War record. Where the dominant family had died out, opportunity was taken to elevate a man who had worked for the Restoration: hence Mordaunt, Grenville, and Monck all became Lord-Lieutenants of the counties in which they owned most land.

As a complement to this work, the leading gentry were restored to the commissions of the peace. The results varied from Anglesey, where not a single Interregnum JP was re-employed, to Devon, where over half survived. In most counties the majority of the bench were changed, and many of the replacements were young men from important families rather than members of pre-war and wartime commissions. To this extent it was a genuine reunion of local communities, but the precise identity of the benches was determined by personal connections. Thus heirs of royalist families represented in pre-war commissions were sometimes left out if they lacked allies at court, and justices who had served the republic were re-employed if they had some: the exceptional continuity in the Devon commission was due partly to the influence of Monck and Morice. We have one insight into the process at work, the case of the Cornishman Edmund Prideaux, who had served the Protectorate. His enemy, the royalist Colonel Arundell, used friendship with Hyde to have the sealing of the commission for the county held up, and began poisoning Sir Edward's mind against Prideaux. The latter was saved by his cousin Sir John Grenville and his brother-in-law Morice, who persuaded the Chancellor to pass the commission and to include Prideaux. Favour at court was not sufficient to obtain a person office without adequate local support: thus, despite royal favour, Cooper failed to become Lord-Lieutenant of

Wiltshire and Monck's protégé Colonel Charles Howard failed to become governor of Carlisle, in the face of gentry hostility.[15] The King certainly made sure that he had more than a superficial knowledge of the issues involved in local appointments. When Hyde asked him why an individual had not been made Lord-Lieutenant of Herefordshire, Charles replied at once that he had found him to be both unpopular in the county and personally unimpressive.[16]

The government attempted to secure the restoration of royalists in corporate bodies by indirect means. Urban corporations in general spent large sums on celebrating Charles's proclamation, made fulsome addresses and presents to him, and restored their fee-farm rents to the royal coffers: the most impressive of the gold and silver gifts are still displayed with the Crown Jewels in the Tower. But the men who did all this were almost always those who had run their communities during the Interregnum. The government's response to this situation was for the King to write to six of the largest councils during the autumn, requiring them to restore their expelled royalists and to remove their replacements, in the name of national unity. They were also urged to administer the Oaths of Allegiance and Supremacy to all members, which would displace not only the disloyal, but religious radicals who objected to oaths in general. Occasionally Charles recommended a royalist for an office. This policy still left a majority of the republic's city fathers in power, but as it was implemented there were hints of retribution to come. Hyde, in private, spoke not of reconciliation but of the need to do things 'by degrees'. In Kent, the government had some direct influence through the persons of the Lord Warden of the Cinque Ports, now James, and the governor of Dover. During the winter these men and the King between them ordered five corporations not merely to restore royalists but to dismiss any men who had petitioned for Charles I's trial, or had been elected during the Interregnum, or merely seemed disaffected.[17]

The legal procedure of the first settlement was carried out alongside the changes in personnel, and to both government and Parliament the most important part of this in England was the Act of Indemnity and Oblivion. The King sent three messages to hasten it and both Houses gave it priority over other business. Designed to be the great gesture to reunite the country, it had from the first an air of ceremonial artificiality in that its principal victims were not the leaders of the republic as such, but the regicides. These included relatively obscure individuals, along with national figures. In his declaration of September 1659, Charles had even offered pardon to all but seven of these, and this was the number fixed by the Commons shortly before the King returned to London. Instead, the Act which received his assent on 29 August put thirty-three men at immediate risk of their lives, but this still represented considerable restraint in the Convention, for over sixty individuals had been exposed to death in the various drafts.

Much of the measure's moderation was due to the tendency of the two Houses to reject each other's victims. At the insistence of the Commons, nineteen regicides who had surrendered themselves were spared execution until a separate Act of Parliament was passed, which the Convention never introduced. The republican general John Lambert and the politician Sir Henry Vane were exposed to death as the Lords wished, but reprieved by Charles as the Commons desired. Generally, the government members in the Lower House argued for moderation in most cases while pursuing their particular enemies. No comparable information survives upon the Lords' debates, but outside Parliament Hyde appears as greedy and unforgiving. He failed to seal the pardon of a former friend, the republican Bulstrode Whitelocke, until he received £250, and he objected to that of another man. By contrast, the rare glimpses of Charles's own attitudes convey an impression of mildness. When a mob hanged an effigy of Cromwell outside Whitehall, he had this removed, and he granted one republican politician a courteous interview, ending with the advice to retire into the country quickly.[18]

The charitable view of Charles's reactions is that they reveal a remarkable moderation and self-restraint. The sceptical one is that he found it easy to forgive individual English republicans because he had no personal grudges against them, and this explanation seems substantiated by the parallel cases of his other kingdoms. He first left the question of indemnity in Ireland to Robartes and then, when the latter's mission aborted, he just forgot about it. At last, in early 1661, he issued two specific pardons, one listing all Coote's allies and clients and one listing all Broghil's, in response to the pleas of these magnates.[19] In Scotland, by contrast, his experiences had left him with livid animosities. As in England, he referred the general question of indemnity to a Parliament, but this time he offered it victims. A month after his return he ordered the arrest of Johnston of Wariston, Sir John Cheisley, and two other leaders of the 'Remonstrants' of 1650. After the insulting diatribes which Charles had suffered, his anger against Johnston was particularly patent, but that individual scuttled overseas leaving the others to be committed. More surprising to many was the arrest of the greatest person of the Kirk party, Argyll himself. The Campbell followed so many others to London in early July, and was taken into custody under the most humiliating possible circumstances, as he stood amid a crowd in the Presence Chamber, awaiting the King. He never got to see Charles personally, but was kept in the Tower until the time came to ship him to Scotland for trial. The King's motives can only be surmised, though explanations are easily offered. He was almost certainly offended by Argyll's uselessness to him in 1650–1, and infuriated when Glencairn rose and the Marquis, far from helping as his monarch asked, joined the Cromwellians. It was said that Charles's anger was fanned by some who told him that the Campbell had expressed approval of the regicide. What is clear is that he acted once he had established that the Scottish nobility were happy to make Argyll a scapegoat for their collective misdeeds and misfortunes. He would not work off his personal dislikes unless public opinion permitted it. Nor, to the disappointment of some, did he bring down the Campbell name. Argyll's heir had defied his father and rebelled with Glencairn, and Charles received him warmly.[20]

All these actions, however, evaded the point that for royalists in all three kingdoms the crucial issue in indemnity was not one of life but of lucre. It was not just a question of having to share a judicial bench or a race-meeting with an old opponent, but of seeing him continue to enjoy the profits of one's plundered goods and cattle, while one continued in the financial difficulties that resulted. The Act in England set the precedent of ignoring this grievance, which would do much to explain the famous accusation, scattered in Whitehall in June, that it was an Act of Indemnity for the King's enemies and oblivion for his friends.[21]

Certainly, Charles was bitterly upset by this jibe.[22] Was his reaction one of outraged innocence or secret guilt? To determine the truth of the matter, it may be helpful initially to ask which were the groups to whom Charles owed personal gratitude at the Restoration. The answer seems to be three: his companions in exile, royalist conspirators of the 1650s, and the people who had brought about the Restoration itself. The failure to reward the last, who actually controlled his kingdoms in early 1660, would have been utter folly, and it is not surprising that they collected the most dramatic honours. Monck, in addition to his three great offices, became Duke of Albemarle and was given a royal palace and land worth £9,000 per year. Montagu, as well as his naval appointments, received the title of Earl of Sandwich and land worth £4,000 per year. Morice became not only Secretary of State but a knight, Governor of Plymouth, and Avenor of the Duchy of Cornwall. Grenville, the crucial message-bearer, was created Earl of Bath, Steward of the Duchy of Cornwall, Rider of Dartmoor, Groom of the Stole, and Underkeeper of St James's Palace. He was promised Monck's title of Duke if the General died without heirs. Charles Howard got the title of Earl of Carlisle and Cooper became Lord Ashley. In Ireland, Coote was made Earl of Mountrath and Constable of

Athlone, and his brother became a baron. Broghil got the title of Earl of Orrery and the post of Governor of Limerick. An important ally of theirs, Sir John Clotworthy, became Lord Masserene, and two more of the ruling Protestant group were made barons. The English 'Presbyterians' whom Monck had restored to power received titles as well as jobs: Annesley became Earl of Anglesey and two others were created barons. In Scotland the heiress of the Hamiltons had followed her father's death from his wound at Worcester by marrying a Douglas cousin. Despite the fact that this young man had collaborated with the Cromwellians, Charles allowed him to take the title of Duke of Hamilton, awarded him a large sum of money, and treated him as one destined for power.

None the less, the King's companions of the 1650s were all cared for. As described, his existing Privy Council was completely incorporated in the enlarged new body, and Hyde remained its leading member. Ormonde was made an Irish duke as well as an English earl, and given land in Somerset to support the title of Lord-Lieutenant of the county. Middeleton and Newburgh became earls in Scotland. Berkeley was considered for the post of Lord Deputy of Ireland, and actually made a commissioner for the navy and Keeper of Nonsuch Palace. Nicholas obtained for himself the post of Keeper of Game at Hampton Court and Ranger of Windsor Park, for his eldest son a knighthood and a Clerkship of the Council, for his second son two financial offices, and for his client Joseph Williamson the Secretaryship of the Latin Tongue. The other Clerks of the Council were Lane, Walker, and Browne. The latter was rewarded for his long penurious stay in Paris with the additional office of Muster Master General. That other unfortunate royalist diplomat, De Vic, received recompense at last as Chancellor of the Order of the Garter and Secretary for the French Tongue. Fox had to yield the major posts of the Household to men of grander birth, but got an office in it as its second Clerk Controller, in addition to the job of Paymaster of the Guards. Despite their quarrels with Charles, Gerard still secured the reversion to a financial post and Balcarres was promoted to an earldom. In addition, the King personally drew up a list of the persons who had assisted his escape after Worcester, and all of them subsequently received rewards if they asked for these.

Charles managed to be almost as generous to the rebels and conspirators who had risked their lives for him during his exile. Mordaunt became Governor of Windsor Castle and received two reversions to Crown lands and one to another office. Every member of the 'Sealed Knot' was granted offices or honours except the presumed traitor Willis, and Booth became Lord Delamere. The surviving leaders of the plots of 1655 and 1658 got posts, stipends, or grants. Glencairn, as said, scooped one of the greatest offices in Scotland. His Highland ally, Macdonald of Glengarry, did not get an earldom as promised in the event of success, but was compensated with a barony. David Leslie, despite having lost the battles of Dunbar and Worcester, was created Lord Newark. There were two posthumous rewards: Hamilton's heiress was granted £15,000 in quittance of her father's loans to Charles I, and Montrose's heir received a grant of money. The severed limbs of the great Marquis were reunited with the torso in a solemn burial in St Giles's Kirk at public expense, upon royal orders.[23]

Compared with all these people, it could be argued that Charles owed little to the great majority of royalists, who had ignored his appeals for active support all through the Interregnum. Yet he attempted to provide for them as well. On his return, he insisted, against the wishes of the Convention and of Monck, that peers created by himself *or* his father since 1642 be allowed into the Lords. He went on to confer two more peerages promised by his father during the wars. Royalists received many more of the baronetcies and knighthoods given at the Restoration than their old opponents. In the three years after his return, Charles rewarded at least 159 former royalist army officers, and at least thirty families of followers now deceased. At least seventy royalists received Crown land, as grants or as leases upon easy terms, and so many were given pensions that the Lord Treasurer Southampton begged the King to be less benevolent. Charles also repaid fifty-four men who had lent money to his father, from his personal income. If Charles I had won Edgehill, the booty would hardly have been greater.

Moreover, individual charges of royal ingratitude collapse upon scrutiny. The poet Abraham Cowley, a former royalist agent, was certainly ignored at the Restoration, and complained of this, but he had abandoned his cause to write praises of Cromwell. When another agent, Samuel Morland, considered himself neglected, this meant that he expected the Garter as well as the ordinary knighthood and pension which he did receive. A Yorkshire royalist, Sir Philip Monckton, stated that he received no reward for seven years but was in fact given three posts in that time. The royalist put in charge of the Post Office declared that most of those who applied for jobs there on grounds of former services to his cause were frauds. Fanshaw had clearly failed to fulfil the terms upon which he was offered the post of Secretary of State, and was instead made a Master of Requests and ambassador to Portugal. But not only did he consider himself ill-treated but actually turned against his former patron Hyde, in vengeance. So many gentry crowded into London to hunt places that prices soared, and even their servants followed in the hope of employment at court. It was a gold-rush atmosphere, with disappointment inevitable for most.

When all this is said, some truth remains in the complaints. The circumstances of the Restoration demanded, as said, that the greatest honours of all were given to non-royalists. A project to found a new order of knighthood, the Royal Oak, for the most distinguished of the King's old adherents was mysteriously dropped, presumably to avoid offence to former parliamentarians. Most of the new knights and baronets were newcomers to politics, the rising men of the shires whose support the government had to confirm. Furthermore, the crowds of impecunious royalists were not a myth, for in 1663 over five thousand needy former officers were identified. Charles was able to reward only 9 per cent of the men who had suffered for his cause in Lancashire and 11 per cent in Yorkshire. The problem was one of means not intentions but a problem it was.[24]

A second great question which the Restoration posed was the fate of the lands confiscated from Crown, bishops, deans, and chapters by the Long Parliament and its purged remnant. The purchasers included many soldiers, London merchants, and gentry, and some former tenants. Together, they constituted a formidable interest group. In his 1659 declaration Charles had offered some unspecified compensation to them, and just before the King's return General Monck proposed that this should consist of long leases on easy terms. Throughout the summer various purchasers held meetings to strengthen their chances of obtaining these by co-ordinated efforts, expressed in addresses to King and Parliament.

As always, the Convention in England proved more royalist than expected. On 22 June a bill which seems to have guaranteed long leases to purchasers was introduced, only to be defeated. Monck's client Howard was among the tellers against it, suggesting that this faction was abandoning the interests of purchasers in general. On the same day the Commons agreed that Henrietta Maria's jointure, which was owed to her by the terms of her marriage treaty, had to be restored entire. The following day Finch introduced a different bill for confirmation or compensation of buyers, and on 11 July, upon the motion of a former royalist agent, Sir Job Charlton, the Crown lands were exempted from its restrictions. The Lords followed this up by voting the King into all his possessions. The Lower House neither concurred with nor challenged this, but continued to the end of the session with desultory discussions of the terms upon which the Church might regain its lands. For both King and ecclesiastics, it was enough that the principle of repossession had been conceded. Nine days after the Lords' vote, the Surveyor-General began to resume control of Crown lands and to negotiate with those who had bought them. Although granted representation in 1641, Durham was traditionally a County Palatine, returning no MPs. The purchasers in it were not men of influence in 1660, and Charles felt able to move swiftly. On 30 July he ordered the seizure of both royal and ecclesiastical land in the county. Nearer the capital more caution was required, as was proved by John Cosin, Dean of Peterborough, who called his chapter together in early August and granted several leases. He provoked a resolution from the Commons that no Church land be disposed of till the bill to regulate this was passed, and a furious letter from Hyde urging him to be tactful. Charles overruled the resolution without provoking any displeasure from MPs, and at its recess the Convention left the problem in his hands. Its only request was that he commission a body of peers and MPs to arbitrate in case of disputes. This, on 7 October, he did.

Both Crown and Church immediately began leasing on a large scale. Charles kept faith with Monck's army, though not as comprehensively as the General had wished. Any officer who had been at Coldstream, and some other military purchasers who had aided the Restoration, were allowed to receive rents up to March 1661 and thereafter became tenants paying nominal rents or were given what they had not yet recouped from their outlay. Other soldiers who had taken the Oath of Allegiance were permitted the rent due in September 1660, and existing or former tenants were given first option of taking the lease. Charles also ordered churchmen to favour purchasers and old tenants in letting their lands anew, and named individuals in the former group for particularly favourable treatment. The southern dioceses settled most of their lands before the end of 1660, while some in the north did not commence the work until the next year. All, however, seem to have worked in most cases according to the King's instructions. There were some illustrious exceptions; the 'Presbyterian' Colonel Birch was supported by Charles, Hyde, and Monck in his desire to lease an episcopal palace which he had bought, yet he required a twelve-year lawsuit to do so because the new bishop was an enemy.

In the land settlement the private individual was sacrificed to the greater good. After the confiscations of public land, many royalists had suffered deprivation to pay for the Commonwealth's wars. A large number of these, varying from almost half in the south-east to two-thirds in the north of England, had rapidly regained some of this property by direct repurchase or the efforts of friends. In 1660 eleven of the most important regained all their estates by private Act of Parliament or orders of the Lords. The remainder were provided for in the Commons' August bill on Church land, which proposed for them a simple restoration of property without compensation or penalty. The failure of this abandoned them to the tedious and expensive business of regaining their estates by lawsuit, as the sales were excepted from the Act of Indemnity. All but a small percentage succeeded, but the process must have irritated men who watched their old masters, sacred and secular, resume their wealth with relative ease. Even less content would have been the far greater number of royalists who had sold land or undergone hardship in order to pay fines. The Earl of Derby, son to the royalist martyr, introduced two private bills in the Lords to regain lands which he claimed to have parted with in the belief that they were held in trust for him. Both failed, from a mixture of lack of time and hostility in the Commons to the reversal of voluntary sales. To such men, as to those who had lost moveable goods, the Restoration offered no redress. The result was privation rather than ruin, and as a group the royalist gentry survived. This was the ominous fact: they were left both powerful and resentful.[25]

The same problem of private land was reproduced upon a gigantic scale in Ireland, as a result of the Long Parliament's confiscation of the estates of Catholic rebels in the 1640s and of Catholics and royalists in the 1650s. About seven-eighths of all Irish landowners who followed the Roman faith had been dispossessed, in addition to many Protestant supporters of the kings. Among the beneficiaries of the transfer were the members of the Irish Convention led by Coote and Broghil and some of Monck's officers: the very people whom Charles needed to conciliate in 1660. They were, moreover, determined to hang on to their acquisitions as far as possible. The commissioners sent over by the Convention first tried to buy off Ormonde by supporting his recovery of all his lands by Act of Parliament. Then they proposed that only two or three other royalists be accorded the same favour and that (save for regicides) those who had held Irish estates in 1659 be left in possession of them. Charles's initial reaction to the problem, as to that of indemnity in Ireland, was to shelve it. The consequences for order were unfortunate, some of the dispossessed reoccupying their lands by force. Insecurity was compounded during the autumn when the King began to order the restoration of certain royalists to their estates without announcing any principles to determine how far the process of restoration might go. Coote sent desperate letters asking for a ruling, and the English Privy Council's committee upon Irish affairs thrashed one out during November. Only traces remain of the views upon the matter of those concerned at Whitehall. Ormonde felt that the Catholics in general should be left too weak ever to rise again, but that individuals among them deserved mercy. The exchanges of notes between Charles and Hyde reveal that the former felt considerably more sympathy for the dispossessed than the latter. At one point the King (brooding yet again over his humiliations in Scotland) commented that he would rather trust a papist than a presbyterian rebel. Hyde replied almost curtly that this reflected Charles's limited experience. Another scribbled exchange provides a tantalizing glimpse of how policy was actually made. The King objected that Annesley sat in the committee upon Irish affairs while representing himself as an interested party in some of the issues discussed. The Chancellor answered that it was Charles himself, and not the committee, who took the important decisions.

The royal declaration of 30 November formally disowned the dealings of the kings with the Catholic Confederacy in the 1640s and confirmed the titles of the new owners of the confiscated land in general. It made special provision for the security of Monck, Broghil, Coote, Annesley, Clotworthy, and their followers. But there were also important qualifications. Church lands had to be returned, and so had those of Protestant royalists and of Catholics not implicated in the rebellion of the 1640s, provided that land was found to compensate those who had purchased their estates. Thirty-eight royalists, including Taaffe, Clancarty, and Belling, were named for immediate restoration by this process, and during early 1661 Charles wrote on behalf of individuals among them, reinforcing these orders. Taaffe and O'Neill were rewarded for their public and private services during exile with a grant of fresh property in addition, and English politicians such as Sir John Grenville and Morice received Irish estates. The problem here was that Charles appeared to think that the supply of land in his western kingdom was almost inexhaustible. Confiscation of regicides' property yielded 36,000 acres in County Dublin, which the King granted away several times over, making a gift of 20,000 acres to one person alone. The lack of property in the royal gift made compensation of the purchasers of royalist and Catholic land virtually impossible and so blocked restoration of the original owners. By 1661 the number of aggrieved former landowners in Ireland greatly exceeded those in England, and so more dragons' teeth were planted in the soil of the restored monarchy.[26]

All these aspects of settlement were expected to cause difficulties, but a fourth was expected to surpass all in its delicacy: the future of the national Churches. Unlike secular conflicts, the religious divisions of Britain transcended any pattern of rewards, penalties, and compensations. Nor was Charles himself equivocally associated with one system of church government. On the one hand, the royalist cause had traditionally been bound up with that of the episcopalian Church of England, and the king had followed its rites upon the Continent. On the other, he had signed both the Covenants and adopted the presbyterian service in Scotland, while despite his appeals the surviving English bishops had been totally passive during the 1650s. At the time of his return, episcopacy had been abolished for over a decade in all three kingdoms, by the Covenanters in Scotland and the Long Parliament in the other realms. Within eighteen months it was restored in all. This apparently remarkable fact used to be ascribed to the machinations of Charles's government. Since the mid-1970s the separate researches of Ian Green in England, Julia Buckroyd in Scotland, and J. I. McGuire in Ireland have instead portrayed a hesitant monarchy acting in response to pressures from outside.[27] It is that story which must be traced now and in the following chapter.

It is easiest to tell in the case of Ireland. Before the King reached London the Convention sitting at Dublin had decided upon the restoration of bishops as a symbol of national order and unity. Its commissioners requested this of Charles at their first audience with him upon 21 June, with toleration of moderate Protestant dissenters. The King and his advisers responded like lightning, naming all archbishops and bishops within two days. Most were royalist clergy, though two had been prominent ministers under the Cromwells. The new Primate of All Ireland, holding the see of Armagh, was John Bramhall, who had been more closely associated with the exiled court than any other Irish cleric and even acted for a while as a commissioner for privateering prizes. Ormonde, while excluded from direct power in his homeland, was given considerable influence in its ecclesiastical settlement. He named almost all of the deans and archdeacons appointed. In November Charles ordered the return of all Church land by its subsequent purchasers, without mentioning compensation.

Thus, when a deputation of Ulster ministers arrived in early July, instructed by their brethren to remind Charles of the Solemn League and Covenant, they were far too late. Most of the Irish commissioners were openly hostile. The Scottish lords, the London presbyterian clergy, Manchester, Annesley, Broghil, Clotworthy, and Monck, while all expressing some fellow-feeling for the Irishmen, felt that their address was unacceptable now that the bishops had been chosen. They watered it down to a mere request for favour, whereupon Annesley presented them to Charles. Probably because he had heard of their original mission, the King treated them very coldly, but did promise protection for their separate religious meetings if they could not accept the episcopalian Church.[28]

Initially, Scotland seemed to be destined as painlessly for a different fate: the preservation of the presbyterian Kirk. At the King's return the majority of its ministers belonged to that 'Resolutioner' faction which had been his allies in 1651. They now had two objectives: to persuade Charles to keep the Covenants and to establish presbyterianism in all three kingdoms, and to shift blame for his humiliations in 1650 firmly on to the Remonstrants. Their agent in London remained James Sharp, whose pointed face, tight mouth, and finely arched eye-sockets preserve in his portraits the supple and canny character of the man. Sharp soon realized that the first hope of his colleagues was unattainable, for the Irish Convention wanted episcopacy and the English ministers were willing to compromise with it. Instead, he concentrated upon securing guarantees for the Kirk, and apparently got them. Three times in June and July Charles received Sharp in private, with every sign of favour, and expressed his willingness to preserve the Scottish Church unaltered. On 10 August he signed a letter, drafted by Lauderdale, which promised the maintenance of the Kirk 'as it is settled by law'. This the ministers generally took to signify their present form of government. There had been a few signs of danger: Middleton had, as said, turned to the Anglican rite in exile and some of the Scottish nobility gathered in London seemed to favour bishops. But Charles dealt with Middleton's possible opposition to the royal letter by the characteristic trick of failing to tell him that he was sending one. The message itself silenced the other lords. It produced a series of grateful addresses from provincial synods, and the King was delighted by these. He apparently did not care what form the Kirk took as long as it was entirely subservient to him.

In their other task the Resolutioners enjoyed total success. Charles's memory of the invectives of Guthrie and Gillespie was as bitter as his recollection of Johnston, and he hardly needed Sharp's whispers to turn his rage upon the Remonstrants. Making it clear that he would receive no petitions from them, he abandoned them to their Scottish enemies. The first act of the revived Committee of Estates, convened upon 23 August, was to arrest a set of clergy led by Guthrie, who were framing an appeal to Charles to keep the Covenants. Gillespie and others of their party soon followed them into prison, to await trial by Parliament. In his letter of 10 August the King prohibited all religious meetings outside the Kirk, and the Committee reinforced this with a ban upon any gatherings not authorized by the government and any petitions intended to direct its policy. By the autumn, in the words of one Resolutioner, the Remonstrants were 'clean run down to the contentment of the most'. Chancellor Glencairn told some of Guthrie's group that Charles wanted them driven out of Scotland.[29]

In England, it seemed as if the 'natural' development would be the revival of episcopacy in a modified form, elected by and operating with the assistance of presbyters. The royalist party had offered this in 1645. From 1656 a group of ministers led by John Gauden had been working for such a model, and in early 1660 one of the most respected members of the Interregnum Church, Richard Baxter, had declared his support for it. Fourteen sees were vacant, and only three were occupied by men who had been associated with the full-blooded prelacy of Archbishop Laud. In May 1660 the leading presbyterian ministers had expressed willingness to use the pre-war Prayer Book, provided that they could omit passages of it. The Convention Parliament was almost evenly split between the supporters of episcopacy and those of presbyterianism and independency, and its favourite preacher was Gauden. The English Privy Council contained men associated with both clerical camps, and Charles appointed a set of chaplains to match. Most of the episcopalian clergy who had rejected the Interregnum Church now preached reconciliation, while their old opponents divided. The majority of presbyterian leaders professed willingness to accept both 'primitive' episcopacy and a Prayer Book revised by a joint conference. Charles pledged himself to work for such a compromise settlement and so, within a month of his return, the way to it seemed open.

There was a possible hitch in the proceedings: that the Declaration of Breda had referred the question of the Church to Parliament, and that the Commons were starting to debate it with an acrimony that boded ill for conciliation. Sittings lasted late into the night, and in one of them the candles were blown out to disrupt proceedings. To an extent, the Privy Counsellors in the House let themselves be divided by the same passions, but increasingly they tended to propose that the matter be settled by churchmen. This not merely offered a means of removing such a difficult issue from their midst but would strengthen Charles's grip upon the Church by giving him the role of arbitrater: it was almost certainly what the King himself wished. In July the Commons conceded it. Instead they bent their energies to settling the titles of ministers to livings. The government members joined the 'Presbyterians' to secure a measure which would guarantee most of the existing clergy their benefices, and the departure of many episcopalians to attend the harvest ensured its passage. The resulting Act restored those royalist ministers who wished to return to their old parishes, and confirmed the titles of all other clergy who were not baptists and had not preached against the King. Hyde, in his speech at the recess, praised the statute while calling for action against ministers who still preached sedition.

In late August, with the Convention preparing for its recess, the government took the next step towards settlement by inviting the bishops to discuss the presbyterian proposals. Charles began to offer the vacant sees to men from both religious groups, just as he was filling the parochial livings in the royal gift, and secular offices, according to the principle of compromise. This time, however, the policy failed because all the presbyterian leaders except one refused the episcopal title. They seem to have done so because the institution had already become insufficiently 'primitive' for their tastes. During July and August cathedral chapters had been reconvening themselves, despite their depleted membership, and provoking no local hostility by this action. Charles took this as a sign to fill up these bodies with a mixture of former royalists, members of Cromwell's Church, and new men, usually without reference to the views of bishops and deans. Although the membership of the chapters was intended as a further symbol of reunification, the mere existence of cathedral clergy was unacceptable to most presbyterians. To fill his sees, Charles had to make do with appointing the widest spectrum of churchmen remaining, from Gauden who had held a living under Cromwell to Cosin who had closely supported Archbishop Laud. Most of those chosen, like most of the surviving bishops, were wartime royalists who had done neither of these things. One of them was George Morley, who had conducted missions for the King during the exile, and another was Gilbert Sheldon, to whom was given the vital see of London. Sheldon had remained in England during the Interregnum and played no part in Charles's affairs, but his power of personality and air of determined efficiency had already marked him out as a man unusually fitted for office. His record and words alike suggested in 1660 that these gifts would be employed in the case of moderation. Canterbury itself was given to William Juxon, who had been Charles I's last Bishop of London and Lord Treasurer, and attended him on the scaffold. He, however, was now too aged to represent more than a feeble and benign figure-head.

Nor did the clerical conference turn out quite as hoped. Charles instructed Hyde to draft a 'treaty' for it and the Chancellor enthusiastically produced one which absolved individual ministers from certain ceremonies favoured by episcopalians. But, it offended the presbyterians with the fervour with which it praised the episcopalian view of the Church. Although the ensuing discussions were held at Hyde's London residence, he was replaced as a mediator by the 'Presbyterians' Holles and Annesley. The result was the Worcester House Declaration of 25 October, an interim settlement which required bishops to ordain and censure with the assistance of presbyters and left clergy to use as much of the Prayer Book as they wished. This corresponded very closely to what the presbyterians had asked in June. It was, however, not an agreement, for it had been imposed upon the churchmen by the decisions of Holles and Annesley. It also led to trouble when the Convention met again, and the 'Presbyterians' in the Commons tried to make it the basis of a parliamentary settlement. This would have wrested control of ecclesiastical developments back out of the government's hands, and its members combined with the episcopalians to get the proposal defeated by thirty-six votes. Here, for the winter, the matter rested.

If Charles's achievement of comprehending presbyterians within the Church of England was more fragile and artificial than at first appeared, so too was his attempt to secure toleration for religious groups outside it. The gathered churches presented only a minor problem, as their close association with the republic made it easy for gentry to arrest their leaders and disperse their meetings on grounds of political security alone. The Privy Council could not risk any discouragement of this activity, which went on across the country during the summer and autumn, and merely required a proper hearing for the accused. The real difficulties arose with the Quakers. These were the most radical of all the religious groups spawned by the Civil Wars, the most numerous, and the most offensive to episcopalians, presbyterians, and independent congregations alike. They rejected all ecclesiastical government, all rituals, all texts, and all oaths, and propagated their views with noisy public demonstrations. Yet their leaders had held aloof from the republican regimes and now hailed Charles as their natural leader, to whom they looked for protection. The receptions of their representatives were a considerable success: he put on the mask of solemn majesty which he had perfected for deputations, graciously permitted them to retain their hats (doffed only for God), and promised that they could meet in safety. Their attitude seems to have flattered him, and in addition he apparently found them entertaining, like the camel drivers and harpers who had brightened his exile. Certainly his word was good, for 700 of them were released from prison on his orders. In November he set up a committee of the Privy Council to find grounds for liberating more. In the following month he promised a Quaker before the Council that their meetings would continue undisturbed, and that they would not be punished for failing to attend church or to remove hats before magistrates.

In this benevolent attitude he parted company with the overwhelming majority of people now in central and local government. His ministers were visibly embarrassed by his interviews with Quakers. Hyde inserted a gratuitous passage criticizing their mode of language into his speech at the Convention's recess. The Commons wanted religious radicals to pay double taxes, while the Lords encouraged the dispersal of separatist meetings. Mobs of commoners attacked Quaker gatherings, while across England many of the new justices ignored Charles's policy and set about locking up Quaker leaders and preachers faster than the King could free them. It was the first unequivocal sign that his principal realm was not wholly amenable to his will.[30]

The winter session of the English Convention Parliament was devoted mainly to an attempt to provide the restored monarchy with a regular revenue. In part, this was the successful culmination, made possible by the shock of the Interregnum, of sixty years of attempts to replace the ancient feudal incomes of the Crown (seigneurial dues, wardship, and purveyance) with something more popular and more predictable. It was also a matter of urgent necessity, for both the remaining traditional sources of royal income were badly depleted—the customs revenue by economic recession and the Crown lands by generosity to former purchasers and supporters. The confiscated estates of regicides had been devoted principally to providing a subsistence for James.

The stabilization of the country took precedence over this work, and although a Commons' committee upon it was set up on 3 May, nothing important was achieved until July. Then the Convention increased the customs dues. Thereafter it became absorbed in the gigantic task of raising sums to pay off and disband the standing army left by the republic. In September the Commons decided that the normal revenue of the government ought to be £1,200,000 a year, an estimate apparently based upon that of the 1630s with 8 per cent added for inflation. Even when taking the higher customs rates into account, the MPs realized that over a third of this needed to be made up. They only had time to vote Charles an interim lump sum before going into recess but upon their return in November they set about debating the deficit. All agreed that the old feudal dues should not be revived but there was much controversy over the substitute. Some argued for a light 'assessment' upon land, but backbenchers generally opposed this, as liable to lead to rating disputes and to discontent among landowners who expected the Restoration to mean the end of direct taxation. As a substitute, they proposed an excise on alcoholic drinks, which promised both to be lucrative and to discourage vice. The government members divided over this, Finch and Cooper coming slowly to support the project while Annesley argued (correctly) that it was a levy inflicted upon the common people in the interests of the landed. It was adopted by just two votes on 21 November, and duly became embodied in an Act. The restored monarchy thereby avoided being associated with continued unpleasantness for the landed classes. The misfortune was that it had provided a nasty shock for any commoner who enjoyed a drink.

The same effect was reproduced in Scotland during the following few months. Middleton persuaded the Parliament there to grant Charles an income of £40,000 a year, from the customs and from an excise imposed upon ale and beer. This was done upon condition that the King never requested a land tax by the efficient new method of 'assessment'. As in England, the gentry were satisfied and Middleton became the villain of the tippling public. In Ireland, as with every other problem, the financial settlement lagged behind developments in Great Britain. As a result, by the end of 1660 the army there was virtually unpaid. Charles gave the Lords Justices an option of recalling the Irish Convention to deal with the emergency or of allowing him to send begging letters for loans to landholders. They chose the former course as the more acceptable to the political nation, and in January 1661 the Convention duly reappeared at Dublin. By this stage the soldiers' wages were twenty months in arrear. A bill for a poll tax was produced, and then a second when the Lords Justices pointed out nervously that the yield of the first would be insufficient. With the passage of these in March, the Convention of Ireland delivered thanks to the King for the religious and land settlement and finally dissolved.[31]

The fiscal achievements of the Restoration were those that gave the new government the least anxiety. Hyde told the English Convention that it had produced a 'noble revenue'. Middleton believed that Scottish public finances were stabilized for an indefinite future. Charles informed the Lords Justices that his income in Ireland was going to improve dramatically with the benefits of peace and security, and that this would solve all problems of supply.[32] In every case this expectation was to be appallingly wrong.

So often during Charles's life, periods of great hope and excitement were succeeded by disaster and disillusion. The Restoration itself was not to reproduce this pattern, but as if to spare him too long an experience of unalloyed happiness, a cruel providence followed it by striking at the royal family. The sequence of tragedy commenced in September 1660, when Henry of Gloucester contracted the great scourge of the century's upper classes, smallpox. His dose was considered mild, and aroused little concern, so that everybody was horrified when, on the 13th, he suddenly died. Charles's grief was patent to all around him, for this brother, having grown into a sweet-tempered youth of twenty, had been his favourite of the two. In some measure he may have been comforted by the arrival of Mary in England on the 25th, but she brought diplomatic troubles in her wake. She had assumed that upon his recovery of his realms, her brother would throw their power behind the House of Orange and re-establish its supremacy in the Netherlands. It was, she felt, high time that he began to repay her and her dead husband's family for all their efforts upon his behalf. Accordingly, Mary spent the summer in a feverish campaign to have her young son Wilhelm made Captain-General of the Dutch republic. Charles wrote in support of this, but when the leaders of Holland refused it he was completely unwilling to pick a fight with them over the issue. His sister, who had threatened the various States with his anger, felt betrayed and furious. She accepted a compromise settlement whereby Holland agreed to pay for the education of Wilhelm for future high office, and crossed the North Sea to confront Charles.³³

The King had been left sorrow by Henry and given bitterness by Mary. A couple of weeks later, James presented him with scandal. In early October, Hyde's daughter Anne was discovered to be heavily pregnant, named the Duke of York as the father, and claimed that they had been secretly married. James denied this, while Charles and his sister were appalled by the notion of the heir presumptive marrying a commoner, and Hyde was determined not to lose royal favour. Henrietta Maria rushed over from France to prevent such a misalliance, while some of the Duke's friends attempted to poison his mind against Anne. There was talk of the matter being raised in the Commons when the Convention regathered, to avoid which Charles made Hyde a baron, securing him the privileges of a peer.

What rescued Anne's cause, despite such powerful opposition, was that she had spoken the truth, and had reliable witnesses to this. During November Charles came to accept the fact. Mary did not, but her opposition was about to collapse for a different reason. In December the smallpox virus reached her, and she died as swiftly and unexpectedly as had Henry, begging the King to act as guardian to her son. It is a mark of how strained relations had become between them that Charles did not seem as broken-hearted by her fate as he had by their brother's. Henrietta Maria, however, was prostrated. Moreover, Mazarin was trying to curry favour with Charles by pressing his mother to accept the marriage between James and Anne and heal the family feud. The Duke, miserable and confused, came to speak to Hyde once more and to recognize his new-born son. When Henrietta Maria returned to France in early January, Anne was recognized by all as the Duchess of York. Hyde was offered a dukedom for himself, but for fear of jealousy, preferred to accept the lesser title by which he has been known ever since, of Earl of Clarendon.³⁴

This great sequence of misfortune had three considerable consequences. James, having been distinguished hitherto by his handsome features, political loyalty, and physical courage, was revealed as foolish and malleable. Hyde's position as favourite minister was cemented by his daughter's marriage, but as he had anticipated he attracted envy and resentment in proportion. And the death of one brother and the discredit of the other made the question of Charles's own marriage, and the heirs expected from it, of some urgency. In fact, secret negotiations for it had been pursued before the end of 1660, and were concluded soon after. Like his other family affairs, they were bedevilled by problems of factional politics and diplomacy.

Upon Charles's return to England, his foreign policy seemed to be predetermined by his experiences towards the end of exile: friendship with Spain, cordial relations with the Dutch, and coldness towards France. The French ambassador was sent packing and the Spanish one received with more pomp than any foreign agent before, and it was agreed to commence talks to achieve a closer friendship with the United Netherlands. As is now well known, this process was halted, and then reversed, by the continuing momentum of policies inherited from the republic. The Commonwealth had passed a law restricting the carriage of English goods in Dutch ships: in the autumn of 1660 the English Convention, without reference to Charles's views and to the consternation of Dutch merchants, produced an act to exclude the latter from England's trade with its colonies. Thus the atmosphere was already slightly strained when a large delegation arrived from The Hague in November, empowered to make a defensive pact between the Dutch, French, and English. To meet it Charles appointed a commission consisting mainly of former Cromwellians and 'Presbyterians', perhaps to draw upon the good relations which had existed between the United Netherlands and the Protectorate. Again, the logic of commercial rivalry foiled good intentions. The English negotiators pointed out that mutual defence would benefit the more vulnerable Dutch, with their land frontier, rather than England, secure behind the Channel. They would only consent to such a pact if it covered the tropical lands from which Holland and Zealand traders were driving all competitors. This the Dutch naturally refused. On 3 January the new English Council of Trade reported that this competition was resulting in a very alarming loss of markets in the East Indies. It recommended not only that the prospective treaty guarantee the safety of English merchants in the tropics, but that it provide for reparations to traders who had already been disturbed or attacked by Dutch rivals. Under Cromwell's treaty of 1654, the English had been ceded the East Indian island of Pulo Run, but the Dutch had subsequently refused to hand this over unless English merchants dropped their complaints of harassment in the region. Soon after his council's report, Charles yielded to pressure of London mercantile opinion, and took his first step away from a policy of greater friendship with the

United Netherlands: he ordered the East India Company to seize Pulo Run.[35]

In the case of Spain, the deterioration in relations was much more spectacular. Soon after the Restoration, both nations prepared for an alliance. Charles, Felipe, de Haro, and Caracena seemed equally enthusiastic for one, and in September the Anglo-Spanish war commenced by Cromwell was formally terminated as a preliminary. Shortly after, the Spanish ambassador, Baron Batteville, presented Felipe's terms. This was the moment at which everything began to go wrong. Charles found himself given a vehement demand for the return of all Spanish territory taken by England since 1630, as he had promised in the event of his restoration by Spanish arms. Next to the Catholic religion, Felipe's driving passion was for the recovery of all the lands which he had inherited in 1621, and his pride would not permit him to write off Dunkirk and Jamaica. For his own part, Charles dared not hand back these prizes for fear of a massive loss of popularity in his newly recovered realm. All he could do was explain this problem in audience after audience with Batteville during the autumn.

By then the English government had been presented with a very severe temptation which, if not resisted, made friendship with Spain impossible. Felipe's sentiments regarding his inheritance applied with particular force to his rebel kingdom of Portugal, and in 1660, with his French and English wars over, he could at last concentrate his strength against it. In their desperation the Portuguese were prepared to bid for help at a fabulous price, and from Charles, who had as yet made no diplomatic commitments, above all. Months before Batteville reached England they had planted an agent there, Francisco de Mello, who systematically bought the goodwill of courtiers from Monck downwards. These investments obtained him a secret meeting with Charles in late July, at which he seems to have offered him the hand of Catherine, daughter of the man whom the Portuguese had crowned. With her, apparently, was dangled the bait of the richest dowry brought by any Queen of England. After more obscure talks, de Mello was sent home to fetch a firm proposition of this match, while Charles announced that England would negotiate a commercial treaty with Portugal, to disguise future bargaining.

De Mello's absence had the effect of leaving the field clear for his rival. By November Batteville had got wind of his negotiation, and commenced counter-measures. Some were negative, such as threatening Charles with war if he married Catherine. But Felipe also empowered him to offer the English King the daughter of Spain's client the ruler of Parma (there being no Spanish princesses available), with a Spanish dowry. At the same time the Madrid government moderated their terms for the treaty projected in the summer, offering valuable commercial concessions and proposing to repurchase Jamaica and Dunkirk for a high price. Bristol had by now returned from Spain, desperate for another opportunity to restore his much-patched political fortunes. He had immediately drawn public attention with a notable speech in the Lords in favour of the Bill of Indemnity. The great diplomatic contest apparently afforded him his chance to regain royal favour by offering his personal and linguistic assets to forward the Parma match. In the New Year, to his delight, the Earl was sent to Italy upon a secret mission to open talks for this alternative marriage. Charles treated Batteville with even greater friendliness. In February de Mello returned with an offer rather less spectacular than that which the English had expected, and a demand that Charles declare war upon Spain as part of the deal. He provoked a corresponding disappointment and irritation.

What tipped the balance once more was the factor which had first established Portuguese credit at Charles's court: a judicious distribution of bribes. De Mello watered the King's Counsellors with money, so carefully and prodigally that his action seemed in itself to guarantee the soundness of his nation's finances. Batteville, fatally, had not been provided with such a fund because Felipe could not spare one. At the same time relations with France dramatically improved. On 28 February the great Mazarin died, affording Charles an opportunity to forget his bitterest memories of French conduct towards him in exile. A month later Henrietta Maria achieved a further link between the Stuart and Bourbon families by completing negotiations for the marriage of her only surviving daughter, young Minette, to the brother of Louis XIV. The French King took advantage of this match to ask Charles for a 'closer union', and the latter eagerly instructed Jermyn (or St Albans, to employ his new title) to open talks for one. Immediately Louis took the opportunity to intervene in the struggle over his English cousin's marriage. The Portuguese reduced their requirement that England ally with them to one that Charles send them some soldiers. The French King now offered to pay for the transportation and upkeep of these. Batteville, sensing that he was losing ground, told the English King that Spain would give the dowry of an Infanta not merely to a princess of Parma but to the Protestant daughters of the rulers of Saxony and Denmark, if Charles preferred these. He also promised a huge sum if England returned Dunkirk and Jamaica and abandoned Portugal. What finally ruined his case was English disbelief that Felipe could actually raise the money needed: the continuing lack of Spanish bribes at court, and royalist memories of neglect in Flanders, combined to reinforce this impression. De Mello meanwhile continued to lay a trail of cash through the Privy Council, which seemed to substantiate his promise that his Princess's dowry would arrive with her, complete. In late April a secret meeting of the Council, lasting four hours, arrived at a decision to accept Portugal's terms.

Batteville, stupefied and furious, blamed Hyde for this result. Indeed, Sir Edward was the most prominent minister in all the convoluted bargaining: he had drafted papers for de Mello, received them from the Spanish, entertained Batteville at his mansion for talks with Charles, and conducted the negotiations with the French. But many others, including Montagu, Morice, Monck, Manchester, and James, had emerged as supporters of the Portuguese match: de Mello's promises, and his presents, had produced a generally favourable reaction. By the agreement, formalized as the Treaty of London in June, Charles promised to send Portugal 10,000 men. For these he was promised Bombay, Tangier, privileges for English merchants in the Portuguese empire, and about £330,000, as well as his bride. The beneficiaries were Portugal, France, and England, in that order. The first secured its survival. The second ensured that its great rival, Spain, was left without allies and forced to continue a debilitating war while Louis nursed his military strength. The third obtained a much-needed injection of funds into the Exchequer, a royal bride, and valuable commercial advantages, at no apparent cost. The absolute losers were the Spanish, who now had reason to curse their patronage of Charles, and the Earl of Bristol, whose expedition to Parma had proved to be yet another of the culs-de-sac of his career.[36]

Charles changed years and Parliaments together. On 29 December he dissolved the English Convention, and on New Year's Day Middleton met the Parliament of Scotland in the King's name. The Earl's instructions, drawn up at a meeting of the 'inner ring' of Counsellors in London, were concerned almost entirely with a reassertion of the royal power. Charles II was determined to regain all the ancient kingly rights which his father had renounced in the hope of winning aid in the Great Civil War. Absolutely nothing was said about the Kirk. According to Hyde, this was because of a dispute between Middleton and Lauderdale at the meeting of royal advisers. The former was convinced that he could obtain the restoration of episcopacy in Scotland, the latter apparently as certain that an attempt to do this would cause nothing but trouble. In the end, the Commissioner was simply left to decide a policy upon the spot.[37]

Middleton certainly fulfilled his brief. He possessed all the best qualities of a soldier, heroism, generosity, and courage, coupled with eloquence, wit, and a capacity for tact and moderate behaviour. If he drank hard, and was said by enemies to have appeared before Parliament not yet sober, this could be taken as a sign of conviviality. Certainly, he rapidly made a favourable impression upon most of the political nation.[38] Even had he not done so, it seems very likely that the Parliament over which he presided would still have acceded with enthusiasm to Charles's request for the 'ancient' royal prerogative. To the nobles and gentry of 1660, the achievements of the Covenanters had resulted first in the exclusion of most of them from office by inferiors and then the conquest of their nation by foreigners. Royal power seemed to represent a bulwark against a repetition of such mistakes, and its restoration a means of wiping out an unhappy past. Thus the assembly began by returning all work of preparation of bills to a committee of Lords of Articles, chosen by itself and presided over by the King's Commissioner. Within a month it had presented Charles with the traditional rights of choosing ministers of state and judges, calling and dismissing Parliaments, and approving statutes. It had denounced any leagues made without royal permission, including the Solemn League and Covenant, and declared that the monarch alone made foreign policy and controlled the armed forces. Charles sent his expressions of delighted gratitude, and the Parliament proceeded during February to approve the Engagement, to declare the statutes of 1649 irregular, and to condemn the delivery of Charles I to the English in 1647. None of this activity provoked opposition, though the declaration against the Solemn League and Covenant caused widespread disquiet. Many absented themselves from Parliament rather than be party to it, and the Kirk in general was seriously perturbed. Cassilis, now a proud and obstinate old man, increasingly eccentric in his dress, refused to take the Oath of Allegiance and Supremacy which recognized the control of royal authority over ecclesiastical affairs. The Earl objected to this last part in particular, wishing to preserve the independence of the Kirk, and seriously expected Charles to dispense him from it. Instead, the King cheerfully accepted his resignation, leaving the Parliament to disable him from office for life. With Rothes now following Middleton in opinions (and drinking habits), this meant that the last spirit of the old Kirk party was now banished from public life.[39]

At the beginning of March, Middleton and Glencairn decided that feeling in Parliament was so hostile to the Covenants that a repeal of all the reforms made since 1637, and a consequent restoration of episcopacy, was possible. On the 4th they wrote to Hyde requesting royal permission to do so. Charles, James, Ormonde, and Lauderdale came to the Chancellor's chamber at Whitehall to debate the proposition for three hours. Lauderdale, still zealous for the Covenanter cause but too ambitious to defend presbyterianism openly, argued that the return of the bishops would be contentious and difficult to achieve. Hyde feared for the impact of such a step upon English 'Presbyterian' opinion. As a result, Middleton was instructed to send Charles the opinions of the most prominent men in Kirk and State before acting. This directive was too late. Even as it travelled north the statute of repeal was passed, in the face of opposition which included Crawford-Lindsay and the new Duke of Hamilton, but with a large majority of votes. An accompanying Act declared Parliament's intention of restoring the pre-war Church. Henchmen of Middleton now scattered to the provinces, to disperse meetings of local presbyteries and prevent them from protesting to the King or anybody else. Charles's ministers in Scotland had effectively snatched the making of religious policy from his hands.[40]

Even as the national assembly of Scotland deliberated, so the King prepared to call Parliaments in his other realms to confirm and contrive the work of settlement. Three events in England in early 1661 had a disturbing influence upon the mood in which the elections were held. One was the final disbanding of the army, which both removed a check upon the proponents of royalist revenge and multiplied fears of plotting. The second was Venner's Rising. Thomas Venner was a London cooper, and leader of a gathered church. Inspired by the speeches of the regicides on the scaffold, he and his flock decided upon an armed rebellion to seize the capital and to impose not only a republic but the rule of the saints predicted in the Book of Daniel. They were, of course, politically, if not medically, insane, but they caught the government totally by surprise. Its spy system, as yet much inferior to Cromwell's, was only capable of reporting rumours without penetrating republican circles. As a result, Charles's regime struck at the wrong target, arresting former army officers, and when Venner's church took arms on Twelfth Night, Charles was at Portsmouth putting his mother aboard her ship. It took four days for the militia and royal guards to kill or capture the thirty-five or so rebels. Fourteen were subsequently executed and their heads placed upon London Bridge.

The truth of the affair was so fantastic that the government, quite naturally, failed at first to understand it and believed that Venner had represented, like the royalist risings of the 1650s, only a corner of a nation-wide conspiracy. The news, spreading out from London to alarm the provinces, was closely followed by a royal proclamation forbidding unauthorized meetings for any purpose and by directives to the militia to arrest all suspected persons and search houses. For those men in all three kingdoms who wished to persecute separatist groups and former republicans, a dream had come true. In England armed gentry reinforced the trained bands in a general round-up of Quakers and sectarian churches, adding (to the catch) former republicans without obvious religious affiliations and some presbyterians. Within six weeks nearly five thousand Quakers were behind bars. In Scotland the Committee of Estates banished all former Remonstrants from the capital and ordered the arrest of any people meeting without authority of Kirk or state. In Ireland the Lord Justices issued a similar proclamation, including presbyterians with all the more radical groups as 'fanatics'.

The Privy Council slowly realized that Venner had led only a tiny group and that the reaction to the rising was itself destabilizing the three kingdoms. On 17 January Charles proclaimed against the searching of houses without warrant, and on the 25th the Council ordered the release of most Quakers confined in the capital. The Lord Mayor, however, protested so vehemently that the order was rescinded. The case of the Irish presbyterians was argued at court by one of their sympathizers, Lord Massarene, who elicited from Charles a promise of toleration for them. When news of this reached Dublin, the Lord Justices received it with patent reluctance and continued to treat the dissenting clergy as potential traitors: the London government was in danger of losing its grip upon ecclesiastical affairs as it had done in Scotland. On 4 March Charles issued a general order for the release of Quakers in England, but compromised with national opinion by allowing the continued confinement of their leaders. In the long term Venner had left two ominous legacies: the decision to retain an unprecedentedly large force of royal guards, and an intensified public fear of rebellion in general and of religious radicals in particular.[41]

The third event which weakened the proponents of conciliation was the London election in March, one of the earliest for the Parliament called to succeed the Convention. The City's new bishop, Sheldon, though still treating leading presbyterian clergy with respect, was enforcing a narrow interpretation of the Worcester House Declaration. London had always been the greatest stronghold of presbyterianism, and its citizens were further irritated by the new excise on alcohol. As a result, four firmly anti-episcopalian MPs were returned at a hustings where the crowd shouted 'No Bishops! No Lord Bishops!' Furthermore, some of the more extreme City presbyterians wrote to allies in the provinces, encouraging them to mount a similar campaign. Charles and his ministers were infuriated by this attempt to overturn their policy, and reacted swiftly. On the one hand, the King commissioned the conference of leading clergy of both persuasions, which had been projected at Worcester House to achieve a lasting compromise. On the other, he ordered the arrest of the men who had urged a general effort against episcopacy, and instructed the Earl of Warwick, patron of the Essex presbyterians, to stay away from the county election. Charles may have leaned upon other magnates of Warwick's views in the same manner, for most of them became curiously passive. At the same time the government ensured that its own supporters found seats. Hyde used his office as Chancellor of Oxford University to secure the return of his own son and of Finch. As Lord Warden, James supplied the Cinque Ports with his clients. The number of influential offices given to royalists and episcopalians had some effect, such as in the Isle of Wight, where its captain, the Earl of Portland, nominated one of the members for Newport, and at Dover where the governor was elected. But the City election also had a wider effect upon public opinion, making presbyterians appear the principal obstacles to a conciliatory religious settlement and awaking memories of the popular demonstrations in London which had preceded the Civil War.[42] When all the returns were in, everybody recognized that the new Parliament would be overwhelmingly episcopalian in its views.

While preoccupied with the complexion of the Parliament which would sit a street away, Charles and the English government had also to consider that which was due to meet in Dublin upon the same day. His Lord Justices, and the Protestants whom they represented, were determined that Catholics, while readmitted to the legal profession and to local government, should not be permitted to seek election as MPs. This was in direct violation of pre-war practice, and the English Privy Council were unable to reach a decision upon it after long debate. Instead, Charles directed his ministers in Ireland to employ all the influence that power afforded to rig the elections in favour of Protestants. The newly appointed Irish Privy Council, which represented the Coote and Broghil groups, accepted this but resolved in addition to exclude former Catholic rebels from the Lords even if the King had restored their lands. They then set to work with every possible machination and secured a House of Commons solidly composed of Protestants. As in Scotland, Charles's major concern was not with the complexion of his government but with his degree of control over it. He shocked the Lord Justices by naming the speaker of the new Commons, against the tradition that the House elect him. When they suggested sending delegates from Ireland to advise him, he replied coldly that he had 'those about him who understand Irish affairs'.[43]

On St George's Day, with both sets of elections safely out of the way, and before the two Parliaments met, the government staged Charles's English coronation. 'Staged' is the appropriate verb, as historical precedent was studied and developed to produce royal pageantry of breath-taking splendour. The robes of one peer were said to have cost £30,000, Hyde 'shone like a diamond', and an onlooker wondered how many ostrich feathers could have been found in England. There were times when current tensions obtruded. The former royalist Ormonde and the former parliamentarian Northumberland quarrelled over precedence in the procession. Although Charles was crowned by Archbishop Juxon, the sermon was preached by Bishop Morley of Winchester, not by the obvious prelate Sheldon of London: after the City election the King wanted Sheldon less visible. The episcopalian citizens of London paid for a supplementary pageant, extolling the virtues of bishops, to counteract the impression of that election. There was a moment of farce, when Charles had to silence the royal trumpeters after a particularly rousing fanfare frightened James's horse into throwing him. But the overall impression was one of royal confidence and magnificence, and, of course, everybody agreed that the monarch himself played his part wonderfully.[44]

It had been a year since the Convention had voted back monarchy, and Charles had been the most obvious beneficiary of its developments. He had regained and secured his three thrones without any of the constitutional concessions made by or demanded of his father. He had resumed his lands and assumed the role of an arbiter between former rival parties. The only doubt that had arisen over his position was whether, although possessed of theoretical supreme authority, he could in practice enforce the policies which he desired. Within the next year, this problem was to give rise to a major struggle.

The Fight for the Settlements, 1661–1664

ON 8 May 1661, Charles rode to open his first English Parliament, wearing the crown so recently placed upon his head and followed by the peers in their scarlet robes. At Westminster he welcomed both Houses with a speech commending the Act of Indemnity. Clarendon followed him by praising the work of the Convention and by asking its successor to confirm it, to honour the spirit of the Declaration of Breda, to improve the royal revenue, and to relieve peaceful nonconformists while repressing sedition. The Houses gave thanks for this with every sign of pleasure, and the Commons elected as Speaker the government favourite, Sir Edward Turner. With little sign of strain, the MPs then set to work to defy much of the advice tendered to them by their monarch and the Lord Chancellor. The result was a growing tension between executive and legislature in England which was to break within two years into open ill will.

One of the first achievements of the 'Cavalier' Parliament was to obliterate most of the constitutional reforms of the previous twenty years. It ordered the public burning of the Solemn League and Covenant and of four other documents, and repealed the statute of 1642 which excluded bishops from the Lords. Another Act declared control of the militia to be vested in the King, followed by yet another to reverse the attainder of Strafford, the great minister for whose life the young Charles had interceded. Thus the two great issues which had divided Charles I from the Long Parliament were decided in his son's favour. The King's security was further increased by an extension of the law of treason to cover attempts to coerce him and both the written and spoken word. As Charles's reward for his apparent fidelity to the Anglican Church during exile, and in response to the rumours which had circulated then, it was made illegal to call him a Catholic. Much of this work could be portrayed as conciliation, but the immolation of the Covenant could not. Not only was it opposed by 103 MPs, but was probably the first issue to produce an open division in the government, for Morice acted as teller against it in the Commons while the Privy Counsellors in the Lords seem to have let that House endorse it without a struggle. Charles appeared indifferent to the fate of the document which he had signed with such reluctance off Garmouth but acclaimed with such fervour at Scone.

What he emphatically had not achieved now was the restoration of his father's monarchy. The Cavalier Parliament only reversed those reforms which had not benefited its members as a class, an estate, or an institution. They revived neither of the great royal prerogative courts, Star Chamber and the Council of the North. They retained the Triennial Act of 1641, denying Charles the power which he had regained in Scotland, of calling and dismissing Parliaments at will. They condemned the memory of the Court of High Commission and the Canons of 1640, denying the new bishops the power that their predecessors had wielded. The immediate reason for declaring the King's formal power over the militia was to indemnify its officers for the many actions committed by them since the Restoration under royal authority. In January 1662 the government asked Parliament for the means to support a new standing army under James. Instead, it got the right to levy £70,000 per year to keep the militia standing in case of an emergency, with the further limitation that this power would lapse in 1665.

The legislation for censorship of publications illustrates particularly well how delicate was the relationship between the Crown and this Parliament, even in the first session and over an issue in which they had common interests. In July 1660, the Privy Council gave a monopoly of the production of newspapers to a pair of reliable and moderately conservative journalists. Over them in turn, Charles seems to have set the man who had run the royalist newspaper during the Civil War, John Berkenhead. Within two months of his return the King, enraged by a pamphlet attacking his ingratitude to old supporters, was demanding firmer control of the press. During the next year a series of arrests of individual authors and printers followed, on the orders of the Council, the Lords, and urban corporations. A formal system of licensing would greatly facilitate such repression, and the Cavalier Parliament provided it in an entirely typical manner. It passed an Act which required the registration of all presses and books, and censorship of the latter by a panel of government ministers and leading ecclesiastics, the heads of Church and State. Yet it also limited its effect to two years, thereby leaving the executive utterly dependent upon Parliament for a renewal of those powers. This may well have been the intention of the House in imposing the limitation.

The attitude of the new House of Commons to public finance was also superficially dutiful but less helpful in practice than was needed. None of the existing sources of royal revenue were producing as much as was expected. Expenditure was swelled by Charles's continuing efforts to reward old and new supporters and to pay off some of the debts incurred by himself before the Restoration and by his father. The government had one of its principal financial officers, Sir Philip Warwick, sitting in the Commons, and the House's other concerns were much less urgent than those which had beset the Convention. Yet while the MPs were willing to admit the problem, they could not easily decide what to do about it. During their first session they did nothing but collect information, hasten the collection of arrears, and arrange for a voluntary contribution to the King which raised very little. At the beginning of the second session, in November, Charles made a personal request for action, and got a lump sum, by an 'assessment' on land, as an interim measure. Nothing was done for the longer term until the third session, in March, when the King reminded them of the problem once more, with complaints. The House now decided to remove the annual shortfall by the crude direct taxation of a levy imposed upon each stove and hearth in a dwelling. Perhaps to mitigate its inevitable unpopularity, the MPs determined upon a means of collection certain to reduce the yield considerably. Householders themselves were to certify the number of their hearths, and to pay the sums due to local constables who forwarded the certificates and money through the JPs to the Exchequer. In financial as in political affairs, the MPs had tried to find a middle way between serving the Crown and protecting themselves and the public. Yet they deserved the gratitude which Charles expressed when he gave assent to the Hearth Tax, for it was a fiscal measure more adventurous than that attempted by any previous Stuart Parliament. Upon its degree of success would hang much of the future goodwill between King and Commons.

In all these fields, therefore, the support of the Cavalier Parliament for the Crown was somewhat qualified. Over the issue of urban corporations it administered a direct rebuff to Charles. During the early part of 1661, his temper was becoming frayed when dealing with town councils, for several reasons. Some failed to restore royalist members as ordered, others ignored royal nominees for offices, and still others became divided by noisy quarrelling. It is not surprising that as soon as the election results for the new Parliament were known, and the government felt secure, a more aggressive royal policy appeared. It was based upon the fact that most towns were in possession of charters conferred by Interregnum regimes, which were open to challenge. In April a writ of *quo warranto* was issued against Bristol's corporation, which had been one of the most obstinate in its failure to grant royalists restitution. This was dropped after negotiations at court which cost the council £584: if it had preserved a list of recipients, then our knowledge of Restoration central politics would be significantly increased. Nevertheless, the new charter was still made conditional upon the removal of all those 'unduly elected', and this was sufficient to purge most of the senior members. On 7 May the Privy Council apparently decided that when issuing any new charters the King would claim the power to nominate the first alderman, recorders, and clerks, and restrict the parliamentary franchise to the corporation. In June, the Attorney-General, Palmer, and a judge recommended that he nominate the entire council, as most of these in existence were still full of 'usurpers'.

Many gentry, however, had other ideas, based upon their resentment of the fact that supporters of the republic had been ejected from power in the counties yet still held it in the towns. Many of the latter contained parliamentary seats, over which county leaders hoped to gain control. In the first nine months of 1661 gentry attempted to dislodge the existing leaders of the corporation of Leeds, Christchurch, and Wallingford, only to be halted by royal orders. It is not surprising, therefore, that on 19 June the Commons introduced a bill whereby municipalities would be purged by commissioners chosen by Parliament. After fierce debate, it was sent up to the Lords by a majority of five votes. Charles saw in this disagreement an opportunity to obtain his ends by statute. He persuaded the Upper House to rewrite the bill completely, removing the proposed commissions and awarding him the powers he had aimed at since May. Three amendments were made in these to make them more palatable to the Commons: he now asked to choose future mayors from a list of six names submitted by the corporation, dropped the clause about the franchise, and permitted county JPs to exercise authority in towns. Apparently to Charles's amazement, the Commons rejected the entire package, with the objections that it would give the Crown too much power and would fail to meet their desire for a purge. The recess intervened, and during it Charles treated corporations as though he expected his plan to operate. He exacted from London itself the right to remove a few aldermen at will as the price of a new charter and named a complete new council for Leeds, where the old charter had been formally suspended in 1643. At the opening of the second session, however, the government backed down. We do not know why it did: perhaps the Lords were wavering or perhaps its financial plight made good relations with the MPs essential. Virtually all of the original bill was restored. The resulting Corporation Act required all members of town councils to sign a declaration against the Solemn League and Covenant and to take an oath against the principle of resistance to the King. These were to be tendered by commissions, who had the power to remove even those who had passed both tests (and usually did). Charles's one victory was to gain the right to nominate the commissioners himself, but he chose royalists and episcopalians of the sort whom the Commons themselves must have intended. The Crown had won a portion of the form and lost all the substance.[1]

Thus, in many ways, the Cavalier House of Commons checked the extension of royal authority during its early sessions. Nevertheless, many MPs would have felt in the same period that the government had inflicted a considerable defeat upon them, by defending the legislation of the Convention. The latter, having never been called by a King, could be deemed an illegal assembly and (as noted) Charles had initially expected to exploit this weakness himself. Instead, ironically, he now found himself protecting statutes which had turned out to be very much in his interest.

Now, as before, the most important of these was the Act of Indemnity. Having opened the Parliament by asking its members to preserve the Act, he had to repeat this request sharply over six weeks later. A bill to confirm it had been produced, but held up by furious debate and by a proviso to exclude more people. Only the King's intervention ensured its passage without amendment. The MPs had to be satisfied with punishing those whom the original act had left vulnerable. They sentenced men who had sat in the regicide court but not signed the warrant, to life imprisonment and loss of property. They also sent up a bill for the execution of the regicides who had surrendered voluntarily, and pushed the government into the trial of John Lambert and Sir Henry Vane, who had been regarded as notable opponents of the Restoration. Yet even here the King thwarted them. He pushed Clarendon a note that he was 'weary of hanging', and so the bill against the captive regicides was 'left to sleep' in the Lords. Vane was indeed executed, but Lambert reprieved again by royal command.

The Convention's Act for the settlement of ministers provoked both a more determined attack by the Commons and a greater effort in its defence by the government. A bill to replace it, with a measure which would remove or punish more clergy, was sent up to the Lords. There it was defeated in February 1662, only because Clarendon mobilized against it the full body of government supporters, including Sheldon and the bishops. Some MPs proposed that the bill for the Hearth Tax be delayed until the rejected measure was revived and passed. This time, however, it was Charles who stood firm, and the Commons backed down. At the same time the government fought to secure the land settlement. This was threatened, not by a general measure but by three private bills introduced by royalists to regain land which they had been forced to sell or to reclaim the profit made out of their estates during the Interregnum. The most important was that of the Earl of Derby, who had already attempted such a measure in the Convention. When it reached the Lords, Clarendon and the government peers mounted a great effort to stop it, but this time were defeated. It was Charles who destroyed the bill, by taking one of the most drastic steps open to a monarch and refusing his assent.

All these developments have been misused, at times, to portray Charles as a man of remarkable natural clemency and breadth of vision. As when considering his actions in 1660, such an interpretation is misleading. The King was utilizing his prerogative of mercy to strengthen his own position. This is strikingly illustrated by the cases of Lambert and Vane. Neither was a regicide, and their actions had been no more culpable than those of many men who had been indemnified. Their real crime was to have proved themselves exceptionally able, and therefore dangerous. At his trial, Lambert chose to ignore the justice of his case, and to beg for his life to Charles. He was duly granted it. Vane, by contrast, defended himself with furious indignation, and so aroused in the King the vindictiveness reserved for those who opposed his will. A royal letter sped to Clarendon insisting upon Sir Henry's death by any means. The means found was to keep the jury without food or drink till it returned the correct verdict. His execution was arranged with finely calculated malice: for the anniversary of the battle of Naseby, upon the spot where Strafford had died, and with musicians under the scaffold to drown his final speech. He spoke none the less, as he offered his neck to the axe, with perfect courage. Significantly, whereas Londoners had exulted over the deaths of the regicides in 1660, now they spoke only in praise of Vane and in criticism of the manner of his destruction. By overplaying his hand, Charles had turned a symbol of treason and schism into one of dignity and law.

As when considering the events of 1660, a look at Scottish affairs reveals much of the King's own attitude towards indemnity. He had formally entrusted this question to the Scottish Parliament and it claimed only three immediate victims. One was the great Argyll, whose head was struck off by a primitive guillotine on 27 May, and fixed where that of Montrose had been. Another was Guthrie, who doomed himself by defending the right of subjects to rebuke their monarch. He was hanged and decapitated a week after the Marquis died, as was an old lay Remonstrant who had similarly failed to express contrition. The others of their party whom the Parliament examined saved their lives by expressing abject apology, and sometimes by bribing influential men as well. The only well-documented case is that of Sir John Cheisley, who dashed to Whitehall before the Parliament met and panted out his repentance to Manchester and other English Privy Counsellors, and to Lauderdale. Perhaps he seasoned his protestations with presents, but certainly all of them sent pleas upon his behalf to Edinburgh. Charles's reaction to the escape of such men was to write to Middleton, rebuking him for permitting this to happen, upon the grounds that it deprived the King of his chance to exercise the prerogative of mercy. This placed the stress upon Charles's concern for his formal authority rather than for vengeance, but there is other evidence for the latter aim. He was said to have been particularly angry at Gillespie's acquittal, and may be held directly responsible for Argyll's death. The evidence against the great Campbell was too slim to sustain the charge of treason, until General Monck sent up some letters written by the Marquis to Cromwell which proved their collaboration in the mid-1650s. It was Monck's own former service of that Protector which had gained him these documents, and it is unthinkable that the cautious General would have intervened with them had not the King given him encouragement. Thus Charles served the man whom, eleven years before, he had promised a dukedom. Nor did Johnston of Wariston long escape the consequences of the King's resentment. At the end of 1662 the government in London received word that the old Scot was at Rouen, and Charles wrote to Louis XIV requesting Johnston's arrest and extradition. On his arrival in the Tower he proved to be a pitiful figure. Abandoned by the God whom he had served with such savage devotion, he was not only terrified and contrite but patently going insane. Yet after examination he was shipped to Scotland, where the Parliament had sentenced him to death in his absence. Although its members were appalled by his mental condition, they upheld the decision in view of Charles's wishes. Johnston's head was fastened beside the skull of Guthrie.[2]

Nor did a reprieve by Charles signify a pardon. The imprisoned regicides were simply left to die in their cells. Lambert may have come to envy Vane's fate during almost a quarter of a century of life which remained to him, penned in island fortresses. Eventually his mind gave way. In Scotland certain of the Remonstrants such as Cheisley, who had satisfied the Parliament, were kept in custody none the less for several years afterwards. Even when the King strove to prevent the English legislature from constricting the terms of the Act of Indemnity, his government considered the same course for himself. In April, when it still expected the Cavalier Parliament to be perfectly compliant, a proclamation was drafted which announced Charles's intention of excepting twelve more people at will. This was not published, and there is no evidence of who proposed and opposed it. But it clearly had a place in the same counsels of royal aggression which produced the Privy Council's ruling concerning corporations.

Furthermore, the government could foster tension while it preached reconciliation. This process became easier in the course of 1661 as, to avoid being surprised again as they had been by Venner, the Secretaries of State constructed a system of spies which spanned the country. It was naturally most active in London, and towards the end of the year it reported there the so-called 'Wildman Plot'. All that can be established of the truth behind this is that a group of former republican soldiers, politicians, and writers had taken to meeting and discussing current affairs. In early winter they were arrested, and Clarendon informed Parliament that these men had been at the centre of a conspiracy to topple the monarchy. It was upon this 'discovery' that the government based its appeal for a standing army. None of the accused were either tried or released after examination, being sent to remote prisons. Among them was James Harrington, the republic's greatest political philosopher. He was eventually set free—after his mind had permanently collapsed. The most pleasant interpretation which one can place upon this episode is that the Privy Council believed that it had found a genuine conspiracy and then exploited it to further its political ends. Some former leaders of the republic retained their liberty, now and later, by discreet presents to those in power. The best documented case is that of Bulstrode Whitelocke, whose old friend Clarendon treated him for years like a sheep to be sheared at will of money and property.[3]

The restored monarchy's dealings with the problem of indemnity and land settlement in Ireland reveal the same sense of self-interest tempered by political reality. The Parliament which sat at Dublin on 8 May consisted overwhelmingly of 'Ancient Protestants', those who had been settled in the country before 1641. The Commons also included about sixty of the 'New English', who had received land from the Long Parliament, and the Lords contained a few Catholics. Although the 'New English' were technically the beneficiaries of the republican land settlement, the 'Ancient Protestants' had two considerable reasons for preserving it. First, many of them had bought confiscated estates from their original grantees. Second, all were horrified by the prospect of Catholics regaining the wealth and power to make a second rebellion by them possible. Their initial problem in confronting the land question was that they were bound to work within the guide-lines of the royal declaration of November 1660, which was unworkable. As mentioned already, there was not enough ownerless land around to provide the compensation due to people restoring estates to their original possessors. Charles further complicated the situation with the carelessness which he often brought to questions not of immediate concern to him: for example, he granted part of a regicide's estate to a Protestant noble, then leased it to the Bishop of Cork, and then gave the whole of it to Taaffe. All three were left uncertain of their title. Furthermore, the commissioners appointed to implement the November

Declaration had proved so divided in their opinions that they had achieved virtually nothing.

That Charles did not have a serious quarrel with the Irish Parliament was due to a heroic work of mediation by the Lord Justices. They persuaded the King to allow the Commons their own choice of Speaker. When Charles sent them an order to readmit Catholics to the towns, from which the Commonwealth had excluded all of that faith, they contested it. They feared for the effect upon Protestant opinion, and the King, again, was talked into concurrence. His effect upon Irish politics at this time was reduced to caring for his favourite Catholic servants of the exile: he promoted Taaffe to the earldom of Carlingford and restored Clancarty to his lands without waiting for compensation to the settlers. This violated his own November Declaration, but everybody chose to ignore the fact. Upon the other hand, Orrery, Mountrath, and Eustace strove to moderate Parliamentary politics. When the Commons wished to expel Catholics from parliament, the Lord Justices warned them of probable royal displeasure, and the measure was dropped. Both Houses then asked that the followers of Rome be confined to Connacht, and were politely ignored. As criticism of the November Declaration mounted the Lord Justices decided to forestall it by offering their own amendments. Most were designed to increase the quantity of land free for compensations, notably by confiscating the estates of more republicans and by reducing those held by the Long Parliament's creditors to the value of their original loans. These were sent over to Westminster in June, and the Committee for Irish Affairs accepted all save that for further confiscations: this was presumably rejected for fear that it would encourage the Cavalier Parliament's attack on the English Act of Indemnity. The government at Whitehall considered narrowing the definition of a 'rebel' in the November Declaration to allow more Catholics to regain their lands. Again, Mountrath raised the spectre of Protestant outrage, and again Charles contented himself with helping Irish supporters from his exile. Orders were sent for the restoration of three more to their lands. Mountrath had not been exaggerating, and the lord who carried these instructions was abused by many Protestants as a 'friend to Teague' (the contemptuous term still applied by Ulster Unionists to Catholics).[4]

In fact, both the royal administration and the Irish Parliament were operating under constraints. The latter needed a land settlement which favoured Protestants, and the former needed money. By the summer of 1661, public expenditure in Ireland was almost treble the public income, and the pay of the army was slipping even further into arrears. The Lord

Justices proposed a package copying the reforms of the English Convention of 1660, whereby Parliament would grant an excise upon alcohol and increase customs duties in exchange for the abolition of wardships and feudal tenures. Even if this were enacted, and retrenchments made, there was still expected to be a deficit which would require parliamentary subsidies, or assistance from the English Exchequer, or both. The two sides therefore had valuable bargaining counters, and the constitutional machinery allowed plenty of opportunity for consultation. Since the 1490s all Irish legislation had to be drafted by the Dublin government, and the drafts submitted to the English Privy Council and to the Irish Parliament before passage into law.[5]

In these circumstances it is remarkable how much obduracy Charles displayed. The Bill of Settlement, incorporating the revised Declaration, was sent to Westminster in August 1661. Orrery spoke for Irish Protestants in general when he called it 'our young Magna Carta'. The King had promised the Irish Parliament in July that he would not receive petitions relating to Irish affairs unless supported by either House, Convocation, or the Lord Justices. As soon as the bill arrived he reneged upon the spirit of this undertaking by instructing the Solicitor-General, Palmer, to receive the objections of Catholics to the measure. In the end it passed back with only minor amendments because the Catholics bungled their opportunity. First, they mishandled Charles, by treating their restoration as a matter of right rather than as an act of his personal mercy, craved with due humility. Then, in March 1662, their credit was ruined by a brilliant coup on the part of the agents of the Irish Parliament. The latter handed Charles a letter sent by the Catholic Confederacy to the Pope in 1647, offering to recognize him as ruler of Ireland in exchange for military aid. The plenipotentiary had been Sir Nicholas Plunket, now the chief spokesperson for the dispossessed. The King lost his temper at this formal treason to his father and himself, banished Sir Nicholas from court, and forbade the Catholics to lodge any more objections to the bill. In a speech to the agents of the Parliament he formally gave his blessing to the Protestant (or as he termed it the 'English') supremacy in Ireland.[6] He did not, however, return the bill itself to Dublin until both Houses there had passed those for four financial subsidies and for the Excise and new customs imposts. He had already refused to abolish wardships as part of the bargain. The Lord Justices, appraised of this by Nicholas, tried to avoid a clash by incorporating the clause for abolition in a separate bill, which Charles simply failed to return. They then devoted all their skill and influence to driving the amended Bill of Settlement through Parliament without further argument, and succeeded.[7]

The question of indemnity was, as has been seen, bound up with that of religion, and the latter was to be the most vexed of all the concerns of Charles's governments in the years 1661–2. In all three kingdoms his aims were consistent: to secure a loyal established Church controlled by himself, and to be accepted as an effective arbiter and protector by nonconformists. In the first of these he was to be only partially successful, in the second to suffer almost total failure.

Among the groups of nonconformists, the Catholics were dealt with most easily. Ever since his sojourn in the priest's hole at Moseley, Charles had repeatedly promised to seek the repeal of the penal laws against them in England, and soon after his restoration he promised that, at the least, the laws would be laxly enforced. The chances of repeal by the Cavalier Parliament were apparently good. The Lords included twenty-five Catholics, and both Houses contained many royalists who might recall the contributions of individual followers of Rome to the Royal cause. In the first session Sir Samuel Tuke, a Catholic and a former royalist colonel, appealed to the Lords to relieve his co-religionists, on the grounds that they had abundantly proved their loyalty to the Crown. The response at first promised limited success, for the peers seemed willing to modify the laws against secular priests, if not the others. At the recess, however, no bill had yet been produced for this purpose, and thereafter the project was quietly dropped. Part of the reason was that support for it had faltered within the government itself, the result not of tensions between the wartime parties but of a feud within the former royalists.

The irrepressible Earl of Bristol had returned from his fruitless expedition to Parma more determined than ever to restore his political fortunes. As ever, his chief asset in this work was his dazzling personality, which he promoted through a series of magnificent parties at which he played host to King and court. Clarendon, sensing a threat to his own pre-eminence, reacted with an almost childish spite, using his new authority as Chancellor of Oxford University to dismiss Bristol from its Stewardship. Clarendon himself had Catholic friends and protégés, such as the former royalist agent Richard Belling, for whom he strove to find work after the Restoration. During the exile he had favoured an alliance with Rome or the Irish, in preference to one with presbyterians. But from his writings and comments it seems that (like many others) he distinguished diplomatic and personal dealings with Catholics from any suggestion that their principles were officially tolerable. These instincts were certainly compounded by the fact that Bristol took up the cause of repeal as a further means of increasing his own importance. The Chancellor, to whom many looked for guidance, withdrew support in proportion. At the opening of the second session the bishops were back in the Lords to reinforce the opposition, while the Catholics were fissuring in a quarrel between regular and secular clergy. Nevertheless, in practice if not in law, the sufferings of the English Catholic community appeared to be over. Magistrates almost all chose to leave the penal laws dormant, and when Bishop Cosin enforced them in his new see of Durham, he was rebuked by Sheldon himself on behalf of the Privy Council. To this extent, Charles had honoured his promise. The principal direct result of the Lords' debates in the summer of 1661 was to turn the relationship between Clarendon and Bristol, which had so long veered between friendship and tension, into permanent hostility.[8]

The principal indirect result was to worsen the position of the Irish Catholics. In early 1661 Charles had intervened to obtain the release of 120 of their priests, and the Protestants were seriously worried that the Cavalier Parliament would champion the cause of those dispossessed of their lands.[9] The disinterest actually shown in Catholic relief by the English legislature made their enemies across the water bold enough to challenge the royal policy of clemency. This process was aided by the same over-confidence among the Pope's adherents which had spoiled their suits against the Bill of Settlement at court. Priests and soldiers were flocking back into the island, meeting and corresponding, while tenants rioted against their new, Protestant landlords. Memories of the rising of 1641 stirred among magistrates from the Lord Justices downwards, and only a slight incident was needed to trigger a panic. It was provided in December by a letter forwarded by Meath justices, purporting to be sent between two priests and speaking of a forthcoming rebellion. Almost certainly it was a forgery, designed to precipitate punitive measures, and it worked. The Dublin government ordered a general round-up of Catholic clergy, the mobilization of the army, and the transplantation of many gentry to Connacht. This sudden persecution inspired Catholics to a great effort to obtain royal protection. The ubiquitous Belling, then in Ireland, drafted an extraordinary document known later as the Irish Remonstrance. The most extreme statement of loyalty ever made by British Catholics to their monarch, it denied the power of Popes to depose him and promised to resist any such attempt. Sent to London, it was signed there by many clergy and nobles, including Taaffe, Clancarty, Inchiquin, and some Englishmen. Charles was understandably delighted, ordered that Belling be restored to his estate at once, and asked for a general subscription. The Holy See was, equally understandably, annoyed and ordered a halt to it. Division now followed persecution for the unhappy Irish Catholic community.[10]

By then the panic in Dublin had subsided, but the Lord Justices had worked out a comprehensive policy towards dissent. Somewhat ashamed by the probability that they had over-reacted, they suspended the law against the mass in February 1662 and released most priests on bonds in March. They granted comparable freedom of worship to Protestant nonconformists. The result was a flurry of protest from the bishops and their supporters amongst the gentry: as Orrery complained, either persecution or toleration meant trouble for the government. In the end, on 30 April, it found a solution, issuing a declaration which withdrew freedom of worship from Catholics, presbyterians, and sectaries alike, but made it clear that discreet nonconformity could be ignored. This made sense of the situation, but it also effectively shifted the initiative in regulating dissent from Charles to his local representatives.[11]

The same process was continuing apace in Scotland. Middleton's group there were only too aware that, by obtaining the Rescissory Act and the declaration in favour of episcopacy, they had directly contravened their instructions through Clarendon. Accordingly, Glencairn and Rothes sped to Whitehall soon after to dispose Charles to view these developments favourably. Events played into their hands. The return of the Cavalier Parliament ensured that English presbyterian opinion need no longer be feared. The Scottish Parliament had not settled the Kirk for the King, but cleared the way, made a recommendation, and then humbly referred the question to him for resolution. Only one Scottish cleric slipped down to Westminster to lend his voice to events: the nimble James Sharp, who came accredited to speak for nobody but himself. His avowed intention was to reconcile Middleton and Lauderdale to working together for the good of the Kirk. The old story that he had always intended the restoration of bishops, believed by his enemies, has been effectively discredited by Julia Buckroyd: her counter-proposal, that having failed to save the presbyterian Kirk he was attempting to ensure the most moderate possible episcopacy, is likely but unproven.[12] What seems certain from the available evidence is that he was determined to profit personally from whatever developed. Under these circumstances it is not surprising that Charles received the news of the Rescissory Act graciously. He may well have made the famous remark to Burnet (much later) that presbyterianism was no religion for a gentleman. Nevertheless, his words and deeds in 1660–1 suggest that he would much have preferred an obedient and stable presbyterian Kirk to an unpopular and fragile episcopalian one. The third alternative, a securely based set of Scottish bishops, was only just starting to seem a possibility.

Royal policy adapted accordingly. Charles thanked the Parliament for its actions but urged it to proceed in all affairs with moderation. Assiduously misinformed by Rothes, he spoke angrily to Sharp of the manner in which local presbyteries and synods seemed to be agitating against the resolutions of Parliament. What he now expected was a 'primitive' episcopacy of the sort which he had been prepared to accept in England in 1660. Everybody at Whitehall agreed that a decision was best postponed, and on 10 June a royal proclamation (drafted by Lauderdale and Sharp) informed the Scots that Charles was taking advice upon the matter. What forced the issue was the return of Middleton from Scotland when its Parliament went into recess in late July, full of confidence and determination to proceed. Charles agreed to call a meeting of the Scottish Privy Counsellors present, plus Clarendon and other English ministers. Middleton, Glencairn, and Rothes argued for an instant restoration of episcopacy, Lauderdale, Crawford-Lindsay, and the new Duke of Hamilton opposed it, and the King decided for the former as they seemed to represent current opinion in Scotland more accurately. On 14 August Charles ordered the Privy Council in Edinburgh to announce the fact.[13]

What the King was hoping to achieve was the compromise that had failed in England: to draft the leading presbyterian clergy into the new Kirk as bishops and to permit peaceful dissent from it. In late August Sharp was sent north to promise the latter, and to offer sees to notable clergy. The primacy, the Archbishopric of St Andrews, was held out to Robert Douglas, who had preached at Charles's coronation at Scone.[14] The result was precisely the same as in England. The most respected presbyterians refused, and Charles had to fill up the bench slowly with a few second-rank figures from the existing Kirk and several royalists and men well-connected to the ruling nobles. All were unimpressive in character and record except Sharp himself who, by process of elimination, became the primate.[15] Middleton now set out to impose these men upon the Kirk with ferocity. It must have been with his advice and encouragement that Charles in December forbade presbyteries, synods, and church courts to meet until the bishops convened them. His fresh instructions as Commissioner to Parliament, issued in January 1662, were silent upon religious affairs, his course being left to himself to determine. In May and June the Scottish legislature confirmed the restoration of episcopacy and invited the bishops to resume their seats in its midst. Other statutes obliged ministers instituted since 1649 to seek episcopal collation, disabled from office all who attacked the change or upheld the Covenants, instructed all clergy to attend the bishops' visitations, and outlawed religious meetings which brought the national Kirk into 'disrepute'. In October the Scottish Privy Council ordered all ministers who had ignored these new laws to vacate their livings, and Middleton and Glencairn went into the covenanting stronghold of the western Lowlands to enforce the command. About two hundred parishes lost their pastor. All this was done in a spirit of calculated belligerence. Newburgh, Middleton's ally since the exile, wrote exultantly to Clarendon that they had 'provoked the fanatic party to the last extremity'.[16]

In this they had been constantly encouraged by events in England. The Cavalier Parliament set out from the beginning to wreck Charles's programme for a toleration of nonconformity regulated by the monarch. He absolved Quakers from oaths, whereupon the Commons responded with a bill to punish all religious radicals for refusing them. Any hope that the government would halt this was destroyed by Clarendon, who now allowed his instinctive loathing of the more extreme Protestant dissenters free expression. Writing to his Vice-Chancellor at Oxford, he described Quakers as 'a sort of people upon whom tenderness and lenity do not at all prevail', and he drove the proposed statute through the Lords in the third session. As in the case of the Catholics, the Chancellor now seems to have felt himself sufficiently indispensable to his royal master to flout the latter's own wishes. His friends and fellow ministers Nicholas and Southampton supported Clarendon in his attitude to 'fanatics' and it is likely, from their past records, that most of the Privy Council did so. The Act that resulted was directed at anybody who refused the Oath of Allegiance and then held or attended a meeting, and the penalties stiffened from fines for the first offence to transportation for the third. Charles tried to mitigate its effects with such intiatives as a proclamation in August for the release of most Quakers awaiting trial in the metropolis. But he was thwarted upon virtually all sides. Clarendon urged on the persecution at Oxford, while the Lieutenant of the Tower conducted round-ups in London. Some assize judges encouraged persecutions, and the government press, run by Berkenhead, applauded the new Act and portrayed religious radicals as criminals and lunatics.

At the same time the Commons were preparing to purge the Church of England of aberrant opinions. In their first session they produced a bill to compel clergy to use the Prayer Book, and their attitude relieved the episcopalian churchmen of any need to make concessions to the presbyterians. When the long-awaited Savoy Conference between the two sides opened in May 1661, the bishops offered none, and so naturally nothing was resolved. The government newspapers, which should have been used to preach conciliation, were employed instead by Berkenhead to voice his own hardline episcopalian views. It seems absurd to conclude that, in view of the general appreciation of the importance of the press, Charles should lack control over his own propaganda machine. Yet this appears the only answer, and Berkenhead himself once insisted that the King never bothered to read the official journals.

On 10 October Charles formally buried the policy of comprehension by entrusting the promised revision of the Prayer Book, not to a joint working-party of episcopalians and presbyterians, but to Convocation. This was the dual assembly of the national Church, meeting at York and Canterbury, and the elections for it had created a body even more episcopalian in character than the Cavalier Parliament: presumably because of the same swing of public opinion which had returned the MPs. In the course of a month this body produced a book altered in hundreds of details but retaining all the ceremonies which presbyterians found unacceptable. This did not mean that Charles had abandoned the presbyterians: on the contrary, he continued to give them comfort and support. His linkman in this work was Clarendon, who met and corresponded with their leaders continually. Throughout his life he made a distinction between Quakers and sectaries, who were enemies to all order, Catholics, who could be forgiven their ideas in practice though not in principle, and presbyterians. These latter, devoted both to monarchy and to a national Church, seemed to him to differ from episcopalians in such trivial respects that, once they had conceded loyalty to some form of bishop, they were worth accommodating. In any case, in such a major issue of policy, it suited his position as the chief minister to manage affairs.

The significant change had been in tactics, from comprehension to the dispensation of loyal nonconformists. As soon as the Lords had received the new Prayer Book, Clarendon proposed an amendment to the Bill of Uniformity which the Commons had sent up and which enjoined use of that book. It empowered the King to relieve clergy from observation of the specific clauses which the presbyterians found repugnant. Behind this the Chancellor arrayed the full set of government peers and several bishops, including Sheldon and Morley. This was the means by which the Commons' attempt to amend the 1660 settlement of ministers had been defeated a month before, and it worked again. This was despite one embarrassing interlude in which Bristol produced a rival proviso granting a much wider dispensation from the bill, which he confidently insisted to represent Charles's true wishes: apparently the King's habit of saying reassuring things to different individuals in private had caused trouble yet again. Clarendon attacked the proposal with venom, and it was defeated. The Lords as a body showed no enthusiasm for toleration and made other parts of the bill more severe, so that their acquiescence derived from a mixture of monarchical sentiment and the sheer strength of Clarendon's team. A great effort was now mounted to persuade the Commons to concur, including Charles's consent to the Act against Quakers and sectaries and the appointment of Clarendon and Sheldon to manage the first conference between the Houses.

All was in vain. As with the Corporation Act, the Commons voted unanimously to deny the King the powers he desired. The government, faced with this defiance, backed down and allowed the bill to pass unamended upon 19 May 1662. It provided for the deprivation of every minister who did not, by 24 August, testify acceptance of the whole Prayer Book, and denounce both the Solemn League and Covenant and the principle of resistance to royal authority. Charles's capitulation was probably from fear that the Lords would waver, but he may already have been considering the dangerous notion that he could dispense individuals under his prerogative without requiring statutory powers. As he assented to the Act of Uniformity, Clarendon urged Parliament to permit the King to decide upon whom it would be enforced. The Chancellor defiantly reiterated the phrase 'tender consciences' which he himself had put into the Declaration of Breda and which the Commons had condemned in the exchanges over the bill. Within two weeks potential nonconformists were being told to expect royal protection, and as soon as 24 August arrived Charles called a conference of advisers to discuss such action. Clarendon and Manchester supported it, but the plan was foiled by Sheldon, who, on behalf of the bishops, utterly refused to co-operate. This division in the government's ranks forced Charles to drop the project. The episcopalian Church of England had just reversed its alliances. Under Charles I it had been increasingly viewed (and resented) as the partner of the Crown in a mission to enhance the power of both. Now it had identified itself with the wishes of the ruling class, embodied in Parliament, against opponents either royal or plebeian. In the process it had provided a crowning humiliation for a sequence of defeats to the King's attempt to act as arbiter in religious affairs. The draconian legislation which had now passed in all three kingdoms was not seriously expected by many of these who produced it to achieve the extermination of dissent. Rather, it left each magistrate the option of dealing gently or severely with local nonconformists, freed from interference by the central government. The additional sting which Sheldon had administered was to make Charles the first English monarch since the Middle Ages to have been successfully defied by his own leading churchmen.

Why did he bring such a snub upon himself? There is, after all, something rather puzzling about the sight of the King and his ministers persisting in trying to help former enemies when a resolutely royalist legislature and dependable armed forces relieved them of any need to do so. One reason was fear of rebellion. As August progressed, and the Corporation and Quaker Acts were also being put into effect, reports of an impending rising poured into Whitehall. The government destroyed the city gates and the walls of four towns with strong presbyterian populations. It also installed two new garrisons, added three foot regiments to the standing army, and kept the militia in arms all autumn. It also kept its intelligence network busy, a precaution which ironically may have produced the very phenomenon that it was designed to prevent. Two spies now took the easy step from agents to *agents provocateurs* and, having located a handful of disaffected London artisans, apparently religious separatists, encouraged them to plan a rising. The result had the inevitability of classical tragedy: the agents reported in November, their dupes were arrested, were shown the rack and confessed, and four more heads joined the impressive collection already rotting on London Bridge. With that perfect circularity common in a process of repression, the affair, called the 'Tong Plot', reinforced the government's belief in the danger of conspiracy. Yet it was the nearest thing to a disturbance that the legislation of 1662 produced. The Act of Uniformity resulted in the resignation of about a tenth of England's ministers, including some of the most able and celebrated, but most of these retired quietly to household religion. The government's preparations for trouble doubtless discouraged it, yet almost certainly the more significant factor was that its evaluation of the ejected clergy had been correct: they were thoroughly loyal.

A more important motivation of royal policy was that already suggested: *raison d'état*. an obedient Church and grateful dissenters meant complete security for the monarchy. A case study of that monarchy at work with minimum restrictions is provided by Oxford University. Charles, as a patron of colleges, and Clarendon, as the university's Chancellor, wielded considerable power there. Magdalen had been the most royalist college in both universities. But when the King imposed an outsider upon it as President in late 1661 and its fellows complained, they received a rebuke of despotic rudeness. The university as a whole resented the way in which it was used as a parliamentary pocket borough and a degree factory for royal clients. Clarendon obtained from Sheldon the money for the beautiful ceremonial centre which bears the latter's name but he also commandeered buildings to house court and Parliament when needed (as will be seen). Charles retained the services of Cromwellian professors who were prepared to transfer their loyalty, and he appointed gifted men such as Christopher Wren to chairs. But too often he then kept protégés like Wren employed in the capital, to the neglect of their classes. In brief, the university was used as it had been by earlier governments, as a machine to render maximum service to the state, and it may be argued that this was a blueprint for the intended fate of the Church.

Having said this, it would still be unwise to rule out the effect, in the last analysis, of Charles's personality. He lacked the profound religious feeling which would have inspired disgust with nonconformity in a ruler. He enjoyed the exotic, and Quakers and sectaries were strange and intriguing creatures to him. He had a strong sense of the order, pomp, and dignity due to monarchy, so was a natural champion of the episcopalian Church. Yet his equally strong insistence upon his royal 'rights' made him susceptible to the flattery of threatened dissenters and unwilling to succumb easily to pressure from a Parliament. It is very difficult to imagine the events of 1661–2 falling out as they did under the supervision of another king.[17]

By the end of 1662 Charles and his ministers had more reasons for discomfort than their humiliation: in England at least, they were becoming patently unpopular. In 1663 Anglesey could comment anxiously upon the hostility of the Londoners, while in Southwark the King's arms were torn down. Charles's old servant and agent Daniel O'Neill was now settled comfortably at court, with a sinecure as head of the Post Office. Yet in the same year he wrote to Ormonde in terms of misery and alienation: 'the King has abandoned himself to his lust and his ministers to their passions against one another'. He then compared the behaviour of the Cavalier Parliament to that of the Long Parliament before the outbreak of the Great Civil War.[18]

What had gone wrong? In part, the development resulted from the recent legislation. Commoners found themselves saddled with the Excise and the Hearth Tax. During the passage of the Act of Uniformity, Charles had irritated the orthodox and disappointed dissenters. But two more factors played an important role, one reflecting badly upon the government, and one upon Charles personally. The former was the sale of Cromwell's greatest foreign acquisition, Dunkirk. The motive was simple: its upkeep cost £321,000 per annum at a time when the public revenue was deficient and had just been further burdened by the acquisition of Tangier and Bombay. It was not easily defensible and had been of no obvious value to trade. It seems that the first suggestion to get rid of it came from Charles's principal active seaman, Sandwich, who told the King that its harbour (its only apparent asset) was second-rate.[19] Clarendon later asserted that he had been persuaded into the project by the Lord Treasurer Southampton, who insisted upon the financial benefits. Certainly the Chancellor made a sudden convert, for he had been tactless enough to tell the Cavalier Parliament in May 1662 that Dunkirk was a jewel in his master's crown. Nevertheless, once he had been given the project he made it his own in an effort to reconfirm his own pre-eminence. As the port lay between French and Spanish territory and Spain's revenue was consumed by the Portuguese war, the obvious customer was Louis XIV. He duly bought it, after fierce bargaining lasting from June till October. Charles and Clarendon persuaded the Privy Council into approval, with the aid of bribes liberally provided by the French. At the Chancellor's request, Louis sent an official letter thanking him for his invaluable part in producing agreement. The transfer was made in November, and the huge garrison either disbanded, shipped home or to Tangier, or loaned to the French and Portuguese.

The response when the news broke was infinitely worse than the government expected. The merchant community feared that Dunkirk would be once more employed as a privateer base, while commoners in general were furious at its loss. In part, this was wounded patriotism, but it also drew upon an intense traditional Francophobia. Bristol and his friends warned Charles that Spain had been provoked but no alliance made with France to compensate. As Clarendon had so carefully advertised his responsibility for the affair, he naturally drew the ensuing anger upon himself. Nor was the money paid in full. Louis had promised nearly $£\frac{1}{2}$ million; but then demanded a discount to pay the whole sum in cash, and got one. He also insisted that the deal had included a clause dispensing him from future responsibility for the English soldiers in Portugal. As a result only £290,000 ended up in Charles's hands, and was easily swallowed up by his public debt. The loss of the port certainly reduced government expense, but this had to be weighed, temporarily, against the cost of the men serving with the Portuguese.[20]

If the English government's greatest weakness at this period was its penury, then its monarch's was his appetite for pleasure. During 1660, when he was on his best behaviour, the epithet most commonly applied to him was 'sober'. It rapidly fell into disuse thereafter. For one thing, he soon gave proof of the enduring stamp that France had put upon his tastes. Before he had been a year in England he was heard to compare its musicians unfavourably with those of Paris. The royalist John Evelyn had his first doubts about the restored monarchy when he visited the Chapel Royal, and found violins accompanying the organ in imitation of the arrangements at the Louvre. When licensing his first theatres Charles insisted that female parts upon the public stage, hitherto played in England by boys, should be taken by their natural performers as in France. A Mrs Norris, who played Desdemona in 1660, became the first professional actress in this country, and her successors soon spread across the land providing consternation among conservatives. French tutors became the fashion among the aristocracy, as did long wigs, face-paint, muffs, and perfume. An observer at Oxford expected to find the ladies in these trappings when the court arrived in 1663, but was taken aback when the royal horse guards appeared in them. The behaviour of the courtiers was as extravagant as their dress. Charles himself set the fashion for gambling, winning £50 on Twelfth Night 1661 but losing £100 at the same revels in 1662. Even the generally decorous Ormonde played hard, and collected £1,000 in one evening. If losses at table were one risk of haunting the court, then syphilis, by late 1661, was regarded as another. In August 1663 the French ambassador (coming from the least innocent court in Europe) could dub the spa of Tunbridge Wells (where the courtiers were in residence), 'L'Eaux de Scandale'. Much of the 'Scandale' was recorded by Pepys, including the particularly unlikely item that a lady-in-waiting had given birth to a baby, anonymously, at a court ball. Even more unlikely (and vivid) tales were hungrily collected in the provinces. Some concerned the heir presumptive, James, who was compensating himself for his enforced marriage by exploiting the shortcomings of other unions. His early mistresses, at least, were considered beauties. One earl in December 1662 packed off his countess to the provinces, out of the ducal reach, as soon as James had been seen in conversation with her.

For Charles to have presided over such a society would have been enough to trouble the virtuous. But worse, he led it in *amours* as in gaming. The Restoration had coincided fairly precisely with the opening of the second great sexual affair of his life. Lucy Walker had been unmarried, relatively obscure, and relatively inept at managing the King. Barbara Palmer possessed none of these politically redeeming qualities. She was born a Villiers, a cousin of the Duke of Buckingham and the daughter of a royalist viscount who had died of his wounds. Despite this noble blood her childhood had been spent in penury resulting from the Great Civil War, engendering in her a ruthless desire for wealth. Her other ruthless desire was whetted at the age of fifteen when she became the mistress of an aristocratic rake. She let herself be married to an honourable and idealistic young royalist squire, Roger Palmer, who was foolish enough to take her with him when he conveyed a gift of money to the King at Breda. Events must have developed so swiftly that, if not premeditation on her part, at least the briefest of courtships must be assumed. In February 1661 she gave birth to a girl, Anne, whom Charles later recognized as his daughter. Thus their partnership must have commenced, at very latest, as the King arrived in England. To any man of easy susceptibilities, Barbara must have been irresistible: she was a ravishing nineteen-year-old now, with auburn hair, deep blue eyes, and a nature passionate in and out of the bedchamber. She was to wear success, like La Châtillon, with a certain magnificent vulgarity. Initially, matters were managed with discretion, but as the King felt more secure this was shed. By the spring of 1661 gossip had begun, and in the autumn it became certainty. At that time Roger Palmer was created Earl of Castlemaine in the Irish peerage, an honour which he had clearly earned by proxy. By the early summer of 1662 a ballad against the Hearth Tax could refer casually to Charles's girlfriend with the hope that she might become England's magdalen. The hope was not a foolish one: at last the King's own bride, the long-awaited Portuguese Infanta, had arrived off Portsmouth.

Catherine of Braganza had been reared in a convent, and spoke no English. Her olive-tinted features were pleasant rather than pretty, and she brought with her 'six frights, who called themselves maids-of-honour'. What she did not bring was more than half the promised money, and some of that in goods not cash. When Charles met her she was suffering from a cold and a heavy period. Incredibly, the wedding night was a success, the King writing rapturously to his ministers of it, and all observers in those first days agreeing upon the patent happiness of the couple. This adds colour to the belief of Charles's apologists that his next move, to install Barbara as his bride's Lady of the Bedchamber, was motivated solely by the need to reward yet another loyal subject for more than usually important past services.

This move ended the connubial atmosphere, for Catherine had been apprised of Lady Castlemaine's record and refused point-blank to accept her. Much of Charles's fondness for his bride seems to have derived from her initial docility. Her defiance provoked much the same fury in him as Sir Henry Vane's, which occurred simultaneously in mid-June, and the consequences of this in turn produced the same public disapproval. By July the rift was complete, and notorious. The King had returned in soul and almost certainly in body to his mistress. The two of them gave their second child, Charles, a public christening. Roger Palmer lost his temper at last, and Barbara walked out on him with most of their possessions. He left the country. The royal couple were now settled at Hampton Court Palace for the official honeymoon, and Clarendon was busy there with the discussions with the imperilled presbyterians. To his distaste, he was employed in a second mediation, with the Queen. The Chancellor performed this with the fidelity with which he followed his master's other direct instructions, advising Catherine to obey the King's will with a lawyer's agility of mind. Charles applied the crueller and cruder pressure of dismissing her beloved maidservants. In August the court sailed down river to Whitehall, with a magnificent flotilla of a thousand barges. Beneath her canopy of cloth of gold, supported on pillars wreathed with flowers, the frightened, isolated Catherine was reaching her breaking point. She accepted her rival into her entourage, and so merely added contempt to her husband's hostile feelings towards her. In the winter of 1662–3 Barbara was at the apogee of her power, the King being utterly devoted to her and courtiers competing for her patronage.

The Queen's misfortunes were still not complete. By winter it had become clear that, despite enthusiastic efforts by Charles after the wedding, and more sporadic attempts thereafter, she had failed in her primary duty of becoming pregnant. In the late summer Henrietta Maria had returned to England on her second visit since the Restoration. She brought with her, as a matter of course, Lord Crofts, and he in turn brought his young ward, the King's son by Lucy. On seeing James again, his father decided to elevate him to the status of a prince. It was a political move, for mere affection would have impelled Charles to keep the boy near him in a less illustrious capacity. In default of any evidence, one can only ascribe it to a desire to parade his potency before the world or (more likely) to a hazy design to secure the Stuart succession in the event of the death of his brother. This second supposition is supported by a search which the King launched in the winter of 1662–3 to find a precedent in Scottish history (English tradition being hostile) for a monarch legitimizing a bastard son.[21] There was no suggestion that he was contemplating the exclusion of his brother from the succession and the object seemed to be to secure young James princely dignities and some eventual claim to the throne. (The final irony of York's marriage had been that the baby which had produced it had expired after a few months.) If nothing else, this attempt suggests powerfully that Charles had not married Lucy and so did not have the means of establishing his son for use in emergency. Nevertheless, rumours that such a union had been contracted were circulating within a month of the boy's appearance.[22] Scottish royalty proved barren of the justification which the King was seeking, but he still loaded the lad with honours. Young James was a favourite at court by September 1662, created Duke of Monmouth and Buccleuch during the next spring, and married to the richest available heiress in April. James, Henrietta Maria, and Barbara were all irritated, but the last of these had the cunning to make a fuss of the boy to consolidate her position.

The two individual victims of this sequence of events were the wretched Queen Catherine, and Clarendon, whose enthusiasm for the Portuguese match was now linked by gossip to his daughter's marriage. It was said that he had deliberately obtained a barren wife for Charles in order to put his descendants on the throne. The main casualty, however, was the King's reputation. By late 1662 an ambassador could quote the Londoners as saying that their sovereign only 'hunts and lusts', and other observers confirmed this opinion less concisely.[23] Charles and Barbara had committed one of the great public adulteries of history, before a nation which a scant twelve years before had made death the penalty for this sin.

To cope with this uneasy situation, Charles led a governing team which underwent changes in all three kingdoms in the course of 1662. In Ireland the Cromwellian leaders were nudged gently from the centre of power by the 'Old Royalists' of the exile. The King instituted this process on 4 November 1661 when he announced to the English Privy Council that Ormonde would be sent to resume active control of his native land as Lord-Lieutenant. Clarendon later ascribed this change to the weakening of the Lord Justices' rule through death, quarrelling, and absenteeism. The explanation will not stand up to the facts. Mountrath indeed died suddenly, of the ubiquitous smallpox, but not until over a month after the return of Ormonde had been announced. At this period the three Lord Justices were co-operating well and working hard, and the two who survived into 1662 were arguably the more popular and able. Charles had no hesitation in commissioning them to act until Ormonde arrived, and they devoted their last months of office to the passage of the crucial statutes for the land settlement and the revenue. It seems that Charles had simply been waiting for a decent interval to elapse before replacing his old servant in his traditional position. Perhaps, also, he had resented the manner in which the Lord Justices had politely contested some of his orders. Certainly, the growing hold of the 'Old Royalists' upon Irish affairs went beyond the appointment of the Duke. After the election results for the Cavalier Parliament came in, Clarendon and Southampton were added to the English Privy Council's committee for that kingdom. Upon Mountrath's death, Charles transferred all his great offices in Connacht to Lord Berkeley, as though the care of this most remote, Gaelic, and Catholic of provinces was merely another sinecure to grant to an English courtier. The King's lack of personal interest in Ireland continued to manifest itself in clumsiness: for example, he ordered the surviving Lord Justices to pass no more patents until Ormonde arrived and then sent them some to be passed. Not only did he show no interest in the Dublin administration's deteriorating finances but he worsened them by ordering a regiment of Irish guards to be raised. To increase the influence of the Butler family over the land, this unit was placed under Ormonde's second son Richard, who was created Earl of Arran. Yet the King remembered to praise Eustace and Orrery warmly for their achievements, and they in turn supported Ormonde loyally when he crossed to Dublin in late July 1662.[24]

These developments almost certainly encouraged Middleton to consolidate the hold of his group, the allies of Ormonde and Clarendon, over Scotland. The former General was growing ever more confident and arrogant, and acquiring the reputation of a tyrant. It was said that when Argyll's daughter knelt before him to beg the burial of her father's head, he threatened to kick her. He was also rumoured to have declared that Lauderdale would pimp for any prince in Europe, and that though he would serve Charles loyally he would not promise the same for his brother.[25] All who stood between him and absolute domination of his native land were Lauderdale himself and Crawford-Lindsay, the men who had opposed his religious policy and who resided at Whitehall, dangerously close to the King. In 1662 he determined to use the Scottish Parliament to force their removal upon Charles, as he had employed it to restore episcopacy. Crawford-Lindsay was easily dealt with, by an act passed on 5 September enjoining all office-holders to denounce the Covenants. The Treasurer's conscience would not stretch to this, and the King obeyed the new law and dismissed him. Lauderdale's conscience, however, could encompass anything which would secure his career. When he made the declaration prescribed by the act, he was reported to have sneered that he could cope with a cartful of others. To topple him, Middleton employed the Act of Indemnity passed on 9 September.

During the previous January, Charles had consented to a proposal by his Commissioner that former Kirk party leaders, Remonstrants, and collaborators with Cromwell should be fined and that the proceeds should be used to compensate royalists for their wartime losses. Middleton's old chum Newburgh sent Charles (through Clarendon) a list of beneficiaries for approval, which included himself and presumably most of his, and the Commissioner's, circle. To this bill, Middleton persuaded the Parliament in June to add a clause requesting the King to disable twelve men from office (as the English Act had disabled forty). This, he assured the Estates, was the royal wish. He had a new protégé, an able, crafty, and ambitious young laird called Sir George Mackenzie of Tarbet. This man was sent to Hampton Court to obtain Charles's consent to the amended bill, with the assurance that the legislature desired it. The King, preoccupied with the English Act of Uniformity and with his marital difficulties, was easily charmed by Mackenzie and ostentatiously shut out Lauderdale from their discussions. Clarendon, Ormonde, and James all supported the new clause. In August, when the laird of Tarbet returned to Edinburgh with the royal approval, all was ready for the final coup. To his existing friends upon the Scottish Privy Council, Middleton had persuaded Charles to add three more: Mackenzie himself, Newburgh, and the King's own remote cousin, the young Duke of Richmond and Lennox. Between them, this group hit on the idea of choosing the twelve names by secret ballot in Parliament, to avoid subsequent personal bitterness. One was duly taken and, thanks to the efforts of the Commissioner's clique, Lauderdale was included. Middleton then gave the royal consent to the whole statute without submitting it to the King first, and Richmond and Mackenzie hurried to Whitehall with it. Newburgh crossed to Ireland to obtain Ormonde's support for the venture.

Middleton had resoundingly miscalculated. He had just committed the same fatal error as his rival Balcarres had done five years before, of making Charles feel coerced. The wily Archbishop Sharp had been careful to play a passive role in the proceedings at Edinburgh, to avoid attracting anybody's hostility. But it was almost certainly he who leaked details of the Commissioner's plot to his brother William Sharp, whom Lauderdale employed as his agent in Scotland. William dispatched to Whitehall by express post a string of reports written in invisible ink on the back of innocuous newsletters. As a result, Lauderdale was able to break the news of the Act of Indemnity to Charles before the smooth-tongued Mackenzie arrived with it. The King was furious. He had assumed that the exceptions from office would consist (as in the English Act) of discredited politicians and not of his own servants. The secret ballot itself was a device which threatened to reduce the supervision of a Parliament by the royal government. Furthermore, Middleton had been reckless enough to couple the passage of the Act with another, prohibiting the children of people convicted of treason from petitioning the monarch for their parents' estates. It was intended to facilitate the designs harboured by the Commissioner and his allies upon Argyll's lands in particular, and represented a restraint upon Charles's prerogative of mercy. This was a matter upon which he had already proved sensitive. Thus, when he was handed the Act, the King threw it into a cabinet with the comment that the list of twelve names was rejected. He then sent Mackenzie back into Scotland, and ordered Middleton to stay there awhile. Instead he summoned Rothes, and other important Scots not closely associated with the Commissioner, to Whitehall to explain what had been happening in Edinburgh. When Middleton was finally allowed to come to court, in the winter, he did so not as a returning conqueror but as a man in danger of disgrace. It was reported that as he passed through Coldstream an old woman shouted that he would never again lord it over Scotland.[26]

At precisely the same time, the influence of Clarendon himself began to wane in England. Like Middleton's, his importance reached its apogee in 1662. Charles had retained his mixed Privy Council of 1660, but soon found the non-royalists upon it, such as Anglesey and Ashley, less amenable than his advisers from the exile. This pattern intensified as 1661 progressed, the King's affair with Barbara developed, his energy declined (!), and his interest in daily government fell off. Clarendon's utility as a work-horse became ever more obvious, and his central position in every royal policy initiative has been noted. He was rewarded with grants of land and the office of Ranger of Wychwood, while his younger son Laurence became Master of the Robes. Four separate urban corporations elected him their High Steward, while the ambitious young poet John Dryden compared Charles to heaven and the Chancellor to the earth.

Nevertheless, Edward Hyde had notable deficiencies as a servant. For one thing, he was a work-horse who frequently went lame, his portly body being confined to bed by attacks of gout. These had incapacitated him during important periods such as the stay at Breda in 1660 and the second session of the Cavalier Parliament. For another, he had ignored the King's views over the questions of the Catholics and the Quakers. For yet another, he had been a remarkably unsuccessful leader at times, so that many royal policies (such as those concerning the standing army, the corporations, and religious toleration) had failed and others (such as the royal marriage and the sale of Dunkirk) had rebounded. But his fundamental fault was one of character: his new responsibilities reinforced an already considerable tendency to self-importance and self-righteousness. His private notes to the King had the tone of a kind but strict schoolmaster. At times he treated the Privy Council like a lecture hall and determined business as though he and not Charles had overall control. For the King's pleasures he had neither sympathy nor approval. In brief, he was not a natural companion to Charles and was accordingly vulnerable to those who were.

Those best placed to take advantage of this opening were not Charles's other ministers, but his courtiers. These tended to be dominated even more obviously by former royalists. His staff in the Bedchamber and Privy Chamber were simply those of the exile—Gerard, Wentworth, Seymour, Elliot, O'Neill, and the rest—reinforced by a very occasional 'Presbyterian' and a few youngsters. The most prominent courtier in 1661–2, however, was a man who held no office at all: that evergreen adventurer, the Earl of Bristol. His brilliant entertainments had predictably become the best in the royal orbit: equally predictably, the Earl's personal interest in them was in the gambling. He and Barbara swiftly became allies, sharing a flamboyant nature and an enmity with Clarendon. The opposition to the latter was reinforced by Henrietta Maria on her return in 1662. This far, the combination was not sufficient to menace the Chancellor. Charles used Bristol for pleasure as he had used Taaffe during exile, leaving the business to Clarendon. Bristol's set, however, became extremely potent when it acquired Sir Henry Bennet.

Bennet had been recalled from his post at Madrid in early 1661, and made Keeper of the Privy Purse. He had returned with a taste for rich clothes and ponderous dignity, the latter enhanced by his heavy figure and the frown imposed by frequent headaches. His friendship seems in retrospect to have been an obvious commodity for Clarendon to cultivate. They had been allies in the attempt to ruin Berkeley in 1656. Bennet was efficient, industrious, and spoke more languages than the existing Privy Council possessed between them. Like Clarendon, he was devoted to the monarchy and fundamentally serious. Yet the Chancellor, with quite appalling shortness of sight, used his newly acquired power to block Sir Henry's advancement to every post he coveted, including that of ambassador to Paris which would have removed him from court. This infantile jealousy had the inevitable effect of pushing him into Bristol's faction, and by the autumn of 1662 Charles was sufficiently impressed by his advice, and disenchanted with Clarendon, to bring Bennet into the government.

In September Sir Henry replaced Clarendon in the informal post of arbitrator between the King and his wife, and in October he replaced Nicholas in the formal one of senior Secretary of State. Nicholas seems to have been selected for sacrifice partly because of his age, which was nearing seventy, and partly because of his unassuming and obedient nature. Indeed, he went quietly enough once he had been assured of his retention of his other posts and a golden handshake of £10,000. Bennet was duly installed, with a large grant of confiscated Irish Catholic land to support the dignities of office. He proved an excellent Secretary, commencing the systematic docketing and filing of correspondence and insisting upon clearly written dispatches. But his appointment created a new feeling of instability in English politics. Clarendon was furious and felt threatened, and Ormonde and Bennet got off to an unfortunate start. The new Secretary belonged to that genial tradition whereby people in high places did favours for each other, and asked the Lord-Lieutenant to give his brother command of an Irish horse troop. Charles supported the request, and so did Orrery, who appreciated the importance of winning Sir Henry's gratitude, but Ormonde was too patriotic and high-principled to appoint a stranger to a position in an already disgruntled army. As bad feeling spread, rumours abounded that other changes within the ministry would follow, but this was specifically not the King's intention. He did begin calling meetings of advisers at his mother's mansion instead of the Chancellor's, and his private notes to the latter almost ceased. But his intention was to multiply his sources of counsel, not to replace them.[27]

In the midsummer of 1662, it seemed as if Charles had settled down to a system of running each of his three kingdoms through an all-powerful minister, drawn from the dominant faction at his court during the later exile. Six months later, this had been abandoned in England and Scotland for a more fluid and pluralist pattern. At best, the new situation promised greater flexibility and opportunities for rising talent. At worst, it would lead to a division and a loss of coherence within government. All depended now upon Charles's skill as a team leader and the wisdom of the policies he chose.

In late December 1662 Charles initiated the first act of policy since the Restoration which can clearly be attributed to him personally: the so-called (and miscalled) Declaration of Indulgence. It did not declare anything except intent, to ask the Cavalier Parliament in its next session to grant him the power to dispense from the Act of Uniformity and to revive the process of removing the laws against Catholics. In fact the King did not wait for Parliament to meet. Before the publication of the Declaration in mid-January he had released most of the religious nonconformists imprisoned in London. One of them was Edmund Calamy, a very distinguished presbyterian who had preached in his former parish church, in flagrant breach of the Act of Uniformity but with the encouragement of several Privy Counsellors. Sheldon had promptly arrested him and the King equally swiftly liberated him. The whole programme seems to have been a fusion of three different preoccupations. One was Bristol's lobbying for the relief of Catholics. Another was a suggestion from Bennet, to prevent a rising following the execution of the Act of Uniformity by holding out hope of amendment of the statute. The third was the wish of former parliamentarians on the Council (notably Ashley) to succour the presbyterian clergy. Perhaps these men made the fusion themselves and then sold the package to Charles. Perhaps the King himself decided to incorporate all these preoccupations into one document, being the only individual who fully shared them all. Certainly, by late January he seemed to be the only man involved who was not seriously worried about Parliament's response.

For one thing, the government was weaker than in 1662. Sheldon was leading most bishops in preparing to fight for uniformity, while observers had doubts about the reliability of Clarendon himself. From November he had been incapacitated by an unusually prolonged agony of gout and left ignorant of the deliberations which had produced the declaration. Bennet had brought it to him for approval, which he only gave with severe qualification, and in early 1663 both ministers were mobilizing supporters, not behind the new bid for indulgence, but to ruin each other. For another thing, the whole policy was absurdly provocative. The arguments for the royal dispensing power had all been deployed a year before, and rejected by the Commons. In addition, Charles had connived in a breach of the Act of Uniformity by Calamy before Parliament had been consulted. Worse, the issue of Protestant nonconformity had been yoked with the different one of Catholic relief. Charles had simply been unable to accept the fact of defeat over the religious issue and was reacting in the most crass possible way. It was a piece of political idiocy, produced by the King responsible for the fiascos of the 'Start' and the rebellion of 1655.

Furthermore, he was seeking to force an unpopular policy upon the Commons at a moment when he depended upon their goodwill for his financial survival. Simply, the regular revenue of the government was still failing to meet its expenses. Some of this problem was certainly due to evasion, obstruction, and corruption. The customs officers faced widespread smuggling operations and were sometimes attacked by mobs. In the autumn of 1662 the Excise had been farmed out to commissioners in each county recommended by the justices, who complained bitterly that local officers either ignored or abetted brewers who dodged payment. The returns made for the Hearth Tax were often ridiculously fradulent: the King informed the City of London, without amusement, that some citizens were reporting themselves dead. On the other hand, the nation plainly felt over-taxed already. It had paid huge sums in direct taxation to pay off the army and to balance the public accounts. Trade remained depressed because the markets lost during years of foreign and civil war could not swiftly be regained. The harvest of 1661 had been spectacularly bad. The new permanent impositions of the Excise and Hearth Tax affected all levels of society, and the latter had produced a furious outcry in the capital.

Nor was the public easily convinced that income, and not expenditure, was the problem. After the years of penury abroad, Charles had viewed England as a cornucopia. He had set the tone of his financial policy on the voyage from Holland, when he ordered that the entire fleet be given an extra month's pay to celebrate the occasion: two months later, the new Navy Board was still wondering where the money was to come from. In 1661 the same board was crippled by lack of funds, and its Clerk, Pepys, wrote that the King was only seeking new ways of spending money. Charles was not throwing away funds upon pleasure so much as seeking to gratify old and new political friends, an essential process in the re-establishment of the monarchy and one which did not prevent the charges of ingratitude from royalists. Nevertheless, the increasing reputation of the court for profligacy gave a general impression of fiscal irresponsibility. By August 1662 it was a proverb in London that 'The bishops get all, the courtiers spend all, the citizens pay for all, the King neglects all, and the Devil take all.' The two great windfalls of the sale of Dunkirk and the Portuguese dowry seemed to many to make further public aid even less necessary. By December 1662 the Treasury was almost empty, and it was obvious that Charles would have to ask Parliament for further assistance.[28]

Meanwhile, trouble was brewing in Ireland. It was not the fault of Ormonde, who was respected and obeyed by all, and who maintained his cautious attitude towards the Catholics. He insisted upon acceptance of the 'Irish Remonstrance' of 1661 by any of them who desired toleration, further deepening the split within their community upon this issue. He protected individual priests who promoted this end, but rebuked Eustace for commissioning two Catholic JPs.[29] Nor did the financial problem cause tension between government and Parliament. On Ormonde's arrival the Lord Justices handed him a scheme whereby the Houses would vote a Hearth Tax like the English one, on the implicit understanding that Charles would then return the bill abolishing wardships. This was successfully implemented. The problems that did arise concerned the implementation of the Act of Settlement. Specifically to avoid controversy, this had been entrusted to seven English gentry, none personally interested in the judgement and all bound by the terms of the Act. They began the reception of claims in September 1662, and by winter had created a furore. The heart of the trouble was that the Protestants had not expected that many Catholics would qualify for restoration, and they were wrong: in a period of eight months the commissioners found 113 persons 'guilty' and 707 'innocent' and deserving of restoration, 566 of whom were Catholics. These judgements represented but a fraction of the claims being lodged, and under the Act of Settlement compensation was not necessarily due to those dispossessed by the successful claimants. Panic soon set in among Protestants. One possible response to the situation was made by the Parliament, which prepared an Explanatory Act sharply narrowing the definition of 'innocence'. Ormonde and the Privy Council rejected this as monstrously unjust, and amended it out of all recognition into a measure which specified the order of precedence among the possible claimants to a piece of land. Indeed, it went into such detail that when it arrived in England for approval Clarendon for one found it unreadable. If his experience was common, this would explain why the Privy Council at

Whitehall sent it back to Dublin unamended. But it was not the measure that the Irish Parliament had prepared, and when it returned, at the end of January 1663, the Dublin government was as frightened about its possible reception as Charles's English ministers were about the fate of their Declaration.[30]

At the same time, the strife between the King's Scottish ministers was growing more bitter. On 5 February Lauderdale formally attacked Middleton in a gathering of Counsellors from both kingdoms at Whitehall, accusing him of having misled the King in the matter of indemnity and exceeded his authority. Middleton was given time to reply. When he did, he was evasive, for his enemy had spoken the truth, and in the meantime he had the wanton folly to offend Charles again. In late January, probably on the advice of Lauderdale, the King wrote to the Scottish Privy Council to suspend the collection of fines due under the Act of Indemnity. On hearing of this, Middleton complained to Clarendon, who saw Charles and reported back that the King had reversed his decision. Two days after being accused of high-handed behaviour, Middleton justified the charge by writing to the Council in his monarch's name to demand the fines. Lauderdale ran immediately to Charles, who denied that he had ever given authority to his Commissioner to instruct the Council, and ordered that bewildered body to suspend the process once more. Some courtiers favoured the opinion that the King had not been listening properly when Clarendon spoke to him, and they may well have been right. Whatever the truth, Charles's fury with both his Scottish Commissioner and his English Chancellor was patent and observers henceforth regarded Middleton as doomed. This further damaged the monarch's popularity in England, where MPs, ignorant of the reasons for Middleton's disgrace, presumed that he was being victimized for his intolerant religious policy. Its possible effects upon Scotland were a matter for anxious speculation.[31]

The fourth session of the Cavalier Parliament opened upon 18 February 1663. As for the previous three, the historian suffers from a frustrating lack of evidence for the workings of personalities and groups within the court and the Houses. But the great effort made by Charles to secure the success of his policy is plain enough. He opened proceedings by reiterating his desire to relieve peaceful nonconformists and Catholics, though he proposed to keep the latter out of office and to stop their numbers from growing. He instructed Clarendon and Bennet to call a meeting of their respective friends and clients in the Commons to ensure a concerted effort. He talked of having Clarendon's son married to Bristol's daughter. As before, the attempt to have the dispensing power recognized was launched in the more compliant Lords, where James introduced a bill for the relief of Protestant dissenters. It carried provocation of the Commons a step further, for it recognized the royal power to dispense not merely with the Act of Uniformity but with any religious legislation.

The reaction of the MPs is equally stark. They rejected the project for dispensation without a division, and replied formally to Charles that toleration would endanger, not produce, domestic peace. Next, they resolved that Calamy's release could not be justified in law, and started a bill not only to exile converts to Catholicism but to facilitate the prosecution of existing recusants. Some of the King's own chaplains denounced nonconformists and Papists to his face, and Berkenhead threw the official newspapers behind this campaign. Nor did royal policy provoke a great swell of gratitude from dissenters themselves, for although a deputation of independent ministers attended Charles to give thanks, the presbyterian clergy were offended by the favour shown to Catholics. This sentiment extended into the Privy Council, for two days before Parliament met, Morice committed to prison a priest captured in Holborn.

On 12 March Clarendon made his long-awaited return from his sick-bed to the Lords. Charles must have been anticipating the moment when he would use his eloquence and influence to assist the bill in the Upper House: indeed, debate of the measure may have been adjourned six days simply to await his reappearance. If so, the result was a surprise, for either from a desire to win favour with the episcopalians to compensate for his decline at court, or from despair of the success of the measure, he neither supported nor opposed it. His abstinence was decisive. The bill was dropped, and the King furious with his Chancellor. Now it was the Catholics' turn to be disappointed. Bristol had been arguing their case in the Lords. When the Commons sent up a proposal to ask Charles to banish priests, the peers were persuaded to insist only that tactless individuals be deported. Clarendon, struggling to mend his relations with his master, spoke strongly on behalf of royalist Catholics and discreet priests. He only lost support among episcopalians without regaining the affection of Charles. In any case all was in vain, for the Commons held firm and on 2 April the King surrendered and duly issued the proclamation. By June the Commons had sent to the Lords not only their bill against Catholics but another to extend the Act of Uniformity to vestry members and a third to extend the penalties of the Quaker Act to all Protestants caught at a nonconformist political meeting.

The principal comfort to Charles in this resounding humiliation may have been the hope that the Commons would be disposed after their victory to deal generously with the public revenue. In mid-March he had drawn their attention to this and obtained a committee of enquiry chaired by one of his own officials, to look into the matter. It heard Sir Philip Warwick explain on the King's behalf that the entire annual revenue was still only £978,000 per annum, while expenditure could not be reduced below £1,085,000. In reality, Warwick was sparing his monarch embarrassment by concealing the actual degree of overspending. A private report which he made simultaneously to Charles put it bluntly: the current expense was double the current income. Unhappily for the King, the bulk of the Commons committee suspected the truth. Not only did it launch an investigation into Warwick's figures, but it took the far more insulting step of enquiring into the grants of royal land made by Charles since the Restoration.

It may be tempting for modern historians to argue that the divisions within Charles's governments could be a source of strength, for they represented a range of views which prevented opponents of royal policies from regarding the regime as a hostile whole. In default of further evidence it is difficult to prove this contention for the first three sessions of the Cavalier Parliament, and the pattern of the fourth one argues against it. By April 1663 the government had failed to preserve a united front over the issue of indulgence and made a series of concessions to the Commons' wishes. But the majority of MPs continued to display hostility and suspicion towards the regime as a whole. The House now launched an attack upon the alleged habit of royal officers of selling junior offices, and in May it prepared a bill to set up an enquiry into this. A proposal to extend the investigation to the sale of honours was prevented by only one vote. In the same week another provocative bill was ordered, to assign public expenditure to particular branches of revenue to reduce the likelihood of misappropriation.

What improved relations in early June was not an effort by the government but a discovery by the Commons: its revenue committee reported that all sources of public income were indeed producing less than expected, and that the new Hearth Tax was the biggest disappointment of all. They set the total revenue at £1,025,000 per annum, still short of the £1,085,000 minimum expenditure suggested by Warwick. Charles decided to risk following this up by personally accusing the Commons of neglecting the public good and offering the account for the expenditure of the previous grant. His tone almost provoked the MPs to defiance, for they resolved to supply him by only forty-eight votes in a House of nearly three hundred. Nevertheless the bills concerning sale of offices and assignation of the revenue were dropped and three statutes were passed to augment the royal income, yet this display of loyalty was less effective than it appeared. Two of the Acts gave Excise farmers and constables receiving Hearth Tax returns power to search properties, but ignored the problems of obstruction and intimidation. The third ordered a direct supply to remove the accumulated public debt, but chose the old method of 'subsidy', based on a percentage of presumed wealth. The efficient 'assessment' had been based upon a fixed sum required from each county. In the end the Act produced less than the voluntary subscription of 1661. Misled by the apparent small size of the gap between income and expenditure, the Commons were determined not to anger their constituents by a heavier and more effective, imposition.[32]

In the same spring, the tension in Ireland exploded into confrontation. On 10 February the House of Commons threw out the Explanatory Act and voted a series of resolutions designed not only to narrow the definition of 'innocent' Catholics but to submit land claims to the verdicts of (Protestant) juries instead of to the royal commissioners. The fear and anger of the Irish Protestant community was clear to observers: as the Speaker of the Commons put it, 'the alarm that Hannibal is at the gates is hot through the Protestant plantations'. What impressed onlookers at the English court was the comparable intensity of the King's reaction. Clarendon commented that he had never seen his master so angry. Charles had, as before, been behaving in such a way as to make the task of his servants in Dublin more difficult. He had bedevilled the work of the Commissioners for Claims by making grants to Catholics and English courtiers of lands to which the title had not yet been decided. As for the problems of the Irish public revenue, far from assisting them with grants from England he had been assigning sums from the Irish Treasury to English purposes. Now he regarded the Irish Parliament's treatment of his commissioners as an insult to his authority, and ordered Ormonde to force the Commons to rescind their votes with the threat of armed action against them supported by the Cavalier Parliament. The Lord-Lieutenant was thus placed in an appalling position. The threat was ludicrous, for this English Commons was never going to coerce fellow Protestants into letting more Irish Catholics regain their estates. Nor could Ormonde count on the unanimous support of his Privy Council, as Massarene, Lane, and others were themselves losing land as a result of the commissioners' decisions. Worst, his army would almost certainly mutiny if instructed to repress a Protestant rebellion. Not only were the soldiers Protestant themselves, but their pay was now so badly in arrears that they begged in the streets. The subsidies granted by the Irish Parliament had still left the government £39,500 in debt. There was no prospect of further aid from the Commons unless their fury was appeased, and little from an English government which was itself in serious deficit.

If the Irish army was to fight anybody, it needed £60,000, and Ormonde did not have a penny of this.[33]

Thus, by early 1663 the monarchy which had been so universally popular two years before was the object of anger and suspicion in England and Ireland and faced possible disaffection among the leading group in Scotland. In part, this situation was due to the carelessness, self-indulgence, and political folly of Charles himself. But it was not to endure. Just as a set of factors had combined to debilitate royal government at this period, so a different set were now to operate to produce a stronger set of regimes.

One of these was that Charles, while capable of rashness, was not totally devoid of political common sense. He could provoke a formidable opposition, but unlike his father he knew better than to defy it for long. Part of the difference lay in the fact that the second Charles had the dreadful warning of the regicide before him. But, in addition, his religious policy was not based upon personal faith. While he was promising the presbyterians relief, he was also laughing at the satirical portrait of them in Butler's *Hudibras*. As for the Catholics, he may have been sincere when he told the French ambassador in April 1663 that he thought 'no other creed matches so well with the absolute dignity of Kings than Catholicism'. But this was a political observation not a profession of belief, and he added that he would nevertheless persecute Catholics if he were forced to.

It was this flexibility which allowed him to keep a working relationship with the Commons during that year. In private he was known to be enraged by the rejection of his religious policy. When Clarendon failed him in March he requested the retired republican lawyer Whitelocke to draft a defence of his power to dispense under the prerogative. But his own replies to the House were at first tactfully evasive and then conceded all that it wished. At the end of the session, on 27 July, he thanked it firmly for its financial help, and promised to economize. He also affected dismay at the failure of the bills against Catholics and dissenters to reach completion in the Lords, and promised to bring in substitutes in the next session and to enforce the existing laws severely in the interim. If his voice lacked sincerity this would not have been apparent, for he always made speeches to Parliament by reading without feeling from a paper in his lap. This was a surprising performance for the man who had declaimed his oaths so resoundingly at Scone, and perhaps reflects his discomfort when dealing with a legislative body. None the less, the words were spoken, and far from punishing Sheldon for his opposition, he made him a Privy Counsellor. When Juxon at last expired in May, the tough-minded bishop was appointed to the supreme see of Canterbury.

Berkenhead was deprived of control of the government newspapers in August, but replaced by another intolerant episcopalian, Roger L'Estrange, and not by an advocate of toleration. The change seems to have been due to invisible personal animosities at court.

This policy was a cosmetic one. Charles's speech hardly concealed the fact that the bills against Catholics and conventicles had perished quietly in the Lords and that this would not have been the case had the King genuinely willed otherwise. The request made by the Commons in response, for royal proclamations to enforce the existing laws instead, was ignored. Two weeks later, Clarendon and Anglesey were already discussing the possibility of relieving loyal nonconformists once more. Though the Privy Council now left most religious radicals to their fate, it did intervene in May to stop some Buckinghamshire magistrates from hanging local baptists by stretching the terms of an Elizabethan statute. Quakers and sects in the capital were in any case enjoying relative peace under a tolerant Lord Mayor. Nevertheless, the monarch had shown a remarkable superficial docility to the Commons' wishes, and reversed his formal policy without a serious struggle. Protestant dissenters were left no better off, and Catholics fared worse, for the pleas made for them only enraged some magistrates into exacting recusancy fines for the first time since the Restoration. As in the previous sessions, so in the fourth, both King and Commons had experienced 'defeats', and the balance between the two was maintained.

Furthermore, Charles kept his promise to make economies at court, to such effect that in the late summer he reduced his Household expenditure by two-thirds. The process, driven on by Southampton and Bennet, was obviously unpopular with those who lost profit or place by it, and Clarendon and Anglesey protested on their behalf. The benefit to the government's solvency, and the potential benefit to its reputation, were nevertheless obvious.

In the same period the factional warfare at court was resolved. During the early summer, this had been hotter than ever, Clarendon's downfall being sought not only by Bristol and Bennet but by Ashley, who had apparently not forgiven the Chancellor for the loss of the toleration bill. What restored stability was that Bristol, once again, ruined himself with a thoroughness beyond the capacity of an enemy. The process by which he achieved this originated in the problems of a young Buckinghamshire squire, Sir Richard Temple MP. Temple was burdened with £12,000 worth of inherited debts, which could be most swiftly paid off with the fruits of office. At the Restoration he lobbied for these with the help of Morice, but apparently exasperated Charles with his sheer importunity.

All that he received was a knighthood, which could not satisfy creditors, and by 1663 he was desperate enough to exploit the differences between King and Commons. Approaching Bristol, he offered his influence in the House to secure the success of Charles's policies, and was accepted. After the ensuing catastrophe, he decided upon the easier course of making himself such a nuisance to the government that it would buy him off. Accordingly, he became a leader of the campaign against sale of office and was a teller for the 'Noes' in the vote to supply the King. Charles, far from being impelled to gratify him, decided to destroy him in June by informing the Commons of his offer to manage them. The tactic rebounded, for Sir Richard denied the charge and the House demanded the name of Charles's informant.

By now, the King's irritation with Temple was starting to spill over to include his former sponsor at court, Bristol. Royal favour flowed back proportionately towards Clarendon, whose establishment as a local magnate was completed with the post of Lord-Lieutenant of Oxfordshire. Bennet, like a true courtier, drew apart from his erstwhile ally and showed affection for the Chancellor again, and Castlemaine turned Bristol from her door. On 26 June Charles named Bristol to the Commons. From this moment, Bristol decided to win popular support sufficient to round upon the government and to force out his rivals. On 1 July he attended the Commons and cleared both his name and Temple's by insisting that a misunderstanding had occurred. When the MPs had finished laughing at his theatrical delivery, they closed the affair. Next, he arranged to impeach Clarendon in the Lords, in alliance with those peers who blamed the Chancellor for the failure of the toleration bill. His list of charges included every popular libel against Clarendon, including that he had arranged the sale of Dunkirk for a huge bribe and obtained a barren queen to strengthen his daughter's position. He deliberately played up to the Londoners, and they in turn made this Catholic courtier their hero.

The attack upon Clarendon occupied the Lords from 10 to 14 July, and represented the last and greatest fiasco of Bristol's public career. Few of his anticipated supporters spoke for the impeachment and some, like Ashley, sensed the course of affairs and commended the Chancellor. The judges ruled that the charges were inadequate and the anger of Charles was plain. Bristol's passage to the Tower was certain as soon as the impeachment failed, and the Earl escaped it only by going into hiding. The King not merely issued a formal proclamation for his arrest but, with exquisite irony, had him proceeded against as a Catholic recusant. When representations were made to Charles on his behalf nine months later they were rejected absolutely, and the Earl had to remain living obscurely for years.

The affair cleared the air at court, as henceforth Clarendon and Bennet gradually accepted that they would have to work together. Charles never returned to his dependence upon the former, for apart from retaining Bennet he immediately elevated in Bristol's place another member of the Earl's faction, a young man of devotedly royalist background called Sir Charles Berkeley. On the day that Bristol's charges failed, Berkeley was made a viscount, and henceforth the King's affection for him was plain to all commentators. His private life was less reputable than Bristol's (indeed, Pepys recorded more scandalous stories about him than any other individual courtier) but unlike the Earl he had no interest in politics. Leaving those to the royal ministers, he preferred to remain the boon companion of Charles's pleasures, and so reinforced the stability of English government.

As Bristol sank from view, so Castlemaine's absolute dominance of the King's sexual affections vanished. In mid-1663 Charles conceived a passion for a virgin of about sixteen years, Frances Stuart, daughter of a Scottish Catholic royalist. Sent to court in 1662, her remarkable elfin beauty soon created comment, and by early 1663 Barbara had befriended her in a desperate effort to reinforce the King's interest in her own company. This failed, for in June Charles's lust for Frances was patent and he was quarrelling with Castlemaine. Throughout the summer and autumn Bennet and other courtiers attempted to use the new favourite to strengthen their own influence with him. What halted this course of events was the personality of Frances herself. The evidence remains unclear as to whether she was at this period a clever and virtuous woman or a feather-headed innocent, but the upshot was clear: she refused absolutely to surrender herself to the King or to take political affairs seriously. Barbara's utility, and survival at court were thereby assured. At the same time, Catherine of Braganza regained some of her husband's affection through a wholly fortuitous piece of good fortune: she almost died. Having spent the late summer being carried from spa to spa in an attempt to cure her infertility, she contracted a fever on her return to Whitehall. Her priests and doctors despaired, and prepared for her end with a medieval concoction of ritual and superstition, giving her the last sacraments, shaving her head, and tying dead pigeons to her feet. In her delirium she expressed such touching devotion to Charles that he wept at her side. The reconciliation survived her recovery, and henceforth the royal affections were divided between the three women, two of whom declined to meddle in public affairs. The area available to political intrigue in court life was thus further circumscribed.[34]

Meanwhile, Charles's ministers in Scotland and Ireland were resolving the problems there with some brilliance. His attention had been distracted from the dispute between Middleton and Lauderdale by events in the English Parliament, and not till late May did he return to it. Then if one can trust the later Bishop Burnet, he called another meeting of Counsellors over the issue, where despite some continued support for Middleton the King declared that he would be replaced. Rothes was chosen Commissioner instead, instructed to investigate the whole process by which the Act of Indemnity had been passed. To increase royal power over the Scottish legislature, the new Commissioner was also expected to have future Lords of the Articles selected according to the 'ancient' procedure. This in fact dated only from 1633, and was a complex system whereby the estates selected representatives for this vital committee, which drafted all legislation, from each other. As the bishops chose first and the King had named these, it meant that the entire membership could reflect the monarch's wishes. Lauderdale was sent with Rothes, to support this work and also to afford himself the opportunity to win supporters in his homeland.[35] At first sight they made a hard-drinking, hard-living, foul-mouthed pair, but both were remarkable. Rothes, still relatively youthful, was commonly described as 'debauched' by contemporaries and never learned how to spell properly. The charge of loose morals, however, merely meant that he could drink prodigiously without showing the effects and carried on a long sexual affair with a young noblewoman. Never a statesman and not industrious by nature, his charming and genuinely pleasant character allied to some shrewdness to make him a born survivor. He had already been made Treasurer in place of Crawford-Lindsay, and now took the highest honour of Commissioner as a result of his prestige and independence from faction. Lauderdale, uncouth in looks and manners as ever, was not only a natural political leader and hard and systematic worker, but a scholar proficient in Hebrew as well as the more orthodox classical languages.

Both succeeded admirably in Scotland. Rothes delivered Charles's message about the Lords of the Articles, and Parliament acquiesced at once. The Scots were still acutely conscious that only the King's grace had delivered them from English occupation, and were anxious not to offend him. The formal parliamentary enquiry into the origins of the secret ballot revealed how Middleton had played off estates and King for his own ends. This, with Charles's displeasure, cost him the support of all but a dozen members. It also completed his disgrace at court. He was reduced, in the words of one observer, to spend his time 'in back lanes among persons obscure and malcontents' until he was sent into honourable and dangerous exile as Governor of Tangier. His old friend Newburgh also lost royal favour, and Mackenzie of Tarbet was deprived of his offices.[36]

Meanwhile, Lauderdale was establishing his credit. Much of the animosity against him in Scotland and England derived from his former reputation as a champion of the presbyterian Kirk. This he now spectacularly dispelled. First, he abjured the Covenants, and then he and Rothes conferred with the bishops about their problems. Most of these concerned the failure of parishioners of the clergy ejected by Middleton to attend the services of their new ministers. Accordingly, they agreed upon a statute which imposed fines on those attending illegal religious meetings and condemned as seditious deprived clergy who continued to preach. Lauderdale launched it in Parliament with a great speech in favour of episcopacy. This assisted the passage of the measure without a vote, and won the Earl the delighted gratitude of the bishops and their supporters in both kingdoms, and the praise of Charles himself.[37]

The two Scots now felt ready to go further, and in early August sent Charles a list of proposals for his consideration. One was to make provision for a Scottish army for use to browbeat his other kingdoms when he required. This greatly excited the King, who saw in it a possible means of putting pressure upon the English in particular, and he endorsed it. He also asked for the razing of references to the ballot from the records of Parliament if Rothes could obtain this. Indeed Rothes could. In quick succession, acts were passed to delete the paragraphs in question, to empower the monarch to levy 22,000 men whenever needed for service in Britain, and, for good measure, to rescind the statute restraining appeals to him. The Commissioner then dissolved the Parliament, leaving Charles overjoyed.[38] Not only had the two nobles continued Middleton's work of strengthening the Crown and episcopal Kirk in Scotland, but unlike their predecessor they had referred back to the King at each turn. They sent dispatches to Lauderdale's agent at Whitehall, Sir Robert Murray, who handed or reported them to Charles in private meetings and received his comments. Hence Lauderdale could tell his master 'you govern this poor kingdom yourself'. This was not quite true: the King was reverting to the closet politics which had come so naturally to him in the 1650s, and carried the danger that he could be persuaded by individuals and not by open debate. So he was, for Murray told Lauderdale smugly of a number of times when he had talked Charles out of objections to the two lords' proposals. In particular, the King was persuaded not to give Middleton a chance to answer the parliamentary enquiry.[39] No more than in England was it Charles's intention to replace one set of ministers with another. Middleton and his two henchmen fell together, and another of the Earl's clients, the Advocate, Fletcher, was sacked for corruption.[40] But the King wrote to Middleton's great ally Glencairn, the

Chancellor, assuring him of continued favour, and praised Lauderdale and Rothes for seeking nobody's ruin.[41] It was not a royal plan, but Glencairn's sudden death in the following May and their own sheer abilities ensured that by mid-1664 Scotland was dominated by the triumvirate of Rothes, Lauderdale, and Archbishop Sharp.

At the same time Ormonde and Orrery were defusing the situation in Ireland. On 9 March the Lord-Lieutenant answered the Commons, appealing to that very concern for public order which was in part responsible for their alarm. He accused them, gently, of having encouraged Protestant fears to the point at which many settlers were abandoning the country, and some hot-headed fools had formed a plot to pre-empt the Papists and to seize Dublin Castle. Orrery was busy with his honeyed tongue among the MPs, cajoling, soothing, and reasoning. Both wisely kept Charles's furious letter private, but leaked rumours of the King's displeasure. On 20 March, swayed by all these efforts, the Commons erased their February resolutions from their journals and agreed to let the commissioners serve out their legal term of office. Orrery went down to Munster to eject all Catholics and Protestant dissenters from the towns.[42] Ormonde stayed at Dublin to watch events. The conspiracy which he had revealed in March had certainly seemed genuine to him but no trials resulted. Either he had been mistaken or he was afraid that judicial action would deter a much larger plot of which he had heard simultaneously and was determined to let develop. For two months his spies kept him informed of its progress, until on the night before its outbreak (another attempt on the castle) he arrested the ringleaders. They represented a small group of Protestant extremists, concerned with winning toleration for dissenters and persecution of Catholics, and only three of them were hanged. But Ormonde gave massive publicity to the conspiracy as a nation-wide affair, revealed by chance and foiled in the nick of time. He savagely harried the dissenters, driving many ministers abroad, and confused, demoralized, and divided Protestant opinion further. Despite Charles, the crisis of February had ended peacefully in victory for the government.[43]

The effect of the revelations in May almost certainly prevented a furore over a ruling by the commissioners in August. It was in the case of Randal Macdonnell, Marquis of Antrim, and represents a study of the way in which Irish affairs could be handled, and mishandled, at court in this period. The Marquis was one of the greatest of the former Gaelic Catholic landowners, and repugnant to the bulk of Irish Protestants both for his personality and what he represented. In 1660, Charles had arrested him, and had him examined upon charges of collaborating with

Cromwell and defaming the late King. Nobody, however, proved these, and the corpulent, vainglorious noble set about claiming his estates. Under the Act of Settlement he was disqualified under three categories of 'guilt', but he could demonstrate that most of the actions in question had been committed while carrying out the commands of Charles I. His services to the royalist cause during the Great Civil War had been considerable and the Queen Mother (who had been involved with them) lobbied unwearyingly for his restoration. Ormonde was both impressed by the Marquis's arguments and unwilling to provoke the Protestants further by supporting him. In January 1663 Antrim got Charles to sign a letter recommending his claim to the consideration of the Irish Privy Council, which rejected it unanimously. The English Privy Council's Committee for Irish Affairs now reopened the matter, and in mid-July it declared unanimously in favour of the Marquis. The King relayed this verdict to the Council in Dublin, which replied that it was based upon inadequate evidence and did not provide for compensation of the present owners. They took till 31 July to frame this letter and Henrietta Maria, sensing trouble in the delay, begged Charles to send a direct order for restoration, to the commissioners. Bennet pleased her by agreeing to dispatch such a command by express messenger, and upon 11 August the King signed one. The commissioners received it, agreed to obey it by a single vote, and so outraged Protestants as Ormonde had feared. A few days after Charles had sent his imperative letter to the Commission, the Irish Privy Council's arguments of 31 July arrived, and left him embarrassed and confused. Carte, Ormonde's biographer, argued from this that Bennet had been bribed by the Marquis and the Queen Mother to conceal the dispatch from Dublin until the King had sent off his order to the commissioners. This view is refuted by Ormonde's own private enquiry into the affair, which noted that both Bennet and Clarendon had written to him on the 15th in apparent ignorance that Charles's order of the 11th had been sent. Bennet could have been disingenuous, but the Duke also discovered that the Secretary who had submitted the royal command for signature was not Sir Henry but Morice, the apparent foe of Catholics. There the evidence, and the puzzle, rests. Few episodes reveal so well the tortuous politics of the Restoration court, and the difficulty of charting them now.[44]

In the second half of 1663 the King continued to trouble his servants in Ireland in other matters than that of Antrim. Until dissuaded by the commissioners, he issued a stream of orders for the restoration of Catholics to urban property. Although just enough in principle, these not only cut across the work of the Commission but undid Orrery's purges in Munster which had reassured local Protestants. Though aware of the absence of free land in his western realm, he none the less ordered Ormonde to find a large piece of it as a gift to his new English favourite, Sir Charles Berkeley. He also instructed the Duke to have a delegation from the Parliament sent over to discuss Irish affairs with him. Ormonde believed that this would lead to direct friction between the King and the Houses, and humiliate the commissioners.[45] Still, Charles let himself be talked out of the first and the last of these projects, and accepted his Lord-Lieutenant's proposal for another Explanatory Bill to complete the settlement. The commissioners' term of office was due to expire in August, with only a fraction of the land claims determined, and nobody felt it politic to renew their powers. Hence the new bill was crucially important.

It was redrafted successively by the best minds present in Dublin, including the commissioners, Orrery and Anglesey. The result was a measure which pleased nobody and which was so technical at points that neither Ormonde nor Clarendon could understand it. None the less, it had many virtues. It provided for a voluntary surrender of one-sixth of their property by all owners of new estates to create enough spare territory to make compensation possible each time an estate was restored. It gave firm legal sanction to the King's grants to Bennet and Anglesey, and to the restoration of Antrim. And, above all, it was the best compromise possible. The bill was sent to Charles in November, and found him already irritated because he claimed to have detected clauses derogatory to the Crown in several minor measures sent over for approval. With more sense of justice than expediency, he entrusted it to a very large committee of the English Privy Council, and invited every interested party, including the Catholics represented by Sir Nicholas Plunket, to comment on it. After a month the committee despaired of the task and got Charles to ask the former Commissioners for Claims to redraft the measure. Another spring of discussions came to nothing and at last, in May 1664, Ormonde was summoned to Whitehall to adjudicate. Thus, four years after the Restoration, the problem of the Irish land settlement was still not resolved, but at least the island was quiet while the talking went on, and on, in England. The army was also calm once more, after a distribution of £50,000, borrowed by the English government from Londoners and shipped over in late 1663. One minor puzzle is left by these transactions. It is provided by the comment left by one young Anglo-Irish gentleman who talked to Charles about the Explanatory Bill and was amazed to find that the King thoroughly understood it. This is so at variance with Charles's usual attitude towards Irish affairs and towards business in general that it requires comment. Had the King, for some reason, taken the time to digest a measure from which his Lord-Lieutenant and Chancellor recoiled? Or was the young man's own knowledge of the measure so imperfect that his sovereign was able to impress him with a smattering of facts? The evidence allows of no answer.[46]

By now the regime at Whitehall had benefited enormously from the same phenomenon which had assisted that in Dublin: a rallying of loyalty following the disclosure of a plot against it. By mid-1663, ironically, England seemed as peaceful as it had ever been before. There were rumours of a projected rising in Durham and Yorkshire, but such stories had come in from the provinces to the Secretaries of State in almost every month since the Restoration. Arrests and searches by justices and militiamen had revealed no substance to any of them, and so it seemed to prove with this northern scare. It is a sign of Charles's feelings of security that he went upon his first provincial progress. He had intended one in 1661, to Boscobel, Moseley, and Worcester, but this was cancelled when the Cavalier Parliament proved unexpectedly difficult.[47] Now, from August to early October, he visited Bath, Bristol, and Oxford, being entertained by local magnates and corporations: the hospitality was magnificent, if the speeches sometimes lengthy.[48] A few days after his return to Whitehall, the warnings from Yorkshire recurred. Bennet commented that 'all circumstances make us conclude it a false alarm'. Anglesey wrote to Ormonde on the 13th that he wished people would stop talking of plots. In reality, during the night before those words were written, groups of rebels had gathered in Yorkshire and Westmorland, convinced that they were part of a great nation-wide rising. They were the dupes of over-imaginative republican die-hards and *agents provocateurs*, and the largest muster of them numbered thirty-one. All dispersed without attempting anything. Nevertheless, an armed uprising had actually occurred, based upon groups of Protestant radicals seeking religious liberty, and it was arguable that only the vigilance of the local gentry had prevented the situation from becoming serious.

Having initially failed to take the northern rebellion seriously, the government proceeded to punish and exploit it to the fullest extent. Despite the small numbers involved, the rebels had spanned the spectrum of dissent from presbyterians to Quakers, and Charles, after his efforts on behalf of these groups, felt personally betrayed. He struck back savagely, and indiscriminately, at nonconformists. When judges left London to try those rounded up in the north, he urged them to proceed with all possible severity. They did, by considering those who had talked of rising to be of equal guilt with those who had taken arms. Twenty-six men were condemned to death and all but two were executed, most being politically unimportant as Charles offered a pardon to leaders who turned

King's Evidence. The gentry of Westmorland succeeded in delaying his messenger carrying a reprieve for the agitator of the local rebels, just long enough to hang the man along with his dupes. The King pressed the northern magistrates and deputy-lieutenants to provide yet more prisoners and examinations, as ammunition for the tremendous publicity given to the event in L'Estrange's press. He explicitly withdrew his protection from Margaret Fell, a Lancashire Quaker leader who had impressed him in 1660 and been spared by local justices since because of his favour. Along with hundreds of other dissenters she was committed to prison. Further south, the Privy Council seized the opportunity to arrest those surviving leaders of the Commonwealth who were still at liberty in England and could be considered dangerous. Some were released upon giving oaths, bonds, or promises to go into exile, but others were detained in fortresses where the squalid conditions killed them.

When the Cavalier Parliament reassembled on 21 March, the government was ready for it with a programme based upon lessons drawn from the rebellion. Charles commenced his speech by alluding to the event and insisting that the danger of further insurrection remained acute. He then demanded the repeal of the Triennial Act of 1641, which obliged a monarch to call a new Parliament within three years of the dissolution of the last. This, he insisted, had encouraged the rebels, who had misunderstood it to mean that the Cavalier Parliament, having lasted longer than three years, was now invalid. He closed by calling attention to the remaining fiscal deficit, but asking for an attack upon tax evasion rather than more taxation. Behind him he now had a united ministry, intent not merely upon working through clients and friends but through every MP holding a royal office or pension, a list of whom was compiled before the reconvention. Clarendon was ill again for the first weeks of the session, but on his recovery worked so hard for royal policies in the Upper House that he declared himself 'absolutely dazed'.

The Commons repealed the Triennial Act within a week, while back-benchers were still arriving. The opposition doubled in size in that time, and was eloquently led. Temple was still trying to bully his way into office, and was joined by John Vaughan, a Welsh royalist who had been rewarded at the Restoration but for unknown reasons now commenced a career of harrying the government. Nevertheless, the measure passed by a comfortable fifty-seven votes, not just because of the determination of the court interest but because many MPs genuinely believed Charles's linking of the Act with the rebellion. It went through the Lords in three days without a division. The statute of repeal declared that no more than three years should intervene between Parliaments, but there now remained no mechanism by which this could be achieved if a monarch chose to disregard it.

Next the MPs attacked the means by which rebellion could be fomented. The prosecutions during the winter had revealed all the more clearly the need for a statute to facilitate the prevention of nonconformist religious meetings. The MPs provided one by reviving the Conventicle Bill which Charles had killed off in 1663. Now he helped it through, turning a deaf ear to Quaker deputations begging for his protection and prolonging the session to ensure that the statute passed. It decreed fines or imprisonment for the first two offences and an enormous fine or seven years' transportation for the third. The only qualification of the Act was that it was limited to four years, either as a gesture of moderation or (in the wake of the repeal of the Triennial Act) a further guarantee of the indispensability of Parliament. It was enforced with ferocity in many counties and cities, urged on by the King, who regarded the Quakers with the same cold fury as he did his other protégé, Bristol. The Privy Council actively encouraged persecution of them, and Charles was anxious that as many as possible should suffer transportation. What saved a large number of dissenters from this fate was the central government's perennial problem of control over its own officers. Not merely were JPs or Lord-Lieutenants frequently too lazy or good-natured to round up nonconformist meetings, but royal judges sometimes showed clemency. One who had served the Protectorate, Sir Matthew Hale, reduced a fine inflicted by a colleague upon a presbyterian from £100 to £2. A former royalist, Sir Orlando Bridgeman, devised a declaration of allegiance for Quakers instead of the oath which their beliefs would not let them take.

Within eight days of Charles's opening speech, the Commons had also set to work on the problem of tax evasion, and this time they tackled it properly. The statute which resulted sliced through the whole web of local loyalty and intimidation, by empowering the King to appoint his own officers to inspect houses. During 1664 the government's financial position was improving in any case, as national prosperity slowly recovered from years of war, insecurity, and heavy taxation. Revenue from the customs and excise grew significantly as the new farmers found it possible to pay their rents. Charles's financial ministers pressed their local officers to punish defaulters and gave cash rewards to those who obeyed. The public debt was still considerable, and the annual revenue about £¼ million short of expenditure, but if the increase in income continued, it seemed likely that a balance would in time be achieved.[49]

In a different sense, a balance had been achieved in the monarch's constitutional position by 1664. Ireland remained unsettled, but some

Catholics had been restored without provoking Protestants to rebellion and the Crown retained the respect of all as an arbitrator. The King's power in Scotland had increased further, and he had prevented it from being wielded by a single faction without close reference to his wishes. In England he had failed to gain a standing army, but the reorganized militia had proved capable of dealing with discontent. He had been thwarted in his attempts to dispense Catholics and dissenters from penal legislation, but for the time being he wished that dissenters be persecuted in any case. The revenue was still inadequate, but was improving naturally. He had received some snubs and humiliations from the Commons, but retained the power to prevent their bills from passing and regained that of choosing when a new Parliament was called without reference to the system appointed by the defunct Triennial Act. He had failed so far to produce an heir, but while his brother survived then the dynasty was safe. The regime had not regained the popularity which it had lost in 1661–2. His morals and those of his court remained the subjects of gossip and censure, and Clarendon remained the most detested of his ministers. The Londoners called the great mansion which he was building in Westminster 'New Dunkirk', believing it was paid for by the sale of the port. As long as the Crown ruled successfully, however, it would remain strong. Its immediate future appeared to be a steady and peaceful growth in security, achieved principally at the expense of religious and political nonconformity. This was not to be. The field of government activity eclipsed since Charles's marriage, foreign affairs, was suddenly to dominate all others, and the course of the reign was to be wrenched into another channel.

Charles's First Dutch War, 1664–1667

⚬⚬⚬

IN the first sixty years of this century, English historians such as David
Ogg and Sir Keith Feiling, and Dutch colleagues such as Pieter Geyl,
assembled a common view of British foreign policy in the years 1661–4.
It was made to seem cautious, amateurish, and unsuccessful. At its centre
were placed three most undiplomatic personalities, Clarendon and his
two protégés Sir George Downing and Baron Holles. Clarendon, while
as ignorant of languages and as peremptory as ever, was also censured
for being so obsessed with domestic dangers that he sought peace abroad
at far too high a price. Downing, sent back to The Hague as envoy
extraordinary, was portrayed as seized by a pathological hatred of the
Dutch which led him to deal with them in a tone certain to produce
resentment. Holles, made ambassador to France, was dismissed as a creaky
old Puritan, interested only in the trivialities of his office and deficient
in French and tact alike. As a result, the British blundered into war
in 1664 without a single ally and faced with a potentially formidable
coalition.

This picture stands in need of revision. Clarendon's papers and the State
Papers Foreign do not seem to suggest that the British were handicapped
by a fear of rebellion. Instead they were constrained by the international
situation itself. They had thrown away their freedom of action by the
treaty with Portugal. King Felipe's immediate impulse at this was to declare
war upon England, but his Council persuaded him to concentrate upon
the Portuguese instead. The Spanish resolved to acquire allies for future
vengeance upon Charles, and to foment insurrections in his kingdoms,
but succeeded in neither. Nevertheless, they recalled their ambassador,
and the two nations attacked each other freely on the oceans and in the
West Indies. In 1663 the British expeditionary force landed in Portugal,
under the old warrior Inchiquin, and played a decisive role in the defeat
of the Spanish army under Charles's former host Juan-José. The friendship
of the Portuguese did not balance the hatred of Felipe, as they rapidly
became an encumbrance to Charles: in default of the promised French
aid he had to pay Inchiquin's men out of his own dowry. An attempt to

cut his losses by mediating peace between the Iberian monarchies received support from neither.

The hostility of Spain hampered the British in their wider diplomacy also. The greatest nightmare of the French was to be opposed by a combination of Britain, Spain, and the United Netherlands. The Anglo-Spanish enmity now removed any chance of this, and meant that for Louis XIV the friendship of the Dutch had become more valuable than that of Charles. If they could be bought off, then Felipe would be isolated and vulnerable to a renewed French attack. As for the Dutch, their greatest fear was to be caught in a pincer between the British and French. Thus they had a vested interest in seeking the goodwill of both, but if a choice became necessary then France, at once more directly menacing and less of a commercial rival, was the more promising ally. This pattern explains the developments of 1661–4. The British tried to win an alliance from the French and trade concessions from the Dutch, and failed. Instead Louis XIV and the United Netherlands made an offensive and defensive pact. All that Britain could win from the Dutch was an agreement to extinguish claims to compensation from their rival merchants dating from before 1654 in European waters and 1659 in the tropics, and to confirm Charles's possession of Pulo Run, the East Indian island gained by Cromwell. A mutual arbitration procedure was set up to deal with commercial disputes. It is difficult to see how, given the weakness of their diplomatic position, Charles's representatives could have done much better.[1]

Nor is it easy to accept all the traditional disparagement of the personalities concerned. Certainly, Clarendon's self-importance offended foreign envoys as well as colleagues, Downing sent home the occasional tirade against the Dutch, and Holles was indeed something of a dinosaur. There was an air of improvisation about aspects of foreign policy: for example, the Chancellor asked Downing to forward no more documents in Dutch because nobody at court could decipher them.[2] But Clarendon's lack of languages did not greatly hamper him, for the Irishman Richard Belling translated French and Spanish papers for him. He forwarded enough money to Downing, despite his government's lack of it, for Sir George to construct a spy system at The Hague and to obtain copies of all the resolutions of the States-General.[3] Downing himself believed that a more efficient revenue would strengthen Charles with far better certainty than war. When he disparaged the Dutch, he did not refer to the whole nation, but to the States of Holland, England's real trade rivals, and their gifted leader Jan de Witt. It was his theory that the inland provinces would not risk war with England for the sake of Holland's interests, and that resolute support for the Orangists would topple de Witt from power. Once Sir George himself had realized the actual strength of de Witt's position, he worked with the man for hours to produce drafts of a mutually satisfactory Anglo-Dutch agreement. It was he who proposed the date 1659 for the acceptance of claims by traders, intending it to cover all regions of the globe. The King's commissioners at Whitehall drove a harder bargain. In a sense, Downing's evaluation of the position of Holland had some truth, for the States-General forced de Witt to grant more to England than he wished.[4]

If Downing was not as obtusely belligerent as has been thought, Clarendon was not as timid. He gathered evidence to support the conspiracy against de Witt, only warning that some treaty with the Dutch should be agreed first in case the coup failed. In 1661 he told the French that if their proposals were to be considered then they would have to be delivered in a less haughty tone. When Louis XIV invited Charles to join the Franco-Dutch alliance, Clarendon noted that the French had guaranteed Dutch fishing rights in British waters and commented that his king saw no point in joining a pact 'against himself'. He told Downing that if the Dutch now felt emboldened to get tougher with the British then they would have to be fought. The Anglo-Dutch trade agreement was made because the United Netherlands, not Britain, resolved deadlock with concessions.[5] But then, although he played a leading part in foreign as in domestic policy, the Chancellor was one of several participants in decision-making. Important questions were submitted to the King's 'inner ring' of advisers, usually Clarendon, James, Southampton, Albemarle, Ashley, and (later) Bennet. The Chancellor and Downing helped shape the Anglo-Dutch agreement, but it was made by the commissioners appointed in 1660, with Morice drafting the papers. On taking the post of Secretary, Bennet assumed the responsibility for briefing envoys to the Iberian lands and apparently persuaded Charles into tentative moves to mend his relations with Spain. These culminated in the appointment of Fanshaw as ambassador there in early 1664.[6]

Charles's part in all this varied with the nation concerned. His only role in the talks with the Dutch was to make occasional stage entrances to urge the respective representatives to complete a treaty. By contrast, he attempted to establish a private correspondence with his fellow monarch and cousin Louis, through the mediation of his sister (and Louis's sister-in-law) Minette. His recorded personal reactions to diplomatic developments consisted of outbursts of anger at infringements of what he considered his rights. The States of Holland provoked a spectacular example by trying to hoodwink him into letting them act as effective guardians of his nephew

Wilhelm. It was prompted by principle not affection, for having won his point and asserted his control over the boy, Charles lost direct interest in him. He was left with another of his joint guardians, the Dowager Princess. Charles had a particularly difficult time with Louis, who not only ignored his invitation to correspond but tried to pare down certain traditional claims of the English. The young French monarch, freed from Mazarin's tutelage, was intent upon asserting himself against all other rulers, and if the Pope was not spared this treatment the King of England certainly would not be. Charles found himself required to shed his antique title of 'King of France' (left over from Edward III), with the demand of English warships to be saluted by all French vessels and the right of the English ambassador to precede French princes upon state occasions. He reacted to these proposals with surprise and irritation, refusing the first and last utterly and only renouncing the right of salute in waters south of Brittany. This business of the respect due to his warships was very close to the King's heart: when one of his captains failed to make a Swedish vessel strike sails to him in the Thames, Charles deprived the man of his command.[7]

There was, overall, no development to British foreign policy in the early 1660s: it existed in a limbo from which it would probably have been wrenched by the renewal of the Franco-Spanish conflict in 1667. What pushed it instead into war with the Dutch was a side-current, the involvement of the court in merchant ventures to the tropics. The process almost certainly began with Charles's cousin Rupert, who despite his quarrel with the King at Paris had crossed to England after the Restoration with clear expectation of being supported. He was not disappointed, for although Charles received him frigidly, he accepted him at court and on to the Privy Council and awarded him a large pension. It is probable that his voyages had inspired him with an idea which became reality a short while after his return: a new chartered company, the Royal African, intended to trade in the products of The Gambia and Guinea. He was joined in this by that other underemployed prince about Whitehall, James, and by the King himself, Bennet, Crofts, Berkeley, Jermyn, Ashley, Albemarle, and Sandwich. All became major shareholders, with James as president.

It remains unclear whether the Company was aware of how strong the Dutch hold had become on the commerce in which it proposed to deal. If not, it was swiftly informed, for its first representatives in West Africa were attacked by their rivals and unable to do business with a native population in awe of the former. Any other English trading organization would have responded by adding to the perennial chorus of merchant complaint. This one instead fitted out a warship under one of Rupert's former captains, Robert Holmes, with instructions to protect its interests.

This sailed in the autumn of 1663, and in the following eight months Holmes cheerfully interpreted his orders by capturing Dutch forts and shipping and loading up with booty. During early 1664, growing still bolder, the shareholders of the Royal African Company set up another, the Corporation of the Royal Fishery, which was intended to operate in the North Sea and again struck at Dutch interests. Simultaneously the government, acting officially this time, decided to put an end to the nuisance created by New Amsterdam, the Dutch colony which represented a smugglers' haven in the midst of England's North American possessions. Charles granted it to his brother and sent a force to seize it. This was duly effected in the summer, and the settlement was rechristened New York in James's honour. For good measure the King granted his governor of Barbados permission to take the island of St Lucia from its French settlers.[8] Apparently Downing was responsible for the notion that Parliament might be utilized to increase the pressure on the Dutch. In March a Commons committee upon trading problems was packed with clients of James and of Bennet. It invited London merchants to submit their grievances, condensed all those concerning the Dutch into a catalogue, and presented the House with a resolution filled with patriotic enthusiasm, inviting the King to demand redress. It was passed unanimously.[9]

None of these actions, however, were intended to produce war. The English government expected the Dutch, confronted with this display of confident aggression, to concede the claims of London merchants to compensation and to a greater share of tropical trade. It was encouraged in this by the new strength of its position at home, and by an outbreak of plague in Holland, which was expected to sap the energies of its rulers. Downing had long advised a policy of resolute pressure to exact concessions from the States-General, and now presented his master's demands with determination. Yet he could not, himself, be held responsible for the English decision to get tough: in the spring of 1664 he was thinking in terms of an alliance between Britain, Spain, and the United Netherlands to contain the French. From April onwards some people were talking of the possibility of real fighting, but in rather fanciful fashion. Most prominent among them was James, who was longing for a return to military service and whom the French ambassador was to call 'the true author' of the war. He was seconded by Albemarle, who had fought the Dutch under the Commonwealth and spoke slightingly of them. But the policy of confrontation was opposed by Clarendon, who feared that it might make Britain more vulnerable to the Spanish and to rebels, and by Southampton, who thought it financially reckless. Their misgivings were shared by James's own secretary William Coventry, a dour, industrious, and clever individual who had been employed by Charles in exile and was now one of the rising men at court. Unhappily, Coventry suffered the moral ailment of the latter breed: whatever he said privately, he encouraged Charles to deal roughly with the Dutch when it was clear that this was what the King wished to do. And indeed it was: he told his sister Minette that he was convinced that the United Netherlands would back down.

During summer and autumn the English sabre-rattling accordingly grew more vigorous. In May Charles decided to parade twelve warships in the Channel, and in August to send them to Guinea under Rupert himself to follow up Holmes's work there. In September the news of the English conquests in Africa and America arrived, sending the Londoners wild with joy. The restored monarchy suddenly seemed to be achieving gains as glorious as Cromwell's at no cost. Clarendon was rewarded for his relative pacifism by being rumoured to be in the pay of the Dutch (instead of, as before, the French), and Charles was delighted to enjoy a brief tremendous popularity. In reality his policy had already borne deadly fruit, on 12 August when the leaders of Holland had persuaded or tricked those of the other provinces into sending their Mediterranean fleet to re-establish Dutch supremacy in African waters. The English did not discover this until mid-October, when Rupert's expedition was only just preparing to sail. By then it was too late for the Prince to intercept the rival force, and the report in itself exposed the fallacy of believing that the United Netherlands would capitulate without a struggle. Charles, feeling unable to withdraw now, made two still more threatening moves: he ordered all available naval forces to concentrate around Rupert's ships at Portsmouth, with James himself in command, and instructed them to seize Dutch vessels.

Only one factor could still curb English aggression: money. Charles I's foreign wars had failed for precisely this reason, his Parliaments voting sums by the ineffective method of 'subsidy'. His war effort had collapsed in a welter of misunderstanding and recrimination. This time a promising start was made when the City corporation expressed its enthusiasm by lending the King £100,000 in June and a similar sum in October. These were, however, relatively small sums compared with what was needed, and only a parliamentary grant could supply that. Accordingly, the government prepared for the new session with the same care and unity with which it had met the last. Charles opened it on 24 November, by portraying the Dutch as aggressors and appealing for £800,000 to put out a fleet capable of saving English trade. The following day a back-bencher primed by the court proposed the sum of £2½ million. In the ensuing debate not a voice was raised agaisnt the principle of sending out a fleet, and even opponents of the government such as Temple and Vaughan felt it expedient to add to the belligerent rhetoric. The huge sum was eventually voted, being not merely the greatest supply ever made to an English monarch but destined to remain so until the next century. Three days later the House decided to raise it by the effective process of 'assessment', over three years. The MPs thus acted precipitately to preserve their country from foreign enemies, as they had done in the spring to defend it from internal foes, and in doing so carried out a reform of extraordinary taxation due for about a hundred years. Coventry called the government 'supernaturally successful', while the French ambassador thought the Londoners 'intoxicated' with the prospect of war.

Events now made a stately progress towards calamity. On 18 December a special committee of the Privy Council, including all the leading ministers except Clarendon, decided to issue a general order to their countrymen to prey upon Dutch shipping. This they declared to be in lieu of the compensation due to English merchants. Simultaneously, news arrived that the Dutch had swept West Africa almost clean of English ships and garrisons, and the credit of the Royal African Company was ruined. At The Hague, Downing's blustering proved to have achieved equally little. The States-General rejected the English claims, demanded the return of New Amsterdam, and was making its own battle-fleet ready for the spring. With a terrible shock, the Privy Council realized that a full-scale war was about to commence, and the royal brothers began clamouring for French arbitration. When Holmes reported back from his expedition he was clapped in the Tower. But it was too late, neither side possessing room for compromise. Having so assiduously whipped his people into a fury of bellicosity, Charles could not be seen to back down, while the States of Holland had their own turbulent citizenry to reckon with. The English government decided at length to put a brave face on things and to get its declaration of war made first. On 4 March 1665 two gorgeously apparelled heralds proclaimed it in London, while the crowds cheered lustily.

As the proclamation was repeated throughout the provinces, reputedly with the same acclamations, Charles set to work to encourage his principal supporters. He had already entrusted the disposal of captured ships and goods to a commission of nine Privy Counsellors rather than one, to prevent jealousy. Now he gave Charles Berkeley a grander peerage, the Earldom of Falmouth, and raised Bennet at last to the Lords. As 'Lady Bennet' was the nickname of a notorious Westminster procuress, Sir Henry delicately selected a territorial title, of Baron Arlington. At the same time the King appealed to royalist sentiment by creating two new peers and promoting three others for services to his cause during the Civil War and Interregnum.[10]

These steps helped to divert attention from the fact that not only was the outbreak of war in itself a failure of English policy but that Charles was without any allies. During the autumn of 1664 he had dispatched envoys to Denmark, Sweden, and France. The discussions with the Scandinavian powers were hampered by carelessness on the part of Clarendon, who allowed his respective agents, in default of clear guidance, to draft mutually incompatible treaties. But what ruined all was the attitude of Louis XIV. The French King's own interests lay in keeping Britain and the United Netherlands hostile to each other and grateful to himself. He had accordingly no wish to fight Charles, but none either to let him increase his power at the expense of Louis's Dutch ally. Thus as soon as the English discussions with the Danish King reached a promising stage, the French reminded him that his interests upon the Continent depended heavily upon their goodwill. The Danes recoiled, and Charles was left isolated. Certainly he had miscalculated in undervaluing Dutch pride, but in the last resort he had been correct in believing that he could fight if necessary. His fatal error had been his failure to realize that his royal cousin would be opposed to him too.[11]

For generations it was the custom among historians to hail Charles as one of the founders of the Royal Navy, both versed and involved in its affairs as few monarchs before or since. In 1975 A. Turnbull provided a more accurate picture, for the first half of the King's 'effective' reign. Charles certainly understood the details of building and sailing ships and of running dockyards. He had his own beloved yachts, and the delight in the sea and its pleasures which he had gained in Jersey never left him. But he intervened little in the running of the navy. He often attended the launching of new warships, received naval officials, and authorized major policy decisions for them. Nevertheless, his chief personal interest in the new ships seems normally to have been in the details of the gilding of their ornate carved sterns. And the decisions which he made were always taken upon the advice of his Privy Council, his brother (who was a conscientious if unimaginative Lord High Admiral), and the Navy Board.[12]

The latter carried most of the burden of daily naval administration. It consisted, by 1665, of a Treasurer, a Comptroller, a Surveyor, and a Clerk, assisted by five 'commissioners' (one of whom was Coventry) and responsible directly to James. The team contained much bad feeling and some incompetence, but its corporate achievement on the outbreak of this Dutch war was praiseworthy. By April they had concentrated a fleet of 107 ships, about forty of which were converted merchantmen compulsorily hired from the real owners. Supplies proved a harder matter, although royal forests provided timber in huge quantities, all the tar, hemp, canvas, guns, and wadding had to be purchased from private contractors. The enormous 'Royal Aid' voted by Parliament only began to be collected in some counties in May, and the loans gained on the security of it were not adequate to the navy's needs. Many suppliers were paid in promises instead of cash, and by summer were refusing further orders. To obtain seamen, orders were sent to the vice-admirals of the maritime counties, and to the government in Edinburgh, to press fixed quotas. These, usually the same magnates who provided Lord-Lieutenants, set the justices and constables to work on the matters, sometimes prompted by agents sent by James. In many ports, rather than face the horrific dangers and the risible pay of the royal service, sailors hid or fled. Magistrates either failed to fulfil their quotas or did so by pressing landsmen, often beggars or criminals. Once brought to the naval bases these 'new ragged men' (as Coventry termed them) deserted in droves.[13]

For all the complaints and recriminations of the officials, by mid-April there rode off Harwich a fleet which was probably the best that any English monarch had ever sent forth. James, Rupert, and Sandwich commanded its three squadrons, and their captains included the best surviving officers from the royalist and republican navies. In May it cruised off Holland for three weeks, challenging the enemy, and then put back to Suffolk to take on victuals. There it was approached by the most powerful fleet that the United Netherlands had ever collected, about its equal in numbers, and on 3 June battle was joined off Lowestoft. All day the guns could be heard faintly, in Whitehall. The following morning definite news arrived of the result: one of the greatest victories in British naval history. Charles's fleet had sunk or captured at least twenty-six ships for the loss of one, chased the enemy to their harbours, and won the mastery of the North Atlantic. Yet the King was one of the few people in his three kingdoms who did not rejoice. A single cannon shot had dismembered three of his courtiers as they stood next to James upon his deck, spraying him with blood and brains. One was Clancarty's heir, another was one of Orrery's family, and the third was the new Earl of Falmouth, the King's best friend. As the bells rang and the bonfires flared through London, Charles retired and wept.

The individual and national rewards of victory were now reaped. The principal beneficiary of the former was not a sea commander but Coventry, thereby recognizing the essential contribution of the naval administration. Getting a knighthood and a seat on the Privy Council, he became a force in national politics. James, despite the outstanding courage and resolution which he had shown as Admiral, was deprived of an active command. Charles was so shaken by his brother's close escape from the ball which had killed his favourite that, to avoid a possible succession crisis, he resolved to keep him ashore. Overall control of the fleet was offered to Rupert and Sandwich, but the Prince refused to accept a divided authority. So the Earl, once the principal seaman of Oliver Cromwell, achieved the sole command. The national benefit of success appeared to be, at last, the acquisition of two foreign allies. One was the most belligerent of the mitred rulers of Germany, the Prince-Bishop of Münster, who had claims in the eastern Netherlands. In June he signed a treaty with Charles whereby he would attack the Dutch with an army paid partly from English subsidies. The King of Denmark, reconsidering his position, offered a pact between his country, England, and Sweden to plunder Dutch shipping. The States-General offered concessions, and their ally Louis XIV, who was still passive in the conflict, was happy to mediate. To increase Dutch eagerness for a treaty, Charles sent off Sandwich with the fleet on 6 July to sweep the North Sea clean of Dutch merchantmen.

At this point, as so often in this King's career, golden prospects began to dissolve in frustration and disappointment. An outbreak of plague in London swelled into one of the greatest epidemics in the capital's history, halting its commerce. Charles and his ministers fled in July to Hampton Court, and then to Salisbury. They settled in that pleasant country town of miniature canals until late September, when they moved to Oxford to meet Parliament. While in Wiltshire, they received news of an unnecessary naval failure. On 2 August an English squadron attacked a rich Dutch merchant convoy in the Danish-held port of Bergen. The governor of the town, having received no instructions from his monarch about the embryo Anglo-Danish alliance, opened fire, beat off the attackers, and inflicted over four hundred casualties. It was a humiliating episode, and damaged the promising talks in Copenhagen. Meanwhile, the Dutch leaders had laboured to rebuild their fleet while offering peace terms. On the day of the Bergen fiasco it set sail, under better commanders, to challenge Sandwich. Instead of fighting, the Earl found his own crews immobilized off the Suffolk coast because of a breakdown in the victualling system. On 30 August they were able to put out, and spent two weeks chasing the Dutch warships and merchant convoy through a series of terrible storms. They managed to capture thirty-two vessels before giving up and dispersing to the dockyards for the winter. Back in Salisbury, the Dutch terms proved to be less of a surrender than Charles had expected. The Hollanders had grabbed Pulo Run at the opening of hostilities, and proposed to keep it in exchange for New York. In addition the States-General would allow the English to maintain two forts in West Africa and would co-operate in the making of regulations to prevent further commercial clashes. Charles demanded all these concessions, plus Pulo Run, a third African fort, an indemnity, and compensation to English merchants. The Dutch found this package utterly unacceptable, and called upon Louis to honour their alliance.

Two more developments completed the public mood of disenchantment. When Sandwich's prizes were brought into the Thames, it was found that he had divided some of the goods among his flag officers. A share was due to them, and Charles approved the action. Nevertheless, rumour soon complained that Sandwich had understated the value of the commodities taken (and the modern evidence indicates that indeed he did) and stories of fraud and theft began to run wild. It was widely felt that the navy had disgraced itself. A few weeks later, the Dutch fleet suddenly reappeared off the Thames. The English warships were by then laid up, and the enemy blockaded the river until they in turn ran into problems of supply and disease and retired. It was a clear signal that, despite Lowestoft, the year had produced a drawn fight.[14]

All the while that it campaigned against the foreign foe, the government continued determined to wipe out internal enemies. In March 1665 Clarendon wrote to all JPs on Charles's instruction, to repress all unauthorized meetings and to report colleagues who seemed lax in the work. On fleeing London, the King sent James to supervise the northern counties and left Albemarle to watch the capital. From the almost deserted palace of Whitehall, the ageing general ruthlessly set his soldiers upon a round of searches and interrogations. In early August they did turn up a real plot, by a small group of former republican soldiers who intended to seize the city. Eight were eventually hanged, and Albemarle carried out a series of mass arrests of religious dissenters, vainly looking for accomplices. The obscure little conspiracy disturbed the government so much that it did not publicize it. Instead, Charles sent urgent orders to his lord-lieutenants to mount guards and to hunt for disaffection. Many obeyed, especially in the North where James led the campaign. Yet no further evidence of conspiracy was found.[15]

The possibility of rebellion in Scotland gave Charles additional reason for concern. This war was essentially an English one, fought for English interests, into which the northern kingdom had been dragged because of the union of crowns. The great bulk of Scottish foreign trade was with the United Netherlands, and the conflict produced immediate economic distress in the land and a sharp drop in customs receipts, with no benefits to be expected from the outcome. Furthermore, the traditional contacts between Dutch and Scottish presbyterianism meant that many of the Scots forced into exile by Middleton's religious policy were now in Holland, providing ideal agents for sedition. To worsen the impression of peril, at the time that the war broke out, the bishops were sending complaints to Whitehall of the increasing numbers and insolence of religious conventicles and the disinterest of many local magistrates in stopping them. The policies which Charles inaugurated in response to these problems have been condemned by the most recent historian of the subject as 'exploitative',[16] but (except in the sense that the whole war was unjust to Scots) they hardly merit the term. All that he required was that the Edinburgh government should be capable of protecting itself against rebellion or invasion. In September 1664 he ordered that the fines due under the Act of Indemnity, which had never been demanded as the King wished to make those vulnerable grateful, should now be collected. They were to be applied to defence. In the autumn the ruling three, Lauderdale, Sharp, and Rothes, met in London and agreed to have a Synod of the Kirk called in 1665 to concert action. Rothes was commissioned to preside over it, and also to command the armed forces of the kingdom. In the following March, Charles sent orders to Edinburgh to disarm all private persons in the Lowlands and to stock up the state magazines with the proceeds. With this instruction came another, to have new taxation imposed upon the nation to pay for defence, preferably by an emergency Convention of Estates rather than a Parliament.

In reacting to these instructions, the people ruling Scotland found themselves in a double bind. On the one hand, the effect of the war upon the public revenue was even worse than feared. Excise as well as customs receipts plummeted, and when Rothes put a garrison in the Shetland Isles he found that he could not pay it. Nor could he (as Lord Treasurer) provide the pensions due to various nobles to encourage their loyalty. On the other hand, the deepening economic recession made discontent, in Rothes's words, 'an epidemical disease', and asking more money was dangerous. The Synod was postponed indefinitely for fear of giving complaints a platform, and the Privy Council was terrified of calling a Convention for the same reason. The fines under the Act of Indemnity had been intended to compensate royalists, so that collecting them and spending them on soldiers meant disappointing old enemies and friends alike. In the event, it was thought wise to demand arms only from known dissenters in the most disaffected area, the south-west, and not many were received. Nevertheless, the Privy Council was forced by sheer necessity to summon a Convention. This proved surprisingly loyal and co-operative. It voted a tax on land, though by a rather inefficient old system, which enabled the regime to meet its costs for the year.

In coping with this crisis, the Scottish ministers had to reckon with a perpetual problem, which equally affected their counterparts in Dublin: that of depending upon a monarch hundreds of miles away. Distance gave enemies a wonderful opportunity for defamation and misrepresentation, if they could reach the King's ear. In 1664–5 two Privy Counsellors flew into a panic on learning that bishops had accused them at Whitehall of tolerating religious dissent. Rothes shared their reaction when told that his proverbial taste for drink had been represented to Charles as a serious weakness. Ambitious politicians could also use physical separation to destroy friendships between ministers, and mutual friends of Sharp, Rothes, and Lauderdale often urged them to ignore reports designed to arouse suspicion of each other. Such warnings were the more necessary in that the triumvirate was based upon convenience, not nature, and the vacant post of Chancellor proved a test of this. The bishops were determined to have it awarded to somebody prepared to campaign against dissent, and Sharp thought that an excellent solution would be to take it himself. Rothes supported his candidature, as did the English Archbishop Sheldon, but Charles himself and Lauderdale seem to have shared an instinctive distrust of the unctuous and ambitious primate. In the end, the post was just left vacant and Rothes was asked to fulfil its political function of sealing state documents. He and Sharp found themselves united again, in horror at the financial exactions ordered by the King, through Lauderdale, for national defence (though who at Whitehall urged Charles to command them, we simply do not know). Yet even the Archbishop and the Commissioner were not wholly of one mind, the latter, with most of the Privy Council, preferring to forgo the great attack on religious dissent urged by Sharp, for fear of making political disaffection worse.

Lauderdale's residence at court obviously made him especially powerful, but he did not have a monopoly of the King's attention. The case of Alexander Burnet, Archbishop of Glasgow and most 'hawkish' of the Scottish episcopate, made that clear. Burnet's province included the most obdurate strongholds of presbyterianism, and he bombarded Sharp, the Scottish Privy Council, and Lauderdale with complaints that only vigorous government action would prevent a total collapse of ecclesiastical and political authority there. Most of the Counsellors thought him an alarmist nuisance, and for his personality as well as his peninsular nose, Lauderdale and his friends nicknamed him 'Long Face'. What made this prelate disconcerting as well as irritating was that he also corresponded with Sheldon, hammer of the English nonconformists, through whom his warnings, and criticism of the Scottish administration, could reach Charles. In August 1665 he invited himself to the court at Salisbury to urge the King to support a package of tough measures, including the internment of dissenting ministers in the Northern Isles, the confiscation of the property of exiles, and the arrest of anybody who refused the Oath of Allegiance. His ally Sheldon had remained heroically in the plague-ridden capital to supervise its spiritual needs, and Lauderdale ensured that the King was kept ignorant of his presence. Eventually Burnet approached Clarendon, that traditional friend of episcopacy, and thus secured a private interview with Charles. The King heard the Archbishop and professed himself convinced by his proposals. He then called him to a meeting with Clarendon, Arlington, and Lauderdale, where the group of measures was given formal approval. Lauderdale was obviously seething with rage but dared not offer opposition, and Burnet went home delighted. But he found that the problem of distance could work to his disadvantage from the other direction as well, for the Scottish Privy Council blithely ignored every part of his scheme, the King's support notwithstanding. In this uneasy manner the northern kingdom's leaders made it through the first year of war.[17]

Before the English government could do the same, it had to face Parliament again at Oxford. Nevertheless, the three-week session in the autumn of 1665 was as much a success for it as the previous two. Because of the danger of travel in time of plague, and the overcrowding in the university town, many MPs stayed away: the highest attendance recorded in the Commons was 160. The court interest must have been disproportionately large, and behaved with most external appearances of unity. Charles opened with a statement that he needed more money to continue the war, Clarendon explained that need in detail, Downing (who had fled Holland) spoke furiously against the Dutch, and Sir Philip Warwick supplied a statement of accounts from the Navy Board. Fifteen minutes after Warwick sat down, the Commons had voted another £1½ million, by 'assessment'. Downing, stealing ideas from the Dutch administration, proposed that the receipt and expenditure of this tax be specially recorded and that loans upon it, at 6 per cent interest, be repaid in the order in which they were made. Both innovations were designed to improve public credit, and were incorporated in the Act.

Despite these successes, the unity of the governing team was superficial. For one thing, they were prepared to use opinion in Parliament against each other. When some MPs spoke against Sandwich for taking the prize goods, James, Albemarle, and Coventry, who all disliked the Admiral, put pressure upon Charles to dismiss him. Sir William seems to have convinced the King that the step would preserve goodwill in the Commons, and in

November Sandwich was suddenly deprived of his command. Another unpleasant incident was the quarrel over Downing's additions to the supply bill. It was occasioned, like so much other trouble, by Charles's taste for making policy in private interviews. He had approved the clauses in such a meeting with Sir George and Coventry, without telling other advisers. As a result, Finch and Ashley opposed them in Parliament, believing that the King would resent the reduction that they made in his control of public funds. To repair the damage, Charles agreed to submit the proposals to a conciliar debate after all and, after some bitter exchanges between Downing and Clarendon, they were upheld. The scene represented a problem corroborated by other evidence: the growing hostility of the Chancellor to Sir George and Sir William. Clarendon's position at court had undergone a notable recovery since his partial disgrace in 1663. When Charles was wondering how to replace his brother as sea commander in June, he called on his old adviser to determine the question. At Oxford, meetings of the 'inner ring' of royal Counsellors were held in Clarendon's lodgings, as of old. Just as, at the zenith of his power, he had needlessly alienated Arlington with his jealousy, so now his suspicion of the two able knights waxed as their influence grew. Coventry sought no feud with the Chancellor because they were both friends of James, but had reason to dislike him. In 1664 the Navy Board had claimed some timber on Crown land which was in the process of being transferred to Clarendon. Rather than lose its value to the nation's profit, he expertly intimidated individual members of the Board into reconsidering the decision. In its avarice and ruthlessness the action was typical of Edward Hyde, and Coventry found it thoroughly distasteful.

Differing viewpoints among advisers were in themselves, of course, no bad thing as long as they did not disrupt executive action: Clarendon, for example, had been unenthusiastic about the war but threw himself into persuading Parliament to support it once it had begun. Even a display of division between Counsellors in the two Houses could be beneficial upon certain issues as it allowed proponents of both sides to remain loyal to the court. An example of such a dispute in this session was the Five Mile Act, which prohibited ejected ministers from residing in their old parishes or corporate towns unless they subscribed oaths neither to resist the King nor to endeavour to alter the government of Church or State. It was decidedly not a government measure. Clarendon had indeed appealed to Parliament for action to increase the regime's security but what was meant by this was almost certainly an increase in royal power: Charles had recently been attracted by a project for a standing army under his brother, stationed in the North. The origins of the statute which he got are lost, though it was almost certainly inspired by a Scottish measure of 1663. How it passed the Commons is unknown, but for once our ignorance of the debates in the early sessions of this Parliament is broken by an account of one in the Lords. The bill was attacked vehemently by the Lord Treasurer, Southampton, seconded by Clarendon and Manchester, who felt that it was far too severe. The leading churchmen, Sheldon and Morley, argued for it, Charles apparently sat back and allowed the peers to decide as they wished, and they voted the measure into law.[18]

Like every wartime winter of the age, that of 1665–6 was spent in feverish diplomacy. As Charles prepared to meet Parliament, the Prince-Bishop of Münster had invaded the eastern Netherlands and swept the Dutch before him. Then his army stopped, for lack of the promised English subsidies. Charles had neither reneged upon the agreement nor been unable to collect the money: his government fully recognized the value of the alliance. The problem had been to convey the funds around the enemy to the Prince-Bishop, which took so much time that too little arrived too late. Then, as the warlike prelate waited for more, Louis XIV moved. The French feared that their Dutch allies might collapse under this landborne attack, and in November they drove the army of Münster back over the frontier. The previous month Louis had laid before Charles the final terms which he was prepared to ask for his English cousin from the Dutch, granting England Pulo Run, New York, and three African forts. The response of the English government was to repeat with the French the same tactics which had failed completely with the Dutch the year before: to try to frighten them into further concessions. Clarendon led the King's servants in a series of speeches designed to whip up feeling in Parliament against Louis, which played their part in gaining that second enormous war grant. On 7 November the formal 'inner ring' of the Council, the Committee for Foreign Affairs, unanimously rejected the French offer. What was missing from it were the two items needed to reassure the public in general and the City in particular that the war had been worth while: compensation to English merchants and an indemnity to help deal swiftly with the public debt. On 1 December the States-General sent their terms, which offered the English a straight choice between the possessions they had on the eve of hostilities and those they had now (which meant deciding between Pulo Run and New York). Charles, Clarendon, and Arlington all agreed that something might be gained by playing off the Dutch against the French in secret approaches. They had instructed Downing in July to impress upon the leaders of Holland the need for Anglo-Dutch co-operation to control French expansion. In the autumn Arlington commenced intrigues with the Dutch Orangists, encouraging them to weaken the position of de Witt's party in exchange for easier peace terms. In February 1666, through one of these men, the English made a covert approach to de Witt himself. Charles now asked only the proper execution of the treaty of 1662 plus an indemnity of £200,000. De Witt's reply was also a marked step down from the public terms asked by his government: he offered an indemnity and Pulo Run if only the English would cancel all their claims outstanding against Dutch merchants. This Charles dared not do, and the exchange ended. In the previous month Louis XIV had at last honoured his alliance, and declared war upon England.[19]

To counterbalance the acquisition of such a formidable new enemy, England had to find new allies, and the obvious one was Spain. In September King Felipe had died, crushed by the latest defeat in Portugal, leaving a sickly heir aged four called Carlos. Louis was anxious to annex certain territories in the Netherlands by right of his Spanish wife, through whom (as her dowry had not been properly paid) he might claim the entire monarchy if the boy-king died in turn. This situation accounts for the reluctance of the French to get involved in the Anglo-Dutch war, and also for the hopes nurtured by the English of playing upon Dutch fears of French ambitions. It also omened well for an Anglo-Spanish agreement. Talks went on warmly all autumn in Madrid and London, but to no effect. The regency government in Spain preferred to exploit France's embroilment in the Dutch war as a means of buying time to make a satisfactory peace with Portugal. Clarendon and Arlington both left their ambassador in Madrid, Fanshaw, inadequately instructed, with the result that he signed a draft commercial treaty so generous to the Spanish that the English government repudiated it. Having menaced Louis since summer with an alliance with his greatest enemy, Charles found himself without one. A second best would be a pact with a powerful German prince, and the obvious one was Friedrich-Wilhelm, the 'Great Elector' of Brandenburg, who arrived on the borders of the Netherlands in November to choose his side in the conflict. A passionate individual, with a dislike of Catholicism and an attachment to the House of Orange, he seemed amenable to an English offer. Charles did promptly send one, of an alliance between the two of them, plus Münster, to restore Wilhelm of Orange to power and gain the Elector fortresses on the Rhine. Again, English high-handedness proved a diplomatic liability, for Clarendon forbade Charles's agent to offer any subsidies, on the grounds that it was beneath the King's dignity to buy support from Brandenburg. The Dutch had no such pride, and in February Friedrich-Wilhelm became their ally in return for a large sum: though in any case he considered them the more reliable partners. Caught between these two powers and the French, the Prince-Bishop of Münster made peace in April. During the same winter Charles's nascent treaty with Denmark perished, as Louis and the States-General systematically bought the support of its ruler as well. In February he declared war upon England, virtually closing the Baltic to her commerce. More Dutch dollars secured the benevolent neutrality of Sweden. Carlingford (Charles's former crony Viscount Taaffe) was sent to the Holy Roman Emperor Leopold, in the hope that his hard-drinking, swashbuckling ways would endear him to the Austrians as Rochester's had done. They certainly did, but Leopold was based too far from the Atlantic to take much interest in the squabbles of its powers. By April, Arlington had to admit that England's only hope lay in its own fleet.[20]

For months it seemed as if it might not even have that. During the financial year from Easter 1665 to Easter 1666 the regular public revenue more than halved, while less than a third of the Royal Aid came in. Dutch-licensed privateers had ruined trade by sea while the plague blocked it by land and stopped its heart at London. Inability to pay was joined to the slight distrust with which many of Charles's subjects had come to regard his administration. When some Derbyshire gentlemen decided to lend money to the King in May, they were told by friends that royal officials would simply pocket the sum. An acquaintance of Pepys informed him in September that half the war taxation which reached the government was not spent upon the navy. In Essex, at midsummer, a man was indicted for saying that the Hearth Tax 'was granted for nothing but to maintain rogues'. These beliefs seem to have been largely unfounded. Evidence survives of slovenly book-keeping and of manipulation of contracts and clients, but very rarely of actual embezzlement. The government's problem was not one of action but of image.

For this the reputation of Charles's court was very much to blame. The King's weaknesses as a monarch at this period were not so much laziness or extravagance. They were, rather, a desire to conciliate and balance different advisers (a theoretical virtue) which led him to keep a dotard like Southampton in charge of the Treasury, and his indulgence of the companions of his pleasures. At a time when some display of austerity would have been tactful, many courtiers provided precisely the opposite. During their stay at Oxford they gambled furiously, Charles's mistress Castlemaine losing £580 (of money ultimately derived from the nation) in one evening. The ladies took to male clothes as a fresh diversion, and one observer noted that although the town was free of plague, the court had brought the 'infection of love' there instead. It was believed at London that Charles was postponing his return there (which happened in February) until Castlemaine had been delivered of their latest child, the fifth of their adulterous union. To the King's fury some erudite critic fixed to her chamber door a Latin inscription which translated into plain English as

> The reason why she is not ducked?
> Because by Caesar she is . . .
>
> (This translation being the
> contemporary, not a modern, one)

It was in Charles's nature not merely to continue the pursuit of pleasure during difficult times, but to accentuate it. From this winter onward he revealed the further trait, of a tendency to prepare rural retreats, far from the hurly-burly of London, and to multiply them with each period of stress. It had been the custom of early Stuart courtiers to sponsor horse-races upon Newmarket Heath, and the Kings had occasionally attended these. In October 1665, when he should have been fully involved with diplomatic and parliamentary affairs, Charles established a prize, and rules, for a race to be held at Newmarket each autumn thereafter. The following spring, as the next round of the war was imminent, he turned up himself to enjoy the sport, and thereafter visited Newmarket for the spring and autumn meetings in almost all of the remaining years of his reign. The race-course was four miles long, over a meadow of short grass, marked by tall white wooden posts. The King and his companions would wait for the racing horses about half-way along it and then follow their progress themselves at full gallop towards the final flag. Upon one occasion, Charles rode in a contest himself. Thus even to spectate at such an event required considerable energy, and in addition the rolling heathlands offered splendid opportunities for walking, hunting, and other recreations. Charles's reasons for liking it are obvious. What should not be forgotten is that he first chose to disport himself there when his subjects were suffering all the horrors of war and plague.

The net result of all these factors was that the Navy Board received no money for two months in the autumn of 1665, at precisely the time that the fleet returned to be paid off. All that it could do was to give the sick seamen tickets to be exchanged for money when it appeared, and to order the rest back to their ships. Some died in front of the Navy Office's doors while others broke its windows. This crisis drove the government to renewed efforts. Charles wrote to chartered companies, urban corporations, peers, JPs, and the clergy, pressing them to provide loans. Sheldon rebuked churchmen who responded feebly, and in total some £300,000 was provided upon the security of the new parliamentary grant. Southampton and Ashley arrested sixteen High Sheriffs for negligence in the collection of the Hearth Tax. Samuel Pepys was

made Surveyor-General to supervise officials placed in each port to ensure
that supplies were maintained ready for the fleet. Accounting procedures
were better regulated. Slowly, the warships were repaired and provisioned.
Their crews remained in the hope of being paid in the end. The money
received by the naval officials in the spring fell £1¼ million short of
their needs and during the early summer they were sent a third of that
necessary. As before, they relied heavily on extended credit. But by April
seventy-nine warships lay in the Thames estuary ready for action. Joint
command was given to Rupert, the last of the squadron commanders
of 1665 left available, and to Albemarle, who was desperate for active
service. Why the Prince accepted the partnership when he had refused one
with Sandwich is unknown: perhaps he simply liked Albemarle more. In
mid-May Arlington's agents reported that Louis had informed the Dutch
that his fleet was on its way to join them. In fact, the French King was
deceiving his allies and holding back his strength while watching events.
The message, however, convinced both Dutch and English with disastrous
results for the latter. Rupert went off with a squadron to beat the French
before they could reach the North Sea, leaving Albemarle to do battle on
1 June with a much more powerful force which had put out from the
Netherlands to meet Louis's vessels. The Prince was recalled in time to
join the fourth day of the fight and converted an outright defeat into
a draw, but the English had lost twice as many ships and men. A week
after their shattered fleet limped back to the Thames, news arrived that
the West Indian colony on St Kitts had been taken by the French. This
meant that England had now made a net territorial loss out of the war. To
complete the fury of its people, ten days later the enemy fleet was back,
blockading the Thames.

   Charles now led his government in a great effort for vengeance. He
called out the militia and commissioned three new foot regiments and sixteen horse troops, to halt any invasion. He requested, and got, a loan from
the City corporation and appealed to gentry for more. Sheldon pressed the
clergy again. The ships were repaired and more hired and a ruthless new
campaign of impressment launched. Had Louis now sent up his ships all
this effort would have been in vain, for the English would have been bot-
tled up by overwhelming numbers. But he had no more desire to see the
Dutch over-mighty than their rivals, and continued to withhold his forces.
On 19 July Charles's navy put out again, exactly their opponents' strength,
and six days later they joined battle east of Suffolk. Once again the guns
were heard at Whitehall, and once again they signified an English victory.
Rupert and Albemarle chased their enemy back to the coast of Holland,
and then landed a party which burned a town and an entire merchant fleet.

From then on, the campaigning season wasted away in frustration and anticlimax as that of 1665 had done. English rejoicing at the bonfire of Dutch shipping was answered by providence with a far bigger conflagration, the Great Fire of London which broke out upon 2 September. It gave Charles his first opportunity since Worcester of playing the hero in person, and he performed the part superbly. He and his brother waded ankle-deep in a conduit, filling buckets and throwing guineas to the fire-fighters to encourage them. Manchester and Ashley were also to be seen against the blaze, directing efforts to halt it. When it did die down, after four days, the financial centre of England and half of its greatest port had been destroyed. Charles, again, took an energetic lead in the first efforts of reconstruction. He appointed new sites for markets and rehoused the Exchange and government offices. He also ordered that public buildings should store the goods of the homeless, while their bodies sheltered in army tents provided without charge, and bread was imported for them.

Meanwhile, observing the new weakness of his allies, Louis XIV at last sent his fleet, forty ships strong, into the Channel and the Dutch came out to join them. Albemarle had been recalled to London to organize his soldiers in fighting the Fire, and Rupert was left to deal with this new menace. To fill up his crews the Prince seized men from a collier fleet, again in defiance of Charles's orders to spare this trade. Then he chased the French back to Brest and the Dutch to their own harbours, before being battered into port himself by a storm on 2 October. Another year's expenditure of energy, money, blood, and misery had achieved no final result.[21]

Another wartime autumn had come, and this meant another session of the Cavalier Parliament. Yet again Charles would have to ask it for money to continue a war which had produced no final decision and no balance of profit. The country was impoverished by the conflict itself, by the existing enormous war grants, and by an agrarian recession which had set in during the early 1660s. This time there was no chance that thin attendance would increase the relative power of the court. The mood of the country was shown in three successive by-elections in the second half of 1666 where the government candidate was defeated. At two of them the crowd shouted 'No courtier'. Rumours of the dissipation of Charles's entourage continued to circulate. Pepys was told that Charles had diverted £400,000 of war funds to private pleasures. An unknown woman, a commoner, wrote to the King to tell him that people generally believed that most of the parliamentary grants had been embezzled. They murmured, she continued, 'Give the King the Countess of Castlemaine and he cares not what the nation suffers.'

The government, accordingly, took pains to manage the Parliament as best it could. Sheldon called in all the bishops to strengthen the court's supporters in the Lords. On 21 September Charles opened the session by appealing for another grant for the war. Coventry then put the naval officials' case in the Commons with eloquence and energy, and the Navy Board itself supplied accounts to substantiate their needs. On 12 October, having checked these figures, the House resolved to supply £1.8 million, a larger sum than that voted at Oxford. Although it took another month to agree upon how to raise this money, it finally decided to employ the efficient 'assessment' for the bulk, and to raise the rest by a reformed variety of poll tax and an imposition upon legal documents. The court was defeated in its proposal of a general excise of the sort used by the Dutch (and by the English republicans) but at least the means chosen were fairly effective. As the MPs debated, Charles tried to make a good impression. He introduced a new mode of court dress which was both inexpensive and made entirely of English textiles: it consisted of a vest and robe which gave rise to the coat and waistcoat of later genteel fashion. The war against Louis, and a rumour that London had been burned by French-inspired Catholic agents, had aroused a feeling against Roman Catholics in England unknown since the early 1640s. On 26 October the Commons proposed that Charles be asked to banish Catholic priests, and to disarm and extract the recusancy fines from their followers. On receiving the address, he concurred at once.[22]

Thus far, the session had promised to repeat the relatively harmonious and productive pattern of the previous three. Two factors were to disrupt this pattern and to bring more bitterness to parliamentary politics than had been seen since the Restoration. One was the return to central political life of Buckingham, bent on mischief. Having been cast off by Charles after their separate escapes from Worcester, he had not been content for long to kick his heels in exile like Grenville, Long, and Herbert. Making peace with the Protectorate, he had married the daughter of Fairfax himself: like his association with Argyll in Scotland, this was partly political expediency but partly a genuine sympathy with presbyterians which was to last all his life and to sit uneasily with his hereditary royalism. At the Restoration he was received by Charles and eventually (as the greatest non-royal peer) allowed back on to the Privy Council. He soon associated himself with Bristol and the enemies of Clarendon, but was given no office and apparently lacked influence with Charles. He became a prominent but dispensable companion of the King's pleasures, noted for his wit and his aptitude for mimicry and building of houses of cards. Slowly, the beautiful and imaginative young grandee was growing into a heavy-jowled, choleric rake. Within three years of the Restoration he had managed to quarrel violently with Bristol, Sandwich, Rupert, and (twice) Northumberland. In 1663 he retired to his vast Yorkshire estates to play the part of a local magnate with apparent success and popularity. At the beginning of the Dutch war he arrived at the fleet expecting a command, and retired in a rage when he was considered untrained for one. This incident must have fuelled his bitterness against the court. It may also have been encouraged by a new mistress, the Countess of Shrewsbury, who combined great beauty with a love of setting men at odds. In the autumn of 1666 he came to Westminster determined to put himself at the head of the men like Temple who were trying to force their way into power. With him came his clients, notably two remarkably clever young gentry of royalist background, Edward Seymour and Sir Thomas Osborne. With them in the Commons they found not only established gadflies like Temple and Vaughan but a former royalist who had gone unrewarded, William Garroway. Coventry had noted Garroway as a man worth buying. Nothing had been done, and another talented malcontent joined the group preparing to harry the government.[23] Fortune delivered to them the second factor in the court's problems, a perfect issue upon which not only to assail the government but to divide it: a collision between the interests of England and Ireland.

Generally, Ireland was the least troubled of Charles's three realms during this war. Indeed, in the first year it actually achieved the land settlement which had eluded it for so long. In July 1664, the English Privy Council committed the Explanatory Bill to the former Commissioners for Claims and the Irish Privy Counsellors present, who included Ormonde and Orrery. Another winter of argument passed, and in April 1665 the Irish Catholics at court, now led by old Clancarty, were still clamouring for a mass restoration. In May, however, they accepted a formula drawn up the previous year, whereby the purchasers of confiscated lands gave up a full third of their property to compensate those of their number who would have to relinquish their estates to Catholics. Twenty more of the latter were named as worthy of restoration, having been selected by Ormonde. In July, at Hampton Court, the bill was put into its final form by the Duke, Orrery, Anglesey, Arlington, Morice, and Finch, and in December Ormonde and Orrery employed all their skill to argue it through the Irish Parliament.[24] As a result of this statute and the previous Act of Settlement, Catholics were left in possession of 22 per cent of the island, as compared with 59 per cent in 1641. The Protestants had secured their dominance, and the great majority of the claims lodged before the commissioners in 1662–3 were never heard. Most of those restored were

Catholics of English descent, and the main losers by the whole process were the 'Old' or Gaelic Irish. Whatever the wider justice of the settlement, it can be said that Charles had followed his personal loyalties as faithfully as in Great Britain. He had owed gratitude to Irish Protestants in general for accepting him as King in 1660, and to a smaller number of Irish Catholics for their service to the royalist cause. Both groups had been provided for in the two states.

Even as vermin thrive among the horrors of trench warfare, so individuals made profits as brokers during the long and complex formation of the Irish land settlement. Courtiers such as St Albans, Carlingford, and Falmouth all accepted sums from dispossessed Catholics to further their claims during the long discussions at Whitehall. The most enterprising of these go-betweens, however, was himself a Catholic, a strikingly handsome and fiery man in his thirties called Richard Talbot. During the exile he had served as a royalist agent and in the army in Flanders, and became a favourite of James who made him a Gentleman of his Bedchamber at the Restoration. Talbot was the youngest son of a baronet from County Dublin, and the brother of the meddlesome Father Peter: intrigue clearly ran in the family. During the debates over the land question, he journeyed indefatigably between the two realms, arguing cases at Whitehall or before the Court of Claims and acting as an agent for Englishmen who wished to purchase Irish land. His key assistant in England was Joseph Williamson, the protégé of Nicholas whom Arlington had inherited and, recognizing the man's administrative acumen, made head of his secretariat. Talbot arranged for Williamson to draw Arlington's attention to the Irishman's clients and to send all the English news to him when he was in Dublin. In return, he secured Williamson an Irish estate and wooed Arlington himself and Coventry by suggesting means to advance their affairs in his country. Ormonde disliked him by instinct, but Orrery supported him despite his general antipathy to Catholics: perhaps one adventurer recognized another. In this manner Talbot not only began to accumulate a fortune but to make himself, like Richard Belling, a figure at court despite the continued Protestant domination of his native land.[25]

During the Dutch war Charles continued to reward the same people whom he had favoured in Ireland since his restoration. The Irish Hearth Tax was farmed to a consortium led by Carlingford and Inchiquin. Berkeley, Arlington, St Albans, and Anglesey were granted Irish pensions, lands, or rents. Belling got a knighthood and a warrant for a lump sum, and Lane was made a Secretary of State and then Secretary at War. Orrery's eldest brother, Cork, was made an English Earl (of Burlington), while another, Michael Boyle, Archbishop of Dublin, became Lord Chancellor on the death of Eustace. As well as a pension and lands, Orrery himself received a warrant for a lump sum, and a seat on the English Privy Council. But it was the Butlers, not the Boyles, who appeared to consolidate their position as the country's ruling dynasty. Belling, Lane, and Archbishop Boyle all owed their recent favours to Ormonde. The Duke's eldest son Thomas, Earl of Ossory, was made Lieutenant-General of the army, while his second, Richard, Earl of Arran, governed Dublin. When Ormonde crossed to England, Ossory was left to rule as his Lord Deputy, and when the Duke was seated in Dublin his heir took up duties as a Gentleman of the Bedchamber to Charles. By this arrangement, a Butler would always be at the King's ear.[26]

Nevertheless, the government in England still sometimes made life harder for that in Ireland. In 1662 Charles had promised Ormonde to consult him over the appointment of all Irish bishops: he refused to do so by 1666. Sometimes the English Privy Council took so long to return draft statutes to the Irish Parliament that the dates in them were all expired. Once it lost a bill completely.[27] But the partnership of Ormonde and Orrery still kept the island tolerably well-governed. The entry of the French into the war carried a danger that their fellow Catholics in Ireland might be launched into rebellion by an invasion force. To prevent it, the two nobles set hard to work raising a militia and fortifying ports.[28] The great weakness of the kingdom, however, remained its public revenue. As in each realm, the income of the government fell because of the war while its expenditure went up. The Irish Parliament proved, in the event, as unexpectedly generous as the Cavalier Parliament and the Scottish Convention, and in 1665–6 it voted £180,000. The money was, however, of necessity spread over years of instalments and because of the wartime depression these were soon in arrears. In January 1665 the annual deficit was £30,800. A year later it was £36,800. This meant, of course, that all those pensions and grants given by Charles could not be paid. Yet more serious, it looked as if, should the French invade, there would be no army to stop them. In January 1666 the unpaid soldiers became restless, and in May the major garrison of Carrickfergus mutinied and had to be suppressed by an expeditionary force. Total collapse was only prevented by two instalments of £15,000 sent over from the English Treasury, which only had the money to hand because the Bishop of Münster, for whom it was destined, had made peace. No more could be hoped for from the Irish Parliament and Ormonde dissolved it in August.[29] It was in this context that the Cavalier House of Commons produced the Irish Cattle Bill of 1666.

By 1663, as mentioned, England was sliding into an agricultural depression which was to outlast the century. As concern grew about falling rents, MPs turned to eliminating foreign competition with English products. One of the obvious examples of this was the cattle trade from Ireland, and in that year 1663 the Cavalier Parliament legislated to restrict it to specified months. In 1665 the Commons passed a bill designed to reduce it to a trickle, but on Charles's instructions this was ignored in the Lords. One day after the King's speech in 1666, a bill to ban the trade outright was proposed in the Lower House. The Irish Privy Council had been dreading this and made it quite clear to Charles that if it became law, the economy of the whole island would suffer severely and the public revenue shrink further. In that situation, the Dublin government would require either large and permanent English subsidies or a loosening of other restrictions on Irish trade. Both being undesirable, the King committed himself to resist the bill. By contrast, the majority of the Cavalier Parliament felt no responsibility towards Ireland other than keeping it Protestant. Ormonde remarked bitterly that some important people in England would have burned or sunk the whole island if this had been possible.[30] As far as many English MPs and peers were concerned, they had sacrificed heavily to support their monarch's war effort during a recession: they could not see why he could not grant their wish in return and put their interests before those of the Irish.

In dealing with this delicate situation, Charles struck an unhappy medium: he made his own opposition to the bill clear but did not commit the members of his government and their clients to resist it. As a result, Finch and Palmer fought it strenuously in the Commons while Coventry, who thought opposition futile and provocative, kept quiet. Temple and Buckingham's group drove the measure on while those back-benchers who normally looked to the court for direction were 'left to the accident of wind and tide'. After three weeks the bill passed by sixty-one votes, containing a clause supplied by Seymour which declared the cattle trade 'a public nuisance' and so rendered Charles technically unable to dispense individuals from the statute by his prerogative powers. In the Lords, the measure was supported (of course) by Buckingham and his friends, but also by Ashley, Southampton, Manchester, and Carlisle. Clarendon, Anglesey, and the bishops opposed it, and Arlington, like Coventry, held his peace. Ashley had invested in the Scottish cattle trade and hated all things Irish, including Ormonde: the other ministers in favour of the bill seem to have feared to anger the Commons. After more than a month of bitter argument, in which Ossory had to be suspended twice from the House, the measure passed by sixteen votes, shorn of the 'nuisance' clause.

The Commons were indeed annoyed. On 27 November they decided by sixteen votes to adhere to the clause: the King was to have no more power over cattle-traders than over corporation members or dissenters. Furthermore, on the suggestion of Garroway, they incorporated into the bill for the poll tax a clause setting up a commission to examine the fate of all the taxes voted for the war. Charles let his violent displeasure be known, but only succeeded in having a separate bill embody the motion for the commission instead of it being attached to a supply. On 15 December the King appealed for the completion of the war grant, but his opponents filibustered away the days till the Christmas recess. Just before this occurred, Charles took Clarendon's advice and offered the compromise which had resulted in the Corporation Act, whereby he would appoint a commission to enquire into the accounts himself, incorporating several of the trouble-making MPs. In January 1667 the Commons reconvened, and rejected the offer. Deadlock had now been achieved over both this and the Irish Cattle Bill. James, Clarendon, Anglesey, and Sheldon urged Charles to remain firm, but to their horror he preferred to follow Arlington's advice and make the war effort his sole priority. On the 14th he told the Lords to accept the entire Cattle Bill, and on the 18th he made a furious speech complaining to both Houses of the lack of progress of supply. This did get the finance bills completed a week later, and on 6 February he prorogued Parliament. The bill for the commission was thereby killed, but as a gesture of conciliation Charles appointed one himself.[31] The Irish economy was saved by the agreement of the English Privy Council to allow Irish merchants freedom of trade with any foreign nations, limited only by the privileges of certain London companies. To bolster the Dublin government, Charles assigned it the proceeds of some captured shipping. In this manner Ormonde's administration survived the war with the pay of its army £80,000 in arrears.[32]

When addressing Parliament in January and February 1667, Charles promised that he was not engaged in any treaty, to allay suspicion that he would make peace and then pocket the latest war grant to keep himself financially independent for years to come. This was exactly what Clarendon, Ormonde, Burlington, and Orrery were secretly urging him to do.[33] The King's speeches were correct to the letter, for he was not yet actually treating, but he was attempting desperately to do so. During 1666 he had made an even more determined attempt to ally with Spain, sending out Sandwich as ambassador extraordinary to replace Fanshaw. What held up his efforts was not only Spanish caution but the inability of Arlington to decide whether first to settle with Spain or to help Portugal to full independence lest the French and the Poruguese make a pact. In

November, he ordered Sandwich to proceed no further, as England and France were now dealing directly with each other.[34]

Long ago, Sir Keith Feiling portrayed the two great English diplomatic initiatives of early 1667 as the product of a clash between Clarendon, who wanted a separate peace with France, and Arlington, who wanted one with the United Netherlands. The sources do not seem to reveal a struggle: rather, the government was desperately seeking an end to the war however it could find one, and the two great ministers pursued the possibilities which opened to them individually. Arlington, as said above, was prepared to back the talks with France and they were reported back to him in full, while Clarendon was by no means trusting of the French. The process began on 4 October, when Charles offered the States-General the treaty of 1662 plus a moderate indemnity and a binding settlement of the East Indian commerce. It replied in November that only a general treaty between all the warring powers would do, and offered only its previous choice: the status quo or the one prevailing before the war. For months St Albans, who still frequently resided in Paris with Henrietta Maria, had insisted that Louis XIV would make peace on easy terms and abandon the Dutch. In January he was empowered to sound out the French King to this end. Meanwhile, the formal talks were opened a week after the prorogation of Parliament, when Charles told the Privy Council that he would send plenipotentiaries to a peace congress. A further week, and St Albans had replied that Louis would end hostilities if Charles promised to make no alliance prejudicial to France for one year, leaving him free to attack Spain. This pledge the King signed, in the absurd belief, shared by his brother but not by Clarendon, that his French cousin would now force the English terms upon the Dutch. In March, as a further compliment to Louis, Charles accepted the French suggestion of Breda as the place for the congress: yet again, this Dutch town was to play a major part in his life. Simultaneously, the English government opened secret talks with de Witt as double insurance. The scheme was the brainchild of the Emperor Leopold's ambassador, Baron de Lisola, a Burgundian with a detestation of the French. He had convinced Arlington of the merits of such an approach and was introduced by him to Charles and James. From them he carried to de Witt in April an offer of a defensive alliance and a guarantee of the Spanish Netherlands against Louis in return for Pulo Run and an indemnity. The last two concessions were refused, and so Charles concentrated upon the French again. Their best offer to him was to lay up their fleet, force the Dutch to treat, and return their West Indian conquests if the English ceded them Nova Scotia and left the Dutch Pulo Run. Upon the basis of this deal the English ambassadors set out for Breda in late April.[35]

Behind Charles's urgency to treat and willingness to make concessions lay a financial crisis. As French privateers had joined those licensed by the Dutch, customs receipts in the financial year 1666–7 fell to a third of their already lamentable level in 1665. Plague and recession affected the brewing business, so the proceeds of the excise continued to decline. The Hearth Tax, however, showed a marked recovery because in late 1665 its collection had been farmed out to local men in each county who demanded it with a new ruthlessness. Unfortunately, this inevitably led to an outbreak of rioting across the country, and more popular resentment of the government. The fall in the regular revenue ought to have been made up by the war taxes granted by Parliament, but these simply did not come in fast enough. By Easter 1667 no more than a third of the total amount voted had been received. Thus in late 1666 there was more money entering the public funds than a year before, but it was all anticipated several times over. The Treasurer of the Navy, Charles's old host in Jersey, Carteret, could afford to pay off less than a quarter of the seamen who returned with Rupert. Many of the remainder rioted in and around London during the winter, and Albemarle had to quell them with soldiers. Charles could offer nothing to them but soothing words. During the same months the English bargaining position was weakened further by the loss of Antigua and Montserrat to the French and Surinam to the Dutch. On 23 February the Navy Board presented James with a complete statement of their position. They had been able to pay £1,315 out of the £150,000 due to suppliers, so could place virtually no contracts for further supplies. They had paid £140,000 to seamen out of the £930,000 due to them. Unless they received over £$\frac{1}{2}$ million immediately, they could not fit out the fleet.

This letter was doubtless the propelling factor behind the order which Charles gave his brother upon 6 March, to lay up the biggest warships and send out the smaller to patrol the coasts. These forays would clear away privateers and capture enemy shipping more effectively than concentrating a fleet could do. As long as the coasts were fortified, even the appearance of a large enemy force would matter little as this would cruise around aimlessly until it ran out of supplies. Thus, it was hoped, the Dutch would be forced to make peace by a continuing pointless expenditure and loss of trade. The decision was not only rational but financially correct, for when all the war taxation finally came in, it proved to cover only the existing expenditure: Charles simply could not have put the fleet out again. Like so many of his decisions it was taken in private, and in a hurry for in the first days of March several Counsellors were still expecting all the ships to set forth. Though there was no formal meeting, the King and

Clarendon separately insisted that Charles had acted upon the advice of his most trusted advisers. The latter could not have included Clarendon himself, James, Finch, Anglesey, and Coventry, for they all opposed the resolution. Who did advise it is simply unknown, despite the importance of the decision and the relative density of the records. It is an illustration, again, of how dim are the inner workings of Restoration politics.

Certainly the decision initially justified itself admirably. English frigates did clear privateers from outside many ports and trade slightly improved. It seemed likely that Charles could meet Parliament again without needing more war taxation. Squadrons were sent to restore English supremacy in the West Indies and Mediterranean. Buckingham was stripped of his offices and driven into hiding with a charge of treason, cooked up by Arlington on the alleged evidence that he had asked an astrologer to draw up Charles's horoscope. An opportunity to reform the financial administration was afforded when the Lord Treasurer Southampton died in agony in 16 May, from a remedy which his doctors had prescribed for urinal stones. To replace him, Clarendon wanted a conservative and unimaginative nobleman, the Earl of Bridgewater, while some of the younger men in the administration hoped for Coventry. Instead Charles agreed to a truly radical innovation, a commission consisting mainly of rising men without ministerial office. Ashley was added as Chancellor of the Exchequer, and Albemarle put in as a compliment. The remaining three were Coventry, an MP loyal to the court called Sir John Duncombe, and a young man with a leonine head of hair and a stubborn mouth called Sir Thomas Clifford. From a royalist family, he was a client of Arlington and through him had been preferred to the plum post of Comptroller of the Household, though he had justified it with the energy he had shown on various diplomatic and administrative tasks. The choice of a commission caused general surprise, and like the laying up of the fleet it is not known who had advised it. Certainly there was a Scottish precedent (to be described) and James encouraged it as he was impressed by the success of the team which ran the ordnance department. But the birth of the scheme remains another lost piece of the Restoration jigsaw. Its consequences are certainly preserved in the series of minute-books which they immediately asked Downing to keep. They embarked upon a systematic review of the state's debts and the money it was to expect, kept a register of all the Exchequer's transactions, and decided to stop in the future the granting of reversions to offices. On the fifth day of their existence they talked Charles out of purchasing a jewel, and on the following day he agreed to let them vet every warrant issued for the payment of public revenue. He had shown the courage to permit the most dramatic overhaul that the English fiscal system had ever received.[36]

In the same period as shifts occurred in the English government's foreign policy and financial administration, its policy towards nonconformity began to alter. In August 1666 he received an appeal from some Quakers for the release of their imprisoned brethren, of the sort which he had stonily rejected since 1663. He chose to receive this one with approval and demonstrated it by liberating the most respected of their surviving leaders, George Fox. Assize judges now became willing to carry other petitions to Charles, and further liberations followed. What we lack is (yet again) the pattern of advice behind the policy, and this time the reasoning as well. Perhaps the passivity or loyalty of most dissenters during the war had made the King reconsider his harsh attitude towards them. Perhaps also he noted that across the country magistrates were slowly ceasing to enforce the Conventicle Act, as they became satiated with persecution, overtired by the various tasks of the war effort, or distracted by the new popular fury against Catholics.[37]

If the alteration of royal treatment of nonconformity in England was quiet and piecemeal, and remains slightly mysterious, the same reversal in Scotland was dramatic and controversial and is well-documented. The sequence of events commenced in November 1666 with the very worst development that royalists and episcopalians in all three kingdoms might have feared. An army of rebels gathered in the south-west, swore the National Covenant anew, and marched upon Edinburgh. The government there was taken totally by surprise, Rothes actually being in London assuring Charles of the security of his northern kingdom. Nevertheless it had the spirit and the means to resist. A year before, Rothes had visited the south-west and had been surprised and appalled by the extent of nonconformity there and the demoralization of the orthodox. He had decided that the Archbishop of Glasgow was correct in advocating a policy of energetic repression, and the Privy Council immediately issued a fresh prohibition of conventicles. To enforce it, parties of soldiers were dispersed from Glasgow to Galloway and during the summer a mobile field force was raised on the proceeds of the fines.[38] It was this which caught and broke the rebel army in pitched battle, and the Scottish Privy Council set to work capturing, interrogating, trying, and executing. In the process they revived the systematic use of torture, which the Covenanters in their days of power had avoided.

Charles had indirectly encouraged the policy of repressing dissent by writing to the leading Counsellors to ask what measures they were taking for the safety of Church and State. Such interest prodded them into reporting back with ideas for yet more tough measures.[39] Naturally, the King also urged on the Council in its work of destroying the rebellion ruthlessly, and he hurried Rothes back to join it with the new office of General-in-Chief of the army.[40] Archbishop Burnet was almost jubilant when he heard of the rising, feeling that it justified all the warnings which he had made for years and had continued to make, to Sheldon as well as to Lauderdale, through 1666. Now at last the Privy Council was treating nonconformity with the savagery which he had pleaded for, and in May 1667 Charles ordered Rothes to send him the names of any Counsellors who spoke on behalf of those brought to trial: this was a direct result of a visit made by Burnet to court to warn once more of laxity in high places.[41] Yet the 'Pentland Rising' led not to an extended persecution and to the admission of men with the Archbishop's views to supreme power, but to the reverse. The story of this remarkable development has been traced in outline,[42] but it should be explained now more fully and firmly than before.

The source of the changes lay in Lauderdale's growing isolation and insecurity at this period. The triumvirate of 1664–6 was in process of disintegration, for he was now bickering openly with Sharp and on uneasy terms with Rothes.[43] Instead, he had formed a friendship with a nobleman from the Borders, John Hay, Earl of Tweeddale, who like him had not welcomed the restoration of episcopacy, had defended some of the Remonstrants in early 1661, and had been detested by Middleton. They were allied, as Lauderdale and Rothes had been in 1663, with the useful Sir Robert Murray. This man had become a regular courtier at Whitehall, establishing a reputation as a scientist and developing his magical way of making each person to whom he spoke feel as though he perfectly understood them and their interests.[44] To the red-haired Earl, the prospect of Sharp and Burnet being recognized as the best analysts of Scottish affairs, and Rothes being treated as the hero who mopped up after the rebellion, was intolerable. From the results, it is clear that he slowly instilled into Charles the belief that the quartering of troops in the south-west had actually driven the people into rebellion, and that persecution had pushed peaceful nonconformists into an alliance with the real radicals (the most recent historians[45] have found some truth both in this version of events and Archbishop Burnet's). At the same time, he moved against his former allies, beginning with Sharp. The primate was the most vulnerable, as Charles had never really liked him, and the most menacing, as he was now canvassing Scottish noblemen for a plan to topple Lauderdale and reinstate Middleton in power. There is no evidence that Lauderdale had him made the scapegoat for the rebellion itself: rather, in January 1667 he showed the King proof of the project for Middleton's return, and some fawning addresses which Sharp had once delivered to Cromwell. Charles confined the Archbishop to St Andrews and spoke of replacing him, but Lauderdale wanted him cowed and eager to please. By July, Sharp was begging for the Earl's friendship.[46]

Rothes had stood aside from the primate's intrigue and assisted in his humiliation: thus he had exposed himself. Lauderdale, Tweeddale, and Murray resolved to have him deprived of his offices very slowly, so that like Sharp he would be politically emasculated. In April Charles was persuaded to appoint him to the honorific but onerous office of Lord Chancellor and, since he could not manage the Treasury as well, to make him head of a commission of four Privy Counsellors to execute his former duties as Lord Treasurer. In early June Murray carried both documents to Edinburgh, taking Rothes completely by surprise. Sir Robert had employed his wonderful charm at Whitehall upon the King: now he turned it upon the horrified Earl, to convince him that as Charles had decided upon the change it would be dangerous to contest it. The argument worked, and so Scotland acquired a chief legal officer who knew neither law not Latin.[47] It remained to revoke Rothes's commission to represent the King in Scotland, the basis of his power there. Charles was inclined to allow the Earl to come to court and to account for himself before this was done and, strangely enough, Lauderdale considered permitting this. From Scotland Tweeddale and Murray sent him anguished letters to impress upon him that if Rothes appeared at Whitehall still in possession of the commission, his pleasant, winning personality would induce the King to confirm it. Murray even considered that the new Chancellor's 'kindness and blandishments' would win over Lauderdale himself. Their ally was persuaded, and went to work on his master again. Doubtless Rothes's misjudgement of the situation before the rebellion was cited against him, as was the fact that he had also been taken by surprise when a Dutch squadron bombarded Burntisland in May. As Charles found it difficult 'to say bleak things', Lauderdale drew up the letter of revocation for his signature. It was sent in September, and Rothes, again advised by Murray, submitted to it tamely.[48]

As the process of his removal neared completion, so it was time for the new triumvirate to execute its ideas, representing the beginning of an attempt to conciliate moderate dissenters and to annihilate extremists. These, like the recall of Rothes's commission, were the brainchildren of Tweeddale and Murray, passed by them through Lauderdale to Charles. First, the standing army had to be disbanded, both as a gesture of moderation and to destroy a potential power base for Rothes and its other officers. In August the King sent the order for this, together with one, solicited by Lauderdale, forbidding its generals to come to court until the process was finished: again, Charles was to be insulated from other advice. To the disgust of the triumvirate, somebody (they suspected Sheldon, primed by Burnet) persuaded the King to make an exception of Lieutenant-General Tam Dalyell, the victor of the battle which had ended the rebellion. Dalyell was a strange-looking man, with a perfectly bald head, a long white beard, and a single tight jerkin instead of the coats and waistcoats of fashion. But he was a savage enemy of nonconformists and determined to keep his forces in being. Lauderdale averted the danger by preparing Charles, so that when the old war-dog appeared the King politely declined to discuss public affairs with him.[49] In September Murray produced proposals for an indemnity to rebels prepared to give bonds, for a militia in place of the army, and for permission for all who declared against the Covenants to keep their arms. They were vetted by Tweeddale and then by Lauderdale, and approved by Charles. With the royal authority behind them they were next adopted by most of the Scottish Privy Council (Burnet and Rothes being among those who refused to do so). On the 13th, as a piece of constitutional formality, the Council recommended them to the King, who as formally consented to them. Sharp obediently crushed an attempt by Burnet to co-ordinate a protest from the bishops. At the end of the year Charles privately empowered Tweeddale to continue the work of hunting down obdurate Covenanters while treating the mass of the people gently. Thus both the new governing team and the new policies were in place. Charles had, once again, been adroitly managed by some of his own Scottish Counsellors, and the grumble of Murray was not that the King intervened too much but too little: he asked Lauderdale if Charles could not, occasionally, encourage his local officers in Scotland by writing them two lines with his own hand.[50]

Thus, by May 1667 Charles appeared to be emerging from his war with neither victory nor defeat. Scotland and Ireland were quiet, his financial and political fortunes in England were on the mend, and the peace congress was in progress at Breda. His representatives there had been instructed, shamelessly, to court both Dutch and French, stressing to each the potential threat of the other and offering English assistance to counter it.[51] This appeared to have the greater prospect of success in that, simultaneously, Louis invaded the Spanish Netherlands with the biggest army that France had ever fielded. As he did so, Sandwich signed a commercial treaty in Madrid granting the English most of the concessions already given to Dutch traders and leaving the West Indies to the fortunes of local warfare. At Breda Charles expected similar success, and told his representatives to demand from the Dutch the treaty of 1662, minus

Pulo Run but with compensation for it and the merchants' claims. From Denmark he wanted reparations.[52] It did not occur to him, or his ministers, that with their fleet laid up they were not bargaining from a position of strength any more. De Witt and his colleagues were indeed anxious to end the war so that they could turn to the conflict in the Netherlands. But they were determined to do so upon their own terms, and resolved to force the English to them by a stunning blow. On 27 May their fleet put out, and on 10 June it bombarded the fort commanding the entrance of the Medway into surrender. Owing to lack of money and of interest by the government, this vital defence had been only half built. Two days later the Dutch sailed upriver, burned three of the biggest vessels of the Royal Navy, and towed off its flagship as a prize. They then retired to the mouth of the Thames, which they settled down to blockade indefinitely as they attempted, with success, the innovation of supplying their ships by sea.

Charles reacted with the energy which he showed in every crisis. On the day after the raid, he and James themselves supervised the sinking of ships in the Thames and its creeks to block them. Rupert planted cannon at Woolwich and along the Medway. The militia of every county were called up and reinforced by a field army of 9,000 men, raised in three weeks. These measures were paid for by loans provided by another tremendous series of government appeals, which added to the enormous public debt. The worst damage, however, was not financial but political. The English had suffered the worst humiliation in their naval history. Throughout the country, people talked of betrayal by Catholics or courtiers. Clarendon's newly finished mansion in Piccadilly had its windows smashed and the trees outside it felled at night. Nobody commented upon Charles's hard work upon the defence of the Thames. Instead it was said in London that he had spent the evening after the disaster supping with his son Monmouth, together with his mistress Castlemaine, and joining the party in hunting a moth around the room. He was paying heavily for his long association with pleasure and negligence.

Crowds at Westminster were shouting for the recall of Parliament, as much to associate it with the Crown in this crisis as to provide funds. James, Clarendon, and Carteret (as Treasurer of the Navy) opposed this, the last two fearing attack and James worrying about his father-in-law. All the rest of the Privy Council urged it, and Charles decided on 25 June to follow their advice. Carteret was allowed to get out of the way by exchanging posts with Anglesey and becoming Vice-Treasurer of Ireland. An official scapegoat was selected, in the person of the commissioner in charge of Chatham dockyard, who was sent to the Tower on 18 June accused of negligence. The obvious way to escape from the predicament, however, was simply to concede everything that the Dutch were demanding, and Charles did. A draft treaty was signed at Breda on 1 July, reluctantly accepted at Whitehall, and concluded at Breda on the 21st. It arrived in London for ratification almost a week later, just in time to enable Charles to dispense with Parliament. Buckingham had emerged from hiding after the Medway disaster, doubting if, in its new weakness, the government would dare to press its charge against him. He was correct: the King dismissed it, and he was free and willing to cause trouble again. The Commons gathered at Westminster as requested, in notably ill humour and, being told that peace was made after all, departed in an even worse mood. The Dutch fleet continued to cruise off the coasts until 24 August, when, the ratifications of the treaty being mutually confirmed, peace with France, Denmark, and the United Netherlands was formally proclaimed.

Charles's first war as an effective king had ended in humiliation and defeat. He kept New York, but had been forced to renounce Pulo Run, Surinam (the only English colony on the South American mainland), Nova Scotia, and the African forts lost in 1664, as well as all the claims to compensation of English merchants and his government's demands for reparations. He had also been forced to concede slight concessions to Dutch traders carrying goods to English ports. The fundamental reason for his failure was that his diplomatic and military pretensions had not been adequately funded. He had been able to spend $£5\frac{1}{4}$ million upon the war, while the Dutch spent the equivalent of $£11$ million and the French in 1667 had an *annual* surplus of $£9$ million upon their *regular* revenue. As during the previous hundred years, the English monarchy was simply priced out of the market of sustained European warfare. The bulk of the Commons, of course, were not to know that: as far as they were concerned, they had been more generous than any of their predecessors, and the funds provided had been as badly used as the war had been badly conducted. Their dismissal in July had only provided the government with a breathing-space in which to prepare to meet their anger. Charles could not afford to prorogue them for long, because his government was left with a debt of $£2$ million which the residue of the war taxes would not cover. Before the date upon which they were due to reassemble, 10 October, the King had to find some dramatic means of satisfying them.[53]

A number were sought. Charles proclaimed that the Irish Cattle Act was to be rigorously enforced, and imposed the Oaths of Allegiance and Supremacy upon all state employees to weed out Catholics. He also forbade the latter his court and ordered the execution of the laws against their priests. The new standing army was disbanded within a month. The King permitted moderate episcopalian clergy and dispossessed presbyterian ministers to agree upon a bill for presentation to the Commons. It would readmit dissenting clerics to the Church without insisting upon their use of the surplice or certain ceremonies, and without involving the royal dispensing power to which the MPs had so much objected. Charles also gave full support to the continued work of his Treasury Commission in gaining control over the expenditure of every other department and over the activity of local financial officers.

But his most celebrated palliative measure was purely negative: his dismissal of Clarendon upon 30 August. Like so many of the key decisions of the reign, this one was taken in private upon the advice of one or two individuals and the reasoning behind it is impossible completely to reconstruct. The precipitating factor is clear enough: the Chancellor's unpopularity was so great that he was the obvious scapegoat to offer Parliament. Charles himself told Clarendon that if he did not retire he would be attacked in the next session, forcing a confrontation between Crown and Commons when one was least needed. Arlington made this the explanation to Ormonde, adding that during August it was generally believed at court that the Earl was worn out by office and ready to go. Certainly, at the time of his dismissal Clarendon was prostrated by grief at the death of his wife and had not attended the Privy Council for three weeks. His son-in-law James thought that he would welcome retirement. Certainly also, Charles's decision was a swift one. In June and July he had supported his greatest servant by making him Lord-Lieutenant of a second county and by dining ostentatiously at Clarendon House.

But in itself the explanation is inadequate, for it does not account for the unmistakable dislike with which the King treated the former Chancellor from the moment of his removal. Coventry was the man who claimed openly to have persuaded Charles into the decision, and although he told Pepys that he had used several arguments, he singled out as most important the one that Clarendon had prevented the King from hearing the advice of others. Lauderdale (guilty of this himself) also thought it the crucial issue, as did Downing. Although Charles told Ormonde that his motives were 'too big for a letter', he did comment that the Earl's 'behaviour and humour' had grown intolerable. Anglesey felt that harmony in the King's Privy Council was essential if Parliament was to be managed. Clarendon himself told Ormonde that the King had accused him of insolence in debates. None the less, there is no evidence that the Chancellor's irritating manner had grown worse in the course of 1667, and as Charles had put up with it for so

long, it is strange that he should have resented it so violently all of a
sudden.

After all, Coventry did tell Pepys that, in addition to Clarendon's political shortcomings, there were 'many things not fit to be spoken' which
counted against him. Perhaps one of these was subsequently spoken by
the later Bishop Burnet, who printed a story gained from Clarendon's
heir. In the previous March one of the three women closest to Charles
had dropped out: Frances Stuart. During the year before she had been as
much in favour as ever, and in February 1667 her form appeared upon
a medal representing Britannia, an image which has endured ever since
upon our coins. A few weeks later she suddenly eloped with Charles's
relative Richmond, whom the King had disliked ever since the affair of
the secret ballot, and married him without royal permission. It was a
genuine love-match, but Frances was rumoured to have told friends that
it was contracted so hastily because she was tired of fending off Charles's
advances. The King was utterly furious, and forbade the couple to return
to court. He did forgive Frances a year later, after an attack of smallpox
threatened her beauty and stirred his pity, and it is possible that the real
casualty of the affair was Clarendon. Burnet's story was that Charles was
told that his Chancellor had encouraged the match, disapproving of the
King's behaviour. It was, after all, precisely such censorious interference
which had cost Edward Hyde the friendship of Berkeley years before. The
tale, if true, would explain the depth of his master's anger now.

But perhaps it is superfluous. When Charles invited Clarendon to
resign upon 25 August, he seems genuinely to have expected him to do
so. Instead, he found himself argued with by his Chancellor, who enlisted
his brother, and his growing anger was patent with both. After five days
he deprived the Earl of his office, whereupon Clarendon made it plain to
everybody that he intended to take an active part in the next session of
Parliament and to oppose royal policies there if he disliked them. James,
continuing to take his father-in-law's part, became on worse terms with
his brother than he had been for ten years. Sheldon, though irritated by
Clarendon's failure to support the persecution of English presbyterians,
none the less remonstrated with Charles for discarding a champion of
episcopacy. It is very likely that by the obstinacy with which he contested
the royal will, Edward Hyde slowly drew upon himself the fury provoked
in this King by those who tried to dictate to him. He had learned nothing
from the fates of Long, Balcarres, and Vane, with which he had been so
intimately associated.

His attitude meant that the King's advisers were even less united after
his fall and that the trouble to be expected in Parliament was even worse.

Slowly, Charles found himself trying to build new support. This had not been his intention upon dropping Clarendon. The post of Chancellor was simply left vacant as it had been for so long in Scotland, and the seals entrusted to Sir Orlando Bridgeman, a gouty old former royalist who had served as a judge since the Restoration and had no political following. But the ambitions of the aggrieved Earl for active opposition, and the quarrel with his brother drove Charles to elevate other men. It was probably his family feud which caused the King to appoint James's potential rival, young Monmouth, to his first office. In September the prince was allowed to buy Gerard out of the command of the Life Guards, and in October an Irish friend of Monmouth's was granted the value of a fireship and a prize ship. Immediately, James's personal enemies Buckingham and Ashley began to talk of having the King's son declared the heir presumptive, and the fact that all James's male children had died in infancy (leaving two girls, Mary and Anne) lent this course some hint of possibility. Charles gave the rumours further support when, most reluctantly, he brought Buckingham into the government to balance Clarendon's new hostility. On 4 September he gave the Duke a private interview and he restored him to all his offices eleven days later. On the 23rd Buckingham resumed his seat on the Privy Council, treated with special favour. Nevertheless, Charles was neither prepared to give office to any of the Duke's friends until they had proved their new loyalty nor willing to endorse Buckingham's proposal to remove Clarendon's challenge by having him impeached.[54] So matters rested until the much-anticipated session opened.

Upon the first day, Charles welcomed the Houses and Bridgeman detailed all that he had done to satisfy them. It was in vain. During the next two weeks the Commons ordered an enquiry into the sale of Dunkirk and introduced a bill for the taking of public accounts stricter than its predecessor. It identified twelve cases of alleged incompetence or corruption in the government's handling of the war, and investigated them both directly and through a committee. Against this criticism, Charles's servants and allies totally failed to show unity. Buckingham's friends drove on the attack, hoping that it would empty offices for them. Albemarle and Rupert condemned Coventry, and the Navy Board and the various naval officials began to blame each other. In response to this situation, the scheme for religious comprehension was shelved and Charles agreed, on 20 October, to the impeachment of Clarendon. This can only be viewed as a desperate measure to rally his supporters and to divert the MPs' rage. Buckingham's set drew up the charges swiftly, aided by the victim's old enemy Bristol, who at last emerged from hiding to offer his services. The King accepted them with the tart comment that Bristol could win a fortune in any kingdom in three years, and lose it again in three months.

The tactic misfired. Seymour presented the charges to the Commons on 26 October, but after more than two weeks the MPs rejected them as inadequate. The impeachment was only rescued by the imperial ambassador de Lisola who tried to win the gratitude of what seemed the rising political group by informing them that Clarendon had betrayed secrets to the French during the war. This persuaded the Commons to vote the measure through. Lisola, however, had not even forged evidence for his claim and the Lords refused to accept the impeachment without it. Even in the Lower House Warwick and Coventry had opposed the charges upon grounds of natural justice and the members who favoured relief of presbyterians did so in the belief that the Earl was their ally. In the Lords, personal feeling for Clarendon was reinforced by a natural rallying to a fellow peer. His impeachment was supported only by Buckingham's friends and by Bristol, the obedient Albemarle, and Arlington. Against them were arrayed James, Sheldon and all but three bishops, Anglesey, Ashley, and the remaining Privy Counsellors. Total deadlock resulted and Parliament became paralysed. Clarendon radiated confidence, determination, and pleasure.

By now Charles himself was seething with rage. He was in the absurd constitutional position of driving on an impeachment against a former servant and opposing that traditional bulwark of monarchy, the Lords. His brother shamed him into denying one of the charges in front of the court. He tried summoning and rebuking some MPs who had defended Clarendon, only for one of them to answer with a defence of free speech. His situation was becoming intolerable, and he extricated himself only by preparing to violate every principle of natural justice. In late November it became known that he was prepared to send Parliament into recess, pick a tribunal of loyal peers, and have them sentence the Earl to death. Clarendon now recognized defeat, and on the 29th he quietly took ship for France, leaving the relieved Houses to banish him for life. With that, Parliament dispersed for Christmas.[55]

The King's mood during that holiday season may be deduced from the fact that for once there were no festivities at court.[56] His ministers were divided and frightened. He had an enormous debt, a regular revenue which had always been inadequate, and a Parliament which did not believe in the problem. He had been defeated by foreign powers and remained without allies. This composite disaster was the result of his own folly and aggression. Ironically, it was in an attempt to learn from his mistakes that he was now to embark on the most extraordinary gamble of his life.

The Ministry of Arlington, 1668–1672

⟨~∾⟩

Two widely held beliefs have coloured histories of the five years following the fall of Clarendon.[1] One is that they were characterized by a
grand governmental strategy, variously interpreted as a design to make
England Catholic, or its monarchy absolute, or to tie it to the rising
fortunes of France, or to obtain vengeance upon the Dutch. The other
is that the government itself was run by five men, Clifford, Arlington, Buckinghan, Ashley, and Lauderdale, whose initials form the word
'Cabal'. A more recent version of this has been to portray the court as
riven between the factions of Arlington and Buckingham, of whom the
latter proved far more influential. It will be argued here that none of
these views is correct. Instead, it is proposed that government policy
remained essentially cautious, defensive, and pragmatic, and that it was
dominated by Arlington just as much as Clarendon had presided over the
period 1660–2. The quiet, portly minister with the black plaster over
his nose attended Parliament, the Privy Council, and the Committee 'for
Foreign Affairs' (the 'inner ring' of advisers) more assiduously than any
other. To foreign ambassadors, men seeking posts, and others requiring
privileges or pardons, Arlington's favour was above all to be courted and
his opposition feared.[2] In April 1667 it was already said at court that
Clarendon only helped his clients for a price, whereas Arlington strove
to lift his into powerful positions where they might do him service.[3]
Certainly, in 1668–70 the relatively young and able men attracted by the
Secretary of State secured every important foreign embassy and a string of
prestigious domestic posts. Yet one aspect of the traditional picture may be
emphasized anew: during these years it was Charles himself who was the
source of important initiatives, and in the last analysis even Arlington was
only his executive agent.

The first fruit of the Secretary of State's new influence was a remarkable diplomatic coup in the New Year of 1668. Like most of Europe's
diplomacy during that winter, it centred upon the conquests made by
Louis in the Netherlands. Faced with the gigantic French army, the Spaniards had been unable to do anything but sit in their towns waiting to be

besieged. By the autumn of 1667 Louis had reduced several garrisons and, unless other powers came to the aid of Spain, there seemed no reason why he should not continue the process in successive seasons until the entire province was his. Charles's government was determined somehow to use this development to repair the humiliation inflicted upon it at Breda. Its first attempt was to fall like a jackal on the carcase of the Spanish Netherlands, signified in December when Arlington and Buckingham visited the French ambassador. They brought an offer of recognition of Louis's conquests providing that he gave England Ostend, Nieuport, and an alliance against the Dutch. Naturally enough, the French monarch refused the former unless Charles attacked Spain himself and the latter unless the Dutch aided his enemies.[4] Clearly, the French would have to be taught that English friendship was worth buying, and they now were. In January Charles suddenly offered de Witt an alliance to force France and Spain to a compromise peace, adding a promise to confirm the commercial concessions made at Breda. The idea for this move came from Arlington, and its vehicle was one of his protégés, an Anglo-Irishman first promoted by Ormonde and named Sir William Temple. Temple possessed the quality of a diplomatic chameleon, for he threw himself into successive missions not only with gusto but with a genuine sympathy and enthusiasm for every state in which he took up residence. He rapidly acquired an intense admiration for the leaders of Holland, and de Witt, already convinced that the French would have to be stopped, was ready to do business. On the 13th he signed a pact to secure Louis his existing conquests or compensation, but nothing more, and to compel France or Spain to accept these terms if either objected to them.[5] Simultaneously, Sandwich negotiated the long-awaited peace between Portugal and Spain, the result of Spanish willingness to concede Portuguese independence to save the Netherlands, and of sheer hard work on his part. The treaty was signed on 13 February.[6] Within two months, England had played a decisive part in ruining the friendship between the French and the Dutch, deprived Louis of two allies, and won the equal regard of both Iberian monarchies. Charles was certainly pleased by the achievement and had contributed to it. In London he turned the full force of his charm on the Dutch ambassador, utterly convincing him of his zeal for the proposed Anglo-Dutch pact. With the sincerity of a great actor throwing himself into a new role, he told the Dutchman that in statecraft straight dealing and sincerity were the best methods. His other interventions, however, were concerned with rather petty points of protocol. He altered the draft proposals to de Witt from 'forcing' to 'persuading' Spain, out of respect for his Spanish fellow-monarch, and was furious with Sandwich for signing the Hispano-Portuguese treaty after the Spanish ambassador. When the Earl returned from his splendid work it was to find himself in disfavour, and he never had his expenses refunded.[7]

Charles and his ministers were in high hopes that these successes would mend their relations with the Cavalier Parliament as well as restoring their influence abroad. Accordingly, the King opened the new session by appealing to the Houses for money to support his new alliance and recommending to them the project shelved in the autumn, of reunifying English Protestants. The results were disappointing, for the Commons still showed more interest in investigating the alleged miscarriages of the Dutch war, and expressed disbelief that all the funds allocated for it had been properly spent. They rejected the principle of religious comprehension after long debate, and sent up a bill to renew the Conventicle Act of 1664, which was expiring. The biggest shock for Charles must have been the utter uselessness of Buckingham's group. The Duke himself destroyed his reputation in the nation at large by killing the Earl of Shrewsbury, husband of his mistress, in the most spectacular duel of the century. It was discussed with horror as far away as western Caernarvonshire, and gossip reported that the Countess had witnessed the fight disguised as a page, or that she and Buckingham had made love afterwards while his clothes were still stained with blood. Seymour, Temple, and his other followers in the Commons found their influence dwindling as soon as they began to support the court, and returned to attacking it again. That things did not go worse for the government must have been due in part to its careful behaviour. Charles twice politely reminded the Houses about his need for funds, but made no intervention in any other matter. After the death of Shrewsbury he pardoned Buckingham but proclaimed that he would never repeat the favour for anybody who committed the same offence. His brother James presented a severe bill against duelling to the Lords. The Commons were allowed to debate religious comprehension without any collective direction from his servants, and the bill for a looser interpretation of the Prayer Book which had been drafted in 1667 was never introduced. When the Houses petitioned the King for a proclamation against conventicles he issued one immediately. The new bill against them was not passed by the Lords, but this, though it doubtless suited Charles as it gave him more freedom of action, could not be attributed to him. It was due to a quarrel between the two Houses over the legal powers of the Lords, which jammed all business. Before this happened, Charles got his supply, the fruit of the eloquence of Finch and Coventry and of an inspection of accounts which revealed that the government had received less in taxation than had been believed. Unfortunately, the grant was not finished till May and consisted of a mere £300,000 by a tax on wines and spirits, enough to put out a small fleet but not to fight a war. After two years, in any case, the levy had produced only two-thirds of the expected total. Charles's lack of enthusiasm may have been reflected in the speech with which he closed the session, which was even more expressionless than most which he made to the Houses, and in which he initially gave the wrong date for reassembly.[8]

In the event a war supply was not needed, but this does not seem to have been for want of will upon Charles's part. Like the Dutch, he attempted to avert an immediate breach with Louis by sending him professions of goodwill, but he also pressed forward with preparations for conflict even though his allies did not. He wrote bitterly to Minette about his French cousin's disdain of him, and when a French privateer attacked Spanish vessels off his coast he arrested the commander and made a furious protest. The Privy Council ordered fifty warships to be fitted out, and Charles asked for money from the Spanish as well as from Parliament. An expeditionary force was discussed, and Arlington's diplomacy was primarily responsible for drawing Sweden, another peripheral power anxious to make its presence felt, into the Anglo-Dutch alliance.[9] In the end, Louis swallowed his rage and made peace at Aix-la-Chapelle on 22 April. It would be hard to argue that Charles's behaviour towards him had been mere bluff, a show of strength designed to make himself a more attractive ally. From the evidence above, his attitude appears more a mixture of pique and determination to secure himself respect, even to the point of fighting. Nevertheless, it does seem that war would have been impossible had the point arrived. Parliament gave too little and too late, Spain sent nothing, and although the new tax enabled Charles to borrow money to put out a fleet in the summer, this was no more than the parade of a small force.

During the remainder of 1668, the English experienced constant minor difficulties with their new friends. The competition with the Dutch for tropical markets continued. Negotiations to regulate it constantly foundered upon the refusal of the rival trading companies to make serious concessions and the reluctance of the respective governments to constrain them to do so. The two regimes also bickered about the terms of evacuation of the English settlers in Surinam. At the same time the Spanish refused to pay Sweden subsidies which were the agreed price for the latter's inclusion in Arlington's 'Triple Alliance' which was now responsible for maintaining the Treaty of Aix.[10] It is not surprising that Louis believed that he could detach Charles from such a ramshackle partnership, and that four months after Aix he offered him the offensive alliance which he had requested in the winter, in return for his withdrawal from the triple league. He was wrong. Charles spoke in honeyed tones of his desire for 'closer union', but insisted, as a prerequisite, that France abandon certain policies which were seriously worrying his subjects:[11] an increase in the French navy and the imposition of tariffs designed to bolster native manufactures.[12] At the same time, the English government worked hard to bolster the Triple Alliance, expressing a readiness to admit other Protestant states to it and proposing that England and the United Netherlands pay Sweden part of the money owed by Spain.[13] It seems impossible to argue that Charles's consistent aim was an alliance with Louis and vengeance on the Dutch. Rather, in 1668 his regime was trying to strengthen itself all round, using its position to win gratitude among its new allies while gaining concessions from France.

The King seems to have attempted to achieve a similar personal power of manœuvre among his own servants, as if to continue the process of emancipation of which the fall of Clarendon was thought by observers to form a beginning. Symbolically, the greatest office, of Lord Chancellor, was kept vacant while Bridgeman wielded the seals. The next most prestigious post, of Lord Treasurer, remained broken into a commission, and the same course was taken in 1668–9 with those of Lord Privy Seal and Treasurer of the Navy. That of Lord-Lieutenant of Ireland almost followed suit, but Charles continued to rule his other realms through individuals, perhaps for fear that at a distance commissions might acquire a dangerous independence. In England, however, division of offices increased the number of men who could be brought into government, while vacancy of office reduced the chance that powerful ministers might put pressure on their monarch. When the greatest military position, of Captain-General, became empty in 1670, no successor was appointed. It seems no coincidence that from April 1668 new judges were issued with patents bearing the dependent formula 'at pleasure' instead of 'during good behaviour' to denote their tenure of office.[14]

A different account of political developments at this period has, however, been common in several recent histories: that Charles, misled by the nefarious advice of the debauchee Buckingham and the adventurer Orrery, was persuaded to dispense with three of his most loyal and able servants, Coventry, Anglesey, and the great Ormonde himself. The evidence, closely inspected, is against this. As has and will be shown, Arlington was by far the most important minister at this time. Second to him was Bridgeman, whose functions as Keeper of the Seals and Speaker of the Lords gave him a central place in public affairs. He was deeply involved in the diplomacy of the Triple Alliance, and though generally associated with Arlington he was quite capable of joining intrigues of which the Secretary disapproved. When he was bedridden with gout, the King, far from contemplating his dismissal, moved important conferences to his chamber. Yet he had no following of clients and was not reckoned to be intimate with Charles. He was really just an important cog in the state machine.[15]

Compared with these two, Buckingham seems an oddly inconsequential figure. He was not made a minister despite constant intriguing, and the only post he obtained was the ornamental one of Master of the Horse, which he bought from old Albemarle for an enormous sum. He was excluded from the secret diplomacy of 1668–70, and only two of his clients were given offices in these years, the positions being comparatively minor.[16] Indeed, the puzzle is why Charles kept him in apparent favour at all. Part of the reason may lie in what he later told a French ambassador: that the Duke was the most useless of men when in power but the most dangerous when out of it.[17] Doubtless the memory of 1666–7 was still uncomfortable. But the two proposals made by Maurice Lee[18] are also cogent, that Charles retained Buckingham as a screen for his more important advisers and activities, and also as a constant threat to Arlington. Thus the clever Secretary could be kept insecure and subservient to the royal will. These considerations between them would account for the wayward Duke's actual impotence coupled with his prominence at court, which led some observers to mistake him for a major influence upon the King at this period.[19]

How then can one account for the changes at court? One of these was fortuitous: the removal of most of the few 'Presbyterians' on the Privy Council. Two died, being Manchester and the man who had brought about the Restoration, Albemarle. Charles honoured him appropriately to the last, with a sumptuous state funeral and the award of the Garter to his young heir. His greatest military office was, as said, left open, while Manchester's post of Lord Chamberlain went to that old royalist and favourite of Henrietta Maria, St Albans. Growing weary of public life, and knowing that his patron Albemarle was ageing, Morice resigned his office of Junior Secretary of State to another client of Arlington's, Sir John Trevor.[20] The fates of Coventry, Anglesey, and Ormonde resulted from more complex problems, concerned with Charles's attitudes rather than those of his advisers. Coventry doomed himself by his treatment of his royal master. He boasted regularly that his unflinching honesty and clarity of vision had left him isolated at court, and reprimanded the King in public. At one point Charles turned his back on him and strode off in fury, and by March 1669 the King was ready to dismiss him upon any pretext. It was provided almost accidentally by Buckingham's group. The habit had just become common of satirizing courtiers upon stage, commenced by the Countess of Castlemaine, who paid an actress to parody an enemy of hers in a production of Jonson's *Catiline*. The aggrieved noblewoman complained to Manchester, who arrested the actress, but on Barbara's plea Charles not only released her but attended and laughed at the play. This was partly, no doubt, to please his mistress but also reflected that strain in his character which enjoyed the sight of his ministers and courtiers being mocked. At the same period he was laughing to watch Buckingham and other followers mimic Arlington in private as they had poked fun at Clarendon before. As a result, the practice grew considerably, and Buckingham and his friends destined Coventry to be impersonated under the name of Sir Cautious Trouble-All in a play which they had composed. Sir William's sense of humour had shrunk as his self-esteem grew, and he challenged the Duke to a duel. Buckingham accepted, but court gossip carried the news to Charles who secured both and deprived Coventry of all offices on the grounds that he sent the challenge.[21] As matters proved, he was dispensable, for within a few weeks the Treasury Commission was operating as effectively as before.[22]

The replacement of Anglesey and Ormonde was intertwined with two great problems of the Irish administration: the continuing deficit upon the public revenue and the breakdown of the important alliance between Ormonde and Orrery. The nominal overseer of the fiscal system was the Lord Treasurer, the Earl of Cork and Burlington, but he tended to spend his summers hawking on his Yorkshire estates and his winters at court. Charles respected him well enough for his agreeable personality, his vast wealth and potential influence in Ireland, and his canny set of marriage alliances between his children and those of English magnates. But nobody expected him to take serious interest in the Irish Treasury.[23] Ormonde confessed to a friend that he himself never understood finance.[24] The actual work of management had fallen to Anglesey as Vice-Treasurer, and he was no better fitted for it than his superior. In 1666 he had bungled the estimates for the pay of the army, pitching the sum needed too low by £8,000.[25] The person with the real genius for figures, who thoroughly understood the details of the land legislation and the public revenue alike, was Orrery. He watched the fumblings at Dublin with mounting disgust, becoming convinced that mismanagement was at least as big a problem as lack of revenue. His ill humour was fuelled by the fact that his Munster army was always sent pay after that commanded from Dublin had been attended to, and suffered severely. Beneath these specific frictions, however, lay a clash of personality. Orrery always had an overplus of energy, and bombarded Ormonde with letters of advice, information, and complaint. These the Duke found a nuisance, if not an impertinence, and they received slow or no replies, while the recommendations made in them were generally ignored. Frustration grew on the Earl's part and irritation on that of the Duke, and the distance between them afforded ill-wishers an opportunity to fan both sentiments into suspicion and then hostility. The surviving evidence, though copious, provides no firm answer to the problems of whether Orrery began to plot against Ormonde from mere ambition or was driven to do so by the latter's distrust of him.[26] The result is clear. In the summer of 1668 Orrery crossed to Whitehall and laid his complaints about the management of the revenue before the King.

Charles at length agreed to a commission of enquiry, representing all factions at court,[27] which found apparent confusion in the accounts. Anglesey had been transferred to the post of treasurer of the English navy in 1667, but the defects belonged to the period of his supervision. When confronted with the problem he 'shuffled in his answers', and thereby incurred suspension from his new office. He then had the wanton folly to challenge Charles's legal right to do this, drawing upon himself the anger always reserved for those who defied the King and being suspended from the Privy Council and forbidden the royal presence as well. His fall was a blessing for the administration, as he had already acquired a reputation for laziness in the navy and was replaced by two energetic men. One was another client of Arlington, the other the most able of Buckingham's followers, Sir Thomas Osborne.[28] Yet Charles's rage often moderated with time, just as it could be concealed if political expediency demanded. He had forgiven Bristol after four years. Once Clarendon was in exile the King made no attempt to harm him there, and he received Frances Stuart back into favour after an illness had almost disfigured her, as said before.[29] Likewise, because Anglesey strove to serve the court in Parliament after his disgrace, he was recalled to the Council in April 1670.[30]

Ormonde in part made Anglesey's classic error of crossing Charles's will. He insisted upon going to England, without a summons, to pre-empt any attack upon himself by Orrery. Once there, he soon irritated the King with the high-handedness with which he treated the Munster Earl and the latter's English allies, Buckingham's group. It was a little reminiscent of Middleton's behaviour, but as his offence was less he was not disgraced. Instead, Charles announced that his services were required in England and delivered a eulogy upon his conduct as Lord-Lieutenant: the Duke had been implicitly reprimanded but his face saved.[31] Thereafter he regularly attended the Committee 'for Foreign Affairs', and retained some influence in policy-making.[32] He was replaced, to everybody's surprise, by Robartes, who had been considered for the post of Lord Deputy in 1660 and whose chief recommendation was that he belonged to no faction.[33] On landing at Dublin, however, he proved that he had learned nothing since he had alien-ated the Irish leaders nine years before, for he was a martinet bereft of tact or courtesy. The gentry at Dublin were soon furious, and when Robartes accorded Charles and Arlington the same brusqueness, he was recalled and forbidden to come to court.[34] He was replaced early in 1670 by Berkeley, another English peer interested in Irish affairs and also relatively detached from faction, being on good social terms with Buckingham and Orrery but not admitted to their intrigues or those of any other group. He was now quite old, and his initially genial and relaxed manner set him off to a good start with the Counsellors at Dublin.[35]

If Charles's political aim at this period was to ensure himself the widest possible freedom of action, with wholly subservient ministers, then his private life followed much the same pattern. In 1668 Barbara was still very prominent at court, festooned with jewels and gambling for huge sums. But she was becoming supplemented as a sexual accessory by a number of other women. Early in that year the King had a brief affair with an actress, Moll Davis, who bore him a daughter christened Mary. Simultaneously, he took up with Moll's more famous colleague upon stage, Nell Gwyn, daughter of a tavern-keeper (who almost certainly ran a brothel as well) and well summed up by Pepys as 'a bold, merry slut'. She had a heart-shaped face, a full-lipped mouth, dimples, bright chestnut hair, hazel eyes, and a small, slender, and shapely body. Her personality was that of a perfect gamine, a compound of wit and urchin looks, and she had made her reputation as a comedienne. By late 1669 she was pregnant by Charles, and in May 1670 she produced a son named for his father. In or about the same years the King may have made love to Winifred Wells (one of the Queen's Maids of Honour), Jane Roberts (a clergyman's daughter), Mrs Knight (a singer), the widow of his unlucky favourite Falmouth, and the Countess of Kildare. Perhaps, in Lady Antonia Fraser's words, there were also 'the nocturnal visitors introduced up the Privy Stairs. . . . Their numbers, like their identities, remain unknown to history.'[36] Certainly there were contemporary rumours that prostitutes were shown secretly into Whitehall for the King's use. In the mid-1670s, as will be seen, one 'official' mistress was to accuse him of consorting with 'trulls'. But it is interesting that not a single professional whore ever boasted of the honour of royal patronage, suggesting that the 'trulls' are more likely to have been ladies of the court. Nor did Charles yield to every beautiful woman who threw herself at him, the Countess of Clanbrassil in 1671 being a notable failure.[37] Nevertheless, during 1668–70 he certainly took to manœuvring between a number of mistresses.

One might expect that the King's enhanced sense of his own authority and independence would have an impact upon government policy and so, notoriously, it did. Two fresh diplomatic initiatives were launched in early 1669. One was a French attempt to do a deal with the Dutch, which provoked a proposal from de Witt to divide the Spanish Netherlands into independent cantons on the Swiss model. This would serve Dutch interests admirably but give nothing to the English, while it would automatically dissolve the Triple Alliance and leave England isolated again.[38] The other approach, equally secret, was by Charles to Louis, and represented the opening of talks which were to culminate in the spectacular Treaty of Dover. It was apparently devised between Charles and his sister Minette in December 1668 and announced to a select group of advisers on 25 January 1669. Our only account of this now famous meeting is from the memoirs of the King's brother James.[39] It tells how Charles called James, Arlington, Clifford, and Lord Arundell of Wardour to a private conference, where he told them with tears in his eyes of his desire to proclaim his belief in the Catholic faith. Then, according to James, the company resolved upon the approach to Louis. The date attributed by him to the meeting perfectly fits the sequence of events reconstructed from other sources, and the names of the participants make sense. Arundell was a minor Catholic courtier of impeccable loyalty, a perfect agent. Arlington was of course the greatest royal minister. Clifford was the latter's favourite client, devoted to the Crown and notably industrious: despite his lack of French, a good secretary. Furthermore, he may already have expressed doubts concerning the validity of the Church of England.[40] This last was certainly true of James himself, who was in the process of undergoing a personal conversion to Catholicism which was arguably to prove the key event in the English political history of his century. Moreover, he consistently expressed hostility to the Triple Alliance and a preference for France.[41] The royal brothers had been estranged since the disgrace of Clarendon and this conference represented a reconciliation.

But did it ever take place? Most historians have accepted James's account at face value, while Professor Lee has considered it totally fictitious.[42] Perhaps a middle course can be proposed here. In general, James's memoirs refer to genuine events, and the precision with which this one is dated and its participants named, plus the circumstantial evidence cited above, induces belief in this one. On the other hand, the memoirs are often confused or dishonest in portraying the details and meaning of affairs. Certainly this meeting did not produce the idea of an approach to Louis, for the letters of Charles to his sister upon the subject date from weeks before.[43] And there is no good reason for believing in the picture of

Charles sobbing out his love for the Church of Rome. But the rest can easily be accepted.

The offer which Arundell carried to France in March has been lost, but its details can easily be surmised from the point-by-point reply.[44] It was for an offensive and defensive alliance, provided that England received men, money, and ships in case of a war, that the Triple Alliance remained, and that Louis suspended his naval programme. It said nothing about attacking the Dutch, but made instead a personal promise from Charles to declare himself a Catholic if Louis gave him £200,000 with which to secure his position. In the context of previous and current diplomacy, this looks like an attempt to achieve complete security and open options, by being secretly allied to France and openly allied to the Dutch. Charles's expression of a change of faith could well have been the bait which would induce Louis to take a serious interest in such a proposal. If accepted, there were financial as well as diplomatic advantages for England in the deal. In July 1668 a committee of the Privy Council produced a plan for cutting expenditure to a level with income, but in October the Treasury Commission pronounced it unworkable.[45] Trade was recovering after the damage of the war, and commitments abroad were reduced by giving Bombay to the East India Company. By the financial year 1669–70 the regular revenue had increased to the point at which it soon seemed possible to cover current expenditure. But there seemed little hope of reducing the accumulated debt and the cost of servicing it.[46] In this situation, the £200,000 asked by Charles before his declaration of Catholicism would have represented a very significant assistance in the struggle to balance his books—and there was of course no means of compelling him actually to make the declaration.

The offer met with partial success. The French King suspended his negotiations with the Dutch, agreed to guarantee the Treaty of Aix and to build no more warships for a year, and consented to send Charles the money for his 'conversion'. He permitted the negotiation of a public treaty to remove commercial rivalry between their nations. But he was adamant that an attack on the Dutch be the basis for any alliance, a proposal which provoked so little enthusiasm at Whitehall that despite much pressure from Louis no formal treating commenced that summer. The talks about tariffs collapsed because the English insisted upon terms too favourable to their own products.[47] Instead, Charles's government continued to strengthen the Triple Alliance. It co-operated with the Dutch to persuade the Swedes to accept their subsidies in instalments and the Spanish to pay the lot in exchange for a guarantee of all their territory by the Alliance.[48] During 1669 also, English diplomats worked feverishly all over

Europe to increase their country's influence and prestige. They talked to German Protestant princes about alliances, carried the Garter to the Elector of Saxony, acted as peacemakers between the Scandinavian powers, and negotiated treaties with Savoy to aid English commerce and with Denmark to act against respective enemies.[49] Charles ordered forty warships to parade through English waters in the summer.[50] This increased activity may have represented growing confidence and ambition, or a feverish search for security, or both. Certainly the Triple Alliance continued to exhibit weaknesses. The Anglo-Dutch disputes over the evacuation of Surinam and tropical trade proved as intractable as before and involved Charles's government in much hard work and frustration. Spain was still withholding the subsidies, insisting now upon a formal blueprint for joint action in the case of a French attack.[51]

Such irritations must have lain in part behind the developments of the autumn. The French approached the Dutch again and received a proposal to partition the Spanish Netherlands between them, giving nothing to the English.[52] Simultaneously, Charles agreed to open a formal (though secret) negotiation with Louis. Our best insight into his own views at this time is provided by a letter to him from Minette in September.[53] She says nothing about his yearning for personal salvation, but is concerned almost wholly with persuading him to destroy the Dutch with French aid. Then, having strengthened himself with the profits of victory, he could ally with Spain and the German princes to contain Louis. Her cold-blooded preoccupation with international power politics is very significant, though even Charles's correspondence with her need not necessarily be taken to represent his personal feelings. His sentiments in these letters generally parallel, at each stage, those which he expressed to the French. They provoke an obvious suspicion that he was taking precautions lest these documents fall into the hands of Louis—which later they did. Nevertheless, in this case Charles began to follow his sister's advice, and by December, though still trying to divert attention to his theoretical declaration of Catholicism, he was at last prepared to offer the French his terms for a new Dutch war. In the ensuing negotiations, papers were drafted by Clifford and translated by that ubiquitous polylingual Catholic Belling. But Arlington did most of the actual talking, managing the affair just as he had been responsible for the Triple Alliance.[54] He may have been acquiescing reluctantly in his master's preference for a pact with France, and although he possibly became a Catholic upon his death-bed many years later he was certainly not one at this time.[55] Yet his correspondence portrays a growing exasperation with the Dutch and Spanish which seems both genuine and understandable.[56] When he later justified the reversal of policy in favour of France to an

English diplomat, he stated simply that England had to make a deal with Louis before the Dutch did so[57]—and it seems that he was correct.

The English conditions presented to Louis[58] commenced with a demand for £1 million beforehand and £600,000 per annum until the war ended. This was not an invented set of figures intended to deter the French, but a realistic one: when the Navy Board was asked for an estimate of its total needs five months later, it stated that about £1 million was needed just to pay its debts and provide for a year's normal expenses.[59] Next, Charles wanted three ports in Zealand as his share of the defeated United Nether-lands, giving him control of the trade of the Rhine delta. To ensure English influence in the portion left to the Dutch, Charles's nephew Wilhelm was to be gratified with land or money. Louis was required to preserve the Treaty of Aix, but if he ever claimed the Spanish throne itself then England was to receive a large share of the Spanish empire. The Dutch war was to be left until after Charles had declared his Catholicism, but Louis was still to pay the money for it within six months of the treaty without requiring a date for the declaration itself.

If these were Charles's terms, what was the domestic background to his negotiations? Certainly he was not promoting Catholics into key military or administrative posts, and in religious affairs his chief preoccupation remained the problem of Protestant dissent. His strategy in this matter was that adopted since the beginning of the reign: to manipulate affairs to yield the maximum possible benefit to his own position. The expiry of the First Conventicle Act had left English nonconformists free to meet. Throughout 1668 and early 1669, reports reached the government that they were taking their impunity for granted rather than as a privilege that might be with-drawn.[60] Royal policy was correspondingly ambivalent. On the one hand, Charles was generally thought to be in favour of toleration and waged no campaign for uniformity.[61] On the other, when he received complaints of the insolence of particular conventicles, he ordered their suppression. He turned a deaf ear to Quaker appeals for a general liberation of their imprisoned brethren and told a deputation of presbyterian ministers to keep their meetings small, infrequent, and discreet. The Privy Council wrote to urban councils warning them to enforce the tests prescribed by the Corporation Act.[62] All through the period 1668–70 he filled sees with churchmen who represented a range of attitudes towards the problem of dissent. This ensured that the bishops were less likely to unite in forcing a particular policy upon him.

In the course of 1669, Charles's attitude hardened. On 15 April he laid the latest complaints of the boldness of local conventicles before the Committee for Foreign Affairs. Bridgeman, Arlington, Buckingham, and James all advised that the report be treated with caution. Ormonde alone urged that an example be made of certain meetings, and yet Charles followed his counsel and had the orders drawn up.[63] Provincial dissenters responded with petitions for toleration, but these backfired. The tone of the largest one, from Wiltshire in July, annoyed most of the Committee for Foreign Affairs, and Charles instructed bishops, judges, and local magistrates to commence a full-scale campaign against conventicles.[64] By the end of the year reports had come in of its effects. In some places it had produced arrests and a decrease in active dissent, while in others it had provoked only derision.[65]

Superficially, policy in Scotland seemed to take an opposite course. In the same month in which Charles launched the drive against English conventicles, Lauderdale pushed Tweeddale into enacting a long-mooted scheme by which some of the most moderate presbyterian ministers were appointed to vacant livings known as the 'First Indulgence'. Charles gave permission for the move, and subsequently spoke to Murray against the persecution of people for their religious beliefs in 'most pungent and unanswerable' terms. Some of Archbishop Burnet's clergy drew up a protest against the new policy, to be delivered directly to Charles and thus to circumvent Lauderdale's group. The latter saw their danger and reacted ruthlessly. As Lauderdale himself was in Scotland, it fell to the silver-tongued Murray to misrepresent the address as a new Western Remonstrance, intended to coerce the King. Charles responded with fury, and ordered Burnet to resign. Lauderdale persuaded the wretched Archbishop to acquiesce meekly, with the promise that he would receive a pension: the order for this was never signed. What the Earl himself was doing in Scotland was enjoying, at last, the supreme office of Commissioner, to a new Parliament, and persuading it to pass an Act drafted by Murray, recognizing the King's complete power over the Kirk. By this, retrospective legal sanction was given to the policy of comprehension.

In fact, the initiatives in the two kingdoms were directed to the same end. Charles was not trying to extirpate dissenters in England but to make them grovel to him. He was not interested in tolerating them in Scotland for the sake of freedom of conscience itself but to separate the most moderate from the extremists in order to facilitate the destruction of the latter. And this, explicitly, was the intention of his Scottish ministers in enacting comprehension. Even as he approved this scheme, the King urged that the 'Remonstrants', as he still termed conventiclers, be crushed. In the same year 1669 the Scottish Privy Council set up a committee to fight dissent and passed acts to increase the responsibility of landowners for meetings on their property. The Parliament passed a statute against the disturbance of orthodox ministers.[66] And the approach to dissent in Ireland was of exactly the same order. Charles directed that 'insolent' Protestant conventicles there be suppressed, and instructed Robartes to divide moderate from obdurate nonconformists as Lauderdale was attempting to do. Both Robartes and Berkeley were directed to encourage the Catholic clergy who subscribed the 'Irish Remonstrance' and to persecute the others if they behaved boldly. In addition, Berkeley was ordered to strengthen the established Church.[67]

Upon contemplating his work in the Scottish Parliament of 1669, Lauderdale told Charles 'Never was king so absolute as you in poor old Scotland.'[68] The remark was probably literally true, but there are two senses in which it should not be misunderstood. The first is an assumption by some modern historians[69] that the King was strengthening his grip upon his northern realm with a view to using the Scots to impose his will on England. Echoing fears expressed at the time, they have pointed to his sponsorship of a Scottish move to unite the two states, and to a Scottish militia act passed in November 1669 which provided for an army for use in other realms. In reality, the project for union had been produced by Lauderdale's group as long ago as 1667, as a means of ensuring that never again would Scotland have to suffer through a war fought for English economic interests without any prospect of reward. Charles was persuaded to favour it at the end of 1669, but it collapsed a year later because representatives of the two nations could not agree upon the nature of a joint Parliament.[70] The militia statute merely re-enacted that of 1663, as part of the reorganization of national security after the disbanding of the standing army—a reversal of the process which a prospective despot would require. Charles himself still thought vaguely of using a Scottish force to defend himself in an emergency, but Lauderdale was surprised that any such notion was now entertained.[71] The second sense in which Charles was not quite 'absolute' master of the Scots was that his view of Scottish affairs continued to be regulated by the small set which dominated them. The fate of Archbishiop Burnet was a spectacular illustration of this fact. On each occasion upon which Lauderdale had to leave his master's side, Murray immediately took his place. Sir Robert was a noted chemist, and Charles took to calling at his laboratory in the evenings, ostensibly to discuss his experiments but in reality to have Scottish affairs interpreted for him among the test tubes. Of one major issue Murray could report to the Earl that 'no creature here knows anything of it but he [the King] and I',[72] and this comment would serve for most.

Certainly, Charles compared the docility of his Parliament in Scotland wistfully with the behaviour of that in England.[73] Both Arlington and Buckingham had urged him to dissolve the latter and to hope that elections would produce a more tractable body. Taking his own line, as over conventicles and foreign policy, the King insisted upon trying to work with the existing one, in the hope that a long 'cooling off' period would have beneficial effects.[74] In October 1669 he opened the new session with an appeal for funds to continue his active foreign policy and to commence the payment of his debts. His tone was friendly and confident. The result was another wretched disappointment. The Commons did eventually decide to supply a larger sum than in 1668, but devoted most of their energies to continuing the inquest into the Dutch war and their quarrel with the Lords. Not only was a government initiative to compose the latter rejected by the Lower House, but once again rivalries within the government worsened the general situation. Before the session Charles had exhorted his servants to show unity, but his words counted for as little as his speech to Parliament. When the Commons proposed that the new supply be raised by another tax on wines, Clifford and Duncombe argued that evasion would result in an inadequate sum. They found themselves opposed by their own colleague Downing, and lost the debate. Ormonde's friends forestalled an expected attack upon the Duke by trying to impeach Orrery. He was defended in turn by his English allies, the Buckingham group, and by Clifford and Finch, who felt that the matter used up valuable time. On 11 December Charles prorogued Parliament once again, apparently because of a rumour that the Commons were going to adjourn themselves. The decision for him to do so was only taken at a hastily called meeting late the previous night, and the King made it on the advice of his brother and of Ormonde and Rupert, against that of Bridgeman and Arlington.[75] 'No man of our Age has seen a time of more expectation which is the next step to confusion', wrote Ashley in disgust.[76]

He was wrong. With his negotiations with Louis at a critical stage, Charles simply had to achieve a working partnership with his English Parliament to increase the apparent strength of his position, and so he did. During the recess he staged a public debate between the Houses' committee of inquiry into the financing of the late war and his naval officials. The latter prepared their case with great skill and he gave them procedural advantages. As a result, they appeared to most observers to emerge with greater credit, and the exchange terminated the long post-mortem upon the war.[77] Long before Parliament remet in February 1670, the Committee for Foreign Affairs agreed 'to frame an entire scheme' of how to handle it.[78] From the results, it is clear that the plan did not include actual bribery of members, nor the forcing through of support when attendance was thin.[79] Instead, Charles successfully wooed the Houses as complete bodies. During the previous two sessions the majority of the Commons had shown themselves to be in favour of a new Conventicle Act. This time the King ignored the appeals of its prospective victims and ensured its passage. The apparent ingratitude of dissenters during the past two years made this course convenient, but the government tempered the potential force of the statute by having a proviso added which emphasized the monarch's ultimate supremacy in ecclesiastical affairs. Similar in terms to the act recently passed in Scotland, it held out the hope that Charles might use his power to relieve individuals as he had done there, and recover some of the ability to regulate dissent which he had lost in 1662–3. In the same session he resolved the legal dispute between the Houses with a judgement which implied favour to the Commons, and when the latter delivered thanks he compounded their goodwill by inviting them to drink their fill in his cellars. He dealt with the Lords by reviving the ancient custom of attending their debates in person, thereby doing them formal honour and forcing any critics to speak under his eyes. A combination of all these devices resulted in a sudden harmony which amazed onlookers and a grant of £400,000, to be raised by taxing wine and vinegar.[80]

Over only one issue did government members divide in this session, and this was unusual in that the principal setting was the Lords and that it suited Charles very well. Baron Roos introduced a bill to divorce his wife, providing an opportunity for the peers to debate the validity of divorce in general. The implications for the King's own position were noted by most observers. For three years gossip had been continuous that he was either about to repudiate his barren queen and remarry, or that he would legitimize Monmouth. From time to time Charles discountenanced such talk, but he continued to lavish favour upon his son and when the Roos bill appeared he supported it and ensured its success. Furiously opposed to him over the issue was James, joined by Manchester and most of the bishops. There is no evidence that the contest was anything but genuine, and yet none that Charles was seriously considering a new marriage. He seems to have been using the question of the royal succession to remind his brother of his dependence upon Charles's goodwill, just as he kept Arlington a little unsure of his position.[81]

Even as the King came to terms with the Cavalier Parliament, so he did with France. The first reaction of Louis to the English terms was shock, his second to outflank them brilliantly by telling Charles that his total contribution to the new war need be only to join thirty ships to the French navy. This was a nasty surprise for the English negotiators, for it reminded them of how great the power of France was and served notice that he was quite prepared to dominate the North Sea for a season if this became necessary. For five months the haggling continued, and once again both sides prepared alternative strategies. France seems to have proposed to Spain that Louis acquire the Spanish Netherlands by an exchange of territory, while England conceded the Spanish demand for a formal 'concert' of forces by the Triple Alliance and began to discuss a commercial treaty at Madrid. Nevertheless, the secret Anglo-French talks produced a compromise acceptable to both sides. Charles agreed to join sixty ships to thirty French vessels, for an annual subsidy of about £230,000. He also promised to send 4,000 infantry to join the French army, whom Louis would pay. These terms were financially realistic, for the Navy Board stated the cost of putting out fifty ships as being about £266,000.[82] The French subsidy would almost cover this, and for the other costs of war Charles would have the latest grant from Parliament and the money advanced by Louis against his declaration of Catholicism, fixed at about £160,000. Furthermore, as the French insisted, the war could itself prove to be a financial asset. Louis expected that the Dutch, assaulted by his army, would neither be able to make a great effort at sea nor to resist for a season. The loot which Charles would secure, particularly in shipping, might solve his financial problems while the glory of the exploit would increase his prestige at home and abroad. It is not surprising that at this point the English King and his confidants took the step of allowing the war to become at least a possibility. Charles's design of making Spain a counterweight to a victorious France was served by a promise from Louis not to attack that other monarchy. And the English kept the ability to postpone the war indefinitely, as it had in theory to follow a declaration of faith by Charles for which he would pick the time. In mid-May Minette met her brother at Dover, ostensibly on a visit motivated by pure affection. On the 22nd, Louis's ambassador Colbert de Croissy signed the secret treaty with Arlington, Arundell, Clifford, and Belling, and Minette subsequently carried back the French copy for ratification. Just over a month later, the English envoy at Madrid completed an Anglo-Spanish agreement which recognized English ownership of Jamaica. The long process of *rapprochement* with Spain was complete.[83] In a sense, this summer represented the apex of the reign, with all the political problems of the previous years apparently solved and glorious opportunities opening abroad. To a great extent the achievement had been Charles's own, as during the years 1668–70 he had assumed an ever larger part in the making of policy and the business of government.

The principal development of the second half of 1670 was the signature of a second treaty with France. The course of events leading to it commenced with what, for Charles, was one of the worst of all possible developments: the death of Minette within weeks of her return to France. Still only twenty-six, she expired suddenly and in agony of what might have been peritonitis. Thus Charles lost his favourite sibling, the third since the Restoration to be struck down by unexpected and rapid illness. As Henrietta Maria had died, in her retirement in France, the previous year, his family was reduced to the difficult James and Rupert, natures quite alien to his own, to a wife for whom he possessed affection devoid of passion, and to his growing number of illegitimate children. Ormonde remarked that he had never known his master so upset: Charles retired to his bedchamber and did not emerge for days, till the arrival of a French marquis, bringing the condolences of Louis and the report of an autopsy which proved that the dead princess had not been poisoned.[84]

The tragedy did provide an opportunity for further secret diplomacy, for as the 'inner ring' met after the King's re-emergence, Buckingham asked to carry the formal reply to Louis. Backed by his allies Lauderdale and Ashley, he further proposed that he make his visit an excuse to offer an alliance to the French. Charles, James, and Arlington were amused and delighted, for it afforded them both a chance to draw these three other chief Counsellors into their own project, and also some delicious play-acting. The Duke duly went, and his master asked Louis to offer him the Treaty of Dover, shorn of the 'Catholicity' clause. Charles regarded his departure with the mixture of amusement and quiet contempt with which he had come to regard Buckingham. When Murray asked the King when he expected to see the Duke again, he received the reply 'at the day of Judgement in the Valley of Jehosophat'.[85] In fact he was back in September, equipped with the draft treaty and all the flattery that his shallow nature required. What now amazed and irritated Louis was the agility with which Charles and his intimates turned the subsequent negotiations to their advantage. Instead of sticking to the terms of the Dover treaty, they used these 'bogus' talks to increase their demands. When the French monarch suggested that the joint attack be launched the following spring, Charles showed reluctance until Louis changed his own mind and then blamed his cousin for the lost opportunity: the technique which he had used upon the Spanish when in exile. The 'Secret Treaty of London' was signed on 21 December, adding two more Dutch islands to the expected English war booty and concealing the money for Charles's declaration of faith as an addition to the subsidies. Louis experienced another shock when he proposed, naturally enough, that the Treaty of Dover be now annulled, and received a denial. As a result, it was left unclear whether the war would follow the declaration or not, and therefore whether it would happen at all.[86] At the same time the English government attempted to persuade the French to reduce their tariffs upon English goods, sending protests through Buckingham and commissioning Rupert to discuss the matter with Colbert de Croissy. But this time Louis held fast and the talks aborted.[87]

This pattern of determined opportunism is clear enough, and forms a continuity with English foreign policy in 1668–70. What is impossible to determine in it is whether Charles had yet committed himself to the war which Louis so clearly wanted. His treatment of the Dutch and Spanish provides no clear evidence on the matter. On the one hand, he followed the signature of the Dover treaty by recalling Sir William Temple from The Hague and treating him coldly, ostensibly for having been too 'soft' in his conduct of the disputes over Surinam and tropical markets. The fact that Temple was not replaced suggests that relations with de Witt were being put 'on hold' until the moment for the attack came. When the Spanish and Dutch proposed in the winter that the Triple Alliance be enlarged to include the Emperor Leopold, Charles politely quashed the scheme. As he was doing so, young Wilhelm of Orange visited England, and Charles told Louis that he had intended to bring the Prince into the scheme for the war, promising him sovereign power over a truncated United Netherlands. According to this letter, it was only because he found his nephew 'so passionate a Dutchman and a Protestant' that he changed his mind. All these details suggest a firm adherence to France after the Treaty of Dover. On the other hand, the English government did conduct long talks with the Dutch ambassador about their current disputes, and Charles himself contributed more energetically to these than mere play-acting would have required. A commercial treaty with Denmark signed in July 1670 benefited English interests at the expense of the French. Leopold's wish to join the Triple Alliance proved on probing to consist in reality of a desire to conclude a pact for mutual defence with all its members, and Charles had no interest in defending Austria. As before, the behaviour of his nominal partners must have pushed him further towards Louis. De Witt threatened to make a deal with the French unless the English gave concessions in the talks about trade, while the Spanish continued to exasperate Arlington by trying to extend the benefits of the Triple Alliance.[88] Perhaps the best summary of English foreign policy in the year after the Treaty of Dover would be as follows: Charles and Arlington continued to edge cautiously towards a new Dutch war, while trying to keep an option of withdrawing from the whole scheme and attempting all the time to win as many concessions from as many nations as possible.

It is easier to divine Charles's true attitude towards his own prospective declaration of Catholicism. He found excuses to refuse offers to put him in touch with the Pope, whether they came from Louis or from Clifford, who, inspired by his own increasing conviction of the faith of Rome, was producing grandiose schemes for the reunion of the Churches. The King's only real interest in the question of his declaration was confined to the money which was to be paid for it, in advance. For that, indeed, he displayed intense concern.[89] He ignored Clifford's proposals for putting Catholics in charge of regular and militia units and for letting Berkeley into the secret to prepare the hosts of Ireland for action.[90] Instead, his policy towards the Roman Church in Ireland remained as before, of encouraging the 'Remonstrant' faction against the more orthodox clergy.[91] As before, also, his personal affection for Catholics was limited to those who had served the royalist cause. In November 1670 Richard Talbot, who had made his name as an agent at court during the Irish land settlement, returned to Whitehall. He carried a petition signed by 58 Catholic nobles and gentry, complaining of the injustice of that settlement and asking for an impartial enquiry into it. Against the advice of Berkeley, the entire Irish Privy Council, Ormonde, Arlington, and Finch, Charles once more yielded to his sentiment for the men who had filled up his army in exile, and appointed one. Yet it consisted of Buckingham, Anglesey, Holles, Ashley, and Trevor, whose atitude to Catholics varied from indifference to hostility, and most of whom supported the project out of enmity to Ormonde, whom they hoped to discredit.[92]

As before, the government was far more concerned with Protestant nonconformity. In June 1670 the Second Conventicle Act went into force in England wherever there were magistrates prepared to execute it, and there turned out to be a great many of them. Once again the prisons were full of dissenters, and once again some of them turned to Charles for help. They got none, for to continue his good relationship with the House of Commons and perhaps also from a genuine bitterness, the King drove on the persecution. His Privy Council employed the Surveyor-General, Christopher Wren, on one of his less-known tasks: to seal up nonconformist meeting-houses in London. It urged provincial justices to harry conventicles and threatened the Stationers' Company with the loss of its charter if it did not make greater efforts to track down 'seditious' literature. Charles supplemented these orders with personal directives, and dismissed a few JPs who had been lax in the work.[93] As the campaign of repression commenced in England, Lauderdale pushed a truly draconian set of measures against conventicles through the Scottish Parliament. All, of course, had the King's approval, and one made death the penalty for open-air meetings, which were the largest. Collectively, they represented an attempt to crush any belief that Charles intended a general toleration,

SEAT OF POWER

Charles and his courtiers walking on Horseguards Parade. These walks became increasingly important in Charles's life, and were an aspect of his famous accessibility. Behind is Whitehall, the warren of rooms in which so much of the reign was set.

RIVAL PRINCES

James, Duke of York, left, and James, Duke of Monmouth, right. Both reveal the same mixture of good looks and not very remarkable intelligence.

RIVAL MINISTERS

Edward, Earl of Clarendon left, and Henry, Earl of Arlington, right. Both were
gifted, but Clarendon is showing all the pomposity which was to assist his fall.

RIVAL POLITICIANS

Thomas, Earl of Danby, left, and Anthony, Earl of Shaftesbury, right. The vulpine
cunning of these great opponents is patent in their faces.

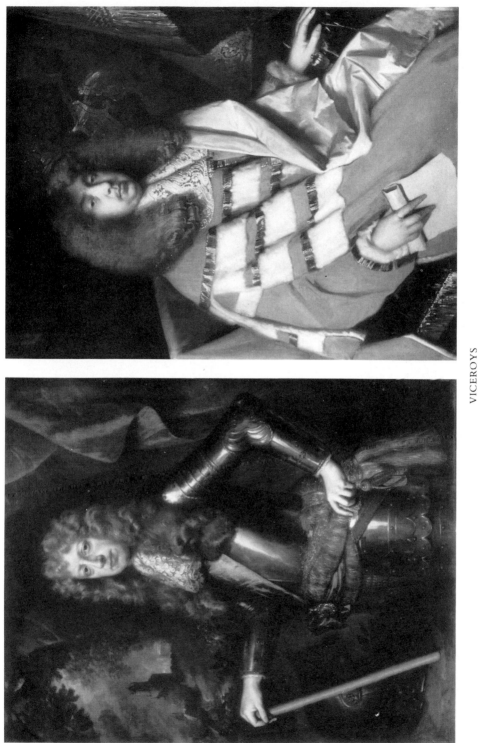

VICEROYS

The courtly James, Duke of Ormonde, left, contrasts with the coarser John, Duke of Lauderdale, right. Yet both dominated their respective kingdoms for most of the reign.

MISTRESSES

Barbara, Duchess of Cleveland, left, worked upon Charles with tantrums while
Louise, Duchess of Portsmouth, right, used tears. But the strongest weapon of each
was her beauty.

PUNISHMENT AND PLEASURE

As illustrated above, the English Republic was quick to laugh at Charles's humiliations by his Scottish allies in 1650. Below, a restored Charles leads the nation in its pastimes. Here he presides over Windsor races, 1684.

THE SACRED MONARCH

An imagined scene in which the alleged Popish Plotters fail to assassinate
Charles in 1678. A silver bullet was needed for a king as for a werewolf.

and to force presbyterian ministers to seek readmission to the Kirk on the terms of the Indulgence of 1669.[94] Only in Ireland, where Berkeley personally inclined to moderation, was there no government-sponsored attack upon dissent.[95]

This is the context for Charles's encounter with one of the age's most romantic characters, Thomas Blood. Blood did not look romantic, being a tall rough-boned man with a pock-marked face and small hollow eyes. Yet his career was undeniably dashing. A former Cromwellian soldier, he had taken part in plots in both England and Ireland in the 1660s, and in December 1670 his gang kidnapped Ormonde at Westminster, apparently with intent to murder him. The ageing Duke succeeded in breaking free, and Charles put a reward of £1,000 upon the heads of each of Blood's group. They survived, and were only finally netted the following May, in the course of an attempt to steal the Crown Jewels. To the wonder of contemporaries and of posterity, the King interviewed Blood and then pardoned him.[96] Admirers of Charles have attributed this to a quixotic romanticism, which caused him to admire the sheer bravado of his captive. Detractors have bewailed the insult thus apparently paid to Ormonde, or suggested that the King could not proceed against Blood without exposing Buckingham, the true author of the attempt upon the Duke. The explanation by Professor Haley[97] fits the evidence far better than these: Blood was released on condition that he use his vast knowledge of the nonconformist and republican 'underground' to act henceforth as a double agent. His son was held as security for this arrangement, and he was forced to keep it for years, supplying much information.[98] As so often, the sort of dramatic story which has made biographies of the 'Merry Monarch' so exciting erodes upon closer inspection into something colder, more 'professionally' political.

Certainly, Charles's attitude towards nonconformity must have contributed towards his continuing splendid relationship with the Cavalier Parliament in its winter session of 1670–1. Nothing had occurred in the recess to vitiate it, and another factor had been working to bolster it: that a number of the court's most outspoken opponents had by now been brought into the government. The process began with Vaughan, knighted and made a judge in 1668, and ended with Sir Richard Temple, given a financial office in 1670. Each was employed only after he had moderated his opposition and spoken for the regime: Charles had avoided the ploy of trying to buy them off directly. In his opening speech, Charles referred to the prevailing mood of harmony and (perhaps not to perjure himself) left it to Bridgeman to go into details of the government's aims. Though ignorant of both the Anglo-French treaties, the ageing Lord Keeper did not misrepresent the situation too badly, calling for a supply to put out a fleet in order to maintain England's active and flexible foreign policy. As usual, the Commons were better able to vote supply in principle than to decide how to raise it in practice, but by early December they were working upon bills for a new excise upon beverages, a tax upon legal documents, and higher rates upon imported goods. On the 10th the King resorted to deceit to obtain more. He informed the House that Louis XIV intended to visit Dunkirk in May, and asked for a total of £800,000 to secure England against a possible surprise attack by the French. The ruse worked admirably, and a bill for an extra subsidy was sent up. A few MPs still opposed the granting of such a large supply, and their ranks now received the addition of Sir William Coventry, who thus began to repay Charles for his dismissal. Almost always, however, the divisions went in favour of the court interest. It was the House of Lords, still smarting from its humiliation in the spring, which caused trouble. One peer complained that the country had never been so heavily taxed, another criticized the habit which Charles had continued of sitting in on debates, and thirty voted against the subsidy bill. But, as in the Commons, this opposition was outnumbered.

Such success depended upon the simple fact that the government was supporting policies favoured by the majority of both Houses. Despite individual strenuous efforts by its members, notably Finch and Clifford, the government did not co-ordinate its speakers much better than in difficult sessions. When Clifford put a valuation upon the supply offered by the Commons, he was contradicted by his colleagues Trevor and Duncombe. Buckingham's client Sir Robert Howard offered to farm all the new taxes and was opposed by Clifford and Downing, only for the latter to discover that Charles had already privately approved the scheme. The most spectacular intervention by courtiers in the session, however, occurred outside the Houses. When the Commons debated taxing theatres, a member remarked upon the pleasure that the players gave the King. Sir John Coventry, a young nephew of Sir William, asked if this service had been performed more by the actors or the actresses. It is not recorded whether this jibe met with laughter or embarrassed silence, but the reaction of some officers of Charles's Life Guard was plain enough. On a night in the following week, they pinned down Sir John in the street, cut him four times in head and body and tried to slice off his nose. The attack created a furore in the capital and in Parliament, and the Commons suspended all work upon supply till they had passed a bill offering the ringleaders trial or exile and making such mutilation a felony. It was rumoured that Charles, or his son Monmouth who now commanded the Life Guard, had ordered the crime. Nevertheless, the storm passed with the statute. The principal culprits escaped abroad, while the King immediately gave permission to local JPs to arrest guardsmen who had assisted the atrocity, and readily assented to the Act. Government peers worked to hurry the latter through the Lords. It is extremely unlikely that he was involved in planning the outrage and there is no real evidence that Monmouth was implicated either.

The session was effectively terminated by another division in the court. The Lords passed most of the fiscal bills sent up, but amended that for increased rates upon imported goods by reducing the proposed duty on sugar. The Commons then challenged their constitutional right to do this and a new dispute between the Houses began. The Committee for Foreign Affairs at first attempted to find a definitive legal ruling upon the issue, but government members in the Houses soon divided upon it, apparently irreconcilably. Buckingham, Ashley, and Sandwich insisted upon the rights of the Lords while Clifford and Finch, reputedly encouraged by Arlington, defended the Lower House. Charles urged the peers to give way, and was ignored. On 22 April he suddenly lost patience and prorogued Parliament. Arlington, who ought to have known, told foreign ambassadors that this was intended to chasten the Houses and dispose them to a reconciliation (and the passage of the controversial statute). Certainly the dispute was highly inconvenient to the King, as it cost him not only a valuable financial resource but an Act of General Pardon with which he was intending to crown the session. This would have been popular in the country, but also have indemnified Sir John Coventry's assailants, and his own ministers for involvement in the secret treaties. Historians have suggested that Charles was disgusted with the smallness of the supply, afraid of offending the French because the new impost would injure their exports, or nervous of other bills pending.[99] There is no evidence for any of these explanations. The two measures pending were one to tighten up the Conventicle Act, of which the Foreign Affairs Committee approved, and one to force Catholics to resign public office. The latter was indeed highly dangerous, as it would have made James declare his new faith. But the Commons had not made supply conditional upon its passage, and Charles was preparing to head it off as he had the proposed Conventicle Act of 1663: he had proclaimed the enforcement of the recusancy laws and the banishment of priests, and the bill was to die in the Lords. So Arlington's word must apparently be taken at face value. It is an indication that Charles did not realize that the session was to be the last before war broke out again.[100]

What of Charles himself in the years 1670–2? The followers over whom he presided retained their reputation for debauchery. John Evelyn found them at Newmarket in October 1671, 'racing, dancing, feasting and revelling, more resembling a luxurious and abandoned rout than a Christian court'. In Buckinghamshire the year before, the gentry were gossiping about how a courtier walked five miles 'stark naked and barefoot' to win a wager while King and nobles watched. In the same month even the demure Queen disguised herself and her ladies as countrywomen to go unnoticed to a fair in Essex: they were discovered and followed by a huge crowd. In the winter of 1670–1 Charles led the court in a fashion of going masked to balls and feasts. He had to ban the practice after a party which included Monmouth and Richmond, thus disguised, clashed with watchmen and accidentally killed one of them.[101] What is difficult to determine is how far the King misbehaved with his followers. In January 1671 Colbert de Croissy wrote to his French sovereign that Charles had supped at his embassy and indulged in 'a gay and unfettered debauch', but that does not seem to have involved more than drinking and telling stories. The following September the ambassador reported that the King hunted every day, 'and occasionally even on his way he stops at a house where he finds other diversions'. This tantalizing allusion seems either to be to tippling at alehouses or to calling at the dwelling in which he had installed Nell Gwyn. It cannot have been to bordellos, or another commentator would surely have remarked upon the fact. The same dispatch records a supper party held by Clifford at which 'everybody', including Charles, James, Monmouth, and Arlington, got drunk. But as soon as the horseplay threatened to get out of control, the King retired.[102] When the young Earl of Rochester, son of the dead general, struck a gentleman in the royal presence, Charles forbade him the court. The victim had made a joke about Rochester's marriage, but to the King this did not excuse the breach of formal propriety.[103] Pepys recorded a rumour that at one entertainment Charles drank too hard to be able to discuss business with Arlington afterwards. Yet this alleged incident can be compared with the King's behaviour during a visit to Harwich three weeks before. The naval commissioner there noted that he arrived, inspected the dockyard, and then supped, refusing all alcohol. The following morning he rose at six, inspected the fortifications and corrected drafts or improvements, and then went for a five-mile solitary walk across the fields. At lunch James of York drank wine, but Charles took only chocolate. Then the royal party sailed for Aldeburgh. It was a performance worthy of a protégé of Baden-Powell, and a firsthand story instead of gossip. At the least, it can be said that Charles's lapses in private were few if any, and his behaviour in public was impeccable.[104]

What characterized him most at this period was a restless energy. He ranged further afield than usual, to Norfolk, the New Forest, and

Plymouth. After the Medway disaster he was repeatedly inspecting coastal fortifications. His solitary hike around Harwich reflected the interest which he was bringing to government since the secret diplomacy began. Likewise the lively diversity of his sexual life, commenced in 1668, continued. In July 1670 Barbara was more or less pensioned off, with the gift of a royal palace (Nonsuch) and the titles of Duchess of Cleveland for herself and of Earl of Southampton for their eldest son. For years she and Charles had been tiring of each other, and rumours abounded that she as well as he had found other partners. She remained prominent at court and received more presents in later years, but by September 1671 Colbert de Croissy could report that her influence was completely gone.[105] In a sense her achievement had been impressive, for at a time when women had few opportunities for advancement she had succeeded in winning herself a fortune, a title, and independence by the age of thirty.

It seemed for a time that her position as favourite mistress would be taken by the woman to whom Barbara apparently referred as 'that pitiful strolling actress'.[106] Nell was enjoying her own more modest success in winning comforts from her royal lover. In the summer of 1670 Charles had set her up in a house in Pall Mall, similar to that into which he had put the discarded Moll Davis and their child. Its value was not good enough for Ms Gwyn, who proceeded to return to her career on the public stage in December. The King was embarrassed enough to persuade her to retire with the outright gift of a much better dwelling in Pall Mall, and for much of 1671 she was his favourite bedfellow: their second son, James, was born at Christmas.[107] By then, however, she had already been eclipsed: Charles had set eyes upon a baby-faced dark-curled Frenchwoman of twenty-one, called Louise-Renée de Penancoët de Kéroualle. Like Barbara, Louise came from impoverished noble stock. Unlike her, she had become nobody's wife or mistress in her teens but obtained a post in waiting to Minette. The latter's death left her without means of support, and she was glad enough when friends found her a position in the entourage of the English queen.[108] By November 1670 she was at Whitehall and her beauty was making a stir. Among the lustful eyes cast at her were those of Charles. But Louise did not want to be a mistress, for like Frances Stuart she preferred courtship and marriage. Unlike Frances, however, her position was too lonely and financially insecure for her to resist severe pressure. Charles coaxed and cajoled her and made her presents. Louis XIV believed that a French lover would further predispose his English cousin to his interests and added his pleas through de Croissy. Arlington professed himself anxious to see his master set up with a polite, sweet-natured woman like Louise, instead of a 'lewd and bouncing orange-girl' or a 'termagant' (clearly both Nell and Barbara had put dents in Arlington's celebrated dignity). The Secretary added that although the King never discussed politics with his mistresses, they could prejudice him against individual ministers, so their identity was of some consequence. He and de Croissy even told Louise that the Queen wished her to submit. They arranged a houseparty at Arlington's mansion at Euston, Suffolk, where the design could be effected. The pregnant Nell was dumped at Newmarket, and Louise transferred to Euston, where she at last gave in. Charles's amazing fertility ensured that exactly nine months later she produced a son. Thus two monarchs, an ambassador, and a great minister had combined to push an unwilling virgin into a royal bed.[109] As before, the English heard of such proceedings with some distaste. The progress of Louise towards her fate was discussed acidly in the manor-houses of Buckinghamshire, while an Oxford man noted of the birth of Nell's second child 'The King is neglected and none of the citizens or other care for him; stupid, heavy.'[110]

There was little change in the governing circle in the last two years before the war. Arlington remained pre-eminent. In May 1671 the Venetian ambassador reported that 'all the interests of the Crown pass through his hands' and praised him for his courtesy, prudence, and lack of a talent for making enemies. He superintended public affairs while other ministers dispersed to their country seats in the summer. When some Hamburg merchants wished Charles to grant them a request, they greased Arlington's palm and duly got what they wished. Clifford remained his loyal follower despite his own increasing stature. His secretary Williamson was made a clerk to the Privy Council even though Charles had earlier promised the place to the diarist John Evelyn. A mayor wanting a royal favour for his corporation or a man wishing to avoid being made sheriff approached Williamson to have their plea passed to his master, and it was effected. One man complained that the crowd of suitors waiting to see Arlington directly was always so large that he equally invariably caught a cold in the queue![111] Buckingham, by contrast, remained prominent at court but excluded from real power. He was, of course, the principal dupe of the secret diplomacy of 1670. His main personal interest in the Secret Treaty of London was the expectation of being made commander of the English expeditionary force, but in the autumn of 1671 Charles gave this prospective honour to Monmouth, Buckingham lost his temper with his monarch, and the latter's true feelings, so rarely displayed in anger, burst forth. He told the Duke that he was worth no more than a dog if he conflicted with the public good, and left him flabbergasted.[112] Monmouth's appointment was a sign that Charles was still intent upon grooming him for a major part in national affairs, but not for the throne. When the lad was summoned to the Lords in October 1670 he was firmly styled 'our natural and illegitimate son'.[113] Lauderdale and Ashley remained active in the Committee of Foreign Affairs, and the latter's local power base was strengthened with the Lord-Lieutenancy of Dorset. Ormonde and Rupert were told of the Treaty of London upon the insistence of James, Arlington, and Clifford in May 1671, and Rupert was turned into a local magnate by being made Lord-Lieutenant of Berkshire and Constable of Windsor Castle. He celebrated his entry into the latter post, characteristically, by hanging 3,000 weapons on the walls.[114] Only Bridgeman slid, unobtrusively, from the centre of affairs at this time.

It was Ireland that saw a significant change of government, as Berkeley in turn fell from power. His fate was partly due to the tensions suffered by any Lord-Lieutenant of that realm when dealing with Charles II. The King had been reminded annually of the inadequacy of the Irish revenue, but even now he was reducing it further by docking it for gifts and pensions for Irish and English courtiers. Berkeley and the Privy Council protested, only to be undercut completely in the matter. Another of the rising generation of smooth and clever young men had come on the scene, Richard Jones, Viscount Ranelagh. He had come to court under the auspices of Ormonde, but in early 1671 formed an alliance with the Catholic adventurer Richard Talbot to assist each other in their respective schemes. Ranelagh proposed to the King that a consortium led by him would take over the entire revenue for five years. He promised to balance income and expenditure and clear all arrears, and then to pay Charles £80,000 at the end of the process. The King snatched at this superficially easy way out of the fiscal problem, baited with a private gift to him of £48,000 from Ranelagh, and informed the Dublin administration of it as a *fait accompli*. The protests made by Berkeley and his Council at the reopening of the land settlement were similarly unavailing. By July 1671 Irish Protestants were thoroughly disconcerted by doubts about their estates and fiscal system, for which the Lord-Lieutenant bore no responsibility.[115] On the other hand, the Lord-Lieutenant made trouble for himself. He reacted to Orrery's inevitable interference as badly as Ormonde had done, and far more swiftly. He tried to deprive the Earl of his military command, only for Orrery to run at once to Charles and obtain full support. Thereafter Berkeley had an enemy at court who blackened his name at every opportunity. He then compounded this mistake by quarrelling, permanently, with Lord Chancellor Boyle, and in his increasing insecurity and isolation he began to earn a reputation for corruption and greed.[116] Furthermore, he ignored his instructions to favour the 'Remonstrant' faction among the

Catholic clergy, because they did not make him humble addresses as the 'orthodox' faction did. The latter were led by the pious and mild-mannered titular Archibishop of Armagh, Oliver Plunket, but their moving spirit at this time was an individual only too familiar to Charles. He was none other than that fertile schemer of the exile, Peter Talbot, who, having fallen out with the Jesuit order, had remade his career as titular Archbishop of Dublin. News that protection was being granted to the 'wrong' group infuriated Ormonde, who told the King. Rebuked and irritated, Berkeley reversed his policy, only to be complained of by both factions.[117] By January 1672 Charles had decided that it was time for him to go, and named his replacement: the youthful Arthur Capel, Earl of Essex, son of a royalist general who had been executed in 1649. His family's record of loyalty and his own patent intelligence, honesty, and vigour seem to have been his recommendations for the post. Again, it is hard to see that he belonged to any court faction at this point.[118]

At some time in the middle of 1671 Charles decided definitely to go to war in the following spring as the Treaty of London had prescribed. In late June Arlington was still worrying Colbert de Croissy by casting doubt upon the project and talking of the need to draw in the Prince of Orange before launching the attack.[119] But during July the decision was clearly taken to commence the picking of a quarrel with the Dutch. Sir William Temple, long detained in England, had his position as ambassador formally revoked, and in early August a royal yacht, the *Merlin*, was sent to collect his wife from Holland. Under the Treaty of Breda, Dutch warships were bound to salute English warships (in the plural). The captain of the *Merlin* was instructed to pass through the States-General's fleet on his way and to demand this honour. As he commanded only a single vessel, and a tiny one, it was not at first given, and Charles was able to claim that he felt insulted. Simultaneously, the English demands over the East Indies and Surinam were increased, and pressed with more vigour.[120] On 10 August the King told de Croissy that he would not be recalling Parliament until the war was won, and in the following month it was prorogued till October 1672.[121] The Dutch offered to negotiate in London, but Charles replied that he would send an ambassador to talk at The Hague. He had been selected long before, in the event of the King provoking a war: Downing, whose bad relations with de Witt had been notorious. Although his appointment was public before the end of September, his departure was carefully delayed until December to allow the campaigning season to draw close. He was instructed to demand the principle of the salute for any English warship and the punishment of the Dutch commander who had refused it to the *Merlin*.[122] Even as he left, James began giving out commissions to officers

in the fleet, and in early January 1672 it was formally announced that
he would lead it in person, as in 1665. Later that month impressment of
seamen commenced, and the French subsidies started secretly to arrive.
To conceal all the previous diplomacy, on 2 February de Croissy signed a
Treaty of Whitehall with the five ministers who had made that of London,
providing for an attack on the Dutch in the same terms.[123]

During these months also the final efforts were being made to isolate
the intended victims. Louis had obtained promises of neutrality from the
princes of western Germany and the Emperor Leopold, and an English
envoy seconded his work to win the Swedes. In the end the Stockholm
government offered an army to guard the French from attack across
Germany, if the French paid it. This would be needed, for at the same
moment the Elector of Brandenburg decided to help the Dutch as he
had done in 1666, as fellow Protestants, and neither English nor French
argument could deter him.[124] His opposition, however, was a small thing
to Charles's government besides that of Spain. The most unrealistic part
of the foreign policy cooked up between the King and his sister was
the belief that the Spanish would sit back and allow the Dutch to be
destroyed, before gratefully recognizing the English as their protectors
against France. The ministers in Madrid recognized that the Dutch were
far more intimately concerned with the fate of the Netherlands than
Charles, and were their obvious allies against Louis. Furthermore, when
Arlington launched a frantic campaign to convince them otherwise, he was
not supported by the French. It suited Louis very well to drive Spain over
to the side of the United Netherlands, thereby opening the way for further
conquests in the Spanish Low Countries as well. To the horror of Charles,
the States-General signed a treaty for mutual defence with the Spanish in
December.[125] Nor, with his cousin now bound to him, did Louis do more
than talk away the requests made by Arlington's diplomats for a reduction
of the tariffs which injured English trade to France.[126] He was starting
to pay Charles back for the agile opportunism displayed by the latter in
previous years.

Nor was the financial prospect as rosy as had been hoped. During
1670–1 ordinary revenue had actually fallen, widening the current deficit. The new parliamentary grants were coming in as slowly as ever. In
August 1671 the navy's victualler had £45,000 worth of unpaid bills, and
in December he and his colleagues were using their private credit to place
any more orders. In September the King had resumed direct collection of
the customs, through a commission, because the new farmers drove their
terms too high. In time this was to become recognized as a step towards
greater efficiency and more 'modern' government, but it cost Charles

the large advance payment expected from the farm. By the end of the year there was little profit accruing from all the main branches of the revenue because they were securing existing loans. Even without a war, the regime was heading for bankruptcy.[127] Charles asked the principal financiers of London (already his main creditors) for a further, unsecured, loan to set out the fleet. He was refused, and the result, on 2 January, was the so-called Stop of the Exchequer. By this, most repayments of government debts were suspended (the King said privately for only ten months), with the promise of an extra 6 per cent interest to creditors as compensation. Long recognized by historians as the work of Clifford, its ruthless simplicity bears the mark of his personality and it was opposed by most of the Privy Council. But the reason for the ineffectuality of this opposition was simply that there was no alternative means of finding the money to fight with.[128]

Two months after the Stop, on 15 March, was published a more spectacular royal pronouncement, the Declaration of Indulgence. It suspended all penal laws against Protestant dissenters and Catholics, and allowed the former to meet for worship if they obtained licences from Charles and the latter to hear mass in private. Although clearly issued in concert with the outbreak of war, it was not presented as an emergency measure but as permanent policy, claiming that toleration would produce a more stable country and encourage immigration. It is difficult to add anything new to the story of the Stop, but there are points about the Declaration which have not been made by previous historians. First, it was preceded by measures to benefit the Irish Catholics. In December Charles ordered Berkeley to appoint some of them as JPs (according to his choice) and followed this on 26 February with an instruction to admit them to corporate towns in order to improve trade. This was certainly done against the advice of Berkeley himself and the Dublin Privy Council, though they promptly obeyed. Their authority had been further undercut since August by the commissioning of most of the English ministers to determine the size of the Irish Establishment so that Ranelagh could fund it. In the process they heard cases concerning inheritance which ought normally to have been settled in Dublin, but they played no formal part in religious matters.[129] In default of evidence one can only say it is likely that the advice to Charles to introduce the new policy came from court Catholics such as Talbot. In charting the course of government in Restoration Ireland, the historian is constantly handicapped by the fact that no Catholic politician left a collection of papers to compare with those assembled by Protestants like Ormonde, Orrery, Essex, and Conway. All that can be said with certainty is that arguments for the new initiative circulated fairly widely within the court and convinced many, for Essex later commented that he, like the King, had been persuaded that the admission of Catholics to towns would greatly benefit the economy, and thus taxation.

By contrast, excellent records exist for the genesis of the English Declaration of Indulgence, and it must be stressed (as it has not been before) how very reluctant Charles was to make it. It was urged upon him by his whole ring of trusted advisers—by Ashley and Buckingham (to aid dissenters), by James and Clifford (to help Catholics), and by Arlington and Lauderdale (presumably to assert royal power and to reduce a risk of nonconformist plotting). Yet clearly his humiliation by Parliament in 1663 and the apparent ingratitude of dissenters in 1663, 1668, and 1669 had left their mark on him. He doubted that he had the constitutional power to issue the Declaration and refused simply to permit nonconformists to meet, for fear of seditious conventicles. It took a search in the records by Ashley, Clifford, and Lauderdale to persuade him on the first point and the proposal to issue licences to convince him on the second. The whole process of argument used up over a week.[130]

Two days after this declaration Charles issued another, of war upon the Dutch. The final steps to this had, after all, been fraught with anxiety. First there was the shock of the opposition by Spain. Then Downing had fluffed his mission at The Hague. His instructions had been to return after three weeks if the States-General did not reply to his demands. These he obeyed to the letter, but by the time of his departure Charles had decided that more time needed to be spun out and instructed Sir George to remain and to keep talking. This fresh direction was sent too late, and to the King's horror Downing reappeared in London. Charles's nerves broke into fury and Sir George was committed briefly to the Tower and permanently lost his position at court.[131] As things turned out, time was used up conveniently by the Dutch, who decided to send one of their best diplomats to London but did not dispatch him till early March. He arrived on the 8th, by which time Charles had already ordered his brother to seize Dutch shipping. The Foreign Affairs Committee hurriedly debated the situation. Lauderdale was all for attacking ships in any case, but Arlington and Buckingham both insisted that some show of treating had to be made. Charles took this more moderate course, and appointed the three of them to deliver an ultimatum to the envoy. When he (naturally enough) failed to concede everything after one week, the declaration was issued.[132] It cited all the familiar grievances—the right of salute, the tropical markets, and Surinam, and accused the United Netherlands for good measure of abetting Charles's enemies. But then the text hardly mattered greatly, for the government was not bidding seriously for allies or domestic support.

Within six months it expected to present its subjects with the *fait accompli* of an astounding victory.

The full tale of British government policy in the years 1668–72 has commonly been seen either as that of a King who almost made a change of faith but got side-tracked into a war, or of a bid by his regime to avenge itself upon foreign and domestic opponents for the humiliations of 1667. Viewed in better perspective, the figure at the centre of the scene should not be Charles II but Louis XIV. The sheer might of the Sun King and the mutual jealousies of the maritime powers were such that sooner or later one of them would make a deal with him and then be forced by him into his schemes for aggrandizement. The English and Dutch both tried to sell each other out, and it was Charles who succeeded. As a result he was caught in a destiny not his own. Whether it would profit him would depend upon whether he had failed to repeat his error of 1664, of underestimating the peoples of Holland and Zealand.

Charles's Second Dutch War, 1672–1674

◦⚬❦⚬◦

THE broad outline of English affairs in the years 1672–4 is well known, and fresh research is unlikely to alter it. On the other hand, the meaning of many of the events has been contested several times over. Likewise, although the naval battles have been studied in detail, there is no proper history of the war in which they were set. The object of this chapter is to weave together the development of diplomatic, military, and political policy more tightly than has been done hitherto, and to contest one or two recent beliefs about the process. One bonding theme runs through all: however cautiously he approached it, Charles made this war his own and fought it with determination till its end was forced upon him.

From March to June 1672 the main business of the Committee for Foreign Affairs consisted of getting the fleet mustered, manned, armed, and supplied. Charles normally presided over this complicated business in silence, although he could not restrain one outburst of anger and incredulity when victuals calculated to last for eight months were consumed in one (Clifford admitted that no accounts existed to explain the error, the Navy Board was duly scolded, and the whole business remained mysterious). In addition, he met naval and financial officials in the Treasury or in Arlington's lodgings, listened to their problems, and issued orders upon their advice. As in the previous war, a period of frenetic activity and anxiety produced (despite the occasional lapse such as the one concerning victualling) a remarkable success. This time the reinforcement from the French meant that the English could put out fewer ships, and of better overall quality. By early May Charles could boast that his fleet was ready, without his having to hire and convert any merchantmen, and with bigger guns and crews than before. He was able to order local officers not to send any more pressed men to it, as it was actually filled up.[1]

The King played a more direct part in strategic planning than he had done before, repeatedly taking his yacht down to the fleet and spending nights upon it between conferences. A pinnace full of armed sailors sometimes guarded him as he slept. These visits enabled him to show off his knowledge of winds and currents, but also to take part in the councils of war aboard the flagships.[2] By March the command structure was completed, with Sandwich acting as James's Vice-Admiral. The Earl was personally most unenthusiastic about the war,[3] but willing to serve, and was presumably a more promising choice than the quarrelsome Rupert. In April the brigade promised to the French, comprising two English regiments, two Irish, and one of Scots, was led to join Louis's muster by Monmouth. On 6 May Charles watched from his yacht at Spithead as the allied fleets united, and made a personal distribution of money amongst the French commanders.[4] Thus the campaigns by land and sea commenced.

As far as Charles was concerned, the naval war soon presented two problems. One was that the admirals frequently ignored advice and orders once under sail. This was certainly sensible in theory, as flexible responses were required of them, but in the event they presented their monarch with the second problem, that they were disastrously unsuccessful. The war began as soon as it was declared, when the Foreign Affairs Committee agreed that Sir Robert Holmes should attack a Dutch merchant fleet before news of the declaration reached it. This was a somewhat despicable act, but Holmes bungled it anyway, by opening fire without awaiting reinforcements. He suffered heavy damage and captured few ships, leaving Charles furious.[5] Contrary to English expectations the Dutch did send forth a navy, which almost trapped James's squadrons in the Thames before they could join their allies. When the junction occurred, the King advised his brother not to seek battle too soon, so that the land invasion could sap the morale of the enemy first, and the French ships could learn to work with his. Instead a council of war resolved to attack at once, and the allies only succeeded in chasing the Dutch into their harbours before they had to put back into Southwold Bay for supplies.[6] Charles afterwards maintained that he had warned James to leave the bay if a wind blew directly from the sea. Whether true or not, when such a wind arose the allied fleet remained, and was taken by surprise on 28 May with little room to manœuvre. When the Dutch withdrew they left James's ships 'miserably shattered' and incapable of campaigning again for weeks. Only one had actually been lost, but that had contained Sandwich. His body was recovered days later, floating with the jewelled star of the Garter still glittering on his chest, and a flock of seagulls screaming over him. Charles ordered the other commanders to the safety of the Thames to refit, joined them, and administered a general rebuke, though he was careful to quash murmuring against the French for their particularly inept part in the battle. For Sandwich he ordered a state funeral, of the sort given to his former comrade under Cromwell, Albemarle.[7] The repairing of the fleet commenced, but suddenly the naval war was momentarily eclipsed by developments upon land.

These were dramatic in the extreme: in the first two weeks of June Louis's gigantic army, outnumbering the Dutch by nine to one, swept across the United Netherlands and occupied most of them. Holland and Zealand were saved by the flooding of their borderlands, but the nerve of the States-General collapsed. Wilhelm of Orange was appointed its supreme officer, while envoys were sent to England and to Louis to ask for terms. When those dispatched to him arrived, Charles opposed all the rest of his Foreign Affairs Committee by insisting that nothing be done to treat with them. Instead, an envoy was rushed to Louis to inform him of their arrival and to assure him that they had not been given a hearing. The man selected was a Yorkshireman of royalist family, George Savile, who had already impressed himself upon the court as extraordinarily able and been created Viscount Halifax in 1668. At worst, Charles may have been motivated by an ingrained respect for and trust in his cousin which, despite everything, remained an instinct in him. At best, he may have feared that the States-General was trying to divide its enemies and that, with Louis now almost in a position to dictate terms, he had to be kept as benign towards England as possible. If the latter was so, then he was correct about the Dutch but wrong about his cousin. Formally, Louis behaved with equal propriety, refusing to conclude a treaty without Charles's participation and inviting the latter to send plenipotentiaries for that purpose. But the terms which he actually offered the Dutch, while exacting vast tracts of territory for himself, provided for England only an unimportant town in Groningen instead of the strategic Zealand ports promised at their alliance: he was determined that the English should gain as little from the war as possible. At least his allies were themselves not wholly ingenuous, for Halifax was instructed to pass through Zealand and quietly to invite its people to put themselves into English hands, giving Charles territory to bargain with.[8]

Shadowing Louis on Charles's behalf was another of the rising generation of clever men whose fathers had been cavaliers, this time from Cornwall and called Sidney Godolphin. His brother William was certainly one of Arlington's protégés, and it was probably by the same favour that Godolphin secured his assignment. In mid-June he sent a series of letters to the Secretary, warning that the English plenipotentiaries had to hasten over before the French army swallowed the remaining Dutch provinces.[9] Accordingly, the government acted fast. Buckingham volunteered for the job, and rather than start an argument Charles appointed him with Arlington himself as his partner. They were instructed to demand that the Dutch salute the Flag in British waters and pay an annual 'rent' to fish in them, that they deliver an indemnity and at least three Zealand towns, that they make Wilhelm their hereditary ruler, and that they satisfy the long-standing complaints about the Indies trade and the evacuation of Surinam. These terms were thrashed out by the Foreign Affairs Committee, and represented a compromise. Clifford wanted to annex most of Zealand or to destroy the Dutch state completely, while Buckingham was happy with a few towns but still expected these to remain English. It was probably Arlington who suggested that the ambiguous word 'cautionary' be applied to the ports demanded, because as soon as he and Buckingham joined Halifax at the French camp, in late June, he seized control of the negotiation. Against their initial suggestions, and apparently against the will of Charles, he insisted that any territory be held only until the indemnity was paid, though that was now fixed at £1 million and five towns were asked. In judging that the Dutch would refuse to give up parts of Zealand he was correct, but they turned out to be unwilling to surrender them even for a few years. The English and Dutch terms were alike rejected, and the best that Arlington and Buckingham could do was to sign a treaty with the French at Heeswijk on 6 July, which stated that neither nation would make peace without the other. In doing so they covered Charles against the fear that his cousin would conquer the remaining Dutch provinces and then ditch him, and for this the agreement has been called an English 'triumph'.[10] But they also bound him to keep on fighting, however unprofitably, until Louis was satisfied. It was an admission of temporary stalemate.

An important sub-plot to these negotiations consisted of Charles's relations with Wilhelm himself. Throughout their mutual history, the English king's dealings with the Dutch prince and the French monarch were conditioned not only by international power politics but by two of his strongest instincts, for royalty and for family. To him it was vitally important that one was a potential sovereign and the other an actual one, and that one was his nephew and the other his cousin. Fundamentally, he seemed to believe that, as a result, their interests were connected and he was always surprised and hurt when one of them crossed him. To Charles, this war was not a division of family loyalties but an alliance with Louis to put Wilhelm on a throne, and from the start he made this plain to his nephew in his letters. He never understood why Wilhelm didn't see it that way. To the young Prince (he was now twenty-one), this war was an invasion of Dutch territory by foreign powers, and from his accession to the supreme magistracy he devoted himself to fighting France and to making peace with England with the minimum of concessions. The latter included most of what Charles was demanding, though Wilhelm secretly offered two instead of five ports as security, or the return of Surinam. However, not only did the King want the full five, but by the time that he received these terms he was bound by the Treaty of Heeswijk not to make a separate peace. An increasingly irritable correspondence between uncle and nephew continued for over two months after the return of Buckingham and Arlington and was then abandoned.[11]

As the land war stagnated, so interest returned to that by sea. In late June Charles and his ministers spent a week with the fleet and decided with its commanders to launch an expedition against the Dutch coast. There the English would summon towns, capture ships, and keep up the pressure on the States-General. As a result, James found himself sailing aimlessly around the North Sea. The enemy would neither fight nor surrender, and there were no merchantmen in sight. In mid-July he was instructed to hunt down the Dutch East India fleet which Sandwich had almost captured in 1665, and duly spent over a month in this quest, battered by frequent storms and having to put in regularly for supplies and repairs. Unsurprisingly, he missed his quarry. In the course of July the Foreign Affairs Committee, having recognized that the Zealanders were not going to claim Charles's protection, decided to land an army under Rupert in the province and reduce its town. The project, however, was as much a dream as the royalist invasion plans made in Flanders in 1657–8. For one thing, the Dutch navy had to be beaten or to be absent in order for the English to put soldiers ashore, and it was at present protecting its coast while refusing battle. For another, there was no expeditionary force to land. In March, Charles had ordered over ten companies of the Irish army, and commissioned a veteran officer from the Tangier garrison, Fitzgerald, to lead them. In the same month Rupert was empowered to raise a regiment, and Buckingham was given the same responsibility in June, while a body of Scots sent by the Privy Council in Edinburgh made up a fourth one. But by the end of July all these units, plus the Guards, made a total of 4,260 infantry, barely enough to defend a bridgehead. By August it was obvious that the war was getting nowhere.[12]

In this predicament, the English government continued to hope, unrealistically, that the Dutch would cave in and make peace. On 31 July the Foreign Affairs Committee debated the wisdom of revising the terms offered to them. Buckingham was still for demanding towns in perpetuity but Arlington, backed by Rupert, felt that the Dutch would never agree. Charles, as usual, followed his cautious and pragmatic Secretary and it was agreed to ask for five ports for ten years. What was absurd about this policy was that, having rejected virtually the same conditions in June, the Dutch were hardly likely to accept them after 25 July, when they acquired their first allies. Upon that date the Emperor Leopold and the 'Great Elector' of Brandenburg, frightened by Louis's success, broke their word to him and united to attack him. In August Arlington persuaded Charles to agree to treat in any place which his ally or enemy named, and told the French ambassador (apparently on his own authority) that the English would not demand any towns if this prevented peace. As, however, Louis was not moderating his terms, which the Dutch found even less acceptable than the English, these gestures were futile.[13] Equally pointless were the efforts of the Foreign Affairs Committee, when James brought the fleet back at the end of August, to make it go forth again to keep pressure up on the Dutch. Charles led these with vehemence, but the commanders replied that their ships required extensive repairs and that another expedition meant more aimless cruising. In the end their common sense prevailed.[14] A myth has grown up among historians that the navy was kept at sea all winter to avoid paying off its crews:[15] in fact copious evidence survives to show that enough money was left in the Treasury to deliver wages to all the seamen in October.[16]

From the diplomatic papers it is clear what sort of gains Charles was hoping to make abroad. But by his Declaration of Indulgence he had also committed himself to a new religious order at home. How did this develop during 1672? The broad answer is that it did along now familiar lines, of a wish to consolidate royal control over religious affairs. The issue of Charles's declaration of Catholicism resurfaced during the early part of the year, taken as seriously as before by the genuine converts James and Clifford, who pressed the King to make it. Arlington and Charles himself continued to employ the project for possible diplomatic and financial gain. They informed the Queen Regent of Spain of it to persuade her to look favourably upon the Dutch war: Her Most Catholic Majesty responded with a stony lack of interest. They asked, with equal lack of success, that money be collected for Charles among the Catholic clergy of France. Nor could they, in early June, persuade the French to give any more for the promise of it. After all these failures, in mid-June, Arlington suddenly told de Croissy that the declaration was postponed until the war was over. And that was the last heard of the matter.[17] Royal policy towards the Irish Catholics remained constant. The King reassured troubled local officers that his orders to readmit the followers of Rome to towns were intended to apply only to merchants and tradesmen, and that all others could be expelled. The new Lord-Lieutenant, Essex, was an Anglican with no personal sympathy for Catholics. His public instructions were to favour those clergy who signed the 'Irish Remonstrance' (as before), his private orders to tolerate only those who seemed useful to the government. And this is what he did. He encouraged the mild and deferential Catholic primate, Archbishop Oliver Plunket, and prosecuted the ever-irritating Peter Talbot, who was claiming erroneously to have authority from Charles over all clerics of his faith in the land. When this affair subsided, Essex gleefully fomented a quarrel between the bishops and the friars.[18]

The English Declaration of Indulgence presented the government with a major administration burden, in the issuing of the licences to dissenters. Most of it fell upon Williamson, who not only demanded fees for each but limited the provisions of the measure by refusing many applications to use chapels, churches, schoolhouses, and town halls for worship. Charles's role in the process consisted of receiving grateful addresses from those successful. The Foreign Affairs Committee resolved that these addresses should be 'driven as high as possible' to magnify the royal power.[19] On 23 March the Committee decided that a logical next step to the Declaration would be to release all dissenters imprisoned merely for their beliefs, leaving inside the large number gaoled for other offences such as refusal to pay fines for not attending church or paying tithes. In late March a Quaker, Thomas Moore, who had formerly impressed Charles at audiences, brought an appeal to him for a specific order to release imprisoned members of his movement. He was promised a favourable response, but the King no longer took such an active part in assisting Quakers and referred the question to the Privy Council. This instructed Bridgeman to report on the matter. Quaker representatives spoke to the Council respectfully, stressing their subservience to the royal will, and Bridgeman recommended on 8 May that those held only for their principles should be given a formal pardon.

The sequel provides an unusually clear example of how the will of the Restoration monarchy was hampered not only by the dilatoriness of its servants but by the processes of its own machinery. After Finch, as Attorney-General, drew up the pardon, it had to pass through the Privy Seal, Patent, and Hanaper Offices before being given the Great Seal. The clerks of those various departments demanded fees for every individual listed in the document, making the cost of it prohibitive. It could only pass in September, when Arlington and Bridgeman not only waived their own payments but ordered the bureaucrats to accept a single one each for the whole pardon. Some members of other dissenting groups, including one John Bunyan of Bedford, were generously included by the Quakers. Even now, weeks were required to haul the great roll of vellum and two copies around the southern counties and to give extracts from it to sheriffs of those further afield. Nor had every prisoner eligible for release under its terms been named in it.[20]

In Scotland Lauderdale pursued the dual policy of comprehending some nonconformist ministers in the Kirk and crushing conventicles. Charles gave him freedom to do both or either. The former was represented by a scheme put together within the Scottish Privy Council in the summer and enacted in September, whereby about eighty presbyterians were simply planted in vacant parishes. Their views were not solicited on the matter and around a quarter refused to co-operate, but it did go some way further towards tackling the problems of leaderless congregations. In the same summer the Parliament remet in Edinburgh and renewed and added to the statutes against dissent. Unhappily, there is simply insufficient evidence to reconstruct the politics behind these developments.[21] More material survives for Ireland, whither Essex went instructed to find a means of framing an Indulgence for Irish nonconformists if possible. In the event, it was not, for the Ulster presbyterians assumed that the measure issued in England gave them freedom of worship by implication. This they took with complete lack of tact, enraging bishops, Lord-Lieutenant, and King alike. Essex responded by strengthening the garrison at Derry (or Londonderry) to cow an especially brash congregation there on Charles's orders. Having thus reduced dissenters to submission, he quietly instructed local officers to tolerate them as long as they behaved with discretion.[22] Toleration for its own sake was never an end for Charles's governments.

But then, indulgence was only half the policy anyway. During 1672 Charles also worked to strengthen the Church of England by promoting men who had opposed toleration before. Such was Henry Coventry, who became the junior Secretary of State when Trevor died suddenly in May. The brother of the gifted and unfortunate Sir William, he had served the King loyally as a diplomat while speaking for the Conventicle Acts in Parliament. The three new bishops chosen in the year were all notable enemies of dissent, though Charles reserved his options by keeping unfilled the greatest vacant see, that of Durham. He also ordered the episcopacy to launch a campaign of catechizing to discourage recruitment by the nonconformists.[23] If one object of these actions was to reconcile the Anglican hierarchy to indulgence, they were a failure. The bishops were sullenly obedient, though by September both Sheldon and Morley of Winchester were so alienated from the government that they suspected its new regiments of being intended to impose despotic rule. They only waited for Parliament to meet before attacking the Declaration. Further-more, the judges, who had not been consulted upon the legality of the matter, were ominously silent concerning it during the summer assizes.[24]

So who were 'the government of England' in 1672? The war involved some further gentle pruning of advisers. Ormonde, who had never been involved in the secret diplomacy, opposed the conflict together with some minor courtiers. He was, accordingly, excluded from most important discussion, though still not disgraced. Indeed, his heir, Ossory, served heroically in the fleet and was given the Garter in September and made a rear-admiral in 1673.[25] Effectively, Charles's advisers consisted of the men who had made the Secret Treaty of London and who have long been denoted 'the Cabal': Clifford, Arlington, Buckingham, Ashley, and Lauderdale. As the war commenced, most were given honours, Clifford becoming a baron, Arlington an earl, and Lauderdale a duke, while Ashley changed rank and name to Earl of Shaftesbury. In addition, Arlington and Lauderdale received the Garter. Yet, as before, it was Arlington who actually functioned as premier minister. He was, after a fashion, linked to the royal family as Clarendon had been before, when Charles requested the hand of his daughter and only child for the King's second son by Castlemaine. His leading part in the policy-making of the summer has been described. De Croissy described him to a French minister in June as Charles's 'other self', and Louis made him a much larger present than Buckingham when they arrived at his camp. The new junior Secretary, Henry Coventry, was yet another of Arlington's clients. In October an Irish peer could consider a suit secured because he had spoken 'both to the King and Lord Arlington'.[26]

Yet the war was to change all this, and the change began rapidly. By August 1672 Charles and his ministers were starting to feel pushed on to the defensive, as the appalling prospect loomed of facing Parliament in the autumn without a glorious victory to appease its probable doubts about the current religious policy. In September the King followed the advice of Arlington, Clifford, Shaftesbury, and Lauderdale (against that of Rupert and Ormonde) and ducked the issue by postponing the reassembly until February. In doing so, he was gambling upon a peace being made before then, and feared that a quarrel with the Houses would weaken his bargaining position. The danger in this (pointed out by its opponents) was that a spring session would provide funds too late to fit out the fleet. The short-term financial position was quite healthy, for the new direct collection of the customs and the distraction of the Dutch by their peril upon land meant that dues upon trade were actually producing a record yield. Thanks to this, the Stop of the Exchequer, and the French subsidies, the Treasury could not only pay off the fleet but had almost half of the £230,000 needed to set it out again.[27] The balance of that sum, however, had to come from Parliament. Accordingly, the English government gratefully accepted the offer of the Swedes, in the autumn, to mediate between it and its enemy. None the less, the best offer made by the Dutch in the winter was still unacceptable. Even in secret discussions initiated by Arlington through an agent, the States-General would not admit the possibility of handing over ports, and Charles would not retrench this demand.[28]

So, potentially, the King had to fight both the Dutch and Parliament, and expected that the agents of the former would encourage the discontent of the latter. To strengthen his governing team for the struggle, he reshuffled it in November. Bridgeman was at last retired, having become an increasing nuisance. Not only was the old Lord Keeper often ill, but he had refused to seal the Declaration of Indulgence because he disapproved of it. He was now delaying injunctions to protect the bankers injured by the Stop from being sued by their own creditors. He affected surprise at the change, but had little cause for it and was promised a pension of £2,000 per annum.[29] The seals went to Shaftesbury with the full title of Lord Chancellor, a promotion which seemed appropriate to all. The tiny earl was an eloquent speaker, a fervent supporter of the current foreign and religious policies, and the man who had actually sealed the Declaration in Bridgeman's place. His existing post, of Chancellor of the Exchequer, passed to Duncombe. This left Clifford as the only member of the original Treasury Commission still alive, in favour, and unpromoted, and he replaced the Commission itself by becoming Lord Treasurer. Expressed like this, the change seems natural, and Clifford's financial experience, honesty, loyalty, and energy doubtless counted greatly towards it. But Arlington had another opinion. Since midsummer he had been expecting the post for himself, together with the title of duke. Clifford had been advanced by him, after all, and when he found himself cheated of his expectation by his erstwhile protégé he was bitterly mortified. James later claimed the credit for persuading his royal brother into the choice, but added that Charles thought Arlington unsuitable anyway.[30] Indeed, it is difficult to see why the Secretary wanted an office for which he had no training and which was so onerous and so politically vulnerable. Perhaps he wanted to balance the appointment of Shaftesbury, friend of his enemy Buckingham, to the other great post. Perhaps he was starting to suffer from hubris. Whatever the reason, this was the first important occasion upon which his influence within the government had been checked. Quite accidentally, it marked the beginning of his decline from power.

Charles's physical restlessness this winter almost certainly expressed the depth of his anxiety. On one frosty day in late January he walked all the way from Whitehall to Hampton Court for recreation.[31] Much of his work was devoted to further preparations for the parliamentary session. He ordered Arlington, Clifford, and Shaftesbury to speak to MPs with whom they had influence, while he showered honours upon Buckingham's group to encourage their efforts. The Duke himself received a pension of £2,400 a year, despite having, in his feckless manner, annoyed Charles by making a pass at Nell Gwyn (who boxed his ears). Of his ablest clients, Seymour was made a commissioner of the navy and Osborne got a Scottish peerage.[32] The Foreign Affairs Committee had a long debate (in the presence of various MPs) to select a Speaker for the Commons. In the end it played safe and chose Sir Job Charlton, a respected lawyer of royalist background and impeccable Anglican beliefs.[33] To prove to the Houses that he was determined to prosecute the war vigorously, Charles preceded their meeting by commissioning eight titled courtiers to raise foot regiments in England and Wales, to fill up the invasion force for Zealand.[34]

When he faced the Houses upon 5 February 1673, the King's tone was confident and assertive, even provocative. He asked for money for the fleet, the army, and his debts, remarked that the supply given in 1671 had been inadequate, referred irritably to rumours that the new regiments were threats to liberty, and warned everybody not to tamper with the Declaration of Indulgence. Shaftesbury followed with a great set piece defence of the war, and in the ensuing debates the government's secular representatives and their clients showed a quite remarkable unity and eloquence. The result had been predicted by Arlington before the session opened. Both Houses showed support for the war. Its proclamation had been cheered by crowds a year before, and MPs who opposed the court in other respects seemed genuinely to accept that the Dutch deserved to be fought. Royal fears that they had been tampered with by enemy agents appeared groundless, and a modern opinion that they made a 'tactical' decision to concentrate upon other issues appears equally without foundation.[35] But the bulk of the Commons proved absolutely determined to force Charles to relinquish his claim to suspend penal laws in religious matters, and they were ready to use the war grants as bargaining counters. In this predicament Shaftesbury, Clifford, Lauderdale, and James all insisted that anything, including the war, had to be sacrificed to maintain the royal power over religion. Buckingham was irresolute. Arlington, Rupert, Ormonde, and Henry Coventry argued for the opposite priority and Charles, who had agreed to the Declaration with such reluctance, was from the first inclined to follow them. Three weeks were spent by the government in trying to evade the issue, by inviting the Commons to embody the Declaration in a bill or by trying to foment a quarrel between the Houses. When the MPs stuck to their point, Charles surrendered to them on 8 March, turning the defeat as much to his advantage as possible with both Parliament and the French. With his natural theatricality, he tore the seal from the Declaration with his own hands and broke it, and made sure that his servants informed both Houses of the fact. This delighted the Commons as much as his gesture of opening his wine-cellar in 1670. Louis had been urging him to concede the issue in the cause of their joint war effort, and Charles managed to convince de Croissy that only this had persuaded him to surrender (an assertion disproved by the minutes of the Foreign Affairs Committee).[36] This, of course, was making the best of a terrible humiliation. Nor was it the end of the government's troubles, for two more issues were to intervene before supply was made. One was the Commons' desire to secure the realm against Catholics as well as to prevent the King from relieving them. The other was that the affairs of Ireland threatened to impinge upon those of the English Parliament, just as the issue of Irish cattle had done during the last war.

On 5 August Essex had replaced Berkeley, who returned to a palace in London built upon the proceeds of his term of office. The young earl soon proved a model Lord-Lieutenant, ruling with energy and a flair for mediation. He delighted Charles and Arlington with the frequency and fullness of his dispatches, and carefully cultivated the great Secretary by informing him of estates which reverted to the Crown. The latter could then be solicited by Arlington from his royal master and added to his great wealth.[37] For all his tact and patience, Essex could treat people ruthlessly when he felt this to be necessary, and his first victim was Orrery. The Munster Earl was not the subject of mere private dislike by the Lord-Lieutenant: rather, he had been officially selected for ill-treatment before Essex set out. His ability to manipulate courts and rulers, which had served him so well before now, had failed him completely as he fell into a classic trap. Orrery's ingrained fear of Catholics was aroused by Charles's order to readmit them to towns. He raised the Munster militia to watch them, and wrote to Anglesey expressing his alarm. This letter was his error. Anglesey showed it to the King, representing Orrery as bent upon wrecking the policy of encouraging Catholic merchants, and as a danger to peace and reconciliation in general. Clifford and James joined their criticisms to these, and Charles was soon persuaded that the Earl was committing the cardinal sin of contesting the royal will. Not only did Orrery receive a stinging rebuke through Arlington, but Essex arrived empowered to abolish his great office of President of Munster, the basis of his power. For good measure, the new Lord-Lieutenant stripped the Earl's homes of cannon, upon the grounds that private subjects had no right to them, and the King approved this. Orrery was sensible enough to submit to the succession of slights, and to grovel to Charles. In the winter, needing every possible supporter in Parliament, the King wrote to him warmly and invited him to Westminster. The Earl, however, wounded in body by gout and in spirit by his disgrace, preferred to remain quietly in Munster.[38]

Nevertheless, Essex himself soon had reason for complaint. This was grounded in the perpetual problem of any Lord-Lieutenant or Deputy, that Ireland was governed from Westminster as well as from Dublin, worsened by the tensions following the Restoration and by the character of Charles. Before the Earl had left Whitehall, the King had spoken soberly to him of the shortfall upon the Irish revenue as the root of all that kingdom's problems, and had recommended economies. Soon after he took up office, Essex found to his amazement that Charles was burdening the same revenue with grants to courtiers exactly as before. The pension for Buckingham and an estate for Monmouth were only the largest of a list of items. In these he glumly acquiesced, but drew the line when the King tried to give Castlemaine Phoenix Park, the residence of the Lord-Lieutenants just outside Dublin. To prevail upon his master to rescind the order, he enlisted the help of Arlington, Shaftesbury, Clifford, and other ministers. Under their combined pressure the King relented, but only on the condition that his former mistress received Crown land of equal value.[39] Other difficulties derived from the sheer carelessness of the English government when dealing with Irish affairs. Essex politely described a series of royal orders about a dispute at Dundalk as 'so contradictory one to the other as by them it appears to be a matter of some intricacy'.[40] But his greatest irritation was with the fact that his authority was constantly being undermined because suitors who had either been discountenanced by him or who expected no favour from him would go to Whitehall to ask satisfaction. That they were allowed to do so was largely a reflection of the King's image of himself as the fount of impartial justice, but it created confusion as well as weakness in the government of Ireland. It was galling enough to Essex when it concerned private persons,[41] but it became an issue of general importance in the matter of the regulation of corporations.

Ireland had been given no Corporation Act. In practice, the urban councils had consisted of Protestants since the Interregnum, but there was no systematic regulation of their membership or powers, and successive Lord-Lieutenants had evaded the problem. Essex was sent over instructed to tackle it, and in August he drew up a code with the help of his Privy Council. In this, they gave themselves the right to approve all leading magistrates, reserving the election of these people to the corporation and demanding that all members take the Oath of Allegiance. The package was sent to the English Council for approval, and the Foreign Affairs

Committee proposed that the Lord-Lieutenant be empowered to dispense individuals from the Oath. Effectively, this meant that Catholics and sectaries would be able to hold municipal office if the Crown's representative willed it. Essex had been hoping for this, and soon after he asked leading Catholics to recommend wealthy co-religionists who might receive the favour and to name bitter enemies amongst Protestant magistrates who might be dismissed. The object of the whole exercise, as Archbishop Boyle made clear to Arlington, was not to promote or repress any religious group, but to increase the power of the government. So far it seemed a masterly illustration of how Whitehall and Dublin Castle could co-operate. Then, in early November, Charles suddenly ordered the suspension of the new rules until Essex had answered certain criticisms. These were the work of what Arlington called 'standers-by who, according to their accustomed liberty, censure this matter as they do all other'. Gallingly for us, the Secretary did not name the 'standers-by', and we are at a loss to know who they might have been, but the gist of their objections was that the rules were unfair to Catholics. Irish municipalities were thus thrown into complete confusion as Essex's reform was enacted and then aborted. In the same fashion the fate of the land settlement was still in doubt, as the commission to enquire into it had not even started work. In the winter of 1671–2, belatedly conscious of the fear that he was causing, Charles added Ormonde to the commission and issued a proclamation that the weaknesses of the settlement, not the settlement itself, were the subject of review. The statement seemed at best opaque, at worst disingenuous.[42] By his bungling, the King was undermining much of the stability which his western kingdom had achieved since his restoration.

At this point several members of the Irish Privy Council decided that it was time to take their monarch in hand and to use the Cavalier Parliament for the purpose as they lacked one of their own. They held seats in the English House of Commons, and proceeded to play there upon the fear of Catholics which had flared up in 1666 and was now fanned again by the Declaration of Indulgence. These men, Ormonde's son Arran, Lords Aungier and O'Brien, Sir Thomas Clarges, and Sir Edward Massey, employed their eloquence and influence to convince the House that Popery was acquiring a dangerous influence both in Irish local government and at Whitehall, and the House addressed the King upon the subject on 25 March. It began by asking for the recall of the commission to enquire into the land settlement. It also wanted Catholics in Ireland to be disarmed and ejected from civil and military office, while their bishops were exiled and their schools dissolved. Those without licences were to be expelled from corporations and Richard Talbot, who had led the agitation against the land settlement, was to be banished from court. Charles could only promise satisfaction in the matter before the next session, and set Essex and the English Privy Council to work upon ways of providing it.[43]

The Commons' new rage against Popery was, of course, chiefly concerned with England, and resulted in two measures. One was a fairly routine request to Charles to order the expulsion of priests and the dismissal of anyone in his army who did not take the Oaths of Allegiance and Supremacy. He readily agreed to this, extended its effects to Scotland, and ordered the execution of the recusancy laws for good measure.[44] The other was the celebrated Test Act, which imposed upon all holders of public office a declaration which no Catholic could accept. This statute was to be a mine which almost blew away the foundations of the regime, for it forced the resignations not only of Clifford but of James, the heir apparent, who thus revealed himself to the nation as a follower of Rome. The shock produced by this rendered English politics unstable for the next two decades. What is peculiar to a biographer of Charles is the apparent insouciance with which he regarded the measure, in comparison with the fight which he had put up over the Declaration. In the Commons, Coventry, Finch, and other courtiers argued that details of the bill were unreasonable, but there was no concerted measure against its substance. In the Lords Clifford delivered a hysterical attack upon it, his nerves starting to break as his dreams dissolved. But Shaftesbury supported it, and the general impression was that Charles did so also. The French ambassador reported that he did, Coventry told the Commons the same thing, and the King urged that House to complete it. The MPs quite explicitly made the war supply conditional upon its success, and certainly the King's public attitude to it derived from this fact. But in view of the appalling implications of his brother's resignation, it seems remarkable that more alarm is not discernible in Charles's demeanour at the time.[45] The answer would probably have been contained in the minutes of the Foreign Affairs Committee, but just at this moment they cease as their author, Williamson, prepared for a diplomatic mission. The end of these crabbed, hurried, and often illegible notes is a terrible blow to the historian, for they recorded not only decisions taken, but views expressed in debate. A unique window into the innermost circle of government, they repeatedly correct the conclusions drawn by ambassadors and courtiers, upon whom we rely for much of the rest of the reign. In default of them, we can only speculate upon the King's reactions in this case. Was he gambling on a great military victory that year which would restore his prestige and enable him to ignore the Test Act? Or did he fail to believe that, at the crisis, poor, stupid, brave James would actually proclaim his faith? Or did he underestimate the likely impact of that revelation upon the country? None of these suggestions seem quite plausible.

As a result of this chain of surrenders, Charles was left in April 1673 with a grant of £1¼ million, and the process of warmaking could resume. The fleet was swiftly armed and supplied but (perhaps after the horrors of Southwold Bay) men were harder to find than before. Press-gangs were reduced to ambushing May Day processions, and the full complements were only made up by seizing sailors from incoming merchant ships, especially colliers, with the King's full approval.[46] The naval administration underwent a major change after James resigned his office of Lord High Admiral in June, when Charles vested it in a commission. It has often been said that following this reform Charles took a considerable personal interest in the running of his senior service.[47] The comment of Pepys, made secretary to the commission, that the King really understood the sea, has often been admiringly quoted. There is truth in both assertions, but they need qualification. In the strategic planning during 1673, Charles often showed a familiarity with the technicalities of ships and harbours.[48] He reserved to himself the dispersal of places and dues, and gave Pepys his instructions directly. He selected ships for special errands, decided whether a commander should fly a pennant, determined a dispute over a prospective dry dock, personally appointed some very minor officials, granted leaves of absence, and judged a porter and a master joiner accused of misconduct. But he rarely attended the commission itself, and the impression is that he was dabbling in such trivial matters partly for a dilettante's pleasure and partly to remind his navy that he was its ultimate commander. The real work was done by the commissioners, who consisted simply of all his principal Counsellors, Ormonde, Anglesey, Henry Coventry, and Arlington being the most diligent.[49] The reform meant neither a delegation to experts nor a 'personal rule' by the King, but an additional burden for already hard-worked servants.

With James disqualifying himself from command and Sandwich dead, Charles had to entrust the fleet to Rupert. Once again it was almost trapped in harbour by the Dutch before putting out, and once again the King watched it unite with the French squadron, this time off Rye.[50] The prospects of success were apparently good. In a brilliant winter campaign Louis's main army had defeated his German enemies and forced them to sue for peace, leaving the Dutch isolated again. For a moment in midwinter it looked as if Spain would enter the struggle, as its governor in Brussels helped Wilhelm attack a French fortress. Charles was forced to withdraw his guarantee of the Treaty of Aix, losing his last hopes of making the Spanish as well as Louis his grateful friends. He also faced the terrible prospect of war with them, but the Queen Regent disowned her viceroy's action and the situation in the Netherlands returned to stalemate. For the English the broad strategic plan was to defeat the Dutch navy and to put the new army into Zealand while Louis attacked the eastern defences of that province. Simultaneously with the campaign, a peace conference would proceed at Cologne.[51]

Initially, Charles had hoped to launch the invasion in March, before the enemy were ready to put to sea, but his own fleet and army proved totally unprepared.[52] Instead, off Rye on 17 May, he and the allied commanders decided that the Dutch navy had to be hunted down and destroyed at once, clearing the way for the army to follow. A week before, he had sent off his plenipotentiaries to Cologne with the same terms as those offered in 1672, save that only two ports were asked as security. These were apparently only to be required if the Dutch made peace unconquered, for Rupert was secretly instructed to take as much of Zealand as possible and to offer the people representation in the English Parliament. As before, Charles was ready to grab what occasion offered.[53] The combined fleets vanished over the horizon, and in early June the sound of guns was heard twice upon the east coast and reported with excitement at Whitehall. Then, on the 9th, Rupert's ships reappeared in the Thames. The Dutch had hit and run, engaging the allies and doing just enough damage to force them to refit, before hiding within their sandbanks again. The Prince was in one of his rages because supplies had not been made ready for him, and talking of hanging officials. Charles said wryly that he himself would get a lambasting from his cousin, and he did. He took it in good part, speaking soothingly to Rupert and enlarging his powers to appoint or deprive officers at will.

Through June, fleet and army were made ready for what was expected to be the final push. Most of the boatmen on the Thames were seized to fill the gaps in Rupert's crews, while a hundred lighters were hired to transport the soldiers. The invasion force was gathered upon Blackheath. It consisted of the Guards, the newly commissioned units, those sent from Scotland and Ireland in 1672, and twelve more companies of the Irish army recently shipped over; in all, fourteen regiments of foot, two of horse, and one of dragoons armed with the new French invention of the bayonet. Of these seventeen units, two were Irish, one Scottish, two Welsh, and the rest English, disproving the contemporary rumours, echoed too uncritically by many historians, that much of the force were Irishmen: even those Irish present were from the regular army used by the Dublin government to watch Catholics. As it assembled, Louis reduced the great isolated Dutch fortress of Maastricht and, though he himself marched on Germany, told

Charles that he was sending an army to draw the Dutch away from the coast of Zealand as arranged. The Stuart king instructed his representatives at Cologne to make no concessions, as the enemy were about to go under.[54]

His optimism was understandable but misfounded. With perfect duplicity, Louis ordered his general in Flanders to stay put, so that the English would arrive in Zealand to face the full force of the Dutch: just as before, he wanted them to make no conquests.[55] As for the army at Blackheath, its units were severely under strength and its quality dreadful. There is no official record of its size and the estimates of observers varied wildly, but it seems to have numbered about 8,000 in all. Charles had vetoed a suggestion of Buckingham that militiamen be conscripted, doubtless to avoid an outcry. As a result, most of the soldiers were totally untrained, and their equipment was deficient. They were the marginal elements of society, who might be tempted by the pay: 'ragged regiments' in Henry Coventry's phrase. Buckingham at first expected to command them and started to drill them from a French textbook, soon winning the disrespect of their officers. When Charles decided that the volatile Duke could not be trusted with such a vital commission, he found that the choice of any other British general would create impossible jealousies and resentments within his court. In the end, he actually had to ask Louis to send him a commander, and got the Count Schomberg, the German son of an English mother and a Protestant. Despite these palliative qualifications, and military ability, he was immediately murmured against as a foreigner. Rupert picked a quarrel with him for good measure. On viewing his charges, he pronounced them a drunken rabble.[56] Had they ever been shipped over to face Prince Wilhelm's veterans, a catastrophe would probably have resulted.

During July, some of the truth of the situation began to occur to Charles's government. At a council of war aboard the fleet on the 16th, Rupert and James, supported by junior admirals, managed to persuade Charles not to launch army and navy together, as the former needed time to train and their transports would encumber the latter. Instead, when the fleet sailed two days later, the soldiers were moved across to Great Yarmouth to await the destruction of the Dutch navy.[57] By now, advised by his brother, the King was starting to realize that the invasion was a very unlikely event. The French in the Netherlands were obviously passive, the Dutch coast was well fortified, and the enemy were unlikely to fight a naval battle unless they had an advantage. Accordingly, his government turned back to the talks at Cologne as its best hope of a successful end to the war. Louis had been suggesting that both he and the Swedes believed the English claim to Zealand ports to be the great stumbling-block to peace. On 28 July Charles gave way at last, and ordered his plenipotentiaries to drop the demand for these in exchange for the restitution of Surinam. To his own irritation, Rupert received new instructions to avoid battle unless upon an exceptional opportunity, as henceforth it was most important just to keep threatening the Dutch until they signed.[58]

On 11 August distant gunfire was heard once more upon the coast of East Anglia. A few days later, five disabled warships brought in the explanation: the Dutch had struck at Rupert's fleet again off the Texel, and vanished once more after a furious fight. The Prince, to the government's relief, did not need to bring back his whole body of vessels for repairs and could continue off the Netherlands. Then, a week later, his navy did reappear off Suffolk and on the 27th he brought it into the Thames. Charles prepared a warm welcome for his cousin, but this rapidly cooled. For one thing, Rupert insisted that the weather was now so bad that the fleet had to be laid up for the winter. The government did recognize that the invasion was now impossible: indeed, it had ordered that the troop transports be discharged and the army dispersed to winter quarters before the warships arrived. Three regiments of it were sent to reinforce the brigade in France, both to show consideration for an ally and to get them off the English payroll. But Charles was anxious to parade the fleet for as long as possible, just in case the enemy were on the point of conceding peace. None the less, the Prince prevailed as James had done in the previous year, and on 6 September he received the desired command. Rupert's principal misdemeanour, however, was to declare loudly that only the ineptitude of the French Admiral had prevented a victory in the Battle of the Texel. When his cousin tried to silence him he protested that he was blaming an individual not a nation, and that his own Vice-Admiral had also been culpable. He completely missed the point: within days it was widely believed in the fleet and the country that the Dutch had escaped because of French cowardice or treachery. Resentment was only increased by Charles's decision to punish Rupert by replacing him with Monmouth for the next campaign.[59]

Charles's diplomacy, like his invasion plans, had been based upon misconceptions. Louis and the Swedes certainly thought that his demand for ports was an obstacle to peace, but they also wanted it to be dropped for their own sake, neither wishing to see the English established upon both sides of the North Sea. The Stuart King's concession did not in fact hasten the treaty, for Louis failed to follow it with more moderate terms of his own. Instead, he tried to confirm the isolation of the Dutch by bullying the German princes into complete subservience. Therein lay a fatal error, for the princes were outraged and infuriated, not frightened, by French incursions. As Rupert returned, the English learned to their horror that the Emperor Leopold had renewed his alliance with the Dutch, this time supported by various lesser rulers—and, at last, by Spain. The latter, moreover, agreed to fight Charles if he did not accept the peace-terms of the States-General. As the Foreign Affairs Committee digested this, two more pieces of news arrived: Wilhelm had won his first victory against the French in the Netherlands, and the States-General had decisively rejected the Anglo-French demands made at Cologne.[60] The war of 1673 was not even ending in stalemate: it was threatening to become a catastrophe.

If the military and diplomatic objectives of the year had been pursued with energy, the religious policy which had accompanied them was left in the shambles created by the reverses of the spring. In June Charles notified the French that his profession of Catholicism was now not merely postponed but abandoned altogether.[61] During the spring session, the Cavalier Parliament had at last abandoned its policy of persecution of Protestant dissenters to concentrate upon a common drive against Catholics. Following an invitation from Charles, the Commons had sent up a bill designed to allow freedom of worship, though only for presbyterians and some independent churches instead of for the broader spectrum indulged by the King. Charles's own interest in this proved to be minimal. His ministers had opposed or supported it according to their personal beliefs, and it failed because the session ended before its completion. There is no evidence that Charles deliberately 'killed' it in this fashion, for he adjourned the session instead of proroguing it specifically so that unfinished bills (of which this was the most important) could be resumed. But it seems obvious that, once religious toleration was uncoupled from the royal prerogative, he became indifferent to it.[62] Thus the status of nonconformity was left confused, as both King and Commons had signalled their desire to end the Conventicle Act, yet this was still technically in force. Ater a long debate in the Privy Council in April, it was decided to advise Lord-Lieutenants to treat dissenters gently unless they misbehaved, leaving open the legal position of dissent as a whole. Anglesey, long a friend to presbyterians, tried in June to find a formula whereby they could be indulged, but Charles ordered him to desist because of the controversy that might be provoked.[63] Thereafter persecution resumed in a few places where the justices were especially intolerant. It is significant that where dissenting preachers were accused of being provocative, the King ordered that they be gaoled until they were humbled.[64]

Meanwhile the consequences of the war continued to have a corrosive effect upon the governing group which had launched it. The truly spectacular event of the summer was the resignation of all their offices, in mid-June, by James and Clifford. Thus both, men of conscience and honour, revealed their recently acquired Catholicism to the world. For Clifford the step was a complete withdrawal. His dreams, his health, and his career all in ruins, he retired from court in great pain of mind and body and died soon after. The King's brother, however, saw no reason to associate loss of post with loss of position. He continued to attend the Privy Council and its committees, to advise naval officials, and to attempt to exert great influence upon the making of policy. For his part, Charles took some time to understand the full implications of the Test Act. He certainly thought James a fool and a liability for having professed his faith at this moment, but within a month he was trying to appoint him as General of the expeditionary force. He was only dissuaded when the judges unanimously informed him that by doing so he would blatantly break the new law.[65] James certainly retained enormous power over ministerial appointments and, indeed, this appeared to increase at this time. Informed observers credited him with the appointment of Anglesey as Lord Privy Seal in April.[66] The most spectacular promotion of all was that of Osborne to succeed Clifford as Lord Treasurer, and although the intrigues to effect this were variously described, the gist of the accounts is that Clifford himself and James were the decisive advocates.[67] The lean, cunning Yorkshireman was succeeded in his job of Treasurer of the Navy by Seymour, another of Buckingham's protégés. But these changes did not signify an increase in the importance of Buckingham himself: rather, his followers were rising because of their own ability. In their respective offices, James and Clifford had enjoyed direct experience of Osborne's amazing acumen in managing naval finances, while Seymour deserved reward for his efforts as Speaker of the Commons. The court's first choice, Charlton, had soon collapsed under the political strain and resigned, but the formidable Devonshire squire had taken over his place and employed it energetically in the royal interest. It was an irony of the age that the wayward, irresponsible Buckingham had attracted clients of real genius, while the sagacious, dignified, and influential Arlington sponsored men of mere ability.

The great Secretary had wanted the Treasury to be put back into commission (doubtless both to achieve greater efficiency and to remove the possibility of a powerful rival). His failure to obtain this reinforced his sense of slipping slowly from pre-eminence, and within a fortnight he was speaking of resigning his office and retiring to the side-lines of politics. Yet he remained very powerful, and even as he spoke of withdrawal a request from him sufficed to keep a man imprisoned in the Tower when Clifford and other courtiers had persuaded Charles to consent to his release.[68] Ormonde, his great ally and Buckingham's enemy, was now invited back to the Foreign Affairs Committee by Charles in an attempt to reassure conservative Anglicans in the wake of James's resignation.[69] The minister who began to lose favour seriously was not the Secretary but the Chancellor, Shaftesbury, whom Charles suspected by May of encouraging opposition to the war. How the King's opinion was formed is a mystery, for Shaftesbury's best biographer has uncovered not a trace, among good records, of any contacts between him and either the Dutch or the English opponents of the court.[70] What was certainly apparent during this summer was a growing hatred between the Chancellor and James. The strongest emotion which animated Shaftesbury's small, sickly frame and inflamed his calculating brain was a detestation of Catholicism. Joined to his long-standing dislike of the Prince, it produced an open rift between them, and it may well have been his brother's whispers which engendered in Charles a belief in Shaftesbury's disloyalty. The King was losing whatever overall vision and sense of purpose that he had possessed in his management of appointments. Increasingly he was propelled into decisions by the ambitions and rivalries of his advisers, as he searched for any means of escaping disaster.

For disaster was approaching, in the shape of the autumn session of Parliament. A grant was necessary to carry on the war, and it was obvious to everybody then, as since, that in the course of 1673 English public opinion swung sharply against that war. What has been less obvious to historians is why this happened. Long ago, Professor Haley proposed that it was the result of Dutch propaganda. Professor Ekberg has correctly pointed out that there is no evidence for the impact of this, and argued instead that sheer military failure produced the shift of feeling.[71] Yet the newsletters of those months[72] indicate that the shift happened long before the crisis of the campaign was reached. Instead, they reveal that one event changed everything: James's public profession of his faith. Charles himself came to realize this.[73] In May, people were still speaking favourably of the war and hoping for conquests. As soon as they became aware that the heir presumptive was a Catholic by conversion, the attack on the Dutch acquired a quite different meaning for many. Thereafter nobody seemed to say anything good of the war in general and the French alliance in particular, most of Charles's ministers were suspected of being Papists, and Catholic uprisings were feared from Yorkshire to Sussex. Some wanted Monmouth to be named heir. In this situation the government had every reason to expect trouble with Parliament but could do no more to avert it than appealing to individual MPs.[74] The regime drifted towards the session like an oarless boat being carried towards a weir. And circumstances continued to worsen. Immediately before the Houses met, James remarried. His union with Anne Hyde, begun in scandal, had ended in tragedy in 1671 when she died of an agonizing disease. The new bride, Mary of Modena, was the daughter of an Italian client of France, with a dowry provided by Louis to strengthen his alliance with England. During the previous two years, James had courted another Catholic princess, of Austria, without arousing any disapproval in England. Nor had the faith of Catherine of Braganza provoked any, ten years before. But again, James's conversion changed everything and the new match was regarded as another stage in England's betrayal to Rome. At the same time, in October 1673, Wilhelm of Orange joined forces with an imperial army and captured Bonn, capital of Louis's principal German ally. The other Rhineland princes began to abandon the French, and they in turn commenced a withdrawal from most of the Dutch territory occupied in 1672. Louis retired, stunned, to his chamber while his provinces grew restless because of the weight of war taxation. Shortly after, news arrived in England that the Dutch had recaptured New York, the only prize of the previous war.

In these appallingly unpropitious circumstances, on 27 October, Charles and Shaftesbury met Parliament with speeches calling for a war supply and blaming the continuation of the struggle upon Dutch intransigence. They found themselves facing an equal intransigence on the part of the Commons. The MPs began by requesting the King to annul his brother's marriage, and when he replied that this was impossible, they voted not to accept his reply. Henry Coventry, Finch, and Duncombe all laboured to persuade the House to grant funds, but the clients of Buckingham and Arlington, who normally supported the court, held back. All that materialized was an offer to supply money if the Dutch failed subsequently to offer reasonable terms. Henry Coventry could only raise three votes against a motion that the standing army was a 'grievance'. When the House began to attack the ministers of state, upon 4 November, Charles declared a prorogation until January, asking the MPs to cool their tempers and promising measures against Popery. For the first time since his restoration, he had totally lost control of a House of Commons and reached an impasse in his dealings with it.[75] This appalling development was associated with another, equally novel for the reign: the problems of all three of his kingdoms seemed to be uniting.

The trouble that arose in Scotland in 1673 had nothing to do with the direct actions of Charles or, indeed, with the policy of his government. It was the result of the behaviour of the man who had slowly and stealthily become a viceroy over that land, the newly promoted Duke of Lauderdale.

The insidious poison of power, which had worked such rapid damage to the character of Middleton, now began to show its effects upon his far more talented enemy. During 1671 he cast off his two allies Murray and Tweeddale, who had played such a useful part in establishing him and in effecting an alteration of policy towards dissent. The process did not stem from a growth of mutual suspicion of the sort which had destroyed the preceding triumvirate. Rather, Lauderdale himself turned unilaterally upon his two clever friends and snubbed, bullied, and insulted them until they withdrew, bewildered and upset, from government.[76] He seems simply to have grown jealous of their obvious ability and fearful that it might come to eclipse his own. Certainly, in their place he promoted two conspicuously less impressive individuals, 'small people' in Tweeddale's phrase. One was the genial Earl of Kincardine, who received grants of money and a monopoly of marketing salt, and represented the Duke at court when he had to leave it for visits to Scotland. The other was Lauderdale's own brother, Charles Maitland of Halton, whom he had hitherto little regarded. His original assessment was apparently correct, for the least partial observers considered the younger Maitland to be distinguished by nothing more than greed and self-interest. In his portraits his long, weak, doleful face is insufficiently concealed by an unfashionable beard and moustache. He was now made his brother's principal henchman in Edinburgh, furnished with grants of land and the offices of Master of the Mint and Deputy Treasurer.[77] The strain of coarseness and brutality in Lauderdale's own nature became more pronounced, as is illustrated by two debates in the Committee for Foreign Affairs. At the opening of the war it was Lauderdale, alone of the Committee, who wanted to attack Dutch shipping without warning and without hearing the final peace offer from the States-General. When two enemy agents were arrested he was, again, alone in suggesting that they be tortured to gain information and then hanged.[78]

Yet the Duke's loss of political finesse can be overstated.[79] He took care to keep the flow of royal favour directed at political opponents, and during 1672 Rothes, Hamilton, and Dalyell all received offices, land, or pensions. It was especially important to reconcile Hamilton, himself a duke and relatively young, ambitious, and underemployed. Lauderdale corresponded warmly with him and attempted to obtain him the Garter, eliciting great appreciation.[80] During the first year of the war the Scottish Privy Council worked effectively to supply soldiers and sailors, and the Parliament voted funds for defence with only slight argument. What disturbed this tranquillity was a combination of factors. One was the strain exerted by a fresh Dutch war upon the

Scottish economy, which made people prone to grumble and to look with unusual disfavour upon the three marketing monopolies held by Lauderdale's friends, of the sale of salt (Kincardine's), tobacco, and brandy. Yet the Scots had suffered more, with more patience, in the previous war. What turned mild discontent into overt opposition was the disaffection of Privy Counsellors with purely personal grievances. One, of course, was Tweeddale, who offered his former friend a reconciliation for the last time in February 1673 and then set out to oppose him. He found ready allies in the current Advocate-General, Sir John Nisbet, who disliked the new ruling set, and (despite all Lauderdale's efforts) in Hamilton. The latter had suffered two nasty shocks. One resulted from a proposal to Lauderdale and the King from the new Archbishop of Glasgow, Robert Leighton, for a small commission of Privy Counsellors led by Hamilton to enforce the laws against nonconformists in the troubled south-west of Scotland. The Duke greeted with horror the notion of being made pre-eminently responsible for what he increasingly saw as a hopeless struggle against dissent. Indeed, he regarded it as a ploy to ruin him, and Charles was certainly angered by his refusal to serve. Hamilton's anger and alarm were compounded by irritation when Charles Maitland demanded accounts for money spent by the Duke in public service. In April 1673 he was already corresponding with Nisbet and Tweeddale to concert plans.[81] Their opportunity was presented when Lauderdale prepared to meet a new session of the Scottish Parliament in November. In England his manner and his reputation for ruthlessness had already made him one of the least popular ministers. Rumours abounded that he had declared Charles's will to be above the law and had made ready Scottish soldiers to intervene in English affairs. Before its prorogation the Cavalier House of Commons had been ready to denounce him. His enemies agreed that if the Parliament of Scotland joined the attack, then Charles would lose confidence in the red-haired Duke and dismiss him. In the circumstances of war, recession, and rule by men such as Charles Maitland, they found many supporters. On 12 November Lauderdale opened the new session, as Commissioner, with a request for a further supply. Hamilton at once moved that none be granted until the King had been informed of the distressing state of the land, and the proposal was carried. To their amazement, the Commissioner and his sovereign found themselves facing obdurate national assemblies on both sides of the Border.[82]

At the same time the problems of Ireland seemed once again likely to be represented at Westminster. In the course of 1673, the English government did indeed labour to satisfy Protestants upon either side of the water. In July its Committee on Irish Affairs persuaded Charles to implement Essex's rules for the regulation of corporations, unaltered. In September it instructed Essex to enact all that the Cavalier Parliament had requested regarding the land settlement, the expulsion of Catholics from the army, local office, and towns, and the exiling of their clergy. Charles ordered that the purge should extend even to minor offices which the MPs had not named. Essex duly issued the necessary orders and proclamations. At the same time Richard Talbot left Whitehall for the Continent, along with other prominent English and Irish Catholics such as Lord Arundell.[83] These concessions were not, however, sufficient to remove the western kingdom from the political agenda at Westminster. On 1 December Essex informed the King that some of the Privy Council at Dublin still wanted to address him formally upon the woes of Ireland.[84] These problems included not only the economic recession produced by the war, but also a belief that the moment for more severe measures against Catholics had come. The Lord-Lieutenant succeeded in quashing this project, but his action only meant that those discontented Privy Counsellors who had seats in the Cavalier Parliament would go to work there once more.

As in the other two kingdoms, the chances of co-operation among Charles's servants in Ireland was vitiated by animosities. In the late 1660s the two great men there who most needed to work together, Ormonde and Orrery, had quarrelled. Now the pattern was being repeated. For the good of the realm, amity was essential between Essex and Ranelagh, the man who now controlled its finances. In 1673 the former turned against the latter and they became bitter enemies. This was in part the result of a clash over policy. Ranelagh's simple and ruthless method for balancing the public revenue was to let the arrears of pay due to the army increase until the soldiers agreed to accept lump sums by way of composition. These were far less than the theoretical amounts due to them, and were given for an agreement to sign away any right to the rest of their back-pay. Essex, who commanded the army, was disgusted by this trick. But a reading of the correspondence gives an impression of a deeper antagonism. The Lord-Lieutenant never reconciled himself to the notion that the finances were beyond his control, while Ranelagh felt that anything less than complete power over them would ruin his chances of managing them, a great gamble in itself. By the end of 1673 the two men, both in Charles's complete confidence, were hoping for each other's replacement.[85]

In scholarship there appears to be such a thing as an orthodoxy by default, signifying an assertion which is made by some authorities and ignored, but not condemned, by others. This definition would fit the belief of two successive American historians[86] that Charles decided from the autumn of 1673 to pull out of the Dutch war and that he engineered this in such a fashion as to give no offence to Louis. It is difficult to disprove the proposal completely, as each warlike action of the English King could be interpreted as another bluff to deceive the French. But one piece of evidence in its favour can be demolished. This is the belief that in October Charles made a secret pact with Spain to overthrow the King of Portugal and to divide his realm, England taking the overseas empire. According to this view, he proved the most perfect actor, feigning near-indifference when a suspicious de Croissy sounded him out concerning his attitude to the Portuguese. Later, however, Louis received confirmation of English involvement in the intrigue, which itself proved abortive. This, to Professor Ekberg, is proof of Charles's willingness and ability to deceive his French allies at this juncture and argues for his employment of similar tactics in the larger matter of the war. Now, it is certainly true that the French did believe that England was implicated in this shady business. But not a scrap of evidence survives upon the English side to confirm that belief. Instead, the regular reports from Charles's agent in Lisbon speak of the plot there as an exclusively Spanish concern,[87] and it seems that the French ambassador in the city was simply mistaken in deciding otherwise. In this case, the English monarch's lack of interest in de Croissy's questions was no more than natural. Once this distortion is removed from the picture, Charles appears in the winter of 1673–4 not so much as a consummate politician carefully moving his nation out of war as a desperate man obsessed with finding any possible means of continuing a conflict upon which his honour had become staked.

His immediate reaction to the disaster of the English parliamentary session was to sack Shaftesbury, whom he suspected, despite his bellicose opening speech, of having given tacit advantages to the court's opponents. As he had every reason to assist the condemnation of the marriage of his enemy the Duke of York, the King's suspicions were probably correct. Observers agreed it was James who, in vengeance, secured his dismissal, a move which horrified Arlington. And it backfired. Charles intended the tiny Earl to be both disgraced and sent out of the capital. Instead, Shaftesbury obstinately remained in London with the clear intention of joining the attack upon the government when Parliament remet.[88] The essentially negative character of Charles's action is indicated by the report that he changed his mind six times in as many hours concerning the identity of Shaftesbury's successor. In the end he chose Sir Heneage Finch, who had been successively Attorney-General and Solicitor-General since the Restoration. With custody of the seals Finch received a barony, but only the lesser office of Lord Keeper. His elevation was due to the sponsorship of the rising men Osborne (himself recently promoted to the title of Viscount Latimer) and Seymour. It appears that by supporting the impeccably episcopalian and well-respected lawyer they hoped to please the conservative and Anglican majority in the Commons. But Finch's success was only part of a wider campaign by Buckingham and his former protégés to win pre-eminence by taming Parliament for the King. The temperament of this Duke was precisely suited to such an over-optimistic venture, and he and his friends set to work distributing French money among likely peers and MPs. There were enough opportunists around, like the now aged Bristol, to offer enthusiastic support and to give the illusion of growing success. Arlington, as ever more sagacious, saw that the only real chance of restoring good relations with the Cavalier Parliament was for the King to end the war and to disown his brother's marriage and perhaps James himself. As Charles found the first course temporarily, and the latter one utterly, unacceptable, the Secretary only earned the dislike of James.[89]

Thus government attempts to reconcile the Commons were restricted by rigid barriers. Charles not only issued a conventional proclamation for the enforcement of laws against Catholics, but banned them from court and ordered the judges to find ways of making the penal legislation more effective. When some Quakers asked him to free two of their leaders from a provincial prison, he replied that he was obliged to leave them to the due process of law. Yet he would not do the two things which were really necessary to allay religious tensions. He kept his brother by his side in high favour, and when Mary of Modena was rowed upriver to Whitehall he welcomed her graciously. City and court marked her arrival with cold silence.[90] And, of course, he did not make peace. He once again moderated his terms, dropping the demands for Surinam and for honours for Wilhelm and reducing the indemnity to £300,000. The States-General were willing to concede the naval salute and a smaller indemnity and to return New York. But division still existed by the end of the year over the fishery rent, the evacuation of the Surinam settlers, and the East Indies trade, and upon these issues Charles would not budge. Furthermore, he wanted negotiations to proceed in partnership with the French at Cologne, while the Dutch wanted to talk at London.[91]

As 1673 ended it seemed that the malcontents of all three kingdoms were gathering at Westminster. The Irish Privy Counsellors were there or on their way, and were being joined by Scots. At Edinburgh the plan to dislodge Lauderdale had failed because of the Duke's great weapon, his control of the flow of information to his monarch. His simple answer to the opposition in the Scottish Parliament was to convince Charles and

James that it had been stirred up by Shaftesbury and the trouble-makers in England. He next obtained royal permission to revoke the monopolies which had been the concrete grievance cited to him. When this failed to satisfy the majority in the Parliament, he informed his sovereign that this was proof that the complaints were merely mischievous, and adjourned the whole institution. Hamilton and Tweeddale bolted for England, both to clear their names to Charles and to abet the attack upon Lauderdale there. When they arrived, they found the King well-primed by their enemy's letters and by his friends such as Kincardine. He believed them to be ambitious self-seekers in league with those in London, and received them frigidly. As a result, they now began to concert plans in earnest with English opponents of the court.[92]

Just before the Cavalier Parliament remet on 7 January, Charles gave French agents at Whitehall the impression of a man losing his grip, at one moment confident of success, at another reduced to despair. This sense of royal weakness was borne out by the well-informed correspondents at court of Essex and Williamson, who found it impossible to determine which ministers were in favour as the King swung wildly from one to the other.[93] It seems to have been Latimer who proposed the main concession to be made to the Houses: to show them the treaty made with the French just before the war and thus to prove that it contained nothing sinister (Latimer himself was probably ignorant of the two earlier secret pacts, of Dover and London). This was accepted by the Foreign Affairs Committee on the night before the session, only Arlington and Ormonde (for unrecorded reasons) opposing it. The two speeches, by Charles and Finch, were repeatedly redrafted, and when delivered they were studiously moderate. The King asked for a war supply, but only to secure a good peace as soon as possible and to keep up the navy thereafter. He invited in return all reasonable proposals to secure the Church and property. Something of his agony of mind was indicated by the fact that he stumbled over his words. Finch then detailed his master's actions against Catholics and blamed Dutch recalcitrance for the continuation of hostilities.[94]

All the hopes of the recess proved false. The recent round of promotions had left virtually only Henry Coventry in the Commons out of all the royal ministers. Although he struggled bravely, 'like the cherubim with his flaming sword, turning it every way to defend his master's cause', he was unsupported. Within five days the Commons had resolved to present grievances before supply, and launched attacks upon Lauderdale, Buckingham, and Arlington. Charles reacted to the first by allowing the Duke to come south to take counter-measures, leaving the Scottish Parliament adjourned. The House asked unanimously for his dismissal. Buckingham next attempted a brilliant coup by appearing in person before the MPs and offering to clear his name. As so often, his talents were not equal to his opinion of them, and he made such a hash of his speech that none of his friends dared to defend him. The Commons asked for his removal from all offices and, as his utility to the King was now at last ended, Charles obliged at once. Equally in character was the fate of Arlington, who also appeared before the House to answer charges, but answered them with admirable clarity and dignity. Despite the efforts of followers of Buckingham and former friends of Clarendon, the attack on him petered out and he retained his posts and his master's esteem.[95]

Charles's attitude through all this was (as he reputedly expressed it to Latimer and James) to 'give the people an open field in order to curb them the better when they were tired with their gallop'. Two private requests of his in early January seem pointless unless he had hoped to continue the war. One was made to John Evelyn, the diarist and man of letters, to pen a tract justifying the struggle against the Dutch in terms of the English grievances still unsatisfied by them. The other was to Samuel Pepys, to draw up a plan for securing English harbours if, as in 1667, there was insufficient money to put out the fleet.[96] Neither project reached fruition, for the States-General now delivered their master-stroke. On 22 January Charles received new terms from them, conceding all his remaining demands save that for the fishery rent. As Arlington confessed to Williamson (who was awaiting further orders at the Cologne congress), there was now virtually no justification for going on with the war. The Dutch had carefully leaked copies of their proposals to MPs, and the government knew that the Commons would soon debate the 'grievances' arising from the conflict. It seemed likely that they would condemn the war itself and so force the King to make peace. Arlington and Ormonde hit upon an obvious means of forestalling this and saving face, by asking the Houses themselves to peruse the terms and to determine whether they were satisfactory. The whole Foreign Affairs Committee agreed to this, and Latimer drafted the speech with which Charles put it before Parliament. As soon as the Commons opened their debate upon the matter Henry Coventry was ready with a condemnation of the Dutch terms, based on the fishery issue: clearly, the government was still hoping thereby to spin out the war. He was completely unsupported, and by the 28th both Houses had voted the proposals to be an adequate basis for a treaty.[97] Even the French now realized that British withdrawal from the war was now inevitable, and Charles's government acted at high speed. All that delayed the process was the need to exchange the formalities of opening negotiations, and these were shortened by allowing the Spanish ambassador to act for the Dutch. The result was the Treaty of Westminster, drafted at Arlington's house by the Secretary himself, James, Finch, Ormonde, the Spaniard, and Charles, and sealed on 9 February. By gaining the salute in British waters, good terms for the Surinam settlers, arbitration of the East Indian trade disputes, and an indemnity, England could be said to have emerged without loss of honour or territory (New York being returned), and to have won 'on points'. Nobody, however, thought that the gains made had been worth the expenditure of lives, limbs, money, and commercial opportunities.[98]

On the 11th, Charles faced the Houses again with new hope of co-operation, promising to reduce the army to the Guards and garrisons and asking for funds to keep up a peacetime navy. He did issue the orders for disbanding within ten days, though thirty-six companies and ten horse troops were shipped over to Ireland along with the soldiers being sent back there: a clever way of reassuring Protestant fears in the island and of keeping the men available.[99] If he seriously expected such measures to remove ill feeling, however, he was deluding himself. The war, and the existence of the army, had essentially been secondary issues. Neither had been opposed in Parliament until James had been revealed as a Catholic; and he remained one, as he remained heir presumptive. The making of peace only allowed Parliament to confront this fact more directly. The Lords were already considering proposals to exclude future princes from the throne if they married Catholics, and to educate any children of James and Mary as Protestants. The Commons concentrated more upon limiting the Crown itself. One member (an Irish Privy Counsellor) declared that it was 'time to take care against our coming under a bad prince', for such James's faith itself now made him. No less than ten bills were in progress by mid-February to reduce royal power over the judiciary, Parliament, taxation, and religion. The alleged laxity of the Irish government against Catholics was discussed, and Ranelagh's enemies among the Privy Counsellors from Dublin opened a full-scale attack upon his management of the revenue.[100] Charles decided, abruptly, that he had nothing more but trouble to expect from the session and prorogued Parliament on 24 February. His action surprised not only both Houses but his own ministers, for he consulted them neither individually nor as the Foreign Affairs Committee. If he was advised by anybody into the action, then it would have been his brother, who reacted to most difficult parliamentary sessions of the reign by advocating defiance, prorogation, or dissolution. Rumours were abroad that James was about to be attacked directly in Parliament, and it seems likely that Charles acted precipitately to prevent this. By doing so, of course, he admitted that, at least in the near future, he could not work with the national assembly of England. For good measure he prorogued that in Scotland, as he had heard that 'mad motions' were being prepared for it also.[101]

For four years Charles's government had been dragged in the wake of the destinies of Louis XIV and of James, Duke of York. It had almost been shaken to pieces in the process. Superficially, the events of 1674 had repeated those of 1667. An unfortunate war had been ended, a great man banished from power (Buckingham instead of Clarendon), and a new start attempted. But the situation in 1674 was fundamentally different. After the Treaty of Westminster Charles was still not free from the onward career of his cousin and brother. As long as Louis remained at war, the English government would be subject to conflicting pressures to lend military or diplomatic aid to the struggle. If he began to defeat his ring of enemies then those pressures would intensify. At home, James had become a nightmare to many Protestants and rendered political life potentially unstable. There was no escaping the sense that during the war years the restored monarchy had entered a new and profoundly uncomfortable era. One of the most calculating observers of the process was Edward, Lord Conway, a crafty and ambitious Anglo-Irishman who was friendly with both Essex and Ranelagh and intended to rise with or without the help of either. In February 1674 he wrote that 'There will be a new game played at court, and the designs and interests of all men will be different from what they were.'[102]

Before turning to this 'new game', it is worth asking one more question about that which was played in British politics between 1670 and 1673. What was really at stake in it? To a pair of very distinguished historians, the answer has been that the government came close to developing into an absolute monarchy.[103] They have proposed that Charles and his ministers in those years had a conscious design to make the Crown independent of Parliament and to reduce the whole political nation to its will. It seems that the surviving sources do not provide proof of this intention. There was plenty of speculation among people outside the 'inner ring' of royal advisers that such a project was afoot. It swelled after the Declaration of Indulgence and the outbreak of war, and became feverish when James resigned his offices. But the papers of those in power, and especially the minutes of the Foreign Affairs Committee, provide no hint of it. When Minette wrote her sole surviving letter to Charles, in 1669, she did speak of his need to be less vulnerable to Parliament, but in view of the exceptional weakness of the Crown during the previous two sessions, this was hardly saying much. In 1672 Finch, as Solicitor-General, did draw up writs against twenty of the most important urban corporations. Yet these were to challenge their power to mint farthings, rather than any more consequential right.[104] The King and his chief ministers certainly expected that the utter defeat of the Dutch would greatly strengthen royal prestige at home and abroad. None, however, seem to have formulated any blueprints for a qualitatively different sort of monarchy, or concerted plans to achieve one. The real visionary among them, Clifford, was only concerned with the reunion of the Churches.

Even had they done so, there seems little chance that any such project would have succeeded. The English prospects of annihilating the Dutch fleet and invading Zealand depended upon the assumption that the enemy would deploy their warships with wanton folly. To thwart an invasion from the sea, the Dutch did not have to fight at all. They needed merely to keep their vessels behind the sandbanks and to strike at the allies when they were off guard. On the other hand, the French came very close indeed to occupying the whole Dutch state by land. Yet had they done so, Louis was determined that his cousin should obtain the minimum of advantage from the operation. Thus it may be suggested that, although this war was indeed a turning-point in British politics, the stakes were less dramatically high than some contemporaries and some historians have thought.

The End of King Louis's War, 1674–1678

⟨✦⟩

THE next four years of Charles's reign are among the best studied, most especially in the publications of Professors Browning and Haley.[1] Their events are well known to scholars, and there are few sources unused which can add substantially to the story. Three different contributions can be made here to a familiar tale. First, this book will of course make its own interpretations of the facts, and add fresh details. Second, it will trace the interpretation of English politics by those of the other realms, as has not fully been done before. And third, it will take up a slightly different perspective upon the whole period. Very often, these years have been seen as an interlude of comparatively peaceful and successful government between two crises, given unity by the leadership of a remarkable minister, Danby. This is quite justifiable. It may, however, be fundamentally more true to regard this time as one in which Britain remained towed in the wake of Louis of France, and to see the period's unity provided by the need to react to the continuing war upon the Continent. From this perspective, the record of government is one of a series of attempts to ward off disaster, culminating in a catastrophe greater than that which had struck it in 1673–4.

Certainly to Charles and his English ministers, the rest of the year 1674 did seem like a blessed relief after the trials of its first two months. There was no project in the King's mind of setting up one adviser over the rest. Rather, it was a matter of settling down with his new team, the men who had survived the war years, Arlington and James, and the men whom those years had brought to power, Latimer, Finch, and Henry Coventry. Until 1679 they formed between them most of the Foreign Affairs Committee. Despite personal dislikes they co-operated as gracefully as any of Charles's teams of advisers before, and generally reached decisions by large majorities. During 1674 they were united in the sentiment that a fresh session of Parliament was best left to another year. Only Henry Coventry opposed this policy, and in September Charles prorogued the Houses until April 1675. He then told the French ambassador that the decision had been a *coup de maître*, taken by him personally without reference to his advisers and done to please Louis.[2] This misinformation was presumably intended to give an impression that royal control over the government was absolute, and to encourage the French to continue to deal with him personally. It is another example of how the reports of ambassadors, even those intimate with Charles, are not to be taken as unsupported evidence for his intentions and actions. Ormonde, who had been restored to prominence as an adviser in 1673, was now pushed gently into the background again, though he, his family, and clients were given more honours to maintain his prestige. One of his firmest supporters, Lord Aungier, was made Earl of Longford.[3]

Thus it looked at first as if Charles was set upon another balancing act, of his former chief minister, Arlington, against the best of the new men, Latimer. Instead, the balance tipped, because the former proved too exhausted and the latter too energetic and ambitious. In the early summer of 1674 Arlington was still regarded as a formidable force and ambassadors and petitioners still sought his aid. One of the latter addressed him as 'one of the Prime Ministers and columns of the government'.[4] But he was worn out by overwork, political exertion, and gout. He became irascible in a way not known before. In March he shocked Charles by launching a savage public attack upon the competence of Anglesey. He displayed towards Latimer the same childish jealousy with which Clarendon had once treated him.[5] His advice during the previous winter had earned him the unwavering hostility of James, who remained as close to his brother as he had been during the war and secured a number of posts for his protégés.[6] In September Arlington resigned his post of Secretary of State to his own client Sir Joseph Williamson, and took the honorific office of Lord Chamberlain. It was a move which he had been contemplating for eighteen months, and was emphatically not intended to mark his departure from politics. Rather, he was shedding a burden of work in order to refresh himself for the fray, an attitude clear enough from his subsequent actions. His successor was unlikely to replace him as a great force, and did not. Williamson was an efficient bureaucrat and a sparkling courtier who could dance six hours at a stretch, play musical instruments, and perform juggling acts.[7] With his new posts, he was admitted to the Foreign Affairs Committee. But he lacked the ambition and the political skill of a statesman. Arlington's error was to believe that, stripped of the administrative importance and the patronage that the post of Secretary had given him, he could provide a match for somebody of the calibre of Latimer.

This man was now rising towards the height of his personal powers, of which his face, lean and cunning with a pencil-line moustache, gives evidence in the portraits. He had the current remarkable fortune to occupy the post of Lord Treasurer at the first point of the reign at which it was possible to make a dramatic success of it. His task was, obviously, to balance the national finances again after the war, and he tackled it ruthlessly. To pay off the fleet, he stopped salaries, and pensions. He renewed the Hearth Tax farm, forcing the new farmers to pay more, and improved the accounting of the Excise. By the end of the year the war had been paid for in full while the regular income had reached £1½ million per annum, which actually exceeded expenditure for the first time in the reign. That this was possible was due to good harvests and a boom in trade, consequent upon the fact that England was suddenly almost the only non-belligerent in western Europe.[8] Nevertheless, Latimer got the credit and was rewarded by an overjoyed royal master with promotion to the title by which he has generally been known ever since, of Earl of Danby.

In Scotland, by contrast, the pre-war administration was confined in power. When the Parliament there was adjourned, Lauderdale returned to a hero's welcome at Whitehall. He was met near London by a great train of nobles and attended to the palace, where Charles and James received him warmly. Hamilton was refused permission to return to court to explain himself, Charles having been thoroughly convinced that he was involved in the trouble in both kingdoms. Under these circumstances it was easy for his mighty rival to consolidate his own position spectacularly, in a string of measures at the end of May. The English Privy Council formally declared that he was innocent of the charges alleged against him by the Commons, and Charles gave him an English earldom to afford him a seat in the Lords and the legal protection that went with it. He persuaded Charles to dissolve first the Scottish Parliament and then the Scottish Privy Council. Hamilton was named for the new Council, but most of his allies were not, including Tweeddale, who was also dropped from the English one. Why their great leader was spared is not known, though from the tone of Charles's letter to him it seems that he was to be left isolated but with the opportunity to seek royal forgiveness and to use his great influence on the government's behalf. Those who were reappointed, and those brought in to fill the places of those purged, almost fell over each other to send messages of gratitude and loyalty to Lauderdale.[9]

'John Red' was now master of Scotland and, as he tended to do every few years, changed his allies. Kincardine was seemingly disturbingly able and energetic, and there was no lack of men anxious to replace him as Lauderdale's lieutenant and willing to implant suspicions of him in the Duke's mind. Like Tweeddale before him, he found himself cast off, by the end of 1674. Charles Maitland was likewise pushed into the background. At once less of an asset and a challenge than Kincardine, he was not 'disgraced' but hereafter played a much less prominent role. Their places were taken initially by Highland nobles, the Earls of Atholl and Argyll (son of the great Covenanter), who wanted more of a part in public affairs.[10] But the mighty Duke was making additional friends, as part of a change in religious policy. Since 1672 he had gradually become frustrated by the results of the Indulgences, which had been intended to divide dissent and make the annihilation of conventicles possible. Instead, illegal religious gatherings had grown in numbers, in size, and in geographical extent. The Duke's impatience conveyed itself to Charles, who declared officially that Indulgence only rendered Scottish nonconformists ungrateful and insolent. The replacement of the Council had been preceded by measures intended to allay discontent after the unfortunate parliamentary session, a remittance of all arrears of taxation levied before 1660, and an amnesty to all hitherto accused of hoarding or attending conventicles. It was followed by a string of commands to the new Council to wipe out any such meetings hereafter. The King insisted that this was not religious persecution, holding that the failure of Indulgence meant that dissenters aimed not at toleration but subversion. The resulting campaign was exactly what the bishops had been demanding ten years before, and opened for Lauderdale the opportunity for a *rapprochement* with them. In the autumn Sharp and Burnet were invited to Whitehall, and the latter reinstated as Archbishop of Glasgow. Both were henceforth the Duke's allies.[11] It only remained for him to secure his position at court Arlington had drifted into enmity with him and tried, unavailingly, to represent Hamilton and Tweeddale well to Charles.[12] Lauderdale took the obvious and easy course and befriended Danby, and thus remained a powerful figure on the Foreign Affairs Committee and in British affairs in general.

In Ireland also the existing leadership was retained, though it was that of a much more limited leader. Of Essex himself, Charles had only good to say. The neatest compliment which he paid him, among many, was that he was a man 'that may be believed blindfold'.[13] But the Earl had to suffer all the old frustrations. The King remained as careless as before of Irish affairs. One public servant obtained a payment from the Irish Treasury with the help of Ormonde, only for Charles to countermand it upon other advice. The countermand actually reached Essex before the original warrant and both were followed (within a week) by a third royal letter cancelling the countermand, as Ormonde's influence was reimposed.[14] And the perennial fear of being undermined at court remained. Essex continually received friendly letters from Ormonde, Conway, Orrery, Ranelagh, and Danby, interspersed with messages from friends that all these men were working to destroy him.[15] While Charles spoke glowingly of the Lord-Lieutenant, he lavished favour upon his potential rivals. Conway was made Governor of Charlemont and Ranelagh became Constable of Athlone and Vice-Treasurer (thus consolidating his grip on the public finances). Orrery received some local privileges in Munster and Danby got the right to vet all grants made from Irish funds before the King sent the orders for them to Ireland.[16] What enabled Essex to carry on under this sort of strain was not merely the assurance of his royal master's support but the knowledge that his real and presumed enemies were as liable to quarrel with each other as with him. In mid-1674 Orrery got a patent submitted to Charles with Danby's support to command all the militia of Munster. Henry Coventry warned Essex, who saw it as an attempt to revive the authority of a president in a new guise, and he enlisted Arlington's help to move the King to refuse it. When Danby felt slighted by this, Essex tried to divide him from Orrery by proving that the latter had lied to him to get his support. Relations between the Lord-Lieutenant and Lord Treasurer improved, and six months later Danby persuaded Charles to give Essex the money to buy a London mansion.[17] In keeping the King's ear, Essex suffered three disadvantages in comparison with Lauderdale. First, his refined aristocratic hauteur was less suited to the business of intrigue than the coarser sensibilities of the great Scot. Like Lauderdale, he kept agents by the King to ensure that his viewpoint was represented. But he disliked it if they immersed themselves too far in the squalid intrigues of the court. Thus, he warned one not to waste his time with 'little people' such as the King's mistresses and Household servants, not noticing that it was precisely with the help of one such servant that his man had got an audience with Charles when necessary.[18] His second handicap was that he simply did not possess the rapport, built up over years, that the red-haired Duke had achieved with his sovereign. Lauderdale, uniquely, combined the qualities of Charles's two categories of favourite: the industry of his trusted ministers and the foul-mouthed, hard-drinking *bonhomie* of his social companions. But last, the case of Restoration Scotland was very different from that of Restoration Ireland. English politicians were happy to let the former look after itself, but the latter represented, from the post of Lord-Lieutenant down, a gigantic spoils system in which all wished a stake.

After each political trauma of his reign, Charles felt the need to retreat further from London. After the humiliations which marked his first Dutch war, he commenced his twice-yearly trips to Newmarket. After those of his second he took to spending his summers at Windsor Castle as well.

It was on his return from there in the autumn of 1674 that his ministers set about trying to solve the remaining problems left over from the war. That of finance had been taken care of for the time being. There remained those of finding a new foreign policy and of re-establishing a working relationship with the Cavalier Parliament, which would make all future things possible. The answer to the diplomatic conundrum was very easy, its achievement extremely difficult. Charles had the strongest possible reasons for mediating an end to the war in Europe. This would leave him with the gratitude of all nations involved and restore his prestige in international affairs, while removing the risk that anti-French feeling in England (and especially in its Parliament) would drive him into co-operation with the coalition against Louis. The obstacle was that none of the combatants in 1674 wanted peace. The allies were out to crush Louis for good, while he was determined to remain uncrushed.

An objective view indicates that it would have been best for Charles if Wilhelm of Orange and his coalition had succeeded, bringing the war to a close and reducing fear of France (and therefore of Catholicism) in England. But the English King's sympathies still lay on the other side. He did not know of his cousin's attempts to double-cross him during the joint attack on the Dutch. He did know (through his espionage network) that his nephew's agents had encouraged the cry for peace in England during the previous winter which had forced him to conclude one. He still felt very bitter about the Treaty of Westminster. When Sir William Temple was called out of retirement to carry the treaty over for ratification he told Charles that he had been ill-advised to commence the war. The King snarled that, on the contrary, he had been ill-served.[19] Accordingly, his policy was double-edged. Remembering how well Temple had won the trust of de Witt, he sent him to reside at The Hague, to try to make the same relationship with Wilhelm, and to persuade him to make a separate peace and thus to break the coalition. At the same time he prevented the Dutch from recruiting in any of his kingdoms while ordering the Scottish Privy Council and Essex to connive at French recruitment in Scotland and Ireland. The gaolbirds in the Edinburgh Tolbooth found themselves being shipped off to serve the Sun King. When a book was published attacking Dutch commercial claims, Charles banned it officially and thanked the author privately.[20]

In the event, the war did not end in 1674. Louis's armies held off attacks in the Netherlands and Rhineland with the loss of only one town, while they conquered the whole province of Spanish Burgundy. At the end of the campaigns, all combatants accepted English mediation and the allies offered peace. But their terms consisted of a French withdrawal from virtually all conquests since 1659, which was clearly not acceptable to Louis. At this stage Arlington attempted a great diplomatic coup which would place foreign policy, and a predominant influence in the government, back in his hands. He persuaded Charles, without consulting the Foreign Affairs Committee, to send him and Ossory (Ormonde's heir) on a personal mission to Prince Wilhelm to persuade him to treat. Clearly the ageing minister's powers were failing, for he was now unrealistic as well as temperamental: Wilhelm saw no reason to reduce the terms which his coalition was offering, and the attempt to detach him from it irritated him. This abysmal failure left the initiative in Danby's hands, and he now guided the government into 1675.

His aim consisted, essentially, of managing Parliament. Before the reassembly in April 1675, Sheldon called up the bishops again to support the Crown, while Coventry wrote to eleven MPs asking them to be present from the beginning of the session.[21] But these measures were insignificant in comparison with the main device, to try to please the Commons by indulging their religious prejudices. During 1674 no one model of ecclesiastical policy prevailed in the British realms. In Scotland, as said, the government was harrying nonconformists to the utmost of its abilities. Lauderdale persuaded Charles to order the raising of more regular forces and to commission one of the Duke's clients, Sir George Munro, to command the whole army. He paraded it through the country to assist the process of arrests and intimidation, while Charles had a brigade of the recently reinforced Irish army sent to Ulster ready to be shipped to Ayrshire. He was fully prepared for the excesses of the military to provoke resistance as in 1666, and to deal with this without sympathy.[22] In Ireland itself, on the other hand, Essex told the bishops to turn a blind eye to dissenters while he satisfied Protestant opinion there, and in England, by driving the Catholic hierarchy overseas or into hiding.[23] In England the situation remained in complete flux. Charles offered a reward for every priest apprehended but ensured that the death penalty was never carried out, commuting it to banishment instead. He forebade Catholics the court once again, but made one of them Governor of Tangier and promoted another to an earldom. The government made no pronouncements whatsoever upon the status of Protestant nonconformity, and some independent churches were expecting another royal Indulgence. Charles appointed two notably moderate men to the sees of Durham and Chichester.[24]

When throwing the weight of the government behind persecution, Danby never troubled to conceal the fact that this was purely done to please the Cavalier Parliament. A simple way to reassure its fears in the wake of the Declaration of Indulgence and James's conversion was to secure the Church against all its enemies, Catholic and Protestant. The Lord Treasurer and Lauderdale initiated informal talks with bishops during the autumn of 1674, which led to a conference in January at which Sheldon and selected prelates met Privy Counsellors to work out a course of action. It was hardly a representative cross-section of Church and State as virtually all the churchmen present were known enemies of toleration and Charles invited them to speak frankly. The Counsellors present consisted of Danby, Lauderdale, Finch, Coventry, and the pliant Williamson, who sat silent while his colleagues urged stern measures. Unsurprisingly, the meeting recommended to the King the full enforcement of the statutes against Catholic and Protestant nonconformity. At the Privy Council, James naturally attacked the project and obtained the cancellation of some of the steps proposed. His brother, however, was convinced by the argument that recusants and conventiclers made easy sacrificial victims to a House of Commons which might otherwise continue its attack upon the powers of the Crown. Counsellors who sympathized with presbyterians, such as Holles and Halifax, stayed away rather than mount opposition, and the result was a proclamation which ordered the execution of the laws and the formal withdrawal of all the licences issued in 1672. It was, and was seen to be, a public relations exercise. London lads called it a 'Declaration of His Majesty for sweetmeats for the Parliament'. Coventry warned a Bristol alderman, who had zealously persecuted the city's dissenters before, that the King was just serving notice that he upheld the law. When the Bishop of Bristol asked for soldiers to round up conventiclers, the Secretary replied that the request was refused and that peaceful nonconformists were to be left alone. Neither alderman nor bishop took this advice, and their subsequent campaign of arrests was halted by royal command, with the admonition that such behaviour led only to bitterness and unrest.[25]

Charles and Finch made this ecclesiastical policy the centre-piece of their speeches to Parliament when the new session opened upon 13 April 1675. Both stressed that Popery was its main target, and the Chancellor invited the Houses to amend the laws as they saw fit (thus emphasizing the government's complete subservience to statute). By permitting the session to happen at all, the King had rejected the impassioned pleas of James and of the French ambassador, who had failed to talk him out of it despite a three-hour interview in which he had offered £100,000 for a further prorogation. Charles's doubts showed in the irritably defensive nature of his speech, during which he denied that he wished to rule without Parliament or that he lacked zeal for the Church. What he asked of the Houses was money to increase the fleet, while he offered them the opportunity to protect religion, liberty, and property as they saw fit. A few days later Danby got a friend to put before the Lords the measure which he thought fitting, a bill prescribing an oath for all Members of Parliament and all office-holders, not to try to alter the government of Church or State. While protecting orthodox Anglicanism, this would deftly secure the traditional powers of the Crown.

The result of all this effort was mixed. The Commons resolved to thank Charles by eleven votes, while the Lords did so by a much larger majority. The shock in this was that those who opposed included not only Shaftesbury and his allies but Arlington and Ormonde, who thereby signalled their unwillingness to co-operate wholeheartedly with Danby. Arlington's clients subsequently played a leading role in an attempt in the Commons to impeach the Lord Treasurer himself. It was defeated, representing the final act in the establishment of the new chief minister and the decline of the old. Charles was furious with his former Secretary for this misbehaviour, and ignored him for a month. Arlington responded by refusing to speak to Danby, even when the King ordered a reconciliation, and subsequently by withdrawing from court for long periods. Thereafter he still attended the Foreign Affairs Committee, and Charles gave him a few long private interviews (one lasting an afternoon), but his influence was gone.[26] What saved him from complete disgrace was probably that he had the sense not to oppose the bill for the oath not to alter government. Nobody among the ministers did, except the morose and high-principled Anglesey, who argued that it would be monstrously unfair to dissenters. To the intense relief of Charles, his brother's feeling for his fellow-Catholics was outweighed by loyalty to his family and the Crown, and James supported not only the bill but Danby himself when that minister was under attack. Lauderdale was less lucky than the Treasurer, less well-defended, and less concerned about the consequences, having his enormous power-base in Scotland. Almost as soon as sitting down, the Commons started work upon another address to Charles for his removal, ignoring in the process the previous year's Order in Council stating his innocence. The King replied (correctly) that the charges laid against him were either incorrect or legally improper. Nevertheless, the rumours that the great minister was preparing his land as a reservoir of royal strength to be loosed upon England were too strong, and another address was voted. Charles ostentatiously drove the Duke in his coach in Hyde Park as a warning (and, unfortunately, a provocation) to the MPs.[27] Another point of friction was over foreign affairs, though, again, it was not a major one. All that the Commons asked of the King was to recall the brigade of British soldiers which he had left in the service of Louis.

Tactlessly, Charles had just drawn further attention to it by making the commander of its Scottish division (a Catholic) an earl.[28] He refused the House's request on the grounds that this would be dishonourable, a message which sounds like his own thoughts rather than those of his ministers. But he did order the recall of all British who had entered the French service since the Anglo-Dutch War, so that the brigade would dwindle away. The work of Louis's agents in Scotland and Ireland made this, in fact, unlikely, but even without knowing of this the House was suspicious enough to resolve on a further address. Nor did it vote any supply.

All this was less than satisfactory to Charles, but, in its way, it was a working partnership. By late May the Houses between them had produced bills to eliminate Catholics and office-holders from Parliament, to educate any future children of James as Protestants, and to prevent non-parliamentary taxation. Not all these, however, need pass, and most would be more than compensated for by the bill for the new oath, which had got through the Lords after protracted argument and amendments. It remains for ever debatable whether the government would have tried to make it pass the Commons, for at that moment all business stuck fast. Another dispute over jurisdiction broke out between the two Houses, encouraged by the court's opponents, and co-operation broke down. Charles called a prorogation on 9 June, commenting bitterly that his enemies had achieved a triumph.

So indeed they had, by rendering the whole session sterile, but the fact that they had been obliged to resort to such tactics indicated how close the government had come to success. So Danby reasoned, and prepared for another try in the autumn. James disagreed. He had compromised his conscience sufficiently already, for an apparent absence of result. His advice to his brother, powerfully seconded by the French, was to scrap the Cavalier Parliament altogether, by dissolution, and to accept a cash reward from a relieved Louis. Charles's response was to play it both ways: to permit a further session while preparing a fall-back position in case it failed. How much enthusiasm he himself had for Danby's policy of trying to tame Parliament, and how much he had to be talked into it, simply cannot be surmised. There is not a scrap of evidence for his 'true' feelings upon the question. Certainly, to achieve a productive partnership with Parliament was the preferable course, and James's argument was not that it was undesirable but that it was impossible. It can be said that the King's response makes perfect sense as a policy of double insurance. In August he made a treaty with Louis whereby he promised to dissolve Parliament if it tried to force him into a war with France or if it refused taxes again. In either case, his cousin would pay him £100,000 per year until fresh elections were held. The figure was achieved as a result of some energetic haggling between Charles and the French ambassador, in which the monarch first asked a much larger sum for postponing the session until the next year, and then wanted £120,000 per annum. Had Charles shown the same solicitude in managing his own money as he did in trying to extract it from others, neither the session nor the subsidy would have been strictly necessary. Instead, he had let his expenditure rise as did his income, so that by late 1675 the latter still covered the former but let no margin sufficient to build warships or to reduce the public debt.[29] To win new parliamentary supplies, Danby now led history's first really systematic attempt to manage the Commons. The Secretaries of State dispatched circular letters to reliable MPs to attend from the beginning. Royal ministers spoke to their friends and clients as usual, but in addition the Treasurer began to construct a bloc of pensioners. By the time that the moment came, on 13 October, he believed that he could count on 179 members and win over a further 90, providing a sufficient majority. He also had reason to hope that fear of France would not yet have increased significantly. That summer Louis had taken three more towns, in the eastern Netherlands, but lost a battle and an important city in Germany, while his best general had been killed. The situation overall appeared still to be stalemate, with the last victories going to the allies. In fact, it had shifted decisively in favour of the French. They had tempted Sweden into the war on their behalf, diverting the power of their German enemies northward. They had sent aid to a revolt in the Spanish province of Sicily, which sapped the already debilitated strength of Spain. As a result, Louis would henceforth enjoy a military superiority in the Netherlands, the war zone about which the British were most acutely sensitive. In 1675 the military situation abroad, like the financial situation, was not yet posing serious problems for the Crown. But this period of grace was not likely to endure. It was all the more essential that the reconciliation with the Commons be effected.

Charles opened the new session with another speech which reflected his trepidations. He asked the Houses not to return to their dispute until they had transacted some public business. He especially asked them to safeguard the Church, and to supply taxes for the fleet (again) and to remove the problem that much of his regular revenue was effectively spent long before it arrived. With an almost embarrassing candour, he admitted that he had been extravagant, but then claimed bitterly that gossip was representing his fault to be much worse than it was. Finch seconded his requests, again making reference to the fraught state of relations by urging the Houses to unity and denying (once more) that his master wished to dispense with Parliament. The response from the Commons was limited and ungracious. They worked hard upon bills to limit royal powers to raise taxes and to imprison, and set up a committee to investigate Danby's efforts to turn MPs into pensioners. They refused by seven votes to do anything about the anticipations on the revenue, finding a variety of excuses for this. They did offer £300,000, but a government attempt to get more was defeated. Still, it was a supply, and might have made the session worth while. It was the Lords, not the Lower House, which suddenly gave serious trouble. To woo the Commons, the government had given the Lower House some countenance in the dispute over jurisdiction, much as it had during the earlier squabble in 1670. The Lords had been left in an ugly mood, which became the more dangerous when James, seeing his advice for a dissolution disregarded, decided to force one by an address from the Lords. Shaftesbury's group was delighted to co-operate, hoping for a new Commons even less tractable by the Crown, and in the end the move was foiled by only two, proxy, votes. The dispute between the Houses now broke out again. Charles had been contributing energetically to the session, attending the debates in the Lords as assiduously as ever, and speaking to a hundred MPs, in batches of twenty, to persuade them to co-operate with the court. But now his patience broke with apparently that of the whole Foreign Affairs Committee. They dared not now intervene in the jurisdictional squabble, which was probably going to jam business again. The supply offered was small, and the bills which accompanied it were irritating. On 22 November the King prorogued Parliament, without any speech, for an unprecedented fifteen months.

The action was a way of administering an obvious rebuke to the Houses without destroying the Parliament. It also provided an opportunity to make a virtue of a necessity by extracting some funds from Louis. Charles succeeded in persuading his cousin that such a long prorogation served French interests as well as a dissolution, and that the promised £100,000 ought therefore to be paid. He did so by telling the French ambassador (correctly) that Danby had been pressing him to ally with the Dutch. It was a third of what the Commons had offered, but in a sense it was money for nothing. Fifteen months would, nevertheless, count for little unless the government could win some prestige during that time, and an obvious way to do it was still to mediate peace in Europe. By the autumn of 1675 both sides were offering terms, but the gap between them was enormous: France wanted the frontier of 1668, plus Spanish Burgundy, while the Spanish demanded the borders of 1659 and the Dutch were pledged to support them. In October Charles had produced his own map of boundaries, based upon the line of 1668 but considerably straightened out by an exchange of towns in the Netherlands. This, he proposed, would be the ideal compromise and would provide defences for France and Spain behind which both would feel secure. In December, he instructed three representatives to take the plan to the peace conference which was about to open at Nijmegen. The British suggestion was soon readily adopted, but in dramatically different ways. Charles asked Louis to acquire two towns, give up three, and retain Spanish Burgundy. Wilhelm wanted the French to surrender either four more or Spanish Burgundy. Louis was determined to wage war until his enemies were prepared to put the new, rationalized frontier where he chose. As the talks at Nijmegen got under way, he launched an army at Flanders, and by the end of 1676 he had taken three more towns. At midsummer Wilhelm asked to visit Charles, but was refused as his uncle saw no profit in a meeting which might jeopardize both his position as a mediator and his secret payments from France. Instead the English King urged the Dutch, as before, to make a speedy peace. Both his consistent preoccupations, with dynasty and monarchy, featured as strongly as before. In July 1676 he told the French ambassador that he rejoiced at a recent defeat suffered by Wilhelm as it would 'correct' the young man and make him more inclined to follow Charles, as head of their family. The way in which the Prince had ruined British plans in 1672 obviously still rankled. At some time earlier he had told the States-General that, should the childless Wilhelm die, he would treat them with continuing favour if they appointed another monarchical figure to lead them.[30] In the upshot, neither Wilhelm nor Louis was disposed to be guided by their relative, but it was an achievement at least that the Prince began to see Charles as a genuine power in Europe, who was worth courting.

As in 1668–70, the English King was trying to have his foreign policy both ways at once: in this case by being a mediator while continuing his lucrative friendship with France. On 16 February he proposed, and got, a new secret treaty with his cousin, binding both not to aid each other's enemies and to treat, especially with the Dutch, only with the participation of each other. The farcical aspect of this transaction lay in the extreme reluctance of Charles's most trusted ministers to become too closely involved in it, after the harrying of their predecessors by Parliament in January 1674. The King let Danby and Lauderdale into the preceding talks, but the former utterly refused to touch the treaty itself. The latter witnessed it after considerable argument when Charles had copied out the text in person and signed it with the French ambassador. The episode demonstrated not only the King's penchant for intrigue but his ingrained carelessness: he had to use a cipher for the signature instead of his signet ring as he wished. The latter, an engraved diamond, had been worn by his father on the scaffold and was one of his most prized possessions, but he had mislaid it before the treaty was drafted and failed to find it in time.[31] The episode has a wider significance, in that it reveals very clearly the limitations of the generally accepted view that after the Treaty of Westminster Charles took, for some years, a back seat in government and allowed Danby to get on with the work. He was no more inactive in the years 1674–8 than in those of 1668–74. He carried on diplomacy with even less assistance from advisers than before, and his personal lobbying of MPs and regular attendance of the Lords marked an attention to parliamentary management greater than in the earlier period.

This said, the year 1676 represented something of a lull in Charles's life. There was plenty to be done, but most of it was in preparation for the future. In 1675 royalist squires and bishops (who supported the new religious policy) had been added to the Privy Council. Now men who had abetted the court's opponents in Parliament, such as Holles and Halifax, were removed from it. The same process was applied in some counties to JPs, and Danby continued his canvassing and listing of MPs. A member of the corporation of London, who called upon it to petition the King for a new Parliament, was sent to the Tower and held without trial. A committee of the Council began to plan for the new parliamentary session eight months early. What was ominously clear was how much that session would be needed. The boom in trade was diminishing, and the opportunity to reduce the debt had been lost. A rebellion in Virginia was only put down after a thousand men had been sent there and £200,000 spent. While it lasted, it disrupted commercial links between America and England and so reduced customs revenue. Trade with New England fell off because of a great Indian war which had broken out there. Moorish pirates operating from Algiers, Tunis, and Tripoli became more than usually destructive, and an expedition had to be mounted to contain them. This situation was made particularly serious by the fact that some of the taxes voted in 1670–1 were due to expire in 1677–8, and without their renewal the public finances would be in deficit once more. The £100,000 which Louis offered for a further prorogation of one year was simply not enough to compensate for the damage that this would do to public opinion and the loss of those sources of revenue. In these circumstances there is no evidence, save for his polite expressions to the French ambassador, that Charles vacillated before rejecting it. Arlington, Ormonde, Williamson, and Rupert now joined his brother James in pressing a more serious temptation upon him, to dissolve Parliament altogether and to try a new one. But in the end the King played safe and followed the advice of Danby, Finch, and Coventry to let the session occur. He believed the Treasurer's confident assertion that he had gained 150 extra votes.

Another, and better founded, statistic provided by Danby at this time must have had an even more decisive effect upon Charles. One of the most powerful arguments used by James against the policy of religious intolerance and in favour of a dissolution had been the presumed gigantic numbers of Catholics and Protestant dissenters combined. According to this view, they were an interest too strong to be offended en bloc. In early 1676, the London aldermen decided to request the Privy Council to end persecution of the City's nonconformists as this harmed trade. Charles's reply was to issue a circular letter denying that he had any intention of altering his present policy, and to order the Lord Mayor to stop all conventicles.[32] Nevertheless, it was obvious to Danby that Charles was seriously worried by the arguments about numbers. It was almost certainly he who was the 'person near to' the King who told Sheldon that his master would approve of an attempt by the bishops to take a census of all Catholics and dissenters in England and Wales. It commenced in January 1676 and was well under way by June,[33] and its findings were conclusive: orthodox Anglicans greatly outnumbered their opponents in every diocese. There is no hard evidence for the assertion, sometimes confidently made,[34] that the survey decided Charles against a new Parliament, though it is possible. But something of the King's reaction can be inferred from results. He never again even toyed with the idea of an Indulgence in England.

A historian has written of Charles's government in the year 1676, 'Every one was busy, except the king.'[35] It is hardly a fair comment, as there was not much to be done then that his ministers could not, and should not, have been doing for him. But it is true that he had more time than usual for his pleasures and for the family and entourage which had largely resulted from these pleasures. Two members of this had risen to greater prominence and power during the war years: Monmouth and Louise de Kéroualle. The former had been given a formal power-base in the court, provincial England, and Scotland, largely with offices taken from the King's cousin Richmond, who had suddenly died, and from the disgraced Buckingham. Thus, by the war's end he was Master of the Horse, Governor of Hull, Chancellor of Cambridge University, Lord High Admiral of Scotland, and Lord-Lieutenant of the East Riding, as well as having the intangible rank of a military hero. Louise's position as the favourite royal mistress had been confirmed with the title of Duchess of Portsmouth. She had celebrated by throwing a tremendous party for the court in a wood near London, with torches placed amongst the trees. Unhappily for her plans, the crowds of onlookers grew so thick that the royal party had to retire, dancing instead upon barges on the Thames.[36]

This pattern of amours did not much alter during the succeeding four years. It has often been said that Charles treated his Queen well, and in the sense that he refused to divorce her and that (at least after 1663) he behaved towards her with kindness and courtesy, this is true. But that is not to say that she was happy. His chronic infidelity continued to hurt her feelings, and from 1674 she began to spend her summers apart, among her own friends, to restore her spirits. The process could not have been assisted by the fact that Louise's apartments at Whitehall were now much more luxuriously furnished than her own. In the mid-1670s a story was told that the King had sent his wife a message that he was ill, and so could not attend her. In fact he was in bed with Nell Gwyn, and when Catherine came to visit him to express solicitude, Nell scuttled behind a wall-hanging. She left a slipper behind her, which unhappily was in the Queen's sight as she entered. With magnificent dignity, Catherine said that she would leave before the pretty fool who owned it fell genuinely ill from cold. If the incident ever happened, one feels that the Queen cannot have enjoyed it as much as story-tellers did.[37]

By any standards, Nell trailed behind Louise in importance at court. We possess some unusually full records of the amounts spent by Charles upon his mistresses in this period, perhaps a reflection of the fact that he had more spare cash, or perhaps just as an accident. In 1670–7 a Treasury Clerk paid Louise a total of £36,073 in royal gifts and Nell a total of £7,938. Nell, however, was only relatively badly off, for in 1674 she received £2,265 for silver ornaments to her bed alone, among several other items.[38] The same imbalance was preserved in political relationships. Danby and Lauderdale, the greatest ministers, took care to ally with Louise. The Treasurer ensured that money was made available for her presents, though he tried to pare some of it out of the revenue of Ireland. Nell retained an old fondness from her stage days for Buckingham, and her friendship was sought by Ormonde. Her detestation of Lauderdale was as great as for Louise, and it was rumoured that she told Charles that the best way to appease the Cavalier Parliament was to 'hang the Scotch dog and the French bitch'. The shrillness of her comments probably derived most from the clear difference in their formal status. Louise was now a Duchess, while Nell, born a commoner, went untitled. A story went the rounds that Finch received a warrant from Nell to make her Countess of Plymouth. He asked the King about it before applying the seals, and was told that it had been given to her as a jest.[39]

Not that life for the new Duchess of Portsmouth was invariably cheerful. For one thing she was intensely unpopular, being both a Catholic and a French subject and also extremely expensive. It has been estimated that between her pension and her presents she cost the nation about £40,000 per year. The Earl of Pembroke told her to her face that she was the realm's greatest grievance.[40] For another, she was unlucky with her health. It was particularly unfortunate that in early 1674 the King presented her with a dose of venereal disease, from which she suffered far worse than he had done: the solid proof that Charles's sexual entertainment extended beyond his 'official' mistresses, though court ladies rather than professional prostitutes may have been the people concerned. He tried to console his wretched Duchess with a gift of jewellery worth £10,000, though seven months later she was still railing at him about his misconduct with 'trulls' (in front of the French ambassador). In late 1677 she had a more polite but also more serious illness. The King imputed her recovery to his favourite medicinal drops, while her confessor attributed it to the Virgin Mary, but whichever was true she required a long convalescence. The merciless Nell nicknamed her 'the weeping willow'.

Her greatest tribulation, of course, was shared with the Queen: she never knew whither Charles's eye would wander next. His impulses were very public, as illustrated when a troupe of comedians performed at Whitehall which included a gorgeous actress aged fifteen. The King sighed to those around him and remarked that probably only Downing or Ranelagh were rich enough to buy her favours.[41] Such passing fancies, however, were dwarfed by the challenge presented by Hortense de Mancini, Duchesse de Mazarin and niece of the great cardinal, who came to Whitehall in November 1675. Like Louise she was a French subject and arrived somewhat short of money. Like Barbara she had abandoned a husband insufficiently exciting for her tastes (hence her lack of funds) and had a powerful, reckless, passionate personality. She was aged thirty, a good deal older than most of Charles's women when they first made his acquaintance, and had the additional allure of self-confidence and experience. She loved to gamble, eat, shoot, and swim, and was noted for her trick of performing a Spanish dance while accompanying herself on a guitar. Her beauty was (needless to say) striking, being composed of a Junoesque figure, full smooth features, jet black hair, and eyes that changed colour with the light. Charles told the French ambassador that she was the finest woman he had ever met. Almost immediately he lodged her at St James's Palace and upon most nights he would go through the official ceremony of retiring in the Bedchamber and then dress and slip across the park to Hortense for the rest of the night. When Louis XIV refused a plea from his cousin to force her deserted husband to send money for her, she received £1,000 from the English Treasury. By the summer of 1676 Charles had ceased to see Louise privately, though he supped and played cards with her in company. She reacted by weeping almost constantly, thereby justifying Nell's cruel sobriquet. Ms Gwyn herself appeared before the astonished French ambassador and offered to replace her rival as Louis's female agent at court, in exchange for a financial consideration. She hoisted up her skirts to show him the beauty of her petticoats, as evidence of Charles's affection. The French were more inclined to hire Hortense herself, and Mary of Modena and Arlington both attempted to promote the flamboyant Duchesse at court, to spite Louise and Danby respectively. How much good this would have done them had they succeeded is debatable; for the King himself told the ambassador that he would not let politicians work on him through women. The truth seems more that the opinions of his mistresses acted as feathers in the scales of his decisions if his mind were genuinely divided. For this they were worth some attention. But Hortense was not to be involved in the process. She had gone on her travels not for riches, not for political influence, but for fun, and in the last analysis Charles did not provide enough of it. By 1677 she was involved with the dashing Prince of Monaco, and, to the fury of Nell, the 'weeping willow' was the favourite concubine again.[42]

The same years also saw a great expansion of honours among the 'unofficial royal family'. In August 1674 Charles gave his third son by Barbara the title of Earl of Northumberland, and created that of Earl of Plymouth for 'Don Carlos', the child of his Spanish exile. This boy, now in his mid-teens, had been brought to court by his mother during the Dutch war and for a while enchanted his father so much that it seemed he might rival Monmouth. Unhappily, he soon proved himself like most of his half-brothers to be a spoiled and irresponsible brat and his opportunity was lost. A year later the King yielded to the importunities of Louise and Barbara and gave his son by the former and his first two sons by the latter equal rank with Monmouth. They became Dukes of Richmond, Southampton, and Grafton respectively. Nell's sons, to her fury, were passed over, save for a pension of £4,000 per annum given to Charles, the elder. Her moment came in 1676 when with Barbara in France and Louise eclipsed by Hortense, a determined campaign of henpecking paid off handsomely. Little Charles became Earl of Burford and his brother James was created Lord Beauclerc. Subsequently Nell herself rounded off her fortune with the help of Ormonde, by getting a grant of Irish land. It only remained for Barbara to close off the sequence in 1678 by having young Northumberland promoted to a dukedom. Nor were the royal daughters neglected. The wedding of the year 1674 was that of Anne Fitzroy, sister of Southampton and Grafton, to Lord Dacre, at Hampton Court. The bride received £20,000 and the groom was made

Earl of Sussex: despite all this lubrication the match was a disaster. None the less, Danby married off his own daughter to 'Don Carlos' in 1678 and thus followed his predecessors Clarendon and Arlington in attaching his family to the royal house.[43]

It has been pointed out by Charles's admirers[44] that those 'pseudo-princes and princesses' cost the nation less than legitimate children would have done. This is true enough but misses three points. First, the King's proclivities meant that as well as paying for the Queen, the nation had to support a string of concubines, some of whom had very expensive tastes. Second, the sheer number of the King's children, made possible by the large number of mothers, did much to counterbalance the expense of a few legitimate offspring. Third, and most important, his subjects on the whole did not want to pay for them. The King's sexual habits continued to create a mixture of disgust and ribaldry, and to sap confidence in the government in general. Charles continued to try to maintain an appearance of dignity—in 1674, for example, he forbade clergymen to wear long wigs or hair according to secular fashion[45]—but this was always undermined by public knowledge of his carnal appetites. A saying was current in the mid-1670s that he had inherited the courage of James I, the constancy of Charles I, and the chastity of Henrietta Maria (the last comparison being grossly unfair to the poor woman). An anecdote of the time related how he had accused Shaftesbury of being the greatest whore-master in the kingdom. Shaftesbury was said to have replied that he supposed he was—among the subjects. Another story was of how an orange-girl presented Charles with a bird taught to talk obscenely. The King, so the tale went, thoroughly enjoyed it, not least when it hopped on to Sheldon's shoulder and said 'Wilt thou have a whore, thou lascivious dog?' When an equestrian statue of Charles was erected in London in 1675, it rapidly acquired a placard reading 'Haste, post-haste, for a midwife'. At the opening of the spring session of Parliament in the same year, a parody of the King's speech was scattered about the Commons. A large part of it was taken up with complaints that the demands of present and past mistresses had emptied the Exchequer. It warned that the money which Charles asked for the fleet would actually be spent on 'cradles and swaddling-clothes'. Such beliefs did nothing to assist Danby's struggle to win supply.[46]

The limbo in which British politics had existed since the end of the Dutch war began to break in 1677. The first, and most gentle, of the changes came in Ireland, with the replacement of Essex. One of the greatest modern Irish historians has drawn a contrast between the fate of the Earl and that of Ormonde in 1668–9, pointing out that Essex faced not one set of enemies but an alliance of groups, that he lasted much longer than Ormonde had done, that he was a much less consequential figure than the Duke, and that he was not attached to a fallen English minister. He has suggested that the Earl only survived so long because of the almost constant need to have the Irish army ready to intervene in Scotland between 1674 and 1676.[47] There is, in fact, no real evidence for the last suggestion, and the similarities between the two cases are much stronger than the differences. Essex was indeed, like Ormonde, severely weakened by the fate of an English minister, in this case the eclipse of Arlington, his great ally at court. The alliance between Buckingham and Orrery to destroy the Duke involved as heterogeneous a collection of individuals as the opposition to Essex. Like his great predecessor, the Earl crossed to Whitehall to pre-empt an attack, and for a time appeared to enjoy success. He arrived in July 1675, for almost a year, having obtained permission to appoint his own deputies as the Duke had done. At the time that he reappeared at court, there was no firm coalition against him, Danby, Coventry, and Lauderdale appearing well disposed towards him while Finch and James seemed hostile. It was Essex who built a coalition against himself by trying to regain control of Irish public finance.

First he discovered that Conway, attempting as before to keep in with both sides, had been showing his letters to Ranelagh. He broke with both, permanently. Then he alienated Danby, by opposing a new agreement of the latter with Ranelagh to divert £20,000 per year of the Irish revenue to the English Treasury. Essex was appalled, as ever, by the condition of the army in Ireland, which the cunning Viscount was prepared to abuse in order to secure his own position and profits. Danby cared very little about the western kingdom, and was desperate for any money to keep the English Treasury afloat. Charles precisely shared his priorities. The same economic expansion which had provided a surplus to the English fisc had made it possible for Ranelagh to keep the books balanced in Ireland, and although the Irish army received only a portion of its wages it was actually being better paid than before. In these circumstances, Essex was inevitably going to lose the dispute. He was not quite isolated at court, because Ormonde and Coventry were still his friends, but he proceeded to commit political suicide. Soon after returning to Dublin, he launched an investigation of Ranelagh's accounts and of the manner in which the army was having to compound for its money. Such an enquiry threatened to ruin the system by which England now profited from Ireland and reveal Charles's own connivance in some rather shady dealings, at a time when the government needed all possible public goodwill. It had become essential to change Lord-Lieutenants.[48]

A further parallel with Ormonde's experience was that the King assiduously failed to appoint a successor from the retiring viceroy's enemies. Danby, Ranelagh, and Lauderdale were ready to have Monmouth made a titular Lord-Lieutenant, with Conway doing the actual work as his deputy. James was extremely unwilling to see his dashing nephew, who had for years been talked of as a potential successor, given such a great honour. It was he who persuaded his brother to play safe and to reinstate Ormonde himself, loyal as ever and now ageing. The Duke got the job on condition that he co-operated with Ranelagh, who was compensated for the partial failure of his scheming by being promoted to the rank of earl. In April 1677 the change was announced, and that summer Ormonde made the crossing. He began his new term of office by passing all accounts without question and allowing the payments to Charles's Privy Purse to be increased by £7,000 to buy more MPs. As had been the case with Ormonde in 1669, Essex was not disgraced. The King officially recalled him as part of a policy of rotating individuals deliberately in his post, and praised his work. He was not ashamed to be replaced by a man as distinguished as Ormonde, and on his return he was added to the Foreign Affairs Committee. It had been a remarkably civilized coup.[49]

An equally gentle and important change occurred at the end of the year, when Archbishop Sheldon died after a long illness. Through the 1670s Charles had continued to appoint men of varying attitudes to important sees, from those of moderation towards Catholics and dissenters such as Nathaniel Crewe, the new Bishop of Durham, and the latest Bishop of Chichester, to notable hardliners such as William Compton, who had once fought in the royalist army and became Bishop of London. On close inspection, however, this appears now to have been not so much a conscious design upon the King's part as the result of the different advice to which he listened. Crewe got named for Durham because of the intercession of James. He had given the formal blessing of his Church to the latter's marriage with Mary of Modena, while Bishop of Oxford, and James was grateful to him ever after. It was, however, necessary for another prelate, Croft of Hereford, to jog the King's memory before the order for Crewe's creation got signed. Compton achieved the great prize of London because of Danby's support. He subsequently infuriated James by his attacks upon Catholics in general and his complaints about the proselytizing habits of the Duke's secretary. Thomas Barlow became Bishop of Lincoln because Williamson and Coventry recommended him. The King objected that he had found the man a flatterer and trimmer, but Lauderdale walked in and denied this, whereupon Charles signed the order. His opinion of churchmen had continued to deteriorate over the years: in 1678 he told one of

Ormonde's sons that 'most bishops would think that gain is great godliness'.[50]

In this context, it is not surprising that when Sheldon died Charles had no idea of whom to appoint to succeed him. Danby wanted Compton and James supported Crewe, though some Catholics preferred the tolerant Archbishop Boyle of Dublin. In addition there were two other candidates. The King failed to make a choice for almost two months, and got so tired of being asked for a decision that at one point he named a notoriously drunken and lecherous Westminster JP. In the end, on the evening of 29 December, he sent for a man who was not even a bishop yet, the solemn, gentle, and learned William Sancroft, Dean of St Pauls. It has been suggested[51] that the King chose him because he would be a more pliant primate after the intimidating Sheldon. It seems more likely that he got the job simply because he was acceptable to all the proponents of the other candidates: after seven weeks of irritation, the King was not so much saving himself trouble in the future as getting rid of it in the present.[52]

In another respect it seemed at first as if the year 1677 would furnish the government with a decisive political breakthrough. On 14 February the King opened the fifteenth session of the Cavalier Parliament with the now customary appeal, for money for ships, and offer, to pass bills to secure religion, liberty, and property. He added the also customary complaint, this time asking how a monarch who had striven to preserve this Parliament could be accused of ambitions to rule arbitrarily. Now Shaftesbury and Buckingham committed a major blunder, by claiming that a prorogation of longer than a year rendered a dissolution automatic. The Lords, urged on by Ormonde and Danby, resolved that this was scandalous and committed them, with the other peers, to the Tower. This disaster for the court's opponents weakened them in both Houses, and the Commons renewed the additional Excise voted in 1671. When the Finance Bill reached the Lords, Charles delightedly measured the yards of it with the Treasurer's staff, as the great roll of parchment was spread across the floor. A measure was also prepared to recall all British subjects from French service, but the King told Louis's ambassador that, with the money bill safely sent up, this other proposal would perish in the Lords. After four years, the problem of working with the English Parliament appeared to be solved and Danby was duly made a Knight of the Garter. At the same time some progress occurred in foreign affairs. During the winter Charles had kept both French and Dutch in play, the former by reminding Louis that he was bound not to make peace without English consent, the latter by offering a defensive alliance when peace was made. Thus he took all possible steps to ensure that any treaty would be beneficial to his interests. In February a commercial pact was made with France which recognized the right of English ships to trade with all combatants and to carry the goods of Louis's enemies. Wilhelm was still unable to agree with the English Foreign Affairs Committee upon how many of his gains the French King should keep, but at least the Prince now recognized the need to end the war. It was one of those moments in Charles's life, as in 1648 and 1667, when all suddenly bid fair, and all was suddenly to be dashed.

In March Louis XIV hurled his full strength against Flanders for the first time during this war. The great fortresses which had held off the French in the 1650s, Valenciennes and Cambrai, now fell within weeks. Like Juan-José in 1658, Wilhelm felt impelled to offer a challenge even in unpropitious circumstances, and at Cassel, where Henry of Gloucester's regiment had been destroyed nineteen years before, his army was routed. Charles was initially delighted by this onslaught, as he thought it would force the Dutch and Spanish to make peace at once. The House of Commons, however, had a very different reaction, embodied in an address to the King upon 10 March, with which the Lords concurred, to make alliances to secure the Spanish Netherlands. The King was surprised and angry at what he regarded as a direct violation of his prerogative to determine foreign policy. The current Spanish ambassador, who had been encouraging the MPs, drew Charles's attention to the address in an interview. The monarch's reaction was to throw his handkerchief in the air and exclaim that he cared that much for Parliament. The ambassador faithfully reported the gesture to hostile MPs, and was expelled by a furious Charles for his pains. The King assiduously informed every representative of the warring nations that he was not in the habit of yielding to pressure from the Houses: the ambassadors were already too interested in the idea of addressing themselves to MPs instead of to Charles. This position, however, was complicated by the fact that Danby himself was adding his promptings to the same end, arguing that a war against France would be an excellent way of rewinning the respect of the political nation.

In all the tergiversations of English foreign policy over the next sixteen months, two impulses seem to be ascertainable in Charles's reasoning. First, he hoped to use a difficult situation to extract the maximum advantages from all involved, and especially from Parliament and Louis. As in 1668–9, he was trying to have things all ways at once, for as long as possible. Second, he was absolutely determined never again to be in the position into which he had fallen in 1673, of having to make to Parliament such concessions as it demanded in return for the funds with which to carry on a war. Accordingly, his responses were complex and hesitant. He ignored the first address by the Houses, but when the Commons followed this with an undertaking to support a French war, he offered on 11 April to act if they supplied the means. Their reply aroused all his suspicions: they invited him to borrow £200,000 on the security of the additional Excise, and promised more later. He pointed out that the additional Excise was already needed for regular expenses, and asked for £600,000. The House refused to give anything until he had made the necessary alliances, motivated by a fear that he would pocket the money and fail to act. Parliament was then adjourned for over a month.

King and Commons were, therefore, both crippled by mutual distrust, but of the two it seems to have been the MPs who made the greater error. From his actions it seems obvious that had the King been granted the war supply which he had asked, he would have tried to use it to push Louis to make peace without actually declaring war upon him. This was not quite what the Commons wanted, but nevertheless would have been a way of halting French progress. At that moment Louis was uncertain whether to offer a compromise peace or to make further conquests,[53] and English pressure would probably have tipped the balance. As it was, the English King lacked the money to make any military preparations, while neither French nor Dutch sent him any offers and the Spanish were demanding, impossibly, a return to the frontier of 1659. When Parliament reconvened on 23 May, he could only deny that he would misuse the money and repeat his request for supply, before he made any alliances. The Commons utterly refused to comply. Charles now lost his temper and informed the Privy Council that this was an intolerable intrusion upon his prerogative. On the 28th he said the same to the House, and adjourned Parliament again. The next day, his birthday, he tactlessly spent watching a performance by a French opera company.[54] The sole satisfaction remaining to the King from the session, apart from the renewed Excise, was the presence of the four peers in the Tower. Of these, Buckingham soon confessed his fault and Charles released him after Nell Gwyn and others of his 'merry gang' and 'ministers of pleasure' interceded for him. James, Monmouth, and Danby all objected furiously, and succeeded at last in getting the dissolute Duke forbidden the court. Two others of the prisoners also made their submissions and earned their liberty. The King rewarded one with particular grace, telling him that they were both now old men and 'should love quietness' (at forty-seven was Charles genuinely feeling tired, or was this an affectation?). This only left Shaftesbury, who refused to grovel and who inevitably earned his full share of his monarch's natural vindictiveness. When the Earl's wife begged clemency for him, Charles refused to speak to her. The King personally struck out most names from a list of persons who had the right to visit him. When Shaftesbury protested that his health was suffering, the Foreign Affairs Committee replied that 'The King will think of some other prison in a better air.' One can imagine the cold smiles in the room as Williamson formally penned those words.[55]

Charles was embittered by the behaviour of the Commons without having any insight into it. He told one MP that those of his fellows who misrepresented the government's intentions were either republicans or ambitious men bidding for popularity in the House. At moments when he recognized that some failure of management might have occurred, he assiduously failed to accept any of the blame. Understandably, though not quite justly, his favourite scapegoat was his brother, and in July he told the current French ambassador that all the anti-French feeling in the country was the result of James's behaviour. Nevertheless, family feeling, as ever, overcame his irritation: Danby confided to an ally at this time that although Charles did not love his brother he would always act indulgently towards him.[56] Furthermore, by the time that he made the complaint to the Frenchman, Honoré Courtin, Charles found events apparently moving in his favour again. Just after the session ended, Wilhelm sent an agent to ask his uncle directly to help make peace, with terms that would leave the French with four Flemish towns and have them return seven. As far as the English King was concerned, his nephew was now behaving impeccably, avoiding working with either the Spanish or the Commons, and Wilhelm duly got an invitation to England for talks. On 7 June Charles met Courtin with James and Danby, and asked the French to return six towns and keep five, plus Spanish Burgundy. He also requested more French money as his reward for mediation. To his surprise Louis's behaviour was as disappointing as Wilhelm's had been gratifying. From now on, his behaviour indicates that Charles was reverting to his tactics of 1668, of forcing his cousin to accept the terms that the English government wanted. In the process he must have hoped, as in 1668, to win more respect from Louis and make himself more worth buying.

He would have been fortified in this belief because, while failing to bring his cousin to a swift treaty, he was once again playing the counter of a parliamentary session with him. The English agent in Paris was a former client of Arlington and cousin to the dead Earl of Sandwich, a young and almost indecently ambitious man called Ralph Montagu. He volunteered enthusiastically to screw huge sums out of France, and despite the grumbles of Danby, Charles gave him his head. Louis empowered Courtin to negotiate a new subsidy for the adjournment of Parliament till April 1678, and the English King made the deal himself while Danby was away from court. Immediately after signing it, Charles took a break himself, sailing in his yacht to Portsmouth and then on to Plymouth and to Pendennis

Castle, with its poignant memories of the Civil War. His itinerary at Plymouth indicates how much of a working holiday this was. He docked in early morning, met the corporation, inspected all the fortifications, wrote a dispatch, and knighted three local worthies. After lunch he went shooting from a boat in the Tamar estuary. The following day he went further up the Tamar, affording not only more opportunity for sport, but meetings with local gentry. Upon the third day he touched for the King's Evil, and then he left. On his return journey, he braved a violent storm before reappearing in the Thames on 22 August and passing through Whitehall on his way to Windsor.[57] This sequence of events, the period of bargaining followed by the crowded journey in the West, should give pause to anybody before making the charge traditionally levelled at this monarch, of laziness. However, it contained one characteristic flaw, which fully substantiates a rather different accusation, of carelessness. Montagu had got the French to agree to a subsidy of £200,000. Courtin, in London, offered 2 million *livres tournois*. Charles blithely assumed that ten *livres* equalled one pound, and signed. He had clearly failed to notice the actual exchange rate, which had been in operation during all the previous secret treaties, and which now left him with only £145,000. Danby and Montagu were bewildered and furious, and unable to do anything immediate as their master was away in his yacht. On his return, an embarrassed Charles promptly declared the treaty void and ordered Danby to renegotiate the sum, thereby adding Louis to the list of people infuriated by the incident. Simultaneously, the engaging Courtin was replaced as ambassador by Paul Barrillon d'Armoncourt, Marquis de Branges, an equally capable man but one who had yet to make a working relationship with the English King.

Thus the circumstances were propitious for Danby and Wilhelm to effect something which they had been cooking up between them since April: an Anglo-Dutch alliance based upon the marriage of the Prince to James's elder daughter Mary. The girl was a Protestant, and her hand would strengthen the 'reversionary' interest in the English throne which Wilhelm had inherited through his mother. In October he arrived at court, and settled down to talks with Charles, James, Danby, and Temple. By sheer stubbornness the Prince of Orange got his way, giving his uncle the choice of the marriage, followed by an agreement upon peace terms, or his departure and an end to all *rapprochement*. Charles let himself be persuaded by his two English advisers that if the latter course were followed it would lose him his role as mediator and his chances of impressing Parliament. James's Duchess was pregnant, reducing his belief that Mary would inherit the crown. In addition, his simple mind was easily convinced by the arguments that his consent to the match would prove to the English that he had no

designs for Catholicism or absolute monarchy. When his brother told him
that he wanted the marriage, on 21 October, James made no trouble. The
Privy Council was informed on the following day and the English and
Scots received the news with gratifying euphoria: Mary herself wept for
eighteen hours but the wedding took place a fortnight later. The King's
ebullient coarseness showed in the exhortation with which he closed the
curtains of the bridal bed: 'Now, nephew, to your work! Hey! St George
for England.'

It did not worry Charles that by allowing this marriage he had broken
a direct promise to Louis. This was natural enough, but it did not seem
to occur to him that it might worry Louis. He told the French that it
was a means to induce Wilhelm to offer reasonable terms to them, and
duly prorogued Parliament in accordance with the subsidy treaty. Four
days after the wedding, he and Wilhelm agreed upon the offer which
they considered would be reasonable, that Louis would return six Flemish
towns and retain four others, plus Spanish Burgundy. These terms were
not much more lenient than those which Wilhelm had offered earlier, but
they were the best that he could be brought to give, and his uncle clearly
considered them to be at least a basis for discussion. Charles sent them to
Louis with a personal plea, and this he clearly considered sufficient, for he
made no alliances or military preparations. The extent of his self-delusion
is revealed by his reaction when his French cousin flatly refused the offer,
made no counter-proposals, and stopped the subsidy. He wept.

Having thus lost Louis, Charles could not afford to lose Wilhelm and
Parliament as well, and thus the time had come to get ready to fight.
He now snubbed Barrillon and led his Foreign Affairs Committee in
preparing for a French war in the most serious and detailed fashion.
Surveys were made of the fortresses and magazines of southern England
and its islands, and the necessary plans were drawn up to launch the
fleet.[58] On 15 December the same committee drafted a treaty for an
alliance with the Dutch, and hastened it to The Hague. It was signed on
New Year's Eve (although bickering over the details spun out ratification
for a month), and provided for joint action to force upon Louis the offer
which he had rejected. At the same time the King still tried to render a
resort to force unnecessary, replying favourably to a French suggestion
of a two-month truce while talks proceeded. After the experiences of
1673–4, Charles was very reluctant to wage war ever again. Nor did his
taste for the culture of Paris, which continually confused and dismayed
his subjects, decrease. Even as he planned for action he was applauding a
troupe of French comedians at Whitehall.[59] Yet all those close to the King
believed that, however sadly, he was actually going to fight unless Louis

backed down. His feelings had genuinely been hurt by his cousin, as by his
nephew in 1672, and his surprise and grief were turning into anger. James
fully shared his brother's feelings, and (as ever) was thoroughly looking
forward to military action. His humour had not been improved by the
fact that his Duchess had indeed presented him with a son, only for the
infant to expire after a month. All that was needed to complete the English
monarch's conversion into the bulwark of an anti-French coalition was the
wholehearted support of Parliament and of his new allies.

To the amazement of the government, this was not forthcoming, in
either case. The English wanted the Spaniards to place Ostend in their
hands as a bridgehead for soldiers to save Flanders. They promised 12,000
of these, and although only 3,500 were ready by mid-January, these would
at the least secure the port against possible attack. The Spanish, however,
had noted Charles's interest in Zealand in his recent Dutch war, and
harboured a suspicion that if they lent him Ostend they would never get
it back. As they procrastinated, Louis acted. He evacuated his army from
Sicily, but this was only to concentrate upon Flanders. On 22 February he
launched the new campaign, and his forces successively invested Ypres,
Brussels, Namur, Luxemburg, and Ghent. As if selecting from a menu,
he decided to take the first and the last of these towns. They fell within
a month, before the Dutch could even mobilize, and Louis then sat back
to let his enemies reconsider their terms. While reeling from these blows,
the Spaniards did allow 2,000 English infantry under Monmouth to cross
to Ostend. But having settled there, he found that the remaining Spanish
garrisons were so demoralized that there was little prospect of them resist-
ing if the French moved forward again.[60] Parliament, brought forward
specially for the purpose of voting a war supply, met on 28 January.
Charles told it that he had now made the alliance which the Commons had
requested, and asked for money to set forth ninety ships and over 30,000
soldiers. He also requested the renewal of the 1670 wine tax, which was
about to expire, to cover the regular revenue. To his amazement, instead
of voting a supply, the Commons replied by advising him to offer Louis no
other terms than the 1659 frontier. It was a militarily impossible request,
which violated the Anglo-Dutch treaty just completed (the details of which
were secret) and made a further intrusion into the royal prerogative. The
King was convinced that all this was a deliberate ploy upon the part of his
opponents in the House to ruin his relations with it again. In this he was
correct. Shaftesbury was now on the point of regaining his freedom, the
government having run out of excuses to curtail it. Arlington was willing
to add his friends in the Lower House to the trouble-makers, in order to
embarrass Danby. Charles also knew (through Montagu) that Louis had

distributed large sums of money amongst MPs hostile to the court to encourage their work: having failed to buy his cousin's will to dispense with Parliament, the French King was spurring on the Commons to wreck it. On 8 February Danby wrote to Wilhelm that, amazingly, the war effort already seemed to be collapsing.

For the next two months, Charles found himself turning within a circle of contradictions. He tried desperately to remake a friendship with Louis, sending expressions of goodwill and protesting that he had been forced into a warlike posture. At the same time he pressed his ministers and diplomats to fashion a powerful alliance between himself, the Dutch, the Spanish, and the Emperor. In this work he seemed for a while, after all, to be aided by Parliament. His fierce response when offered advice instead of money had shamed the Commons into voting, by a large majority, to supply him. In mid-February the House estimated that £1 million would be needed, and sent up a bill for a poll tax as the first instalment. They also renewed the wine tax. As soon as the MPs drew up their estimate, Charles commissioned fifteen new regiments of infantry, four of cavalry, and three of dragoons,[61] and within a few weeks he had 15,000 men under arms. In early March also, a permanent defensive alliance was negotiated with the Dutch. But it was never ratified, for now a new result of Louis's marvellous diplomacy manifested itself. His victories, and his gold, had brought about the appearance of an increasingly powerful party in the States-General, devoted to making peace virtually upon French terms. Wilhelm was losing the support of his own national representative body. As a result the grand plans for a coalition hung fire, and the Commons grew impatient. The MPs hostile to the court had now altered their charge. They admitted that their King was going to use the supply to pay soldiers, but spread the rumour that he would use the soldiers, not for war but to curtail his subjects' liberties. The House as a body could not understand why, if an alliance had been made in December, more active steps were not being taken to concert it. The result was an address on 15 March for an immediate declaration of war upon France, which the Lords, despite all the eloquence of the government peers, only amended to the extent of deleting 'immediately'. The MPs also tacked to the Poll Tax an insistence that all French goods be banned for three years, which would reduce customs receipts. When the Lords would not concur with the address for war, the Commons requested a recess until mid-April, to let the King 'perfect' his alliances. Charles's prospects of a successful foreign policy and of popularity at home were slipping away together. Furthermore, just as in 1673, the pressures of war were producing or accentuating problems in his other realms and these were once again converging upon Westminster.

The imminence of a French war, as in 1666, put Ireland in the front line of the military problem, after years in which, thanks to Ranelagh's priorities in financing, magazines and fortifications had been allowed to run down. As soon as he took charge, Ormonde had been determined to build up the army, not because he yet feared a foreign foe, but because he wanted to curb Protestant dissent once more. Essex had been inclined to see the Catholics as the greater problem, but the old Duke believed them harmless unless the French invaded, and was inclined to stress the threat from republicans and Covenanters. When the prospect of fighting Louis loomed, he set about improving the defences of the southern coast, beginning by building a fort at Kinsale. To provide money for greater military expenditure, he hoped both to keep the whole revenue in Ireland, as Essex had tried to do, and to increase the revenue itself. To strengthen himself politically, he was shrewd enough to take the step which would have prevented his dismissal in 1669, and to cultivate Orrery consistently. The Munster earl, also now ageing, co-operated readily and agreed that Irish money should not be diverted to England. So did Lord Chancellor Boyle, and of course Essex, but even in unison they were not enough to shake Ranelagh's arrangement as long as Danby dominated English policy. The tragicomic aspect of the situation was that the revenue had not yet in fact produced a surplus, to be used anywhere, and the preparations for war made it likely that it would go back into deficit. Hence the sagacity, and success, of Ormonde's proposed solution to the problem: to call an Irish Parliament which would vote extra revenue and specify that it was to be used in Ireland. Ranelagh and Danby naturally disliked the scheme, not only because it so neatly circumvented their arrangement, but because the prospective Parliament might want to look at some accounts. But in February, with war apparently imminent, Charles agreed to it. Characteristically, having adopted Ormonde's scheme, he empowered Ranelagh, Danby, and Conway to devise the measures to be presented to the Houses when they met. It remained to be seen whether discontent in a Parliament in Dublin would exacerbate that of the existing one in London. While his ministers speculated, the King thought nothing of docking the Irish revenue further by ordering pensions from it for Monmouth and other courtiers.[62]

The problems of Scotland were less directly concerned with the diplomatic crisis, but touched the court more closely. They arose from Lauderdale's techniques of government. Since 1674 he had continued to rule triumphantly with his new set of friends. In the Cavalier Parliament's autumn session of 1675 there was an attempt to continue the campaign in the Commons for his removal. It was fomented, in large part, by Scots who waited at the House's door daily 'like as many porters'. After the session ended, Hamilton invited himself to Whitehall to rehabilitate himself, and failed disastrously. As maladroit as ever, he chose both to criticize Lauderdale to Charles and to ask for a renewal of the discredited policy of religious indulgence. The King was only angered further. An attack upon the red-haired Duke's regime was published in England, while others were sent anonymously to the English ministers of state, to equally little effect. That they did not have more was due in large part to a bevy of Lauderdale's allies, led by Archbishop Burnet and the Earl of Atholl, who came down to London to represent him well to both MPs and monarch. Their work was appreciated by their great leader, and Atholl swiftly found himself promoted to a marquisate. Conversely, Hamilton was finally put out of the Scottish Privy Council, as Lauderdale convinced Charles that his soft attitude towards dissent made him a liability there. The great Duke's grip upon his native land was strengthened further in July 1677, when the King notified the Scottish Privy Council that in future all offices of state were to be held not for life but during royal pleasure. Given the prevailing circumstances, this more or less meant at Lauderdale's pleasure, and placed ministers such as Rothes at his mercy. Rothes, as ever, survived by bending: he read the signs, behaved impeccably to the all-powerful Secretary, and avoided discussions with Hamilton.[63]

The long crisis which was to alter everything began suddenly, and was brought about by Lauderdale himself. Since 1674 the Council had repeatedly reissued proclamations against dissent, and as often found the problem intractable because of the unwillingness of local magnates to enforce them. This resistance was almost always covert and passive, but in late October 1677 the gentry of Ayrshire, led by the young Earl of Loudon, son of the Covenanting Chancellor, called the Council's bluff. They collectively refused to apply the latest round of coercive measures, and told the Counsellors that toleration was the only practicable solution. Lauderdale took this defiance as an excuse to settle with the nonconformists of the west once and for all. He convinced Charles that a rebellion was about to break out in the south-west of Scotland, by religious fanatics tending to republicanism, and that the local leaders had lost control. Thus he obtained royal permission for massive pre-emptive action. In November the King instructed Ormonde to send a brigade of the Irish army to the Ulster coast once more, ready for action in Scotland. The Foreign Affairs Committee resolved to replenish the magazines of northern English garrisons and to prepare a task force for action over the border. But Lauderdale's main blow against dissent was to be an army of militia drawn from elsewhere in Scotland, notably from Highland clansmen, which would descend upon the south-west.

There it would force landlords to give bonds for the behaviour of their tenantry, disarm the local people, and weaken the authority of Hamilton and several of his friends by proving them incapable of intervening. If they tried to prevent the process they could themselves be proceeded against for disloyalty. To stop them from complaining to Charles, the Council proclaimed that nobody could leave Scotland without their permission. Lauderdale himself came up to supervise the process, bringing the royal order for the harrying of the south-west to commence. It was signed upon 11 December, as the King prepared for war with France: at this moment it was all the more important to Charles to have Scotland pacified, and he was not going to be squeamish about the methods employed.[64]

In January 1678 what was to be known as the 'Highland Host' entered Ayrshire. That became the first of a series of counties to be put to the experience of supporting soldiers who deprived the people of weapons, cross-examined them, extorted bonds and fines from them, and generally plundered them as well. When these irregulars left a shire they towed away cartloads of booty, like an army retiring from a city which it had stormed.[65] The young Earl of Cassilis, son of the Kirk party leader, became the first nobleman to be made into an example: when he refused to be made responsible for his tenants' behaviour, he was declared a traitor by the Council. His reaction took them by surprise, for despite the proclamation he bolted for Whitehall to beg the mercy of the King, accompanied by Hamilton. They were attempting in political terms the same desperate stroke which Charles himself had tried in military terms in 1651: leaving Scotland in Lauderdale's power, they were trying to get behind him to court and so sever the charmed connection with their sovereign which had been the secret of his success. Had the Council not succeeded in making them so desperate, they would never have dared it. The great Secretary was still more shaken when his own ally Atholl turned against him, apparently appalled by what he had seen in the south-west, and himself set out for Whitehall to warn Charles. Lauderdale made the obvious response. He got the Council to empower two of his trusted henchmen to rush to court and to try to head off his enemies from the royal presence. All of them reached Whitehall at the end of March. The Secretary's cronies commenced a game of cat and mouse around the corridors and chambers, intervening at every point at which it seemed that the others might obtain a meeting with Charles. The King himself behaved very well from the Council's point of view, sending it a letter of commendation for all its actions and refusing to accord the malcontents any formal reception. What disturbed Lauderdale was that he did not send Hamilton and Cassilis back to Scotland for trial as the Council asked. Part of the reason seems to have been that, with a suspicious English parliament soon to remeet, he wanted no dramatic gestures likely to provoke mutters about tyranny. In addition, however, it appears that the appeals of the two nobles flattered his vanity: they were asking him to exercise his prerogative of mercy, and the King was generally pleased to have any of his prerogatives magnified.[66]

For the next two months, Charles continued his attempts to deal successfully with Louis, Wilhelm, the States-General, the Spanish, the Cavalier Parliament, and different groups of indignant Scotsmen. For most of April, with the diplomatic talks hanging fire and the Houses in recess, his positive measures tended to be concerned with Scotland. The contest for his attention heated up, Kincardine and others arriving to swell the numbers of malcontents and Archbishop Burnet and more Counsellors reinforcing the supporters of Lauderdale. The latter had another ugly surprise when, having presumed that the English government was composed of friends of their leader, they found Monmouth and Williamson inclined to listen sympathetically to Hamilton and to represent him to the King. For both men this marked a major departure from a hitherto consistent acquiescence in the prevailing political line. James, who remained Lauderdale's fast friend, was understandably worried by the new boldness of his nephew: the wind blowing from Scotland was starting to open cracks in the English regime. Under these conflicting pressures, the King took a middle line. He invited Hamilton and his friends to present their complaints to the Foreign Affairs Committee, who would then relay them to Charles himself. He told the Scottish Privy Council that he still approved of its policies, but wanted them to withdraw the Highland Host before the Cavalier Parliament remet because of the stories of its misbehaviour now circulating. The stories themselves did not worry him at all, and his memory of the now distant Western Remonstrance was as bitter as ever. He told Monmouth (before a gathering) that he could go and 'wink and shit' in that part of Scotland, for the people there were all bad.[67]

When Parliament remet on 29 April, all that Charles could do was offer sincerity and hope for loyalty. Finch opened (truthfully) to the Houses the full story of the negotiations with the Dutch since early 1677, gave them the December treaty to peruse, and invited them to advise him on how to proceed in view of the increasingly uncooperative attitude of the States-General. Two days later, in a gesture of optimism, he commissioned Gerard and the Earl of Craven to command under Monmouth in a projected campaign in Flanders.[68] On 4 May the Commons returned their reply, which could scarcely have been less helpful. They condemned the December treaty (by sixteen votes) and advised the King to make another: all the efforts of the two Secretaries and Danby's henchmen had not quite prevailed over the rhetoric of the opposition. For all his sabre-rattling, Charles was in no position to fight anybody, for the Poll Tax had all been spent upon paying the army and he now did not even have funds to fortify the coast.[69] A new ambassador arrived from the States-General to inform him that Louis was now offering to keep three towns in Flanders and to return five. This appeared to the Dutch to signify the end of the war, and they had no more interest in alliances. On the 7th the Commons requested the removal of the ministers who had advised the King that some of their previous addresses had infringed his prerogative. For good measure, urged on by Hamilton and his friends, they again desired the dismissal of Lauderdale. The chemical effect of these addresses upon Charles shocked all around him: he turned pale and shook violently with rage. His feelings were only slightly better controlled when the Dutch ambassador, with astonishing insolence, told him that he no longer knew whether to apply to King or Parliament.[70] James was at hand with a suggestion as to how to extricate himself from the predicament. It was simply to realize the worst fears of the 'opposition', by scrapping Parliament and ruling with the new army.[71] Another recent activity of the Commons had been to discuss new measures against Catholics, robbing the heir presumptive of illusions that his daughter's marriage had secured the position of his co-religionists. Charles was instinctively against such radical courses, and from now on pursued a fairly consistent policy, of using the existence of the army and the bellicosity of Parliament to get money from Louis. He would attempt to make his cousin pay for neutrality, disbandment, and prorogation, the three courses into which he was being forced anyway.

The secret treaty which he hurriedly signed with Barrillon on 17 May promised all these things if the Dutch and Spanish did not accept Louis's terms within two months. In return, he was to get £540,000. On the same day Danby wrote sorrowfully to Wilhelm that their hopes were ruined, and that the Prince had to make peace. The treaty was made in the nick of time, for on the 22nd the Dutch agreed to a truce. The King now had the greatest of difficulty in keeping his army in being in order to retain credibility in the eyes of any of the combatants. On the 11th the Commons refused any supply to maintain the armed forces, by one vote. During late May, in a series of exchanges, he asked the House to postpone the disbanding of the army until a general peace was made. Each time it refused, and the most that he could obtain was an agreement on 11 June, by three votes, to give the government until 27 July to accomplish the task. It provided the money for the purpose, but when Charles appealed for an extra £300,000 per year to refloat the regular revenue, it refused without a division. Nor would it give any compensation for the loss of French trade to the customs. When 5,000 more soldiers were shipped to Flanders at this time, it was as much in the hope that Spain would pay them as to keep up pressure upon Louis. Twenty foot companies were sent to Ireland, to be supported by that nation.[72]

Apart from his subsidy treaty, in fact, the King's sole achievement at this period was to send the rival Scots home. At first sight, this was done entirely upon the terms of Lauderdale and his friends. They proposed to Charles that a Convention of Estates be summoned, with the Duke acting as Commissioner, to vote money to cover the costs of the Highland Host. This would also have the effect of drawing their enemies back up to Scotland. The King agreed, and signed a letter which they presented to him, declaring his dissatisfaction with Hamilton and his friends and his vindication of the Council's actions. He did at last give the malcontents a formal hearing, but treated them with great coldness. When Lauderdale's friends left court at the beginning of June, they believed themselves to have been wholly successful.[73] The Convention opened at the end of the month, and despite strenuous efforts by Hamilton it was a complete triumph for its Commissioner. The money was voted with the minimum of fuss, and Charles and James sent their congratulations and gratitude.[74] Yet neither of the rival Dukes saw things quite in this light. Just before the Convention, Lauderdale had received a letter from his sovereign dated 14 June. It commenced with the usual assurances of kindness and support, but went on to order him to treat Hamilton better in future and to allow him to come to court, to suspend the taking of bonds, and to leave the armed forces alone. When he read this, the Secretary fell into a deep depression and gave instructions that the missive be hung round his neck when he died and buried with him (it was). In that moment he had recognized that some of his enemies' complaints had gone home to Charles, that he no longer had a monopoly of his attention, and that his control of policy had been partially fractured. In brief, his power was starting to crumble. Hamilton also knew what had happened: despite his humiliation in the Convention, he wrote to a friend at the end of July that they could now expect to play a part in government.[75]

The alteration in English affairs in July was still more dramatic, and remains rather mysterious. The outline is clear. At the end of June the talks between Louis and his enemies suddenly collapsed, because the French King, as a point of honour, insisted upon the return of all the territory lost in the war by his ally Sweden. Both sides mobilized once more. The English government, just as swiftly, stopped the disbanding of its army and sent Temple to The Hague to make a new alliance with the Dutch. This was conditional upon their consent to pay the expeditionary force in Flanders and not to make peace without English permission. The first would have partially removed the problem of fighting without adequate support from Parliament, while the second would have restored Charles's diplomatic position. On 15 July Temple signed an agreement promising to declare war on Louis if he did not abandon the Swedes within two weeks. By then three more English regiments had been shipped to Flanders. Yet on the day that the treaty was made, the King prorogued the Houses in accordance with his deal with France. Perhaps the Commons now seemed useless anyway as they had resolved to give no more supply that session, but the vote could have been rescinded. And the Foreign Affairs Committee sent a secret message to Wilhelm that it could not field its army without a parliamentary grant.[76] So all this was posturing, but it was posturing on the grand scale. Five more regiments and twelve horse troops were drawn down to eastern ports ready to be shipped to the Netherlands. On the 23rd, Henry Coventry wrote to Ormonde that measures for war were being concerted with the Dutch and Spanish generals.[77] It was in vain. The Swedes rescued Louis from his predicament by volunteering to write off their losses. Temple had not persuaded the Dutch to concede Charles's request about not making a separate peace, and on 31 July they signed the Treaty of Nijmegen with the French. Charles found himself abandoned, and also bereft of the promised French subsidy, as he had broken the agreement in May by failing to remain neutral.

What was the English King aiming at? It has been suggested[78] that he and Danby had begun to toy with James's proposal of ruling with the authority of his army. According to this school of thought, the foreign policy of July was simply an excuse to halt the disbanding. The problem with this interpretation is that there is not a scrap of real evidence for it, and that during the crucial weeks the soldiers were being shipped to Flanders or Ireland instead of concentrated for domestic use. They were certainly not employed for any such purpose after the treaty. Another explanation[79] which has been offered is that Charles genuinely cared about the fate of western Europe and intervened to check Louis's power when he might have contemplated further conquests. This is at variance with the whole drift of the English King's thought, as interpreted in this chapter, which was both cautious and opportunist. An alternative proposal may be made here from two kinds of evidence. One is a letter sent from Temple to Ormonde,[80] in which he said (unhelpfully) that he could not put the reasons for Charles's change of heart on paper. But, he added, the King was now convinced that he was going to get nothing out of France, and his only hope lay in a Dutch alliance. Now, Temple presumably did not know about the subsidy treaty, but the tendency of his monarch's fears is clear: he thought that, so close to a peace, Louis was not going to accord him any gratitude (or funds) after all, unless reminded of his power to make trouble. This must have been mixed with a feeling that the war had gone on for too long and caused far too much trouble, and had to be ended. Certainly, this accords with the second clutch of evidence, his conversations with Barrillon and his instructions to an envoy to Paris in which Charles used the threat of invervention to the full, and pressed his cousin to abandon the Swedes and to sign the treaty.

And now the war was over at last, and all the British governments were left in serious difficulties. The standing of that in Scotland had been severely undermined, and its leaders left unsure of their position at home or at court. Ormonde found himself given an enlarged armed force without the extra revenue which he needed to maintain it. The situation in England was worst of all. Charles had spent upon keeping up his army the funds voted to Parliament to pay it off. He could now neither afford to pay it nor to disband it, and had no use for it. By retaining it in July he had directly thwarted the wishes of the Commons, who could be expected to be extremely angry. He dreaded having to face them again, but unless he did so he could not get rid of the soldiers. In the interim they made a steadily more complete mess of the national finances, which had already been pushed back into deficit. Their presence would also multiply fears about the government's intentions, worsening the already embittered relationship between the Crown and the political nation. The ministry in England was probably doomed, and it only remained to be seen how it might collapse. But nobody in the summer of 1678 could have visualized quite how dramatic its end was actually to be.

Collapse of a System, 1678–1679

∽✦∼

THE period of Charles's reign which commenced with the Peace of Nijmegen has also been very intensively studied. And from those studies, a fairly consistent portrait has emerged of an 'Exclusion Crisis' which paralysed foreign and domestic policy and threatened a breakdown of government for two years. This, so the traditional tale runs, was first contained and then resolved by a display of extraordinary political skill and courage on the part of Charles himself.[1] In the next two chapters this long-established orthodoxy will be challenged twice over. In the first place, it will be proposed that the position of the monarchy was fundamentally so strong that, only providing that he did not show consistent folly, Charles's control of his realms was never in doubt. In this sense, there was no 'Exclusion Crisis' at all. Some contemporaries did think that the situation was 'critical', but it will be suggested here that they were wrong. Second, it will be argued that Charles was responsible for a string of mistakes amounting in some cases to real idiocy, which created many of the problems which he did face in 1678–81. Their immediate effect was to demolish the system by which he had run England and Scotland since the Treaty of Westminster.

The storm that was about to break approached like tempests in nature, by stealthy degrees and upon a landscape of more than normal calm. Whatever the seriousness of the predicament in which the English government now lay, for the time being Parliament was in recess and the harvest engaging the nation's attention. Charles and his Counsellors spent August and September attempting to tackle two issues. One was to prolong the European war so that they might yet win some glory or profit from it. Agents hurried to the Spanish and German rulers appealing to them not to imitate what Henry Coventry called 'the ugly treaty' between the French and Dutch. All through August thousands of soldiers were still being shipped over to reinforce the English army in the Netherlands. To ward off financial collapse in the short term, Danby farmed out the Hearth Tax collection a year in advance of the expiry of the existing contract. By closing off his future options in this matter he got a lump sum, but this did not avert the need for further borrowing to keep the regime afloat. And the great effort was in vain, for one by one Louis's opponents came to terms during the autumn, and Charles was reduced to salvaging what reputation he could by functioning as a mediator. At least, decided the Foreign Affairs Committee, it would provide an excuse to Parliament for keeping up the army. Charles persuaded the Spanish to request him formally to maintain his troops until the treaties were all ratified, which he could then disclose to the Houses.[2]

The Committee's other great business was to try to settle the affairs of Ireland, so that one realm at least would be quiet when the Cavalier Parliament reassembled. There was even a hope that money might, once again, be sent from the Irish to the English Treasury. Accordingly, Charles and Danby now enthusiastically supported Ormonde's scheme for a Parliament to vote new funds, and the Irish Privy Council sent eighteen bills over in August for appraisal. Ranelagh began trying to sell his office of Vice-Treasurer before the long-threatened enquiry was launched into his accounts. But the bills themselves produced time-destroying controversy at court like so many Irish measures before. Two were for a subsidy and an increased Excise, but the Foreign Affairs Committee agreed that the sums required were too small. Charles was irritated by clauses appropriating the proceeds for use in Ireland alone, which for him destroyed most of the point of the exercise. But the real trouble was caused, as so often before, by the technicalities of the land settlement. Among the bills sent over was one to confirm and explain these further, and Orrery, Conway, and Anglesey united in denouncing it as too favourable to Catholics. Ranelagh joined the cry in the hope of averting the session which he dreaded, while Finch worried that in view of these objections the measure would not pass an Irish House of Commons. The arguments, conducted by post between Dublin and London, frittered away the time until the Cavalier Parliament met and the chance of a swift success in Ireland had gone. Nobody at Whitehall wanted two Parliaments to sit simultaneously and to encourage each other's malcontents.[3] But by then, in any case, the storm had broken over both kingdoms.

The 'Popish Plot' has been described as 'an extraordinary tale of human credulity, knavery and folly'.[4] It might be added that it would have been extraordinary if those three qualities had not characterized most of the politics of Charles's reign. The first action of the tale, however, illustrated some of the most genial traits of the King, his dilettante interests, easy familiarity with the public, and utter accessibility. His hobby of watching chemical experiments had given him the acquaintance of a keen practitioner of the science, Christopher Kirby. On the morning of 13 August this individual accosted Charles as he was walking through Whitehall towards the park, and asked him for a private meeting. Kirby intimated that this concerned a plot to kill him, and the King showed his degree of alarm by appointing the interview and then taking his stroll alone as usual. He displayed no more concern when the amateur chemist duly introduced him to a wild-eyed (and wild-brained) clergyman called Israel Tongue. This individual presented his monarch with a fat document, detailing a plot by Jesuits to assassinate him and Ormonde and to raise a rebellion in all three kingdoms with French aid. Charles clearly thought this ludicrously unlikely, and went off to Windsor having turned the papers over to Danby for a routine investigation.

Danby's reaction remains more opaque. Since Roger North[5] wrote in 1740, it has been a historical orthodoxy that he pretended to take the fantastic story seriously in the hope of rallying sympathy to the government in Parliament and country. In fact there is nothing to show that he did not merely carry out the examination of the facts which his master required. He certainly proceeded very slowly, so much that Tongue and his 'informant' tried to expedite matters by sending forged and incriminating letters to the Duke of York's confessor. These were so clumsy that Charles completely lost patience with the whole business. When he decided to refer it to the Privy Council, on 28 September, it was simply to get rid of it once and for all. He even went off to Newmarket, with his brother, instead of seeing the hearing through. The following day he was amazed to find himself invited back by an excited and frightened Council. Before it had appeared a remarkable human apparition, a man with a low forehead, tiny eyes and nose, a gigantic chin (like a pedestal) and a high-pitched, curiously affected voice. This was Tongue's informant, Titus Oates, who proceeded to capture the attention and sympathy of the Counsellors with his minutely detailed account of a conspiracy which had now been expanded to include monks, friars, some of the Catholic peerage, and a former secretary of James, Edward Coleman. Hurrying back, Charles's mood could not have been improved by the fact that one of the lords accused was his confidant in the diplomacy leading to the Secret Treaty of Dover, Arundell of Wardour. He applied a simple test to Oates. The man had claimed to have met Charles's old host in exile, Juan-José. The King asked him to describe the prince. Oates confidently did so, and got both his height and his complexion wrong. This, for Charles, ought to have finished the matter but to most of the Council it was only a detail among a crowd of precise and circumstantial accusations. The King sanctioned a range of measures to follow them up, and went back to the horse-races.

At this point events commenced an appalling escalation. One of the measures taken by the Council was to order all lord-lieutenants to mobilize militia for a round of searches of Catholic homes for arms, informing them that a dangerous conspiracy had been uncovered.[6] This startling announcement, barren of detail, triggered the greatest of those paroxysms of panic to which Stuart England was prone. Soon all over the country people were reporting mysterious horsemen and sinister conversations. Another of the Council's instructions was to search Coleman's house. There its agents found a series of letters written by the owner in the mid-1670s, to the confessor of Louis XIV. In them he spoke blisteringly of Charles's weaknesses and detailed the (utterly ineffectual) intrigues which he had conducted about the court to advance the Catholic faith. They revealed nothing more than that James's former secretary was a self-important fool, but technically they were treasonable. Furthermore, Coleman had burned all his correspondence of more recent years, producing the obvious suspicion that it had contained proof of Oates's assertions. Finally, and most disastrous to the forces of sanity and stability, there occurred one of the great unsolved crimes of history. Before attending the Council Oates had sworn to some of his 'evidence' in front of a JP, Sir Edmund Berry Godfrey. On 17 October Godfrey was found dead, apparently murdered. The case remains utterly mysterious, but in the heightened atmosphere of the time most who heard the news (and it spread with fury) attributed his demise to the Catholic 'plotters'. Only four days later the Cavalier Parliament remet.

The government's predicament was, of course, that it could neither disprove the 'Plot' nor punish the perpetrators. Charles now had a group of Jesuits behind bars, who denied all, and Coleman's letters, which were not evidence. In Ireland Ormonde at first proved very willing to believe the story, and arrested the chief individual named by Oates.[7] This was none other than the ever-meddling Archbishop Peter Talbot, whose desire for importance had just rebounded appallingly upon him. Over twenty years before, that other maladroit adventurer, Bristol, had wished that Talbot would get martyred. Now, a few years after Bristol himself had quietly expired, his wish came true, to a degree. The Archbishop could tell Ormonde nothing, and, being an ailing and elderly man, died in prison after a period of confinement. As for the Godfrey murder, there was only time before Parliament met to offer a reward for information.[8] The King himself never gave anybody around him the impression that he believed Oates, and he told the French ambassador Barrillon that he thought him to be a tool for others. In this last comment he was wrong, for Titus Oates was a liar and scoundrel employed and motivated entirely by himself, drawing upon knowledge gained during a failed career in the Catholic

Church. Coleman's letters angered Charles enough for him to wish the author dead, and he now spoke of Jesuits as a nuisance, but beyond that he would not go.[9] Thus a disbelieving King faced an all too credulous Parliament.

It has been suggested[10] that when Charles made his opening speech to the Houses his references to the 'Plot' were ambiguous, to please both Danby, who wanted to magnify interest in it, and James who wanted the reverse. There is no evidence for this, and the speech seems totally plain. It told Parliament to attend to disbanding the army and increasing the ordinary revenue, and to leave the 'Plot' to the normal processes of law. He might have saved his breath because both Houses immediately launched their own enquiries and within twenty-four hours the King had to agree to hand over all the 'evidence' to them. Most of the Commons were only too happy to swallow Oates's story whole, and the House committed Arundell and four other aged Catholic peers to prison on the strength of it. The great perjurer had originally intended his tale to persuade the King, not his legislature, and so had been careful to exonerate James from blame. But it made common sense to conclude that the religion of the heir presumptive must be an encouragement to Catholic plotters, and Coleman's letters proved that in 1675–6 the royal Duke had worked to get Parliament dissolved in exchange for French money. He was soon denounced in the Commons, and when Shaftesbury opened the attack upon him in the Lords it was joined by two Privy Counsellors and five bishops. Charles now moved to pre-empt further action. Speakers in the Houses had called for his brother to be banished from court or realm. On 3 November, with the overwhelming advice of his Counsellors behind him, the King required the minimum from James, of withdrawing from the Privy Council and Foreign Affairs Committee. Six days later he tried to narrow the frame of debate by offering Parliament to pass any laws to secure the country as long as they did not affect the powers of the Crown or the succession to the throne.[11] He then maintained this attitude. When the Commons wanted him to exile Catholics from London and confine them within five miles of their homes, he agreed but did not regard these measures as applying to his court. When they asked that everybody in that, including James, take the Oaths of Supremacy and Allegiance, or leave, he exempted his brother from it. The great test of strength came when the MPs sent up a bill to remove Catholics from Parliament. The government first mobilized its supporters in the Lords to delete James from the measure's provisions, and then all its strength in the Commons to have this amendment accepted. On 21 November this was accomplished, by two votes. Only the King's utter determination could have called forth such a united response from his servants and their friends.

The shock-waves of the 'Plot', which had so nearly injured James, came close to achieving the same impact upon Ormonde. They had immediately ruptured the newly reformed alliance between the now ageing Duke and the increasingly ailing Orrery. Exactly as in 1666, the latter bombarded the former with proposals for drastic action, which Ormonde thought alarmist and liable to produce worse trouble among Catholics than they prevented. Racked by pain and frustration, feeling that his grip upon life and politics was slipping away, the Munster Earl retaliated by sending letters to London accusing the Lord-Lieutenant of negligence, which were shown around the court and the Houses of Parliament. In dealing with this potentially nasty situation, Ormonde had a number of strengths. First was the unstinting support of Charles, who was only too glad to have his western realm in such trusted and loyal hands. Second was the Duke's own remarkable stoical courage, which had carried him through adversity so often before. He described Orrery's behaviour as 'but a storm in a cream bowl' (instead of a teacup), and led the Irish Privy Council in enforcing a moderate and practicable round of actions against Catholics. They were ordered to disarm, their bishops and regular clergy were formally exiled, and a few more were arrested on Charles's orders including Peter Talbot's enterprising brother Richard, who had now been denounced in England. The great majority, however, were left in peace. Ormonde's final asset was that he had a network of friends at Westminster, headed by Coventry, Anglesey, and Longford, who worked hard on his behalf.[12]

No sooner did his brother seem safe and the potential menace to his Lord-Lieutenant contained, than Charles found his wife under attack. Legally, Oates's testimony alone was not sufficient to convict anybody of treason. Coleman was condemned by his own letters, and was duly hanged, but a second witness was required in order to proceed against the clergy and nobles in custody. The position was going for the asking to any crook willing to take it, and it was grabbed in early November by William Bedloe, a self-confessed scoundrel from the Welsh Border. Less adroit than Oates, his confirmation of the latter's testimony was none the less enough for all who were longing to proceed against Catholics or simply to bring the matter of the 'Plot' to an end. He delivered it to Council and Parliament and was taken up as a hero by the Commons. In the last week of the month both 'informers' made a considerable misjudgement and tried to please both the MPs and her apparently faithless husband by implicating Queen Catherine in the conspiracy. In the event this was easily dealt with. The Commons asked the Lords to join them in an address to have her banished from court, and the Lords, in the face of Charles's patent fury, refused.[13] That was that, and lesser victims were to be offered. The government ordered the arrest and trial of all priests and the disarming and binding over of all laity who would not take the Oaths of Allegiance and Supremacy. The evidence of Oates and Bedloe was sufficient to secure the conviction of three men in December who had been named as principal plotters.

Thus far the government might be said to have suffered an extraordinary run of bad luck, which it had coped with rather well. It had been dealt no real damage by the 'Plot', which may indeed have distracted attention from the question of Charles's misappropriation of the funds to disband the army in July. By the end of November the Commons were at work on another supply bill for this purpose. But by then Charles and his Counsellors had begun to commit a series of blunders, for which they had no excuse other than sheer overwork. First there was the affair of Dongan's regiment. As part of his menacing gestures towards France in the spring, the King had recalled all the British who had been in Louis's service. The largest number of these were Catholic Irish officers, and Charles felt bound to provide for them, by employing them to lead a newly raised regiment in their homeland. This body was recruited during the autumn, and had no purpose other than as a dumping-ground for the returning soldiers. Ormonde begged the Foreign Affairs Committee to send it to Flanders or into another state's service and was consistently ignored. Thus, even as the English and Irish governments were disarming and watching their Catholic populations, Charles was ordering Williamson to sign commissions for experienced Catholic military men to command a new force, almost wholly composed of their co-religionists. On 18 November the Commons found out about this, and sent Williamson to the Tower, from which the King as promptly released him, with a sarcastic message to the MPs. The regiment was disbanded with full speed, but the damage was done. The Secretary dared not resume his seat in the House, costing his master a spokesman, and political tensions were further increased.[14] Twelve days later came the matter of the Militia Bill. This was a measure proposed by the Commons, to raise the militia for as long as the 'Plot' scare required. It passed both Houses without any fuss, and was about to get the royal assent when somebody warned Charles that it contravened his right to control the armed forces. He vetoed it, leaving the MPs feeling insulted and understandably aggrieved because no Crown spokesman had warned them of the problem until that point. They subsequently insulted him by directing that the money to disband the army be lodged with the City of London and not the Treasury, as a sign of lack of faith.

Thus, by mid-December English politics seemed to be drifting amid an atmosphere poisoned by ill will. Coventry told Ormonde 'we are all, I think, in a mist as yet'.[15] The government appeared to have offered Parliament one way out, by proposing that any Catholic successor should be deprived of control of the army, the revenue, and all appointments in Church and State. This was the first appearance of the option of 'Limitations' which was to feature prominently in future debates upon the succession. But it was made not by Charles but by Seymour, usually regarded (as Speaker) as a court spokesman but in this case acting without royal confirmation and flatly contradicting the King's recent refusal to have the monarchy's powers amended. The Commons did not know what to make of it and nor, for complete lack of evidence, can we. Charles tried to negotiate a fall-back position with the French, by asking Louis for money which would enable him to live without Parliament. He made this approach to Barillon alone, without informing Danby or James. As before, he used the threat that the Commons would force him into anti-French measures, and also as before, he tried to exploit a necessity. In this case it was obvious to him that his army would have to be disbanded, so he represented his intention to disband it as a gesture of goodwill towards Louis.[16] Barrillon was not deceived. He knew perfectly well that if Commons and King quarrelled with sufficient bitterness then the army would fall apart for lack of pay. He had been giving money to those MPs who most fiercely opposed the government, to encourage their work. He also knew that those MPs had, since the opening of the session, possessed a device which might, if properly employed, blow away the foundations of the government itself. It had been presented to them by Charles himself, not as a result of ill fortune or necessity but as an act of crass stupidity resulting from fundamental traits in his nature.

The trouble centred upon Ralph Montagu, the ambitious young ambassador to France. He was as energetic an adventurer in the boudoir as in the Council chamber, and as such made a kindred spirit with Charles's former mistress the Countess of Castlemaine. The two had conducted a passionate affair in Paris in early 1678, which ended abruptly when Montagu seduced Barbara's daughter Anne. The Countess stormed over to England to complain to Charles, and the ambassador panicked. Without applying for permission to leave his post, he dashed to Whitehall in July to defend himself, and so precipitated his ruin. The King was already unamused by Montagu's gambols with the 'unofficial' royal family, but it was the technical infringement of protocol which infuriated him. The hapless rake encountered the same testy sense of ceremony which Sandwich had injured by signing a treaty in the wrong place, and lost not only his diplomatic office but every other post which he held in court or Council. It was unwise of Charles thus to cast off an able and ruthless servant. It was suicidally foolish to make an enemy of one who possessed letters proving that Danby had been involved in secret negotiations with France while asking Parliament for money to fight it. Montagu promptly got himself elected to the Commons and joined the malcontents there. Charles and his Lord Treasurer were aware of their danger and only exacerbated it by clumsy acts of aggression. First, they tried, and failed, to prevent their new enemy's election. Then, on 19 December, their nerves finally broke and they ordered his arrest upon a trumped up charge of treason. He coolly produced the fatal letters in the middle of the House, which went into a rage and resolved upon Danby's impeachment. It has been pointed out[17] that Montagu's revelation, not those of Oates, wrecked the Cavalier Parliament. It should be added that Charles himself was completely responsible for this disaster.

It had cost the government control of the Commons but not of the Lords. The latter refused to commit Danby to prison, and he always maintained that he had wanted to see the impeachment through and to defeat it. Charles preferred to prorogue Parliament for over a month, which he did on 30 December. Neither his sources of advice nor his reasoning have left any traces in archives. The decision was a rushed one, taken late at night[18] but it clearly had many possible motives. The attack upon Danby threatened to reveal the King's own role in the shady diplomacy of the spring. The supply bill was held up by the government's (and thus the Lords') refusal to let the money be entrusted to the City. New 'informers' upon the 'Plot' were appearing, following the gratitude (and pensions) accorded to Oates and Bedloe, and their information needed to be processed. In brief, whatever the precise weight given to all these factors, historians have agreed that Charles wanted a breathing-space. But many at court, and outside it, were shocked by the action. It was feared that the public would interpret it as a device to protect a guilty Danby, to keep the army in being, or to prevent further investigation of the 'Plot'. These worries were compounded by the King's obstinate and noble refusal to execute the three Catholics condemned a few weeks earlier. Most of the Privy Council, led by Danby, Lauderdale, and Finch, begged him to do so, but Charles replied that he could not, in conscience, sign death warrants for men convicted upon the evidence of imposters.[19] The fact that not a single public disturbance resulted indicates the respect in which the English held the restored monarchy, whatever feelings some might express about the monarch and his actions.

But then, those actions swiftly became palliative again. As soon as he announced the prorogation, the King summoned the Lord Mayor and aldermen of London and assured them that he would secure the Church and disband the army. The latter task was commenced at once, solely with the government's existing resources. Part of the money was provided by halting virtually all pensions, and part by renewing the lease of the Excise farm a full eighteen months before it was due to run out. But most was simply borrowed, once again.[20] At the same time a major source of friction between King and political nation was removed, when Charles at last became convinced of the reality of the 'Popish Plot'. One of the new 'informers' who had appeared was a smooth, genteel young Catholic called Stephen Dugdale, who confirmed the evidence against the three condemned men and three of the five lords in custody. Nothing was different about Dugdale except his neat appearance and educated manner, but it was enough to persuade the King. Charles told everybody around him of his 'conversion', the Council breathed a sigh of relief, and the three men were hanged. Three more followed within a fortnight. At the same time the government made a gesture to its opponents in Parliament by appointing one of them, the Earl of Salisbury, to the Privy Council.[21]

A much more significant act of conciliation was apparently under way in private between Charles and those opponents. According to both the later Bishop Burnet and Barrillon, Danby made a pact with a 'moderate' group of his enemies, led by Holles, to get a new Parliament called and to resign himself in exchange for a promise to supply the King and to drop his own impeachment. That both these writers reported the deal indicates that it occurred, and at just this period. Charles was considering moving Danby, like Arlington before, to an 'honorific' court office. What seems odd is that both should have imagined that a faction among his opponents could guarantee to speak for all of them. Still, this evidence bears out the impression around the court that Danby, who had apparently resisted the prorogation, became the strongest proponent of a dissolution.[22] James (as ever) made his approval of the idea clear, but (in a private letter to Wilhelm[23]) claimed no credit for it. Certainly, Charles's behaviour in the matter suggests confusion and impulse. On 17 January he told the Privy Council that he wished to prorogue Parliament for a further three weeks, to allow time to disband the army and investigate the 'Plot'. The idea provoked such disagreement, especially from Lauderdale, that it was taken back to the Foreign Affairs Committee, which in turn totally failed to reach a consensus. Discussions went on in private until Danby apparently persuaded the King to dissolve. On the 24th Charles announced the decision to the Council, adding, as gratuitous rudeness, that he did not think debate worth while as his Counsellors all appeared to fear Parliament more than they did him. If the comment was true of anybody, it was only true of Williamson, and it would hardly have been helpful even if just. Everybody was shocked, Lauderdale was angry because he had not been party to the secret arguments, and Finch remarked gruffly that the King had been misadvised.[24]

Indeed he had. Ormonde's son Ossory mildly described the subsequent elections as 'untowardly'. Charles himself reputedly put it more bluntly: that a dog would be elected if it stood against a courtier.[25] The government did its best to win seats, but the English monarchy had not, so far, developed more than rudimentary electoral techniques. The King and his ministers asked notable supporters to stand and tried to stop them from competing with each other. As a gesture of scrupulous legality, Charles had units of the army not yet disbanded drawn out of towns lest they be suspected of influencing contests held there.[26] On the whole, the regime was at the mercy of public opinion and public opinion was at this juncture against it. Most of the MPs upon whom Danby had counted in the Cavalier Parliament were not re-elected. As one failure succeeded another, the King worked upon the only factors in the situation over which he had control: the people and policies with which he would face the new Commons. All his changes in personnel indicated a determination to strengthen his existing team rather than to bring parliamentary opponents into it. After the Cavalier House of Commons had resolved to impeach Danby, Charles had dismissed every office-holder who had voted for this measure. The most notable was Sir Stephen Fox, who had served him since exile. In February he tried to replace both Secretaries of State. Williamson had lost his influence in the old House of Commons since the affair of the commissions (which was Charles's own fault). He had also annoyed his royal master by searching the Queen's residence for evidence of the 'Plot' without permission, in an effort to mend his reputation with the MPs, and now he went. His successor was Robert Spencer, Earl of Sunderland, who had served as a diplomat in Madrid and Paris and was friendly with Danby and the 'opposition' groups alike. This dexterity in the matter of political friendships revealed one aspect of the personality who was to prove as seductive, brilliant, and dangerous a political gambler as Bristol had once been. His manners and appearance were that of the perfect young aristocrat, endowed with strong, handsome features and a drawling speech which belied the hyperactivity he displayed in the Council chamber and at the gaming tables. Coventry had by now assumed the role of his predecessor Nicholas: aged, respected, and usually disregarded. He was marked down for replacement by Temple, the architect of two anti-French alliances and acceptable to the court's opponents, but the diplomat refused the burden and the old man carried on.

There remained the problem of policies. At one of his last Foreign Affairs committee meetings, Williamson scribbled the minute 'Parliament—to think of heads. The great matter is Popery. All imaginable satisfaction must be given.'[27] As an analysis it had two defects. One was that it ignored the question of Danby, and Montagu's revelations. The other was that not much more could actually be done about it. On 31 January the King proclaimed his intention of dismissing any JPs who did not proceed against Catholics.[28] But the only other 'satisfaction' offered was Charles's instruction to his brother James to go abroad, on 28 February. James had not been consulted about the matter and went, to Brussels, obediently but with an ill grace. The order was drafted by Danby himself, following an unsuccessful attempt, orchestrated by the Treasurer, to argue the royal Duke back into the Church of England by beleaguering him with bishops.[29] Though James himself did not know who had advised his exile,[30] the evidence suggests that Danby was offering him up as a sacrifice to appease those who wanted the Earl himself prosecuted. Doubtless the King was brought to believe that the move would protect his brother from attack: he was wrong, but it is impossible now to say whether it did not prevent a yet more direct attack than that which did develop, such as impeachment.[31] Certainly, the letter requiring James to depart became one of the best-circulated documents of the age, copies surviving today in most archives. In all this planning, only one initiative can be attributed to Charles himself, and that was mercifully aborted. He wished to put Montagu under arrest, but the Privy Council advised him that this would only provoke public opinion, and might violate the privileges due to an MP. The King had to make do with inveighing against his former ambassador to all who would listen.[32]

Still, when the new Commons assembled on 6 March, there was some chance of co-operation between them and the government. Half of them were completely inexperienced, and if the court could win them over then it would replace its missing supporters. Charles's opening speech was one of the longest which he ever made, though it cannot have contained any surprises: he recited his actions to reassure concern about Catholics and the army, and asked for a supply to complete the disbanding, improve the fleet, and remove the anticipations on the revenue. Finch added that the five Catholic lords remained to be tried and that the law regulating the press needed renewing. The King now participated in a measure which guaranteed that relations with the Commons would be strained from the start. Danby had quarrelled with Seymour, and did not want him to be

Speaker of the newly elected House. Charles allowed himself, at the last moment,[33] to be persuaded into supporting an alternative candidate to please his Treasurer. The court spokesmen in the Commons did not move fast enough, Seymour got elected, and when the MPs addressed the King to retain him, Charles replied 'You do but lose time: return to the House and do as I have directed.'[34] His constitutional right to direct it at all was debatable, and this high-handed treatment merely drove the MPs into a rage which only subsided when a third candidate, acceptable to everybody, took the chair.

This dispute convinced both the King and Danby that the latter had to retire. The step had been occurring to them ever since the returns for the new Parliament had come in and made its complexion clear. Before it met, Charles had decided, or agreed, to indemnify his great minister for all past actions by granting him a pardon. The episode represented another example of the intensely 'personal' nature of the restored monarchy, in the sense that the King carried out policies with which few of his servants were either willing or invited to co-operate. Charles summoned Finch in secret to fix the Great Seal to the pardon: he refused, on the grounds that the action would be an admission of the Treasurer's guilt, and the sealing was done by a servant.[35] On 13 March, as the battle over the speakership was being resolved, Danby's resignation was resolved upon by what seems to have been mutual agreement.[36] Instead of moving him to a less important office, Charles compensated him with a huge pension and promotion to a marquisate. It has generally been assumed,[37] as Barrillon reported (from court gossip)[38] that Danby insisted upon these rewards, and Charles gave way to his appeals. But in the fallen Treasurer's own private notes he recorded that the idea for the compensation came from the King himself, and this is confirmed by one of Ormonde's agents at court, who added that Danby accepted it with great reluctance.[39] Thus there is at least a good case for blaming Charles himself for another of the government's blunders of the year. Both Houses were scandalized by the mixture of profit and honour accorded to one whom many regarded as a criminal. As the Commons rushed into a new impeachment, the King resolved to take a strong line with them of the sort that had failed so totally in the matter of the speakership. On the 22nd he told the House that Danby had acted upon royal instructions, and that as he had in any case been pardoned the affair was now closed. Charles spoke with such feeling that, for once, he did not need to use a script,[40] but the MPs only challenged his right to give pardons in such cases. Two days later, he sent a written order to the wretched Danby, to hide before the Lords arrested him.

Charles has customarily been praised for his treatment of Danby, which appears to contrast so pleasantly with his betrayal of Clarendon. Until the point at which both Houses turned against the former minister, he had indeed stood by him (even if his mistakes had helped to ruin the man). From then on, it must be stressed, he looked only to himself. It suited him, now that Danby was apparently bound to stand trial, that he should vanish abroad, taking with him his embarrassing fund of knowledge concerning royal secret diplomacy. Accordingly, his instruction to go into hiding contained a supplementary order, to go into exile. The fallen Treasurer obeyed the first part but not the second, whereupon his monarch gave full support to a bill in the Lords to banish him as Clarendon had been. A series of appeals from Danby himself, smuggled into Whitehall by friends, failed to move the King,[41] but the Commons threw out the bill. On 14 April the two Houses agreed to proceed against the former minister directly, by attainder, and two days later he surrendered, with Charles's permission, to avert this.

As in 1667, it was expected that the fall of the supreme minister in England would be followed by that of the Lord-Lieutenant of Ireland, and for months after Danby's resignation Ormonde expected that he would be recalled. This possibility was the fervent hope of many in England, notably Shaftesbury, who had always disliked him, and Essex, who wanted his office back. The fact that the old Duke had been restored because of the influence of James was remembered and in late March Shaftesbury opened an attack upon him in the Lords. It was based upon the expected charge, that Ormonde either favoured or tolerated Catholics, and was defeated because the Lord-Lieutenant retained all his old strengths. His sons Ossory and Arran mobilized his friends in the Upper House and the Irish Privy Council sent the peers a list of its measures to secure the island. As a result, the Lords were content to ask for a small package of further actions, notably the removal of Catholics from the Irish Parliament. With his Lord-Lieutenant so well defended in both kingdoms, Charles had no need to worry about him, and was only too happy to laugh at the rumours about his impending dismissal. To improve the security of his western realm, he sent it a regiment from the army which was in the process of being disbanded in England. Unhappily, like so many of the Restoration monarchy's gestures towards Ireland, it proved more of a hindrance. The regiment sent over was Scottish, and as such seemed especially alien and unwelcome to the Irish. More important, there was, of course, no provision made to pay it, and the Treasury in Dublin was further encumbered.[42]

Speculation about Ormonde's survival, though baseless, seemed the more worth while because of a marked change of policy regarding

English appointments. It commenced with the replacement of Danby by a Treasury Commission, a device intended, as in 1667, to gratify as many people as possible and to get several brains working on the fiscal system at a tough time. Initially, Charles's instinct was to take a step backwards from Danby and put Arlington at its head, thereby apologizing, after a fashion, for his failure to make the man Lord Treasurer in 1672. In the event, he made the very different choice of Essex, who had been his loyal servant in Ireland but who had, in the course of 1678, begun to oppose the government in Parliament.[43] The alteration of course may be ascribed to the fact that the vacuum created by Danby's loss of influence was being filled by men like Sunderland, Temple, and, to a lesser extent, Monmouth. Connected to both the King and his erstwhile opponents, they favoured a stabilization of central politics by the bringing of leading enemies of Danby into the government. Even though the rest of the commission were minor courtiers with no influence in Parliament, Essex's appointment sufficed to ensure that when the Commons voted funds to complete the disbanding of the army, these were directed to the Treasury and not the City as before. Having gone this far, Charles was emboldened to receive other former critics at court and to restore to office men such as Fox, who had voted against Danby. There was thus a period of preparation for the gigantic alteration made upon 20 April.

Credit for it has been attributed to Temple, Sunderland, Essex, Monmouth, Holles, or the King's mistress Louise: the consensus now seems to be that Temple had the original idea but the others talked the King into it.[44] It consisted of the dissolution and reformation of the English Privy Council (as the Scottish one had been served in 1674). The new body numbered thirty, instead of forty-six, was divided equally between those who held offices and those who didn't, and contained a majority of men who had opposed the court in recent months. Shaftesbury himself was its Lord President. Moreover, Charles made it clear that this body was supposed to be the English government in fact as well as theory, by promising to do away with the Foreign Affairs Committee and with informal consultations. A 'Committee for Intelligence' was formed, but it merely prepared important items for submission to the full board. At the same time the King replaced the Admiralty Commission with one also headed by Shaftesbury and containing a similar mixture of members. Having done this, he ceased to interfere in naval matters in the manner in which he had done since 1673.[45] In agreeing to these reforms Charles was swallowing a great deal, especially in the inclusion in the new Council of Halifax, whose deadly wit had infuriated the King as he stood watching the debates in the Lords. But the attractions of the package for him seem obvious: he was apparently removing for ever any accusations that he was subject to evil counsel, and thereby restoring a perfect harmony between executive and legislature.

In view of what was to follow, it must be stressed that Charles did gain some positive advantages from the change. It divided, for ever, the coalition which had felled Danby, and some of the new Counsellors, especially Halifax, became invaluable royal servants. Initially, it promised to reconcile even the most obdurate of the court's opponents: six days after his appointment, Shaftesbury successfully asserted to the Lords the King's right to term any relations whom he pleased 'princes of the blood'.[46] Essex led the Treasury Commission with tremendous energy, investigating every branch of the revenue and the spending departments. Thanks to this work, the record £2.4 million debt left by Danby was contained and solvency preserved.[47] Charles enjoyed working with a smaller Council, and kept down its numbers until the end of his reign. In late May he suggested to Ormonde that the Irish Privy Council be reformed in the same fashion, only to be told that, with so many members regularly absent in England, a reduced body would probably be inquorate.[48] With a splendid irony, it was Ormonde, whose political demise was being so eagerly and fatuously discussed, who was the geatest beneficiary of the alterations in England. Essex may have used his new position at the Treasury to hound the Lord-Lieutenant, sending him stringent directions and demands for accounts, but at least, unlike Danby, he agreed that Irish revenue should be spent in Ireland. And, in their respective positions, the two rivals now had trapped between them the man who had been such a great irritation to both, the agile Earl of Ranelagh. In May the new Privy Council at Whitehall launched a campaign to force the Earl to account at last, and Charles felt obliged to order him to Dublin to face the Council there. He showed his personal favour to the Vice-Treasurer by giving him a place in the Bedchamber, a gesture which reproduced in miniature his disastrous 'compensation' to Danby. But, to Ormonde's glee, his friend Longford could now announce to him that Ranelagh was 'wholly in your power'.[49] The position of the Lord-Lieutenant was made yet more comfortable as, during the spring and summer, Orrery's health failed at last. He died in September, removing from Restoration Ireland a figure whose talents should have made him one of its greatest ornaments, but whom fortune forced increasingly into the role of a mere trouble-maker.

When all this is said, the 'experiment' of the new round of appointments failed dismally for both 'sides', and the reasons are plain and well known. Charles expected that now he had given his opponents office, they would do his will. Men like Shaftesbury expected that, having obtained power, they could carry out the policies which they wanted. Both he and they seemed to share the illusion that, now that the King had 'good' advisers, the Commons would become much more compliant. Instead, the House turned upon the exiled James. On 27 April it resolved that his religion had encouraged the 'Popish Plot'. Charles instantly made a final great concession, by proposing, in person, that the powers of a Catholic successor be limited in the fashion which Seymour had intimated in November. The details of the offer were muddled in a way which probably reflects the haste in which they were drafted, for they left such a successor in charge of the army, navy, and Household. Presumably they were cobbled together by the new Privy Council, an idea which is supported by the fact that only Shaftesbury and Temple among the Counsellors opposed them.[50] What must have staggered Charles is that the majority of the Commons shared Shaftesbury's views, and that on 21 May a bill to exclude James from the throne passed its second reading by seventy-nine votes. Nor was any supply forthcoming other than the funds to disband the army. When, on the 14th, the King asked for more to keep up the fleet, he was ignored despite the efforts of every Counsellor in the House. This left him with absolutely nothing to gain from this parliamentay session and, having both the Exclusion Bill and the trial of Danby to reckon with, a great deal potentially to lose.

It is difficult to chart the development of Charles's attitudes in these weeks. Years afterwards a courtier recorded that the King had remarked of the new Privy Council, 'God's fish! They have put a set of men about me, but they shall know nothing.'[51] It is unfortunate, and important, that we do not know if this was said right at the beginning or during the period of disenchantment which followed. As late as the day upon which the Exclusion Bill passed its second reading, Charles agreed to a request from the Council, proposed by Shaftesbury, for a purge of JPs which would have allowed former opponents of the court to remodel several county benches at will. There is a charming anecdote, in a much later source, that the King thwarted this exercise by finding specious reasons for retaining each individual whom the Counsellors wanted put out. The Council records, however, indicate that the project never actually reached the stage of naming justices, being overtaken by events.[52] What is clear is that during May the leading Counsellors divided, with Essex, Halifax, Sunderland, and Temple upon one side and Shaftesbury and Monmouth on the other. The former group, being opposed to Exclusion, tended to form a new 'inner ring' of royal advisers, and by late May they had become as alarmed as Charles by developments in the Commons. On hearing that further inflammatory addresses were intended by MPs, they supported him in his now ardent desire for a prorogation. Essex, Halifax, and Sunderland, who were becoming known as 'the Triumvirate', proved sufficiently worried to advise him to do so, on 27 May, without waiting to consult the Council. Thus the decline in the standing of that body, which had commenced with the King's insult in January, continued despite the reform in April.[53]

Charles's bitterness was made clear when he told a circle of courtiers that he 'would rather submit to anything than endure the gentlemen of the Commons any longer'.[54] In fact, he did not have to submit to more than to listen to his Counsellors lamely trying to find ways of improving the government's reputation before Parliament remet. Neither of the means adopted was novel or promising. One was to conclude an alliance with the Dutch, at least to guarantee the Treaty of Nijmegen. A draft agreement to this effect was approved by the 'Committee for Intelligence' on 17 June. The initiative was driven on by the 'Triumvirate' and Temple, partly for the general good and partly to improve their personal standing with Wilhelm, who might inherit the throne. An uncomplaining and uninterested Charles approved it, but the Dutch showed no enthusiasm.[55] The other initiative was to resume official persecution of Catholics, by permitting the execution of the priests condemned at the spring assizes. The King plainly disliked the destruction of men who had committed no other offence than to practise their religion, but he offered little opposition when most of the Council urged this.[56] He made his disillusion with the course of events since April clearer by his attitude than his actions, treating his Counsellors with such contempt that even Halifax and Temple thought of resigning.[57] Meanwhile, Danby and the five Catholic lords were kept in political refrigeration in the Tower. This unpleasant but undramatic state of affairs might have gone on for months, had not the affairs of Scotland impinged upon those of its southern neighbour with more impact than they had done for thirty years.

Since the confrontations of mid-1678 an uneasy peace had been maintained between the rival factions of noble Scots. North of the Tweed, Lauderdale seemed as all-powerful as ever. After the Convention had been dissolved, he rewarded his latest circle of allies like a potentate distributing the spoils of war. The two greatest, the Earls of Argyll and Moray, were both linked to the Duke's family by marriages. Argyll was given official support in his appropriation of the island of Mull, while Moray got a place on the Treasury Commission removed from Lauderdale's newly made enemy, Atholl. The alliance between Privy Council and bishops, to extirpate conventicles by employing soldiers, was maintained with full royal support.[58] Yet Hamilton and his friends were now received by Charles with warmth and allowed to speak freely, and all Lauderdale's attempts to dislodge them were of no avail, the King just directing him to put his complaints in writing. A friend of the Secretary's could describe Hamilton in October, as 'the only key that can usher in great concerns'.[59] Charles seems to have been treating Hamilton as he had once done Buckingham, trying to keep him out of mischief and using him as a reminder to a chief minister of the latter's vulnerability. The balancing act became more difficult in May 1679, when Hamilton once again allied with Lauderdale's English enemies in an attempt to oust him. The struggle was intensified after the 3rd, when Archbishop Sharp was removed from his coach near St Andrews by a group of aggrieved presbyterians, and stabbed many more times than was medically necessary for his departure to another life. The incident was atrocious, especially as he died beneath his daughter's eyes, but there is a grim irony in the fact that a politician as subtle and crafty as Sharp should have met so crude an end. At London, Hamilton blamed Lauderdale's misgovernment for it, while Lauderdale accused his rival of fomenting unrest. Charles resolutely stood by his Secretary, ignoring alike the addresses of the House of Commons and the pleas of the 'Triumvirate' for his removal. It was only after the prorogation that he decided to deal with the problem as before, by hearing out both groups of Scots.[60] Preparations were being made for the conference when, on 9 June, an express dispatch arrived from the Scottish Privy Council. The presbyterians of the western Lowlands had risen, in greater force than in 1666, and the Council had lost control of the country west of Stirling.

In retrospect, it seems that both Hamilton and Lauderdale were right. It was the dual policy pursued by Charles, of encouraging the Scottish government to persecute presbyterians while showing advocates of toleration favour at court, which had produced the escalation of unrest. The rebels had reason to believe that an armed demonstration would cause the King to abandon Lauderdale, his allies, and their policies.[61] Indeed, when the dispatch reached Whitehall, the English Privy Council begged Charles to sack Lauderdale, without a voice being raised in his defence, and a majority of it advised him to treat with the rebels instead of trying to crush them. Hamilton's group insisted that the rising would collapse as soon as the Scottish government was altered. To the amazement of his advisers, the King refused once again to dismiss the Duke, and determined that an English expeditionary force be sent against the rebels. Halifax and Sunderland supported the latter wish, and the rest of the Council glumly began to work out the details of the expedition with them.[62] Having stuck by these two fundamental points, Charles returned to treading a political tightrope. He gave the command of the expeditionary force to Monmouth, who was associated with Shaftesbury and Hamilton, and commissions to command its six regiments to Monmouth's friends. He made Lauderdale's old enemy Tam Dalyell the Lieutenant-General. Charles instructed his son to fight or treat with the rebels as he wished, but two days later he sent an order to the Scottish Privy Council to punish them with exemplary severity. Lauderdale drafted both documents.[63] On the 25th the best possible news reached the King, that Monmouth had routed the rebels without requiring most of the new units from England. This meant that the latter could be disbanded at once, with minimum damage to the royal finances and without needing to ask Parliament for funds which would have been conditional upon Exclusion.[64] It had apparently been a narrow escape, and Charles himself may be blamed for the policy which had encouraged the trouble to break out. It had cost 1,200 lives.

And that policy remained ambiguous for some time. In mid-June Temple was convinced that the King had promised him to dismiss Lauderdale within a few weeks. In mid-July, Halifax could only be confident that this would happen at some point in the future.[65] After the defeat of the rebellion, Charles issued what became known as the Third Indulgence of Restoration Scotland, legalizing conventicles in private houses and pardoning most of the insurgents. It was an initiative of the sort which Hamilton had long urged, and was undertaken without consulting the Scottish Privy Council and against the pleas of English churchmen. But it is possible that Lauderdale was behind it, seeking to steal his enemies' arguments. The long-awaited conference between the rival factions was held in early July, and afterwards both sides were convinced that Charles had decided in their favour: the King's ingrained habit of saying opposite things to different people at different times was showing its effects again. Lauderdale got him to sign a letter to the Privy Council in Edinburgh, declaring unequivocally that Hamilton's complaints had been unjust. Two weeks later he signed another, instructing the Council to abandon the policies which Hamilton had criticized and to govern moderately. A fortnight after that, he replaced the dead primate Sharp with Archbishop Burnet who had been associated more firmly than any other churchman with the persecution which was now supposed to be ended.[66] By August 1679 it was no longer clear to anybody who was in charge of Scottish affairs. But, after twelve years of his supremacy it did not seem now to be Lauderdale.

In England the repercussions of the rebellion were more immediately decisive: it ended the 'First Exclusion Parliament'. The process began with the great (and deserved) credit which Monmouth had gained with his lightning victory. In his actions he had remained a loyal servant to his father throughout the crowded events of the previous year, but his associations had begun to trouble many. As soon as James had come under attack in November, friends of the young Duke had begun to canvass the possibility that he might inherit the throne instead. Before going into exile, his uncle had insisted that Charles declare before the council that Monmouth was illegitimate. Since then, the King's dashing son had sided with Shaftesbury against the 'Triumvirate' (and Charles) in Council debates, while his companions had continued to talk wildly. When he departed for Scotland, relations with his father were still overtly friendly but the latter was getting worried about him.[67] So, to an even greater extent, were the 'Triumvirate' and Temple. On hearing of his victory, they decided to get the English Parliament dissolved before Monmouth returned in triumph and enhanced the power of Shaftesbury's group. The result was a piece of bungling as remarkable as any which had gone before.

Temple began the process by persuading Charles to agree to put the question to the Council. Instantly, the King launched a secret initiative of his own, by trying to coax money out of Louis in exchange for a dissolution which now seemed likely anyway. He told Barrillon, melodramatically, that only the French could prevent the collapse of the English monarchy. On 3 July he met the Council, only to find that the 'Triumvirate' and Temple had all failed to prepare their fellow Counsellors for the question. As a result, only they supported dissolution and Charles postponed a decision. When the meeting broke up, Sunderland remained with the King and persuaded him to dissolve as a display of royal authority. As the Secretary in turn departed, Charles ruined the crucial element of surprise by sending for Finch and Anglesey to enlist their support. They not only refused it but told the rest of the Council, which remet on the 10th in vile temper. Against a barrage of hostile advice, the King insisted upon dissolution and the calling of a new Parliament for October. In yet worse mood, the Counsellors dispersed again.[68] Charles was doubtless pleased to be rid of these particular 'gentlemen of the Commons' for good, but had achieved this in circumstances calculated to ensure the greatest odium for himself and his preferred Counsellors. Nor had he got any money from the French.

As it happened, the King had something to worry about which probably drove these other considerations to the back of his mind. During that summer the testimony of the various 'informers' upon the 'Popish Plot' had continued to claim victims, and Charles to permit their execution despite returning doubts.[69] But the trial of a man was pending whose conviction the King would find very alarming: that of Sir George Wakeman, physician to the Queen. If he were found guilty, then she would be exposed to calumny, if not accusation, once more. In late June Charles was closeting himself with the 'Triumvirate' and Arlington to discuss ways out of the predicament.[70] All the 'informers' were brought before the Council to state any evidence which they might have relating to the Queen, and it proved quite inadequate to form a charge. Nevertheless, it was still desirable to have Wakeman acquitted, and during his trial he received considerable help from high places. The journal of the House of Lords and a clerk of the Council were both made available to him to formulate his defence, and on 18 July he was acquitted. In the process the first serious doubt was cast upon the credibility of Oates and Bedloe. How much Charles personally played a part in helping Wakeman is unknown, but he wept with joy at the result.[71] The capacity of the 'Popish Plot' to damage the government directly was now much reduced.

There remained little to be done now until the autumn. The King intervened even less in the new General Election than he had in the last,[72] and the results would take months to come in. With a sense of mopping up at the end of a season, he promoted three men for recent services. Halifax was made an earl like the rest of the 'Triumvirate', a move of dubious political wisdom as it gave the impression that he was being rewarded for advising the dissolution of Parliament. That old Counsellor from the exile, Lord Gerard, became Earl of Macclesfield for his efforts to second Monmouth in putting down the rebellion: he was one of the young Duke's closest friends. That sour nobleman, Lord Robartes, had redeemed his disgraceful performance in Ireland by persuading the Lords to let Danby's allies, the bishops, sit in judgement at his trial: he became Earl of Radnor. None of these men had been associated with the 'court' in Danby's time, and by honouring them Charles was continuing the tactic of trying to broaden the basis of his support. Yet at the same time one of his most steadfast traditional supporters in the Lords, Viscount Yarmouth, became a fourth new earl, showing that the King would reward upon all sides.[73] With his usual opportunism, he made another attempt to entice money from Louis, asking for a free gift of £350,000. He got only an offer of £40,000 for postponing the approaching Parliament until 1680, which he considered too little for a provocative move which would worsen his situation. So there was not much to be done other than to go on holiday.

That, at least, was something at which Charles excelled, and one of his strengths in coping with periods of severe tension was precisely that quality of insouciance which was such a handicap in other respects. As the First Exclusion Parliament prepared its attack on James, the King was watching greyhound-racing. As soon as it was prorogued he moved to Windsor and conducted most of his conferences there, filling in the time between by fishing.[74] In early August he adjourned the Council for two months and went on a yachting trip from London to Portsmouth before heading back overland to Windsor for some falconry, tennis, and more angling.[75] In truth, there was nothing fundamentally wrong with his position. He could not at present make war, and it was detrimental to his reputation at home and abroad that he could not, apparently, work with an English Parliament. But his rule was not at present likely to be challenged by anybody in his three kingdoms, and he did not need a grant of money. Under the careful supervision of the new commission and with a wholehearted royal support not given to any previous initiative, state expenditure had been cut to its lowest level yet known in the reign. The Treasury was able to pay off the summer fleet while covering all its regular commitments.[76] In brief, in order to land himself in real trouble, Charles would have had to behave in a grossly provocative and insensitive manner. Danby (from the Tower) had in fact advised him to do this, by dissolving the First Exclusion Parliament in May, increasing the army again, and (of course) releasing Danby himself. Such enormous strategic gambles were alien to the King's nature, which tended instead to tactical carelessness and misjudgement of the sort which provoked difficulty and distaste but not massive public disobedience. When reviewing the past year's events to Barrillon in the summer,[77] Charles blamed all their miscarriages furiously upon James's religion and Danby's bad advice. He had some excuse, yet, as this chapter has suggested, he himself bore the major responsibility for converting difficulties into disasters (principally for others). It was another of this monarch's double-edged qualities that he could barely conceive of being personally in error.

In mid-August he showed signs of launching a new initiative before the next Parliament met. As in 1667, he followed a rebuff from Louis by trying to build an anti-French coalition, telling the 'Triumvirate' that he wanted to ally firmly with the Dutch, Spanish, and Emperor. At the same time a new bitterness entered his attitude to those who had opposed his wishes in Parliament. He refused to receive Buckingham, saying that he had supported the election to the new Commons of men 'who would cut his throat'. Likewise he began to get tough with recalcitrant servants, by summoning Shaftesbury to give pledges of his future co-operation or to resign from the Council.[78] Before the tiny Earl could reach Windsor, however, an entirely unexpected event brought the atmosphere of vacation and the leisurely pace of politics to an end. On the 21st Charles took a long walk by the Thames after playing tennis and hawking. The next day he felt dizzy, and then fell into a high fever, perhaps malarial.[79] Within a few hours he was in danger of his life.

During the 1670s, Charles had implemented the system which he had almost instituted in the early 1660s, of ruling through a chief minister in all three kingdoms: Danby in England, Lauderdale in Scotland, and Essex and then Ormonde in Ireland. The effect of the crowded politics from mid-1678 till mid-1679 had been to collapse that system in the two most powerful of the three realms. The result was not a 'crisis' but a near-complete confusion. From the moment of the King's physical breakdown onwards, a new means of governing was very slowly to emerge. The structures left tottering in 1678 had been felled: the rebuilding could now commence.

The Quest for Men and Measures, 1679–1681

THE King's illness did not turn out to be as serious as had at first been feared. Although he took months to regain his full strength, the crisis passed within three days and within a week more he was tucking into mutton and partridges and walking in Windsor Park. The political consequences, however, turned out to be both dramatic and protracted. The first of them became apparent on 2 September, when his brother James suddenly appeared at Charles's bedside, having crossed the Channel disguised in a black wig. He fell upon his knees and both burst into tears of joy. We have it upon the authority of two such different memoir-writers as Temple and James himself that this touching scene was the result of more than a fraternal impulse upon the part of the royal Duke. The 'Triumvirate', Sunderland, Essex, and Halifax, had panicked at the prospect that the King might die and Monmouth, who controlled the armed forces, seize the throne. Hence they had extended a strictly secret and verbal invitation to James and so brought him back into English affairs.[1] One of the finest historians of the period has repeatedly suggested that he now, indeed, dominated those affairs and was responsible for the series of measures which his brother now adopted.[2] Against this three points may be argued. First, as noted earlier, Charles was preparing to adopt a tougher policy just before he fell ill. Second, James's subsequent letters radiate a sense of impotence, anger, and confusion about the situation in England, not one of power or control. And third, as will be illustrated, the government's approach to problems in the years 1679 to 1681 developed week by week, reacting to events. It might be suggested that from August 1679 Charles had an attitude towards the questions of rulership, religion, and the succession, but had great difficulty in finding the servants or formulating the precise measures by which to implement it.

Certainly James was heavily involved in one initiative which followed swiftly in September, the ordering of Monmouth into exile abroad. The King told his son that his brother had refused to leave the country again himself unless Monmouth went too.[3] But James recorded later that he only insisted upon this because 'The Triumvirate' put him up to it, being anxious never again to be caught in the situation in which they had found themselves when Charles's death seemed imminent.[4] And nor was the King himself a passive participant in these plans. He had encouraged the invitation to his brother to return, and courtiers recognized that he had resented his son's increasing association with Shaftesbury and others among James's enemies.[5] Thus, although he spoke gently to Monmouth, and promised to preserve his many offices for him, he broke this undertaking in one spectacular case by revoking his great dual commission as Captain-General in England and Scotland. The Scottish army was put under old Tam Dalyell again,[6] while the supreme command of the English one was left vacant. One more step was needed to complete the precautionary measures: to ensure that James was closer at hand than Monmouth in the event of the King's death, and with his own power-base. In secret discussions Henry Coventry urged Charles to let his brother remain at court, seconded by Sunderland, who was apparently seeking to establish himself with the heir apparent now that his interest in the throne seemed secure. But Essex and Halifax were opposed to this, and Charles clearly decided that it would be unwise to provoke the new Parliament by exiling Monmouth but retaining James. It was apparently Coventry and Lauderdale who proposed a compromise, that James be sent to supervise Scotland. This immediately proved acceptable to everybody except Halifax, who was talked round. In late September the two rival dukes crossed to the Netherlands. On 7 October James, to his delight and relief, received an invitation to return and to pass on to the northern kingdom.[7] In all this, Charles had been consistent. By sending his brother away in March he had tried to stabilize the politics of England, while by opposing James's exclusion in May he had demonstrated his support for him as heir. Now he had taken steps to ensure his inheritance in the now conceivable event of Charles's own sudden death. At the same time, with both dukes absent, the prospects for domestic peace must have seemed further improved.

Certainly by October the King had some reason for optimism. The London Lieutenancy had voted formally not to regard James's presence as a danger to the public peace. When Charles returned to Whitehall in mid-September, the city erupted into bonfires and celebrations in a massive communal gesture of loyalty and congratulation upon his recovery.[8] This is the background to another meeting which he had with Barrillon, in which he appeared very frightened, informed him that England was on the point of revolt, and asked for a gift of money again.[9] Either Charles was being remarkably alarmist or (again) he was misrepresenting something to a Frenchman for his own potential profit. His next action was certainly in keeping with previous practice, for he postponed the opening of Parliament for three weeks with the announcement that he intended in the interval to complete a treaty with the Dutch.[10] No doubt the action also gave time for James to get off to Scotland, but its significance in the old game with his foreign neighbours is clear enough. Though it was proposed by the King, given the ostensible reason his Privy Council cheerfully endorsed it. Charles and his Queen now went off to Newmarket, to enjoy comedies and races by day and dances at night.[11]

In their absence, Shaftesbury provided the King with a new piece of provocation. The project of disciplining him, formed in August, had been shelved because of the new preoccupation with James and Monmouth. In early October, the Earl called a Privy Council with his authority as Lord President, to discuss growing rumours that the Duke of York was going to Scotland. Charles's reaction was first, to inform the Council that the story was true and did not require discussion, and then, to sack Shaftesbury. Just before the latter announcement was made, and while James was passing through England, a new problem arose. It has been said that history is played once as tragedy and once as farce. If so, the 'Popish Plot' of 1678 was certainly the former and the 'Meal Tub Plot' of 1679 as clearly the latter. It was an inept attempt by a group of upper-class Catholics to gain vengeance upon Shaftesbury and his allies by accusing them of plotting to seize power. Not only did they let themselves be duped by an 'informer' whose fabrications collapsed upon the first proper inspection, but the rogue concerned changed his story when the investigating magistrates turned upon him. Now he reinforced the original lies of Oates and Bedloe. The news of all this broke when the new Parliament was due to meet within a fortnight, ruining Charles's hopes of a calmer political climate. His reaction was clearly one of panic, for the very next day, when he met the Privy Council again, he not only dismissed Shaftesbury as planned but informed the other members flatly that Parliament was prorogued till January. He had always hated argument, and until now had generally avoided it by appearing to agree with most of what was proposed to him. Now, in his growing bitterness and aggression, he was adopting the tactic of forbidding discussion to occur. Most of the Counsellors were horrified by his behaviour upon this occasion, and reports of it soon circulated widely. It made final nonsense of his promise in April to rule with advice tendered after formal debate.[12] Yet even this appeared to do him little political harm. On 21 October, six days after the prorogation, he and James attended a banquet held by the Honourable Artillery Company, a body of wealthy London militiamen of whom James was titular colonel. Not only was the event well attended, but among the guests were the Lord Mayor and some of the chief aldermen. These pledged support to the royal Duke, followed by others of the important citizens there.[13] It must have seemed to Charles that his policy of obduracy could arouse significant support.

The King's actions effectively destroyed the team with whom he had worked through the summer. Essex, Halifax, Temple, Anglesey, Radnor and the MPs who had been appointed to the Privy Council in April, all begged him to allow the council to discuss the prorogation, the decision to send James to Scotland, or both. He peremptorily refused them all. As a result, Temple and Halifax retired from court, no longer wishing to participate in a government in which they had lost influence. Shaftesbury was replaced as Lord President by the aged Radnor, who had neither the energy nor the talent to act as a leader. Essex resigned his post at the head of the Treasury Commission, and although Arlington tried to make a political come-back by bidding for it, Charles appointed the efficient but unimportant Fox instead.[14] It was easier for observers (and is for us) to say who was losing power at court at this time than to tell who was exerting it. James doubtless encouraged the prorogation and the dismissal of Shaftesbury, but, much to his disgust, he was still packed off to Edinburgh.[15] Among the courtiers, there were three men who seemed to be gaining prominence during this autumn and winter. Collectively they were known as 'the Second Triumvirate' or (more rudely) as 'the Chits' because of their relative youth. This quality, with ambition, intelligence, and vitality, was all that they did have in common. The first was Sunderland, who remained the image of the polished, scheming, and unprincipled aristocrat, his smooth manner occasionally punctured by out-bursts of rage. The second was Laurence Hyde, the second son of the dead Earl of Clarendon. In his choleric temperament, appetite for work, and devotion to the episcopal Church of England, he was very recognizably his father's child. He drank, quarrelled, debated, and administered with equal zest. He had become increasingly associated with his brother-in-law James, and was now the latter's principal contact and ally at Whitehall. The third was the Cornishman Sidney Godolphin, who had first made his mark in the Anglo-Dutch war (as shown above) and, like the other two, served on various diplomatic missions since. Godolphin made many people nervous by combining a brilliant mind with an almost impenetrably silent manner. We cannot know whether Charles described him as 'never in the way and never out of it', for this famous remark does not appear in any contemporary source. But the witticism fits. Only at the gambling table did his usual reticence and modesty fracture, for there he ventured huge sums with glee. These, then, were the new favourites, and their disparaging nickname 'the Chits' says something more about them than their ages. They were until this moment insignificant in national life and had been brought into prominence now purely by the royal will. It was as if, having taken up a position, and cast round for ministers to support it, Charles found that they were the best he could come up with.[16]

With the assistance of this loyal and industrious, but somewhat insubstantial, trio, the King set about trying to pursue a policy. Part of it consisted of attempting to locate and encourage supporters. That evergreen political entrepreneur, Conway, obviously volunteered as one, for in November he was promoted to an earldom. At the same time, toying with the idea of calling yet another new Parliament, Charles began appointing trusted individuals as sheriffs, who would be responsible for election returns. In early December, Finch, Radnor, Coventry, and Sunderland were made a committee to consider the JPs in each county. Local loyalists as well as courtiers sent suggestions, and in January and February Charles reviewed the results with Radnor and Finch. Before May every county bench had been remodelled to ensure that, although the most prestigious supporters of the First Exclusion Bill were all still present, their faction was in a minority.[17] But, as before, the King was still trying to pursue popular measures. He drove on the continued persecution of Roman Catholics and took further action to drive them from court and capital, and when James protested about this he was ignored. The advice of the royal Duke was also neglected in foreign policy, for he continued to urge an alliance with France. Charles, Sunderland, and Hyde were prepared to talk to Barrillon and Louis was prepared to offer some money. But the Englishmen demanded a huge sum plus a guarantee that the French would not break the peace in the Netherlands. When these terms were refused, Charles returned to wooing the Dutch, and in December his government scored a tremendous negative success by persuading the States-General not to accept a French offer of alliance. A personal letter from the English King swung the debate in the great assembly and so kept his foreign neighbours divided. By January relations between Charles and Louis were so bad that Barrillon was forbidden to come to court. And all this while Danby and the five Catholic lords, despite their appeals, remained in the Tower.[18]

That such measures did little to calm English politics was attributable to the court's opponents, who set up with Charles a process of action and reaction which only increased bitterness. Their respective positions were made clear in early November, when Sunderland tried to mediate an agreement between Shaftesbury and the King. The former demanded that the latter repudiate both his brother and his wife, which Charles did not regard as negotiable.[19] Three weeks later, Monmouth returned from exile uninvited and refused to leave. Biographers of this prince have apparently failed to notice that when he went abroad he was assured by his father that he could come back once the session of Parliament was over.[20] Now it was postponed, and yet he had received no summons. Moreover, James had been allowed to go to Scotland, something which Monmouth had asked to do and had been refused.[21] The young Duke plainly felt unfairly treated. But then Charles's feelings are also comprehendable. His son had tainted himself by association with men whom the King increasingly regarded as intractable enemies, and any favour to Monmouth (especially given his potential as an heir) was a gift to them. Furthermore, he made an increasingly unfortunate contrast with James. The latter did not keep compromising company, however inconvenient his religion, and always submitted to his brother's wishes, however opposed to his own.[22] A mixture of political necessity and personal pique dictated Charles's response to his son's behaviour: to strip him of all his offices save that of Master of the Horse, and ban him from court.

Such behaviour only encouraged Shaftesbury and his allies to increase pressure upon their monarch. On 7 December Charles was not unduly worried when these men presented him with a petition for Parliament to sit without further prorogations. But two days later it was printed, and a newspaper published two similar documents with an advertisement to the public to subscribe them. At the same moment news arrived of more petitions to the same end being prepared in the provinces, and it became obvious that the King was to be the target of a nation-wide campaign. In an icy rage Charles called a Privy Council the next day, the 10th, and told it that he was proroguing the new Parliament for a whole eleven months. The result was uproar, in which every Counsellor argued against this except Radnor, Sunderland, Lauderdale, and a staunchly loyalist peer, the Marquis of Worcester, who all said nothing. Even Finch, who normally supported whatever his royal master desired, begged him to reconsider his decision. But Charles simply silenced the outcry and the proclamation was made. That evening, still seething, the King summoned the Lord Mayor and aldermen of London and ordered them to stop subscription of any such petitions. Having consulted Finch and selected Counsellors, he pronounced that these documents were illegal, and seditious, unless they were subscribed by people of substantial property, such as gentry and freeholders. Two days later a proclamation ordered justices to prosecute any promoters.[23]

The response of Shaftesbury and his allies was to promote petitions with undiminished zest, and to present a series of them in January, calling upon the King to let Parliament sit and to follow its will. The presentations afforded him an opportunity for a display of magisterial rudeness, his remarks consisting of variations upon the theme that such policy decisions were not the concern of subjects. He also took pains to point out that the addresses represented private persons within certain communities and not the public institutions which he held could alone speak on their behalf.[24] He remained consistent to this notion. It has been noticed that he spoke with unusual grace to the presenters of the Berkshire petition, telling them that they were neighbours of his at Windsor and should share a cup of ale with him.[25] What has not been remarked is that this was the only one to have an 'official' character, being subscribed by the county's Grand Jury and presented by its MPs. Throughout this period his display of confidence and cheerfulness was constant: only a disordered stomach gave some indication of the strain which he was feeling.[26] His attitude provoked the resignation of four MPs from the Privy Council, and he responded to their departure with sarcastic delight. The Council was being transformed back steadily into what it had been for most of the 1670s, a loyal administrative body for the enactment of decisions already taken. On 28 January Charles informed it that, as James's absence had produced no good effects, he had invited his brother back to his side.

During his three months in Scotland James had, in fact, done splendidly. In September it was by no means obvious that Lauderdale would not eventually reimpose his grip upon the country. One man asking for a favour described him as somebody 'able to dare any storm'.[27] More than one observer counted him among those who had suggested that James go to Edinburgh,[28] and the two men had repeatedly defended each other before. It seems likely that Lauderdale expected that the Catholic Prince would re-establish his own authority in the northern kingdom. If so, he was very disappointed, for the royal Duke at once set out to make up what one Scot called 'a mongrel party of his own'. He treated Lauderdale's clients well, but took the Marquis of Atholl north with him and invited other opponents of the great Secretary to participate in government. Hamilton himself foolishly chose to remain aloof, sulking because his rivals were still in favour, but several of his clients joined James. His industry and tact impressed many. Although his authoritarian nature caused him instinctively to dislike the new tolerance granted to presbyterians, he maintained it. When he left Edinburgh for Whitehall, he did so to enthusiastic congratulation from the Privy Council and the bishops. In one winter, he had built himself a huge new power-base.[29]

Perhaps by now advancing years would in any case have taken their toll of Lauderdale. Perhaps the realization that he was now finally eclipsed, by a presumed friend, was the final blow to his long-overworked constitution. Whichever the case, in March 1680 courtiers suddenly became aware that the ebullient, ruthless, brilliant Duke, the greatest Scot of the age, was a broken old man. He had a stroke, and thereafter both his strength and his memory were palpably declining. His advice was still sought by the King on Scottish affairs, but only as one among several sources. Sunderland wanted to have him replaced by the son of Lauderdale's old enemy Middleton, but Charles preferred, generously, to let the once-magnificent Secretary choose his own time for retirement and his successor. James also supported him in this respect.[30] Still, it was now very obvious that the way was clear for the next man to become the most important in Scotland after the royal brothers.

In April some of the leading Privy Counsellors, and the Bishop of Edinburgh, arrived at court to settle this question, and also that of the policy which would now be followed. The answer to the first matter was provided in May, the man turning out to be the Chancellor, Rothes, whose genial nature and readiness to submit to fortune now handsomely paid off at last. He was made a duke and given a huge pension. Behind him were grouped a new 'inner ring' for the Council. The Bishop was in it, and so were two clients of Lauderdale, the Earl of Argyll and Alexander Stewart, Earl of Moray, who had been the Secretary's chief agent at Whitehall in 1678. With them was the most able of Hamilton's former allies, William Douglas, Earl of Queensberry. Rothes's misfortune was that some of his political stoicism may have been made possible by his habitual application to the bottle, and observers wondered if he could remain sober enough to fulfil his new position. This would certainly be required, as with these changes went a development in policy. The body of Scots visiting the King convinced him that Indulgence had failed and only provided an opportunity for further rebellion. They were supported in this view by James, whose distaste for the measure has already been mentioned, and the leaders of the English Church, who wanted a drive against dissent in both countries. Suffering, as usual, from a carefully monitored flow of information, the King was not to know, as modern historians do, that unrest among presbyterians was in fact now confined to a tiny radical minority detested by their fellows. Instead, he was deceived by a group of men who wished to try, once more, to extirpate all active nonconformity. He signed orders to wage war against field conventicles and greatly to limit the activities or places of residence permitted to indulged ministers. With these the Scots returned home in June, to launch a campaign of repression. Behind them, Lauderdale's will finally failed. In September he resigned his post of Secretary, to his loyal friend Moray, and henceforth intervened only sporadically in the political scene.[31]

Charles, as usual, was of course far more concerned with English affairs. In the first half of 1680 his actions there remained of a piece with those during late 1679. On his return James continued to lobby for a French alliance and toleration of Catholics and again got neither. His brother continued to try to punish Louis for not offering generous enough terms and for attempting to ally with the Dutch. In April, with the full support of the Council's 'Committee for Intelligence', the King insulted his French cousin by neglecting to congratulate him on the birth of a grandson. The 'Chits', like the 'Triumvirate' before, were in favour of building an anti-French coalition and Charles fully endorsed this policy: as it would please his subjects and as he had no reason for gratitude to Louis it was the obvious step. He berated the French to James and firmly supported diplomatic initiatives to build the new alliances. He and 'the Chits' decided to begin with the Scandinavian and German powers, leaving Spain and the Emperor, who had more complex interests, till last. As his agents went out to these northern courts, he reassured the Dutch that if Louis attacked them he would declare war and meet Parliament at once. However, these projects failed to ripen as the summer did. For one thing, after the war which had ended at Nijmegen none of the powers approached were keen to oppose the French again, and some were making their own secret deals with Louis. The Dutch themselves were less enthusiastic about such a coalition than Charles had temporarily become. For another, many foreign states doubted that England could wage war if its King depended upon grants from Parliaments with which he appeared incapable of co-operating. As a result, the only powers who did respond to the idea of an alliance with Charles were precisely the most dangerous with whom to become tangled. The Emperor Leopold offered an offensive partnership, which was completely out of the question to the English. This left the Spanish. In May Charles was still telling courtiers that a league against France was certain, and a momentum grew up in the idea which made it imperative to ally with somebody to avoid losing face. Sunderland was the man most active in the negotiations, but on 8 June the whole Privy Council decided that a pact with Spain was better than with nobody. Two days later a strictly defensive alliance was made, and the delighted Spanish ambassador threw his arms around the immaculate Sunderland and kissed him. Charles was reported to be pleased to be making 'a figure in Europe' again, but at the same time he tried as usual to have it both ways: to gain prestige abroad without getting involved in an actual war with France. Thus, he took care to remake his relations with Barrillon and to assure him that the treaty was purely defensive and intended principally to impress his own subjects.[32]

This emphasis on domestic problems was real enough, and in the same period Charles pressed on with measures more directly related to them.

He continued to refurbish his governing team, and in April the ailing and exhausted Henry Coventry was finally succeeded as Secretary of State by Sir Leoline Jenkins. It was not so much a replacement as a resurrection, for Jenkins was a man formed exactly in the mould of his predecessor, being solemn, industrious, devoted to the episcopal Church of England, and of marginal political importance. His talent as a speaker was less, but his experience as a diplomat greater. Charles had initially wanted Godolphin to take the post, but the latter, now part of the Treasury Commission, recommended Jenkins as a 'safe' substitute.[33] In June, Sunderland per-suaded Halifax to come back to court, though Hyde had less success in winning back men who had supported it in 1679 and were now drifting into opposition.[34] James played a notably small part in matters of either policy or patronage. When people applied themselves to him, he referred them back to his brother.[35]

As before, his submissive conduct contrasted sharply with the actions of Monmouth. In early 1680 Charles made two offers of forgiveness to his son, on condition either that he returned to exile or that he provided information upon his compromising friends. The young Duke refused both. During the spring rumours thickened that evidence existed of Monmouth's legitimacy. In mid-April the King set his Counsellors and judges to work investigating the source of these, but nothing was revealed. In mid-May he cut short the examinations, saying bitterly that 'he would have no more of that farce',[36] and two weeks later he published a denial of his marriage to Lucy Walter. At the same time he invited Macclesfield, his old Counsellor in exile, to recall in public how Lucy was 'a whore to other people'. Macclesfield, being a friend to Monmouth, refused to do so, and the prince himself responded by touring the West to encourage supporters of the campaign against James. His father looked on, both furious and powerless to stop him.

The winter's package of policies was continued in every other respect. The Council forbade the execution of priests, but urged on financial persecution of Catholics, which would help the Treasury as well as the government's image. It also tried to ensure the enforcement of the 1662 Corporation Act, as part of its promise to maintain the Church of England: this tended to reinforce an existing tendency for dissenters to join James's enemies, which in turn strengthened royal antagonism towards them. The same effect of polarization attended the continuing efforts by Charles to encourage his supporters. The replacement of justices was associated with similar treatment of militia officers. Charles's dismissal of the petitions for Parliament to sit provoked loyal addresses from people anxious to win his esteem and embodied in the institutions which he claimed to respect, such as benches of the peace and Grand Juries. Six had been presented by May, three of which congratulated Charles upon his brother's return.[37] In March the King set out boldly to rally opinion in London by inviting himself to dine with the new Lord Mayor, and bringing James. The Mayor entertained them magnificently, and, as they returned, crowds in the streets, for the first time, shouted for the Catholic Duke. There is some evidence that Charles continued to sup with the Mayor privately during April to maintain close relations.[38] Having obtained the opinion of the judges that he could act against libels, he issued a proclamation against unlicensed tracts in May.[39] These actions, as is well known, did not win over the nation so much as divide it into increasingly recognizable groups. Those who wished Charles to accept the will of Parliament (which, to them, effectively meant to abandon James) were called Whigs by their opponents, after the Scottish rebels of 1679. Those who were prepared to support him in what he willed, which also increasingly meant supporting an intolerant episcopal Church, were by April distinguished as 'the cavalier or church party'.[40] Their enemies named them Tories, after dispossessed Irish Catholics turned bandit. To compensate for the strains of this process, Charles became physically more isolated. As early as mid-April he withdrew to the peace of Windsor, only leaving it for Newmarket and the very occasional trip to the capital. In mid-May he suffered another fit of fever after a series of solitary walks in the chill of dawn and evening.[41] But this passed, and by midsummer he was perfectly healthy and ready to carry on the contest.

This was as well, for the Whigs were prepared for it. If James had called in the Scots to assist his cause, then Shaftesbury would exploit Ireland. Memories of the great Catholic rebellion of 1641 were still fresh in all three realms: as interest in the 'Popish Plot' waned in England, the tiny Earl sent over agents to hire 'witnesses' to a new uprising being planned in the western kingdom. As well as fanning hatred of Catholics, this would enable him to accuse Ormonde of negligence and undermine his position. Essex was only too happy to co-operate with him in this work from within the Privy Council, apparently hoping to regain the post of Lord-Lieutenant. During the winter the preoccupations of Ormonde himself, Charles, and most of the Councils of both realms had remained as they had been all through 1679, with the question of an Irish Parliament. No further progress had been made in this, as they had still proved unable to agree upon either the time or the measures for it.[42] On 5 March the King finally resolved to call one for May and ordered the Irish Privy Council to hurry over a new set of draft bills.[43] He then went off to Newmarket, and in his absence Shaftesbury and Essex presented their 'evidence' of the

'Irish Plot' to the Council at Whitehall. They must have been gratified by the result. Essex, Radnor, Coventry, Hyde, and an old and conservative peer, the Earl of Bridgewater, were appointed a committee to consider it. Bridgewater, Radnor, and Coventry were soon convinced that the danger was real, and Finch, though not on the committee, agreed. To the alarm of Coventry and Hyde, the council resolved to send for the 'witnesses' without putting the matter to Ormonde or the King. When Coventry told him of this, Charles hurried back, angered by the proceedings but unwilling to countermand them for fear of being accused of endangering Irish Protestants.[44] The prospective Irish Parliament was again postponed. In May there duly arrived a set of ragged Catholic renegades, later dubbed 'the MacShams'. Their brogue proved unintelligible to King and Council, and when their written depositions were studied they accused one man, Oliver Plunket, the Pope's primate in Ireland. This inoffensive individual, liked by successive Lord-Lieutenants, had been selected simply because of his rank. Charles and his Counsellors directed that he be tried in Ireland, where his popularity would ensure his acquittal even by Protestants. This, of course, suited Shaftesbury well enough, for it would further his charges of wilful negligence when an English Parliament met.

On 26 June 'that little man' (as James termed him) delivered his next stroke, by presenting the Catholic Duke as a recusant and the royal mistress Louise as a prostitute, to the Grand Jury of Middlesex. At once Charles rushed from Windsor and had a judge disperse the jury before it pronounced upon the bill, but the public insult to the government had been made. On 22 July Whig strength in London was proved by the election of two passionately partisan sheriffs, though the court of aldermen remained predominantly Tory. In response, royal policy became a little more conciliatory. The judges going upon assize were ordered to execute the laws against Catholics severely and to assure people that Parliament would meet in the autumn.[45] On 13 August the King told his Counsellors that he had fixed the date of assembly for October. He shelved a plan to apply the Corporation Act to the London livery companies, and ordered a Tory propagandist not to write tracts which would increase the divisions of the nation.[46] And he agreed to a suggestion from the 'Chits' to invite Wilhelm, Europe's Protestant hero, to England for consultations. All this, none the less, did not involve any moderation of his hostility to the Whigs. He refused to knight the new Sheriffs of London, depriving them of a traditional honour, and when a Whig Lord Mayor was elected in September, Charles administered a comparable snub by declining to attend his feast. Likewise, Jenkins wrote to prominent gentry along the route of Monmouth's summer tour, offering royal congratulations to those who did not entertain the young Duke.[47]

The same relative caution was observed in regard to Irish affairs. When Ormonde's heir Ossory, the Lord-General of the Irish army, died in the summer, Ormonde wanted this vital office given to his next son, Arran. Charles preferred to let it remain vacant.[48] The great Irishman's main ally at court during this period was Arlington, still by no means a spent force and one of the dominant members of the committee of Council which debated the prospective bills for a Parliament at Dublin. Ormonde's principal agent in England was his old client Longford, who reported that Halifax, Radnor, Sunderland, and Louise had joined Essex as his enemies, and were determined to prevent such an assembly lest it give him a triumph. The Irish revenue farmers opposed the project also as the finance bills promised them nothing. Against them were pitted the arguments of Coventry, Jenkins, Finch, and Temple as well as old Arlington, and the King inclined to them. But with the approach of the English Parliament, Charles decided to play safe and to suspend the matter yet again. His only interventions in Ireland turned out to be purely negative. Although the whole point of calling a Parliament in Dublin was to supplement a small revenue, he continued to multiply demands upon that revenue. These could take a small form, such as a pension to Sunderland, or a gigantic one, such as the transfer of the upkeep of Tangier, under heavy attack by Berbers, from the English to the Irish budget. In mid-August Ranelagh suddenly reappeared at court, having bolted from Dublin when the Privy Council there finally cut through the thicket of his accounts and decided that he owed the state over £100,000. Charles remembered the Earl kindly for the fidelity which he had shown (and might yet show) to their private financial arrangements, and blandly ignored the charges which Ormonde sent after him. Meanwhile, on 16 September, Shaftesbury's 'informers' upon the 'Irish Plot' reappeared in London, now fourteen strong and complaining bitterly of the Lord-Lieutenant's behaviour. They were given shoes and settled down to perfect their lines. Ormonde's friends began to prepare for a defence against his impeachment when the Parliament met.[49]

Charles's personal involvement in all this activity had been spasmodic, most of his time being passed in the solitary occupations of fishing and walking, far from 'the hurry of the gay and busy world'.[50] It did not seem to occur to him that, with political tensions rising as Parliament approached, he might forgo the pleasures of Newmarket. Nor did he respond to the appeals of Jenkins, to return to Whitehall ahead of schedule to prevent his Council from behaving rashly. By post, he agreed with the Secretary's suggestion that an Irish Parliament be called to take Shaftesbury's 'Plot' off the agenda of the English one. He was still watching the races when, on 6 October, the Council decided instead to buckle to Whig pressure and have old Archbishop Plunket brought to England for trial. On his own initiative, Anglesey wrote to the Mayor of Gloucester who had gaoled a dissenting preacher. The Earl told him that the King's directions to persecute Protestant nonconformists were a sham, and that all Protestants should unite against the Catholic menace.[51]

Since July, then, the King's behaviour had shown a characteristic mixture of caution and carelessness, which could be mistaken by some observers for weakness. The same was true of his last great action before Parliament met, to send his brother back to Scotland. James had wanted to stay and face his enemies boldly, and Seymour, Hyde, Jenkins, and the leaders of the English Church were all prepared to support him. Together, these men mustered a majority in the Council. Charles, however, had been persuaded by Sunderland that the Catholic Duke would certainly be impeached by the new Commons. The King could not find Counsellors who denied this and Sunderland, Halifax, Godolphin, and Essex all implored him to send his brother to safety. Charles first pressed James to reconvert, and when this was again refused, he faced the Council and asked it if he should dissolve Parliament if the impeachment were tabled. This drove over waverers like Finch and Radnor to join 'the Triumvirate', and a majority of Counsellors voted against the idea on 16 October. Three days later, having promised not to assent to any bill against him and having ordered the Scots to prepare a joyous reception, the King waved the Duke off to Edinburgh. In the same week Charles met Monmouth for private conferences, apparently intended to woo the prince away from the Whigs. They were an utter failure, but news of them did make some people suspect that the King would not stand by James.[52]

A number of important courtiers decided at about this stage that it would be best if Charles did sacrifice his brother, thus at a stroke restoring a partnership with the full political nation. They included Sunderland, Godolphin, Essex, Anglesey, and the favourite royal mistress, Louise. The King's position was by no means desperate if he failed to take this course, for he had Ireland, Scotland, the Guards, the garrisons, and the Tories, who included a majority of local officers of most counties and towns including London. He did not need parliamentary supply to survive financially. This situation was due partly to ruthless economies, administered by a Treasury Commission now including Hyde, Fox, and Godolphin. Apart from shifting some items on to the Irish budget, the commissioners left many salaries and pensions unpaid, ran down the navy and fortresses, and had the King create unwaged posts in his Household. Overall, the civil expenses of government were reduced by more than half. During 1680 some of the extra duties granted by Parliament in the 1670s expired, but the buoyancy of the national economy prevented more than a slight net decline of revenue. Thus the public account was almost in balance as the MPs gathered.[53] So, the government's problem was not one of isolation or imminent collapse, but that it faced the opposition of an important section of the nation. For a year it had been trying to deal with this by soothing it away. Since the Whigs would not budge, they had either to be fought or given what they wished. Some, including Halifax, believed that matters might come to civil war and to individuals such as Sunderland and Louise, James was simply not worth that trouble. By spreading stories that Charles was secretly of their mind, they encouraged the Whigs, and increased pressure on the King, still further.

On 21 October, Charles opened the new Parliament, by boasting of his alliance with Spain and calling upon the Houses to secure the Church, investigate the 'Popish Plot' further, try the five Catholic lords still in the Tower, supply money for Tangier, and reunite the nation. He warned them plainly not to touch the royal succession and did not mention Danby. The response was utterly disappointing. Nothing was done for supply, nor to thank the King for his foreign policy. In their first week the Commons resolved to exclude James from the throne, informed the King that the true dividers of the nation were those who had advised him to postpone the session, and set about condemning individual Tories. The King's fury was patent to those around him, and he assured one Tory MP 'I will stick by you and my old friends; for if I do not, I shall have nobody to stick by me.'[54] He then set out to cultivate an air of stoical determination and to fight the Exclusion Bill with all his power. He appointed those of the Council's Committee for Intelligence who were MPs to report the Commons' debates to him in detail.[55] On the evening of 8 November he summoned the most important Counsellors and asked them to draft a message to the Lower House that he would pass any bills against Popery except that for Exclusion. Halifax and Hyde co-operated enthusiastically with this, and the King followed this initiative by writing to individual lords to ensure their attendance to fight the Exclusion Bill if it was set up. This it was, upon 15 November, without even a division in the Commons. Many who had opposed the same measure in the former Parliament, including Temple and Godolphin, now turned to it as a panacea for the nation's disagreements. So all now depended upon the Lords, and to make his feelings utterly plain to them Charles attended the entire debate, having his meals brought to him in a portable cabinet.[56] Aided by his great height, he put on a virtuoso performance of nods, smiles, grimaces, and scowls at each speech, crowned by his loud comment when Monmouth spoke of his solicitude for his father: 'It is a Judas kiss which he gives me.'[57] His presence was decisive. Finch was 'ill' upon the crucial day and Sunderland, Anglesey, and two lesser Privy Counsellors voted for the bill. But, led by the magnificent eloquence of Halifax, the rest of the Council turned out to oppose it and it was defeated by a large majority. Had it passed, the situation would indeed have been a grave defeat for Charles and perhaps caused a constitutional crisis. But it did not.

In their frustration and fury, the Commons blamed Halifax himself for the resolution which Charles had shown. But the Marquis complained to a friend in terms which most royal advisers might have used during the reign: that while the King 'seemed perfectly to approve of the counsel you give him, he hearkened to others from a back door'.[58] Observers named Hyde and Seymour as Halifax's colleagues in Charles's confidence,[59] but how far these men were 'influential' may be doubted. As a year before, having struck a posture the King favoured those who would support it. In Scotland, once again, James's letters reveal his sense of utter helplessness in the face of the events at Westminster, and utter lack of purchase upon his brother's actions.[60] He certainly had cause to complain after the defeat of the Exclusion Bill, when the Lords set to work upon alternative measures. Against one of these the King set his face (literally) as clearly as against Exclusion: a proposal by Shaftesbury to force him to remarry. But when Halifax revived the proposal of depriving a Catholic successor of most royal powers, for that monarch's lifetime, Charles accorded it a benevolent neutrality, and it went forward. Wilhelm as well as James expressed horror at even a temporary diminution of the Crown's rights, but the only comfort which the King offered in reply was that he would try to limit the damage as far as possible.[61] He adopted the same attitude to the trial of the first of the five Catholic peers accused of the 'Popish Plot', William Howard, Viscount Stafford. This man was selected before his fellows because the 'evidence' against him seemed most plausible and because of his choleric personality which had made him many enemies. The case was heard by his peers and Charles remained studiously aloof while Finch presided with a scrupulous regard for the law. Bereft of royal instructions, Council and courtiers divided over the issue, Halifax and Arlington believing the Viscount innocent while most of their colleagues disagreed, as did all but one Gentleman of the Bedchamber. Stafford was found guilty and, faced with this, the King ignored James's appeals and his own doubts and signed a warrant for the man's beheading.[62]

Thus far, Charles and the Whig House of Commons had fought a drawn battle. He had obtained nothing from the Parliament, and neither had they. His expectation, and that of the Tories, had been that the defeat of Exclusion would force them to turn to measures which all could endorse, and so bring about the reunification of the nation of which he had spoken. This they now set out to frustrate, by ignoring the project for limitations, and informing the King in repeated messages that they would do nothing for him until he abandoned his brother. They also demanded the dismissal of a succession of Tory Counsellors and courtiers. Charles's temper, and that of his Council, was further tried when the Dutch States-General sent him a message asking him to come to terms with the MPs. He responded by excluding the Dutch ambassador from his presence and forbidding his own man at The Hague, the Whig Henry Sidney, to forward any more such documents. Meanwhile, Shaftesbury's Irish 'witnesses' had delivered their tale to the Lords, who could understand their accents no better than the Privy Council had done. This slowed up the impact of their 'revelations', but on paper these proved plausible enough to persuade the peers to vote their belief in an 'Irish Plot' on 4 January.

For six weeks the King tried to continue sparring with the Commons. When they demanded the dismissal of Halifax, he replied that their reasons were inadequate. When they told him that Catholics were behind most of his government's recent measures, he put the address in his pocket and ignored it thereafter. Their message insisting upon James's exclusion, on 20 December, provoked him to call first the Committee for Intelligence, and then a full Council, to discuss possible replies. The debates went on in secret for two weeks, and Charles prepared Hyde to go to his brother with an ultimatum to abandon either Catholicism or his hopes of the throne. It may have been a mere threat, but it was not used. Instead, on 4 January, the King returned a simple refusal to the MPs. On the 7th the latter responded with further attacks upon royal advisers, and the Council resolved to prorogue Parliament for ten days to cool tempers.[63] The Commons were given fifteen minutes' notice of this decision, on the 9th, and the Houses had only one bill of political importance ready to pass, a measure to repeal a savage Elizabethan law against Protestant dissenters, which had rarely been invoked in Charles's reign. Finch and Halifax supported the reform. Nevertheless, it did not suit the King that nonconformists should obtain any relief from a Parliament and not from his own prerogative, and he prevented the enaction of the bill by a dirty and rather dangerous trick. He ordered the clerk to 'lose' it, so that it was not presented with others for his assent or rejection.[64]

For a week longer discussions continued in public and private about the next course to be followed, and then on the 18th Charles settled the matter by declaring Parliament dissolved and calling a new one to meet at Oxford. The latter choice served notice that if violence did result, it would be in a city easily dominated by the royal guards. Who advised him in reaching this decision remains a mystery. Once again, he merely announced it to his Council, and the action ran contrary to the opinion of most of its members. One of them, the Earl of Salisbury, tried to protest. When Charles silenced him, the Earl offered to resign, whereupon the King had his name struck off the register at once.[65] Charles followed this by a purge which served notice to the Whigs that he remained obdurate over the issue of Exclusion. Most who had voted for it were turned out of the Council and the Household, and also lost their posts in local government. Among those thus kicked out were Essex, Sunderland, Temple, and Macclesfield. It was typical of this King that he waved off Temple to a country holiday with expressions of kindness and that Sir William learned of his dismissal by post: Charles still kept personal unpleasantness to a minimum.[66] The vacant positions on the Council and in the counties were filled with Tory noblemen. To replace Sunderland as Secretary of State, James recommended Hyde's elder brother, the second Earl of Clarendon, while the King wanted Finch's heir. The old Chancellor, however, thought his son not yet ready for the burden, and in the end the office went to the Earl of Conway, who was proposed by Seymour and to whom nobody took exception. Thus, after ten years of observing and intriguing, this Anglo-Irishman at last came into his own.[67]

It has often been believed[68] that in proceeding in such a decisive fashion Charles's nerve had been steeled by the support of the French. This was not an impression which the French themselves possessed. During the course of the 'Second Exclusion Parliament', Barrillon admitted that he had totally failed to understand the English monarch, and that he might be capable of anything including abandoning his brother. The defection of such major figures as Sunderland and Louise strengthened this latter possibility in French eyes, and the ambassador began to worry that the English political scene might lose the Prince who was the firmest friend to both his nation and his Church. In late November, Barrillon sent Charles a message that Louis would now come to his aid, as the English sovereign had begged, so histrionically, a year before. To his amazement, the Frenchman provoked no interest, the King now having more serious things on his mind. Barrillon renewed his proposals, employing the man who long before had been the favourite courtier of Henrietta Maria, St Albans. The latter was now very aged and blind, but retained a hearty appetite for food, drink, gambling, and attempts to reconcile the Stuarts with France. By January he was forwarding to Charles an offer of about £200,000 if he gave up his Spanish alliance and his attempts to work with Parliaments. This was politely refused, and Louis ordered Barrillon to redouble his efforts to save James's succession. James himself begged his brother to accept the deal and to cancel the new Parliament called to Oxford. Barrillon raised the sum, asking in addition for the recall of the Catholic Duke and the relaxation of the laws against his co-religionists. Charles refused even to see him. As March came, and the King prepared to leave for Oxford, he agreed at last to a secret meeting in the Queen's apartments. There he appointed Hyde to discuss matters further with the ambassador, revealing who had become his most trusted adviser. It must have seemed sweet to him suddenly to be importuned by the French, for no effort of his own.[69]

Charles went to Oxford equipped with a symmetrical ideology of politics which he had developed during the previous two years. In the first decade after the Restoration, he had stressed the reconciliation of all previous parties, and all creeds, under the monarch. In the 1670s, as described, he had found it politically expedient to stress his role as defender of the established Church, but had not gone on from this to regard dissenters as his natural opponents. It was this latter step which he had now taken. In Scotland, he had treated presbyterians as political rebels from 1674 until 1679, qualified this attitude for a year, and then reverted to it in 1680. In Ireland he accepted that Protestant nonconformists were at once too numerous and too peaceable for persecution to be a wise policy, but in late 1679 he ordered an army brigade into their stronghold of Ulster, to overawe them and to cut their links with Scotland.[70] When he received the Whig petitions in January 1680, he began in reply to make explicit comparisons between the presenters and the Civil War parliamentarians who had fought against his father. At the same time, when nominations were being made to him for the vacant post of Attorney-General, he announced that he would never again give office to the son of a rebel, meaning an old-time parliamentarian or republican.[71] Just before he left for Oxford he attended a lunch party held by one of his Household officers, and told the guests that he would do his utmost to extirpate Popery. One of them replied 'Amen, and Presbytery too', whereupon Charles answered in turn 'With all my heart.'[72] It was a reversal of the ideology of the Restoration decade, and one which he must have known was based upon false premises, for some Whigs had a Civil War royalist background and many presbyterians had proved conspicuously loyal to the monarchy. But there it was: for the sake of political simplicity, former parliamentarians, former republicans, and present dissenters had all officially been turned into enemies of the Crown. Right up until the opening of the Second Exclusion Parliament the King had continued at times to talk of unity and conciliation, but now he fully appropriated the language of division for his own uses.

For once, he deprived himself of the pleasures of Newmarket, but was compensated in part by a trip to the horse-races and hawking country near Burford, Oxfordshire. On 14 March he entered the university city to a most gratifying reception. The elaborate panegyrics of the scholars were inevitable, but the townspeople, many of them youths, added their own enthusiastic plaudits. Some hung from the windows of the royal coach, shouting 'Let the King live and the devil hang up all Roundheads!'[73] Parliament opened on the 21st, with an invitation by Charles to the Houses to try the remaining Catholic lords and to act against their co-religionists, and to accept a new alternative which he was offering to Exclusion. The speech which he had originally drafted was longer and more acerbic, but the Privy Council had persuaded him to moderate it, and from the appreciative hum which it provoked, it appeared to have made a good impact. He did not specify the compromise which he was offering, but it was soon presented by his Counsellors in the Commons. He had talked excitedly of it for a month, as an expedient likely to satisfy everybody: its sponsors among his advisers were Halifax, Finch, Seymour, and Arlington. It proposed to establish a regency when Charles died, making his brother King in name but appointing Wilhelm and Mary as joint Protectors to rule in reality.[74] James was utterly appalled by the news, but Charles was almost as shaken by the reaction of the Commons. Despite all the government's efforts, and growing evidence of Tory feeling in the nation, the elections had returned a House as Whig as the last one. Its reply was to begin work on a new Exclusion Bill, while in the Lords Shaftesbury accosted the King and proposed, for the first time, that Monmouth be named as his successor. The little Earl did not trouble to revive interest in the 'Irish Plot' for this session, having a more convenient instrument to hand for the purpose of stoking popular hatred of Catholics. This was Edmund Fitzharris, himself an Irishman and a former agent of Louise's, who had originally intended to curry favour with Charles by accusing the Whig leaders of treason. On finding that this project threatened to misfire like the 'Meal Tub Plot', he changed sides and deponed against James, Louise, the Queen, and some Tories as conspirators inspired by Rome. The King reacted swiftly, placing Fitzharris in the Tower incommunicado before the session began. But the Whig Commons soon voted his impeachment, which if endorsed by the Lords would give him a parliamentary stage upon which to be heard.[75]

Three days before the session, Charles had concluded the last secret Anglo-French treaty of his reign. It has always been assumed that this was intimately connected with the King's attitude to the new Parliament, but the relevance is difficult to find. The talks between Barrillon and Hyde had culminated at Oxford in an agreement which left the King a completely free hand with the approaching assembly. It stipulated that Charles would receive about £385,000 over three years if he did not support Spain against France and call a Parliament for that purpose. It left him free to call one for any other purpose, and Louis promised not to attack the Spanish Netherlands, so that it seemed as if the Anglo-Spanish pact would not be invoked in any case. The Englishmen tried to add a French undertaking not to expand into Germany and in this they failed, but that, to the British, was not an area of vital importance. The Sun King seems to have thought that his cousin needed the money to survive without a parliamentary grant, and that he was saving James with it. We know now that this was wrong, and so should Charles have done: indeed, he did not ask for supply at Oxford. The French *livres* which would now be delivered were, in many ways, simply a gratuity.[76]

So the English monarch was left to judge the session upon its own merits, and these seemed very few. The Lords threw out the proposed impeachment, and would doubtless do the same to the new Exclusion Bill. But then, the Commons seemed as set into an attitude of intransigence as their predecessors, and on the 26th the Lords set up a committee to investigate the 'loss' of the bill at the end of the previous Parliament. The King's worsening humour was apparent. When Shaftesbury proposed Monmouth to him as an heir, he denied this (as expected) but also launched into another, public, attack on presbyterians, whom he described as ten times worse than the Pope. As evidence of this he cited his experiences among the Scottish Covenanters, choosing to forget the support of the Resolutioners whom he had remembered so fondly in 1660.[77] When the new Parliament was less than a week old, he and all his leading Counsellors met secretly in Finch's lodgings and decided, unanimously, that to proceed was pointless.[78] To avoid disorder, and also to humiliate the Whigs, the dissolution was sprung as a complete surprise. On the 28th Charles was carried to the Lords in a sedan-chair, his royal robes and crown concealed in it. He donned them in an antechamber and summoned the Commons as they gave the new Exclusion Bill a first reading. Stumbling up the narrow staircase to Christ Church hall, they were confronted by their monarch in his regalia, and heard him finish the Parliament with one sentence. He then lunched and drove away to Windsor, leaving the two Houses to disperse, watched by his Guards.

This moment has often been represented by historians as the end of the 'Exclusion Crisis', with Charles's 'triumph' over the Whigs. It was nothing of the kind. For one thing, as has been said, the situation of the government had never been 'critical'. For another, it was a moment of profound failure. Before the eyes of Europe the English sovereign had admitted his inability to work with his national assembly. He had proved himself to be the ruler of a disunited nation, incapable of pooling its strength in a communal effort. He had thereby demonstrated his incapacity, at least for the time being, to fight a foreign war. Only parliamentary subsidies could permit this, and his regular income merely allowed him to survive in peacetime by a narrow margin maintained by rigorous economy. Even this achievement had ultimately only been made possible by an upswing in the economy. Put like this, March 1681 was not a victory for Charles so much as a nadir.

And, of course, this unfamiliar verdict begs a familiar question: why did he bring himself to this, by standing by an unpopular brother and a barren wife? As has been pointed out many times, it could hardly have been from deep personal affection. He complained regularly (especially to Barrillon) of his brother's stupidity in adhering publicly to the Roman faith, and James had always been the sibling whom he had loved least. As for Catherine, it surprised courtiers when, in November 1680, he spent enough time alone with her for an afternoon nap.[79] Instead, it must be sensible to stress once more something that has often been said before: that the Whigs expected Charles to accept their demands, without offering anything concrete to him in exchange. Rather than tempting him, they tried to bully him. In this context, it may be useful to return to a much-misquoted remark of Barrillon's penned in July 1681.[80] Reviewing the previous two years and his conversations with Charles, the Frenchman hazarded the opinion that the English monarch would have passed an Exclusion Bill had its promoters offered him generous grants of money and not tried to gain control of the armed forces and other powers of the Crown. This was only the ambassador's guess, and not (as is often asserted) an admission by Charles himself. What is so interesting about it is that the Whigs did not, in fact, ever attempt to gain such control. It was the King, and the Tories, who offered it in the projects to limit a Catholic successor, while the Whigs wanted to pass on the royal prerogatives intact to a Protestant. It seems as if Charles had convinced himself that Exclusion was but a first step towards the dismantling of the monarchy, just as he seemed to be brainwashing himself into equating religious dissent with rebellion. His most recent biographers[81] have indeed explained his attitude to the matter by suggesting that he saw the right of descent as a prerogative in itself which, if tampered with, opened the way for the destruction of others. This is extremely likely, but, without claiming to read the King's mind, it may be suggested here that the Whigs' hopes may have foundered upon no less than three different traits in his personality, in proportions which we cannot ascertain. One was his sense of the sanctity of kingship, expressed in his sensitivity about the formal dignities of his office and his marked attention to the 'King's Evil'. As he himself had taken the throne because of his descent in blood, he may have felt a superstitious repugnance when invited to tamper with that descent to another. The second was his sense of family, sharpened by the experiences of exile. It has been suggested that this complicated his relations with Louis and Wilhelm. Perhaps his brother and wife were precious to him, whatever their failings, simply because they were his. The third was the appreciation with which he always tried to reward loyalty and obedience, and its converse, the hatred with which he regarded those who crossed his will, or failed him. James and Catherine always submitted to his wishes in all matters except their faith, while the Tories were the official incarnation of the qualities which he expected in subjects. By contrast, Monmouth and the Whigs came increasingly to represent disobedience and disrespect, and to treat him in a manner to which he had almost always reacted savagely. Only a fourth trait, his political caution, can explain why he continued to work for agreement for as long as he did.

Towards a New Way of Ruling, 1681–1685

IN retrospect, March 1681 was to mark a dividing-line in Charles's reign, between politics which were centred principally upon Parliaments and politics which operated without them. Historians have conventionally used that point to close the chapter titled 'The Exclusion Crisis' and open that christened 'The Tory Reaction'. The utility of the first term has been questioned before, and it may now be pointed out that the second phenomenon had been under way since 1679. To Charles himself, the dissolution of the 'Third Exclusion Parliament' did not, at first, seem to mark a change of eras. Not only did he tell the nation, in April, that he intended to call another Parliament soon, but he was sincere in this. His battle with the Whigs was as bitter as ever. Only with the passage of time did it become obvious that something had changed, and that a new system of government was, at last, emerging.

The winter of 1680–1 had left the King with yet another team of advisers. Towering over the rest were Halifax and Hyde, who duplicated to a great extent the relationship between Buckingham and Arlington a decade before. To many observers the Marquis was patently the chief minister and influence upon the government, and certainly Charles summoned him to comment upon all major issues. But, like that of the dissolute Duke before him, his power was more apparent than tangible. He held no great office, occupied only 'a little garret' in Whitehall, knew nothing of the secret diplomacy with France, and (as shall be seen) had remarkably little success in getting his advice followed. The King valued him for his intelligence and his stand over Exclusion, and his useful habit of telling people that he only supported Charles because the latter was the champion of the Church and the law.[1] Hyde made a less prominent and self-confident figure than Halifax, but was far more central to the administration. He had, of course, been Charles's only agent in the dealings with the French and continued to be so. In April 1681 he was rewarded with the title of Viscount and promotion to the head of the Treasury Commission. His appetite for work remained even greater than his appetite for drink, and when the Privy Council convened he was always found to be the first in the chamber, 'plodding' over accounts as the other Counsellors arrived.[2] Both extraordinarily capable and hot-tempered men, their political beliefs were fundamentally different. Halifax had many instincts in common with the Whigs. He wanted the King to rule in partnership with Parliaments, sympathized with Protestant dissenters, and had a visceral distrust of Catholics and the French. By contrast, Hyde was an aboriginal Tory, who cared not greatly how the King ruled as long as he maintained an intolerant episcopalian Church and the traditional social order. Yet, initially, these men co-operated very well.

A third force within the Council consisted of the partnership between Seymour and Conway, but it counted for less. Choleric, clever, and libidinous, Seymour somehow never managed to make much impression upon Charles, while Conway failed to exploit the potential of his new office of Secretary. This Earl has been the object of unmerited abuse by modern historians.[3] He certainly did not know much about the Continent, took a country holiday at an inconvenient moment, and on one day at Newmarket was too drunk to receive a deputation of city councillors. Yet his letters show intelligence and a pleasing wit. He did write dispatches as frequently as his predecessors, while an efficient clerk in London received incoming post and forwarded the most important items to him. There were times when he was the only minister whom diplomats or petitioners could locate in a hurry. Given his amiable personality, it is hardly surprising that Charles liked to keep him by his side while Jenkins, whom one observer described as 'a faithful drudge', manned the office at Whitehall. But Conway simply had no appetite for administration and no real ideas, so could make little impact.[4] Thus, although he and Seymour were the most aggressively ambitious Counsellors in 1681,[5] the administration in that year was essentially a team superintended by the King. The greatest honour was given to old Finch, who was elevated to the earldom of Nottingham in April. This was clearly a matter of gilding a figure-head.

During this spring and summer, indeed, Charles was much more concerned with levels of government below the Privy Council. In April the Chief Justice who had presided at Wakeman's trial, and been vilified by the Whigs ever since, was replaced. This was, however, to make way for a successor determined to demonstrate his loyalty to the King by helping to destroy Edmund Fitzharris, while the retiring man got a large pension and public thanks.[6] At the same time the replacement of JPs continued, and in the summer Nottingham, Halifax, Conway, Hyde, and Seymour were instructed to review and complete the process. How they obtained their information is unknown, though some Tory magnates certainly sent up suggestions, but the end result was impressive. A series

of new commissions in July and August left Tories dominant in every
English and Welsh county. Parallel to this was the remodelling of the
militia commands. For this, again, the central government depended to
some extent upon the advice of Tory worthies, and it tried to beware
of accepting it too uncritically. Charles took a personal part in this,
informing one Tory Lord-Lieutenant that he would do nothing until
he had discussed 'every particular man' in his lieutenancy with him. In
this and other letters it is obvious that local men, rather than the King
or Council, were forcing the pace in some purges, and perhaps in all. By
the end of the year the same magnates were sending up names for sheriffs,
but Charles was not sure how to act. Tory sheriffs were only desirable if
a Parliament was to be called, as they would make election returns, for
otherwise the job was a nuisance for its holder. As the King did not
know whether he wanted a Parliament or not in late 1681, he settled
for a compromise.[7] Appointments in the Church were handed over in
July to a commission consisting of Archbishop Sancroft, Bishop Compton
of London, Halifax, Hyde, Seymour, and Radnor. This probably had its
origins in a characteristic piece of royal carelessness, when in January
Charles agreed to Anglesey's plea to make one of his sons the Dean
of Exeter, without ascertaining the likely effect upon other churchmen.
Sancroft and the Bishop of Exeter protested furiously that the new Dean
was unfit for the office and its was apparently in response that Charles
promised not to make future appointments without the advice of the
Archbishop and Compton. It was this responsiblity which was widened
to include the lay Counsellors in July, and the commission set about
ensuring that sound Tories got the jobs, Sancroft and Hyde exerting most
influence.[8]

It was this team which carried on the struggle with the Whigs as soon as
the Third Exclusion Parliament dispersed. In April the government issued
a declaration justifying the dissolution, to be read in all churches. The
Whigs riposted by persuading London's Common Council, by a narrow
majority, to petition Charles to call a new Parliament at once and let it
complete some legislation. The government responded adroitly to this in
turn. The King asked for the names of all Common Council members who
had spoken against the petition, to congratulate them. Nottingham then
administered a ferocious snub to the petitioners upon his master's behalf,
which was printed with loyal addresses from London Tories.[9] Meanwhile
the work was progressing to make an example of that foolish crook
Fitzharris, still held in the Tower. Charles perused all the papers relating to
the case and then ordered his Attorney-General to prepare an indictment
for treason, and to ensure a Grand Jury which would endorse it. Jenkins

was given the job of keeping the witnesses 'sweetened'.[10] The principal of these turned out to be none other than the 'MacShams', whom Shaftesbury had brought over to prove the existence of the 'Irish Plot' and whom the Whigs had foolishly left underemployed. The government was only too happy to hire them, and their testimony was sufficient to send Fitzharris to the scaffold in July. With him had to go the wretched Archbishop Oliver Plunket. When Barrillon interceded for the Catholic primate's life, Charles replied smoothly that the matter troubled his conscience, but that as the 'MacShams' were witnesses against both men, he could not spare one without undermining their ability to destroy the other. He added that it might blight the Crown's reviving fortunes if he pardoned a Catholic condemned by law.[11] Plunket's trial had been a travesty, because he was not given time to fetch over friendly witnesses from Ireland, but nobody in England was much bothered about his fate: there are few comparable cases in our history of an utterly harmless man caught up in the wheels of politics and crushed. He received a curious compensation from his Church recently by being made a saint, although he did not really die for his faith and was a most unwilling victim. Because Charles returned his head and quarters to his friends, the former, withered and grey, survives today to decorate his shrine at Drogheda.

By the time of the double execution the government was hunting bigger game. On the very next morning Shaftesbury was arrested at dawn, and taken before the Council, which the King had just joined from Windsor. After interrogation he was committed to the Tower and preparations commenced to try him for treason, Halifax, Hyde, and Seymour all being equally active in this work.[12] Charles was now announcing to bystanders at court that the whole 'Popish Plot' had been a fraud, and personally asked that 'evidence' be found to indict Oates of blasphemy.[13] None, however, was forthcoming, and instead the dress rehearsal for Shaftesbury's fate was made the trial of a Whig propagandist, Stephen College. The legal problem confronting the government was that both men were said to have committed their crimes in Middlesex, where (uniquely) the sher-iffs were elected not appointed. These men chose the Grand Juries to consider indictments and both the current officials were Whigs. Thus, when College was accused at Westminster, the jury promptly threw out the indictment. The government took a petty revenge by having Jenkins arrest the foreman and bring him before the Council to be examined on suspicion of 'collusion' with College. A more effective response was devised by Halifax, Hyde, Seymour, Jenkins, and Conway, who between them advised Charles to have College retried at Oxford, where he could also be accused of having uttered treasonable words.[14] Jenkins wrote to the county's Lord-Lieutenant to empanel a Tory jury, and College was convicted and executed in August. However, when Hyde and Halifax talked to the judges about ways to get Shaftesbury tried out of Middlesex, none could be found. As the autumn came on, the government hired more 'witnesses' against the Earl and then got them to swear before the Council that they were not acting for profit. Charles denied to a Scots cleric that he had corrupted any of these men and quoted the proverb 'At doomsday we shall see whose arse is blackest.'[15] All this hypocrisy availed nothing; nor did a series of public invectives by the King against London's Whigs and in praise of its Tories.[16] On 24 November Shaftesbury appeared before a solidly Whig Grand Jury, which rejected the indictment against him. Charles made a great many self-pitying statements about the lack of justice in England, although at moments his attractive resilient good humour still resurfaced. When the Whigs struck a medal to celebrate their leader's escape, the King remarked that his brother ought to wear it instead of the Garter insignia.[17] Paid off, the 'MacShams' went happily home. Ormonde remarked sourly that having left Ireland 'with bad English and worse clothes' they had 'returned wellbred gentlemen'.[18]

By the end of 1681 the grip of the Whigs upon London was only one of the problems facing the government, for foreign policy had suddenly become a matter for urgent consultation once again. During the spring and summer Europe had seemed quiet enough to allow Charles and Wilhelm to meet and to take the measure of each other again. During the winter the Prince had, overtly, behaved perfectly from the King's point of view. He had formally disapproved of Exclusion, and even begged his uncle not to consent to limitations, as a bad precedent for the monarchy. But Charles was a little irritated that Wilhelm gave advice at all, and this sentiment strengthened when the Prince made clear his alarm at the dissolutions of Parliaments in January and March. To Wilhelm, few results were less desirable than an English monarchy unable to get parliamentary supplies and thus incapable of joining the next war against France.[19] Charles made a gesture of friendship in April by permitting the Dutch to recruit Englishmen to fill up English regiments left in their service since 1678. But this was negated when Wilhelm decided to appoint the English ambassador at The Hague, Henry Sidney, to command these units. Not only did he do so without consulting his uncle, but Sidney, being a Whig, was holding on to his post only on the very best of behaviour. Charles's response was to recall him, although without formal disgrace, and propose as his successor a man whom Wilhelm disliked, without asking the Prince's opinion in the matter as he had formerly promised to do. At this point Hyde and Halifax agreed that it would be best for English interests if the King and the Prince met and reconciled their differences swiftly. Charles listened to them and invited Wilhelm to visit him in July.[20]

Anxious to keep his French pension flowing, Charles (seconded by Hyde) assured a worried Barrillon that the talks were just a blind to cover the secret Anglo-French pact. It did not, however, require any effort from the King to render them abortive. Wilhelm had precisely the sort of personality which grated upon Charles: tactless, humourless, determined, and quarrelsome. His wishes were, moreover, unacceptable not merely to his uncle but to the entire present administration, for he wanted the King to call a Parliament, come to terms with the Whigs, and send an army to the Netherlands. He hinted that the Dutch fleet might blockade the Thames if Charles refused. The King appointed Halifax, Hyde, Seymour, Conway, and Jenkins to confer with the Prince and the Spanish and Dutch ambassadors.[21] All these Englishmen rejected Wilhelm's proposals, and in August the Prince had to go home, gracelessly, with an assurance that Charles would summon a Parliament and declare war upon France if Louis invaded the Netherlands.

The English monarch had, of course, his cousin's promise that he would do no such thing, which Charles described to Barrillon in July as 'the foundation of our union'. Nevertheless, the treaties of 1678 had left the Franco-Spanish frontier ill-defined at certain points in the Netherlands, and in mid-1681 Louis began to claim the districts left in dispute. Formally, the English King had his ambassador in Paris deliver a protest with the Dutch, while informally he and Hyde begged the French to compose the matter peacefully.[22] The matter hung fire during Wilhelm's visit, and still did so as Charles went off to Newmarket in September. It was the English King's fortune to suffer nasty shocks while at the horse-races, and the pattern held on this occasion, when Jenkins forwarded a message from the Spanish ambassador that Louis had declared war upon Spain. This was an exaggeration. It turned out that the Sun King had occupied the 'free' city of Strasburg in Alsace and given Spain six weeks to sign over the border districts in dispute. Charles found it difficult to get worked up about Strasburg, a distant place to which Louis had some legal claim, but the Dutch, Spanish, and Germans were all understandably more agitated. The English government was in no position to wage war, and its King grumbled that he 'did not care to show his teeth when he could not bite'. Formally, he warned Louis to leave the Netherlands alone, and privately he begged him to do so.[23] In fact, the French sovereign was no longer greatly interested in his northern frontier, but determined to strengthen his eastern one to the point of risking war. In October his soldiers surrounded the Spanish-owned city of Luxemburg, situated where France, Germany, and the Netherlands met. This, he announced, would represent an acceptable compensation for the disputed districts.

In reacting to the ensuing international crisis, Charles found himself surrounded by conflicting constraints. He did not want to lose his French pension. He did not want to call a Parliament to obtain war funds, or to risk being cajoled by continental allies into menacing France and then being abandoned, as in 1678. But nor could he suffer the loss of face at home and abroad consequent upon doing nothing while Louis went onto the offensive. Thus the weeks leading up to Shaftesbury's indictment were also spent in frenzied manœuvring to escape from this trap. Charles was slightly hampered in this by the fact that he had now no representative at The Hague, as he had left the choice of Sidney's successor to Wilhelm as a gesture of conciliation, and the Prince had named nobody. Still, the States-General did send him a batch of envoys, empowered to discuss a guarantee of the Treaty of Nijmegen by their two countries and Sweden. The King empowered Halifax, Hyde, Jenkins, and Conway to discuss the project, and it was soon apparent to the Dutch that the Englishmen were prepared to protect the Spanish Netherlands, but that none were keen upon guaranteeing the German provisions of the treaty, which hardly affected English interests. The whole Privy Council discussed the issue into November, when it resolved upon a formal reply. In this, Charles promised to call a Parliament if France attacked the Netherlands, and to enter a league to guarantee the whole treaty if Denmark and the major German powers did so. It was a sensible position to take. Meanwhile, the King was bombarding his French cousin with appeals to withdraw from Luxemburg. Instead, Louis secretly offered him £77,000 on top of his pension if he helped the French to obtain it. After weeks of discussion, Charles and Hyde accepted this, but only on the condition that the walls of the city were razed to render it militarily useless. The French were happy to make this proposal, and Charles devoted December to pressing his cousin to make him arbitrator of his claims on Spain (enhancing his international position) and to allow food into Luxemburg. In both these projects he was successful, having convinced Barrillon that if the city fell he would be forced to call a Parliament by the public outcry. By way of reciprocity he accepted Louis's wish when the English government agreed to a Dutch request for a joint protest against the blockade and the French insisted that it be delivered separately.

For all these efforts, by January 1682 the circle of options seemed to be narrowing further. Charles had sent diplomats to all the German princes to discover if they were interested in a league against France, and none would make firm commitments. The Spanish refused to cede Luxemburg under any conditions, and they and the Dutch pressed him to call a Parliament and declare war (without yet having done so themselves). On the 21st, Charles invited his leading Counsellors to discuss these requests. Halifax now supported them, but Hyde, Jenkins, Seymour, and the majority preferred caution. The deadlock continued, and by March the English monarch was convinced that war was coming because of the inflexibility of his would-be allies. He blamed Wilhelm bitterly for having encouraged them. The Spanish were considering plans to coerce him by suspending trade with England. Faced with this appalling situation, Charles went off to Newmarket to console himself, and for once was the recipient of miraculously good news while there. On the 21st he heard that Louis had called off his army, and referred the whole dispute to his cousin's good offices.[24] The French King gave as his official reason the fact that the Turks were advancing upon Austria, and he wanted to free the attention of the German powers to deal with them. Charles and his ministers anounced that it was their pressure which had forced the French back, and Charles's biographers have accepted this. The Spanish preferred to give credit to the Dutch efforts. Wilhelm's principal biographer ascribes the action to Louis's fear that his cousin actually would be forced to call a bellicose Whig Parliament.[25] The author of the standard life of Louis himself states firmly that the great Frenchman had been distracted by the prospect of becoming Holy Roman Emperor if Leopold went down before the Turks.[26] None have firm evidence to buttress their cases, and it seems that we shall never know to what Charles owed his escape. He had not got the extra £77,000, but the regular pension continued, he had not suffered disgrace, and he could now regain the initiative in domestic affairs.

At Newmarket, he received not only glad tidings but a welcome visitor, his brother, who returned to England for the first time in seventeen months. Every one of those had been spent by James fretting to get back, and the knowledge of his feelings provoked intense, if obscure, debate in England. James himself thought that his true friends upon the Council were Hyde and Jenkins, with Seymour and Conway well-disposed but cautious, and Halifax, Nottingham, and Radnor determined to keep him in Scotland. In early summer the King debated the issue with Hyde, Halifax, and Seymour and decided to let him return once Shaftesbury had been convicted. All of them agreed to try out the threat which had been mooted in the winter, of telling James to revert to Anglicanism or expect to be abandoned. It failed. With the survival of Shaftesbury and the prospect of a Parliament to deal with the Luxemburg crisis, the leading ministers at last sharply divided. Halifax felt that it would be needlessly provocative to fetch James home at such a time, while Seymour and Hyde advised that the moment had come to get the Duke back for a direct confrontation with the Whigs. Charles, true to character, took the cautious way. In the end, James's reappearance was almost an accident. If we can trust his own statement, the King's mistress Louise, anxious to rewin the Catholic Duke's goodwill, persuaded the King to let his brother meet him briefly at Newmarket. Once there, James aroused such fraternal affection in Charles that, in the more relaxed atmosphere following the French withdrawal, he was allowed to remain.[27]

Behind him he left a Scotland in which he had consolidated his standing. Its nobles had asked for a Parliament to provide further funds for the army, and Charles, having denied his brother so much else, was happy to appoint James his Commissioner to it. His prominence was accentuated by the fact that Rothes, having worn himself out with dissipation, died just as the session was about to open, leaving the Duke to ask loyal old Atholl to officiate in his place. Formally, the King instructed his brother to get himself declared heir to the Scottish throne and to obtain new laws against dissent. Secretly, he empowered him to declare anybody whom he wished a rebel and to break up any conferences of public men of whom he did not approve. Such extreme measures were not needed, for with little debate the Parliament voted the money, recognized the Duke's claim to the throne, and produced an Act imposing a declaration to preserve Church and State upon all office-holders. Charles was transported with joy when he heard of his brother's recognition, but the new Scottish Test had unforeseen consequences.[28] Five noblemen, including Hamilton, expressed scruples about the wording of the declaration. Four of them eventually made it when they were on the brink of losing their offices, but the fifth, the Earl of Argyll, not only refused it but attacked it on constitutional grounds. As a result he was tried, and condemned to death in December, amid much rejoicing on the part of Scots who felt that Lauderdale's favour had, once more, allowed the Campbells to grow overmighty. James had certainly not contrived this result, having protected Argyll against his enemies in the summer. Neither he nor his brother sought the Earl's life, and on hearing of the sentence Charles instantly had a pardon prepared. But Argyll did not wait for it, for he escaped from prison, reached London, and then slipped across to Holland. His actions provoked a fierce debate at Whitehall. James was by now furious with the Earl and wanted his estates confiscated. To put his view he sent down Charles, Earl of Middleton, son of the great leader of the early 1660s and a rising courtier who, having served as a diplomat, had become a favourite of the Catholic Duke. James wanted him to replace Lauderdale's man Moray as Secretary of State. Opposing Middleton, Halifax and Lauderdale argued that Argyll was a loyal servant against whom the Scots had massively over-reacted. Most of the English court agreed, and Charles compromised. He did not order a search for the fugitive Earl while he was hiding in London, and let the Campbell estates pass to his son. But he shared out Argyll's jurisdictions among other Highland chiefs and offered him no pardon. Nor did he make Middleton Secretary.[29] A bare few weeks after this affair had been settled, James was back in England, with another massive vote of confidence from the Scottish Church and laity.

With him came a bevy of important Scots, intent upon having the new leadership of their nation settled after Rothes's death. Their determination grew more marked when it became apparent that the Duke of York would be staying in England. On the whole, Charles was content to follow his brother's advice in the matter. To the fury of Atholl in particular, and the Scottish aristocracy in general, James chose as Chancellor a mere gentleman, Sir George Gordon of Haddo. Gordon came from impeccably royalist lineage and was a distinguished lawyer, but nobody could remember when the seals had been held by somebody neither a noble nor a prelate. It was obvious that the Duke had selected a man totally dependent upon himself, and nobody was much impressed when, after some months, the new Chancellor received the title of Earl of Aberdeen. To balance him, James had the far more distinguished and respected Queensberry raised to the rank of Marquis and made Lord Treasurer. This promotion led Queensberry in turn to vacate the post of Justice-General, and into this was put the Earl of Perth, chief of the Drummonds, who had opposed Lauderdale in 1678 and was now friends with Atholl, Queensberry, and James himself. As part of the latter's plan to reconcile the Scottish leadership after the divisions provoked by Lauderdale's rule, Hamilton and Tweeddale were restored to the Privy Council, and young Middleton added to it. All the new officers got generous pensions, and Atholl received one as a consolation prize. Thus equipped, they returned north in May.[30]

It is difficult, at this distance, to distinguish Scotland's new leaders by traits of personality: they all seem hard-faced, ambitious, and energetic. There was a rift within them, between Aberdeen and the rest, but in 1682 it was concealed as they united to destroy Lauderdale's brother Charles. The waning of the great Duke's influence had left the younger Maitland increasingly isolated, holding the plum job of Treasurer-Depute. With Queensberry as his new boss, it was easy to organize an enquiry into Maitland's administration of the Mint, which of course found irregularities. James knew that the wretched man had served him well, and was loyal to the Crown and the bishops, but with the rest of the Scottish government so determined on his ruin, James could not be bothered to save him. Both royal brothers acted in character. The Duke of York encouraged Maitland to leave London for Scotland with assurances that he would be safe. The Treasurer-Depute (correctly) distrusted this and enlisted his once-mighty brother's good offices with the King, who avoided the problem by bolting down the back stairs when both arrived to see him. The ailing Lauderdale read the signs and abandoned his sibling. He then died, suddenly in August. Charles Maitland lost his job, some lands, and the right to inherit the ducal title. The office went to John Drummond of Lundin, a cousin of Perth who was as young and avid for promotion as Middleton, and had also recommended himself to James. Lauderdale's posts were shared out between Perth himself, Middleton, and Queensberry. His place in the Order of the Garter was sought by both Louise and Nell Gwyn for their sons, but James persuaded Charles to use it to gratify Hamilton, who was thus wholly reconciled to the regime. Finally, to cope with both his own tastes and the renewed importunities of his brother, Charles made Moray and Middleton joint Secretaries of State.[31] With this, the new rulers of Scotland settled down to size each other up and to prepare for a new struggle for supremacy.

The year 1682 saw the end of two great figures of Stuart Britain. Lauderdale was one. The other was Prince Rupert, who died in November. His final years had been embittered not only by an ulcerated leg but by a conflict between loyalty to his royal cousins and sympathy with the Whigs. His last public action, in July 1681, had been to leave the Council Chamber rather than sign the warrant for Shaftesbury's arrest. Yet a third towering personality of the same vintage not only continued in power but became even more prominent. This was Ormonde, who, like James, re-entered English politics directly in this year. For the previous fourteen months he had looked on while the seemingly endless question of the Irish revenue was debated in England. One aspect of this consisted of the last stage in the pursuit of that wily quarry, the Earl of Ranelagh. The latter had sought to secure himself in early 1681 by an alliance with Seymour (who shared his taste for womanizing as well as for politics) and with that other disreputable courtier, Louise. None the less, in July the combined pleas of Ormonde, the Irish Privy Council, and several (nameless) English Counsellors, pushed Charles to renew the enquiry into the slippery Earl's acounts. In October a new commission of the Dublin Council reported a total of £93,000 unaccounted for. The King's reaction was a classic compromise of the sort to which his nature tended: he dismissed Ranelagh from his post of Vice-Treasurer in March 1682, but ordered that the amount he owed be written off in compensation. Thus both monarch and Earl sidled out of the predicament, leaving the latter at court to await a time when his genius for manipulating money and pleasing royalty would be called upon again. Even as all this was going on, Ranelagh was performing a great service for Ireland by thwarting the schemes of a fellow crook, Sir James Shaan. Honour, it appeared, might exist among thieves, but sympathy among rival thieves was in short supply. In June 1681 Charles had called the English Treasury Commission and his chief English Counsellors to Windsor to discuss projects to improve the Irish public finances. One submitted by Ormonde's son Arran was considered and rejected. Then the King coolly produced another from his pocket and placed it before the meeting with his blessing. This had been given to him in private by Shaan, another Anglo-Irishman and a financial speculator who had farmed the revenue under Ranelagh since 1676. It is easy to see why Charles warmed to him, for in exchange for complete power over the Irish Treaty he and his partners promised to pay for all the current expenses plus Tangier, and ship a surplus to England. What Ranelagh pointed out afterwards, when the star-struck gathering had given support to the offer, was that Shaan had not actually explained how he was going to do all this. All through the winter, as his own enemies harried him, the Earl harried the man who promised to be his successor in fraud. The arguments were still going on as Ormonde arrived.

He came because James and Hyde, who regarded the old Duke as a natural ally, wanted him at court to bolster their own position. The split that had developed between Hyde and Halifax over foreign policy and the recall of James had developed into the beginning of real enmity. The Marquis had started to work for a reconciliation between Charles and Monmouth as soon as it was plain that the heir presumptive was staying in England. In May 1682, therefore the royal Duke and his supporter first persuaded the King to call Ormonde over, then to get him to marry his grandson (and heir) to Hyde's daughter, and then to honour him with an English dukedom. Soon after the greatest Anglo-Irishman arrived, the affairs of his homeland suddenly began to be settled one after another, in ways which had little to do with the Duke himself. First, in July, Hyde suddenly lost patience with Shaan because he had still not provided any detailed breakdown of his project. The English Treasury Commission decided, with Charles's concurrence, to have the Irish revenue managed directly by a fellow commission. The resulting body was a model of checks and balances, consisting of Ormonde's client Longford, two friends of Ranelagh, and two protégés of Hyde. All were experienced financiers, some English and some Anglo-Irish. They were entirely responsible to the English Treasury, but their instructions were redrafted by the Irish Privy Council and they immediately determined to have no money sent to England. The whole Privy Council in Dublin expected them to fail, but instead they set to work in 1683 with wonderful efficiency, and within one year had pushed receipts to record levels. Next, in May 1683, somebody proposed to Charles that he set up a royal commission to remedy defects in the Irish land settlement, in the way that a Parliament had been intended to do in 1678–80. The King asked the opinion of the Irish Privy Council, who cautiously agreed and sent a draft proposal which was amended successively by the English law officers and Treasury Commission. In March 1684 it was sealed, empowering the chief officers of the Irish government to check titles to land and to issue new patents to all. They were soon doing a roaring trade, and by the end of the year were giving general satisfaction. Another great issue of contention seemed to be evaporating, as a result of genuine co-operation between London and Dublin.[32]

On arriving at court, Ormonde grumbled to his son Arran that the royal mistresses, ex-mistresses, and their children were too numerous and 'overdignified'. He also told him that he intended to waste no time paying respects to Louise, who was still the most prominent of this ménage. Yet a few months later he reconsidered, commenting that since the pretty Breton could not be removed, use might as well be made of her.[33] These remarks between them sum up the position of the 'alternative' royal family in the 1680s. There had been no additions to it since 1672, and it was slightly depleted by the disgrace of Monmouth and the death of 'Don Carlos', the Earl of Plymouth. This poor lad, trying hard to win military glory by joining the Tangier garrison, had died there of dysentery in 1680.[34] But the King continued to establish his remaining sons as illegitimate princes, making Richmond Master of the Horse and Grafton colonel of a Guards regiment and Vice-Admiral, while Richmond and Northumberland both got the Garter. In January 1684 old St Albans died at last, and Nell's son Burford got his title with the rank of Duke. Ms Gwyn herself remained in favour, with lodgings at Westminster and Windsor and substantial grants from the Exchequer.[35]

But the supremacy of Louise also remained absolutely patent, and from 1682 she functioned almost as an alternative queen. She entertained ambassadors to sumptuous banquets, at which several of Charles's children were guests. Louis XIV made her a Duchesse and sent her rich presents. The King fondled her in public in a way that he had not done before, and went to her apartments to relax among the company there after his meals. When Halifax expressed resentment of her in 1681, Charles forced them to a public reconciliation as if they were feuding ministers. Her influence had proved negligible in the matter of Exclusion, but it has been described how she played an important part in bringing back James to court. Henceforth she was his close ally, both being Catholic and supporters of the French interest, and together they could be very potent, as shall be illustrated.[36] Again, the King's reputation suffered from his extramarital attachments, most notably in late 1683 when observers from Halifax downwards believed that Louise was deceiving him with the Chevalier de Vendôme, Grand Prior of France. The rumours were sufficient to enrage Charles, especially when the cheeky Frenchman ignored his orders, first to stay away from her and then to quit the country. Only the threat of being escorted out by the Guards induced him to depart, leaving behind him the nation's gossips convulsed with mirth or indignation.[37] It has been claimed that the Queen was content and comfortable with her husband's other loyalties,[38] but this is manifestly untrue. In April 1683 she rounded upon Charles at Windsor and told him that his mistresses dominated him while she was humiliated. Showing as much dignity as gallantry, he went straight to Louise's apartments and complained of the incident to a gathering there. In May 1684 the great mistress amused herself by insinuating herself among Catherine's maids and waiting upon the Queen at dinner. Catherine broke down and wept in public.[39] Her husband may not have repudiated her, but her lot was hardly happy.

Thus, by a process of interaction, James, Ormonde, and La Kéroualle all moved closer to the centre of political affairs in 1682. And the same process restored a fourth figure, the brilliant adventurer Sunderland. The latter, since his grievous error over Exclusion, had never lost his friendship with his partner in that error, Louise herself. She nagged both the royal brothers to obtain forgiveness for him, while Sunderland himself cultivated Hyde and grovelled to James. Charles himself was probably missing the Earl's smooth manners and quick wits, and when his brother asked for his reinstatement it followed swiftly. In July he was received at court, in September he re-entered the Privy Council, and in January he was made Secretary of State once more. Conway got a large pension and the promise of succeeding Arlington as Lord Chamberlain, and retired apparently well satisfied. As things turned out, Arlington survived both Charles and Conway, for the latter died suddenly only seven months later.[40]

The former Secretary was one of three individuals displaced by this regrouping. A second was Anglesey. Ever since 1680 he had been an anomaly on the Council, being to all intents and purposes a Whig. He had voted for Exclusion, remained friends with Monmouth, Shaftesbury, and Essex,[41] and preserved a sympathy for Protestant dissenters. When the

King was absent at Newmarket and the Privy Council thinly attended, he persuaded it to order the Mayor of Bristol not to persecute nonconformists: a furious Charles subsequently had this countermanded.[42] That Anglesey survived as long as he did was due to the lack of importance which the King attributed to him. But the royal patience wore out in early 1682, when Charles heard that the Earl had published a history of the Irish civil war of the 1640s which was unflattering both to Charles I and to Ormonde. It was one of the few books which the King troubled to read himself, and it left him snarling. Just after his return, Ormonde formally accused Anglesey in Council of defamation. The Earl, as in 1668, made matters worse for himself by denying the authority of the Counsellors to proceed against him, and he was duly stripped of the Privy Seal in August.[43] Charles intended at once to employ the office to build up a counterweight to the formidable faction which was growing around Hyde. Courtiers confidently expected that Seymour would be made Lord Privy Seal and a baron, while Halifax was promoted to a marquisate. Seymour himself was so certain of this that he sold his existing post of Treasurer of the Navy to clear time for his new duties. Instead, Halifax begged for both the office and the marquisate and Charles gave them to him. Seymour was horrified, and immediately started intriguing for another post by persuading the aged Radnor that the King wanted him to retire from his position of Lord President. Charles got wind of this, reassured the doddering old Earl, and expressed his displeasure to Seymour. The latter flew into one of his characteristic passions, stormed away from the court, and thereby completed his loss of favour.[44] Thus a third figure was removed from central politics. The former Speaker's petulance almost certainly prevented him from sharing in the bonanza of honours which the King provided in November 1682, whereby eleven individuals received new peerages or promotions of title. Nine were Tory magnates who were being rewarded for service in the localities, but one was a client of James and another was Hyde himself. To balance Halifax's elevation, he was advanced to the earldom of Rochester. A final alteration occurred in December, when Nottingham died. Competition for his place was fierce, but eventually the seals were entrusted to Sir Francis North, a judge not associated with any faction and respected by all. In September 1683 he was made Baron Guildford, with the full title of Lord Chancellor.[45]

There seems no reason to question the traditional view that, having restored his self-confidence by holding out against the Whigs, Charles was now deliberately balancing his ministers against each other. The hatred between Sunderland and Rochester, on one side, and Halifax, upon the other, was patent, and the King fostered it. In January the new Marquis paid back Rochester for befriending Sunderland and trying to make Seymour Lord Privy Seal, by accusing him of conniving at frauds in the Hearth Tax collection. The new Earl was cleared by an inquiry, but aghast that his royal master had let him be attacked at all. Privately, Charles reassured Halifax that he would never reward Rochester for his patient work on the Treasury Commission by making him Lord Treasurer. The King also resisted pleas by Louise and Sunderland to admit James to policy-making discussion, and he encouraged Ormonde to act as a conciliator rather than reinforcing his brother's faction as James had expected. Despite their divisions, the Royal Counsellors still functioned well as a team. It was the logic of his situation, not the advice to which he listened, which made Charles follow the policy favoured by James, Rochester, Louise, and Sunderland, of avoiding a Parliament, remaining friendly with France, and encouraging intolerant episcopalians and former royalists.[46]

The solidarity which the new governing team could show to external observers was illustrated by the continuing contest with the Whigs. After the disaster of Shaftesbury's trial, this focused upon control of the officers of London. Feeling there continued to move in Charles's favour, more Tories than Whigs being elected to the Common Council in December 1681 and crowds welcoming James back to the city in April. The militia, which the King controlled through Tory deputy lieutenants, watched the streets nightly to prevent disturbances. Charles himself worked off his feelings by singing a ballad composed by one Thomas D'Urfey, holding part of the script while the composer held the rest. In the song, the Whig sheriffs were described (among other things) as thieves, rats, baboons, cuckolds, and Jews.[47] The current Lord Mayor, though not a Tory, was a pliable man in awe of the Crown. Thus all bid relatively fair for the great trial of strength in June 1682, the election of the new sheriffs. The King called the existing officers several times before the Privy Council to warn them not to resist the return of Tories. Ormonde dined with the Mayor two or three times a week 'to keep him fixed', while Jenkins dined with a selection of City Tories, and most of the ministry ate with the Tory candidates. The result of all this political gastronomy was a riotous meeting at which both parties declared their men elected. Charles had come down from Windsor for the event. He immediately called the Mayor and aldermen before the Council, and after hearing them the Counsellors committed the existing Whig sheriffs to the Tower. A new election in July duly returned the Tories, and the Guards reinforced the militia to keep order as the latter took office. In September the election of the new mayor came round. Charles went off to Newmarket saying that if a Whig were elected he would overrule the decision and continue the existing mayor. This threat had a very dubious basis in law, but (mercifully) it was not required in practice. The Bishop of London ordered his clergy to campaign for the Tories, the Council warned keepers of ale and coffee-houses that they would lose their licences if they allowed Whig meetings or tracts on their premises, and Tories in the corporation disallowed many Whig voters as unqualified. A full-blooded Tory was duly returned. Control of the sheriffs now meant that the King could get Shaftesbury tried and convicted. Faced with this, the little Earl fled abroad, where he collapsed and died.[48]

So, Charles had won, but, as Ormonde pointed out, the victory could be reversed later unless lasting control was gained over the whole City corporation.[49] This was the next step. As soon as Shaftesbury had escaped indictment, in 1681, the King had asked whether the validity of the charter might not be challenged by a writ of *quo warranto*. In the winter of 1682–3 he reorganized the Court of King's Bench to secure new and compliant judges who would unanimously declare that the charter was defective and had to be surrendered. This, in June 1683, they did. Halifax tried in private, and without success, to persuade Charles to delay this verdict to allow for further negotiation, but in public the government preserved a united front. From October the Mayor and aldermen were reconstituted as a royal commission to run the city, once the Whigs among them had been removed. In early 1684 writs of *quo warranto* were issued against all livery companies, Tory or Whig, and they were given new charters in turn, naming the chief officers and purging them of religious dissenters. The capital was now firmly under Crown control, making even the goodwill of the Tories not strictly necessary.[50] Yet this success gave the King no inclination to spend more time in the metropolis. In 1682 he formed the resolution of spending a month at Winchester every year in early autumn before going to Newmarket. The climate, the hunting, and the horse-racing there all suited him, and he resolved to build a palace. Thus his sequence of provincial retreats was further elaborated.[51]

But then, Charles had special reason for feeling uncomfortable in 1683. In mid-June, as the King was at Windsor, awaiting the judgement upon the City's charter, a messenger panted up from the Privy Council in London. Jenkins had been approached by an oil merchant and a brewer, who told him, in frightening detail, of a plot which had been formed to kill both royal brothers during their return from Newmarket that spring. It had been foiled, they said, only by the return of the court to London in advance of the projected date. Charles and James moved to Whitehall to interrogate the informers personally, and the Council began making arrests on the 23rd. It soon became obvious that two plots had been discovered, the murder project, discussed by former Cromwellians from London of insignificant social and political rank, and a scheme to overpower the Guards and seize custody of the King, mooted by leading Whigs. For the first of these, three men were hanged and for the second Lord Russell and Algernon Sidney were beheaded, and John Hampden heavily fined. Essex, to everybody's surprise and horror, cut his throat with a razor in a latrine rather than face trial. In this sordid and tragic way died the high-minded statesman, who had endeavoured so much good for both Ireland and England. It has been recently agreed that both conspiracies were genuine, although there is less evidence for what the royal brothers and courtiers certainly believed, that but for accident they would have been implemented. The confessions left Charles very melancholy and prone to unusual security measures: he took attendants upon all walks and barred St James's Park, his normal London promenade, to the public. He seems to have found it genuinely shocking that anybody would want to kill him. Under these circumstances his behaviour was very restrained. He asked examiners no leading questions, and did not allow informers to 'remember' details later. Although he pardoned nobody who was convicted, he commuted the sentences of Russell and Sidney from the more horrific hanging and quartering. As with the executions of 1681, he generally let the families of the dead have their heads and quarters for decent burial. Although entitled to Russell's estates and Essex's chattels, he left both to their families. The only burst of his occasional vindictiveness came when a messenger allowed one Whig noble to escape from his custody. Charles ordered that the wretched man be put in a dungeon at the Tower where mud and water came up to his waist. He was only removed to better conditions when the Lieutenant of the Tower reported that he was dying.[52]

One additional reason for the King's melancholy must have been that his son Monmouth had been implicated in the plot to seize power. Since 1680 their relations had been, overtly, very bad. When the young Duke congratulated Shaftesbury upon his acquittal in 1681, Charles removed his last remaining offices. When James returned to court, Monmouth declared that he would never submit to him, whereupon the King forbade any courtier to have dealings with his son. Charles remarked with fervent bitterness upon young James's spurious claims to legitimacy. The prince retaliated with a tour of Cheshire to encourage the Whigs there and woo the populace. The government arrested him on his return, the King refusing to see him, and tried hard to gather information to convict him of seditious activities. But none could be found and he was released. And

yet, through all this bickering Charles's paternal affection remained patent.
He ensured that his son received regular payments from the Treasury to
help him subsist, and when a play was written in July 1682, satirizing
Monmouth, the King forbade its performance.[53] From the time that James
of York returned to court, also, Halifax was always seeking an opportunity
to reconcile father and son and so bring the young prince back to court
as his ally.[54] When the news of the plotting broke, Monmouth asked his
father whether he was under suspicion. Charles, with his penchant for
crude sayings, replied that if the Queen went daily to a brothel then
he would be justified in believing her a whore. So, as his son kept bad
company he must be presumed party to its schemes. But when the Duke
reponded by hiding at his mistress's house in Bedfordshire, although the
Council knew perfectly well where he was,[55] he was left in peace. In
November Halifax at last engineered the reconciliation, the young Duke
apologizing to both his father and uncle and being received again at court.
The King wept with joy—until Monmouth refused to admit publicly to
the reality of the plot and so worsen the position of his Whig friends. Then
Charles's mood changed to bitter anger, and he called his son a 'beast and
a blockhead' before sending him from court again. In January 1684 the
prince was summoned to give evidence against Hampden, and fled to the
Netherlands.[56]

Who gained by the 'Rye House Plot', as the two conspiracies have been
known to history? Charles's government certainly benefited as a whole, for
the news of it, carefully publicized, produced a series of loyal addresses
and demonstrations. The arrests and trials broke the Whig party. But
individuals did especially well out of the affair. One was James, whom
the King readmitted both to the Privy Council and its 'inner ring' of policy
advisers which was becoming known as the 'cabinet council'. Charles felt
that since his brother had also been a target of the would-be assassins,
he deserved to be brought back into government, and in the revulsion
of feeling against the Whigs no voices were raised in protest.[57] James
had further cause for rejoicing in seeing his rival Monmouth once more
in exile, and Halifax's scheming thwarted. The Marquis suffered another
defeat shortly after. He had urged the King to follow the destruction of
his opponents by calling a Parliament, especially since, under the terms
of the 1664 Triennial Act, he was legally bound to do so in March 1684.
James, with his instinctual dislike of Parliaments, advised his brother to
ignore the Act, relying on the same swing of feeling towards the Crown
to prevent an outcry. His allies supported this, and to Charles it seemed the
less risky course.[58] True to his nature, he took it, and there was, indeed no
public reaction. But there were four other notable beneficiaries from the

Plot than the Duke of York. They were Danby and the three surviving Catholic peers charged with the 'Popish Plot' (one having been executed and one now dead) who were still in the Tower. Since 1681 Charles had repeatedly asked the judges whether he could grant Danby bail, and as repeatedly they had denied the legality of this. In February 1684, given the new security and confidence of the government, James implored his brother to release his co-religionists, while Halifax, still trying to find allies, asked the same for Danby. Eventually the two of them combined, with James's friends Rochester and Sunderland, to press for all four to be granted bail. When the judges again protested, the King just bullied half of them into reconsideration and ignored the other half. And so the four prisoners at last found liberty, and the judges showed signs of a decline in power comparable to that suffered by the Privy Council.[59]

There was one important group apart from the Whigs which was injured as a consequence of the Plot's exposure: Protestant dissenters. In Scotland the persecution which had been resumed in 1680 intensified during the following years. The more extreme presbyterians were further alienated by Parliament's positive endorsement of a Catholic successor, while the new Test forced more clergy out of the Kirk. This broadening of the basis of nonconformity only inspired James's new team to more rigorous repression, with an intensification of fining and the quartering of troops. The confessions of the plotters in England revealed that a parallel rising, under Argyll, had been discussed in Scotland. A series of arrests, with torture of suspects, followed, and between these and the general escalation of state terrorism, the year 1683 saw more executions than the aftermath of the rebellion of 1679. By the end of 1684 immediate death was ordered for any who denied royal authority, and gaol for all who denied that of the bishops, while the last ministers brought back into the Kirk by the Indulgences were deprived. With Charles's full blessing, 'the Killing Time' had begun. The Scottish bishops ensured that one of them regularly visited the King to tell him of the wonderful results which violence was achieving. There was nobody at court to contradict them, Hamilton, the former spokesman for moderation, being silenced by his new honours.[60] In Ireland, Ormonde slowly began to toughen his attitude towards Protestant dissent. In July 1682 he instructed the bishops to announce that the laws against it were to be enforced, though he told them that in practice they should still overlook peaceful worship. But when news of the 'Rye House' conspiracy broke, he ordered his son and deputy, Arran, to repress nonconformity vigorously. All over Ireland ministers were bound over and meeting-houses closed, while units of the army were quartered in presbyterian strongholds in Ulster. By 1684 the policy that was nominally in force was the same as that in Scotland, and only the relative restraint and good sense of both sides prevented the bloodshed which was now commonplace in the northern kingdom.[61]

In England, likewise, Charles intensified the campaign against dissent. In part, this was the product of abstract principle: nonconformity was restrained by a set of statutes, and by ordering the observation of these the Crown could appear as the defender of the law as well as of the Church. But, as described earlier, by identifying dissenters with Whigs Charles was encouraging an actual association between the two which would inflame further his resentment of the former. In September 1682 he was furious to note that many London Quakers campaigned against his candidate for the post of Mayor. In his public pronouncements he began to use the term 'fanatic' interchangeably to describe radical Whigs or Protestant nonconformists. Accordingly, from 1681 onward, he and the Privy Council repeatedly called for the execution of the penal laws, praised magistrates who responded, and rebuked those who did not. Any man ambitious for royal favour now knew that he might obtain it by turning savagely upon the local presbyterians, sectaries, or Quakers. The persecution which followed was, for all these groups, the most sustained of the reign and, indeed, in history. In his directives, Charles informed officials that to tolerate nonconformists would mean a rebellion by them leading to a new civil war. At the same time his attitude to the original war became more explicit. When the people of Taunton celebrated the anniversary of the relief of their town in 1645, as they had done for thirty-eight years, the Council ordered the Mayor to punish them for commemorating 'the crime of that place'.[62]

The laws of the land, to which the King was now so ostentatiously devoted, were of course even harsher to Catholic than to Protestant nonconformists. On the other hand, having become convinced that all the people convicted of the 'Popish Plot' had been innocent, Charles was guiltily aware that the English and Irish Catholics had already suffered far beyond their deserts. The tensions produced by this situation are visible in policy-making during the last years of the reign. In November 1682 Ormonde reported to his master that friars in County Clare were insolently flouting the laws against their activities. The King's reaction was to ask that news of their behaviour, not the behaviour itself, be suppressed. Ormonde decided on his own authority to have their leader arrested as well. The next year he ordered prosecutions elsewhere in Ireland to reassure Protestants, and to avoid touching Charles's conscience upon the matter he simply did not inform him of it at all. In January 1685, some Irish Catholics complained to the King that their chapels in

Dublin had been closed, whereupon he mildly asked the Lord-Lieutenant for information. The reply was that it was good policy to shut the chapels if Protestant conventicles were also being dispersed. Charles's likely response to this remains an open matter, for he did not live to read it.[63] But events upon his own side of the water suggest that he would have accepted the situation. The English Privy Council had continued to urge the persecution of Catholics until the return to court of their champion James, after which their fate was left to local inclination. This was not nearly good enough for the royal Duke, who put considerable pressure upon his brother in late 1684 to release many of those in prison. Sunderland supported him loyally in this, and the King put the issue before a 'cabinet council' in October. There Sunderland, Rochester, and Jenkins all called for an end to the persecution of English Catholics, opposed by Halifax and Guildford. Charles said that he wanted to relieve those who had served himself and his father during the Civil War and Interregnum (something which he had said repeatedly at the Restoration). Halifax agreed that this was just, and Guildford pointed out that individual pardons were quite legally practicable. In January 1685 several Catholics with a royalist past were freed in this way, though Charles still proceeded more slowly and selectively than James had wanted. Essentially, he had taken a middle course in the matter, which most of his Counsellors endorsed.[64]

This intense preoccupation with real and imagined domestic opponents was made easier by the absence of any further crises involving foreign policy. It has been traditional to assume that during his last years Charles was happy to conduct his diplomacy by reference to the wishes of his French paymaster,[65] but things were a little more complicated than that. The English King had emerged from the events of 1681–2 with a deep resentment of the Spanish and Dutch, including Wilhelm, for having tried to coerce him, and a gratitude to Louis for having resolved the crisis and honoured Charles with the position of arbitrator. The Spanish immediately compounded these sentiments by refusing to accept his arbitration. In late 1682 they offered to change their minds if his awards were not binding and if the French frontier with Germany, as well as with the Netherlands, was the subject of the discussions. All Charles's trusted Counsellors, including Halifax, who was still the proponent of co-operation with France's enemies, were unwilling to go that far and grew furious with Spain. Their irritation, and his, worsened when the Spanish administered a series of insults. In December they ejected the English ambassador from Madrid and in June 1683 a Spanish fleet surrounded an English warship off Cadiz and shot away its rigging until it gave a salute.[66]

In these circumstances, English policy consisted of a patient insistence upon avoiding involvements. Charles continued to talk to the Dutch, but refrained from concerting measures with them, either against France or to intervene in rivalries between the Baltic powers.[67] When Louis demolished the walls of Wilhelm's ancestral possession of Orange, as a personal insult, his English cousin made a formal protest to Barrillon but refused to present a joint one at Paris with the States-General. Privately, he told the French ambassador that the affair was a trivial one and that Wilhelm deserved humiliation: this probably reflected his true feelings.[68] In the following spring, the Prince of Orange sent a Dutch fleet to the Baltic to support Sweden in the current squabble there. He did not bother to consult the States-General, annoying many of its members even as he irritated Louis, who had decided to send a squadron to help Denmark. The French monarch asked his cousin to let these ships shelter in English harbours in case of storms. James and Sunderland supported this request, but the other Counsellors were doubtful of the effect upon public opinion. Charles decided to give Louis permission, but only on condition that the squadron passed swiftly and avoided all contact with English ships. This it did, and the need to enter harbour never arose.[69] Denmark, searching for more allies, offered a commercial treaty to England, cemented by the marriage of James's younger daughter Anne to the Danish King's brother George. Charles commissioned Sunderland and Rochester to negotiate this, but there is no evidence that they pressed him into agreeing to it, or that any other royal adviser objected. The benefits to English trade were clear, and Prince George was a Protestant prepared to live in England. The marriage, performed in July 1683, turned out to be notably happy, and the husband to be a plump, jolly, and simple man with no interest in politics. With his usual Rabelaisian good humour, Charles instructed him in public to 'walk with him, hunt with his brother and do justice on his niece'. But when the Danes followed this success by offering a military alliance, it was utterly refused.[70] A further dramatic manifestation of the policy of disengagement was the abandonment of Tangier. English historians have invariably spoken of this as an attempt to improve the English finances, ignoring the fact that since 1680 it had been paid for by Ireland. But the Irish revenue itself needed consideration, and the port had proved of little value to trade, was difficult to defend, and was now constantly blockaded by Berbers. In December 1682 James, Sunderland, and Rochester persuaded Charles to get rid of it by selling it to Portugal or Spain (even they realized that offering it to France would create a dreadful impression). It turned out that neither of the Iberian powers wanted it, and in August 1683 the decision was taken simply to evacuate the inhabitants and demolish the town, which was done the next winter. Though the work of James's faction, the decision was opposed only by Halifax among the Counsellors, and that not because of the intrinsic worth of the place but because of the likely effect on patriotic opinion. In the event, the news was received with apparent equanimity in the nation, and the action seems to have been a sensible one.[71]

By late 1683 Charles was pointing out to the Dutch that, with the Emperor fully preoccupied with the Turks, the other princes of Germany unwilling to act, and Spain so weak, the only sensible outcome to the Franco-Spanish dispute was for the Spanish to cede the territory concerned. This was in fact no more than common sense, and the States-General refused Wilhelm's plea for more expenditure upon his army. In the event, Spain reacted with a heroic idiocy which nobody had quite expected: its government refused to yield an inch, and in December it declared war upon France. The Anglo-Spanish treaty of 1680 had been purely defensive, and so Charles was not required to lend assistance. Nor, of course, did he, apart from permitting the Spanish to recruit in Ireland. Neither did any other power intervene. Louis took Luxemburg in the summer of 1684 and pronounced himself satisfied, offering his European neighbours a twenty-year truce after which the final status of his recent acquisition would be decided. Charles supported this proposal, as did the most important German princes and Dutch cities, and in June Louis formally agreed to work for it with the States-General. In August Spain and the Emperor accepted it, and an indefinite peace was given to western Europe. The English King, of course, declined to act as a guarantor of the treaty when the Spanish invited him to do so. The French pension had expired in early 1684, but Charles redoubled his private protestation of devotion to Louis, fearing (as Barrillon came to learn) that the French and Dutch might draw together again.[72]

It was Wilhelm, not Charles, who was left high and dry by these events, having lost credit in both the States-General and the English court. On learning of Anne's marriage, he asked to come over to England again for consultations, and was refused point blank. Charles snarled to James that he did not want his nephew trying to push him around again. At the time of the twenty-year truce, the Prince of Orange compounded his offence with his uncles by giving a great welcome to Monmouth and making him his guest. Furious remonstrances from both the King and his brother produced no effect, and by October 1684 Charles was telling courtiers that he now believed Wilhelm to have been party to the 'Rye House Plot'. Given his present situation, it might be suspected that the Prince of Orange had welcomed the Whig Duke simply from pique. Yet the Governor of the Spanish Netherlands and the Elector of Brandenburg both gave hospitality to Monmouth as well, and when English diplomats protested they were told that Charles's affection for his son was so notorious that he was presumed to be shamming anger. That Wilhelm believed this also is indicated by the fact that he sent the young Duke away as soon as Charles died. In the winter of 1684–5, while formal relations were embittered, agents of Wilhelm kept passing to Whitehall for private talks. It is possible that foreigners simply misjudged the King's feelings towards his erring offspring, but it could equally be the case that Charles's tendency to seek double insurance, to run rival lines of policy, was at work again. Was he saying one thing in public and another in private? The evidence does not permit an answer.[73]

The removal of any risk of foreign war made it all the easier for the English government to celebrate a parallel development, a steady improvement in the finances. In the years 1681–5 all the main branches of the revenue showed increased receipts, and despite the expiry of the last supplementary grants of the 1670s the total annual income reached £1,370,000. In the same period the national debt was reduced by nearly £½ million, the margin for this work being provided by keeping expenditure down to £1,175,000 per annum. Most of this improvement resulted from an increasingly healthy economy, consequent upon the way in which the King had kept his realms out of war. But some was the consequence of improved administration. During the early 1680s the Treasury Commission was given control over all departmental spending, and direct collection of the Excise and Hearth Tax was resumed as the farms expired.[74] The crucial moment in this latter process came in April 1683, when all the more important Counsellors came down to the Treasury with Charles to debate whether or not to farm out the Hearth Tax again. Halifax was strongly in favour of this, perhaps simply because Rochester was not, but Radnor, Ormonde, Arlington, Jenkins, Sunderland, and the King himself were all swayed by the arguments in favour of direct collection.[75] In this, they turned out to be perfectly correct. Because of the Glorious Revolution, and the intelligence of his writings, historians have tended to warm to Halifax, while regarding James's friends with suspicion and dislike. It is worth pointing out that the advice of the Marquis upon both financial and foreign affairs in the early 1680s was unsound and might have been disastrous. It is a tribute to caution and common sense on the part of Charles and most of his Counsellors, rather than to the influence of a sinister clique upon a pliable King, that it was not followed.

The King himself was delighted by the upturn in his financial fortunes, and during his last year he often dropped in at the Treasury to look at estimates and dispositions:[76] how much of these he understood it is impossible to judge. His newly learned frugality, though adequate to the situation, was only relative. Louise's apartments continued to fill with French tapestries, Japanese vases, ornate clocks, and gold and silver vessels. The new palace at Winchester, so blithely ordered, was to cost £36,000. Money saved by direct administration of the army's pay was at once reallocated to founding Chelsea Hospital for crippled soldiers, an idea put forward by Charles himself, in emulation of Les Invalides, the foundation of Louis XIV.[77] But the most significant item of expenditure which he could now afford was a standing army. When Tangier was evacuated, the Irish units serving there were sent home to reinforce their own homeland, while the best regiment, a body of Scottish infantry, was shipped to London. In October 1684 the King appointed a review of it, with the various Guards units, on Putney Heath. The event itself was a failure, heavy rain causing the court and other spectators to withdraw, but the number of soldiers mustered was noted: six thousand.[78] This was quite a powerful striking-force, capable of dealing with any foreseeable form of domestic unrest, and supported entirely without the need of further parliamentary supply. What role Charles envisaged for it, and whether he observed any political implications, we cannot now say. If he had any plans, then they are obscured by his death as completely as the autumn rain veiled the parade at Putney.

So we come, at last, to the cluster of riddles which hang over the final year of Charles's life. Over thirty years ago, John Kenyon provided a complete answer to these by suggesting that policy-making was controlled by James and Sunderland, who initiated a series of developments.[79] These were intended to produce a much more powerful monarchy in all three kingdoms. In England, they got themselves and their clients into still greater power in government, and directed a policy of repression which included the remodelling of many borough charters to give the Crown control of membership. James obtained the recall of the Scottish Parliament to pass Acts confiscating the property of those accused of treason and fled. He prepared to meet it himself, as Commissioner. In Ireland, James and Sunderland obtained the replacement of Ormonde as Lord-Lieutenant by Rochester, while reserving to the King and a Secretary of State (meaning Sunderland) power over military appointments. This was used at once to commission Catholics as army officers. To Professor Kenyon, Charles's complete passivity is shown by the affair of the young Earl of Clancarty, one of the greatest Gaelic landowners. This lad had been sent to Oxford to be educated as a Protestant. In December 1684 the King allowed him to be removed from the university, furtively married to Sunderland's daughter, and then permitted to return to Ireland, where he reverted to Catholicism.

Professor Kenyon's views have been challenged directly twice. The first time was a decade ago, by Lady Antonia Fraser, who stated that Charles's continued vigour was not that of a monarch in decline, and that he himself initiated James's policies because he considered that the time was ripe for them.[80] Very recently J. R. Jones[81] has also declared that all political initiatives came from the King, who was intent upon an unadventurous and safe existence. He asserts that the only significant development was in Ireland, where Charles had the limited objectives of helping old royalists and removing old opponents. Of these three authorities, only Professor Kenyon has considered all three kingdoms and underpinned his ideas with extensive research. Nevertheless, my own conclusions correspond most closely with those of Professor Jones, although the events concerned appear more complex than had been thought before, and the influences upon both the King and his advisers more significant.

It must be said at once that there are three major, and celebrated, bodies of material which support Professor Kenyon's view and may have conditioned it. One is the dispatches of Barrillon, who relied heavily for his knowledge of court politics upon information given by his natural allies, James's faction. The second is the later *History* of the Whig Gilbert Burnet, who represented an evil brother working upon a pliable King. The third is the memoirs of James himself, which survive only in a form glossed by a loyal follower years afterwards. All, it can be seen, may be suspected of distortion, but this suspicion does not in itself invalidate them. Nor can much be surmised from Charles's own comments on his brother. The King continued to say unflattering things about James's intelligence and aptitude to rule. A playwright claimed later that he had come across the two having a quarrel, in which Charles said that he wanted a quiet life with no dangerous policy changes, and James stormed out. But, as Professor Kenyon points out, these may have been no more than 'the ramblings of a querulous old man'.[82] To judge the truth of the matter it is necessary to dissect the policy initiatives one by one.

Let us deal with Scotland first. There the new men installed by James did not view themselves as the agents of a master who would also control the King. They hoped to control James himself, and through him his brother. They succeeded in the first part of this scheme and failed in the second. The royal Duke promised Queensberry and Aberdeen not to put anything before Charles unless they had sent or vetted it, and they produced a series of requests for grants and titles which James readily endorsed. But Charles seemed almost to take a perverse pleasure in refusing them.[83] All that the chief men in Scotland did secure was a further narrowing of power at the top. In late 1683 they persuaded the

Duke of York, and through him the King, to let all policy be proposed by a 'secret committee' of the Scottish Privy Council and submitted to the two Secretaries and through them to the royal brothers. This body consisted of Aberdeen, Queensberry, Atholl, Perth, John Drummond, and two others. Having got it established, Queensberry, Perth, and Drummond allied to destroy Aberdeen, just as they had joined Aberdeen in ruining Maitland the year before. The new Chancellor had never been forgiven for his relatively low birth, and had no powerful friends other than James himself. In 1683 John Drummond went down to court for the purpose of misrepresenting Aberdeen to the Duke and undermining his credit. The process took six months, being applied slowly but relentlessly and assisted by Middleton, and by early 1684 it was complete. James now believed that the Chancellor was too unpopular, incompetent, and unreliable to be maintained, and Charles, who had only accepted the man on his brother's recommendation, was happy to drop him. Too late, Aberdeen came to England in May to defend himself, trailed by Queensberry and his clients, who thus reinforced his enemies at court. Finding a chilly reception, the wretched Chancellor went home, leaving the spoils of his defeat to be divided. Perth got his great office, Drummond became a Secretary of State for Scotland, and Queensberry was made a Duke. So was the Marquis of Huntly, chief of the Gordons and the greatest Scottish Catholic magnate. Observers credited James, naturally, enough, with his elevation, but in fact this too was the work of Queensberry and the Drummonds, who had made the Gordon their ally. The Privy Council was reconstructed to throw out Aberdeen and his few supporters on it. The next, and obvious, stage of this political gladiatorial contest was for the Drummonds to turn on Queensbury, and this slowly commenced. But first there was some other mopping up to be done. It was the 'secret committee' in Edinburgh which proposed the recall of the Parliament in order to confiscate estates, especially of Scots implicated in the 'Rye House Plot'. The same committee drafted the necessary measures and instructions for James. Both royal brothers agreed upon the practical necessity of the step, and the royal Duke scheduled his departure for 15 February 1685.[84] So, Scottish policy in 1682–5 was made more from Edinburgh than from the court, and of the royal brothers it was James who functioned more as a puppet for others.

In England the changes began with a Secretary of State. For some time Jenkins had been very 'slow in business' and by late 1683 he was frequently too ill to attend to any. His replacement had become necessary, and in April 1684 his post was given to Godolphin. James and Louise both supported him, but Charles was already sufficiently impressed by his talents. He had not, after all, dismissed him from the Treasury even after he had voted for Exclusion.[85] In May the King terminated the Admiralty Commission which had existed since 1679, in theory resuming their powers himself but in practice delegating them to his brother. This, of course, increased James's importance but was also a matter of practical efficiency. The royal Duke had been a popular Lord High Admiral and was welcomed back by the navy, while the Commission had grown so quarrelsome and detested that its supersession or reconstitution was necessary. Charles's personal way of balancing his brother's growing power was to allow him to be 'very familiarly used' by guests at private suppers which James did not attend.[86] Just as he had let Clarendon and Arlington be mocked behind their backs in their days of influence so now he exposed the Duke to such treatment.

The dramatic alterations which followed in that summer had their origins in the personality of Rochester. Over the previous two years the King's one-time confidant had become ever more discontented and cantankerous. He had a point, for he was the mainstay of a Treasury Commission dwindling because of deaths and transfers. Increasingly, the burdens of the Commission's work fell upon him and he grumbled about the lack of appropriate reward which he was receiving. At times he spoke of resignation. To bolster him, Sunderland and James sent him frequent encouragement while Louise aided them in trying to get him first the Garter and then the post of Lord Treasurer. Instead, in July 1684, Charles took the advice of Halifax to remove some of the work from Rochester and to provide a balance of factions upon the Commission by enlarging it to include clients of Halifax himself and of Guildford. Rochester and all his allies were naturally horrified, but the King took this as an advertisement to the world of how little he was controlled by any one faction. At this, Rochester himself drove James, Louise, and Sunderland almost crazy with tantrums and threats of retirement. To pacify him, they persuaded Charles to give him first a grant of royal land and then the honorific post of Lord President, from which old Radnor was at last retired with a pension. This carried virtually no duties, gave Rochester formal precedence over Halifax, and appeared to be very much what the tired and crotchety Earl had been waiting for. Halifax affected great delight at seeing his rival transferred to a position of little practical importance, but James's group saw it as a defeat for the Marquis and believed that Halifax himself had asked Charles for the office now granted to Rochester. To fill the vacant position at the head of the Treasury Commission, both the royal brothers agreed that the experienced Godolphin was the only man. That in turn created a need for a new Secretary of State. Here James had a candidate, Rochester's brother Clarendon, but Charles utterly rejected him. The King turned out to like a range of other candidates no better, and in the end he decided to transfer Middleton, already Secretary for Scotland, to the English position. Intelligent, generous, and superficially easy-going, and by upbringing an Englishman, the young Earl was equally liked by both brothers. Godolphin was made a baron, to encourage him in his new responsibilities. Finally, the King invited into the 'cabinet council' one of the new judges, an energetic and ferocious London Tory called Sir George Jeffreys. The man had been recommended to Charles by James and Sunderland. The King was initially worried about promoting him over the heads of his colleagues but during the summer of 1684 Jeffreys's services made him a favourite of Charles himself. The 'cabinet council' stood in need of another sharp lawyer, and so the judge was admitted in September.[87] Thus, in sum, it can be seen that the King was receiving advice from different quarters and, in the last analysis, following his own inclinations. If James and his allies tended to get more of their protégés into posts, it was simply because their men were both more numerous and more talented than the clients of others.

One of the services for which Judge Jeffreys was promoted was his encouragement of the surrender and regrant of borough charters. It was a systematic intrusion of royal power into municipal government of a sort never known before. At the time of Charles's death fifty-one new charters had been issued since 1681 and forty-seven more were in the process of preparation. Recently, a body of excellent work has been carried out upon this subject, and we now know a great deal about how the policy towards the boroughs developed and how local politics promoted it. What has been left mysterious is who, among the governing team, was responsible. It appears to have been a gigantic effort by the central government, with nobody in particular behind that effort. All the 'cabinet council' approved of it, and many were directly involved in it either through virtue of their offices or because of local influence. In 1689, after the 'Glorious Revolution', the House of Lords investigated the process and recorded that all the new charters in the winter of 1684–5 were 'procured' by the Secretaries, Sunderland or Middleton. This, however, need reflect nothing more than the peculiar administrative importance of their posts.[88] Charles himself took a direct interest in only two cases: that of London (of course), and that of York, whose corporation he never forgave for having snubbed his brother in October 1679.[89] Overall, the story of the charters went as follows.[90] In 1681 the government contented itself with rejecting a Whig town clerk where a charter allowed it to do so, and encouraging the election of Tories as mayors or recorders. In January 1682 Jenkins said that the Crown would claim no more powers in future charters than before. But that year changes began. In most cases there were indeed no novelties, but in one the King gained the right to approve aldermen, in another the right to remove them, while three others empowered him to eject the steward, the clerk, or JPs. In early 1683 two charters were at last issued which allowed the Crown to remove any of the corporation. Until 1684 this formula was interspersed with one limiting the power to the principal officers, but thereafter a general right of removal became the rule. In the winter of 1684–5 there was a great acceleration, thirty-one charters being renewed between 1 November and 31 January, and the surrenders procured of thirty-four more. Charles's death effectively halted the process. It had left more than a third of the parliamentary boroughs untouched, including some of the greatest Whig strongholds. Indeed, many of those given new charters were dominated by Tories. The result of such a new charter was not necessarily a purge. Some corporations were left unchanged, more lost one of two obdurate Whigs, and a few suffered several deprivations.

What is one to make of this? Perhaps the role of central government seems so mysterious because we are looking at it from the wrong angle. The proper perspective could be from below, from the localities. Something revealed by the recent research[91] is how much the campaign was powered by Tories concerned with the communities involved, whether councillors, bishops, peers, gentry, or garrison governors. To these people a change of charter was at once a way of getting rid of local opponents, gaining a few extra privileges for a town, and (by encouraging a writ of *quo warranto* and then manœuvring the surrender of the old charter) gaining credit at court for themselves. The member of the court itself who was most active was Charles's Groom of the State and agent at the Restoration, the Earl of Bath, who obtained the surrender of twenty-one charters in Devon and Cornwall. This, a record individual effort, at once confirmed his credit with the King and consolidated his own grip on the south-west. Such a process would explain the erratic progress of regrant in the years 1681–4, in which the contents of charters varied so much and the Crown's legal officers often behaved more cautiously than local Tories wished. It would explain the incomplete nature of the whole exercise. The sudden acceleration of the process in late 1684, and the standardization of the powers claimed, may perhaps be attributed to Jeffreys. In the summer he rode the northern Circuit, and made a habit, as no judge or Privy Counsellor had done before, of urging corporations to seek royal favour by offering up their charters. His impact was compared to that of the trumpets upon Jericho, for he returned having obtained fourteen surrenders. Charles was so little concerned in the campaign that the judge had difficulty in finding times in the King's schedule when the charters might be presented to him. Yet the royal pleasure was obvious and marked by his promotion of Jeffreys to the 'cabinet council' to use his legal skill there in 'vigorous resolutions' to be taken. These, it seems, can only be the systematic policy of challenges to charters which followed swiftly, and was applied wherever it seemed that a surrender could easily be obtained. Again, local politics probably determined the pattern, the difference now being that the government actively encouraged the process and it snow-balled. Certainly, the idea for such an exercise had arisen since Ormonde returned to Ireland in August, for in September he wrote asking for details of the 'standard' new charters being proposed. He intended to issue them to Irish boroughs when the opportunity arose.[92] One thing can be said with certainty: that James was not greatly concerned with the issue. He did not refer to it in his chats with Barrillon, and on his accession to the throne it died away as he found more pressing concerns.

By contrast, the Duke was greatly interested in the developments in Ireland. To the end of his life, Charles could never identify personally with his western realm. When loyal addresses from Dublin and Cork were read to him in 1682 he found them a subject for amusement and got his Secretaries to discourage any more, on the grounds that declarations from places so 'out of the road' were of little propaganda value.[93] But he did like Ireland to be well run, and to be a source of strength to him. In the early 1680s he had seen how two major aspects of its government, the revenue and the land question, had been greatly improved by closer co-operation between Dublin and Westminster. This left the army as the major problem requiring attention. The increase in the revenue provided Ormonde with an opportunity both to increase and to remodel it as he had long wished, without waiting for a parliamentary supply. It was he who repeatedly drew the matter to the attention of the royal brothers. In July 1683 he discussed his plans with James and that December he gave a list of proposed regi-ments to the King. Characteristically, Charles lost it and Ormonde had not kept a copy, but during the next year the plan went ahead. The size of the army was increased by a fifth and a proper regimental structure imposed by the time that the Lord-Lieutenant returned to Dublin.[94] He had been wishing to go back for a long time, and was happy when, in June 1684, he finally received permission to do so. If he had played little part in the developments concerning the fiscal system and the land settlement, it was because he had never, from the 1660s, understood the technicalities of these. But the reform of the army was very much his business, and he also retained during his stay in England the essential ability to get his clients in Ireland titles and plum jobs.[95]

None the less, he should have been given ample reason for unease. In 1680 the King commented that too many Irish offices seemed to be held by absentees or children. In 1681 he asked for a clean sweep of all sympathizers or friends of the Whigs from the Dublin Privy Council and army. He suggested names but left the job to Ormonde. The Lord-Lieutenant apparently ignored both royal suggestions. At times Ormonde's son and Deputy, Arran, was himself worried by the behaviour of Privy Counsellors, such as when, in 1683, he discovered that one, Lord Massarene, was not only protecting presbyterian meetings but was attending them. Yet father and son preferred to remonstrate gently with such offenders and try to keep their cases from the royal ear. Before Ormonde left court, both royal brothers complained that they had heard that Irish army officers kept returning false musters, and that military stores were poorly kept. Charles also believed that commissions were being sold to the highest bidder. The old Duke did not take these stories seriously, in which he was possibly correct, but he attached equally little weight to his master's concern, which was foolish. He should have remembered a letter which he had written to Charles in 1681, saying that he would soon be too old to fulfil his duties, and that when that became apparent he asked to be replaced. In the summer of 1684 he was prostrated by grief because of the death of his wife. He might later have recalled that such a private tragedy had afflicted Clarendon, forcing him to suspend business in a fashion which helped persuade the King to dismiss him.[96]

In that same summer somebody drew the conclusion that these affairs could, if properly handled, be used to suit both James's principles and his friends. The germ of the idea may have arrived at court in the brain of that resourceful adventurer Richard Talbot, the Catholic Palesman who had once enjoyed the favour of the royal brothers. Talbot's imprisonment in 1678 had been ended after some months by permission to go into exile. In 1683, with the 'Popish Plot' long exploded, the English 'cabinet council' allowed him to go home to Leinster.[97] From there he reappeared in England a year later, full of the accounts of corruption which so worried Charles and James. For those who wished to utilize them, however, Talbot's word alone was not enough. The man most directly concerned with the Irish army was Arthur Forbes, Lord Granard, an old royalist who was responsible for the training of the soldiers and would lead any expeditions which they might make. He had been friendly with Argyll, and since the latter's disgrace had been dreading that the association might have tainted him. His nightmares seemed to be coming true when, in the late summer, he was summoned to court by a letter from Middleton. Once there, however, he was welcomed by the Earl and by Talbot, who told him that if he co-operated, he would not merely be forgiven but promoted. Co-operation meant adding the weight of his respected testimony to Talbot's. This he did, and soon the King heard that not only was corruption rife because of the negligence of Ormonde and Arran, but that several officers were actually politically untrustworthy. Charles was indeed made to feel grateful for this, and Granard returned to Ireland promoted to an earldom. On 19 October the King wrote to the Lord-Lieutenant that he wanted to remove several men from both the army and the civil administration. As some were clients of the Duke, rather than impose the job upon him he was replacing him with Rochester. He then sent assurances of his continued favour and friendship, as did James. Rochester, for his part, professed both his affection for Ormonde and his surprise at his own elevation, perhaps disingenuously. It was a magnificently prestigious and lucrative office that had come his way, after all, which he was apparently going to hold concurrently with that of Lord President.[98] In modern parlance, Ormonde had been 'framed', and Charles manipulated. What cannot now be judged is whether James had been also.

Rochester was certainly not happy with the next step in the process, announced in December. This was to take all power to give army commissions away from the Lord-Lieutenant and vest it directly in the King, acting through Sunderland as Secretary of State. Contemporaries were in no doubt as to where this idea came from, all naming Sunderland himself, whose powers were thus dramatically enlarged.[99] Professor Kenyon has asserted that James and the Secretary were managing Charles in this affair, while Professor Jones believes that Charles was using Sunderland. It is neither possible nor profitable to determine the truth, for all three were plainly happy with what they got out of the arrangement. Just as in the case of the Irish Treasury Commission, affairs promised both to be better run and to be more closely controlled from England. The immediate consequence of the change soon became news: former parliamentarians or Cromwellians were to be put out of command and to be replaced, in some cases, by Catholic former royalists. Here, however, Professor Jones's distinction does seem appropriate: for James the importance of the incoming men was that they were Catholic, and for Charles that they were former royalists. After much wild rumour, the changes made in January 1685 were minimal. Only two officers failed to satisfy the King of their loyalty, and only two Catholics were commissioned. One was inevitably Talbot, who was thus restored to the organization from which he had been ejected, against Charles's will, in 1673. The other was Justin MacCarthy, who like Talbot had served in the royalist army in Flanders. He was the principal of the soldiers for whom Dongan's regiment had been intended in 1678, and whom the King believed had been so shabbily treated then. Halifax begged his sovereign to give him a pension instead, but Charles did not want to fob off McCarthy with anything less than employment.[100] How much further the process would have gone had the King lived longer, it is impossible to say. Perhaps nowhere, as Charles had no other favourite Irish Catholics left to reward.

Against this perspective, the episode involving young Clancarty seems an irrelevancy, and the gloss which Professor Kenyon puts on it appears to have been inspired by the malicious Gilbert Burnet. The issue with the young Earl was not to get him away from Protestantism but from the influence of his mother, who was believed to have presbyterian and Whig sympathies. Two years earlier his relative Justin MacCarthy had tried to solve the problem by having Ormonde himself made the lad's guardian. The Duke had claimed to be too busy, and now the problem seemed to be resolved by having MacCarthy fetch Clancarty and marry him into the family of the (recently) impeccably loyal and episcopalian Sunderland. The fact that the youth would subsequently abandon his wife (insulting his father-in-law) and then revert to Catholicism could hardly have occurred to most, if any, of the actors in this little family drama.[101]

At the same time Charles and the English government first became seriously concerned with possessions of his a good deal further away than Ireland.[102] Until now, the King had shown no personal interest in the colonies. Their steering body, the Privy Council's Committee for Trade and the Plantations, included some of the greatest names in English politics but had to have its quorum reduced from five to three in 1676. The King had no difficulty in finding aristocrats willing to take the posts of colonial governors, but often frequent trouble in making them leave England to take up their duties. The government's financial troubles left it incapable of maintaining posts which required regular subventions from the motherland: thus, Dunkirk was sold, Tangier deserted, and Bombay handed over to the East India Company. Some possessions were lost in war, Surinam to the Dutch and Nova Scotia to the French (both in 1667). Against these failures, however, could be set a tremendous expansion of English North America. Of the original Thirteen Colonies of the Revolution, no less than six were established in Charles's reign, and the territory for a seventh acquired. In the 1660s the Carolinas were settled by a consortium led by Shaftesbury, and New York and New Jersey carved out of land conquered from the Dutch which would later include Delaware. Pennsylvania was granted to proprietors, and New Hampshire made a Crown Colony, in 1679–81. If the Crown had a consistent policy, it was to get as much of

North America as possible not merely under its suzerainty but settled with English people. Only this can explain the charter granted to the Quaker William Penn in February 1681 to settle Pennsylvania. It gave him absolute authority to order the new colony, and he promptly established liberty of conscience, freedom from arbitrary arrest, and control of taxation by voters. This was, in effect a radical Whig Utopia and was established by a man who had, two years before, attacked Danby, declared the truth of the 'Popish Plot', personally supported Algernon Sidney, and called for relief of dissenters and provision for frequent Parliaments. To explain this anomaly, sentimental writers once believed in a personal friendship between the Quaker, Charles, and James. This does not stand up. What credit Penn possessed with the royal brothers derived from his status as a prospective colonial developer, not vice versa. His grant was processed by the Committee for Trade, the Crown's legal officers, and Bishop Compton, and Penn had to obtain the help of both Hyde and Halifax to get it through. A similar experience had been enjoyed by his fellow Quaker Edward Billing, who, having been arrested repeatedly in the 1660s, bought a section of New Jersey with a partner in the early 1670s. James, the overall proprietor, was happy to let them establish there the same liberties as were later instituted in Pennsylvania, and to separate New Jersey from New York. He was led to believe that the alteration would improve the security of the area and therefore its wealth (from which he would benefit). Likewise, the new colony of Pennsylvania would close a gap in the existing pattern of settlement, act as a shield to older colonies, and represent a new trading mart. James would be paid rent for it, and a debt of £16,000 owed by the Crown to Penn's father, an admiral, was cancelled as part of the agreement. In 1684 Penn himself remarked upon the oddity of returning to England to be fêted at court as a proprietor at one moment, and persecuted as a former Whig and a Quaker at the next. The British Empire up till 1680 was very much a 'sublet' affair, two-thirds of both the mainland and island colonies being run by private companies or individuals.

From the mid-1670s the Crown's attitude towards this situation began to alter, fitfully, because of the increasing difficulties which it represented. During that decade a rebellion broke out in Virginia, Jamaican privateers threatened to disrupt relations with Spain, and the New Englanders seemed to be paying steadily less attention to English law, especially in regard to trade. In 1678 the Privy Council resolved upon two initiatives to tackle these problems. To Virginia and Jamaica it proposed to extend a model already in use in Ireland and Barbados, whereby the colonial Councils had to submit all prospective legislation to that in England before it was put before assemblies. To browbeat Massachusetts, it considered challenging the charter of the company which ran it. This initiative lost a great deal of force in the next year, as the colonists campaigned vehemently against the proposed reform, Danby's ministry fell, new Counsellors such as Shaftesbury and Halifax showed sympathy for colonial liberties, and the government had to face constant distractions. A compromise was worked out eventually with Jamaica and Virginia whereby the assemblies made legislation but the Crown retained a right to veto it. The attack upon Massachusetts was not pressed, but New Hampshire was established under direct royal rule to cut off its expansion. Still, as the royal government acquired growing confidence in the early 1680s, reasons for further intervention multiplied. Reports assured the Council that the colonies were full of Whig sympathizers, that New Englanders were still breaking the Navigation Acts, that Marylanders were refusing to pay customs dues, that the New Yorkers were on tax strike until they were granted an assembly, that the Bermudans were desperate to get rid of their proprietory company, and that the proprietors of the Bahamas were sending out their own privateering raids. Many of the people who sent this information were the exact equivalent of the English Tories, anxious to provoke imperial intervention to enhance their own standing.

Exactly as with the English municipalities, the Crown's response began fitfully and then suddenly gained a mighty momentum. In November 1682 a writ was issued against the charter of Bermuda. During the following year another was threatened against that of the Bahamas, but dropped when they put their own colony in order. Likewise the long-discussed *quo warranto* was sent to challenge Massachusetts, but enclosed with a message that a compromise would be preferred. Jenkins and the Attorney-General urged Charles to send out a governor to Bermuda, but he preferred to await the issue of the lawsuit. This was determined in June 1684, and a governor instructed at once. Meanwhile, the people of Massachusetts remained obdurate, and in October the principal royal customs collector in Maryland was murdered. The next month, just as the English government launched the great series of writs against borough charters, it commenced proceedings to attack those of Maryland, the Carolinas, New Jersey, Delaware, Connecticut, and Rhode Island. That of Massachusetts was at last declared void in the Court of Chancery, and James and Penn prepared to surrender their proprietorships to the Crown. The Privy Council ordered the navy rigorously to enforce the trade laws. In December the secretary to the Committee for Trade told the Governor of Virginia that the government had begun 'to bring about that necessary union of all the English colonies in America which will make the King great and extend his real empire in those parts'. A truly imperial vision had suddenly appeared. The content of that vision was debated by the 'cabinet council' when it discussed the extent of royal power in the projected combined colony of New England. Halifax wanted this to be constitutionally limited, on the grounds that the best form of monarchy was that bound by law and consent. All the other Counsellors present, especially James, contested this in favour of a governor and council accountable only to the King. Charles, who did not himself contribute, accepted the decision of the majority.[103]

So, from this lengthy analysis, it can be seen that during his last year the King was selecting men and measures after consultation with a range of advisers, according to his own tastes. At times he was hoodwinked, but so had he been at intervals throughout his reign, especially when dealing with his two more remote realms. If he tended to choose servants and ideas most frequently from James's circle, it was because his brother had surrounded himself with more and cleverer followers than any other power broker at court. It must also be obvious that in every British kingdom, and the colonies, not only was the strength of the Crown growing notably in 1684 but its servants were conscious of this fact. In England and Ireland it could, for the first time in history, maintain formidable standing armies without recourse to parliamentary taxation. In Scotland there was a comparable force, kept in being by occasional grants from a tame Parliament. A drive had begun, backed by naval power, to reduce the colonies to obedience and uniformity. The English judiciary was increasingly subservient, many of the English municipalities were under an unprecedented degree of royal control, and there were plans to extend this pattern to Ireland. In every British realm and some of the colonies the Crown had enthusiastic local collaborators. On the other hand, much of this progress had itself been propelled by those collaborators or in reaction to a challenge by formidable adversaries. It was only in the last few months of Charles's life that his servants began to realize the potential of the advantages that they now enjoyed. Until now the King's own comments upon the process had been purely defensive, and during the last winter he continued to speak in terms of security and repair rather than expansion and aggression. How much longer this would have continued, we cannot say. Perhaps he would have seen the opportunity to construct an absolute monarchy, or perhaps he would have viewed his new strength merely as an opportunity to spend more time hawking at Winchester and forgetting business.

If it seems that many of the issues discussed have ended in questions, then the biggest one of all still hangs over the politics of that last winter. H. C. Foxcroft, long ago, hypothesized that Charles was about to demote James and his allies, make Halifax his principal minister, and recall Monmouth. John Kenyon insists that, on the contrary, the Catholic Duke was about to complete his hold on the government by obtaining the dismissal of Halifax. Some historians have supported the one, and some the other, while still others have confessed themselves to be utterly baffled.[104] At the heart of the problem lie some passages printed in a history published by a Whig in 1700, claimed to be extracts from Monmouth's pocket-book.[105] The names are in code, but the personalities concerned may be easily identified. According to this, the young Duke received a letter from Halifax, initialled by Charles, in January 1685, telling him to expect to be recalled in February. This was confirmed by a second a few weeks later, adding that James suspected nothing and would be sent into exile, probably to Scotland. The original document has vanished, and it would be tempting to dismiss it as a Whig invention. But immediately above this extract is another in the same code, telling Monmouth's side of his abortive reconciliation with his father in late 1683. It fits perfectly with all that the other participants recorded of those events. And there were the rumours to the same effect as those 'letters', circulating in Wilhelm's entourage at the time, as mentioned earlier. Perhaps Monmouth himself invented the lot. There is a pocket-book in his handwriting preserved in the British Library, but it does not contain these notes. Instead, it includes the route which he took on a secret visit to England during the previous November and December.[106] Lots of people knew that he was in London at that time, but not what he was doing. The Whig Burnet later said that he departed contented, but did not see the King.[107] Was Charles preparing to receive his son at court while his brother was busy in Scotland? James himself was preparing not for the test of strength but for final victory, as in December the King promised him and Louise that he would dismiss Halifax as soon as the latter provided the slightest pretext. In public he continued to speak resentfully of both Wilhelm and Monmouth, and in January he appointed a client of his brother's to be Master of the Rolls, against claims made by Danby, Seymour, and the Attorney-General. Court gossip said that both Halifax and Guildford would be sacked on the eve of James's departure for Scotland. Yet Charles was also telling Danby soon to expect a return to high office. Halifax made a further charge against Rochester of financial maladministration, and the case was appointed to be investigated upon 2 February. Never had this monarch's favourite tactic, of telling everybody what they wanted to hear, created greater bewilderment. On the evening before Rochester was to answer the charge, Charles and Halifax strolled together laughing merrily. The next morning the King was taken fatally ill at dawn.[108]

Nobody was expecting such a development. In May 1682 Charles had a brief fit of the fever which had struck him in 1679 and 1680,[109] but since then had enjoyed his traditional excellent health. He ate heartily and drank only for thirst, and when not hunting he walked twice daily. In July 1682 he went yachting upon a sea so rough that it broke the bowsprit and threw everybody off their seats at lunch. The King put his seasick and terrified pages ashore and carried on, with tremendous enjoyment.[110] The illness which struck him so terribly on 2 February 1685 must, at this distance, remain undiagnosable, although the symptoms are similar to those of chronic glandular kidney disease with uraemic convulsions.[111] He took four days to die, in which the royal physicians bled and blistered him repeatedly and filled his urine with scalding cantharides. Such measures hastened his demise, but added considerably to the intensity of his suffering. All observers agreed that he withstood it with incredible courage, though he wished that the end would come. It was one of the best-chronicled death agonies in history, several observers having left accounts of these last days. Yet it is chiefly remembered not for a medical but a religious event, and, as so often in Charles's story, the details of this are not as straightforward as they at first appear.

It is certain that on the last evening of his life, Charles II was received into the Roman Catholic Church. James obtained the consent of his brother for this act, and then cleared the bedchamber of everybody except two Protestants high in his confidence, the Earls of Bath and Feversham, to act as witnesses. Father John Hudleston, the priest whom Charles had met at Moseley thirty-three years before, was admitted to the chamber by a side-door and performed the necessary rites. He then departed and the rest of the court was allowed back in, mystified by their brief exclusion. If various people involved had been content to record that, then there would be no problem. Unfortunately, they went on to say and write too much. The freshest account was Barrillon's dispatch to Louis. In this, the Frenchman claimed to have had the idea of making Charles Catholic. On being given it, James went to his brother and, although fifteen minutes and much repetition were required to get an answer out of the sinking Charles, obtained his consent. Barrillon was cleared from the room with the rest, and after all was done the royal Duke told him that his brother had not only undergone the necessary rituals but promised to make his new faith public if he recovered. At some time soon after, James himself wrote an account in which he took credit for the idea. He recorded that the King received the sacrament joyfully, but did not mention any promise in the event of recovery. At a later stage still, he went back to his statement and inserted a sentence that, a few days before he fell ill, his brother had shown him a testimony of faith in the Catholic Church which he himself had written, and asked the Duke to have him received into it soon. The following year James published not one, but two, defences of Catholicism, which he claimed to have found in his brother's strong-box and to have been written entirely in Charles's own hand. Significantly, the original papers were never produced, nor found later. Contemporaries noted that neither sounded like the style in which the dead King had spoken or written, and that he had never shown any interest in theology: the historian has to agree. Seven years later, James told the nuns of Chaillot, in France, of that fateful evening. Although he still claimed to have thought of fetching a priest, he said no more about papers or promises. All he said was that his brother had cheerfully consented to be received. Meanwhile, soon after Charles's death, an English priest called Benedict Gibbon published a tract in which he claimed to have conceived the idea of fetching the dying King a priest. He also included the Earl of Peterborough among the witnesses in the Bedchamber and put rousing speeches of praise for his new Church into Charles's mouth. Finally, in 1688, Father Hudleston published his own account. It is remarkably sparse and brief, recording that the King declared his willingness to be received and listing the necessary rites which he underwent.[112] Interestingly, neither of the Protestant witnesses, Bath and Feversham, seem either to have made any statement or to have been called upon to make one.

What is clear from all this is that a few important Catholics wanted to make as much personal and political capital as possible from Charles's reception into their Church. We need not doubt that he was received, for not only do all the accounts of his new co-believers agree upon that, but some of the Protestants at court noted their suspicious exclusion from the Bedchamber for that interval and the fact that the King refused to take the Anglican communion thereafter.[113] What we can never know is the spirit in which he embraced Catholicism. One of the things upon which all the accounts agree is that the idea for his admission did not come from Charles himself. Was his action the triumphant climax to years in which he had longed for such a moment but dared not, for political reasons, bring it to pass? Or was the King indifferent to forms of religion and, so far gone that at first he could barely comprehend what was being asked, humouring his brother? It is typical of him that such a mystery should hang over the very death-bed of the man who has been known as the 'Merry Monarch' but could equally be dubbed the 'Slippery Sovereign'.

His last words were not 'Let not poor Nelly starve.' This is a paraphrase, made in one account, of words which he spoke in the course of a recitation of wishes. On the last night his strength rallied a little and he devoted it to his family. He expressed love for his wife and his brother, and commended to James's financial care his two surviving mistresses and all his sons—except Monmouth. The person for whom he had particular solicitude, according to every observer, was not Nell but Louise, his favourite companion. Some remembered that he had prayed for his country, others insisted that he did not. His final words were spoken at dawn on the 6th, when he asked to have the curtains drawn so that he could see the day: like many a dying person he was instinctively reaching for the light. He lost consciousness soon after, and at the end of the morning he ceased to breathe. The courtiers went off to inaugurate the reign of King James II, leaving the body covered by a single sheet and watched by a page. Curious visitors raised the covering from time to time to gaze upon the corpse: in death, as life, Charles was on stage. The slices, blisters, and pricks left all over the body by the doctors had already begun to fester before death came, and in the succeeding hours they rapidly began to stink. The odour of human corruption rose to mingle with the perfume of the heavy velvet hangings of the royal bed.[114]

Conclusion: Monarch in a Masquerade

UPON completing this biography I was strongly tempted to invite readers to supply their own conclusions upon the virtues, vices, and achievements of Charles II. I had offered a mass of evidence upon the matter, some of it conflicting, and thought it a worthwhile innovation to forgo the usual authorial verdict and to leave others the room to draw together their own opinions. Such an impulse I resisted in the end, from the suspicion that many might consider it a failure of duty and imagination greater than its opposite. Thus, with some qualms, I shall now draw my own portrait of this complex man.

First, it must be said that upon conducting research into the subject, I soon realized that I was dealing with a legendary figure. Other kings had inspired more respect, but perhaps only Henry VIII had endeared himself to the popular imagination as much as this one. He was the playboy monarch, naughty but nice, the hero of all who prized urbanity, tolerance, good humour, and the pursuit of pleasure above the more earnest, sober, or martial virtues. The process of creating the legend really began with the writings of Tories during the age of Walpole, who delighted in collecting anecdotes to illustrate the amiable qualities of the greatest Tory king (which could be set against the boorishness of the early Hanoverians). These stories multiplied into the next century, even though both Charles's morals and his diplomacy shocked many historians. It remained for George Bernard Shaw to establish him, after a fashion, as a philosopher sovereign and for Sir Arthur Bryant to rehabilitate him, it seems permanently, as a monarch fit for the company of gentlemen.

In constructing my own picture of Charles, I took care to use only anecdotes attested by his contemporaries, omitting in the process much material of life and colour which might have been apocryphal. He was a person who clearly fascinated those who knew him and at least four of these (Halifax, Gilbert Burnet, the Earl of Ailesbury, and the first Sheffield Duke of Buckingham) wrote pen-portraits of him after his death. I have tried to use these to corroborate the evidence of his actions during life, rather than lifting their comments wholesale as has so often been done in the past. If I could use one example to illustrate the hold exercised by these well-known narratives, it would be the assertion, read repeatedly in books and quoted to me by colleagues, that Charles grew to be rather a bore, retelling his favourite stories far too often in the same company. It originates in the *History* of the malicious Burnet. Why is he so often copied uncritically when Ailesbury, who knew the King better, noted that he never told the same tale twice?[1] Or while nobody commented upon any of Charles's defects as an entertainer (even in private notes and diaries) during his lifetime?

With these caveats, it is time to assemble a balance-sheet of his qualities. The least tangible is that of sheer good fortune. He arguably defeats even Henry VII to claim the title of the luckiest monarch in English history. The two greatest examples of his guardian angel in action are the escape after Worcester and the Restoration itself, an event resulting from a compound of accidents. But there are many others, such as the repeated crossings of the Channel and North Sea made by Charles in 1646–51 without once being intercepted by hostile vessels, or his unconscious evasion of the trap set for him and his fleet in 1648, or the fact that he emerged from fusillades at Worcester and a bombardment at Mardyke without a scratch, or that the Secret Treaties which he made with the French (especially that at Dover) were never disclosed, or that chance kept him from sailing off to get captured with Booth in 1649. He certainly had a wretched time as an exiled prince and king, but he was returned to his three thrones on a wave of reverence and adulation which seated him with more security than previous monarchs. The only real problem which the Restoration bequeathed him was financial, and that eased with time. The greatest misfortune which struck him in later life was his brother's change of religion, yet the contrast which he made with James enhanced his own standing. Most of the real troubles of his reign after 1660 were caused by himself, by challenging the religious policies of the Cavalier Parliament, starting two needless wars, promoting his son Monmouth, and enjoying a lifestyle which brought his court into disrepute.

To undoubted personal luck he coupled an unmistakable charm. From childhood he learned how to exert it, and everybody who came into contact with it was captivated, whether the French court, the Dutch States-General, the corporation of Cologne, the leaders of Spain and of the Spanish Netherlands, the Scottish Covenanters, the population of Jersey, or deputations from English political, municipal, or religious bodies. The man was a seducer, in a much broader sense than that normally attributed to him. It is easy to reconstruct the components of this gift. One was a capacity for almost constant good humour, so that he could meet most situations with a smile or a jest. Another was a punctilious courtesy. A visiting potentate, the Duke of Tuscany, noted with interest how carefully Charles returned the salutes of all whom he encountered, whatever their rank. Yet another was his readiness, which Evelyn especially recorded, to listen with apparent rapt attention to a range of conversational topics and to ask advice upon them. The diarist thought this to be 'an extraordinary talent', and the subjects which he alone covered with the King included shipping, architecture, bee-keeping, gardening, and urban pollution.[2] Charles possessed one of the most potent of all social assets, the ability to make every individual whom he encountered feel to be of special interest to him. Furthermore, his affability was accompanied by a rigid self-control. When he felt anger he tended to internalize it, even (as has been recorded) to the point of shaking with it. When he felt great grief he tended to retire into privacy. His losses of temper were so rare that they stunned those (such as Rupert and Buckingham) who were the targets.

This tremendous gift was closely allied with the fact that he was, like other English kings loved or respected by their subjects (such as Edward III, Henry V, or Henry VIII), a 'participating' monarch. He enjoyed every pastime of the ruling class, including tennis, pall-mall (a form of croquet), swimming, angling, dancing, riding, hunting (his quarry included hares, stags, foxes, and otters), hawking, horse-racing, bowling, sailing, gambling, and going to the theatre. All these activities he executed well, but he was a really superb dancer, rider, and sailor. His recreations clearly did not consist merely of joining the aristocracy at their pursuits, for they were too numerous and some (notably fishing and yachting) were somewhat unorthodox. They reflected genuine personal enthusiasm, propelled by an extraordinary restless energy and usually perfect good health. When in later life he wearied of the more sociable activities, he took to the solitary walks which feature so much in accounts of the last years of his reign. This compulsive need to be active is of a piece with his obviously strong libido and his celebrated loquacity. All who knew him agreed upon how talkative he was,[3] and he, in turn, needed a variety of company. His interest in so many topics, which impressed Evelyn, was in large part genuine, reflecting a considerable curiosity about the world and its phenomena. He was especially attracted by the novel and the exotic. Such interests are reflected in his expenditure upon purchases and pastimes while in exile, in his initial reaction to Highland bagpipers, in his desire to follow in the latest fashions in clothes and entertainment (which generally meant those of France), in his readiness to listen to the projects and observe the experiments of scientists, and, indeed, in the mixture of amusement and sympathy which he at first accorded to Quakers. It was a trait closely associated with his famous accessibility. Although he took guards with him upon his progresses as a matter of form, except at moments of presumed acute danger he could be approached by perfect strangers in his walks around his residences or their vicinity. The manner in which Kirby accosted him to break the news of the 'Popish Plot' was typical of the casualness and informality of many of his encounters. Such physical and mental vitality was maintained quite self-consciously by a personal regime of remarkable rigour for one so often associated with his pleasures. He rose at five or six upon most mornings, and breakfasted only upon whisky and water.[4] For much of his life he hunted whenever opportunity presented itself, and in middle age he went for walks twice a day, timing them with a pocket-watch. He always ate heartily yet was very seldom reported to have been drunk, and in his last years he drank only to quench his thirst.[5] He took pains to find good tobacco, but nobody observed him to use it heavily.[6]

With abounding physical energy he coupled undoubted physical courage. The reckless bravery which he showed as a prince, at Edgehill and in the Thames estuary, did not diminish with maturity. He longed to lead an army in his youth, and when his chance came in 1651, Henry V could hardly have done better. He lived in the camp, inspected its guards himself, and led a cavalry charge uphill, against enclosures, at the crisis of the battle of Worcester. During his escape after that battle, he always seems to have kept his nerve. At Mardyke in 1657 he exposed himself to a cannon bombardment apparently without a thought. After the Restoration there were fewer opportunities for him to display this aspect of his nature, but a supreme test was administered to him in his last few days. Physical pain makes cowards of most of us, but he endured his prolonged death agony with a stoicism which won admiration from all who observed it.

He was also fairly intelligent. This may seem tepid praise to accord to one traditionally regarded as the wittiest of English monarchs, whose sayings were collected by admirers during the two centuries after his death. The trouble with such material is that some of it is certainly apocryphal, and most may be so. If we confine ourselves to the remarks of Charles which were recorded by contemporaries, then there is much lively good humour in them, but virtually nothing which is actually memorable. The best moment was probably when the Moroccan ambassador presented thirty ostriches to the King in January 1682, and Charles wondered aloud if he should send a flock of geese in return.[7] It is possible that he gave an expression to the English language when he termed the new-born son of Lord Bruce a 'chip off the old block'.[8] Halifax, who was himself unmistakably clever, probably came closest to evaluating his master by attributing to him a 'plain, gaining, well-bred, recommending kind of wit'.[9] His letters are of a piece with his reported words, being vivacious rather than brilliant. He had the trick of varying his style according to his recipient, being plain and functional to ministers, boisterous to friends, and charmingly childlike to Minette in her adolescence. He was neither dull nor dazzling.

Charles was not as great an aesthete as his father and not as much an intellectual as his grandfather James. Newcastle's determination that his pupil should not be too bookish left the King with little appetite for reading of any sort. In the course of his youth and early manhood Charles tried to learn French, Italian, and Spanish. Yet he never seems to have attained any proficiency in the last two tongues. The Earl of Ailesbury, who served him as a page in his last years, noted that the King did understand French. This was clearly so, but he had confessed to Minette two decades before that he found it 'troublesome' to employ the tongue himself, even in a short letter.[10] As for his appreciation of the arts, it is obvious that his admiration of beautiful things, evident in his boyish response to the books at Little Gidding, was a lifelong trait. His 'Closet' was stocked with paintings and statues, as has been said, and when a cardinal living in France wanted to dispose of a collection of such works, he found an enthusiastic purchaser in Charles. In 1671 Evelyn told the King of a superbly executed crucifix produced by the great woodcarver Grinling Gibbons, whereupon Charles insisted upon seeing it at once.[11] Yet, neither as a patron nor a collector, does he rank highly among monarchs. Nor does his appreciation of music seem to have been above average, and although he regularly attended the theatre his favourite works there were comedies or epic dramas with stunning special effects. His mind seems to have been of a scientific rather than a literary bent. Burnet noted his knowledge of chemistry and mathematics, Halifax thought that he had a 'mechanical head', and Ailesbury agreed with both of them.[12] He took an interest in the experiments of certain savants, such as Murray and Kirby. Yet his personal contribution to the sciences seems to have been as shallow as that to the arts, and the fact that the Royal Society was founded during his reign owed more to initiatives of the nation's learned men than any views on the part of the sovereign. His curiosity concerning the natural world was shared by many members of the ruling class, most notably Rupert and Buckingham: in this, as in many other respects, Charles was following fashion. This was, of course, only to his advantage, as was the lack of any passionate commitment to learning or aesthetics which would have set him off from the bulk of his subjects. Ailesbury doubtless represented the viewpoint of many when he commended the King for speaking 'more like a gentleman than a learned pedant'.[13]

Three other traits must complete the list of his positive qualities. One was the fidelity which he showed to loyal servants, only qualified by his own impulses and needs and by political expediency. At the Restoration, as has been shown, he made great efforts to reward as many former royalists as possible, including every member of the exiled court. His golden handshake to Danby, and his protection of Ranelagh, were expressions of gratitude which had most unfortunate political consequences. This instinct became overwhelming when his family was involved. As has been seen, his emotional attachment to both his brother James and his son Monmouth bedevilled national affairs for two decades. And only this impulse can account for his refusal to discard the Queen, whom he so often betrayed and made unhappy. This characteristic must be obvious enough at a glance. Equally significant for his political career, and less easy to notice, was his ability to divide his ministers from his playthings. The real jobs in the administration were bestowed upon men such as Clarendon, Ormonde, Arlington, Danby, and Laurence Hyde, all able, industrious, and serious-minded. By contrast, the delightfully entertaining and mercurial personalities such as Taaffe and Buckingham were kept in high favour but never given high political or military commands. Halifax, though an intellectual heavyweight in comparison with these two, was still relegated to the same category. Bristol, whose aptitudes spanned both, accordingly oscillated between them. The King was as loyal to his companions of pleasure as to his workhorses and influential advisers, but none the less kept the distinction between them fairly clear. His most intimate companions of pleasure were, of course, his mistresses. At the time it was widely assumed that they had great influence upon policy-making, but this narrative has indicated that, on the whole, such a notion was false. Rather, as Arlington and Ormonde observed, they were worth cultivating because their opinion might count as a crucial feather's weight in otherwise equal scales. All agreed that Louise was at once the best-loved by Charles and the most involved in politics. Yet all her tears and arguments could not move him to agree to Exclusion. She was only potent when her advice coincided with her royal lover's wishes or when she became part of a powerful faction, as in the last years of the reign.

His third 'political' virtue was caution. Again and again, as has been shown in the course of this book, Charles chose to reject bold and provocative methods being urged upon him by some or most of his advisers. Although it is impossible in many of these cases to say positively that he chose wisely, it is at least likely that the number of occasions upon which he resorted to conciliation or surrender prevented his already febrile reign from suffering disaster. Until the battle of Worcester he was certainly ready to throw himself into rash and exciting courses, but after his escape from that the new attitude was apparent. Even the greatest gamble which he took after the Restoration, the foreign policy centred upon the Secret Treaty of Dover, was, it has been suggested, originally an attempt to obtain double insurance. This trait is the more remarkable in that he lived in an age of flamboyant royal adventurers, such as Louis XIV, Wilhelm of Orange, Friedrich-Wilhelm of Brandenburg, Peter the Great of Russia, Karl XII of Sweden, and (indeed) his own brother James. Yet, as the Whigs discovered, he could be quite unyielding when he believed that it was politically possible to be so.

It is time now to turn to a pair of acusations often levelled at him, which require qualification even if they must be upheld. One is that he was financially extravagant. There is indeed no evidence that, until his last few years, he understood the problems of his financial officers. He repeatedly made demands upon an English or an Irish revenue which he had already agreed to be overburdened. He spent lavishly upon jewels, *objets d'art*, and mistresses. Yet it is unjust to suggest that this weakness was responsible for the considerable fiscal problems of his regime. Rather, it accentuated, and postponed the solution of, a situation created by an initial shortfall in the revenue and greatly worsened by two wars. The latter, the true extravagance of the reign, were at first enthusiastically supported by his subjects. Furthermore, after 1667 he appointed gifted men to take charge of his revenue and in England at least he gave considerable support to their efforts. In peacetime virtually all his excess expenditure was represented by grants to men whom the government wished to reward or to gratify. This largess was greatest at the Restoration, yet it did not prevent a chorus of complaints that the King was being niggardly, ungracious, and negligent. It is, again, very difficult to judge how much greater, and more damaging, this chorus might have been if Charles had been more provident.

The other traditional accusation which needs amendment is that he was easy-going. His good humour and accessibility do much to account for, and justify, such a reputation. So does the rather childish delight which he took in bawdy talk and crude expressions. Examples of the latter have peppered the pages of this book. Most were uttered or written to men, and worldly men at that, but he did not scruple to observe to his sister Minette, 'You know the old saying in England, the more a turd is stirred the more it stinks.'[14] Halifax was disturbed by the indecency of his daily talk.[15] In the last year of his life, Charles asked the playwright, Thomas Crowne, to adapt a Spanish work for the English stage. When he read Crowne's draft, he faulted it only for not having enough 'smut'.[16] Having endorsed a proclamation against profane oaths at the Restoration, his favourite expletive remained 'Od's Fish!' He was, however, pedantically conscious of the dignity which was due to monarchy even if he could not quite personify it himself. The intense interest which he took in disputes over the salute due to his flag, his treatment of Sandwich after the signature of the Hispano-Portuguese treaty of 1668, and the fate of Rochester for striking a man in the royal presence during the same year, are all examples of this. Even to insult another man in front of the King was sufficient to earn banishment from court.[17] Charles's antipathy to the second Earl of Clarendon, heir to the great Chancellor, had its origins in such an incident. The Earl forced his way past a porter to see a play at Whitehall after the King had directed that no more should be admitted to the auditorium. As a result, his royal master sacked him from his existing court post and refused his brother's entreaties to have Clarendon made Secretary of State almost ten years later.[18] It was not wise to relax too much in the company of the monarch.

So we proceed to his main personal and political shortcomings. One was his dislike of paperwork. It would be utterly misguided to term him lazy. As has been said above, he was hyperactive by nature. He fulfilled ceremonial functions, and those which involved action or debate, with exceptional assiduity. He attended the Privy Council almost constantly, in sharp contrast to his four predecessors as sovereigns of England and Scotland. He also sat in every or virtually every meeting of its policy-making 'inner ring', the Foreign Affairs Committee or 'cabinet council'. In Scotland he attended the Committee of Estates and Parliament as soon as he was allowed to do so and then as often as military affairs permitted. He was also the first monarch for over a century to attend the English House of Lords, and once he had revived this custom he, again, fulfilled it regularly. His love of purely symbolic functions, such as touching for the King's Evil, imposed a further burden upon his time unusual for an English monarch. Williamson's notes upon proceedings in the Foreign Affairs Committee in 1668–73 make certain what every other source suggests: that Charles participated actively in debates and frequently led the discussion. Rupert commented upon how punctually he arrived for all meetings.[19]

By contrast, he could never overcome his distaste for reading or writing. To this King, any letter of more than five hundred words was a long one,[20] a cause of congratulation if he had written it himself or of dismay if another were the author. Indeed, he rarely set eyes upon dispatches or addresses if somebody else would read them to him aloud, and he equally rarely looked at the drafts which his ministers and officials prepared in reply. It was this trait, not his attitude to business in general, which must have provoked Halifax's famous comment that Charles had to be offered work like medicine, coated in something pleasant to persuade him to swallow it.[21] The impatience expressed by the Marquis reflects the agony felt by generations of royal servants from the moment that Charles claimed the title of King, in trying to talk their sovereign into paying attention to deskwork. Through the history of his exile, and of his effective reign in all three kingdoms, runs a trail of documents lost or misunderstood, and instructions delayed, forgotten, duplicated, or muddled. It was a miserably bad performance compared with that of his contemporary rulers, and especially that of his cousin Louis and his nephew Wilhelm.

This political shortcoming was accompanied by a moral cowardice as remarkable as his physical courage. Charles could face a hostile deputation (such as Whig petitioners) with as much resilience as he could cannon balls, but he fled from personal unpleasantness. Halifax judged that 'the motive of his giving bounties was to make men less uneasy to him than more easy to themselves'.[22] This habit of agreeing to importunities rather than to have the bother of refusing them resulted in worse problems than overstrained national treasuries. As has been shown, he sometimes promised things that could not possibly be given or had already been guaranteed by him to others. He extended the same attitude to the making of policy. In the 1650s he would cope with the probable opposition of his mother to actions by initiating them without informing her, thereby ensuring himself even greater troubles when she found out what had been done. He continued to employ this tactic with his ministers, and also with Parliament. His classic way of ruling, especially in foreign affairs, was to have different lines of policy running at once, conceived with different groups of advisers and often mutually contradictory. For all his assiduous attendance of the Privy Council, he loved to hatch schemes in private discussions with one or a few confidants, and to inform the whole government of them later, if at all. Likewise, he would assure ministers to their faces of his affection and support and then allow them to be criticized, or dismiss them, in their absence. Instead of dominating and leading, he preferred to ensure his supremacy by setting Counsellor against Counsellor and mistress against mistress. Such practices provoked confusion, demoralization, and distrust, among his servants, in Parliament, and in foreign states. They also multiplied occasions upon which, while conceiving himself to be a puppet-master, he was manipulated by his advisers.

Somewhere in the heart of his psyche, this weakness was intertwined with his desire (generally achieved) to charm everybody, and a vindictive cruelty to those who failed or opposed him. The list of victims of this last trait is extensive and obvious: it includes Long, Argyll, Johnston of

Wariston, Vane, his own wife (in 1662), the Quakers, Clarendon, and Shaftesbury. He could spare those who thwarted him if they were too powerful to attack (like Sheldon), or forgive some with time (like Frances Stuart and Bristol), or leave others in peace once they had ceased to be a direct problem (like Clarendon), or be generous to others after years in which they had tried to expiate their offence (like Balcarres). But the cold, venomous fury of this monarch was a terrible thing to provoke. Lying beneath his cultivated, good-humoured composure, so rarely unleashed upon a victim's face, reserved for the weakened and vulnerable, it represents his least appealing personal characteristic. It must be associated with the consistent pleasure which he took in seeing his chief ministers mocked behind their backs, and in embarrassing his courtiers.[23]

So we arrive at the most complex question to hang over this king, the nature of his religion. Until now, historians who have agreed in little else have formed a consensus upon this point. Charles has been seen as an individual without strong personal piety but with a considerable commitment to the principle of religious toleration, based in great part upon his attraction to the Roman Catholic Church, and a corresponding feeling for its persecuted followers. Most have gone as far as calling him a 'secret Catholic' while remaining undecided upon the date or depth of his commitment to that faith. A hundred years ago a formidable body of evidence had been assembled to testify to it. There was the certain fact that as a small boy he had been taken to mass by his mother, an episode which he recalled wistfully at Moseley. There was a letter written privately to him by that same mother as soon as he succeeded to the title of King, referring to his expressed longing to join her Church. Then came the great emotional experience of his rescue by Catholics after Worcester and his confession at Moseley Hall that he found their tenets unanswerable. The political damage consequent upon his open adoption of their faith would, of course, be great enough to deter it but (as the famous Gardiner pointed out) he did offer it to the Pope in secret in exchange for aid. None was provided, and the insecurity of the years after the Restoration would have discouraged further efforts for a time. But in view of this personal history, it is not surprising to come across the 'De la Cloche letters', written by him in secret to Rome in 1668 on behalf of a natural son and repeating his longing to declare his true allegiance. No wonder we find him weeping in front of a group of confidants the next January, as his brother James attested, and repeating this wish. The result was the Secret Treaty of Dover, which provided for such an eventuality and might have achieved it had it not been for ill fortune. After that, facing a political nation ferociously hostile to Catholics, Charles had once again to conceal his feelings to keep his throne. But upon his death-bed he was free, at last, to achieve his dearest wish. Thus expressed, the sequence of events makes a logical and coherent progression. Yet upon proper inspection it falls to pieces.

As pointed out in Chapter 1 of this book, nobody at the time thought that his brief attendance at mass in his childhood made any impression on him. The letter from his mother in 1649 is actually an English translation of an Italian version of an original which, if it ever existed, has been lost. It could not have been the work of Henrietta Maria, for it makes errors about the circumstances of the exiled royalist courts which would be astounding if committed by the Queen Mother.[24] It must therefore be considered to be a forgery. There are good reasons, likewise, for being suspicious about the words which he is alleged to have spoken at Moseley, expressed in Chapter 4. In Chapter 5 Gardiner's belief in the offer to the Pope in 1654 is shown to have been mistaken. As mentioned in Chapter 2, the 'De la Cloche letters' are rather clumsy forgeries. In Chapter 10, it has been explained why James's testimony as to the events of 25 January 1669 is unreliable, and why the Treaty of Dover had little to do with religion. Finally, although it is certain that Charles was received into the Church of Rome upon his death-bed, the quantity of forgery and contradiction in the accounts of that event makes it impossible to establish its true significance. Thus, the whole story of this king's relationship with Catholicism has been clouded by a regrettable, and somewhat amazing, quantity of proven or suspected falsification.

Once this has been stripped away, what can be said of Charles's attitude to religion? Bluntly, that it centred upon his own interests. He had no sympathy for Catholics as such, but felt powerfully the need to reward those who had served him or his father loyally. He also wanted preferential treatment for those, notably the signatories of the 'Irish Remonstrance', who declared that in political matters they owed allegiance to him rather than to the Pope. It is equally difficult, in view of the evidence presented in this book, to claim that he had much of a commitment to religious toleration, as such. He certainly spoke at times against the persecution of people for their beliefs, but he increasingly made it plain that people who put beliefs into practice, by acts of worship, had no automatic right to be left undisturbed. It is perfectly true that at the Restoration he favoured a far less repressive regime than that which was subsequently imposed by the Cavalier Parliament. He accepted a moral undertaking to see the repeal of the penal laws against English Catholics because of the services of so many to the royalist cause, not least the preservation of his own life in 1651. He also believed the protestations of loyalty made by Protestant nonconformists, especially the Quakers, who addressed him in the most flattering terms. It was not of much moment to Charles whether people held strange theological dogmas as long as they supported his authority. None the less, when his Parliament proved unwilling to ameliorate the condition of Catholics, he proved quite prepared repeatedly to encourage repression of them when he wished to curry favour with a House of Commons. More important, and less observed, the rebellion of 1663 permanently altered his attitude towards Protestant dissent. It turned him for a while into one of the dissenters' worst enemies, and thereafter he remained much more suspicious of the benefits of clemency than most of his inner circle of advisers. It was they who talked him, with some difficulty, into issuing the Declaration of Indulgence of 1672, and he was prepared to repeal it when most of them were still counselling obstinacy. No wonder he subsequently turned to encouraging enforcement of the laws against nonconformity when there seemed to be political capital to be made out of this. No wonder, also, that when such a policy drove the dissenters and the Whigs together, he campaigned against the former with genuine bitterness.

The results of these campaigns were impressive. It has long been recognized that the last years of Charles's reign witnessed the most savage religious repression in the history of Scotland. What has not been adequately appreciated is the impact of his policies upon England. The greatest persecutor to sit upon the English throne has traditionally been considered to have been 'Bloody' Mary Tudor, who burned over three hundred Protestants. As a body count of victims upon the scaffold, suffering for conscience, it remains a record. On the other hand, under Charles II, more than four hundred members of the Quaker sect *alone* died in prison, of diseases consequent upon being confined in such an environment and as a result of charges relating directly to their principles. It is a matter of personal taste whether a moment of agony at a stake is a worse end than a slow decline, penned upon stinking and verminous straw. To those who would prefer the former, the supposedly genial and cynical Charles must rank as the most savage persecutor of all.

So, how can the man be summarized? It must be left to those better qualified than myself to decide whether Charles's personality was characterized by a deep insecurity produced in the course of a disturbed childhood, or by defects and strengths associated with over-indulgence when young. If, indeed, the evidence is sufficient to reach a conclusion of this sort. But we surely have enough to confirm the traditional verdict that, judged as both man and monarch, he was a remarkable individual but lacked greatness. He could act a part magnificently, whether that of guest, seigneur, warlord, or sacred monarch. In the theatre of kingship in the age of baroque, he was a star. Yet so many of his virtues were like costuming or gilding, finest at one remove and upon public occasions. The more intimate that his contemporaries became with him, the longer that they were associated with him, the more a sensation of distrust and alienation runs through their accounts. More than anything else, he was monumentally selfish. In an important sense monarchs of his time were paid to be egomaniacs. But it is rare to find one with Charles's utter inability to admit himself privately to be in error and his unhesitating anger and scorn towards individuals and nations like the Scots and the Spanish, whom he blamed for his own mistakes. At his core there lay a vacuum, and what emerges most powerfully from the accounts of those who knew him is a feeling of unreachability, a frustrating instinct that the man inside the king eluded the observer. He suffered no apparent fears of inadequacy. Nor was he, as some have thought, a private melancholic, for he genuinely enjoyed his many pleasures with the same carelessness which he brought to much of the business of ruling and to some of his personal relationships. Yet he remains, for us as for contemporaries, a set of strongly marked characteristics with a cold void at the centre of them. He was a monarch who loved masks, whether of ceremony, of role-playing, or of intrigue. Behind those coverings, something was always missing.

References

THE following abbreviations have been employed when attributing texts:

AAE CP (A)   Archives des Affaires Étrangères, Quai D'Orsay, Paris, Correspondance Politique (Angleterre)

APS   *The Acts of the Parliaments of Scotland* (ed. T. Thomson and C. Innes)

BIHR   *Bulletin of the Institute of Historical Research*

BL   British Library

Bod.L.   Bodleian Library

CJ   Journals of the House of Commons

CSP   *State Papers Collected by Edward, Earl of Clarendon* (Oxford, 1786)

CSPD   *Calendar of State Papers, Domestic Series*

CSPV   *Calendar of State Papers, Venetian Series*

CTB   *Calendar of Treasury Books*

EHR   *English Historical Review*

HJ   *Historical Journal*

HMC   The Royal Commission for Historical Manuscripts

JBS   *Journal of British Studies*

L.   Library

LJ   Journals of the House of Lords

NLI   National Library of Ireland

NLS   National Library of Scotland

P/C   Privy Council Registers (in the Public Record Office)

PRO   Public Record Office

RCGA   *Records of the Commissioners of the General Assemblies of the Church of Scotland* (ed. A. F. Mitchell and J. Christie, SHS 1896 and 1909)

RO   Record Office

RPCS   *The Register of the Privy Council of Scotland* (ed. P. Hume Brown, 3rd ser. 1908)

SHS   Scottish History Society

SO   Signet Office Papers (in the Public Record Office)

SP   State Papers (in the Public Record Office)

SRO   Scottish Record Office

| Thurloe State Papers | *State Papers of John Thurloe* (ed. Thomas Birch, 1742) |
| TRHS | *Transactions of the Royal Historical Society* |

I have consulted the following unpublished dissertations, with great profit and gratitude to the authors:

Allen, D. F., 'The Crown and the Corporation of London in the Exclusion Crisis, 1678–1681' (Cambridge Ph.D., 1977).

Aydelotte, James Ernest, 'The Duke of Ormond and the English Government of Ireland, 1677–1685' (Iowa Ph.D., 1975).

Dow, F. D., 'The English Army and the Government of Scotland, 1651–1660' (York D.Phil., 1976).

Egan, Sean, 'Finance and the Government of Ireland, 1660–85' (Trinity College, Dublin, Ph.D., 1983).

Fowler, William J., 'The Crown and Municipal Corporations, 1679–88' (Reading MA, 1935).

Norrey, P. J., 'The Relationship between Central Government and Local Government in Somerset, Dorset and Wiltshire, 1660–1688' (Bristol Ph.D., 1988).

O'Donoghue, Fergus, 'Parliament in Ireland under Charles II' (University College, Dublin, MA, 1970).

Pickavance, Robert, 'The English Boroughs and the King's Government: A Study of the Tory Reaction, 1681–1685' (Oxford D.Phil., 1976).

Reece, Henry, 'The Military Presence in England, 1649–1660' (Oxford D.Phil., 1981).

Roseveare, H. G., 'The Advancement of the King's Credit, 1660–1672' (Cambridge Ph.D., 1972).

Roy, Ian, 'The Royalist Army in the First Civil War (Oxford D.Phil., 1963).

Seaward, Paul, 'Court and Parliament: The Making of Government Policy, 1661–1665' (Oxford D.Phil., 1985).

Smith, A. G., 'London and the Crown, 1681–1685' (Wisconsin Ph.D., 1967).

Stradling, Robert, 'Anglo-Spanish Relations from the Restoration of Charles II to the Peace of Aix-la-Chapelle' (Wales Ph.D., 1968).

Turnbull, A., 'The Administration of the Royal Navy from 1660 to 1673' (Hull Ph.D., 1975).

Wanklyn, Malcolm, 'The King's Armies in the West of England' (Manchester MA, 1966).

Notes

∽⋙∾

All titles cited below were published in London, unless otherwise indicated.

Chapter 1

1. Francis Eglesfield, *Monarchy Revived* (1661, repr. 1822), p. 1; Edward Chamberlayne, *Angliae Notitia* (1671), p. 123; references to the star occur in the poems by John Dryden, *Astraea Redux*, lines 288–9; by Abraham Cowley, *Ode on His Majesties Restoration*, stanza 1; and by Edmund Waller, *On St. James's Park*, line 128.
2. *CSPV* (1629–32), p. 350.
3. SP 16/168/64 and 169/50 (orders for ceremony); HMC Portland MSS, iii. 27 (Conway to Harley family); *CSPV* (1629–32), p. 372; Francis Peck, *Desiderata Curiosa* (1736), ii. 36 (Meddus to Meade); BL Harl. MS 791, fo. 40 (account of event).
4. SP 16/172/81 and 234/83 (lists of personnel and expenditure).
5. Sir Oliver Millar, *Van Dyck in England* (1982), pp. 60–1.
6. SP 16/328/104 (letter from Duppa, clearly to Wyndham, in 1639), and see below, in 1645.
7. *CSPV* (1632–6), p. 438, and (1636–9), pp. 288, 418; SP 16/392/60 (letter from Arundell).
8. *CSPV* (1629–32), p. 350; SP 16/168, *passim*; Mary E. Green (ed.), *Letters of Queen Henrietta Maria* (1857), pp. 17–18 (to Madame St George).
9. *CSPV* (1632–6), pp. 118, 445–7; HMC Cowper MSS, ii. 11–12 (Chambers to King); SP 16/481/33 (Queen of Bohemia to Roe).
10. *Letters of Henrietta Maria*, pp. 17–18.
11. Ibid.; HMC Cowper MSS, ii. 18 (Goring to Coke).
12. William Knowler (ed.), *The Earl of Strafforde's Letters and Dispatches* (Dublin, 1740), ii. 57, 148, 166–7 (Garrard to Strafford), and 174–5 (Strafford to Newcastle); SP 16/387/62 (Smith to Pennington); Sir C. H. Firth (ed.), *Life of Newcastle* (1886), pp. 9–10, 324–6.
13. *Life of Newcastle*, pp. 326–30; BL Harl. MS 6988, fos. 97–106.
14. Sir Henry Ellis (ed.), *Original Letters* (1825), 1st ser., iii. 285–6.
15. Both stories are in John E. B. Mayor, *Two Lives of Nicholas Ferrar* (1855), pp. 115–294.
16. The fullest description of these negotiations is in Gordon Albion, *Charles I and the Court of Rome* (1935), ch. 2.

17. *CSPV* (1629–32), pp. 368–82.
18. Ibid., p. 350; Peter Heylyn, *Cyprianus Anglicus* (1668), p. 209.
19. BL Add. MS 15391, fo. 235 (Con to Barberini); PRO, PRO/31/10, five dispatches of Panzani dated from 27 Mar. 1635 to 25 Feb. 1636.
20. See the Vicar of Loughborough before the Court of High Commission in SP 16/261, fo. 119ᵛ.
21. *CSPV* (1640–2), pp. 5, 66.
22. SP 16/453/63 (Privy Council to Lord-Lieutenants of Surrey) and 485/61 (Robinson to Mildmay).
23. LJ iv. 245.
24. *Life of Newcastle*, pp. 13–14; BL Harl. MS 478, fos. 668ᵛ–669 (John More's parliamentary diary), and MS 5047, fo. 23ᵛ ('Short Observations on the Long Parliament').
25. This is the judgement of Edward Hyde, Earl of Clarendon, *History of the Rebellion* (ed. W. Dunn Macray, Oxford, 1888), iv. 294–6. As Hertford was politically quite convenient to Hyde, this may be trusted more than many of his character-sketches.
26. BL Harl. MS 6424, fos. 89ᵛ, 98ᵛ (extracts from parliamentary journals), and MS 162, fos. 325–327ᵛ (Sir Symonds D'Ewes's parliamentary diary); W. H. Coates (ed.), *The Journal of Sir Symonds D'Ewes* (1942), pp. 58–9; CJ ii. 379; LJ iv. 513.
27. CJ ii. 450–9; LJ iv. 608–17; BL Add. MS 14827, fo. 53 (Sir Framlingham Gawdy's parliamentary notes).
28. *A Diurnall of the North* [July] (1642).
29. *A Loving and Loyal Speech spoken unto our Noble Prince* [2 Oct.] (1642). My suspicions of the authenticity of the events described in this tract are growing, but I am still prepared to accept them as possible for lack of positive refutation.
30. The letter is to Prince Rupert: BL Add. MS 18980, fo. 78. In June 1641 Sir Hugh Cholmley and Sir John Culpeper had proposed him in the Commons for the office of governor: BL Harl. MS 478, fos. 668ᵛ–669. He grew more embittered and pessimistic later in the war, but with reason: see his letter to the Earl of Bath on 6 June 1645, in the Kent RO, De La Warre MSS. Thus Clarendon's contemptuous dismissal of him, in the *History*, vi. 324, 390, needs to be treated with caution.
31. Traquair House Collection, Charles to Earl of Roxburgh, Oxford, 29 Feb. 1645.
32. This is recorded in *Miraculum Basilicon* (1664), pp. 64–5, and in Sir John Hinton, *Memoires* (1679), pp. 7–13, and must be true as Hinton presented his book to Charles himself. Other accounts of the escape of the princes, confirming some aspects of those above, are in Ellis (ed.), *Original Letters*, 2nd ser., iii. 304, and in the Revd J. S. Clarke (ed.), *The Life of James II* (1816), i. 15–16. The only accessible copy of *Miraculum Basilicon* that I could trace is in the library of University College, Cardiff.

33. Both are in G. Elliot (ed.), *Diary of Dr. Edward Lake, Camden Miscellany*, i (1846), pp. 26–7. The narrator claimed, very credibly, to have been a witness.

34. P/C 2/53, fo. 227; BL Add. MS 18981, fo. 170 (Elliot to Rupert).

35. John Latimer, *The Annals of Bristol in the Seventeenth Century* (Bristol, 1900), p. 194.

36. Clarendon, *History*, viii. 179, 253–4, 279–80.

37. The Hyde group were described by Ian Roy, in his pioneering thesis, pp. 79–85, as 'The Civilians'. In 'The Structure of the Royalist Party, 1642–1646', *HJ* 24 (1981), pp. 553–69, I defined them, more loosely, as 'moderates'. Between my interpretation and that of J. Daly, 'The Implications of Royalist Politics 1642–1646', *HJ* 27 (1984), pp. 745–56, I leave others to judge.

38. What was said in the fierce debate recorded in the sources at note 33? And why was the man who proposed the idea of a Western Council the 'ultra-royalist' Lord Digby?

39. An evaluation based upon his portraiture and the whole mass of evidence cited below.

40. Bod. L., Clarendon MS 24, fos. 56–127 (letters of Prince, Digby, Goring, Culpeper, Berkeley, Grenville, and Mackworth); Eliot Warburton (ed.), *Memoirs of Prince Rupert and the Cavaliers* (1849), iii. 66 (Digby to Rupert); William Salt L., Stafford, Salt MS 45, fos. 1–54 (minute-book of Prince's Council); Bod. L., Tanner MS 60, fos. 15–63 (letters of Waller, Culpeper, Dyve, and Digby).

41. Clarendon, *History*, ix. 19.

42. William Salt L., Salt MS 45, fos. 1–54.

43. Bod. L., Clarendon MS 24, fos. 79 (Goring's proclamation), and 129 (unsigned note); Bod. L., Firth MS C8, fo. 25, and BL Add. MS 18982, fo. 36 (letters to Rupert from officers in West); Clarendon, *History*, ix. 20, 46.

44. Wanklyn, thesis, pp. 141–6; Bod. L., Tanner MS 60, fo. 36 (Digby to Goring); Staffordshire RO, D (W), 1778, li/44 (Rupert to Legge).

45. Clarendon, *History*, ix. 15–28, corrected by Bod. L., Clarendon MS 24, fos. 134–8 (letters of Digby, Goring, Council), and MS 26, fo. 77ᵛ (Grenville's defence); Bod. L., Rawlinson MS C125, fo. 12ᵛ (letter by Fanshawe); Warburton, *Memoirs of Prince Rupert*, iii. 79–80 (resolution of Western Association); William Salt L., Salt MS 45, fos. 33–13 (the latter part of the book being paginated backwards); Bod. L., Firth MS C7, fo. 325 (Trevor to Rupert).

46. Clarendon, *History*, ix. 18.

47. Bod. L., Clarendon MS 26, fo. 77ᵛ (Grenville's defence); Bod. L., Firth MS C7, fos. 310–11 (Goring to Digby).

48. Clarendon, *History*, ix. 18–19.

49. Ibid., ix. 43–7, corrected by Bod. L., Clarendon MS 24, fos. 149–67 (letters of Goring, Culpeper, Council, and Digby), Tanner MS 60, fo. 624 (Culpeper

to Goring), and Firth MS C7, fos. 298 (Goring's report) and 308–11 (Goring to Digby); Warburton, *Memoirs*, iii. 92–123 (letters of Hyde, Goring, King, and Digby); LJ vii. 374 (Weldon to Fairfax); HMC Portland MSS, i. 222, 224 (letters of Prince and Digby); Wanklyn, thesis, pp. 195–218; SP 16/507/70, 74, 79 (letters of Digby, Goring, Culpeper).

50. Clarendon, *History*, ix. 22–7, 52–6, 59–65, corrected by Roger Granville, *The King's General in the West* (1904), pp. 116–17 (Grenville to treasurer); Bod. L., Clarendon MS 24, fo. 172 (Grenville to Culpeper), MS 25, fo. 5 (Grenville to Council), and MS 27, fos. 77–8 (Grenville's defence).

51. Clarendon, *History*, ix. 48–51, 57, corrected by Bod. L., Clarendon MS 24, fos. 163, 175, 178–200 (letters of Prince, Goring, and Hyde), and MS 25, fo. 44 (Goring to Digby); Wanklyn, thesis, pp. 235–7.

52. Clarendon, *History*, ix. 73–84, 92–102, corrected by Bod. L., Clarendon MS 25, fos. 19–237 (letters of Goring, Culpeper, Council, Prideaux, Grenville, Berkeley, Triplett), and MS 26, fos. 3–61 (letters of Fanshawe, Culpeper, and Goring); HMC Portland MSS, i. 262, 278, 292 (letters of Massey, Culpeper, and Fairfax); Joshua Sprigge, *Anglia Rediviva* (repr. 1854), pp. 138–9, 145–8, 154–9.

53. Clarendon, ix. 103–60, corrected by Sir Richard Bulstrode, *Memoirs and Reflections* (1721), pp. 149–52; Sprigge, *Anglia Rediviva*, pp. 149–223; Bod. L., Clarendon MS 26, fos. 11, 81–191 (letters of Wentworth, Culpeper, Grenville, and Hyde), and MS 27, fos. 3–15 (letters of Grenville and Prince) and 78–9 (Grenville's defence); Thomas Carte (ed.), *Original Letters* (1739), pp. 109–26. (Hopton's account); *Report and Transactions of the Devonshire Association*, 85 (1953), pp. 97–102 (Council to King).

Chapter 2

1. Clarendon, *History*, ix. 149, x. 3; Bod. L., Carte MS 16, fos. 609–10 (Hyde to Ormonde, Digby); Bod. L., Clarendon MS 28, fo. 156 (Hyde to Berkeley); Charles Robert Fanshawe (ed.), *Memoirs of Lady Fanshawe* (1829), pp. 59–60.

2. Clarendon, *History*, x. 3–5; Bod. L., Clarendon MS 28, fos. 15–16 (Hyde to Arundell); CJ iv. 478–94; LJ viii. 216–46; Chevalier's Journal, quoted in S. Elliot Hoskins, *Charles II in the Channel Islands* (1854), i. 351–3, 413.

3. Hoskins, *Channel Islands*, vol. i, *passim*; Fanshawe, *Memoirs*, pp. 60–1; LJ viii. 295–315; CJ iv. 554.

4. Printed in Clarendon, *History*, ix. 74, 95, 112, 114.

5. Bod. L., Clarendon MS 27, fos. 116, 158, 160, and MS 28, fo. 23.

6. As the Venetian ambassador pointed out: *CSPV* (1643–7), p. 264.

7. Bod. L., Clarendon MS 27, fo. 90, and MS 28, fo. 95; Sir Charles Petrie (ed.), *The Letters of King Charles I* (1968), p. 180, J. G. Fotheringham (ed.), *The Diplomatic Correspondence of Jean De Montereul and the Brothers De Bellièvre* (Scottish History Soc., 1898), i. 219–20.

8. My general observations upon France in the 1640s, here and below, are based on Geoffrey Parker, *The Thirty Years War* (1985); A. Lloyd Moote, *The Revolt of the Judges* (Princeton, 1971); Pierre-Georges Lorris, *La Fronde* (Paris, 1961); Ernst H. Kossman, *La Fronde* (Leiden, 1954); and John B. Wolf, *Louis XIV* (1968).

9. Chevalier's Journal, in Hoskins, *Channel Islands*, i. 374.

10. I have drawn Digby's portrait twice before, in 'The Structure of the Royalist Party, 1642–1646', *HJ*, 24 (1981), pp. 553–69, and *The Restoration* (1985), p. 167. For Irish affairs in these years, the staple detailed work still seems to be Thomas L. Coonan, *The Irish Catholic Confederacy and the Puritan Revolution* (1954), though I dissent from its conclusions.

11. All in his frank letter to Ormonde, printed in Thomas Carte, *The Life of James, Duke of Ormonde* (1735–6), iii. 475–6.

12. Bod. L., Clarendon MS 28, fos. 37–9 (Hyde to Jermyn).

13. As noted in *CSPV* (1643–7), p. 258.

14. Chevalier's Journal in Hoskins, *Channel Islands*, i. 382; HMC Beaufort MSS, pp. 16–17 (Capel's memorial).

15. Carte, *Ormonde*, iii. 476–7; HMC Beaufort MSS, pp. 17–18; Henry Cary (ed.), *Memorials of the Great Civil War in England* (1842), i. 32–3, 42, 56, 72 (reports of parliamentarian agent in France); Leopold von Ranke, *Englische Geschichte* (Berlin, 1859–69), viii. 169, 175 (instructions to Bellièvre).

16. Chevalier's Journal and Osborne Papers, in Hoskins, *Channel Islands*, i. 351–413.

17. HMC Beaufort MSS, pp. 18–19.

18. Bod. L., Clarendon MS 28, fos. 95 (Queen to Prince), 114 (Counsellors to Queen), and 116–18 (notes of debate); Hoskins, *Channel Islands*, i. 427, 442–4 (Chevalier's Journal).

19. CSP ii. 242–329 (letters of King, Queen, Jermyn, Culpeper, and Ashburnham).

20. Coonan, *Irish Catholic Confederacy*, chs. xv–xvii, and sources listed there, plus Carte, *Ormonde*, iii. 481–559 (letters of Prince, Queen, and Ormonde).

21. Pierre Adolphe Cheruel, *Histoire de France pendant la Minorité de Louis XIV* (Paris, 1879), ii. 278.

22. *CSPV* (1643–7), pp. 272–3.

23. Bod. L., Clarendon MS 28, fo. 229 (newsletter from London).

24. *CSPV* (1643–7), p. 275.

25. Ibid., pp. 269–70, 275–6; Grace Hart Seely (trans.), *The Memoirs of La Grande Mademoiselle* (New York, 1928), pp. 68–71; Bod. L., Clarendon MS 28, fo. 262 (minutes of conversation with Dr Johnson). There is a suggestion in George F. Warner (ed.), *The Nicholas Papers* (Camden Soc., 1886), i. 117 (Hatton to Nicholas), that Charles was offended by the French royal family at their parting from him in 1648, but no trace of earlier friction.

26. *CSPV* (1643–7), pp. 269–70; Bod. L., Clarendon MS 28, fo. 200 (financial memorandum); BL Add. MS 34702, fo. 12 (letter from Browne).

27. CSP ii. 345 (Hyde to Nicholas).
28. *CSPV* (1643–7), p. 256.
29. Osborne Papers, in Hoskins, *Channel Islands*, i. 354–5.
30. CSP ii. 329 (Hyde to Earle).
31. Ibid., ii. 253 (King to Prince).
32. She reveals herself wonderfully in her own Memoirs.
33. *CSPV* (1643–7), pp. 40–1, 151, 232.
34. Mademoiselle, *Memoirs*, pp. 69–75.
35. Fotheringham (ed.), *Correspondence of Jean de Montereul*, i. 447–8; CSP ii. 346 (Hyde to Nicholas). The latter reference is almost certainly to this courtship, though often misinterpreted to refer to Lucy Walter.
36. Mademoiselle, *Memoirs*, pp. 69–78.
37. Katherine Prescott Wormeley (trans.), *Memoirs of Madame de Motteville* (1902), i. 211.
38. Ibid., i. 174; Mademoiselle, *Memoirs*, pp. 69–75; *CSPV* (1643–7), p. 293; Bod. L., Clarendon MS 29, fo. 144 (newsletter from Paris).
39. Examples are in *CSPV* (1643–7), p. 267; HMC Beaufort MSS, pp. 16–17; CSP ii. 312 (Jermyn, Culpeper, to King); and Mademoiselle, *Memoirs*, pp. 72–5.
40. Wiltshire RO, MS 'A', fo. 57, and MS 'B', fo. 11 (accounts of Rupert's Civil War career by a friend or friends); CSP ii. 301 (Jermyn, Culpeper, to King) and 351 (letter from Rupert). There is no real evidence that Charles felt any special admiration for Rupert as a boy, or that the two were ever close. The only hint of warmth between them is the story in Clarendon that Rupert used Charles as an intermediary with the King to deliver a petition on behalf of an officer condemned to death. On the other hand, Charles certainly appreciated Rupert's abilities and advice.
41. Thomas Carte (ed.), *A Collection of Original Letters* (1739), i. 152–8 (O'Neill to Ormonde); Samuel Rawson Gardiner (ed.), *The Hamilton Papers* (Camden Soc., 1880), p. 178 (letter to Lanark); Bod. L., Carte MS 29, fos. 113, 143 (newsletters from Paris).
42. Fotheringham (ed.), *Correspondence of Jean de Montereul*, ii. 161–3, 187, 192. I cannot accept Gardiner's belief, in his *History of the Great Civil War*, iii. 294 and note, and 326–7 and note, that Cromwell and St John made secret overtures to the Queen in January 1648 to have the Prince crowned. The evidence, gossip in London, is simply too flimsy.
43. Samuel Rawson Gardiner (ed.), *Constitutional Documents of the Puritan Revolution* (Oxford, 1962), p. 350.
44. Carte, *Ormonde*, iii. 545–6, 549, 574 (letters of Queen, Prince, and Ormonde); Bod. L., Carte MS 22, fo. 585 (Ormonde to Inchiquin).
45. Carte, *Ormonde*, ii. 20–1; Coonan, *Irish Catholic Confederacy*, ch. xix.
46. Fotheringham (ed.), *Correspondence of Jean de Montereul*, ii. 385–491.
47. Bod. L., Carte MS 22, fos. 58–60, 76, 87–9 (exchange of papers).
48. The best study of Scottish affairs in these years is David Stevenson, *Revolution*

and *Counter-Revolution in Scotland, 1644–1651* (1977); pp. 97–109 cover the events under discussion.

49. Gilbert Burnet, *The Memoires of the Lives and Actions of James and William, Dukes of Hamilton* (1677), pp. 346–7; 'Royal Letters and Instructions, and Other Documents, from the Archives of the Earls of Wigton', *Maitland Club Miscellany*, II. ii (1840), pp. 457–9.

50. Bod. L., Clarendon MS 31, fo. 66 (newsletter from Honslaerdyck); *Colonel Joseph Bamfeild's Apologie* (The Hague, 1685), pp. 41–2; the Revd J. S. Clarke (ed.), *The Life of James II* (1816), i. 34–8.

51. J. R. Powell, *The Navy in the English Civil war* (1962), ch. x.

52. *Hamilton Papers*, pp. 171, 175, 226 (letters to Lanark); Firth, *Life of Newcastle*, pp. 90–1; S. R. Gardiner (ed.), 'Hamilton Papers. Addenda', in *Camden Miscellany*, ix (1895), pp. 1–35 (letters to Lanark).

53. *CSPV* (1647–52), p. 61; Bod. L., Clarendon MS 31, fo. 116 (Prince to Hyde); BL Add. MS 34702, fo. 26 (Browne to Nicholas); *Hamilton Papers*, p. 207 (Murray to Lanark); 'Royal Letters and Instructions', *Maitland Club Miscellany*, II. ii. 459–63.

54. *Hamilton Papers. Addenda*, p. 39 (Murray to Lanark); *CSPV* (1647–52), p. 64; Bod. L., Clarendon MS 31, fos. 118–48 (various letters to Hyde); *Prince Charles Sailing from Callice* [17 July] (1648); *The Perfect Weekly Account* (12–19 July 1648); HMC Pepys MSS, p. 210 (Prince to Willoughby).

55. Bod. L., Clarendon MS 31, fo. 141 (newsletter to Hyde); *Nicholas Papers*, i. 92–3.

56. Clarendon MS 31, fos. 112 (Nicholas to King), 119 (Hyde to Queen and Prince).

57. *A Remonstrance of His Highness the Prince of Wales* [19 July] (1648).

58. Clarendon, *History*, xi. 33–6; *Dumfeild's Apologie*, pp. 43–5; Clarke (ed.), *Life of James II*, i. 43–4; BL Add. MS 18982, fo. 118 (Bampfield to Rupert); *CSPV* (1647–52), p. 66.

59. Ibid., p. 69; *A Remonstrance to His Highness*; Bod. L., Carte MS 22, fo. 140 (the oath); *The Moderate Intelligencer* (13–20 July 1648).

60. Clarendon, *History*, xi. 35; *Hamilton Papers*, pp. 228 (Bellenden to Lanark), 232 (Prince to Scots); *CSPV* (1647–52), p. 69.

61. Motteville, *Memoirs*, i. 211.

62. The case against them is made in A. Lang, 'The Master Hoaxer: James de la Cloche', *Fortnightly Review* (Sept. 1909), and the whole dispute reviewed in Arthur Irwin Dasent, *The Private Life of Charles the Second* (1927), ch. 11, while some of the papers (deposited in the Vatican) were imperfectly printed in *The Gentleman's Magazine* (1866), pt. 1, pp. 531–4, and pt. 2, pp. 65–8. My own feeling about the latter is that they entirely fail to fit into the English political context of the dates upon them, and in at least one point are factually wrong about it. So they are indeed very suspicious.

63. All the extant sources are printed and discussed by Lucy's apologists, G. D. Gilbert, in an appendix to his addition of Baron D'Aulnoy, *Memoirs of the*

Court of England in 1675 (1913), and Lord George Scott, *Lucy Walter: Wife or Mistress* (1947).

64. *The Heroic Life and Magnanimous Actions of the Most Illustrious Protestant Prince* (1683).

65. LJ x. 399–400 (bailiffs to Derby House Committee); Bod. L., Clarendon MS 31, fo. 171 (draft of declaration); *The Prince of Wales His Coming to Yarmouth* (27 July 1648); *The Resolution of the Prince of Wales* [31 July] (1648); *The Kingdomes Weekly Intelligencer* (25 July–1 Aug. 1648).

66. *The Resolution of the Prince of Wales*; LJ x. 414 (Warwick to Derby House Committee); Clarendon, *History*, xi. 36.

67. Wiltshire RO, 413/444, MS 'B', fo. 22 (notes upon Rupert's career).

68. LJ x. 415; Corporation of London RO, Journal 40, fo. 291^v; *CSPV* (1647–52), p. 72; Bod. L., Clarendon MS 31, fos. 241 (Dr Stewart's relation) and 242 ('A Relation of the Prince's Motions'); *The Declaration of his Highnesse Prince Charles* [8 Aug.] (1648).

69. HMC Portland MSS, i. 494 (Livesey to Lenthall); *Packets of Letters from Scotland* (14 Aug. 1648); *Colonel Rich's Letter To The House of Commons* (16 Aug. 1648); *The Princes First Fruits* [18 Aug.] (1648); *Hamilton Papers*, p. 247 (Lauderdale to Lanark).

70. *The Designs and Correspondencies of the present Committee of Estates* (16 Aug. 1648), pp. 12–15 (letters to Lanark); Scottish RO, PA 11/6, fos. 92^v, 156–61 (register of Committee of Estates).

71. *Hamilton Papers*, pp. 232–48; Bod. L., Clarendon MS 31, fo. 202 (draft replies of Prince to Scots).

72. This is to accept the story in University L., Cardiff, A(braham) J(ennings), *Miraculum Basilicon* (1664), pp. 67–8, that the first news of Preston was brought to Charles in the Downs by Dr John Hinton.

73. Bod. L., Clarendon MS 31, fos. 233 ('A Journal of the Movements of the Fleet'), 241 (Dr Stewart's Relation), 242–3 ('A Relation of the Prince's Motions'), and 246 ('Relation Concerning The Management of the Fleet'); Clarendon MS 40, fos. 172–6 ('Mr Causabons Paper'); Wiltshire RO, 413/444, MS 'B', fos. 23–4 (account of Rupert's actions); LJ x. 483–95 (Warwick's dispatches); *Miraculum Basilicon*, pp. 67–73 (Hinton's account); *A Perfect Remonstrance and Narrative Of All The Proceedings of the Right Honourable Robert Earl of Warwick* [1 Jan.] 1649; *The Copie of A Letter From A Commander in the Fleet* [20 Sept.] (1648) (a royalist version); *A true Relation of what past betweene the Fleet of his Highnes the Prince. . . .* (1648) (Batten's account); *The Diary of Samuel Pepys* (ed. Robert Latham and William Matthews, 1971), v. 169 (Charles's reminiscence).

74. Bod. L., Clarendon MS 31, fo. 247 (Hyde to Queen); Bod. L., Firth MS C8, fo. 76a (Jermyn to Rupert); Clarendon, *History*, xi. 86–90; *A Letter Sent From The States of Holland*, 22 Sept. (1648).

75. Stevenson, *Revolution and Counter-Revolution*, pp. 115–24.

76. Bod. L., Clarendon MS 31, fo. 282 (Committee of Estates to Prince).

77. LJ x. 495–523 (Warwick's dispatches); *A Perfect Remonstrance and Narrative*, pp. 3–4.

78. Pieter Geyl, *Orange and Stuart* (1969), pp. 41–3.

79. Ibid., p. 44 and n. 10; Clarendon, *History*, xi. 78–84, 127–30; Carte, *Ormonde*, iii. 597–8 (Prince to Ormonde); *Nicholas Papers*, i. 107 (Nicholas to Oudart); Fanshawe, *Memoirs*, p. 70; Bod. L., Carte MS 22, fos. 263 (Wentworth to Ormonde) and 619 (Digby to Ormonde). Charles's Counsellors in the autumn of 1648 were Rupert, Culpeper, Hyde, Cottington, Hopton, Willoughby, and Brentford, with Robert Long as secretary to the Council. Also at his court were Lords Percy, Gerard, Wentworth, Wilmot, and Widdrington, and the Duke of Buckingham, and some of these certainly exercised influence at times; sources at nn. 71, 73, 79, and 80.

80. *CSPV* (1647–52), pp. 79–80; BL Add. MS 18982, fos. 138–9 (Hyde to Rupert).

81. Warburton (ed.), *Memoirs of Prince Rupert and the Cavaliers* (1849), i. 532 (Hyde to Rupert, 29 Nov. 1648); Bod. L., Firth MS C8, fo. 82 (Batten to Rupert); Clarendon MS 31, fo. 322 (Rupert to Batten); BL Add. MS 18982, fo. 152 (letter to Queen); *A Fight at Sea* (6 Nov. 1648).

82. Clarendon, *History*, xi. 32, 142; BL Add. MS 18982, fos. 138–9 (Hyde to Rupert); *Nicholas Papers*, i. 97 (Hatton to Nicholas); Carte, *Ormonde*, iii. 582, 584 (Nicholas to Ormonde).

83. Warburton, *Memoirs*, iii. 263–4 (lost notes upon Rupert's life); Bod. L., Carte MS C8, fo. 78 (Hyde to Rupert).

84. LJ xi. 595 (Warwick's dispatch); *Two Letters* [Nov.] (1648); *A Letter From The Navy with the Earle of Warwick* (1648); *A Perfect Remonstrance and Narrative*, pp. 6–7; Wiltshire RO, MS 'B', fos. 24–5; *CSPV* (1647–52), pp. 81–2.

85. BL Add. MS 18982, fos. 138–9 (Hyde to Rupert); Clarendon, *History*, xi. 141; Warburton, *Memoirs*, iii. 279–80 (Hyde to Fanshaw); Bod. L., Clarendon MS 31, fos. 301, 305 (Charles to James).

86. Bod. L., Firth MS C8, fo. 85 (Culpeper to Rupert); Clarendon MS 31, fo. 310 (Hopton to Hyde), and MS 32, fo. 57 (accounts).

87. LJ xi. 625–6 (Warwick's dispatch); *A Perfect Remonstrance and Narrative*, pp. 7–8.

88. Warburton, *Memoirs*, iii. 273–5, 280–1 (lost royalist narratives); Bod. L., Firth MS C8, fo. 142 (Hyde to Rupert); BL Add. MS 18982, fo. 161 (Hyde to Rupert), and Add. MS 21506, fo. 52 (Hyde to Rupert).

89. Clarendon, *History*, xi. 138–40.

90. *A Letter Sent From The States*; Carte, *Ormonde*, iii. 576–7, 581 (Prince to Ormonde); Bod. L., Clarendon MS 31, fos. 278 (Jermyn to Hyde), 319 (Hyde to Digby), and MS 32, fo. 68 (Massey to Prince); Carte MS 22, fos. 259–60 (Hyde to Ormonde), 371 (Long to Ormonde), and 415–16 (Digby to Ormonde).

91. Carte MSS 67, fo. 315 (Inchiquin's commission) and 273, fos. 5–8 (Ormonde's commissions); Carte, *Ormonde*, iii. 577–83 (letters from Ormonde).

92. Coonan, *Irish Catholic Confederacy*, ch. xxi.
93. Warburton, *Memoirs*, iii. 266, 281 (lost royalist narrative); Bod. L., Carte MS 23, fo. 288 (Prince to Ormonde); Clarendon, *History*, xi. 150. Prince Maurice and Sir John Mennes were made junior admirals and Sir Richard Fielding and Sir Thomas Kittleby were among the captains.
94. Carte, *Ormonde*, iii. 601 (Ormonde to Prince); HMC Pepys MSS, pp. 248–9 (instructions to Byron).
95. Carte, *Ormonde*, iii. 584 (Nicholas to Ormonde); Bod. L., Carte MS 22, fos. 433 and 438, and MS 63, fo. 562 (letters of Digby, Jermyn, and Long to Ormonde); *CSPV* (1647–52), pp. 83–4; Clarke (ed.), *Life of James II*, p. 45; Clarendon, *History*, xi. 150 n. 2.
96. Petrie, *Letters of Charles I*, pp. 239–40; Clarendon, *History*, xi. 189–92.
97. *CSPD* (1648–9), p. 347 (Prince to Queen Regent, and to Mazarin); Bod. L., Clarendon MS 32, fos. 82 (Prince to army) and 83–4 (draft of circular letter).
98. Clarendon, *History*, xi. 212–15; Bod. L., Carte MS 23, fo. 311 (Prince to States-General); SP 16/516/143 (Boswell's speech). The traditional story of the Prince's *carte blanche* offer to Parliament has been exploded by C. V. Wedgwood, *The Trial of Charles I* (1964), p. 170.
99. Ellis, *Original Letters*, 2nd ser., iii. 347.

Chapter 3

All studies of Scotland in the period 1649–51 must be based on David Stevenson's book *Revolution and Counter-Revolution*, cited ch. 2 n. 48. He provided in that a framework for events and a number of reinterpretations which I have entirely accepted. My work in parts of this and the next chapter has been to refocus, to extend, and sometimes to redevelop some of the points within his framework.

1. Carte, *Original Letters*, i. 301–2 (Jermyn to Ormonde); *Nicholas Papers*, i. 116–17, 123–5, 128 (Hatton and Hyde to Nicholas). Most potent among the unofficial advisers were reckoned the Gentlemen of the Bedchamber, Lords Wentworth, Gerard, Wilmot, and Andover, but these were apparently themselves divided upon the question of concessions.
2. CSP ii. 523–5, iii. 13–16 (Hyde to Nicholas).
3. The permanent agents were Sir William Boswell at The Hague, Sir Henry De Vic in Brussels, and Sir Richard Browne in Paris. Those employed on missions, other than the Privy Counsellors named, were William Curtius (to German states); Sir John Cochrane (to German states, Denmark, Poland, and Courland); Sir William Vavasour (to Oldenburg); William Swan (to Emperor and Saxony); Thomas Killigrew (to Italian states); Robert Meynell (to Pope); Sir William Bellenden (to Sweden); Thomas Elliot (to Portugal); and Johann von Karpfen (to German states). The diplomats of 1649–50

were therefore a mixed set of important royal advisers, household officers, and military men who knew the countries concerned, selected *ad hoc*: BL Add. MS 37047, fos. 1–2, 60, 72, 76 (letters of Browne, De Vic, Culpeper, and Curtius to Long); HMC 2nd Report, p. 176 (Cochrane to Montrose); Carte, *Original Letters*, i. 231–2 (newsletter from The Hague), 311, 313 (Nicholas to Ormonde); S. R. Gardiner, *Charles II and Scotland in 1650* (Scottish History Soc., 1894), pp. 124–6 (notes by Long), 128–9 (Meynell to Cottington); *Nicholas Papers*, i. 123–5 (Hyde to Nicholas), 182–5 (account of Culpeper's embassy); CSP ii. 481–532 (instructions to and letters from Hyde, Cottington, and Meynell); HMC Hodgkin MSS, pp. 120–1 (Elliot to Portuguese king); 'Civil War Papers' (ed. H. Simpson) in Scottish History Soc., *Miscellany*, 1 (1893), pp. 169–202; the Revd W. D. Macray (ed.), *Ruthven Correspondence* (Roxburgh Club, 1868), pp. 97–103 (instructions to and letters from Brentford); HMC Pepys MSS, pp. 252–3 (instructions to Bramshall), 292 (Brentford to King); *CSPV* (1647–52), pp. 119, 136–7; Clarendon, *History*, xii. 48–50; BL Add. MS 15857, fos. 126–8 (King to Browne); Scottish RO, GD 40, Old Classification 6/16, Nos. 1–16 (abstracts of Von Karpfen's dispatches). Reimbursement, and advances, for missions, are recorded in BL Add. MS 37047, fos. 5–10, and MS 38854, fos. 30–51, and Royal Archives, Stuart Papers Add. 1/19.

4. Carte, *Original Letters*, i. 237–8, 240 (Byron to Ormonde), 242–4 (Hamilton, Lauderdale, to Ormonde), 247 (King to Ormonde); Bod. L., Carte MS 24, fos. 97 (King to Ormonde), 575–6 (instructions to Legge); *Nicholas Papers*, i. 120–1 (Hatton to Cottington); CSP ii. 473 (Hyde to Jermyn).

5. Bod. L., Carte MS 23, fo. 400 (King to Ormonde), MS 24, fos. 107 (King to Ormonde), 709–10 (instructions to Steward), and MS 25, fo. 45 (King to Ormonde).

6. Bod. L., Carte MS 23, fo. 534 (offer to O'Neill), and MS 25, fo. 498 (instructions for Talbot).

7. APS vi. ii. 157, 161, 211–12, 300; *RCGA* (1896), pp. 197–8, 212–15, 236.

8. HMC Leybourne-Popham MSS, pp. 9–11 (letter to Thomas Kynaston); CSP ii. 476–8 (Hyde to Berkeley); HMC Pepys MSS, pp. 250–1 (Argyll, Loudoun, to King).

9. The description of Hamilton is from Burnet, *Dukes of Hamilton*, p. 417. The best current life of Montrose seems to be Edward J. Cowan, *Montrose: For Covenant and King* (1977). Lesser Scottish figures present at court were the Earls of Callander (for the Engagers) and of Seaforth and Kinnoul, plus Lord Sinclair and Lord Napier (allies of Montrose).

10. HMC Leybourne-Popham MSS, pp. 9–11 (letter to Kynaston); David Laing (ed.), *The Letters and Journals of Robert Baillie* (Edinburgh, 1842), iii. 71–90, 511–14; HMC 2nd Report, p. 170 (Queen to Montrose); Carte, *Original Letters*, i. 231–2 (newsletter), 238 (Byron to Ormonde); *Nicholas Papers*, i.

126–7 (Edgeman to Nicholas); HMC Pepys MSS, p. 252 (King to Loudoun); Bod. L., Carte MS 24, fo. 407, and MS 27, fos. 10–11 (Long to Ormonde); Clarendon, *History*, xii. 15–22, 30–1.

11. J. Maclean, 'Montrose's Preparations for the Invasion of Scotland', in Ragnhild Hatton and M. S. Anderson (eds.), *Studies in Diplomatic History* (1970), pp. 7–9.

12. Ibid., pp. 9–10; SP 18/1/80 (Von Karpfen's commission); Baillie, *Letters*, iii. 515–20; Bod. L., Clarendon MS 37, fos. 104–5 ('Papers read in Council' and note by Hyde on reply of 19 May); Mark Napier, *Memorials of Montrose and his Times* (Maitland Club, 1850), ii. 376–83 (Montrose to King), 416 (King to Napier); BL Add. MS 40132, fos. 7–10 (imperfect copy of King's 'express' to Scottish Parliament); HMC 2nd Report, p. 173 (commissions to Montrose); Carte, *Original Letters*, i. 260–3 (memorial to States-General); Clarendon, *History*, xii. 27.

13. Geyl, *Orange and Stuart*, pp. 50–2; Bod. L., Carte MS 25, fo. 6 (Wandesforde to Ormonde); Carte, *Original Letters*, i. 237–8 (Byron to Ormonde), 265–6 (Long to Ormonde), and 279 (newsletter); Clarendon, *History*, xii. 23–7; Cary, *Memorials*, ii. 131 (Strickland to Council of State); *CSPV* (1647–52), p. 89.

14. Geyl, *Orange and Stuart*, p. 52. On 6 June Charles ordered the payment of 29,900 guilders to 48 individuals, and on 13 June he divided 26,738 guilders among 98 people. These payments included salaries to Privy Counsellors, household officers and servants, and reimbursement of diplomats: BL Add. MS 37047, fos. 5–10. But he still owed 187,126 guilders to a variety of individuals including jewellers, tailors, an apothecary, and several royalist gentry, which may or may not have been paid off: BL Add. MS 38854, fos. 30–51.

15. Bod. L., Carte MS 24, fos. 575–6 (instructions to Legge).

16. Clarendon, *History*, xii. 55–8; M. Guizot, *History of Oliver Cromwell* (trans. A. R. Scoble, 1854), i. 389–402 (letters of Council, Cardeñas, Penaranda, and Archduke); BL Add. MS 37047, fo. 15 (instructions for De Vic); *CSPV* (1647–52), pp. 109–10.

17. Motteville, *Memoirs*, ii. 131–44; *Memoirs of Mademoiselle de Montpensier* (1848), i. 125–45; Sir James Balfour, *The Historical Works* (1825), iii. 415.

18. *Memoirs of Sophia, Electress of Hanover* (trans. H. Forester, 1888), pp. 23–5; *The Diary of John Evelyn* (ed. E. S. De Beer, Oxford, 1955), ii. 561–2; *The Heroic Life*, pp. 1–2. The previous biographies of Charles have references, without sources given, to a daughter born to him in 1651, by Elizabeth, wife of Francis Boyle and Maid of Honour to Henrietta Maria. The girl was baptized Charlotte Jemima Henrietta Maria Fitzroy and later married James Howard. I have been unable to uncover any contemporary details of this affair whatever.

19. Bod. L., Carte MS 25, fos. 56–7, 195, 380, 597–8.

20. Apparently coined by Eva Scott, but expressed most succinctly by David

Underdown, *Royalist Conspiracy in England, 1649–1660* (New Haven, 1960), pp. 10–11.

21. Sources at nn. 1–3, plus Clarendon, *History*, xii. 59, xiii. 41; CSP ii. 516–20 (Hyde to Morley); *Nicholas Papers*, i. 138–9 (Hyde's paper on Levellers); *A Complete Collection of State Trials* (ed. T. B. Howell), v (1817), pp. 68–9.

22. Clarendon, *History*, xii. 60–4, which seems confirmed by Carte, *Original Letters*, i. 301–2 (Jermyn to Ormonde); Bod. L., Carte MS 25, fos. 175–6 (Nicholas to Ormonde) and 302 (Radcliffe to Ormonde).

23. *Nicholas Papers*, i. 133–4 (Oudart to Nicholas); *The Diary of John Evelyn* (ed. Henry B. Wheatley, 1879), iv. 195–8 (Nicholas to King, King to Nicholas).

24. Clarendon, *History*, xii. 60. It is odd that nothing in the Nicholas or Ormonde papers refers to Elliot's malign influence: perhaps Hyde exaggerates. Elliot departed for Portugal in February 1650: Royal Archives (Windsor Castle), Stuart Papers Add. 1/19, 1 Feb. 1650. Perhaps Elliot's departure may be connected with his rigid disapproval of negotiation with the Scots: CSP ii. 530–1 (Berkeley to Hyde).

25. Clarendon, *History*, xii. 75–7; Hoskins, *Charles II in the Channel Islands*, ii. 310–57 (quoting Chevalier's Journal).

26. Hoskins, ii. 320–1, 350–1; SP 18/3/85–9, 5/15 (letters to royalists and to servants); Sir Arthur Bryant (ed.), *Letters of Charles II* (2nd edn., New York, 1968), pp. 14–15 (to Progers); BL Lansdowne MS 1236, fos. 89–97 (letters to royalists).

27. Hoskins, *Channel Islands*, ii. 340, 371, 381; Carte, *Original Letters*, i. 314 (Nicholas to Ormonde); Bod. L., Carte MS 25, fo. 557 (King to Ormonde); SP 18/3/14 (King to Buckingham).

28. Hoskins, *Channel Islands*, ii. 385; BL Add. MS 37047, fo. 25 (grant to seven individuals)

29. Carte, *Original Letters*, i. 314–38 (letters to Ormonde from Nicholas, Long, Byron, Jermyn); Hoskins, *Channel Islands*, ii. 345–6 (King to Rupert); Carte, *Ormonde*, ii. 86–7, 106–7 (Ormonde to King); Bod. L., Carte MS 25, fos. 597–8, 728–48, MS 26, fos. 289, 304, 412, MS 31, fo. 275 (letters from Ormonde, King, Long, and Nicholas), and MS 213, fos. 12–13 (Seymour to Ormonde).

30. BL Egerton MS 2542, fos. 14–15 (Whitley's instructions); SP 18/3/23–4 (King to western royalists); HMC Portland MSS, i. 577 (Cooke's confession).

31. Bod. L., Carte MS 26, fo. 289.

32. Balfour, *Historical Works*, iii. 417, 432; Baillie, *Letters*, iii. 99–103 (to Spang, Wynrame); APS vi. ii. 535, 739–41; Scottish RO, PA 11/8, fos. 146–7 (register of Committee of Estates); Carte, *Original Letters*, i. 332–3 (Jermyn to Ormonde); Hoskins, *Channel Islands*, ii. 358–9; *State Trials*, v. 69.

33. Carte, *Original Letters*, i. 337–9 (Byron to Ormonde); Hoskins, *Channel Islands*, ii. 358–63 (Chevalier's Journal); Bod. L., Carte MS 26, fo. 498 (King to Ormonde); RCGA (1896), pp. 354–5; *Nicholas Papers*, i. 160–1 (Council resolution).

34. Napier, *Memorials of Montrose*, ii. 410–12; HMC 6th Report app., p. 612 (King to Argyll, 12 Jan. 1650); Maclean, 'Montrose's Preparations', pp. 11–20; *Hamilton Papers*, p. 254 (King to Hamilton); BL Egerton MS 1533, fo. 18 (King to Presbyterians); BL Harl. MS 6852, fos. 335–50 (Newcastle's commission).

35. Balfour, *Historical Works*, iv. 2; *APS* VI. ii. 557–60; *RCGA* (1896), pp. 367–73; John Nickolls, *Original Letters and Papers of State* (1743), pp. 3–4 (newsletter); Scottish RO, PA 11/9, fo. 65ᵛ (register of Committee of Estates).

36. Hoskins, *Channel Islands*, ii. 377–81 ('Journal of the King's motions'); *RCGA* (1896), pp. 381–2; Gardiner, *Charles II and Scotland*, pp. 15–40. I lack Gardiner's faith in his principal source: *A Brief Relation*, because although racy and detailed, it is an accomplished work of hostile propaganda. Hence I have been able to employ it little.

37. *RCGA* (1896), pp. 381–92; Baillie, *Letters*, iii. 523–4 (Wynrame to Douglas); *A Brief Historical Relation of the Life of Mr. John Livingstone* (ed. the Revd Thomas Houston, 1848), pp. 115–23; HMC Hamilton MSS, p. 131 (Privy Council minute); Gardiner, *Charles II and Scotland*, pp. 60–88; *Nicholas Papers*, i. 186–7 (Nicholas to Hyde); Carte, *Original Letters*, i. 378–9 (Nicholas to Ormonde); CSP, vol. ii, pp. li–lix (papers exchanged for treaty); Bod. L., Clarendon MS 39, fos. 99–101 (King to commissioners, 17 Apr.; Cassilis's copy of the note on Ireland is in the Scottish RO, GD/9/30); SP 18/9/25 (Privy Council note).

38. Bod. L., Clarendon MS 40, fos. 20–40 (letters of Hyde, Cottington); CSP ii. 530–1 (Berkeley to Hyde); Gardiner, *Charles II and Scotland*, pp. 106–8 (Queen Mother to King); *Nicholas Papers*, i. 172 (Nicholas to Hyde).

39. Gardiner, *Charles II and Scotland*, p. 154 (Coke's confession); SP 18/9/27 (answer to Colonel Keane); *State Trials*, v. 69–70, 78, 89–90, 105; *Nicholas Papers*, i. 180–1 (King to Lord Beauchamp); HMC 6th Report, app., p. 613 (King to Ormonde).

40. There is a real problem of evidence here. The letters and instructions dated from 3 to 9 May, all in the *Maitland Club Miscellany*, II. ii. 472–81, are perfectly compatible and comprehensible. The instructions of 12 May, printed in the *Proceedings of the Society of Antiquaries of Scotland*, 34 (1899–1900), pp. 199–202, direct the concealment of a letter to Parliament if Montrose had been defeated (and fled) or never landed, but its presentation if he had invaded and enjoyed success. This is also just about compatible with the letter dated 8 May, asking Parliament for a safe-conduct for Montrose out of Scotland. The trouble is that Fleming did present a letter to the Parliament on 25 May, dated the 12th (or, if New Style, the 2nd), but in which, according to those present, Charles denied that he had ever sanctioned Montrose's invasion. With this he delivered the copy of the order to the Marquis to disband. Gardiner proposed that Argyll and his friends either forged this letter or misrepresented that of the 8th in order to dissociate the

King from Montrose: *History of the Commonwealth and Protectorate* (1894), i. 259–60. Stevenson suggests that Charles wrote another letter to Parliament on 12 May, now lost, coupled with the instructions of that date, and Fleming decided, in the unforeseen circumstances of Montrose's capture, to deliver it: *Revolution and Counter-Revolution*, pp. 165–8. The latter explanation is more logical, but slightly weakened by the fact that drafts of the 'public' order to Montrose to disband and of the letter of 8 May survive in Long's papers in Bod. L., Carte MS 130, but that none exists there of the presumed letter of the 12th. As things stand, the matter is an insoluble puzzle.

41. Napier, *Memorials of Montrose*, ii. 444–5, 448.
42. HMC 2nd Report, app., p. 172 (King to Montrose's son); Gardiner, *Charles II and Scotland*, p. 111 (*A Brief Relation*), 115–16 (North to Edgeman); SP 18/9/94 (Samborne to Nicholas).
43. Balfour, *Historical Works*, iv. 15; *Correspondence of Sir Robert Kerr, First Earl of Ancrum, and his son William, Third Earl of Lothian* (ed. D. Laing, Edinburgh, 1875), p. 262 (Argyll to Lothian).
44. *APS* vi. ii. 562–6; *RCGA* (1896), pp. 399–402.
45. CSP, vol. ii, pp. lxii–lxiii; BL Add. MS 37047, fo. 142.
46. Livingstone, *Relation*, pp. 124–30; Gardiner, *Charles II and Scotland*, pp. 140–2 (Dean of Tuam to Ormonde); CSP, vol. ii, pp. lxiii–lxv (commissioners to King); Sir Edward Walker, *Historical Discourses* (1705), pp. 158–9; *The Journal of Thomas Cunningham* (ed. E. J. Courthope, Scottish History Society, 1928, pp. 231–3); Bod. L., Clarendon MS 40, fo. 80 (the Covenants signed by Charles); *RCGA* (1896), pp. 436–8.
47. *Diary of Alexander Jaffray* (ed. John Barclay, 1833), p. 33.

Chapter 4

1. *APS* vi. ii. 601–3; *RCGA* (1896), pp. 439–40; John Nicoll, *A Diary of Public Transactions* (ed. David Laing, Bannatyne Club, 1836), pp. 16–17; James Fraser, *Chronicles of the Frasers* (ed. W. MacKay, Scottish History Soc., 1894), pp. 365–6; *The Diary of Mr. John Lamont* (ed. G. R. Kinloch, Maitland Club, 1830), pp. 19–20; Balfour, *Historical Works*, iv. 61–2; Walker, *Historical Discourses*, pp. 158–60; SP 18/9/126 ('Jonsonus' to Nicholas).
2. Chiddingstone Castle Collection, King to Argyll and King's instructions to Dunfermline, both 26 June 1650.
3. *The Life of Mr. Robert Blair* (ed. T. M'Crie, Wodrow Soc., 1848), p. 231; *APS* vi. ii. 594–604.
4. Scottish RO, PA 12/5, 3 July 1650 (Lauderdale to Loudoun) and GD 25/9/30 (Hamilton to Cassilis, 2 July 1650); *Hamilton Papers*, p. 254 (King to Hamilton); Gardiner, *Charles II and Scotland*, p. 130 (Loudoun to King); Balfour, *Historical Works*, iv. 66–76; Walker, *Historical Discourses*, pp. 159–62; Bod. L., Clarendon MS 40, fo. 103 (King to General Assembly); Bod. L., Carte MS 130, fo. 179 (General Assembly to King).

5. *The Autobiography of Anne Lady Halkett* (ed. J. G. Nichols, Camden Soc., 1875), pp. 58–65. There is absolutely no reason to link this episode (as Hester Chapman does) to the scurrilous anecdote in *Memoirs of Ewan Cameron* (ed. J. MacKnight, Abbotsford Club, 1842), pp. 91–2, which seems apocryphal. Nor can I substantiate most of the colourful stories given without sources in the Revd C. J. Lyon, *Personal History of King Charles the Second* (Edinburgh, 1851).

6. Livingstone, *Brief Relation*, p. 133.

7. To be precise, 16,354: Cromwell's dispatch in *A Perfect Diurnall* (22–9 July 1650).

8. *APS* vi. ii. 587–600; Balfour, *Historical Works*, iv. 80.

9. W. C. Abbott (ed.), *The Writings and Speeches of Oliver Cromwell* (Cambridge, Mass., 1939), ii. 299–301; *A Perfect Diurnall* (22–9 July 1650); *Mercurius Politicus* (25 July–1 Aug. 1650); *Nicholas Papers*, i. 198–9 (Letter from Cassilis).

10. Chiddingstone Castle Collection, King's instructions to Dunfermline, 26 June 1650.

11. Scottish RO, PA 12/5, 17 July 1650; HMC 6th report, p. 613 (King to Argyll, 19 July).

12. *Charles . . . Whereas The Lord Hath Been Pleased . . .* (1650); Bod. L., Clarendon MS 40, fo. 154ᵛ (the declaration with note appended); Walker, *Historical Discourses*, pp. 163–4.

13. *Diary of Sir Archibald Johnston of Wariston*, ii (ed. D. H. Fleming, Scottish History Soc., 1919), pp. 5–6; Scottish RO, PA 7/24, fo. 7 (paper of Committee); *Hamilton Papers*, p. 255 (King to Hamilton); SP 18/11/5 (letter to Nicholas); *Nicholas Papers*, i. 193–4 (letter from Lauderdale); Balfour, *Historical Works*, iv. 86–7; Walker, *Historical Discourses*, pp.162–3, 165; *Writings of Cromwell*, ii. 300–1; *Mercurius Politicus* (15–22 Aug. 1650); *A Large Relation of the Fight at Leith* [7 Aug.] (1650).

14. *RCGA* (1909), pp. 9–46; Scottish RO, PA 12/5, 8–14 Aug. 1650 (warrants of committee); *Mercurius Politicus* (19–26 Sept. 1650), pp. 269–70 (letters from Loudoun to King); SP 18/11/2, 5 (Radcliffe to Nicholas, unsigned letter to Nicholas); Johnston, *Diary*, pp. 8–20; Bod. L., Carte MS 130, fos. 114–18 (draft of declaration with Long's amendments); Balfour, *Historical Works*, iv. 89–96; Walker, *Historical Discourses*, pp. 167–9; Blair, *Life*, p. 236: *Ancrum and Lothian Correspondence*, pp. 280–94 (letter of committee, Loudoun, Johnston): *A Declaration By The King's Majesty* (16 Aug. 1650).

15. Evelyn, *Diary* (ed. Wheatley), iv. 198–9.

16. HMC Earl of Eglinton MSS, pp. 57–8 (Montgomery to Eglinton); *Nicholas Papers*, i. 193–4 (letter from Lauderdale); Balfour, *Historical Works*, iv. 89; Johnston, *Diary*, pp. 18–20; *Writings of Cromwell*, ii. 311–12; *Mercurius Politicus* (3 issues, 15 Aug.–5 Sept. 1650); *A True Relation of the Daily Proceedings and Transactions of the Army in Scotland* [30 Aug.] (1650); *Several*

letters from Scotland [7 Sept.] (1650); *A Brief Relation* (20 Aug.–10 Sept. 1650), pp. 809–11.

17. The best account is still C. Firth, 'The Battle of Dunbar', *TRHS* NS 14 (1900), pp. 19–52, though Stevenson, *Revolution and Counter-Revolution*, pp. 178–9, has important comments.

18. Walker, *Historical Discourses*, pp. 187–9; Nicoll, *Diary*, p. 29; *Ancrum and Lothian Correspondence*; pp. 305–6; *Writings of Cromwell*, ii. 345–6; *Mercurius Politicus* (2 issues, 19 Sept.–3 Oct. 1650): *The Lord General Cromwell His March to Sterling* [2. Oct.] (1650).

19. *RCGA* (1909), pp. 46–8; *Ancrum and Lothian Correspondence*, pp. 499*–500*; Thurloe State Papers, i. 163–4.

20. *RCGA* (1909), pp. 44–69; Balfour, *Historical Works*, iv. 107–11; Lamont, *Diary*, p. 23; *Ancrum and Lothian Correspondence*, pp. 300 (Balcarres to Lothian), 301–3 (Committee to King); Blair, *Life*, p. 239.

21. Baillie, *Letters*, iii. 111–16; Walker, *Historical Discourses*, pp. 181–9; Scottish RO, PA 7/24, fo. 14 (2) (paper of Committee).

22. HMC 6th Report, p. 606.

23. Baillie, *Letters*, iii. 117–18; *Hamilton Papers*, p. 256 (King to Hamilton); John, 7th Duke of Atholl, *Chronicles of the Atholl and Tullibardine Families* (Edinburgh, 1908), i. 140 (King to Atholl); Clarendon, *History*, xiii. 47; Scottish RO, PA 7/24, fos. V30–32 (papers of committee); *RCGA* (1909), pp. 74–5; HMC Laing MSS, i. 250–1 (Erskine to Middleton); Carte, *Original Letters*, i. 389–90 (O'Neill to Marchioness of Ormonde); Balfour, *Historical Works*, iv. 112–21; Walker, *Historical Discourses*, pp. 196–201; *Ancrum and Lothian Correspondence*, pp. 306–7 (instructions of Committee), 500*–501* (King to heritors); Blair, *Life*, p. 245.

24. *RCGA* (1909), pp. 74–90; Baillie, *Letters*, iii. 118; Thurloe State Papers, i. 165 (Committee to Leslie); Balfour, *Historical Works*, iv. 121–32; Walker, *Historical Discourses*, pp. 200–3; *Ancrum and Lothian Correspondence*, pp. 317 (Committee to Lothian), 501*–502* (Middleton to King).

25. Baillie, *Letters*, iii. 112–13, 118–20; Balfour, *Historical Works*, iv. 120–3, 160; Nicoll, *Diary*, pp. 30–6; *RCGA* (1909), pp. 94–106.

26. Balfour, *Historical Works*, iv. 128–60.

27. *RCGA* (1652–7) (1909), pp. 108–57; Scottish RO, PA 7/24, fos. 42–60 (papers of committee); Baillie, *Letters*, iii. 121–4; the Revd W. Stephen (ed.), *Register of the Consultations of the Ministers of Edinburgh* (Scottish History Soc., 1921), pp. 298–9; Balfour, *Historical Works*, iv. 160–74; 'Memoirs by James Burns', in J. Maidment (ed.), *Historical Fragments Relative to Scottish Affairs* (Edinburgh, 1833), pp. 16–17; Johnston, *Diary*, pp. 28–30.

28. Baillie, *Letters*, iii. 124–5; Balfour, *Historical Works*, iv. 192–5; *Writings of Cromwell*, i. 364–5; *Mercurius Politicus* (2 issues, 12–26 Dec. 1650).

29. *Diary*, p. 29.

30. *Mercurius Politicus* (19–26 Dec. 1650).

31. *APS* VI. ii. 609–33; *RCGA* (1909), pp. 157–60, 267–70; Baillie, *Letters*, iii. 126–7; Balfour, *Historical Works*, iv. 196–228.

32. John, 3rd Marquess of Bute, *Scottish Coronations* (1912), pp. 141–220, plus Baillie, *Letters*, iii. 128.

33. *APS* VI. ii. 631–3; Scottish RO, PA 11/10, fos. 1–100 *passim* (register of Committee); BL Egerton MS 1533, fos. 20, 28 (instructions to Titus); Johnston, *Diary*, pp. 97–8, 218.

34. *RCGA* (1909), pp. 161–355, *passim*.

35. Carte, *Original Letters*, i. 445–6 (newsletter from Montrose); Balfour, *Historical Works*, iv. 246–7; Lamont, *Diary*, pp. 27–8; *Ancrum and Lothian Correspondence*, pp. 502*–503* (instructions for commissioners), 344 (Committee to King).

36. *APS* VI. ii. 647–63; *RCGA* (1909), pp. 345–61; HMC Laing MSS, pp. 257–9 (letters to Halket and Johnston); Baillie, *Letters*, iii. 160; Balfour, *Historical Works*, iv. 268–81.

37. *Nicholas Papers*, i. 254 (Nicholas to Hatton); Carte, *Original Letters*, ii. 25–9 (newsletter from Perth).

38. Scottish RO, PA 11/10, fos. 54ᵛ–55ᵛ (register of committee); Balfour, *Historical Works*, iv. 297–300; 'Memoirs by Burns' in Maidment (ed.), *Historical Fragments*, p. 19; Blair, *Life*, pp. 270–1.

39. *APS* VI. ii. 672–84; *RCGA* (1909), pp. 440–79; Lamont, *Diary*, p. 33; Blair, *Life*, pp. 274–8.

40. Scottish RO, PA 11/10, fos. 23ᵛ, 24ᵛ (register of Committee of Estates); Balfour, *Historical Works*, iv. 238–46; Carte, *Original Letters*, i. 410–11 (newsletter from Perth).

41. Recorded in successive issues of *Mercurius Politicus*.

42. Scottish RO, PA 11/11, fos. 3ᵛ, 19–20, 25ᵛ, 29ᵛ–31ᵛ, 40 (register of Committee); Thurloe State Papers, i. 168–9 (letters from Dunbar, Urquhart), 173 (Leslie to committee); *Ancrum and Lothian Correspondence*, pp. 347 (Sutherland to King), 358–9 (heritors to King), and 360 (Leslie to Lothian); David Stevenson (ed.), *The Government of Scotland under the Covenanters* (Scottish History Soc., 1982), pp. 112–41.

43. *Chronicles of the Frasers*, pp. 378–80.

44. Ibid., p. 380; Carte, *Original Letters*, ii. 25–6 (newsletter from Perth); *Writings of Cromwell*, i. 428–34; Nicoll, *Diary*, pp. 52–3; 'Memoirs by Burns', p. 21, and 'Collections by A Private Hand', pp. 34–7 in Maidment (ed.), *Historical Fragments*; *Mercurius Politicus* (3 issues, 10–27 July 1651).

45. *Mercurius Politicus* (6–13 Mar., 20–7 Mar., 29 May–5 June, 12–19 June 1651); BL Egerton Charter 422 (Buckingham's commission); Clarendon, *History*, xiii. 58; *Writings of Cromwell*, i. 411–12; BL Egerton MS 2542, fo. 56 (blank commissions); Evelyn, *Diary* (ed. Wheatley), iv. 201–2 (King to Grenvilles).

46. *Nicholas Papers*, i. 264 (Nicholas to Hatton) gives 12,500. CSP ii. 560 ('Relation of the Business of Worcester') gives 10,000. Sir James Turner, *Memoirs of His Own Life and Times* (ed. T. Thomson, Bannatyne Club, 1829), p. 94,

gives 4,000 horse and 9,000 foot. *The Weekly Intelligencer* (26 Aug.–2 Sept. 1651) gives 12,000, as does Thomas Blount, *Boscobel* (3rd edn., 1680), p. 3.

47. *Chronicles of the Frasers*, p. 384; HMC Portland MSS, i. 610–11 (King to Crawford-Lindsey etc.); HMC Hamilton MSS, Supplementary Report, pp. 77–8 ('Worcester Fight'); Cary, *Memorials*, ii. 283–94 (letters of Buckingham, Smith, Cromwell); Burnet, *Dukes of Hamilton*, p. 426 (Hamilton to niece).

48. *His Majestyes Declaration to all His Loving Subjects* (5 Aug. 1651); HMC Portland MSS, i. 613 (King to Derby); HMC Hamilton MSS, Supplementary Report, p. 78; Cary, *Memorials*, ii. 299–337 (letters from Lauderdale, Wentworth, Hamilton, Whitley, Derby, Worcestershire committee); Burnet, *Dukes of Hamilton*, pp. 426–7; CSP ii. 560–1; Turner, *Memoirs*, pp. 94–5; Clarendon, *History*, xiii. 63–5; Bod. L., Tanner MS 54, fo. 170 (royal declaration, 16 Aug. 1651); *Mercurius Politicus* (3 issues, 7–28 Aug. 1651); *Perfect Diurnall* (18–25 Aug. 1651), p. 1225; Blount, *Boscobel*, pp. 4–6. I have not repeated Clarendon's famous story about Buckingham's tantrum (*History*, xiii. 72). It is not recorded in any contemporary source, was written twenty years later when the author had reason to hate Buckingham, and looks like a classic piece of Clarendonian nastiness.

49. Turner, *Memoirs*, p. 94; *Weekly Intelligencer* (26 Aug.–2 Sept. 1651); J. W. Willis-Bond, *The Civil War in Worcestershire* (1905), pp. 225–6 (warrant to Salwarpe); HMC 10th Report, app., VI. 175 (Berkeley to Cave); *Writings of Cromwell*, i. 455; Clarendon, *History*, xiii. 64–5; C. Green, 'Charles II and the Battle of Worcester', *EHR* 5 (1890), pp. 115–18; HMC 5th report, p. 299 (Lechmere's Journal); *Weekly Intelligencer* (26 Aug.–2 Sept. 1651); A. M. Broadley, *The Royal Miracle* (1912), section of Worcester Chamber Accounts. In keeping with Charles's promise of indemnity, all the absent republicans in the corporation were re-elected when the annual choice of members was held on 24 August: Worcestershire RO, A14, Chamber Order Book, 1650–76, p. 7.

50. Reece, thesis, pp. 1–10.

51. *A Great Victory by the Blessing of God* (1651); *Two Letters from Colonel Robert Lilburne* (1651); *Mercurius Politicus* (28 Aug.–4 Sept. 1651); Cary, *Memorials*, ii. 338–41 (Lilburne to Cromwell).

52. Underdown, *Royalist Conspiracy*, ch. 3; L. Carlson, 'A History of the Presbyterian Party from Pride's Purge to the Dissolution of the Long Parliament', *Church History*, 11 (1942), pp. 108–22.

53. HMC Hamilton MSS, Supplementary Report, p. 79 ('Worcester Fight'); Cary, *Memorials*, pp. 348–60 (letters from Stapylton, Scott and Salway, Cromwell and Downing); Burnet, *Dukes of Hamilton*, pp. 430–1; CSP ii. 561–3; Bod. L., Clarendon MS 42, fos. 149–50 (royalist account); HMC 5th Report, p. 299 (Lechmere's Journal); *Mercurius Politicus* (4–11 Sept. 1651); *Another Victory in Lancashire* (1651); Blunt, *Boscobel*, pp. 15–19.

54. Richard Ollard, *The Escape of Charles II After the Battle of Worcester* (1966),

which also lists every extant source. I have used all of these, and failed to add to their number.

Chapter 5

1. *The Memoirs and Letters of Ulick, Marquis of Clanricarde* (1757), app., pp. 50–2 (King to Clanricarde and Lorraine); Bod. L., Clarendon MS 42, fo. 354 (instructions to Norwich), and MS 43, fo. 66 (Lorraine to Irish commissioners); HMC Ormonde MSS, os i. 10–11.

2. SP 78/113, fos. 16–19 (letter from MM); Montpensier, *Memoirs* (translation of 1848), i. 169–70; *Mercurius Politicus* (30 Oct.–6 Nov. 1651); *CSPV* (1647–52), pp. 202–3; Evelyn, *Diary* (ed. De Beer), iii. 147–52.

3. BL Add. MS 15856, fos. 41–3.

4. Bod. L., Clarendon MS 42, fos. 280–381, *passim* (papers on the Long case); CSP iii. 36–46 (letters of Hyde to Nicholas); *Nicholas Papers*, i. 279–85, 315 (letters from Nicholas, Gerard, and Ormonde); Bod. L., Carte MS 130, fo. 167 (King to Long); BL Add. MS 37047, fo. 221^v (Long's notes on his disgrace).

5. CSP iii. 45–8, 59, 67, 77, 86–8, 106 (letters of Hyde to Nicholas); *Nicholas Papers*, i. 283, 285–6, 298, 304 (Nicholas to Hyde and Hatton); HMC Bath MSS, i. 99–103 (Radcliffe to Holles).

6. CSP iii. 52, 162 (Hyde to Nicholas); Bod. L., Clarendon MS 45, fos. 35 (patent for Bristol), 48 (Hyde to Nicholas); Evelyn, *Diary* (ed. Wheatley), iv. 257–8 (Hyde to Browne).

7. CSP iii. 82–4, 99, 125, 158, 161–2 (Hyde to Nicholas); Warburton, *Memoirs*, iii. 418–20 (letters of King and Hyde to Rupert); BL Add. MS 18982, fo. 236 (Jermyn to Rupert); Evelyn, *Diary* (ed. Wheatley), iv. 280 (Hyde to Browne); Bod. L., Clarendon MS 45, fos. 384–5 (Hyde to Nicholas).

8. Clarendon, *History*, xiii. 107, 122, 129; CSP iii. 43–6, 52, 58, 80–1, 124, 174 (Hyde to Nicholas); Bod. L., Clarendon MS 44, fo. 61 (note of pension due); SP 78/113, fo. 18 (letter from MM); BL Add. MS 38091, fo. 114 (letter from King); Bod. L., Carte MS 29, fo. 324 (Ormonde to Clanricarde). For this chapter I have used the exchange rates given in Fox's papers in Dorset RO, D124.

9. Clarendon, *History*, xiii. 122–3, 148–53; CSP iii. 41 (Hyde to Nicholas); Montpensier, *Memoirs*, i. 168–81; Bod. L., Clarendon MS 43, fo. 48 (Hyde to Nicholas); *Life of James II* (ed. Clarke), i. 53–4; *CSPV* (1647–52), p. 207; SP 78/113, fo. 24 (King to Von Karpfen); Royal Archives, Stuart Papers Add. MS 5/2/2 (King to Queen of Bohemia).

10. *Nicholas Papers*, ii. 14 (Nicholas to Hyde); Bod. L., Clarendon MS. 47, fos. 80–1 (Bunce to Ormonde).

11. Clarendon MS 47, fo. 77, MS 48, fos. 234–5, and MS 50, fo. 72.

12. Clarendon MS 47, fo. 241.

13. BL Add. MS 18738, fo. 85 (model privateer commission); SP 78/113, fo. 37

(the list of captains); HMC Ormonde MSS, NS i. 292–8 (letters on success of voyages); SP 77/31, fos. 392–4 (commissions from De Vic); SP 18/16/92a (Whittington to Bramhall); Bod. L., Clarendon MS 48, fos. 131 (Wyndham to Fleming) and 244 (King to Wyndham); Evelyn, *Diary* (ed. Wheatley), iv. 292–300, 307–10 (Browne to Nicholas).

14. *History of the Commonwealth*, iii. 137.

15. Sir John Reresby, *Memoirs* (ed. James Cartwright, 1875), p. 7; Bod. L., Clarendon MS 45, fo. 488 (Hyde to Nicholas); Clarendon, *History*, xiv. 67; Thurloe State Papers, i. 306 (Wogan to Massey) and 471 (spy's report); *The Complete Peerage*, vi. 706.

16. Edward Hyde, Earl of Clarendon, *The Life of Edward, Earl of Clarendon* (3 vols.; Oxford edn., 1826), i. 255–6 and ii. 19.

17. *Nicholas Papers*, ii. 110 (Hatton to Nicholas); Scott, *Lucy Walter*, ch. XI, lists the few sources for the life of Lucy's daughter Mary.

18. Clarendon, *History*, xiv. 96–7; Montpensier, *Memoirs*, ii. 41.

19. Bod. L., Clarendon MS 45, fo. 488.

20. Ibid., fos. 199–200, 442; Bryant, *Letters of Charles II*, pp. 35–6 (to Hyde); Evelyn, *Diary* (ed. Wheatley), iv. 205 (Mary to Nicholas); *Nicholas Papers*, i. 293 (Nicholas to Hyde).

21. Evelyn, *Diary* (ed. Wheatley), iv. 260; Geyl, *Orange and Stuart*, pp. 91–111; Bod. L., Clarendon MS 43, fos. 284 (Hyde to Nicholas) and 337 (paper on Guernsey), and MS 49, fos. 49 (Boreel to King) and 57 (King to Macdowell); CSP iii. 105 (Hyde to Nicholas), 141 (King to Boreel); Herbert Rowen, *John De Witt* (Princeton, 1978), chs. 4, 10; HMC Ormonde MSS, NS i. 273 (Massey to Ormonde).

22. *CSPD* (1651–2), p. 103 (minute of Council of State); CSP iii. 56 (Hyde to Nicholas); Bod. L., Clarendon MS 43, fo. 1 (instructions to Vandruske); Turner, *Memoirs*, p. 103.

23. Bod. L., Clarendon MS 43, fos. 266 (King to Moderator), and 247–8 (instructions to Middleton); BL Add. MS 15856, fo. 480 (Middleton's commission).

24. Bod. L., Clarendon MS 44, fos. 223–5 (draft commission and instructions); MS 45, fos. 128, 176, and 193 (Hyde to Middleton), 56, 130, 149–51, 229–31, 237 (King to Courland, Smith, Balcarres, Glencairn, chiefs, Wentworth, Middleton), 244 (Wentworth's commission), and 370 ('Sum of the Scotch business'); CSP iii. 119, 126 (Hyde to Nicholas).

25. Bod. L., Clarendon MS 46, fos. 138 (Hyde to Wentworth), 216–17 (Middleton to States-General); MS 47, fos. 7–9 (instructions to Drummond, Shaw, Macleod), 30 (Danes to King), 51 (Hyde to Middleton), 337–45 (instructions to Middleton); Geyl, *Orange and Stuart*, pp. 111–25. For my knowledge of the nature of 'Glencairn's Rising' I have relied heavily upon F. D. Dow, *Cromwellian Scotland* (Edinburgh, 1979), pp. 69–96.

26. Underdown, *Royalist Conspiracy*, ch. 4 and pp. 67–70. While I differ marginally from Professor Underdown in my interpretation of royalist court politics, I depend firmly upon him for my view of conspiracy in England. I

would also have taken infinitely longer to understand many letters were it not for his collection of the ciphers in an appendix.

27. BL Add. MS 4180, fo. 107^v. By my reading this letter seems to clear up Professor Underdown's doubt as to whether the initiative to found the 'Sealed Knot' came from England or from the court.

28. Underdown, *Royalist Conspiracy*, ch. 6.

29. SP 18/24/15.

30. Bod. L., Clarendon MS 48, fo. 240 (intelligence to Hyde); Thurloe State Papers, ii. 248–9 (the proclamation), 257–8 (report from Paris), 510, 533 (Bampfield to Thurloe). I follow entirely the reasoning in Gardiner, *History of the Commonwealth*, iii. 141, n. 2, save that I cannot be as certain (in default of evidence) that Herbert drafted the proclamation.

31. Underdown, *Royalist Conspiracy*, ch. 6.

32. Thurloe State Papers, ii. 322 (O'Neill to Ashburnham); Bod. L., Clarendon MS 48, fo. 328 (King to Villiers).

33. CSP iii. 65, 71–2, 75 (Hyde to Nicholas); Montpensier, *Memoirs*, i. 181–293; *CSPV* (1647–52), p. 223; Bod. L., Clarendon MS 44, fo. 61 (note of pension); HMC Bath MSS, ii. 103 (Radcliffe to Holles).

34. Bod. L., Clarendon MS 43, fo. 141 (Louis to Charles); Montpensier, *Memoirs*, i. 247–50; CSP iii. 77–84 (Hyde to Nicholas); Turner, *Memoirs*, p. 104; *Life of James II* (ed. Clarke), i. 83–9.

35. CSP iii. 84 (Hyde to Nicholas); *CSPV* (1647–52), pp. 272–3.

36. *Nicholas Papers*, i. 312 (to Hyde).

37. Bod. L., Clarendon MS 47, fo. 187 (King to Rupert).

38. In 1649 it had been intended to make Lord Hatton a Viscount and ambassador to Sweden: BL Add. MS 15856, fo. 84. But the embassy was cancelled and so was the promotion.

39. Bod. L., Clarendon MS 43, fos. 109–309, *passim* (King to eight rulers, and replies), 339 (Hyde to Taylor); MS 44, fo. 27 (Hyde to Taylor), 53 (Hyde to Nicholas), 66–112 (Letters to many states), 114, 154–7, 229–30 (Rochester's patent, commission and instructions); MS 45, fo. 134 (Hyde to Belling); MS 46, fos. 48 (speech by Brandenburgers), 116 (Hyde to Rochester); MS 47, fo. 231 (Hyde to Clement); CSP iii. 99, 118, 121, 128–9, 146, 196 (Hyde to Nicholas); Thurloe State papers, i. 238, 399 (reports from Ratisbon).

40. CSP iii. 111–12, 191, 211, 217–18 (Hyde to Nicholas); Clarendon, *History*, xv. 73–7; Thurloe State Papers, ii. 57 (report from Paris); *Nicholas Papers*, ii. 19 (Nicholas to Hyde), 35 (Lovell to Nicholas), 37–40, 49–50 (Hatton to Nicholas); Bod. L., Carte MS 130, fos. 148, 150, 161–2 (letters between Massonett, Long, and Grenville); Clarendon MS 46, fos. 146 (Grenville to King), 294 (Grenville to Ormonde), 318 (Ormonde to Bramhall), 333 (Wyndham to Ormonde); MS 47, fos. 103–4 (Ormonde to Grenville), 156 (Gerard to King), 263–5 (Long to King), 266 (royal declaration); BL Add. MS 37047, fos. 183 (Massonett to Long), 221–38 (papers on charge).

41. Bod. L., Clarendon MS 47, fo. 187 (King to Rupert); MS 48, fo. 224 (King to

Queen of Bohemia); CSP iii. 222, 224, 229, 245–6, 253 (Hyde to Nicholas); Thurloe State Papers, ii. 270, 327, 398 (reports from Paris), 322 (O'Neill to Ashburnham).

42. Clarendon MS 48, fo. 173 (letter from King); CSP iii. 245 (Hyde to Nicholas); Thurloe State Papers, ii. 322 (O'Neill to Ashburnham).

43. Dorset RO, D124, Box 267, General Household Accounts, 1654–5.

44. Ibid.; Clarendon, *History*, xv. 93–115; Thurloe State Papers, ii. 436–694, *passim* (many spy reports from Paris, Spa, Aachen, and Cologne); Bod. L., Rawlinson MSS A16, fo. 483 and A17, pp. 175–7 (spy reports from Spa and Aachen); BL Lansdowne MS 1236 (King to Queen of Bohemia).

45. Thurloe State Papers, ii. 502 (report from Spa); *Nicholas Papers*, ii. 156–7 (Hatton to Nicholas).

46. BL Lansdowne MS 1236, fo. 113.

47. Thurloe State Papers, i. 553 (King to Atholl); Bod. L., Clarendon MS 46, fo. 364 (Hyde to Middleton); MS 47, fos. 8, 49–50 (instructions for Shaw), 258 (King to Middleton); CSP iii. 196 (Hyde to Nicholas); T. Brown, *Miscellanea Aulica* (1702), p. 108 (instructions for James).

48. Bod. L., Clarendon MS 48, fos. 247, 271–3 (Middleton, Atholl, Macdonald to King); Thurloe State Papers, ii. 502, 556, 567, 585–6 (reports from Spa, Aachen); *Nicholas Papers*, ii. 79–80 (Nicholas to Norwich); Clarendon, *History*, xv. 108–9.

49. Dow, *Cromwellian Scotland*, pp. 115–34.

50. Turner, *Memoirs*, pp. 114–15; Thurloe State Papers, ii. 609–10 (report from Aachen), iii. 100 (report from Cologne); Bod. L., Clarendon MS 49, fos. 39–44 (letters to Middleton and Glencairn, instructions to Colonel Borthwick), 67 (Middleton to Hyde), 259 (King to Middleton), 264 (Hyde to Middleton).

51. Dow, *Cromwellian Scotland*, pp. 134–41.

52. Bod. L., Clarendon MS 48, fos. 326–8.

53. Underdown, *Royalist Conspiracy*, pp. 105–15. I have adopted the exiles' own nickname instead of Professor Underdown's term, 'The Action Party', as the new conspirators do not seem to have possessed most of the characteristics of a political party.

54. Thurloe State Papers, ii. 626 (report from Aachen), BL Add. MS 15856, fo. 46 (Rochester's commission); Bod. L., Clarendon MS 49, fos. 22, 33–7.

55. BL Lansdowne MS 1236, fo. 113 (King to Queen of Bohemia); Thurloe State Papers, ii. 544 (report from Aachen).

56. SP 81/54, fos. 96–101 (the accounts).

57. BL Add. MS 18827, fo. 15 (letter from Taylor).

58. CSP iii. 293–4 (Hyde to King); Carte, *Original Letters*, ii. 78 (Radcliffe to Ormonde).

59. Dorset RO, D124, Box 267, General Household Accounts, 1654–5, and Box 237, Fox's Autobiography; BL Add. MS 51318 (Kitchen accounts, 1654–5); *Memoirs of Sir Stephen Fox* (1717), pp. 14–19; HMC Ormonde MSS, NS

i. 313 (Hyde to Ormonde); Bod. L., Clarendon MS 49, fo. 152 (Hyde to Culpeper).

60. BL Egerton MS 2829, fo. 3 (King to Rumbold); Bod. L., Clarendon MS 49, fos. 345–6 (Edgeman's accounts); MS 50, fo. 72 (Halsall's account).

61. Thurloe State Papers, ii. 609–10, 694, iii. 19, 44 (reports from Aachen and Cologne), 425 (Armorer to Wood); SP 81/54, fo. 118 (Council minute); Bod. L., Clarendon MS 45, fo. 209 (Hyde to Rochester).

62. SP 81/54, fo. 118 (Council minute); Bod. L., Clarendon MS 50, fo. 77 (Hyde to De Vic).

63. Royal Archives, Stuart Papers, Add. MS 5/2/5, 8 (Hyde to Cottrell); Dorset RO, D124, Box 267, General Household Accounts, 1654–5; Thurloe State Papers, i. 681–3 (O'Neill to King).

64. CSP iii. 293–4 (Hyde to King).

65. Dorset RO, D124, Box 267, General Household Accounts, 1654–5; Lambeth Palace L., MS 645, fo. 14 (Mary to King); Thurloe State Papers, ii. 732, iii. 19, 465 (reports from Cologne); Brown, *Miscellanea Aulica*, pp. 116, 123 (King to Bennet); Bryant, *Letters of Charles II*, pp. 45–5; BL MS Loan 37/1, James to King, 27 Apr. 1655; Royal Archives, Stuart Papers, Add. MS 5/2/11, 12 (Morley, Nicholas, to Cottrell).

66. Royal Archives, Stuart Papers, Add. MS 5/2/9, 16, 18 (Hyde, Morley to Cottrell); Thurloe State Papers, iv. 88 (report from Cologne); Brown, *Miscellanea Aulica*, pp. 119–21 (King to Bennet); SP 84/159, Nicholas to Jane, 2 Oct. 1655.

67. *Miscellanea Aulica*, p. 123 (to Bennet).

68. BL Stowe MS 677, fos. 80–1 (lists of Council and Household); Thurloe State Papers, ii. 502, 556, 567, 586, 602 (reports from Spa, Aachen, Cologne); CSP iii. 234, 237 (Hyde to Nicholas); *Nicholas Papers*, ii. 80 (Nicholas to Norwich); Evelyn, *Diary* (ed. Wheatley), iv. 210–11 (Queen of Bohemia to Nicholas); SP 18/97/109, and 18/99/16, 33–4 (Manning to Thurloe).

69. SP 18/77/52, 124/39, 76, 125/4 (Nicholas to Jane); *Nicholas Papers*, ii. 279–80 (Norwich to Nicholas); Thurloe State Papers, iii. 617 (report from Cologne). No details survive of the actual membership of the 'inner ring'.

70. Clarendon, *History*, xv. 67; Bryant, *Letters of Charles II*, pp. 43–4; Bod. L., Clarendon MS 51, fo. 242 (King to Hyde); Royal Archives, Stuart Papers, Add. MS 5/2/9 (Hyde to Cottrell).

71. *Nicholas Papers*, ii. 90–1 (Hatton to Nicholas).

72. CSP iii. 256–60 (letters of Hyde, Ormonde, and Mary); Thurloe State Papers, i. 661 (King to Henry); *Nicholas Papers*, ii. 109–14 (letters of Hatton, Ratcliffe, and Ormonde); BL MS Loan 37/1, Henrietta Maria to King, 6 Apr. 1655; HMC Ormonde MSS, NS i. 306–7 (letters of Hyde and Hatton); *An Exact Narrative of the Attempts made upon the Duke of Gloucester* (1655); Bod. L., Clarendon MS 48, fo. 324 (instructions to Henry); MS 49, fos. 76–206 (letters of Lovell, Henry, Henrietta Maria, Jermyn, Mary, Ormonde, Percy, and Hyde).

73. Clarendon MS 44, fo. 141 (Holder to King); MS 45, fos. 36–45 (papers between Pope and King, 1652–3); MS 49, fo. 46 (Hyde to Weston).
74. *CSPV* (1653–4), p. 283; Thurloe State Papers, iii. 44 (report from Cologne); SP 18/77/52 (Nicholas to Jane).
75. PRO, PRO/31/9/95, Nuncio to Pope, 20 Dec. 1654.
76. Bod. L., Clarendon MS 49, fo. 204.
77. CSP iii. 270–1 (instructions to agent); Carte, *Original Letters*, ii. 52 (King to Philippe-Wilhelm); Bod. L., Clarendon MS 49, fo. 257 (draft terms); MS 50, fo. 133 (King to Philippe-Wilhelm).
78. Thurloe State Papers, i. 744. Lady Antonia Fraser, *Charles II* (1979), pp. 150–1, discards other stories and assertions concerning Charles' warmth towards Catholicism during the exile.
79. Underdown, *Royalist Conspiracy*, pp. 127–33, and sources there, plus Bod. L., Clarendon MS 49, fo. 347 (King to republicans).
80. Underdown, *Royalist Conspiracy*, pp. 135–58.
81. Clarendon MS 50, fos. 1–31, *passim* (letters of Ormonde and Hyde); CSP iii. 266–7 (States-General to Mary); Thurloe State Papers, iii. 190, 301 (Manning to Thurloe); *Nicholas Papers*, ii. 236 (Jane to Nicholas).
82. *Nicholas Papers*, ii. 273–4 (Hume to Nicholas), 284–5 (Jane to Nicholas).
83. Dorset RO, D124, Box 267, General Household Accounts, 1654–5; *Nicholas Papers*, ii. 278 (Nicholas to Norwich).
84. Clarendon, *History*, xv. 123–37.
85. Bod. L., Clarendon MS 50, fo. 121 (instructions for Borthwick); Brown, *Miscellanea Aulica*, pp. 111–12 (King to Bennet).
86. Lambeth Palace L., MS 645, fo. 84 (Queen of Bohemia to King); Thurloe State Papers, iv. 249, 286, 290–1 (reports from Cologne); SP 89/159, Nicholas to Jane, 25 Dec. 1655; *Nicholas Papers*, iii. 149–87, 196 201 (examination and pleas of Manning); *CSPV* (1654–6), pp. 168–9.
87. Bod. L., Clarendon MS 47, fo. 240 (Hyde to Middleton); MS 48, fo. 202 (Hyde to Nicholas); Thurloe State Papers, i. 502 (Newburgh to Balcarres).
88. His surviving dispatches are in Thurloe State Papers, vol. iii, and SP 18/97–9.
89. HMC Ormonde MSS, NS i. 303 (Bennet to Ormonde); *Nicholas Papers*, ii. 110 (Ratcliffe to Nicholas); Thurloe State Papers, iii. 100 (report from Cologne); *Mercurius Politicus* (10–17 July 1655), p. 7108.
90. Lambeth Palace L., MS 645, fos. 14, 26; Timothy Crist, *Charles II to Lord Taaffe* (Cambridge, 1974), No. 1.
91. Bod. L., Clarendon MS 46, fo. 361 (Hyde to O'Neill); MS 47, fo. 93–4 (Hyde to Nicholas); MS 48, fo. 126 (Hyde to Wentworth); MS 52, fo. 118 (Hyde to Ormonde); SP 18/125/4 (Nicholas to Jane).
92. Thurloe State Papers, i. 683–4.
93. CSP iii. 275–6 (Hyde to de Haro); Thurloe State Papers, iii. 617; Carte, *Original Letters*, ii. 53–7 (King to Philippe-Wilhelm), 59–60 (Philippe-Wilhelm to Ormonde).
94. Bod. L., Clarendon MS 50, fos. 160–2, 219, 232–3, 250; MS 51, fos. 1, 32, 37,

59, 89 (letters of Hyde, Talbot, Norwich, and De Vic); CSP iii. 279–81, 286–7 (letters of Hyde and Talbot); Carte, *Original Letters*, ii. 84–7 (Talbot to Ormonde), 99–101 (unsigned letter from English Catholic); *Nicholas Papers*, iii. 214 (Jane to Nicholas), 217 (Norwich to Nicholas), 243 (Ormonde to King); Bryant, *Letters of Charles II*, pp. 43–5; SP 18/124/14 (Nicholas to Jane); SP 84/159, Nicholas to Jane, 23 Nov. 1655; Thurloe State Papers, ii. 694 (Rupert to King).

95. Bod. L., Clarendon MS 51, fos. 89 (Hyde to De Vic), 94 (King to Ormonde), 147–54 (the treaty); Thurloe State Papers, iv. 592, 677 (reports from Brussels and Lille); CSP iii. 288–92 (King to Ormonde and Hyde).

Chapter 6

1. There seems to be no proper history of either the Spanish monarchy or the Spanish Netherlands in the 1650s. For my portrait I have relied upon more general works: Pieter Geyl, *The Netherlands in the Seventeenth Century* (1964); John Stoye, *Europe Unfolding* (1969); Geoffrey Parker, *The Army of Flanders and the Spanish Road, 1597–1659* (Cambridge, 1972); R. A. Stradling, *Europe and the Decline of Spain* (1981); Jonathan I. Israel, *The Dutch Republic and the Hispanic World, 1606–1661* (Oxford, 1982); Henry Kamen, *Spain, 1469–1714* (1983).

2. Charles's aims will be obvious from the sources cited below. The Spanish viewpoint is neatly captured in Guizot, *History of Oliver Cromwell*, ii. 537–9 (Cardeñas to Felipe), 540–8 (Consultas of Council of State).

3. Ibid., CSP iii. 294–6 (Hyde to Ormonde), 298, 302–3 (Hyde to King), 303–4 (paper to Cardeñas); Brown, *Miscellanea Aulica*, pp. 127–8 (King to Bennet); Bod. L., Clarendon MS 51, fos. 208–9, 215, 242, 293, 315 (letters of King, De Vic, Taaffe, and Juan-José), MS 52, fos. 31, 52, 93, 97, 119, 132, 141, 144–5, 158 (letters of Cardeñas, Hyde, Talbot, Juan-José, and Ormonde).

4. Thurloe State Papers, v. 119–20 (reports from Dunkirk), 131 (Berkeley to Davis), 145 (letter from Ratcliffe), 219, 250 (reports from Paris), 369 (Lockhart to Thurloe), 447 (report from Bruges); *Miscellanea Aulica*, pp. 125–6 (instructions for Bennet); *Life of James II* (ed. Clarke), i. 265–6, 275–9.

5. CSP iii. 302–3 (Hyde to King); Bod. L., Clarendon MS 52, fo. 254 (Bristol to Hyde).

6. Ibid., Clarendon, *History*, xv. 79; *Life of James II* (ed. Clarke), i. 293.

7. BL Add. MS 15856, fo. 52.

8. Thurloe State Papers, v. 315–16, 334, 351–2, 362, 391–2, 431, 447, 521–2, 575, 596, 609, 645–6, 709, 724, vi. 31, 43, 88 (spy reports to Thurloe); Guizot, *Oliver Cromwell*, ii. 542–8 (Consulta of Council of State); CSP iii. 306–8 (Ormonde to Bishop of Dromore), 311–12 (Bristol to Hyde), 313 (Bristol to King), 317 (King to Cardeñas); SP 77/31, fo. 437 (report from

Bruges); BL MS Loan 37/1, King to Irish at Courtrai, 16 Dec. 1656; Bod. L., Clarendon MS 52, fos. 185 (Bristol to Ormonde), 219 (Ormonde to Hyde), 273–4, 289 (Bristol to Ormonde), 292 (Ormonde to Hyde), 314–15 (Bristol to Hyde), 351–2 (Hyde to Bristol); MS 53, fos. 3–4, 7–8 (Hyde to Bristol), 25–6 (King to Spaniards), 31–2, 55, 83–5, 179, 261 (Bristol to Hyde); MS 54, fos. 37 (Hyde to Ormonde), 42 (report from Flushing); Bod. L., Carte MS 213, fos. 90–2 (Ormonde to De Vic) and MS 30, fos. 415–16, 427–34 (De Vic to Ormonde); BL Add. MS 61484, King to Grace, 10 Sept. 1656.

9. HMC Laing MSS, i. 301–4 (instructions to Middleton); SP 77/31, fos. 480, 488 (Middleton to Hyde), 482 (Hyde to Nicholas); CSP iii. 348 (Middleton to Hyde); Thurloe State Papers, v. 315 (report from Cowyn), 604–5 ('Heads of a Discourse'), and vi. 52–3 (Monck to Thurloe). This seems to refute the view of Dow, *Cromwellian Scotland*, p. 194, and in her thesis, pp. 557–63, that Charles never seriously planned an invasion of Scotland in his Flemish years.

10. Thurloe State Papers, v. 319 (Lockhart to Thurloe), vi. 33 (report from Flanders); CSP iii. 301–2 (Talbot to Hyde), 310 (Bristol to Hyde), 311 (Talbot to King), 319–21 (Bristol to Hyde, to King); Bod. L., Clarendon MS 53, fo. 107 (royalist paper on Sexby's proposals).

11. Underdown, *Royalist Conspiracy*, pp. 181–214.

12. Thurloe State Papers, v. 488 (Lockhart to Thurloe); CSP iii. 311–12 (Bristol to Hyde); Bod. L., Clarendon MS 52, fos. 273–4 (Bristol to Ormonde), 314–15 (letter from Bristol), 351–2 (Hyde to Bristol); MS 53, fos. 25–6 (paper to Spaniards).

13. Clarendon MS 53, fos. 62 (Bristol to Hyde), 122 (memorial to Juan-José); MS 54, fos. 44 (Ormonde to Hyde), 164 (memorial to Juan-José), 214 (reply); Thurloe State Papers, v. 151 (report from Bruges); CSP iii. 330–1 (memorandum to Ormonde); *Nicholas Papers*, iv. 2 (Nicholas to Middleton), 3–4 (Nicholas to Roper), 4 (Nicholas to Bennet), 4–5 (Ormonde to Nicholas); SP 77/31, fos. 460 (Belling to Nicholas), 462, 470, 490 (Hyde to Nicholas), 474 (De Vic to Nicholas).

14. Clarendon, *History*, xv. 80; Thurloe State Papers, v. 11414 (Barrière to Stouppe), 136 (report from Bruges); SP 77/31, fo. 462 (Hyde to Nicholas); *Mercurius Politicus* (2 issues, 12–26 Mar. 1657); BL Add. MS 61484, seven documents on St Ghislain affair, dated 2–20 Feb. 1657; HMC Various Collections, iii. 355 (Nicholas to Langdale); BL Add. MS 32102, fo. 84^v (Lane's knighthood).

15. Thurloe State Papers, vi. 286, 336, 338, 384 (reports from Maastricht, Flushing, and Bruges); CSP iii. 342–3 (Hyde to Nicholas); C. H. Firth (ed.), *The Clarke Papers* (Camden Soc., 1899), iii. 119; Bod. L., Clarendon MS 54, fo. 189 (Somer to Thurloe); MS 55, fos. 50, 121 (Ormonde to Hyde); HMC Bath MSS, ii. 117–18 (Ross to Holles).

16. Lambeth Palace L., MS 645, fo. 42 (James to King); Thurloe State Papers, vi. 326 (Nicholas to Culpeper), 397, 435, 463–4, 478, 547 (spy reports

from Brussels, Ghent, Bruges, Flanders); *Life of James II* (ed. Clarke), i. 299–322; *Mercurius Politicus* (4–11 June, 9 issues 25 June–3 Sept. 1657); *Clarke Papers*, iii. 110–11 (officer to Monck), 116–17 (Morgan to Monck), 119–21 (reports from Flanders, Sowkirk).

17. Bod. L., Clarendon MS 54, fo. 214.
18. SP 81/54, fos. 149–92 (Roper's reports).
19. Bod. L., Clarendon MS 54, fo. 177 (King to Muskerry); MS 56, fo. 36 (Bennet to Hyde).
20. CSP iii. 348–9 (Hyde to King), 349–50 (Hyde to Ormonde); Thurloe State Papers, v. 301 (Broghil to Thurloe).
21. Underdown, *Royalist Conspiracy*, pp. 190–214.
22. CSP iii. 351.
23. CSP iii. 346 (King to Hyde), 347 (Ormonde to Hyde), 352 (Hyde to Ormonde); Bod. L., Clarendon MS 55, fos. 52 (King to Hyde), 50, 116, 160 (Ormonde to Hyde), 162 (Bristol to King); MS 56, fo. 152 (Bristol to Ormonde).
24. CSP iii. 354 (Hyde to King), 359 (Bristol to King); BL Add. MS 61484, Paper for Juan-José, 12 Aug. 1657; Bod. L., Clarendon MS 55, fo. 125 (Hyde to King).
25. CSP iii. 374–5 (Hyde to King); Thurloe State Papers, vi. 578 (report from Bruges); *Life of James II* (ed. Clarke), i. 323–5; *Clarke Papers*, iii. 121–2 (letter from Calais), 124–5 (Hughes to Monck); HMC Various Collections, ii. 358 (Hyde to Langdale); *Nicholas Papers*, iv. 17 (Ormonde to Nicholas).
26. Bod. L., Clarendon MS 56, fos. 41–2, 62–3, 115–21, 125, 138, 152 (Bristol to King and Ormonde), 154 (Hyde to Nicholas), 190 (Hyde to King), 224–5 (Bristol to Ormonde), 282 (Hyde to Mottet); *Calendar of the Clarendon State Papers* (ed. F. Routledge, Oxford, 1932), iii. 383, 394–5 (Mary to Heenvliet); CSP iii. 366 (Hyde to Nicholas), 367 (Bristol to Ormonde), 374–5 (Hyde to King), 378–9 (King to Mary); BL Add. MS 61484, 'Memoir pour l'entreprise d'Angleterre'.
27. Underdown, *Royalist Conspiracy*, pp. 215–19, and sources there.
28. Ibid. 219–28; Thurloe State Papers, vi. 842 (intelligence); *Nicholas Papers*, iv. 34 (Nicholas to Bennet); *Life of James II* (ed. Clarke), i. 330–4; Carte, *Original letters*, ii. 126–7, 132–3 (Hyde to Ormonde), 135 (Bristol to Ormonde); SP 77/32, fos. 29, 86 (Walker to Nicholas), 44, 75–6 (Culpeper to Nicholas), 49, 52, 64–5 (Talbot to Nicholas), 57, 71 (Fox to Nicholas), 70 (De Vic to Nicholas), 77 (Wentworth to Nicholas), 78 (Ross to Nicholas); Bod. L., Clarendon MS 57, fos. 16–17 (King to Juan-José), 52–3, 86–7 (Bristol to Hyde), 124–5 (Bristol to Ormonde); BL Add. MS 61484, Memoir from King to Juan-José, and reply.
29. SP 77/32, fos. 29, 61, 86 (Walker to Nicholas), 50 (Newburgh to Nicholas), 84 (Fox to Nicholas), 89 (Mewes to Nicholas); *CSPD* (1657–8), p. 300 (Prince to Nicholas); *Life of James II*, i. 322; *Nicholas Papers*, iv. 37 (Blagge to Nicholas); Thurloe State papers, vi. 578 (report from Bruges);

The Military Memoirs of John Gwynne (ed. Sir Walter Scott, Edinburgh, 1821), pp. 118–19.

30. Thurloe State Papers, vii. 156, 183, 230, 243–4, 254, 262, 280, 304–6, 317–18, 337, 353–4 (reports from Mardyke, Antwerp, Bruges, Ghent, Brussels, Nieuport); *Nicholas Papers*, iv. 40, 51–5 (Jane to Nicholas), 48–9 (Bristol to Nicholas), 49–50 (Cotterell to Nicholas), 56–61 (Mewes to Nicholas); *Life of James II*, i. 334–67; *Clarke Papers*, iii. 148–53, 156–8 (Hughes to Monck), 153–6 (Drummond to Monck), 159–60 (newsletter), 160 (Morgan to Monck); *Mercurius Politicus* (17–24 June, 1–8 July, 19–26 Aug., 16–30 Sept., 1658); Bod. L., Clarendon MS 57, fos. 256–7 (Nicholas to Hyde), 258–60 (Newburgh to Hyde), 318–19 (Slingsby to Hyde); CSP iii. 407 (James to Hyde).

31. CSP iii. 403–4 (King to Hyde), 404–5 (Bristol to Hyde); *Nicholas Papers*, iv. 34 (Nicholas to Bennet); SP 77/32, fo. 98 (Fox to Nicholas); Bod. L., Clarendon MS 57, fo. 247 (King to Juan-José); Dorset RO, D124, Box 268, General Household Accounts, 1658–9; Clarendon MS 60, fo. 127 (accounts of agent).

32. Thurloe State Papers, vii. 221, 247–8, 280, 321–2, 337, 353–4 (various spy reports), 360–2 (Downing to Thurloe); SP 77/32, fo. 170 (Nicholas to King); Dorset RO, D124, Box 268, General Household Accounts, 1658–9.

33. Clarendon, *History*, xv. 142; Carte, *Original Letters*, ii. 154–6 (King to Princess Dowager); Thurloe State Papers, vii. 379 (Downing to Thurloe).

34. Geyl, *Orange and Stuart*, p. 133; Clarendon, *History*, xvi. 2; Thurloe State Papers, vii. 419, 428 (Downing to Thurloe); Bod. L., Clarendon MS 58, fos. 330–1 (Belling to Hyde); MS 59, fos. 132–3 (Bennet to Hyde); CSP iii. 409–10 (Hyde to Ormonde), 410–11 (Hyde to Rumbold), 421 (reply).

35. Dorset RO, D124, Box 268, General Household Accounts, 1658–9; Bod. L., Clarendon MS 57, fos. 147–8 (King to Juan-José), 286–7 (Bennet to Hyde).

36. Clarendon MS 58, fo. 379 (Marcés to Hyde).

37. SP 77/32, fos. 203, 209 (Nicholas to Middleton, and reply); Clarendon MS 58, fo. 306 (Lane to Hyde); BL Egerton MS 2551, fo. 10 (Clancarty's creation).

38. Underdown, *Royalist Conspiracy*, pp. 233–5.

39. Dorset RO, D124, Box 268, General Household Accounts, 1658–9.

40. HMC Hodgkin MSS, pp. 124–5 (ordinance of James of York); Bod. L., Clarendon MS 62, fo. 201 (King to Caracena); HMC Leybourne-Popham MSS, pp. 119–20 (Lawson to Monck). Dispatches like the last have provoked mistaken accounts in some histories of Charles having 6,000–8,000 soldiers available in July 1659. In fact Lawson was referring to broken Spanish regiments, not royalist troops. James of York could only regather 1,000 of the latter in August 1658, and lacking money or attention it is difficult to see how the King could have gathered more since.

41. Underdown, *Royalist Conspiracy*, pp. 247–8; *Nicholas Papers*, iv. 174–5 (King to James); HMC Heathcote MSS, p. 14 (Hyde to Fanshaw); Bod. L.,

Clarendon MS 61, fos. 233–4 (King to Montagu and Queen Mother); CSP iii. 530 (King to Hyde); Dorset RO, D. 124, Box 268, General Household Accounts, 1658–9.

42. Underdown, *Royalist Conspiracy*, pp. 248–9, 301; CSP iii. 534 (Hyde to Mordaunt), 536–8 (King to Mordaunt).

43. Bod. L., Clarendon MS 56, fos. 365–8 (declaration of 1656–8); MS 62, fos. 170–1 (declaration of 19 July); *Nicholas Papers*, iv. 72–4 (declaration after Cromwell's death), 180–1 (King to royalists).

44. SP 77/32, fos. 287 (Nicholas to Marcés), 288 (Hyde to Marcés), 292 (letter from Brussels).

45. *Life of James II*, i. 372; Bod. L., Clarendon MS 63, fo. 240 (Bristol to Hyde); MS 64, fo. 275 (O'Neill to Hyde).

46. Bod. L., Clarendon MS 63, fo. 274 (Bennet to Hyde); MS 64, fos. 275, 324 (O'Neill to Hyde), 306 (Bennet to Hyde); MS 65, fos. 14 (O'Neil to Hyde), 39, 203 (Bennet to Hyde), 135 (King to Hyde), 263 (Culpeper to Hyde); *Nicholas Papers*, iv. 183–4, 186–7 (Culpeper to Nicholas); SP 77/32, fos. 301, 321 (Nicholas to James); SP 78/114, fo. 333 (Taaffe to Inchiquin).

47. *Nicholas Papers*, iv. 185, 188 (Culpeper to Nicholas); Bryant, *Letters of Charles II*, pp. 77–8; HMC Bath MSS, ii. 140 (Ross to Holles); *CSPV* (1659–61), pp. 91, 95–6; SP 77/32, fos. 333 (Nicholas to Mordaunt), 337 (Nicholas to James), 351 (Nicholas to Johnson); SP 77/33, fo. 1 (Nicholas to Mills); Bod. L., Clarendon MS 65, fo. 263 (Culpeper to Hyde); MS 66, fos. 3 (Bennet to Hyde), 5, 30, 95, 147 (O'Neill to Hyde), 200 (Bristol to Hyde), 255 (Culpeper to Hyde); MS 67, fos. 50 (O'Neill to Hyde), 263 (Hyde to 'Bird'); Bod. L., Carte MS 30, fo. 496 (Bristol to Condé); MS 213, fos. 433–4 (Ormonde to Mordaunt); HMC Various Collections, ii. 362 (Hyde to Langdale); Dorset RO, D124, Box 268, General Household Accounts, 1658–9.

48. SP 77/32, fo. 52 (Talbot to Nicholas); CSP iii. 367–8 (Ormonde to Hyde); Thurloe State Papers, v. 227 (letter from Ratcliffe), 362 (spy report).

49. *Life of James II*, i. 333.

50. BL Add. MS 15856, fo. 54ᵛ (Walker's commission).

51. *Nicholas Papers*, iv. 77–8 (Knatchbull to Nicholas).

52. Ibid. iv. 280–2 (Hatton to Nicholas); SP 77/32, fo. 9 (Culpeper to Nicholas).

53. Thurloe State Papers, v. 160 (report from Hague); CSP iii. 363 (King to Mary); *Nicholas Papers*, iv. 3 (Nicholas to Middleton), 8 (Ormonde to Nicholas); SP 77/32, fo. 156 (Balcarres to King); Bod. L., Clarendon MS 58, fos. 166–7 (Hyde to King), 189–90 (King to Henrietta Maria).

54. Bod. L., Clarendon MS 60, fo. 283 (Talbot to friend); MS 66, fo. 30 and MS 67, fo. 132 (O'Neill to Hyde); SP 77/32, fo. 346 (Nicholas to Browne).

55. Ibid.; F. Routledge, 'The Negotiations between Charles II and the Cardinal De Retz, 1658–9', *TRHS* 5th ser. 6 (1956), pp. 49–68.

56. *Life of James II*, i. 265–93; CSP iii. 317–18 (James to King), 318–21 (Bristol to Hyde), 321–4 (James's instructions to Blagge), 359 (Bristol to Ormonde); *Nicholas Papers*, iv. 1–2 (Nicholas to Culpeper), 4, 21–2

(Nicholas to Bennet); Bod. L., Clarendon MS 53, fos. 160, 187, 205 (Bristol to Hyde); *Calendar of the Clarendon State Papers*, iii. 223, 223–4 (Mary to Heenvliet).

57. Ibid.; CSP iii. 360 (Hyde to Nicholas), 361 (Mary to King), 363 (reply), 369 (Mary to King); Bod. L., Clarendon MS 58, fos. 122 (Mary to King), 158–9 (James to King), 160–1 (reply); MS 59, fo. 408 (Cotterell to Hyde); MS 60, fos. 517–18 (O'Neill to Hyde); Lambeth Palace L., MS 645, fos. 6–9 (letters between King and Mary), 105 (Henrietta Maria to King).

58. Bod. L., Clarendon MS 58, fos. 112–13, 128–9 (Jermyn to King), 124–7 (Henrietta Maria to King), 131–2 (replies).

59. Bryant, *Letters of Charles II*, pp. 79–80, 89–90.

60. Thurloe State Papers, vi. 724 (spy report); *Nicholas Papers*, iv. 32–3 (Church to Nicholas); SP 77/3, fo. 61 (Walker to Nicholas); *Life of James II*, i. 293; BL Egerton MS 2551, fos. 6–7 (warrants for Langdale and Berkeley); MS 2542, fo. 254 (warrant for Norwich); Sir William Dugdale, *The Baronage of England* (1675), p. 476.

61. BL Egerton MS 2551, fo. 8 (warrant for John Nicholas); Bod. L., Clarendon MS 59, fos. 306–7 (patents for Lane); MS 67, fos. 136–9 (draft warrant and memorandum for Fanshaw); HMC Heathcote MSS, pp. 9–11, 16 (Hyde to Fanshaw); CSP iii. 296–8 (Hyde to King).

62. Thurloe State Papers, v. 646, 673–5.

63. Crist, *Charles II to Lord Taaffe*, No. 1; CSP iii. 157 (Hyde to Nicholas); MS Diary of Corfitz Braem, 28 May (a photocopy of this diary, in private hands in Denmark, was lent to me by Lady Antonia Fraser).

64. Thurloe State Papers, ii. 586 (spy report).

65. *CSPD* (1657–8), pp. 310–11 (Cotterell to Nicholas); Thurloe State Papers, vii. 337, 353 (spy reports from Bruges); HMC Bath MSS, ii. 130–1 (Ross to Holles); Bod. L., Clarendon MS 54, fo. 54 (Bristol to Hyde); MS 56, fo. 31 (Taaffe to King); MS 58, fos. 181–2 (Taaffe to King), 183–4 ('from Mr. Hartop's'); BL Egerton MS 2542, fo. 278 (declaration against duels); Crist, *Charles II to Lord Taaffe*, No. 21; Carte, *Original Letters*, ii. 287 (Hyde to Ormonde).

66. *Nicholas Papers*, iv. 13 (Nicholas to Hyde); Bod. L., Clarendon MS 54, fo. 225 (Hyde to Ormonde); CSP iii. 387 (Ormonde to Hyde).

67. Crist, *Charles II to Lord Taaffe*, No. 8; Bod. L., Clarendon MS 54, fo. 52 (Hyde to Taaffe); Bryant, *Letters of Charles II*, pp. 79–80; Dorset RO, D124, Box 268, General Household Accounts, 1658–9; Brown, *Miscellanea Aulica*, pp. 128–9.

68. It translates as 'I am so in love with you that I cannot crap.' The remark echoes Rabelais and was probably a direct quotation: Crist, *Charles II to Lord Taaffe*, No. 1.

69. Ibid., Nos. 4–7, 17–20. I cannot understand why Timothy Crist considers the affair to refer to the wooing of Henrietta Catherine of Orange. The setting is clearly Brussels, Taaffe would have been a peculiar mediator with

the House of Orange, and Charles would not have given a princess his second-best gloves or referred to the Dowager Princess with the obscenity with which he pelts the head of the 'infanta's' family. Once this distortion is removed, the true sequence of the letters should probably be 5, 6, 7, 19, 20, 16, 17, 18 and all dated 1657.

70. The known facts are collected in *The Complete Peerage*, vi. 706 and x. 559–60.

71. Bod. L., Clarendon MS 51, fos. 293–4.

72. Thurloe State Papers, v. 169 (Barkstead to Thurloe, Howard's examination), 178 (Anne Hill's examination); *CSPD* (1656–7), p. 4 (Council order); *Mercurius Politicus* (10–17 July 1656), p. 7108.

73. CSP iii. 354–5 (Hyde to Ormonde), 357–8 (Hyde to Nicholas); Thurloe State Papers, vi. 463 (report from Brussels), vii. 347 (Downing to Thurloe); Bod. L., Clarendon MS 56, fo. 7 (Bristol to Hyde).

74. Clarendon MS 56, fo. 278 (Cardeñas to King); MS 57, fo. 27 (Cardeñas to Hyde); MS 59, fo. 306 (Slingsby's patent); CSP iii. 382–3 (exchange of three letters between Ormonde and Mottet), 384–5 (Slingsby to King); SP 77/32, fo. 85 (Ross to Nicholas); Crist, *Charles II to Lord Taaffe*, No. 13.

75. The evidence is reviewed in Elizabeth D'Oyley, *James, Duke of Monmouth* (1938), p. 26, and see Thurloe State Papers, vii. 337 (report from Bruges).

76. See Hutton, *The Restoration*, pp. 68–79.

77. SP 77/33, fo. 5 (Nicholas to Heath).

78. Ibid.; Clarendon, *History*, xvi. 73–6, 137; *Life of James II*, p. 381; HMC Various Collections, ii. 362 (King to Caracena); Bod. L., Clarendon MS 68, fos. 34, 187 (Hyde to Bennet); MS 69, fos. 47 (Bennet to Hyde), 67 (Hyde to Willoughby); Underdown, *Royalist Conspiracy*, pp. 296–304; CSP iii. 642–92 (letters between court and conspirators).

79. Clarendon, *History*, xvi. 137–8; Bod. L., Clarendon MS 69, fo. 186 (Hyde to Mordaunt).

80. Hutton, *The Restoration*, pp. 106–7, and sources there.

81. Ibid., plus Bod. L., Clarendon MS 70, fos. 218–19 ('reasons for the King's removal'), and MS 71, fos. 53–4 (King to Prince of Orange and Monck); West Suffolk RO, Grafton Correspondence, King to Grenville, 14 Apr. 1660.

82. Hutton, *The Restoration*, pp. 105–6, 117, plus Bod. L., Clarendon MS 70, fos. 46–7, 93, 159–60, 208; MS 71, fos. 7–8, 43, 212, 368 (letters from King to prospective supporters); Carte, *Original Letters*, ii. 319–22 (Howard to Ormonde, and reply).

83. Hutton, *The Restoration*, pp. 110–11, plus Bod. L., Clarendon MS 71, fo. 124 (King to Crawford, Lauderdale).

84. SP 18/220/89–90, 111–13, 119–31 (responses to petitions); SP 18/221/17 (grant to O'Neill); BL Add. MS 32102, fo. 84ᵛ (Fanshaw's knighthood); BL Egerton MS 2551, fos. 16–17 (warrants for St Albans and Rumbold).

85. Hutton, *The Restoration*, pp. 111–13, 117–18; Bod. L., Clarendon MS 72, fo. 257 (King to Inch); Bryant, *Letters of Charles II*, pp. 90–1.

86. Sir William Lower, *A Relation in the Form of a Journal* (1660), pp. 5–108;
    Nicholas Papers, iv. 210–11 (King to de Haro and Caracena); Clarendon,
    History, xvi, 234–45; Scottish RO, CH/1/1/11, fo. 155 (Sharp to Douglas);
    MS Diary of Corfitz Braem, 24 May–1 June (NS); *The Diary of Samuel Pepys*
    (ed. Robert Latham and William Matthews, 1970), i. 143–56.

Chapter 7

1. 'The image of virtue', in David Starkey (ed.), *The English Court* (1987),
   p. 230.
2. E. S. De Beer (ed.), *The Diary of John Evelyn* (Oxford, 1955), iii. 299–
   300; Osmund Airy (ed.), *The Lauderdale Papers* (Camden Soc., 1885),
   i. 146 (Murray to Lauderdale); Pepys, *Diary*, viii. 64; 'Last Moments of
   an English King', *Household Words*, 9 (1854), p. 278; Royal Archives,
   SP1/14 (James's account of Charles's death); E. M. Thompson (ed.), *Correspondence of the Family of Hatton* (Camden Soc., 1878), ii. 21–2, 24 (Lyttleton
   to Hatton); G. M. Colvin (ed.), *The History of the King's Works* (1976), v. 266–
   70.
3. Thurloe State Papers, vii. 225 (report from Brussels); Lower, *A Relation*,
   p. 108.
4. *The Diurnal of Thomas Rugge* (ed. W. L. Sachse, Camden Soc., 1961),
   pp. 88–122; *CSPV* (1659–61), pp. 155–82; Pepys, *Diary*, i. 144;
   Mercurius Publicus (19–20 July 1660), p. 465; Staffordshire RO, D
   868/4/46–7 (newsletters); Shakespeare's Birthplace Centre, Stratford-upon-
   Avon, Commonplace Book of Sir Francis Fane, fo. 145; and there are
   the comments of Whitelocke and the Quakers, below.
5. PRO, P/C 2/54, pp. 1–144.
6. Ibid., p. 91; Clarendon, *Life*, i. 364–70; *Camden Miscellany*, ix (1895), p. 2
   (a life of Nathaniel Crew); *CSPD* (1660–1), pp. 59–604, *passim*; PRO,
   ADM/2/1725, fo. 21ᵛ (Montagu's commission).
7. J. C. Sainty, 'A Reform in the Tenure of Offices during the Reign of
   Charles II', *BIHR* 41 (1968), pp. 155–6; Pepys, *Diary*, i. 199–236, *passim*;
   SP 29/1/63–6, 68, 90–110 (grants and reports on petitions).
8. P/C 2/54; W. D. Macray (ed.), *Notes which passed at meetings of the Privy
   Council* (1896), p. 7.
9. SP 29/23/93–104 (minutes of committee).
10. Clarendon, *Life*, i. 362–3; Bod. L., MS Eng. Hist. d. 279 (the petitions);
    Macray (ed.), *Notes*; P/C 2/54, p.31; Pepys, *Diary*, i. 236; Scottish RO,
    CH 1/1/11, pp. 185–7 (Sharp to Douglas).
11. Ibid., pp. 155–7, 163, 171–2, 175–6, 185–7, 191–2; Clarendon, *Life*,
    i. 365–7; Baillie, *Letters*, iii. 443; *Lauderdale Papers*, i. 32–3 (petition of
    Scots nobles); Bod. L., Clarendon MS 73, fo. 380 (King's reply); Blair, *Life*
    (ed. M'Crie), pp. 353–5; Revd James Kirkton, *The Secret and True History of
    the Church of Scotland* (Edinburgh, 1817), pp. 68–9; Sir George Mackenzie,

Memoirs of the Affairs of Scotland (Edinburgh, 1821), pp. 8–13; BL Add. MS 23114, fo. 50 (Leven to Lauderdale).

12. In 1669 he claimed that he and Coote had invited Charles to Ireland in February 1660 (SP 63/326/67). It seems incredible that such an offer should have left no trace either in the contemporary or the retrospective sources, and it is contradicted by Coote's letter to Charles, cited earlier. In March Broghil wrote to Thurloe that he was anxious that Ireland would not be a 'back door' for the King (Thurloe State Papers, vii. 859). But some less spectacular approach may have been made.

13. Clarendon, *Life*, i. 376–9, 394–8; Pepys, *Diary*, i. 227–9; Robert Steele (ed.), *Tudor and Stuart Proclamations* (Oxford, 1910), vol. ii, No. 2177; *Public Intelligencer* (4–11 June 1660), p. 384; *Mercurius Politicus* (26 July–2 Aug. 1660), pp. 484–7; SP 63/303/82 (instructions to Robartes), and 83 (King to Chief Justices); Bod. L., Carte MS 48, fo. 4 (anonymous letter); Macray (ed.), *Notes*, p. 8; P/C 2/54, pp. 34, 91, 124.

14. Clarendon, *Life*, i. 394, 461–3; *Mercurius Politicus* (1–8 Nov. 1660), p. 711, and (20–7 Dec. 1660), p. 839; SP 63/304/89 (warrant for Lords Justices), 305/56 (list of Council); Bod. L., Clarendon MS 74, fo. 99 (Broghil to Hyde).

15. Hutton, *Restoration*, pp. 128–9, and sources there, plus A. F. Havighurst, 'The Judiciary and Politics in the Reign of Charles II', *Law Quarterly Review*, 66 (1950), pp. 63–4; Prideaux Place, Padstow, 'Old Letters', Morice to Prideaux, 2 Sept. 1662.

16. Bryant, *Letters of Charles II*, p. 99 (exchange of notes).

17. Hutton, *Restoration*, p. 130.

18. Ibid., pp. 132–4.

19. P/C 2/54, p. 124; SP 63/305/18 (pardon to Coote set); SO 1/4, pp. 625–6 (pardon to Broghil etc.).

20. Clarendon, *Life*, i. 367–70; Scottish RO, CH 1/1/11, pp. 175, 189–91, 192–4, 203 (Sharp to Douglas); Steele, *Proclamations*, vol. ii, Nos. 2180, 2191a; *Mercurius Politicus* (5–12 July 1660), p. 484 and (19–26 July 1660), p. 460; Nicoll, *Diary*, p. 295; Mackenzie, *Memoirs*, p. 13; Bryant, *Letters of Charles II*, p. 98 (exchange of notes).

21. Hutton, *Restoration*, pp. 134–5.

22. Bryant, *Letters of Charles II*, p. 98 (exchange of notes with Hyde).

23. Hutton, *Restoration*, pp. 136–8 and sources there; Donald Nicholas, *Mr. Secretary Nicholas* (1955), pp. 298–302; *CSPD* (1660–1), pp. 73–546, *passim*; West Suffolk RO, Grafton Correspondence, King to Bath, 13 June 1667; Bod. L., Clarendon MS 75, fo. 176 (list by King); Bod. L., Carte MS 59, fos. 4–7 (list of Household appointments); Underdown, *Royalist Conspiracy*, pp. 333–8; *APS* vii. 8, 181; *Mercurius Publicus* (20–7 Sept.), p. 623, and (13–20 Dec.), p. 810, and (28 Mar.–4 Apr. 1661), p. 194.

24. Hutton, *Restoration*, pp. 137–8; Fanshawe, *Memoirs*, pp. 119–27.

25. Hutton, *Restoration*, pp. 139–42.

26. Bod. L., Carte MS 70, fo. 28 (paper from commissioners); MS 31, fo. 101 (Clanricarde to Ormonde); MS 49, fos. 4 (Ormonde to Coote), 48 (Ormonde to Montgomery); SP 63/304/71, 131 (Coote and Bury to Nicholas), 63/305/5 (Cashel corporation to commissioners); P/C 2/54, p. 126; P/C 2/55, pp. 28–47; Bryant, *Letters of Charles II*, pp. 108–9 (exchange with Hyde); Carte MS 66, fos. 493–512 (November Declaration); MS 45, fo. 465 (appeal of new landlords); SO 1/4, *passim* (orders concerning property); SP 63/307/4 (Eustace to Nicholas).

27. I. M. Green, *The Re-Establishment of the Church of England, 1660–1663* (Oxford, 1978); Julia Buckroyd, *Church and State in Scotland, 1660–1681* (Edinburgh, 1980); J. I. McGuire, 'The Dublin Convention, the protestant community and the emergence of an ecclesiastical settlement in 1660', in Art Cosgrove and J. I. McGuire (eds.), *Parliament and Community* (Belfast, 1983).

28. Trinity College, Dublin, MS 808, fos. 156–8 ('The further humble desires of the General Convention'); P/C 2/54, p. 125; SP 63/304/154, p. 160 (King to Lord Justices); Scottish RO, CH 1/1/11, pp. 188–205 (Sharp to Douglas); Revd Patrick Adair, *A True Narrative of the Rise and Progress of the Presbyterian Church in Ireland* (ed. W. D. Killen, Belfast, 1866), pp. 243–4.

29. Scottish RO, CH 1/1/11, pp. 156–205 (Sharp to Scottish ministers and replies); *Mercurius Publicus* (30 Aug.–6 Sept.), pp. 562–5, and (13–20 Sept.), p. 580, and (20–7 Sept.), p. 602; Robert Wodrow, *The History of the Sufferings of the Church of Scotland* (Glasgow edn., 1836–8), i. 68–81; Baillie, *Letters*, iii. 410–11, 446–8; *Lauderdale Papers*, i. 34–5 (ministers to Lauderdale), 52–5 (Sharp to Drummond); Blair, *Life*, p. 240; Gilbert Burnet, *History of My Own Time* (ed. Osmund Airy, Oxford, 1897), i. 198; Scottish RO, PA 11/12, *passim* (register of Committee of Estates).

30. Hutton, *Restoration*, pp. 143–8, 172–3, and sources cited there.

31. Mackenzie, *Memoirs*, pp. 29–33; SP 63/305/22 (Rawdon to Conway), 51 (King to Lord Justices); *Mercurius Publicus* (21–7 Feb.), p. 114, and (28 Feb.–7 Mar.), p. 130, and (7–14 Mar.), pp. 145, 155, 160.

32. LJ ix. 236; Mackenzie, *Memoirs*, p. 31; SO 1/4, pp. 361–5 (King to Lord Justices).

33. Hutton, *Restoration*, p. 149; Geyl, *Orange and Stuart*, pp. 138–44, and English sources cited there; SP 84/163, fos. 35, 50, 72, and 84/164, fo. 29 (memorial of Mary and replies of States of Holland).

34. Hutton, *Restoration*, pp. 149–50.

35. SP 103/302 (the discussions); Keith Feiling, *British Foreign Policy, 1660–1672* (1930), pp. 85, 93–4, 96, 104.

36. I have been unable to add substantially to the story pieced together by Stradling, thesis, pp. 23–63, and G. L. Belcher, 'Spain and the Anglo-Portuguese Alliance of 1661', *JBS* 15 (1975), pp. 67–88. I have merely contributed details from Bod. L., Clarendon MS 73, fo. 215 (King to Queen of Portugal); MS 74, fos. 111 (Portuguese to King), 284–7 (Batteville to King), 288 (St Albans to King), 340 (reply); MS 75, fos. 99–103 (papers

between Hyde and French), 207 (King to Portuguese), 217 (draft treaty), 381–3 (Batteville to King); and SP 78/115, fo. 193 (instructions to St Albans).

37. Clarendon, *Life*, i. 370–6; *Lauderdale Papers*, i. 39–40 (the instructions).
38. Mackenzie, *Memoirs*, pp. 6–7; Kirkton, *Secret and True History*, p. 114; *Lauderdale Papers*, i. 61–2 (Sharp to Drummond); Nicoll, *Diary*, p. 311; Bod. L., Clarendon MS 74, fo. 222 (Glencairn to Hyde).
39. *APS* vii. 8–45, 162–3; Bod. L., Clarendon MS 74, fos. 64, 67 (Middleton to Hyde), 291–2 (reply); *Lauderdale Papers*, i. 72 (Sharp to Drummond); Osmund Airy (ed.), 'Letters Addressed to the Earl of Lauderdale', *Camden Miscellany*, viii (1883), pp. 2–7 (Cassilis to Lauderdale); Mackenzie, *Memoirs*, p.23.
40. Bod. L., Clarendon MS 74, fos. 220 (Middleton to Hyde), 222 (Glencairn to Hyde), 290–2 (Hyde to Middleton); MS 75, fo. 400 (Lauderdale to Glencairn); *APS* vii. 86–8; Wodrow, *Sufferings*, i. 110–30; *Lauderdale Papers*, i. 77, 80 (Sharp to Drummond), 91 (Rothes to Lauderdale); Blair, *Life*, p. 381; Burnet, *History*, i. 196–8, 215–16; NLS MS 2512, fo. 6 (Sharp to Lauderdale). This account differs from Buckroyd, *Church and State*, pp. 27–36, principally in stressing the absolute impotence of the English government. I cannot, like her, see Middleton as a 'protégé' of Hyde, and the evidence cited above is against any influence by Hyde over the developments in Scotland.
41. Hutton, *Restoration*, pp. 150–2; Steele, *Proclamations*, vol. ii, No. 2198; Nicoll, *Diary*, p. 320; Adair, *True Narrative*, pp. 246–7.
42. Hutton, *Restoration*, pp. 152–3.
43. SP 63/305/62 (questions for King), 63/308/15, 22–3, 28–31 (Nicholas to Lord Justices).
44. Hutton, *Restoration*, pp. 153–4, and sources there.

Chapter 8

1. All this is based upon Hutton, *Restoration*, pp. 154–61, and sources there. During this chapter in particular, and also in those before and after, I have not only used this previous book of mine as a sole reference but have taken passages from it for interpolation into the text. If this irritates any reader, then I apologize. The book in question was published only a year before these chapters were written, and at the time of going to press I have had no reason to revise it. I listed the sources used for every part of its text in very lengthy footnotes and decided not to reproduce them here. It is my hope that the quantity of information upon Scotland and Ireland, and a little more upon England, will redeem this part of the present book to anybody who knows the former one well. But I would strongly recommend to those who have access to doctoral theses, the one recently deposited by Paul Seaward. It is a work which I much admire and look forward to seeing published, and which

he posted to me, with great generosity, at my request. Several of its arguments conflict with mine. I do not wish to take issue with them until they appear in print, but neither do I wish to take account of them in this present work. It is my belief that these areas of disagreement are based upon sources which could support the conclusion of either one of us, and leave it to colleagues to judge between them.

2. Ibid., pp. 162–3; Wodrow, *Sufferings*, i. 130–96; Baillie, *Letters*, iii. 465–6; *Lauderdale Papers*, i. 92–32 (King to Middleton); Burnet, *History*, i. 224–6; SP 29/65/11 (examination of Robert Johnston), 29/68/6 (examination of Archibald Johnston); SP 44/15, pp. 18–19 (warrant for shipment); *Lauderdale Papers*, i. 135, 151–2 (Lauderdale to Murray), 153 (reply); *RPCS* i. 370–1; Kirkton, *Secret and True History*, p. 216.

3. Hutton, *Restoration*, pp. 164–5.

4. Bod. L., Clarendon MS 74, fos. 345 (Lord Justices to Clarendon), 383–5, 408, 460 (Orrery to Clarendon); SP 63/307/55 (speech of Eustace), 61 (Eustace to Nicholas), 73 (Orrery to Nicholas), 171–2 (Lord Justices to Nicholas), 181 (reply); SO 4, p. 634, and 5, pp. 93, 267 (King to Lord Justices); Bod. L., Carte MS 31, fos. 155, 167, 172, 176, 232, 254 (Aungier to Ormonde), 185 (Montgomery to Ormonde), 223 (Mountrath to Ormonde); MS 221, fo. 186 (Bramhall to Ormonde); MS 42, fo. 276 (Carlingford's creation); MS 69, fos. 255ᵛ–259 (order by English Privy Council); MS 64, fos. 235–9, 316 (Irish Commons' Journals).

5. Bod. L., Clarendon MS 75, fos. 171–2 (Orrery to Clarendon), 263–70 (Dublin government to Clarendon); SP 63/307/179 (Lord Justices to Nicholas), 200, 232 (Orrery to Nicholas); Orrery State Letters, p. 23 (Orrery to Ormonde).

6. Orrery State Letters, p. 21 (Orrery to Ormonde); P/C 2/55, pp. 368, 405, 488–9, 530, 540, 548, 569, 575–6; Bod. L., Carte MS 49, fos. 75–6 (Ormonde to Eustace).

7. Orrery State Letters, pp. 28–9, 37–8 (Orrery to Ormonde); SP 63/310/31 (order in Council); Bod. L., Carte MS 31, fo. 526 (Mervyn to Ormonde); P/C 2/55, p. 627; P/C 2/56, p. 6.

8. Hutton, *Restoration*, pp. 166–7, and sources there; John Miller, *Popery and Politics in England, 1660–1688* (Cambridge, 1973), pp. 95–8, and sources there.

9. NLI MS 13217, fo. 2 (Anglesey to Orrery); NLI MS 13223, fo. 6 (Petty to Orrery).

10. Steele, *Proclamations*, vol. ii, No. 667; SP 63/307/194 (Lord Justices to Nicholas); Bod. L., Carte MS 214, fos. 309, 315 (Belling to Ormonde); Peter Walsh, *The History and Vindication of the Loyal Formulary, or Irish Remonstrance* (1674), pp. 4–19; SP 63/308, p. 119 (warrant for Belling).

11. Steele, *Proclamations*, vol. ii, Nos. 674, 677; Bod. L., Clarendon MS 76, fos. 178 (draft declaration), 205–7 (Orrery to Clarendon); Orrery State Letters, pp. 47, 55–6 (Orrery to Ormonde).

12. *Church and State in Scotland*, pp. 35–8.
13. *APS* vii. 188–9, 197, 271–2; *RPCS* i. 28–32; Burnet, *History*, i. 217–19, 2133–6; Mackenzie, *Memoirs*, pp. 53–6, 59; Kirkton, *Secret and True History*, pp. 133–4; *Lauderdale Papers*, i. 98 (Bellenden to Lauderdale) and ii, app. C (Sharp to Middleton); NLS MS 2512, fos. 6 (Sharp to Lauderdale), 8 (Sharp to Wood). I can find no proof in the evidence cited here for Julia Buckroyd's belief that Clarendon tipped the balance at the meeting: it seems to be an extrapolation from Burnet, who is wrong in other details, such as his assertion that Charles consulted the Scottish Privy Council. Nor can I endorse her suggestion that the English government put pressure upon the Scottish Parliament to accept episcopacy by delaying the withdrawal of English garrisons, the passage of the Act of Indemnity, and the exemption of Scotland from the Navigation Act. There is no proof that the Parliament felt under any such pressure. Charles had resolved to remove the garrisons in May 1661, having work for the men in Portugal, and his delay was for fear of the reaction of the Cavalier Parliament: *Lauderdale Papers*, ii, app. C. Middleton and the Parliament itself, not Charles, delayed an Act of Indemnity, and in June 1661 the King promised one in the next session and ordered that nobody be challenged for their past in the interim: *APS* vii. 344–7. The exemption from the Navigation Act was held up because English Privy Counsellors feared the effect upon customs receipts: SP 29/44/12–13, 66 (various reports). As before, I am inclined to stress the passive reaction of the English government to Scottish developments, in contrast to Dr Buckroyd's sense of royal intervention: *Church and State in Scotland*, pp. 39–40.
14. NLS MS 3922, fo. 17 (Lauderdale to ministers); Kirkton, *Secret and True History*, p. 135; Burnet, *History*, i. 236–7; NLS MS 2512, fo. 10 (letter from Sharp).
15. Buckroyd, *Church and State*, pp. 42–4.
16. *RPCS* i. 125–6, 260–1, 269–70; *APS* vii. 370–9; *Lauderdale Papers*, i. 103–5 (Middleton's instructions); Buckroyd, *Church and State*, p. 50; Bod. L., Clarendon MS 77, fo. 373 (Newburgh to Clarendon).
17. All based upon Hutton, *Restoration*, pp. 168–80, and sources there; plus Chatsworth House, Burlington's Diary (1659–66), 1 May 1662.
18. Hutton, *Restoration*, p. 185.
19. Letter from Southwell to 2nd Earl of Clarendon, 25 Apr. 1700, pasted to end-paper of first volume of edition of Clarendon, *Life*, held in library of University College, London. I owe this reference to Robert Latham, Esq.
20. Hutton, *Restoration*, pp. 190–1, and sources there.
21. 'Letters from John, Earl of Lauderdale, and others, to Sir John Gilmour', SHS *Miscellany*, V (1933), pp. 144–5 (David to George Stewart), 150–1 (Gilmour to Lauderdale).
22. Pepys, *Diary*, iii. 238.
23. All save above references from Hutton, *Restoration*, pp. 186–90.
24. Clarendon, *Life*, i. 490–4; SP 63/308, pp. 78^v (Nicholas to Lord Justices),

135, 140–1 (warrants for Arran); SP 63/307/272 (Orrery to Nicholas), 278 (King to Irish Privy Council); Bod. L., Carte MS 48, fo. 79 (Ormonde to Lord Justices); P/C 2/55, pp. 193, 206, 475; SP 63/310/14 (Ormonde's commission); Orrery State Letters, p. 47 (Orrery to Ormonde); BL Sloane MS 1008, fo. 185 (Orrery's speech to Ormonde).

25. Kirkton, *Secret and True History*, pp. 156–9.
26. *APS* vii. 415–29; 'Letters to Gilmour', SHS 1933, pp. 139–40 (Lauderdale to Gilmour), 141–2 (Roxburgh to Gilmour); *Lauderdale Papers*, i. 103–5 (instructions to Middleton), 108–18, 123–4 (William Sharp to Lauderdale); Bod. L., Clarendon MS 76, fo. 256 (Newburgh to Clarendon); Blair, *Life* (ed. M'Crie), pp. 413–17; Mackenzie, *Memoirs*, pp. 64–77; Kirkton, *Secret and True History*, p. 155; Bod. L., Carte MS 32, fos. 68 (O'Neill to Ormonde), 69 (Middleton to Ormonde); NLS MS 2512, fo. 13 (James Sharp to Lauderdale); *RPCS* i. 216, 248, 250. There is no evidence for Dr Buckroyd's suggestion (*Church and State*, p. 50), that Clarendon proposed the tactic of the 'disablement' clause, having been involved with the English precedent in 1660. The latter had in any case been suggested by Commons back-benchers while Clarendon was busy in the Lords.
27. Hutton, *Restoration*, pp. 191–3, and sources there; 'A list of the department of the Lord Chamberlain of the Household, autumn 1663', *BIHR* 19 (1942–3), pp. 13–24; SP 63/313/14, 147 (Ormonde to Bennet), 128 (reply); Bod. L., Carte MS 42, fos. 744–5 (King to Ormonde).
28. Hutton, *Restoration*, pp. 193–6, and sources there.
29. Bod. L., Carte MS 31, fo. 358 (Ormonde to Eustace); MS 143, fos. 9, 57–9 (Ormonde to Clarendon); MS 47, fo. 18 (Clarendon to Ormonde); Orrery State Letters, p. 21 (Orrery to Ormonde); Walsh, *History and Vindication*, pp. 85–6.
30. Steele, *Proclamations*, vol. ii, Nos. 689, 691, 705; Bod. L., Clarendon MS 78, fos. 81 (Orrery to Clarendon), 83 (Ormonde to Clarendon); MS 79, fo. 55 (Orrery to Clarendon); SP 63/310/121 (Dumville to Bennet); Orrery State Letters, pp. 63–4 (paper for Ormonde); Bod. L., Carte MS 47, fo. 16 (Clarendon to Ormonde); MS 78, fo. 18 (Ormonde to Clarendon); MS 143, fos. 28–9, 36 (Ormonde to Bennet, to Clarendon); MS 64, fos. 243–249ᵛ (journals of Irish Parliament); P/C 2/56, pp. 26, 192, 238; BL Egerton MS 789 (judgements of commissioners).
31. Burnet, *History*, i. 361–2; *Lauderdale Papers*, i. 132–3 (Sharp to Lauderdale); 'Letters from Lauderdale', SHS 1933, pp. 156–63 (Lauderdale to Gilmour); *RPCS* i. 329–48; Brown, *Miscellanea Aulica*, pp. 206–36; Mackenzie, *Memoirs*, pp. 112–14; Bod. L., Carte MS 32, fo. 368 (O'Neill to Ormonde).
32. Hutton, *Restoration*, pp. 196–9, and sources there.
33. Bod. L., Clarendon MS 79, fos. 55, 104–9 (Orrery to Clarendon), 16–19, 80, 90 (Ormonde to Clarendon), 88 (Mervyn to Clarendon), 92 (reply); SP 63/313/22 (Coventry to Bennet), 25 (Ormonde to Bennet), 33 (Ormonde

to King), 43 (speech by Mervyn), 46 (Bennet to Ormonde); SP 63/313, pp. 19–24 (King to commissioners, Ormonde); Bod. L., Carte MS 32, fo. 257 (Berkeley to Ormonde); MS 47, fo. 39 (Clarendon to Ormonde).

34. Hutton, *Restoration*, pp. 200–4, and sources there.

35. Burnet, *History*, i. 363–4; *Lauderdale Papers*, i. 134–5 (Sharp to Lauderdale); 'Letters from Lauderdale', SHS 1933, pp. 171–2 (Lauderdale to Gilmour); NLS MS 597, fo. 85 (Rothes's commission); *RPCS* i. 380–2.

36. Kirkton, *Secret and True History*, p. 159; *APS* vii. 448–51, 459–61; *Lauderdale Papers*, i. 136–7, 141, 146–8, 177–9, 188–9 (Murray to Lauderdale), 139–40, 163–8 (Lauderdale to Murray); Mackenzie, *Memoirs*, pp. 116–33.

37. *APS* vii. 455–6; SP 29/75/81 (Meni to Muddiman); *Lauderdale Papers*, i. 154–7 (Lauderdale to Murray), 162–3 (reply); BL Add. MS 23119, fo. 86 (Lauderdale to King). Julia Buckroyd follows Burnet in believing that the Scottish Conventicle Act copied that in England. There may have been some influence, but the English Act did not pass till the next year, and both that and the failed bill of 1663 were far more savage than the Scottish measure.

38. *APS* vii. 463–81; *Lauderdale Papers*, i. 166–74 (Lauderdale to King), 177–8 (Murray to Lauderdale); NLS MS 597, fo. 96 (instructions to Rothes).

39. *Lauderdale Papers*, i. 177–8, 181 (Murray to Lauderdale), 184 (Lauderdale to King).

40. Only tangentially did he fall for being associated with Middleton: 'Letters from Lauderdale', SHS 1933, pp. 147–8 (Lauderdale to Gilmour); *Lauderdale Papers*, i. 183 (Murray to Lauderdale).

41. NLS MS 573, fo. 77 (King to Glencairn): *Lauderdale Papers*, i. 184 (Murray to Lauderdale).

42. Carte, *Ormonde*, vol. iii, app., pp. 28–30 (Ormonde's speech); Bod. L., Clarendon MS 79, fos. 90, 102 (Ormonde to Clarendon), 104–9, 113, 125, 181 (Orrery to Clarendon); SP 63/313/54 (Ormonde to Bennet), 58 (Commons' address), 61, 82 (Ormonde to King); SP 63/307/76 (Kingston to Nicholas); Orrery State Letters, p. 68 (Orrery to Ormonde).

43. Bod. L., Clarendon MS 79, fo. 251 (Anglesey to Ormonde); Adair, *True Narrative*, pp. 280–1; SP 63/313/156 (Ormonde to King), 170 (Ormonde to Bennet).

44. Bod. L., Carte MS 143, fos. 25, 70 (Ormonde to King); MS 44, fos. 351 (Queen Mother to Ormonde), 390 (Ormonde to St Albans); MS 219, fos. 369–70 (the same); Clarendon MS 80, fos. 203–5 (Broderick to Clarendon); Carte MS 31, fo. 165 (St Albans to Ormonde); MS 32, fo. 719 (Clarendon to Ormonde); *Murder Will Out* (1663); Carte, *Ormonde*, ii. 277–93; SP 63/314/62 (Antrim to Williamson), 68 (Irish Privy Council to Bennet and Ormonde's notes).

45. SP 63/313/219 (Bennet to Ormonde), 233 (reply), 227 (Vernon to Bennet); SP 63/314/39 (Order to Council); SP 63/312, pp. 144–7 (Bennet to Ormonde).

46. Bod. L., Clarendon MS 80, fos. 116 (Broderick to Clarendon), 254, 262, 290

(Ormonde to Clarendon); MS 81, fos. 147, 164, 193, 211, 247 (the same);
SP 63/313/233 (Ormonde to Bennet); SP 63/314/5, 9, 59 (Ormonde to
Bennet); SP 63/312, pp. 144–7, 171–2, 179–96 (Bennet to Ormonde); SP
63/314/102 (Dumville to Bennet), 104 (Orrery to Bennet), 9, 81 (Ormonde
to Bennet); Bod. L., Carte MS 49, fos. 242–3 (Ormonde to Talbot), 255–6
(Ormonde to O'Neill); MS 47, fos. 73–5, 94 (Clarendon to Ormonde); MS
33, fo. 227 (Broderick to Ormonde); MS 43, fo. 655 (King to Ormonde); MS
46, fo. 189 (Bennet to Ormonde); P/C 2/56, pp. 607, 619, 640; Bod. L., Carte
MS 214, fos. 576–7 (Carlingford to Ormonde); K. H. D. Haley, *An English
Diplomat in the Low Countries* (Oxford, 1986), pp. 23–4.
47. Baillie, *Letters*, iii. 471, 473; SP 63/308, p. 55 (Nicholas to Eustace).
48. *CSPD* (1663–4), pp. 264, 271 (newsletters to Williamson); Bod. L., Carte MS
33, fos. 69 (O'Neill to Ormonde), 118 (Boys to Ormonde); *The Intelligencer*
(31 Aug., 7 Sept., 28 Sept., 5 Oct. 1663); *The Newes* (10 Sept., 1 Oct. 1663).
49. Hutton, *Restoration*, pp. 204–13, and sources there.

Chapter 9

1. As well as the two great archives mentioned in the text, this panorama is based
   upon HMC Heathcote MSS (Fanshaw's papers); Stradling, thesis, pp. 55–6;
   Herbert H. Rowen, *John De Witt* (Princeton, 1978), chs. 23–7.
2. Bod. L., Clarendon MS 104, fo. 81.
3. Ibid., fos. 88, 230 (Clarendon to Downing).
4. Ibid., fos. 10–88, 230, 252–8 (Clarendon to Downing); Clarendon MS 105,
   fos. 13–140, and MS 106, fos. 6–16 (Downing to Clarendon); Rowen, *De
   Witt*, pp. 453, 457–8.
5. Bod. L., Clarendon MS 75, fo. 156 (Clarendon to Bastide); MS 76, fos. 28–33
   (Louis XIV to D'Estrades); Ms 104, fos. 59, 67 (Clarendon to Downing); MS
   77, fos, 64, 122–5 (Dutch envoys to States-General).
6. Heathcote MSS, pp. 44–74 (letters of Bennet to Fanshaw); Clarendon MS
   77, fos. 128–34 (Downing to Clarendon); Stradling, thesis, pp. 94–7.
7. Clarendon MS 104, fo. 75 (Clarendon to Downing); Geyl, *Orange and Stuart*,
   pp. 165–74; Bryant, *Letters of Charles II*, pp. 122–50; SP 78/116–17,
   passim; BL Egerton MS 2071 (D'Estrades's dispatches); Clarendon MS 105,
   fo. 122 (newsletter).
8. Hutton, *Restoration*, pp. 214–16, and sources there, plus Sir Allan Burns,
   History of the British West Indies (1965), pp. 301–2.
9. Paul Seaward, 'The House of Commons Committee of Trade and the Origins
   of the Second Anglo-Dutch War', *HJ* 30 (1987), pp. 437–52.
10. Hutton, *Restoration*, pp. 216–19; plus Clarendon MS 107, fos. 210–13
    (Downing to Clarendon); Bryant, *Letters of Charles II*, pp. 159–61.
11. SP 78/119, 31–64 (dispatches and instructions of Fitzharding); H. L.
    Schoolcraft, 'England and Denmark, 1660–1667', *EHR* 25 (1910), pp. 462–6.
12. Turnbull, thesis, pp. 13–36.

13. Hutton, *Restoration*, pp. 220–1; *RPCS* (1661–4), pp. 600–7.

14. Hutton, *Restoration*, pp. 222–5; Schoolcraft, *EHR* 1910, pp. 471–2; PRO/31/3/114–15 (dispatches of French ambassadors); C. Brinkmann, 'Charles II and the Bishop of Munster in the Anglo-Dutch War of 1665–1666', *EHR* 21 (1906), pp. 686–90.

15. Hutton, *Restoration*, pp. 232–3.

16. Buckroyd, *Church and State*, p. 64.

17. Ibid., pp. 61–4; *Lauderdale Papers*, i. 199–233 (letters from Rothes, Hamilton, Tweeddale, Bellenden, and Kincardine), and vol. ii, app. A, pp. ix–xxvi (letters from Burnet and Sharp); Burnet, *History*, i. 379–87; HMC Laing MSS, i. 342 (letter from Dalrymple); HMC 4th Report, app., pp. 505–6 (commissions to Rothes); *RPCS* (1661–4), pp. 608–13; *RPCS* (1665–9), pp. 60–1; NLS MS 2512, fos. 54–76 (letters from Sharp and Burnet); NLS MS 7023, fos. 1–4 (Lauderdale to Tweeddale).

18. Hutton, *Restoration*, pp. 225, 233–6; Pepys, *Diary*, v. 203–19.

19. Hutton, *Restoration*, sources listed at p. 240 n. 102; BL Add. MS 22920, fo. 132 (Arlington to Downing); PRO/31/3/114–15 (dispatches of French ambassadors); Geyl, *Orange and Stuart*, pp. 215–29; Brinkmann, *EHR* 1906, pp. 690–2.

20. Stradling, thesis, pp. 168–96; Schoolcraft, *EHR* 1910, pp. 474–8; Brinkmann, *EHR* 1906, pp. 693–4; Bryant, *Letters of Charles II*, p. 183; Bod. L., Carte MS 47, fo. 424 (Coventry to Ormonde); MS 231, fo. 98 (Arlington to Ormonde); SP 81/57 (Vane's dispatches); SP 80/11, fos. 30–51 (Carlingford's dispatches); BL Add. MS 16272, fos. 8–31 (Clarendon to Vane).

21. Hutton, *Restoration*, pp. 237–48; J. P. Hore, *The History of Newmarket* (1886), ii. 220–88.

22. Hutton, *Restoration*, pp. 251–4.

23. Ibid., pp. 252–3; Chatsworth House, Burlington's Diary (1659–66), 25 Jan. 1662.

24. SP 63/316/98 (Orrery to Bennet), 317/6 (Dumville to Ormonde); Bod. L., Carte MS 48, fo. 172 (Ormonde to Ossory); MS 33, fo. 510 (Order in Council); MS 70, fo. 219 (minutes of committee); MS 59, fo. 268 (Orrery to Ossory); Orrery State Letters, p. 98; O'Donoghue, thesis, pp. 196–223; Chatsworth House, Burlington's Diary (1659–66), 13 May 1665.

25. SP 63/319/116 (letter to Orrery), 131, 212 (Talbot to Williamson); SP 63/321/129 (Orrery to Arlington); Bod. L., Carte MS 47, fo. 454 (Coventry to Ormond).

26. SP 63/319/83 (warrant for Hearth Tax farm), 146 (petition of Belling), 161 (letters-patent for Lane), 234 (warrant for St Albans); SP 63/318, pp. 113, 117, 122, 130 (royal orders); SO 6, pp. 103^v, 146, 160^v, 177–82^v (royal orders); Orrery State Letters, pp. 199–200 (Orrery to Ormonde); Kathleen M. Lynch, *Roger Boyle, Earl of Orrery* (Knoxville, 1965), p. 123; Bod. L., Carte MS 43, fo. 452 (King to Ormonde); SP 63/320/85 (Duchess of Ormonde to Arlington);

SP 63/321/10 (Ormonde to Arlington); Bod. L., Carte MS 162, fo. 9 (Arran's commission).

27. SP 63/320/72 (Irish Privy Council to Arlington); Bod. L., Carte MS 48, fo. 374 (Ormonde to Clarendon).

28. Upon which activity there are thousands of pages in the Carte MSS, Orrery State Letters, and SP 63.

29. SP 63/319/44 (Dumville to Bennet), 160 (Ormonde to Bennet), 163 (Anglesey to Bennet), 237 (Leigh to Williamson); SP 63/320/13, 81 (Irish Privy Council to Bennet), 24, 55, 58, 84, 95 (Ormonde to Bennet); SP 63/321/10, 11, 17, 33, 69, 91 (Ormonde to Bennet), 20 (Anglesey to Bennet); O'Donoghue, thesis, ch. 6.

30. Bod. L., Carte MS 48, fo. 382 (to Clarendon).

31. Hutton, *Restoration*, pp. 250–7, 262.

32. SP 63/322/45 (Irish Privy Council to King), 50, 99, 166 (Ormonde to Arlington), 152 (proclamation); SP 63/318, pp. 166–9 (King to Ormonde); SP 63/323/10, 29 (Ormonde to Arlington), 42 (Irish Privy Council to Arlington).

33. SP 63/322/42 (Orrery to Conway).

34. Stradling, thesis, pp. 209–43.

35. Bod. L., Carte MS 215, fos. 259–61 (St Albans to Ormonde); Feiling, *British Foreign Policy*, pp. 209–19; Geyl, *Orange and Stuart*, pp. 257–60; P/C 2/59, pp. 160–1; Clarendon MS 84, fos. 43–4 (instructions to St Albans); MS 85, fos. 72 (St Albans to Arlington), 84 (St Albans to King), 86–90, 118–19, 197, 217–19, 237 (St Albans to Clarendon), 100, 102–6, 145, 156, 203, 227 (Clarendon to St Albans); SP 95/6, fo. 135 (Lisola's account of talk with King); SP 78/119 (dispatches of St Albans to Arlington).

36. Hutton, *Restoration*, pp. 257–63, and sources there.

37. Ibid., pp. 263–6.

38. *Lauderdale Papers*, i. 235–9 (Rothes to Lauderdale), 242–3 (Bellenden to Lauderdale), and vol. ii, app. A, pp. xxviii–xxix, xxxiv–xxxv (Burnet to Sheldon); *RPCS* (1665–9), pp. 108–9; NLS MS 2512, fo. 84 (Burnet to Lauderdale).

39. *Lauderdale Papers*, vol. ii, app. B, pp. xxiv–xxv (Privy Council to King); *RPCS* (1665–9), pp. 202–5; HMC Laing MSS, i. 352 (Argyll to Lauderdale).

40. *RPCS* (1665–9), pp. 225, 234–5, 267–8, 284–5.

41. Ibid., pp. 285–6; *Lauderdale Papers*, vol. ii, app. A, pp. xxx–xxxviii (Burnet or Sharp to Sheldon); NLS MS 2512, fo. 87 (Burnet to Lauderdale); NLS MS 7023, fo. 34 (Lauderdale to Tweeddale).

42. Most recently and fully by Buckroyd, *Church and State*, pp. 65–74. My account overlaps with hers at many points while differing in details and emphases.

43. *Lauderdale Papers*, i. 241–2 (Rothes to Lauderdale); NLS MS 2512, fos. 74, 76 (Sharp to Lauderdale).

44. Buckroyd, *Church and State*, pp. 68–70, sketches their background. On Murray, see also Pepys, *Diary*, viii. 64.
45. Buckroyd, *Church and State*, pp. 66–7; Ian B. Cowan, *The Scottish Covenanters* (1976), ch. 4.
46. *Lauderdale Papers*, i. 244–5 (Bellenden to Lauderdale), 269, 276 (Rothes to Lauderdale), 274–6 (William Sharp to Lauderdale), ii. 17, 22–3 (Tweeddale to Lauderdale), 28–30 (Sharp to Lauderdale); Burnet, *History*, i. 438.
47. *Lauderdale Papers*, ii. 1–2, 16 (Rothes to Lauderdale), 2–4, 13 (Murray to Lauderdale); HMC Laing MSS, i. 358 (Rothes to King); *RPCS* (1665–9), p. 294; Blair, *Life* (ed. M'Crie), p. 510; HMC 4th report, app., p. 506 (Rothes's commission).
48. *Lauderdale Papers*, ii. 45 (Tweeddale to Lauderdale), 47–9, 66–8, 71, 78 (Murray to Lauderdale), 71 (Rothes to Lauderdale); Burnet, *History*, i. 441–3; HMC Laing MSS, i. 259–61 (Murray to Lauderdale); *RPCS* (1665–9), p. 343; NLS MS 3136, fo. 25 (Lauderdale to Tweeddale).
49. *Lauderdale Papers*, ii. 32–5, 35 (Tweeddale to Lauderdale), 36–7, 41–2 (Murray to Lauderdale); *RPCS* (1665–6), p. 334; Kirkton, *Secret History*, pp. 226–7; NLS MS 3136, fo. 24 (Lauderdale to Tweeddale); NLS MS 7023, fo. 72 (the same).
50. *Lauderdale Papers*, ii. 49, 55–6, 69–71, 84, 86, 90 (Murray to Lauderdale), 51 (William Sharp to Lauderdale), 52–3 (Council to King), 54 (Tweeddale to Lauderdale), 59–61 (bishops to Lauderdale), app. A, pp. xlvi–liii, lxix (Burnet to Sheldon), and pp. liii–lvii (Sharp to Sheldon); SHS *Miscellany*, I, pp. 261–3 (Lauderdale to Sharp); *RPCS* (1665–9), pp. 343–6; NLS MS 2512, fos. 104, 106, 110 (Sharp to Lauderdale); NLS MS 14488, fo. 46 (instructions for Tweeddale); NLS MS 7024, fo. 64 (Tweeddale to Murray).
51. Bod. L., Clarendon MS 85, fos. 441–4.
52. Stradling, thesis, pp. 246–60; Clarendon MS 85, fos. 311 (letter from Lionne), 301, 313 (Clarendon to Jermyn).
53. Hutton, *Restoration*, pp. 268–76, and sources listed there.
54. Ibid., pp. 276–81, 284–5, and sources listed there; Pepys, *Diary*, viii. 83, 432, 436 n. 3, 489 n. 4; NLS MS 7023, fo. 88 (Lauderdale to Tweeddale).
55. Hutton, *Restoration*, pp. 281–4.
56. SP 29/253, fo. 6ᵛ (Williamson's journal).

Chapter 10

1. The historiography is reviewed in my essay 'The Making of the Secret Treaty of Dover', *HJ* 29 (1986), pp. 297–318, which prefigured many of the arguments of this chapter.
2. PRO/31/3/118, fo. 210, and 123, fo. 2 (dispatches of Ruvigny and de Croissy); *CSPV* (1666–8), *passim*; SP 29/233–66, *passim* (letters to Williamson and Sir John Finch); Matthew Sylvester (ed.), *Reliquiae Baxterianae* (1696), b. i, pt. III, pp. 50–1.

3. Pepys, *Diary*, viii. 185–6.
4. F. A. Mignet, *Négociations rélatives à la succession d'Espagne* (Paris, 1835–42), ii. 505–46; Feiling, *British Foreign Policy*, pp. 371–2; Thomas Peregrine Courtenay, *Memoirs of Sir William Temple* (1836), i. 133–40; Thomas Bebington (ed.), *The . . . Earl of Arlington's Letters to Sir William Temple* (1701), 189–90.
5. Haley, *English Diplomat*, pp. 155–70.
6. Stradling, thesis, pp. 273–86.
7. Bryant (ed.), *Letters of Charles II*, pp. 214–15 (instructions to Temple); Mapperton House, 'Letters from Ministers', vol. ii, fo. 114 (Carteret to Sandwich), and Journal of the First Earl of Sandwich, viii. 568–76; Haley, *English Diplomat*, p. 164.
8. Caroline Robbins (ed.), *The Diary of John Milward* (Cambridge, 1938), pp. 179–301; Pepys, *Diary*, ix. 47–192; Anchitell Grey, *Debates of the House of Commons* (1763), i. 70–121; CJ ix. 53–98; LJ xii. 180–247; Buckinghamshire RO, M11/22, Denton to Verney, 12 Mar., and 26 Mar. 1668; HMC 8th report, pt. 1, pp. 122, 126 (draft bills); National Library of Wales, Wynn MSS, Lady Sarah to Sir Richard Wynn, 22 Mar. 1668; BL Add. Ms 36916, fo. 104 (Starkey to Aston); W. A. Shaw (ed.), *Calendar of Treasury Books* (1669–72), p. x; *Statutes of the Realm*, v. 630–5; Bebington (ed.), *Arlington's Letters*, pp. 310–11.
9. Mignet, *Négociations*, ii. 562–630; Courtenay, *Memoirs*, i. 192–7; Bebington (ed.), *Arlington's Letters*, i. 201–37; Feiling, *British Foreign Policy*, pp. 262–4 and app. vii; Bryant, *Letters of Charles II*, pp. 215–16; *The Works of Sir William Temple* (Edinburgh, 1754), iii. 115–247; PRO (Kew), ADM/106/15, fo. 407^v (Wren to Admiralty Board); SP 29/234/156–90, 29/235/7–123, *passim* (numerous papers on La Roche affair); Bod. L., Carte MS 46, fo.s. 598–606 (Arlington to Ormonde); Bod. L., Rawlinson MS A255, fos. 47–50^v (instructions to Trevor), P/C 2/60, pp. 124, 153, 218; SP 104/176 (Foreign Affairs Committee); BL Add. MS 9796, fos. 45–6 (instructions to Temple).
10. Courtenay, *Memoirs*, i. 265–6, 276–83, and app. B, No. 5; Temple, *Works*, iii. 248–342; Bebington, *Arlington's Letters*, pp. 347–77; Rowen, *De Witt*, pp. 709–19; SP 29/247/178 (Bridgeman to Williamson); P/C 2/60, pp. 387–8; SP 103/74, 'Maritime Treaty 1668'; BL Add. MS 9796, fos. 102–3 (papers of Privy Council).
11. To judge from Pepys, *Diary*, ix. 7, 38; SP 29/243/111 (Bridgeman to Williamson); BL Egerton MS 2539, fo. 195 (Sir John to Sir Edward Nicholas); BL Add. MS 36916, fo. 103 (Starkey to Aston); BL Add. MS 28093, fos. 168–77 (Temple's summary of commercial talks).
12. Mignet, *Négociations*, iii. 14–54; Bryant, *Letters of Charles II*, pp. 357–80.
13. SP 104/176, fos. 78–119 (Foreign Affairs Committee); Courtenay, *Memoirs*, vol. i, app. B, No. 5; Bebington, *Arlington's Letters*, pp. 357–80.
14. SP 44/31, fo. 35 (warrant for Privy Seal commission); Pepys, *Diary*, ix. 253–360, 438, 446–7, 525; Waldemar Westergaard (ed.), *The First Triple*

Alliance (New Haven, 1947), p. 134; Edward Berwick (ed.), *The Rawdon Papers*, (1819), pp. 236–8; Bod. L., Carte MS 221, fos. 116–17 (Arlington to Ossory); MS 36, fo. 593 (Broderick to Ormonde); SP 44/20, fo. 205, and 44/30, fo. 188 (division of Monck's offices); Havighurst, *Law Quarterly Review*, 1950, p. 65.

15. Pepys, *Diary*, ix. 425; SP 29/245/74 (newsletter to Saunders); SP 106/176, fos. 1–225ᵛ (Foreign Affairs Committee); SP 63/325/20 (Orrery to Conway); Bod. L., Carte MS 48, fo. 226 (Ormonde to Ossory); MS 36, fo. 406 (Knight to Ormonde); Andrew Browning, *Thomas Osborne, Earl of Danby* (Glasgow, 1951), ii. 21–2; BL Add. MS 28040, fo. 4 (Osborne's diary).

16. SP 29/240/160 (patent of office); HMC Le Fleming MSS, p. 56; BL Egerton MS 2539, fo. 218 (Sir John to Sir Edward Nicholas); Buckinghamshire RO, M11/22, Denton to Verney, 26 Aug. and 4 Nov. 1668; SP 44/30, fo. 87 (warrant for office).

17. Mignet, *Négociations*, iv. 240.

18. *The Cabal* (Urbana, 1965), pp. 104, 167.

19. Pepys, *Diary*, ix. 26, 293–5, 335–6, 360, 466–8; SP 29/234/215 (Morland to Tempest); BL Add. MS 36916, fo. 124 (Starkey to Aston).

20. SP 29/235/140 (letter to Finch), 29/289/187 (newsletter to Kirke); *CSPD* (1668–9), p. 89 (Trevor's warrant); HMC Le Fleming MSS, p. 59 (newsletter); BL Add. MS 36916, fos. 161, 223 (Starkey to Aston).

21. Pepys, *Diary*, ix. 7, 40–2, 205, 323, 386–7, 462–91; PRO/31/3/121, fos. 198–200 (de Croissy to Lionne); BL Egerton MS 2539, fos. 327–31 (Sir John to Sir Edward Nicholas); BL Add. MS 36916, fo. 129 (Starkey to Aston); Mapperton House, Journal of First Earl of Sandwich, ix. 120–6; HMC Buccleuch MSS, i. 442 (Montagu to Arlington).

22. *Calendar of Treasury Books* (1669–72), pt. 1, pp. 1–77.

23. All plain enough from his diaries at Chatsworth House.

24. Bod. L., Carte MS 70, fo. 449 (Ormonde to Southwell).

25. Orrery State Letters, p. 184 (to Ormonde).

26. Ibid., pp. 142–320; Bod. L., Carte MS 36, fos. 351–2; MS 48, fos. 155–237; MS 49, fos. 537–612; MS 69, fos. 138–40; MS 70, fos. 419–20; MS 141, fos. 74–200; MS 220, fos. 310–18 (all letters by Ormonde, Orrery, Ossory, and Archbishop Boyle). If Carte's *Ormonde* is too much of a panegyric, the life of Orrery by Morice, preserved in full in NLI MS 473, seems utterly untrustworthy when read alongside contemporary sources for the events described.

27. SP 29/245/8, 74 (newsletters); SP 29/239/55 (commission's warrant); Browning, *Danby*, ii. 21–4; Carte, *Ormonde*, iii. 62–5; Bod. L., Carte MS 36, fo. 418; MS 48, fos. 237–82; MS 59, fos. 555–612; MS 51, fos. 86, 396; MS 52, fo. 183; MS 217, fo. 434; MS 220, fos. 341–91 (all letters from Ormonde, Ossory, Richard Jones, Anglesey, and Privy Council); BL Egerton MS 2539, fos. 238–60 (Sir John to Sir Edward Nicholas).

28. Pepys, *Diary*, ix. 310, 340–1; SP 44/18, fos. 345, 608 (Anglesey to King,

and reply); *The Collection of Autograph Letters and Historical Documents formed by Alfred Morison: The Bulstrode Papers* i (1897), pp. 71–2; Bod. L., Carte MS 36, fo. 367 (paper of commission of enquiry); MS 48, fos. 280–313 (letters from Ormonde); NLS MS 3136, fo. 48 (Lauderdale to Tweeddale); BL Egerton MS 2539, fos. 238–60 (Sir John to Sir Edward Nicholas); Mapperton House, Journal of the First Earl of Sandwich, ix. 20–2, 34.

29. Bryant, *Letters of Charles II*, pp. 219–20 (to Minette).

30. Mapperton House, Journal of First Earl of Sandwich, ix. 268.

31. HMC Le Fleming MSS, p. 61; Carte, *Ormonde*, iii. 69; SP 29/271, note by Williamson, 14 Feb. 1669; SP 63/325/103 (King to Ossory and Irish Privy Council); PRO/31/3/121, fos. 182–3 (de Croissy to Louis).

32. SP 106/176 (minutes of committee); SP 63/325/23 (Rawdon to Conway) and 106 (Ormonde's comment on instructions to Robartes).

33. SP 63/325/20 (Orrery to Conway); Bod. L., Carte MS 48, fos. 338–46 (Ormonde to Ossory), and MS 220, fos. 445–6 (reply).

34. Carte MS 37, fo. 488 (Ranelagh to Ormonde), and MS 48, fos. 350–4 (Ormonde to Ossory); SP 63/324/14–327/108 (letters of Lane, Ford, O'Brien, Herbert, Leigh, Armourer, Frowde, Orrery, Robartes, Arlington, and Charles); Mapperton House, Journal of First Earl of Sandwich, ix. 282.

35. SP 63/318/224 and 327/14–121 (letters of Leigh, Frowde, Orrery, Leighton, and Charles).

36. Fraser, *Charles II*, p. 285; John Harold Wilson, *Nell Gwyn* (1952).

37. Berwick, *Rawdon Papers*, p. 251 (Conway to Rawdon).

38. Rowen, *De Witt*, pp. 715–16, for Dutch sources.

39. As edited by J. S. Clarke, i. 441–3, and in Carte MS 198, fo. 47.

40. The evidence is considered in Feiling, *British Foreign Policy*, pp. 267–9, and Cyril Hughes Hartmann, *Clifford of the Cabal* (1937), p. 137.

41. PRO/31/3/121, fos. 247–8 (de Croissy to Louis); *CSPV* (1669–70), p. 60.

42. *The Cabal*, p. 102.

43. Bryant, *Letters of Charles II*, pp. 227–30.

44. Ugbrooke Park, STD Papers, 'First Paper'.

45. BL Egerton MS 2543, fo. 129; SP 29/243/102; BL Add. MS 28078, fo. 14.

46. C. D. Chandaman, *The English Public Revenue, 1660–1688* (Oxford, 1975), pp. 218–71.

47. Ugbrooke Park, STD Papers, 'First Paper', 'Second Paper', 'Their Reply to First Paper', 'Third Letter', French memoir, 10 Sept. 1669; P. de Segur-Dupeyron, *Histoire des Négociations Commerciales du Regne de Louis XIV*, n.d., pp. 246–54; *CSPV* (1669–70), pp. 103–4; Westergaard, *First Triple Alliance*, p. 134.

48. Feiling, *British Foreign Policy*, pp. 277–9, for Dutch and Spanish sources; Rowen, *De Witt*, pp. 717–21, for Dutch sources; Courtenay, *Memoirs*, vol. ii, app. B, No. 6; Bebington, *Arlington's Letters*, pp. 391–402; *CSPV* (1669–70), pp. 37, 62–3; Bod. L., Rawlinson MS A255, fos. 85–90 (instructions to Godolphin).

49. Feiling, *British Foreign Policy*, pp. 280–1, for German sources; BL Stowe MS 191, fo. 16 (instructions to envoy to Saxony); BL Sloane MS 1519, fo. 231 (Elector to Charles); J. Dumont (ed.), *Corps Universel Diplomatique* (Paris, 1726–31), vol. vii, pt. 1, pp. 119–30, 126–30.

50. BL Add. MS 36916, fo. 124 (Starkey to Aston); BL Add. MS 32094, fos. 212–13 (list of ships); Pepys, *Diary*, ix. 425; SP 29/259/20 (Wren to Pepys).

51. Bebington, *Arlington's Letters*, i. 389–417; Courtenay, *Memoirs*, vol. i, app. B, No. 7; *CSPV* (1669–70), p. 87; P/C 2/61, p. 145; SP 104/175, fos. 191–201 (English note to Dutch); SP 104/176, fos. 170–86 (Foreign Affairs Committee); BL Sloane MS 1003, fos. 1–55 (Trevor to Temple); SP 84/185 (Temple's dispatches to Arlington); Temple, *Works*, iii. 355–428.

52. Rowen, *De Witt*, pp. 725–30.

53. Ugbrooke Park, STD Papers, dated 23 Sept. 1669.

54. Mignet, *Négociations*, iii. 100–24; PRO/31/3/123, fos. 49–72 (dispatches of de Croissy and replies); Ugbrooke Park, STD Papers, memoir to Madame, memoir to Abbé Montagu, commissions to treat.

55. Feiling, *British Foreign Policy*, pp. 267–70, reviews the evidence.

56. Bebington, *Arlington's Letters*, pp. 227, 250, 300, 305–7, 336, 407–9, 417.

57. Longleat House, Coventry MS lxv, fo. 5 (to Henry Coventry).

58. Ugbrooke Park, STD Papers, 'The Project'.

59. SP 29/284/22.

60. SP 29/232/70 and 187, 234/35, 245/20, and 247/133 (letters from Yarmouth, Staffordshire, and Westmorland).

61. Pepys, *Diary*, ix. 278; BL Add. MS 36916, fos. 107, 116 (Starkey to Aston); BL Add. 10117, fo. 225[v] (Rugge's Diurnall).

62. Sylvester (ed.), *Reliquiae Baxterianae*, bk. i, pt. iii, p. 36; Durham Cathedral L., Hunter MS 137, note by Isaac Basire, 25 Nov. 1668; SP 44/25, fo. 78 (King to Newcastle corporation); Revd G. Ornsby (ed.), *The Correspondence of John Cosin* (Surtees Soc. iv, 1872), pp. 197–201; Bod. L., C305, fo. 205 (Sparrow to Sheldon); B. W. Quintrell (ed.), *Proceedings of the Lancashire Justices of the Peace* (Lancashire and Cheshire Record Soc. cxxi, 1981), p. 126; A. R. Barclay (ed.), *Letters, etc. of Early Friends* (1811), p. 165; Friends House L., Swarthmore MS 4, fo. 103 (Salthouse to Fell); HMC 8th Report, pp. 389, 439 (letters to corporations); P/C 2/60, p. 107, and 2/61, pp. 26–42.

63. SP 104/176, fos. 139–145[v]; BL Add. MS 36916, fo. 311 (Starkey to Aston).

64. SP 104/176, fo. 181; PRO/31/3/121, fo. 338 (de Croissy to Louis); Bod. L., Tanner MS 44, fos. 121, 127, 140 (Hacket to Sheldon); Steele, *Proclamations*, vol. i, No. 3529; G. Lyon Turner (ed.), *Original Records of Early Nonconformity* (1911), iii. 69–140; P/C 2/61, pp. 348–415.

65. SP 29/263/54–127, 265–15 (letters to Williamson from Cumberland, Coventry, Lincoln, Portsmouth, Yarmouth, Chester, and Bristol).

66. Buckroyd, *Church and State*, pp. 74–90; NLS MS 2512, fo. 143 (Burnet to Lauderdale); *Lauderdale Papers*, ii. 168–71 (Murray to Lauderdale); NLS MS 7023, fo. 165 (Lauderdale to Tweeddale).

67. Bod. L., Carte MS 49, fo. 667 (Ormonde to Dungannon); SP 63/325/95–7, 63/318, pp. 190–6, 222, and 63/327/36, 64, 121 (instructions to Robartes and Berkeley); Bod. L., Carte MS 45, fo. 366 (Ormonde to Boyle).
68. *Lauderdale Papers*, ii. 163–4.
69. Professor Lee, followed by Professor J. R. Jones.
70. C. S. Terry, *The Cromwellian Union* (Scottish History Society, lx, 1902), pp. 188–218; SP 104/176, fos. 245, 251 (Foreign Affairs Committee); E. Hughes, *The Negotiations for a Commercial Union between England and Scotland in 1668* (SHR xxiv, 1927); NLS MS 7023, fo. 100 (Lauderdale to Tweeddale); *Lauderdale Papers*, ii. 140–66 (letters between Lauderdale and Murray); 184 (instructions for Lauderdale); NLS MS 3136, fos. 49, 58, 116, 117 (Lauderdale to Tweeddale and Rothes).
71. *Lauderdale Papers*, ii. 101–3, 140–1, 150–64 (letters between Lauderdale and Murray); *RPCS* (1665–9), pp. 389–548; Mackenzie, *Memoirs*, pp. 165–7; NLS MS 7024, fos. 181–97 (Tweeddale to Murray).
72. *Lauderdale Papers*, ii. 166.
73. Ibid., ii. 165.
74. PRO/31/3/121, fo. 235 (de Croissy).
75. CJ ix. 97–120; Grey, *Debates*, i. 157–210; LJ xii. 252–85; F. R. Harris, *The Life of Edward Montagu K.G., First Earl of Sandwich* (1912), vol. ii, appendices D, F, G; HMC 8th Report, pt. 1, pp. 128a–133b (report of Committee for Accounts); *CSPV* (1669–70), pp. 127–44; H. M. Margoliouth (ed.), *The Papers and Letters of Andrew Marvell* (Oxford, 1971), ii. 95–6; *Lauderdale Papers*, ii. 165 (Murray to Lauderdale); PRO/31/3/123, fos. 17–60 (de Croissy to Louis); SP 104/176, fos. 215–20 (Foreign Affairs Committee); BL Add. MS 36916, fo. 159 (Starkey to Aston).
76. PRO/30/24/4, fo. 178 (to Morice).
77. Magdalene College, Pepys L., MS ?874, fos. 388–505 (Pepys's notes upon debate); BL Stowe MS 489, fos. 255–60 (other notes on event); CJ ix. 121–2.
78. SP 104/176, fo. 225^v.
79. As alleged by Marvell in his *Letters*, ii. 313–16. This is directly contradicted by Bryant, *Letters of Charles II*, p. 241; Steele, *Proclamations*, vol. i, No. 3531; CJ ix. 123 (for the division figures).
80. CJ ix. 121–54; Grey, *Debates*, i. 220–65; LJ xii. 298–351; SP 29/274/126 (Lerie to King); Margoliouth, *Letters of Marvell*, ii. 97, 101–2, 313–17; Bod. L., Carte MS 77, fo. 592 (Lord Wharton's notes); Westergaard, *First Triple Alliance*, p. 205; Barclay (ed.), *Letters*, pp. 169–71; Friends House L., Swarthmore MS 1, fo. 386 (Hooke to Fox); *CSPV* (1669–70), pp. 173–80; Harris, *Sandwich*, ii. 202–4; John Rylands L., Richard Legh to wife, 22 Feb. 1670; PRO/31/3/123, fos. 41–124 (de Croissy's dispatches to Louis).
81. SP 29/235/140 (letter to Finch); BL Egerton MS 2539, fo. 292 (Sir John to Sir Edward Nicholas); *CSPV* (1669–70), pp. 79–80, 174–5; BL Add. MS 36916, fo. 121 (Starkey to Aston); HMC 10th Report, iv. 114 (Longueville

to Moore); Bryant, *Letters of Charles II*, pp. 212–14; SP 44/30, fo. 7, and 44/34, fo. 22 (warrants for Monmouth); LJ xii. 311, 329; Harris, *Sandwich*, vol. ii, app. 1; PRO/31/3/123, fos. 55–66 (de Croissy to Louis); Berwick, *Rawdon Papers*, pp. 239–41; SP 63/327/44, 51, 66 (Orrery to Conway); Margoliouth, *Letters of Marvell*, ii. 313–16.

82. SP 29/284/22.

83. Mignet, *Négociations*, ii. 124–201; Bryant, *Letters of Charles II*, pp. 242–3; PRO/31/3/124, fos. 44–99 (de Croissy's dispatches); Feiling, *British Foreign Policy*, pp. 298–9; Rowen, *De Witt*, pp. 729–30; Bebington, *Arlington's Letters*, pp. 423–30; Courtenay, *Memoirs*, vol. i, app. B, Nos. 7–8; BL Add. MS 9797, fos. 95–112 (papers concerning 'concert'); SP 104/176, fos. 207–303 (Foreign Affairs Committee); *CSPV* (1669–70), pp. 158–9; Dumont, *Corps Universel*, vol. vii, pt. 1, pp. 137–9; SP 103/34 (papers concerning 'concert'); BL Sloane MS 1003, fos. 44–82 (Trevor's letters to Temple); Stradling, thesis, pp. 271–90.

84. Mignet, *Négociations*, iii. 207–13; PRO/31/3/125, fos. 210–12 (de Crossy to Louis); SP 29/276/208 (newsletter to Staplehill); Westergaard, *First Triple Alliance*, pp. 261–8; *CSPV* (1669–70), p. 219; Bod. L., Carte MS 219, fo. 104 (Ormonde to Berkeley); BL Add. MS 36916, fo. 185 (Starkey to Aston).

85. PRO/31/3/125, fos. 213–24 (de Croissy to Louis); *Lauderdale Papers*, ii. 202 (Murray to Lauderdale).

86. BL Add. MS 28040, fo. 5 (Osborne's journal); PRO/31/3/125, fos. 225–316 (de Croissy's dispatches); Mignet, *Négociations*, ii. 221–4, 230, 233–40, 249–52; Sir John Dalrymple, *Memoirs of Great Britain and Ireland* (1790), i. 115–19 (letters of Buckingham).

87. HMC Buccleuch and Queensberry MSS, i. 479–87 (letters of Montagu to Arlington); SP 44/34, fo. 55 (warrant for Rupert's commission); SP 78/130, fo. 221 (order in Council).

88. PRO/31/3/125, fos. 198–201, 259–63; Jonathan Swift (ed.), *Letters Written by Sir William Temple* (1700), ii. 278–98; Feiling, *British Foreign Policy*, pp. 316–24, for Dutch and German sources; Dalrymple, *Memoirs*, i. 122 (de Crossy to Louis); Evelyn, *Diary* (ed. De Beer), iii. 559; Bebington, *Arlington's Letters*, ii. 298–313; Rowen, *De Witt*, pp. 731–6; SP 94/57, fo. 47 (conference with Dutch ambassador); SP 104/176, fos. 259, 269, 271 (Foreign Affairs Committee); BL Add. MS 35852, fos. 1–61 (Boreel's negotiation); *CSPV* (1671–2), pp. 11–22; SP 105/100, fos. 587–667 (papers on talks with Leopold). Sir John Reresby's story that young Wilhelm got drunk at Whitehall and tried to climb into the rooms of the Queen's maids has often been repeated. Like many such beloved anecdotes, it now seems very doubtful. The incident is not recorded anywhere else, including the copious contemporary newsletters. Reresby was a Tory and a supporter of James II, and he is wrong in other details of his account of Wilhelm's visit: *Memoirs*, ed. Andrew Browning (Glasgow, 1936), p. 82. For an interesting recent account of English diplomacy in these years, which contrasts with

mine, see Haley, *English Diplomat*. Professor Haley believes that Charles was determined upon a French alliance from 1667 onwards, and a Dutch war from 1669. 'Hence' he refused to limit the number of evacuees from Surinam, protested at a Dutch medal glorifying the Chatham victory and insulting him, and instructed Temple not to discuss the co-ordination of military measures within the Triple Alliance in any detail (pp. 243–5). Yet such touchiness about points of personal and national honour were typical of Charles, while the instruction to Temple must be set in the context of doubts by the whole Foreign Affairs Committee, that to press ahead rapidly with co-ordinating measures simply encouraged the Spaniards to make fresh demands.

89. Mignet, *Négociations*, ii. 230–2; PRO/31/3/125, fos. 248–74, 294–7 (de Croissy to Louis); Ugbrooke Park, 'Cressy Papers', various projects for religious reunion.

90. Ugbrooke Park, STD Papers, 'The Scheme'.

91. SP 63/330/34 (instructions to Berkeley); P/C 2/62, p. 321.

92. P/C 2/62, pp. 363–74; Trinity College, Dublin, MSS 844–9 (papers concerning petition and enquiry); SP 63/330/26 (Irish Privy Council to King); Bod. L., Carte MSS 69, 70 (papers concerning enquiry); PRO/31/3/126, fo. 27 (de Croissy to Louis).

93. P/C 2/62, pp. 190–361, *passim*; SP 29/278/56 (newsletter to Scawen), 137 (Ward to Justices); SP 29/294/15 (notes by Williamson); *Reliquiae Baxterianae*, Pt. III, p. 87; SP 104/176, fo. 241 (Foreign Affairs Committee).

94. Buckroyd, *Church and State*, pp. 91–100.

95. Adair, *True Narrative*, pp. 292–300.

96. Norfolk RO, Bradfer-Lawrence lc (i), letters to Sir Robert Paston, 13 May and 5 Aug. 1671; Steele, *Proclamations*, vol. i, No. 3541; Berwick, *Rawdon Papers*, pp. 246–7 (Conway to Rawdon); *Remarks on the Life and Death of the Fam'd Mr. Blood* (1680), pp. 1–10; HMC Le Fleming MSS, p. 78 (newsletter); Buckinghamshire RO, M11, Denton to Verney, 8 Dec. 1671; *CSPV* (1669–70), p. 314; BL Add. MS 36916, fos. 200, 223 (Starkey to Aston); SP 29/289/187 (newsletter to Kirke).

97. K. H. D. Haley, *William of Orange and the English Opposition, 1672–4* (Oxford, 1953), pp. 65–6.

98. Ibid., SP 44/34, fos. 84, 110 (warrants for committal and pardon); SP 29/290/11 (Blood's petition); SP 29/291/207 (Robinson to Williamson); SP 29/293/28, 135 (Blood to Williamson).

99. David Ogg, *England in the Reign of Charles II* (2nd edn., Oxford, 1956), i. 350; D. T. Witcombe, *Charles II and the Cavalier House of Commons, 1663–1674* (Manchester, 1966), p. 125.

100. Margoliouth, *Letters of Marvell*, ii. 110–37, 304–8; Basil Duke Henning (ed.), *The Parliamentary Diary of Sir Edward Dering* (New Haven, 1940), pp. 2–73; *CSPV* (1669–70), p. 310. (1671–2), pp. 2–43; HMC Finch

MSS, ii. 2 (warrant to Finch); Grey, *Debates*, i. 294–467; CJ ix. 160–244; LJ xii. 351–516; *Statutes of the Realm*, v. 691–719; BL Add. MS 36916, fos. 193–221 (Starkey to Aston); SP 104/176, fos. 261, 275, 293 (Foreign Affairs Committee); Harris, *Sandwich*, vol. ii. app. J; HMC 9th Report, ii. 2–15 (draft bills); Steele, *Proclamations*, vol. i, No. 3545; PRO/31/3/126, fo. 28 (de Croissy to Louis).

101. Evelyn, *Diary* (ed. De Beer), iii. 596; Buckinghamshire RO, M11, Denton to Verney, 20 Oct. and 24 Nov. 1670; Norfolk RO, Bradfer-Lawrence 1c (i), unsigned letter to Paston, 13 Oct. 1670; HMC Rutland MSS, ii. 23 (Bertie to Noel); Lancashire RO, DDHu/47/55 (letter from Jessop); BL Add. MS 36916, fos. 199, 207–8 (Starkey to Aston); HMC Le Fleming MSS, p. 73 (newsletter).

102. PRO/31/3/126, fos. 9–10, 98.

103. Mapperton House, Journal of First Earl of Sandwich, ix. 117–18.

104. Pepys, *Diary*, ix. 335–6; SP 29/247/127 (Taylor to Pepys).

105. SP 29/277/56 (newsletter to Staplehill), 136a (newsletter); Westergaard, *First Triple Alliance*, p. 429; John Harold Wilson, *A Rake and his Times* (1954), pp. 144–6; Buckinghamshire RO, M11, Denton to Verney, 4 May 1671; Anthony, Count Hamilton, *Memoirs of Count Gramont* (ed. Allan Fea, 1906), pp. 266–8; PRO/31/3/126, fo. 101 (de Croissy to Louvois).

106. *Memoirs of Gramont*, p. 268.

107. Wilson, *Nell Gwyn*, pp. 91–2.

108. Jeanine Delpech, *The Life and Times of the Duchess of Portsmouth* (1953), ch. 1.

109. Evelyn, *Diary* (ed. De Beer), iii. 564, 589; Buckinghamshire RO, M11, Denton to Verney, 4 and 19 Oct. 1671; PRO/31/3/126, fos. 100–34 (de Croissy to Louis, Louvois, and Lionne); AAE CP A 102, fos. 283, 290 (Louvois to de Croissy).

110. Denton to Verney, above; Andrew Clark (ed.), *The Life and Times of Anthony Wood* (Oxford History Soc., 1892), ii. 237.

111. *CSPV* (1671–2), pp. 52, 67–8, 98; Evelyn, *Diary* (ed. De Beer), iii. 601; E. M. Thompson (ed.), *Correspondence of the Family of Hatton* (Camden Soc., NS xxii, 1878), i. 79; SP 29/278/123, 132 (Morton, Nicholls, to Williamson), 280/18 (Noell to Williamson), 75 (amended list of sheriffs), 294/100 (Brouncker to Arlington); Westergaard, *First Triple Alliance*, p. 450.

112. PRO/31/3/126, fos. 137–40 (de Croissy to Louis).

113. SP 29/279/104 (Bridgeman to Arlington).

114. SP 44/35A, fo. 32 (warrant for Ashley); PRO/31/3/126, fos. 57–9 (de Croissy to Louis); SP 29/280/1 (newsletter to Aldworth).

115. *CSPD* (1671), p. 1 (King to Berkeley); SP 63/330/24, 26 (Council to King), 58 (King to Berkeley), 97 (Council to King), 160 (Armorer to Williamson); SO 1/8, Nos. 313–14 (King to Council); 83, 97 (King to Berkeley); SP 29/292/45 (newsletter to Stanton); Bod. L., Carte MS 37, fos. 542–3 (Ranelagh to Ormonde); Egan, thesis, pp. 231–40.

116. SP 63/330/58 (King to Berkeley), 165a (Orrery to Conway); HMC Hastings MSS, ii. 378 (letters from Conway).
117. W. Maziere Brady, *The Episcopal Succession in England, Scotland and Ireland* (Rome, 1876), i. 227–8; Bod. L., Carte MS 221, fos. 349–50 (letter from Gearman); MS 45, fos. 385–6 (Gearman to Walsh); MS 37, fos. 544–5 (Berkeley to Ormonde); P/C 2/62, p. 321.
118. SO 1/8, p. 101 (King to Berkeley); *Hatton Correspondence*, i. 76 (Lyttleton to Hatton), and see below.
119. PRO/31.3.126, fo. 63 (de Croissy to Louis).
120. *Letters by Temple* (ed. Swift), ii. 302–8; *Hatton Correspondence*, i. 66 (Lyttleton to Hatton); Norfolk RO, Bradfer-Lawrence lc (i), Brockenden to Paston, 9 Sept. 1671; PRO/31/3/126, fos. 82–6 (de Croissy to Louis); SP 104/176, fos. 301^v, 307 (Foreign Affairs Committee).
121. PRO/31/3/126, fos. 82–3 (de Croissy to Louis); Steele, *Proclamations*, vol. i, No. 3552.
122. PRO/31/126, fo. 53 (de Croissy to Louis); SP 44/24, p. 54 (Downing's instructions); Longleat House, Coventry MS lxv, fos. 11–12 (Trevor to Coventry); BL Add. MS 35852, fos. 78–94^v (Boreel's dispatches); BL Add. MS 36916, fo. 231 (Starkey to Aston); SP 104/176, fo. 323 (Foreign Affairs Committee).
123. Mignet, *Négociations*, ii. 700–2; SP 44/31, fo. 82 (King to James); *CSPV* (1671–2), p. 165; BL Add. MS 36916, fo. 237 (Starkey to Aston); PRO/31/3/127, fo. 4 (de Croissy to Louis); P/C 2/63, pp. 141–65.
124. Mignet, *Négociations*, ii. 269–558; Feiling, *British Foreign Policy*, pp. 320–34; Longleat House, Coventry MS lxv, fos. 1–130 (letters to Henry Coventry).
125. Feiling, *British Foreign Policy*, pp. 325–7, 334–7, for Spanish sources; SP 94/59 (dispatches from Sunderland, 30 Dec. 1671 20 May 1672); Bebington, *Arlington's Letters*, pp. 319–35; Paul Sonnino, 'Louis XIV and the Dutch War', pp. 153–7, in Ragnhild Hatton (ed.), *Louis XIV and Europe* (1976); Longleat House, Coventry MS lxv, fo. 126 (Trevor to Coventry); Bod. L., Rawlinson MS A265, fos. 152–4 (instructions to Southwell).
126. Feiling, *British Foreign Policy*, p. 328; HMC Buccleuch and Queensberry MSS, i. 511 (Montagu to Arlington).
127. Chandaman, *English Public Revue*, pp. 223–5; SP 29/292/121 (Gauden to Navy Board), 29/302/7 (victualling commission to Navy Board); *CTB* iii. 935; HMC 13th Report, iv. 6 (Ryder to Treby).
128. A. Browning, 'The Stop of the Exchequer', *History*, NS 14 (1929–30), pp. 333–7; Lee, *The Cabal*, pp. 150–5; Roseveare, thesis, pp. 194–5; BL Add. MS 36916, fo. 236 (Starkey to Aston); Chandaman, *English Public Revenue*, pp. 224–8.
129. SO 1/8, p. 216; P/C 6/13 (register of the commission on the Establishment); *Essex Papers* (ed. Osmund Airy, Camden Soc., 1890), p. 19; Steele, *Proclamations*, vol. ii, No. 821.

130. SP 29/294/15, 36 (notes by Williamson, which I take to represent Arlington's views); Ugbrooke Park, STD Papers, 'The Scheme'; W. D. Christie, *A
Life of Anthony Ashley Cooper* (1871), vol. ii, app. i, pp. vii–viii; SP 104/177,
fos. 12–17ᵛ (Foreign Affairs Committee).
131. SP 44/24, p. 54 (instructions to Downing); *CSPV* (1671–2), pp. 168, 170;
Bryant, *Letters of Charles II*, pp. 245–6; Longleat House, Coventry MS
lxv, fo. 113 (Trevor to Coventry); SP 84/188, fos. 2, 32 (Downing to
Williamson), 16, 84–5 (King to States-General).
132. SP 84/188, fos. 39–43, 131–2 (Dutch memorials to Charles); SP 104/21,
p. 1 (King to James); SP 104/177, fos. 13, 15, 18 (Foreign Affairs Committee); P/C 2/63, pp. 195–6.

Chapter 11

1. SP 104/177, fos. 21–52 (Committee for Foreign Affairs); BL Add. MS
28040, fos. 21–4 (Osborne's diary); Harold A. Hansen, 'Opening Phase of
the Third Dutch War', *Journal of Modern History*, 21 (1949), p. 101; SP
29/309/80 (Order in Council).
2. *Journals and Narratives of the Third Anglo-Dutch War* (ed. R. C. Anderson,
Navy Records Society, 1946), *passim*; HMC Hastings MSS, ii. 157–8
(Woodruffe to Huntingdon); PRO/31/3/127, fo. 249 (de Croissy to Louis).
3. Evelyn, *Diary* (ed. De Beer), i. 618.
4. J. N. P. Watson, *Captain General and Rebel Chief* (1979), pp. 42–4; SP
29/307/102 (Arlington to Williamson); Hansen, *Journal of Modern History*,
1949, p. 101.
5. SP 104/177, fo. 15; *Correspondence of the Family of Hatton* (ed. E. M.
Thompson, Camden Soc., 1878), i. 81–3 (Lyttleton to Hatton); Hansen,
Journal of Modern History, 1949, p. 99.
6. Ibid., p. 101; BL Harl. MS 7006, fos. 164, 166 (King to James); PRO/31/3/
127, fos. 249–52 (de Croissy to Louis).
7. *CSPV* (1671–2), pp. 232–7; Hansen, *Journal of Modern History*, 1949,
p. 106; Evelyn, *Diary* (ed De Beer), i. 620; SP 84/189, fo. 16 (spy report);
PRO/31/3/127, fo. 256 (de Croissy to Louis); SP 29/311/137 (Lyttleton to
Newport); Bryant, *Letters of Charles II*, pp. 250–1.
8. SP 104/77, fos. 57–60; SP 78/134, fos. 73–5 (Halifax's instructions); BL
Add. MS 17677, vol. BB, fo. 484 (envoys to States-General); SP 84/189, fos.
125–6 (Halifax to Arlington); *London Gazette* (20–4 June 1672); Mary
Caroline Trevelyan, *William the Third and the Defence of Holland, 1672–4*
(1930), pp. 214–16, for Dutch sources; Mignet, *Négociations*, iv. 35, 44.
9. BL Stowe MS 191, fo. 34 (Godolphin's instructions); SP 78/134, fos. 64, 71,
89, 103 (Godolphin to Arlington).
10. K. H. D. Haley, *William of Orange and the English Opposition, 1672–4*
(Oxford, 1953), p. 302.
11. SP 84/189, fos. 48–50 (Buckingham to Clifford), 67–9 (the instructions),

107–8 (Williamson to Clifford), 117–19 (Arlington to Clifford), 143–51 (plenipotentiaries to Clifford); SP 84/190, fos. 1–2 (Williamson's notes), 24–5 (the treaty), 26 (letter from Williamson), 52–5 (plenipotentiaries to Clifford); PRO/31/3/127, fos. 262–3, 266, 272, 273 (de Croissy to Louis); SP 29/101, fo. 37 (Arlington to King); Mignet, *Négociations*, iv. 48 (English terms); Trevelyan, *William the Third*, pp. 216–75, for Dutch sources; Bryant, *Letters of Charles II*, pp. 249, 257–9; SP 104/177, fos. 69–70, 77–8; BL Add. MS 28053, fo. 63 (Seymour to Osborne); Longleat House, Coventry MS ii, fo. 29 (Seymour to Coventry).

12. *CSPV* (1671–2), pp. 243–4, 268–9; BL Harl. MS 7006, fos. 168, 170 (Clifford to James), 170 (Coventry to James); *Hatton Correspondence*, i. 83 (Lyttleton to Hatton); SP 63/331/21, 27 (King to Berkeley); *RPCS* (1669–72), pp. 473–80, 487, 510–13; SP 57/2, p. 101 (King to Scottish Privy Council); Christie, *Life of Cooper*, vol. ii, app. ii, p. xviii (de Croissy to Louis); Bryant, *Letters of Charles II*, pp. 251–5; Ugbrooke Park, seven letters from James to Clifford 24 June–8 Aug. 1672; SP 104/177, fos. 60–9, 76; BL Add. MS 21948, fo. 292 (Copplestone to Richmond). These sources cast doubt upon Clarke (ed.), *Life of James II*, i. 477–8, and Charles Dalton, *English Army Lists and Commission Registers* (1892), i. 119–22.

13. SP 104/177, fos. 70, 77; SP 84/191, fos. 7–9, 36, 44 (spy reports); PRO/31/3/127, fos. 276–7 (de Croissy to Louis).

14. *Lauderdale Papers*, ii, 229 (Clifford to Lauderdale); *Hatton Correspondence*, i. 95–6 (Lyttleton to Hatton); *CSPV* (1671–2), p. 281; Clarke (ed.), *Life of James II*, pp. 480–1.

15. Stated most recently by J. R. Jones, *Country and Court* (1978), p. 176.

16. *CSPV* (1671–2), pp. 295, 300; BL Add. MS 28040, fos. 26–7 (Osborne's diary); Ugbrooke Park, 'Resolutions for payment of fleet'.

17. PRO/31/3/127, fos. 236–7, 244, 249–52, 263 (de Croissy to Louis); Christie, *Life of Cooper*, vol. ii, app. ii. pp. xiv–xix (the same).

18. BL Add. MS 28053, fo. 48 (Orrery to Osborne); Longleat House, Coventry MS xxii, fo. 56ᵛ (Essex's instructions); BL Add. MS 21505, fo. 29 (Essex's private instructions); SP 63/333/160 (Essex to Arlington); *Essex Papers*, i. 126 (Essex to brother), 137–8 (Essex to Ormonde).

19. Frank Bate, *The Declaration of Indulgence 1672* (Liverpool, 1908), pp. 92–8; SP 104/177, fo. 19ᵛ (Foreign Affairs Committee).

20. Ibid., fo. 20ᵛ; P/C 2/63, pp. 109, 230; Barclay (ed.), *Letters of Early Friends*, pp. 184 (Whitbread to Crisp), 184–5 (Rous to Fox), 185–91 (Hooke to Fox); *The Christian Progress of ... George Whitehead* (1725), pp. 347–66.

21. Buckroyd, *Church and State*, pp. 102–3, 106–7; *RPCS* (1673–6), pp. 56–7; Burnet, *History*, i. 605–6; *Lauderdale Papers*, ii. 223–4 (instructions to Lauderdale), 225–6 (Leighton to Lauderdale); HMC Hamilton MSS, p. 142 (Hamilton to Lauderdale).

22. Longleat House, Coventry MS xxii, fo. 55, and BL Add. MS 21505, fo. 29 (instructions to Essex); *Essex Papers*, i. 33 (Mossom to Essex), 122–3 (Essex

to Arlington); SP 63/331/130 (Essex to Arlington), 168 (Mossom to King); SP 63/335/11 (Rawdon to Coventry); BL Stowe Ms 200, fo. 287 (Arlington to Essex).

23. Longleat House, Coventry MS vii. fo. 3 (Morley to Coventry); Bod. L., Tanner MS 43, fos. 27, 36, 90 (Morley to Sheldon); HMC Fleming MSS, p. 92 (newsletter); BL Harl. MS 7377, fos. 41ᵛ–43 (Sheldon to bishops).

24. BL Harl. MS 7377, fos. 37ᵛ–39ᵛ (Sheldon to bishops); Bod. L., Tanner MS 43, fo. 32 (Morley to Sheldon); SP 104/77, fos. 106, 120 (Foreign Affairs Committee).

25. PRO/31/3/127 fos. 242–4, 265 (de Croissy to Louis); Evelyn, *Diary* (ed. De Beer), i. 629.

26. Christie, *Life of Cooper*, vol. ii, app. ii, p. xiii (de Croissy to Louis); AAE CP (A) 104, fo. 275 (de Croissy to Pomponne); Bod. L., Carte MS 70, fo. 445 (Ormonde to Southwell); SP 63/332/11 (Ranelagh to Conway); *Hatton Correspondence*, i. 89 (Lyttleton to Hatton); BL Add. MS 25122, fo. 1 (Coventry to Arlington).

27. SP 104/177, fos. 77ᵛ–85ᵛ; PRO/31/3/127, fos. 276–7, 287–91; Chandaman, *English Public Revenue*, p. 31.

28. SP 84/193, fos. 69–72 (Howard's report); Brown, *Miscellanea Aulica*, p. 8 (Arlington to Gascoigne); SP 104/177, fos. 98–100; BL Add. Ms 25122, fos. 30–1 (Coventry to Arlington).

29. K. H. D. Haley, *The First Earl of Shaftesbury* (Oxford, 1968), pp. 305–6, is sensible enough, but more conclusive information can be found in BL Add. MS 21948, fo. 427 (Copplestone to Richmond) and Add. MS 29571, fo. 195 (Hatton to Hatton).

30. AAE CP (A) 104, fos. 210–11 (de Croissy to Pomponne); *Hatton Correspondence*, i. 90 (Lyttleton to Hatton); Clarke (ed.), *Life of James II*, i. 481–2.

31. HMC Hastings MSS, ii. 161 (Woodruffe to Huntingdon).

32. Browning, *Danby*, i. 94–5; *CSPV* (1671–2), p. 321; PRO/31/3/128 fos. 1ᵛ–2, 13 (de Croissy to Louis); SP 104/177, fo. 140ᵛ.

33. SP 104/177, fos. 101, 107.

34. Dalton, *English Army Lists*, i. 134–7; *CSPV* (1673–5), p. 9.

35. Witcombe, *Cavalier House of Commons*, pp. 131–2.

36. Grey, *Debates*, ii. 9–69; LJ xii. 521–49; Eveline Legh, Lady Newton, *The House of Lyme* (1917), p. 252 (Richard to Thomas Legh); SP 104/177, fos. 143ᵛ–150; PRO/31/3/128, fos. 45–6 (de Croissy to Louis); CJ ix. 245–66; AAE CP (A) 106, fos. 94–6 (Louis to de Croissy), 123 (de Croissy to Pomponne), 126 (reply); *CSPV* (1671–2), p. 195, and (1673–5), pp. 13, 19; BL Add. MS 29571, fo. 195 (Hatton to Hatton).

37. Evelyn, *Diary* (ed. De Beer), i. 625; SP 63/133/117–332/16, *passim*.

38. SP 63/331/89 (Arlington to Orrery), 114 (King to Orrery), 192 (Essex to King); *Essex Papers*, i. 5, 9–10, 12 (Orrery to Essex), 20–1 (Essex to Arlington), 24–5 (King to Essex); Petworth House, Leconfield MSS, Orrery to Anglesey, 20 May and 23 July 1672; Ugbrooke Park, Clifford Papers,

James to Clifford, 24 June 1672; BL Stowe MS 200, fos. 195, 214 (Arlington to Essex); BL Add. MS 28055, fos. 48–53 (Orrery to Osborne); SP 63/333/52 (Orrery to Conway); Bod. L., Add. MS C33, fo. 2 (Essex to Orrery).

39. SO 1/8, pp. 358, 403 (King to Essex); SP 63/333/90 (royal warrant), 120, 176 (Essex to Arlington); *Essex Papers*, i. 60–84, 122–3 (Essex's letters to Clifford, Arlington, King).

40. SP 63/332/1 (Essex to Arlington).

41. SP 63/332/30, 333/76 (Essex to Arlington); SP 63/333/29 (Boyle to Arlington).

42. SP 63/309, pp. 305–28 (the regulations); SP 63/332/1 ('copy of Lord Conway's letter'), 42 (King to Essex), 88 (Boyle to Arlington), 86, 105 (Essex to Arlington); *Essex Papers*, i. 12, 17–18, 36, 42–3 (Essex to Arlington), 41 (Arlington to Essex); SP 104/177, fo. 80; BL Stowe MS 200, fos. 351, 367 (Arlington to Essex), and MS 201, fo. 58 (Godolphin to Essex).

43. CJ ix. 270–8; Grey, *Debates*, ii. 118–19; SP 63/333/109 (Ranelagh to Conway); HMC Hastings MSS, ii. 381 (Conway to Rawdon).

44. CJ ix. 261, 265–6; Steele, *Proclamations*, vol. i, No. 3579, and vol. ii, No. 2367.

45. CJ ix. 259–74; LJ xii. 554–84; PRO/31/3/128, fos. 49–65 (de Croissy to Louis); Grey, *Debates*, ii. 74–8, 83–5, 97–100, 137–9, 150; HMC 9th Report, ii. 30 (Lords' committee paper).

46. Lady Newton, *House of Lyme*, pp. 255–7 (Richard to Thomas Legh); SP 44/31, p. 308 (King to Lord Mayor); SP 29/335/94, 97, 103 (Rupert to Arlington).

47. Even in Turnbull's thesis, which disproves the same belief for the earlier period.

48. Bryant, *Letters of Charles II*, pp. 266–8.

49. J. R. Tanner (ed.), *A Descriptive Catalogue of the Naval Manuscripts in the Pepysian Library* (Navy Records Soc., 1903–29), vols. i–iii, *passim*.

50. SP 29/335/121, 127, 148 (Rupert to Arlington); Lady Newton, *House of Lyme*, pp. 257–8 (Richard to Thomas Legh); Anderson (ed.), *Journals and Narratives*, pp. 298–9, 315–17.

51. Carl J. Ekberg, *The Failure of Louis XIV's Dutch War* (Chapel Hill, 1979), pp. 1–85; Mignet, *Négociations*, iv. 176–7; *CSPV* (1671–2), p. 328, and (1673–5), p. 9; Brown, *Miscellanea Aulica*, pp. 89–91; SP 104/177, fo. 113; PRO/31/3/128, fos. 1ᵛ–2 (de Croissy to Louis).

52. SP 29/334/141 ('Zealand. The design.').

53. Anderson, *Journals and Narratives*, pp. 317–18; Bryant, *Letters of Charles II*, p. 266; William Wynne, *The Life of Sir Leoline Jenkins* (1724), pp. 3–8 (instructions for plenipotentiaries); SP 29/335/91 (Rupert's instructions).

54. SP 29/335/225, 230, 231, 261, 267 (Rupert to Arlington), 229 (list of regiments); *Letters Addressed from London to Sir Joseph Williamson* (ed. W. D. Christie, Camden Soc., 1874), i. 22, 39, 52; SP 78/137, fo. 231 (Lockhart to Arlington); SP 105/221, pp. 57–9 (Arlington to envoys at Cologne).

55. Ekberg, *Louis XIV's Dutch War*, pp. 24, 157.

56. SP 29/335/281 (Yard to Williamson); SP 44/35A, fo. 70 (Schomberg's commission); *Letters to Williamson*, i. 4–102; *CSPV* (1673–5), pp. 67–72;

HMC 9th Report, ii. 448–9 (letter from Buckingham); SP 29/336/149 (Schomberg to Arlington).

57. Anderson, *Journals and Narratives*, pp. 324, 342; SP 29/336/96, 106 (Rupert to Arlington); H. T. Colenbrander (ed.), *Bescheiden vit Vreemde Archieven omtrent de Groote Nederlansche Zeeoorlager* ('s-Gravenhage, 1919), ii. 288 (council of war).

58. Colenbrander, *Bescheiden*, ii. 197–8 (Charles to Rupert); SP 29/336/170 (Rupert to Arlington); *CSPV* (1673–5), pp. 71–2; Bryant, *Letters of Charles II*, pp. 268–9; SP 105/221, pp. 120–3, 163 (Arlington to envoys).

59. Tanner, *Naval Manuscripts*, ii. 33 (Admiralty Commission to Navy Board); *Essex Papers*, p. 121 (Temple to Essex); SP 29/336/242, 247, 259, 270, 286, 288 (Rupert's dispatches), 251, 265 (newsletters to Williamson); SP 29/337/3, 35 (the same), 16, 24 (Rupert's dispatches); Bibliothèque Nationale, Paris, Mélanges Colbert 165 bis, fos. 502, 558–60, 631 (de Croissy to Colbert), 592–3 (de Croissy to Seignelay); *Letters to Williamson*, i. 191, ii. 2–21; Anderson *Journals and Narratives*, pp. 365–9.

60. Ekberg, *Louis XIV's Dutch War*, pp. 85–93; *CSPV* (1673–5), pp. 127–8; SP 105/221, p. 217 (Arlington to envoys).

61. PRO/31/3/128, fos. 49–55, 56–65, 88–9 (de Croissy to Louis).

62. CJ ix. 252–81; Grey, *Debates*, ii. 38–54, 69–74, 92–117; LJ xii. 561–79.

63. P/C 2/64, p. 6; *Letters of Williamson*, i. 33.

64. Bate, *Declaration of Indulgence*, pp. 130–6; Lady Newton, *House of Lyme*, p. 249 (Richard to Thomas Legh).

65. *Letters to Williamson*, i. 55–6, 60.

66. *CSPV* (1673–5), p. 40; BL Add. MS 40860, fo. 45 (Anglesey's diary).

67. Browning, *Danby*, i. 100–1.

68. PRO/31/3/128, fos. 80–2 (de Croissy to Louis); *Letters to Williamson*, i. 73; *Hatton Correspondence*, i. 107–8.

69. *Letters to Williamson*, i. 56, 58; Tanner, *Naval Manuscripts*, vols. ii–iii, *passim*.

70. Haley, *Shaftesbury*, pp. 330–3.

71. Ekberg, *Louis XIV's Dutch War*, pp. 153–4.

72. Especially *Letters to Williamson*, but also those in SP 29/334–6.

73. PRO/31/3/129, fos. 154–9, (de Croissy to Louis); Bod. L., Tanner MS 42, fo. 34 (Sir John to John Hobart).

74. PRO/31/3/129, fos. 134–59 (de Croissy to Louis); AAE CP (A) 108, fo. 41 (de Croissy to Pomponne).

75. The familiar story from LJ xii. 588–93; CJ ix. 281–6; and Grey, *Debates*, ii. 182–222.

76. Buckroyd, *Church and State*, p. 103, is inadequate as an account of this development. Much closer to the mark is John Patrick, 'The Origins of the Opposition to Lauderdale', *Scottish Historical Review*, 53 (1974), pp. 12–13, though NLS MS 7005, fos. 110 (Murray to Tweeddale) and 192 (Kincardine to Tweeddale), and MS 7006, fo. 10 (Murray to Tweeddale), disclose more of the story.

77. SP 57/2, pp. 16, 25, 92, 118 (the grants); NLS MS 7025, fo. 127 (Tweeddale to King).

78. SP 104/177, fos. 135–6 (Foreign Affairs Committee).

79. As I believe that it has been by Patrick, *SHR* 1974, pp. 10, 15.

80. SP 57/2, pp. 15, 30, 71 (grants); HMC Hamilton MSS, pp. 143–4 (Hamilton to Lauderdale and replies). And see BL Add. MS 32094, fo. 262 (Mackenzie to Lauderdale).

81. NLS MS 7006, fo. 10 (Murray to Tweeddale), and MS 7025, fos. 104–11 (Tweeddale to Murray); HMC Hamilton MSS, pp. 144–6 (letters between Lauderdale and Hamilton), 147–8 (letters between Lauderdale and Kincardine).

82. Kirkton, *Secret and True History*, pp. 339–40; Mackenzie, *Memoirs*, pp. 251–6; *Lauderdale Papers*, ii. 234–6 (instructions to Lauderdale), 237 (Lauderdale to King), 241–3 (Lauderdale to Maitland); *APS* viii. 210; BL Add. MS 32094, fo. 296 (Lauderdale's speech).

83. P/C 2/64, pp. 53, 62–3, 104–5; *Letters to Williamson*, ii. 24; *Essex Papers*, ii. 133–6 (Essex to Arlington); Steele, *Proclamations*, vol. ii, No. 844; SP 63/334/84 (Essex to Arlington); SP 63/335/9 (Essex to Conway).

84. *Essex Papers*, i. 146–8.

85. SP 63/333/104, 133 (Essex to Arlington), 156 (Ranelagh to Conway); SP 63/334/11 (Essex to Arlington); *Essex Papers*, i. 152 (Conway to Essex); Bod. L., Carte MS 218, fos. 76, 79 (Aungier to Ormonde and Arlington); MS 70, fos. 427, 430 (Ranelagh to partners).

86. Lee, *Cabal*, pp. 237, 243–4; Ekberg, *Louis XIV's Dutch War*, pp. 169–71.

87. SP 89/12, fos. 229–79.

88. Haley, *Shaftesbury*, pp. 335–44; PRO/31/3/129, fos. 183–90 (de Croissy to Louis); *Essex Papers*, i. 141 (Conway to Essex); *CSPV* (1673–5), pp. 175–6; Burnet, *History*, ii. 36.

89. PRO/31/3/129, fos. 183–235 (de Croissy to Louis); AAE CP (A) 108, fo. 128 (de Croissy to Pomponne); *Essex Papers*, i. 140–1, 150, 152–3 (Conway to Essex), 155 (Temple to Essex); *Letters to Williamson*, ii. 92, 101, 105.

90. PC/2/64, p. 132; Steele, *Proclamations*, vol. i, No. 3584; Friends House L., Spence MS 3, fos. 169–70 (Moore to Parke) and Abraham MS 17 (Lower to wife); Barclay, *Letters of Early Friends*, pp. 191–3; *Essex Papers*, i. 145 (Conway to Essex); *Letters to Williamson*, ii. 88.

91. Bebington, *Arlington's Letters*, ii. 450–7; *CSPV* (1673–5), pp. 190–1; SP 105/221, p. 419 (Arlington to envoys).

92. Kirkton, *Secret and True History*, pp. 341–2; Mackenzie, *Memoirs*, pp. 263–4; *Letters to Williamson*, ii. 100, 104; *Lauderdale Papers*, ii. 237 (Lauderdale to King), 240 (James to Lauderdale), 241–6 (Lauderdale to Maitland), and iii. 1 (instructions to Lauderdale), 2–3, 16–17 (Lauderdale to King), 5–6, 14, 21 (James to Lauderdale), 6–7 (Yester to Tweeddale), 11, 14–15, 18 (Kincardine to Lauderdale); *APS* viii. 210–12; Bryant, *Letters of Charles II*, pp. 272–3; NLS MS 7025, fo. 127 (Tweeddale's notes).

93. PRO/31/3/129, fos. 267–9 (Ruvigny to Pomponne); *Essex Papers*, i.

152–4, 159 (Conway to Essex), 155 (Temple to Essex); *Letters to Williamson*, ii. 92–105.

94. PRO/31/3/129, fos. 267–9 (Ruvigny to Pomponne); *Essex Papers*, i. 159–60 (Conway to Essex); LJ xii. 594–8.

95. *Letters to Williamson*, ii. 131; Grey, *Debates*, ii. 225–339; LJ xii. 601–8; *RPCS* (1673–6), p. 130; *Essex Papers*, i. 164–5 (Harbord to Essex); *Lauderdale Papers*, iii. 23, 25, 28 (Kincardine to Lauderdale), 26–7 (Lauderdale to King); CJ ix. 291–8.

96. *CSPV* (1673–5), p. 206; Evelyn, *Diary* (ed De Beer), iii. 30, 41; Bod. L., Rawlinson MS A191, fo. 114 (Pepys's report).

97. LJ xii. 616–22; PRO/31/3/130, fos. 280–4 (Ruvigny to Pomponne), 285–96 (Ruvigny to Louis); *Essex Papers*, i. 167–8 (Conway to Essex); *CSPV* (1673–5), p. 211; CJ ix. 298–9; Grey, *Debates*, ii. 339; SP 105/221, p. 508 (Arlington to envoys); BL Add. MS 29571, fo. 267 (Hatton to Hatton). Put together, this evidence seems to refute the view of Haley, *Shaftesbury*, p. 358, that the idea to ask Parliament's advice was devised by Charles and typical of his ingenuity. And that of Browning, *Danby*, i. 121–2, and Jones, *Country and Court*, p. 183, that it may (with most policies of the time) be attributed to Latimer.

98. PRO/31/3/130, fos. 315–20 (Ruvigny to Louis); *Letters to Williamson*, ii. 143; *CSPV* (1673–5), p. 214; HMC Kenyon MSS, p. 99 (newsletter).

99. *Essex Papers*, i. 176–7 (Herbert to Essex), 178 (Orrery to Essex); LJ xii. 632; HMC 6th Report, p. 454 (newsletter).

100. LJ xii. 626–47; *Essex Papers*, i. 177–8 (Orrery to Essex); *CSPV* (1673–5), pp. 220–1; James Macpherson, *Original Papers* (1775), i. 71–2; CJ ix. 296–314; Grey, *Debates*, ii. 329–445; *Lauderdale Papers*, iii. 35 (Kincardine to Lauderdale).

101. LJ xii. 649; *Letters to Williamson*, ii. 154–5; *Essex Papers*, i. 179 (Conway to Essex); *CSPV* (1673–5), p. 232; *Lauderdale Papers*, iii. 36 (Lauderdale to King); Macpherson, *Original Papers*, i. 72; BL Add. MS 25123, fo. 26 (Coventry to Sylvius).

102. *Essex Papers*, i. 180.

103. This is the prime theme of Lee, *The Cabal*, and has recently been powerfully restated in J. R. Jones, *Charles II: Royal Politician* (1987), p. 8 and ch. 5.

104. PRO, E. 148/8, pt. 2.

Chapter 12

1. Thus, to save space, there will be no references in this chapter to material extracted from the following works and the sources upon which they rely (which I have reread for myself without gaining more than these predecessors); Browning, *Danby*, i. 128, 285; Haley, *Shaftesbury*, pp. 371–448, and 'The Anglo-Dutch Rapprochement of 1677', *EHR* 73 (1958), pp. 614–46; C. L. Grose, 'The Anglo-Dutch Alliance of 1678', *EHR*

39 (1924), pp. 350–69, 526–50; and Ogg, *England in the Reign of Charles II*, ii. 524–57.

2. BL Stowe MS 206, fo. 565 (Harbord to Essex); Mignet, *Négociations*, iv. 320–1 (Ruvigny to Paris); *CSPV* (1673–5), pp. 297–8.

3. Also Ormonde was made constable of Tutbury in 1674 (Bod. L., Carte MS 40, fo. 36), while in 1676 his son John was made an Irish earl (Bod. L., Carte MS 118, fo. 62ᵛ) and his long-standing client Lane became an Irish viscount (Bod. L., Carte MS 120, fo. 215).

4. SP 29/360/203 (Onslow to Norwich); SP 29/361/3 (Turner to Arlington); *CSPV* (1673–5), p. 233; AAE CP (A) 113, fos. 20–1 (Ruvigny to Louis).

5. BL Add. MS 40860, fo. 66ᵛ (Anglesey's diary); *Essex Papers*, i. 197 (Harbord to Essex); Temple, *Works*, iv. 27–9 (Temple to father).

6. *CSPV* (1673–5), p. 279; 'Memoirs of Nathaniel, Lord Crewe', *Camden Miscellany*, ix (1895), pp. 13–14; *Essex Papers*, i. 228 (Conway to Essex).

7. The French ambassadors at London and Cologne reported his social accomplishments with admiration, and see Evelyn, *Diary* (ed. De Beer), iv. 39.

8. Chandaman, *English Public Revenue*, pp. 64–5, 235.

9. *The Bulstrode Papers*, i. 267 (newsletter); *Lauderdale Papers*, iii. 40–1 (Kincardine to Lauderdale), 45 (Atholl to Lauderdale); NLS MS 597, fo. 259 (Order in Council); NLS MS 7034, fo. 53 (Tweeddale to James); SP 57/2, pp. 394 and 401 (warrants from Privy Council and Treasury Commission); BL Add. MS 25123, fo. 81 (Coventry to Essex); *CSPD* (1673–5), p. 272 (warrant for earldom); HMC Hamilton MSS, pp. 149–50 (Hamilton to King and reply); *Essex Papers*, i. 234 (Aungier to Essex).

10. Burnet, *History*, ii. 66; Mackenzie, *Memoirs*, pp. 314–15.

11. The facts and the sources are in Buckroyd, *Church and State*, pp. 112–15, though I have made slightly different use of the sources and chosen a different interpretation. The sequence of events suggests to me that Lauderdale's alliances with the bishops and Danby followed his change in religious policy. Thus the chain of causation is reversed.

12. HMC Hamilton MSS, pp. 150 (Arlington to Hamilton and reply); NLS MS 7007, fo. 39 (Arlington to Tweeddale); *Essex Papers*, i. 228 (Conway to Essex).

13. *Essex Papers*, i. 195 (Harbord to Essex), and see ibid. i. 219–20 and 237.

14. Bod. L., Carte MS 38, fo. 67, and MS 70, fos. 196–8 (Lane to Ormonde).

15. Only BL Stowe MSS 204–6, *passim*, give a notion of the sheer wealth of rumour, gossip, and assertion.

16. SO 1/9, pp. 87, 97–101, 120 (orders for Ranelagh, Conway, and Orrery); BL Stowe MS 205, fo. 368 (order for Danby).

17. Bod. L., Carte MS 38, fo. 107 (Lane to Ormonde); *Essex Papers*, i. 238–9 (Essex to Coventry), 245–6 (Essex to Arlington), 250–1, 303 (Essex to Danby); Browning, *Danby*, ii. 53–4 (Danby to Essex).

18. *Essex Papers*, i. 272, 280 (Essex to Harbord, and reply).

19. Temple, *Works*, i. 182–4.
20. *RPCS* (1673–6), pp. 161–2, 178; *Essex Papers*, i. 313 (Essex to Ranelagh); Evelyn, *Diary* (ed. De Beer), iv. 41.
21. BL Add. MS 25124, fos. 25–9 (Coventry to MPs); BL Harl. MS 7377, fo. 58 (Sheldon to bishops).
22. SP 57/3, pp. 30 (King to Council), 88 (Lauderdale to Monro); HMC Hastings MSS, ii. 383–4 (Conway to Rawdon); BL Add. MS 4106, fo. 258ᵛ (complaint against Lauderdale's rule).
23. Steele, *Proclamations*, vol. ii, No. 850; *Essex Papers*, i. 193 (Essex to Harbord), 223 (Essex to Capel), 202 (Essex to Bishop of Down).
24. Steel, *Proclamations*, vol. i, No. 3597; SP 29/362/67 (Bowyer to Williamson); *Bulstrode Papers*, i. 273–4.
25. The outline of this story is familiar, but I have told it with more accuracy than before, the key sources being BL Add. MS 25124, fos. 14–16, 33, 67 (the letters from Coventry); Bod. L., Carte MS 72, fo. 229 (letter to Ormonde); P/C 264, pp. 364–5, 372; Sylvester, *Reliquiae Baxterianae*, pt. III, pp. 156–7; *CSPV* (1673–5), pp. 357, 366; SP 44/43, p. 11 (Williamson to bishops); SP 29/367/131–8 (conference recommendations); 'Letters written to James Sharp', pp. 279–80, SHS *Miscellany*, I. I cannot find any evidence for Professor Browning's assertion that Lauderdale insisted upon intervening in Danby's work: *Danby*, i. 147–8. Nor for that of Professor Jones, that Williamson was a valuable link-man for Danby with the clergy (as Secretary of State, he wrote out the invitations to them, and that was all): *Country and Court*, p. 185. Nor that of Victor Sutch, that the change of policy meant that Charles's 'humiliation and subordination to the Church was complete' (rather, he was using the Church for his own purposes): *Gilbert Sheldon* (The Hague, 1973), p. 127.
26. AAE CP (A) 115, fo. 204, and 116, fos. 46–7 (Ruvigny to Louis); BL Stowe MS 208, fo. 109 (Harbord to Essex); Temple, *Works*, I. 230–1.
27. CJ ix. 316–48; Grey, *Debates*, iii. 24–8; *Bulstrode Papers*, i. 291.
28. SP 57/3, p. 220 (warrant for earldom).
29. Chandaman, *English Public Revenue*, pp. 235–6.
30. BL Add. MS 9798, fos. 198–9 (instructions to plenipotentiaries); *CSPV* (1673–5), p. 441; Temple, *Works*, i. 339–43; BL Add. MS 39672, fos. 38, 41 (King to Temple); Dalrymple, *Memoirs*, i. 99–100 (Ruvigny to Louis).
31. Dalrymple, *Memoirs*, i. 106 (Ruvigny to Louis).
32. HMC 7th Report, p. 467 (John to Sir Ralph Verney); HMC Laing MSS, i. 409–10 (circular letter); HMC Fleming MSS, p. 125 (newsletter).
33. BL Harl. MS 7377, fo. 66 (Sheldon to Archbishop of York); HMC Leeds MSS, p. 14 (Morley to Danby).
34. Browning, *Danby*, i. 197; Miller, *Popery and Politics*, p. 143.
35. Ogg, *England in the Reign of Charles II*, p. 541.
36. *Letters to Williamson*, pp. 127, 130; SP 38/25, No. 321 (warrant for Monmouth).

37. *CSPV* (1673–5), p. 305; Evelyn, *Diary* (ed De Beer), iv. 74; Stratford-upon-Avon, Shakespeare Birthplace Centre, Commonplace Book of Sir Francis Fane, fo. 170.

38. BL Add. MS 28094, fo. 54; HMC 3rd Report, p. 265.

39. *Essex Papers*, i. 199 (Conway to Essex), 255–6 (Harbord to Essex); HMC 9th Report, pp. 450–1 (Louise to Danby); BL Add. MS 27192, fo. 20 (Buckingham to Charles); Shakespeare Birthplace Centre, Fane's Commonplace Book, fos. 179ᵛ, 182ᵛ; HMC 6th Report, p. 721 (Ormonde to Arran).

40. Henri Forneron, *Louis de Kéroualle* (1887), p. 204; HMC 7th Report, p. 466 (John to Sir Ralph Verney).

41. Forneron, *Kéroualle*, pp. 108–10; J. H. Wilson (ed.), *The Rochester–Savile Letters* (1941), pp. 52–3.

42. All this is reported in tremendous detail in Courtin's many dispatches in PRO/31/3/132–6.

43. HMC 7th Report, p. 465 (John to Sir Ralph Verney); SP 44/40, p. 430 (warrant for creation); *CSPD* (1673–5), pp. 343–4, and (1675–6), p. 221 (the same); HMC Leeds MSS, p. 18 (Mrs Green to Danby); BL Egerton MS 3330, fo. 82 (Greves to Danby); Wilson, *Nell Gwyn*, pp. 157–63; HMC Hastings MSS, ii. 165 (Stanhope to Huntingdon); *Rochester–Savile Letters*, p. 55; *Hatton Correspondence*, p. 167 (Charles to Lord Hatton).

44. First by Sir Arthur Bryant, *Charles II* (1935), p. 240, which has been quoted approvingly many times since.

45. SP 29/36/7 (Monmouth to Vice-Chancellor of Cambridge); Wood, *Life and Times* (ed. Clark), ii. 297–8.

46. Shakespeare's Birthplace Centre, Fane's Commonplace Book, fos. 178ᵛ, 185ᵛ, 186ᵛ; Wood, *Life and Times*, ii. 33; Lady Newton, *House of Lyme*, pp. 273–4 (the parody).

47. J. C. Beckett, 'The Irish Viceroyalty in the Restoration Period', in *Confrontations: Studies in Irish History* (1972), pp. 75–80.

48. *Essex Papers*, ii. 31–2 (Harbord to Essex); Egan, thesis, pp. 29–71.

49. Revd C. E. Pike, 'The Intrigue to Deprive the Earl of Essex of the Lord Lieutenancy of Ireland', *TRHS* 3rd ser. 5 (1911), pp. 95–103; Egan, thesis, pp. 72–5; *Essex Papers*, ii. 124 (Essex to Ormonde), 125 (Coventry to Essex); BL Stowe MS 217, fo. 142ᵛ (Essex to Capel); Bod. L., Carte MS 79, fo. 150ᵛ (newsletter to Ormonde); SP 104/180 (register of Foreign Affairs Committee).

50. Lady Newton, *House of Lyme*, pp. 273–4 (parody of King's speech); 'Memoirs of Nathaniel, Lord Crewe', *Camden Miscellany*, ix (1895), pp. 13–14; Burnet, *History*, ii. 98–9; Lake, *Diary*, *Camden Miscellany*, I, p. 11; Wood, *Life and Times*, ii. 312; HMC Ormonde MS, NS iv. 149 (Arran to Ormonde).

51. Bryant, *Charles II*, p. 260; Sutch, *Sheldon*, p. 166.

52. HMC Portland MSS, ii. 357 (Marvell to Harley); *Hatton Correspondence*, i. 156–7 (Charles Hatton to Lord Hatton); HMC Rutland MSS, ii. 42 (Lady

Charworth to Lord Roos); Burnet, *History*, ii. 98–100; 'Memoirs of Lord Crewe', pp. 16–17; Wood, *Life and Times*, ii. 395–7; Lake, *Diary*, pp. 18–20.

53. Sonnino, in Hatton (ed.), *Louis XIV and Europe*, p. 167.
54. HMC 7th Report, p. 469 (John Verney to Sir Ralph Verney).
55. HMC Portland MSS, ii. 355 (Marvell to Harley); BL Add. MS 27872, fo. 20 (Buckingham to King); Haley, *Shaftesbury*, p. 430; SP 104/179, p. 146 (Foreign Affairs Committee).
56. PRO/31/3/136, fo. 36 (Courtin to Louis); Sir John Reresby, *Memoirs* (ed. Andrew Browning, Glasgow, 1936), 162–3, 167.
57. SP 29/396/8, 14, 20, 40 (reports to Williamson from Talbot, Lanyon and Holden, and newsletter).
58. BL Add. MS 10115, fos. 1–66, plus SP 29/398/106 and SP 29/366, pp. 433–7 (Williamson's notes).
59. *Rochester–Savile Letters*, pp. 52–3.
60. Browning, *Danby*, ii. 415–19 (Danby to Wilhelm); Sonnino, in Hatton (ed.), *Louis XIV and Europe*, p. 170; BL Add. MS 32095, fo. 81 (Monmouth to King); BL Add. MS 25119, fos. 21–7, 34 (instructions for Godolphin, Monmouth).
61. Dalton, *English Army Lists*, i. 201–20.
62. HMC Ormonde MSS, NS iv. 35–7, 123–5 (Ormonde to Coventry), 41–3, 48–52, 100–1 (Orrery to Ormonde), 46–7 (reply), 55–6 (Ormonde to King), 89 (Essex to Ormonde), 105 (Danby to Ormonde); HMC 6th Report, p. 720 (Ormonde to Arran), 730–1 (Boyle to Ormonde); Edward MacLysaght (ed.), *Calendar of the Orrery Papers* (Dublin, 1941), p. 183 (Boyle to Orrery); BL Add. MS 21484, fos. 10–12, 18 (Ormonde to Southwell); SP 61/336, pp. 70, 79 (warrants for pensions).
63. HMC Atholl MSS, p. 33 (Alexander Murray to Charles Murray); Buckroyd, *Church and State*, pp. 120–1; *Life of Blair* (ed. M'Crie, 1848), pp. 564–5; HMC Hamilton MSS, p. 151 (Hamilton to Rothes); Turner, *Memoirs*, pp. 255, 258–61; HMC Hamilton Supplement, pp. 89, 91 (Burnet to Hamilton); BL Add. MS 4106, fos. 255–9 (complaint of Lauderdale's rule); *An Account of Scotland's Grievances* (1675); HMC Buccleuch MSS (Drumlanrig), pp. 221–9 (Hamilton to Queensberry); Mackenzie, *Memoirs*, pp. 325–6, Revd Mr Robert Law, *Memorialls* (ed. C. K. Sharpe, Edinburgh, 1818), pp. 87–8.
64. Buckroyd, *Church and State*, pp. 124–7, fails to notice the importance of the Ayrshire petition in precipitating the Highland Host: RPCS (1676–8), pp. 250–396; Kirkton, *Secret and True History*, pp. 377–8; SP61/338/141 (Rawdon to Conway); *Lauderdale Papers*, iii. 89–92 (Lauderdale to Danby, and reply); HMC Ormonde MSS, NS i. 21–2 (misdated instructions to Ormonde); NLS MS 597, fo. 270 (letter from Lauderdale); SP 104/179, p. 172 (Foreign Affairs Committee).
65. John Rawson Elder, *The Highland Host of 1678* (Aberdeen, 1914).

66. SRO GD 157/1659 (Cassilis to King); HMC Portland MSS, ii. 44–50 (Hickes to Patrick); *Hatton Correspondence*, i. 158 (Charles Hatton to Lord Hatton); HMC Buccleuch MSS (Drumlanrig), pp. 234–5 (Hamilton to Queensberry); *RPCS* (1676–8), pp. 406–14; *Lauderdale Papers*, iii. 99–102 (Arran to Lauderdale).

67. HMC Hamilton MSS, Supplement, pp. 95–6 (Hamilton's complaint); *Lauderdale Papers*, iii. 103–25 (Moray to Lauderdale); NLS MS 7034, fo. 84 (Scottish bishops to King); BL Add. MS 32095, fo. 88 (Mackenzie to Lauderdale); BL Add. MS 12068, fo. 58 (Duchess of Hamilton to Turner).

68. SP 44/44, p. 92.

69. BL Add. MS 25124, fo. 139 (Coventry to Holmes).

70. *Lauderdale Papers*, iii. 131–2, 145–6 (Murray to Lauderdale), 133–4 (Forrester to Lauderdale).

71. PRO/31/3/139, fo. 76 (Barillon to Louis).

72. HMC Ormonde MSS, NS iv. 150, 154 (Arran to Ormonde and reply); HMC Rutland MSS, ii. 51 (Smith to Roos).

73. HMC Hamilton MSS, Supplement, pp. 97–8 (Hamilton's hearing); *Lauderdale Papers*, iii. 147–53 (Moray to Lauderdale); HMC Buccleuch MSS (Drumlanrig), pp. 236–7 (Hamilton to Queensberry); *RPCS* (1676–8), pp. 459–67; Steele, *Proclamations*, vol. ii, No. 2441; BL Add. MS 32095, fos. 98–104 (Murray etc. to Lauderdale).

74. HMC Portland MSS, ii. 50–1 (Hickes to Patrick); *Lauderdale Papers*, iii. 154–9 (account of Convention), 159 (King to Lauderdale), 247–56 (Lauderdale to Moray); NLS MS 597, fo. 272 (Moray to Lauderdale).

75. Bod. L., MS Eng. Hist. b. 2, fo. 72 (the letter); Bod. L., MS Eng. Misc. 4, fos. 11–12 (Hickes's notes); HMC Buccleuch MSS (Drumlanrig), p. 238 (Hamilton to Queensberry).

76. BL Add. MS 25119, fos. 35–6 (instructions for Feversham).

77. HMC Ormonde MSS, NS iv. 172–3 (Longford to Ormonde).

78. Jones, *Country and Court*, p. 195; Browning, *Danby*, i. 282; Grose, *EHR* 1924, p. 542.

79. Bryant, *Charles II*, p. 266.

80. HMC Ormonde MSS, NS iv. 160.

Chapter 13

1. The orthodoxy has been most recently, and triumphantly, restated in J. R. Jones, *Charles II: Royal Politician* (1987). Nevertheless, both J. P. Kenyon, *Stuart England* (2nd edn., 1985), pp. 229–30, and John Miller, *James II* (Hove, 1978), p. 77, have considered Charles's skill in handling the crisis overrated. What prevents me from adopting their views wholesale is that neither develops them at length and that I disagree with details of both their cases. To save over-wieldy footnotes, I shall not provide references in this chapter to facts already known from (among others) the following works:

John Kenyon, *The Popish Plot* (edn. of 1984) and *Robert Spencer, Earl of Sunderland* (1958); Browning, *Danby*; J. R. Jones, *The First Whigs* (Oxford, 1961) and *Charles II*; and Haley, *Shaftesbury*. I have checked all the sources cited in these.

2. Chandaman, *English Public Revenue*, p. 101; BL Add. MS 25142, *passim* (instructions to agents); HMC Ormonde MSS, NS iv. 181 (Coventry to Ormonde); SP 8/3/59, 61 (James to Wilhelm); SP 29/336, pp. 571–5 (Williamson's notebook).

3. Aydelotte, thesis, pp. 62–93; Egan, thesis, pp. 92–3. I have checked the sources for both these.

4. From the review of Kenyon, *Popish Plot*, in *The Times* newspaper, quoted on the cover of the 1984 paperback edn.

5. *Examen*, p. 175.

6. P/C 2/66, p. 409.

7. HMC Ormonde MSS, NS iv. 211 (Ormonde to Boyle).

8. Which was the obvious step to take: there is no evidence for the assertion in Jones, *Charles II*, p. 130, that Danby talked him into it.

9. PRO/31/3/141, fos. 3ᵛ, 44ᵛ, 55 (Barrillon to Louis); Reresby, *Memoirs*, p. 180.

10. Haley, *Shaftesbury*, p. 468.

11. CJ ix. 516 (of course).

12. Lynch, *Orrery*, pp. 224–7; Bod. L., Carte MS 146, fo. 11 (Ormonde to Coventry); MS 70, fos. 475–6 (Ormonde to Southwell); HMC Ormonde MSS, NS iv. 233, 268–9 (Coventry to Ormonde), 254 (Ormonde to Ossory), 262 (Cooke to Ormonde), 270 (Wyche to Ormonde), 292 (Arlington to Ormonde); MS 38, fo. 662 (Southwell to Ormonde).

13. There is no evidence for the statement in Jones, *Charles II*, p. 131, that the King acted precipitately to save Catherine because her secretary was Belling, whose arrest might uncover the Dover treaty. Her household was to be banished, not seized, and Belling in any case was leaving the country.

14. The Irish dimension of this is summarized neatly by HMC Ormonde MSS, NS iv. 299 (Ormonde to Coventry), 245 (reply), 246 (Ossory to Ormonde).

15. HMC Ormonde MSS, NS iv. 268–9.

16. PRO/31/3/141, fos. 83–84ᵛ, 99 (Barrillon to Louis).

17. Kenyon, *Stuart England*, p. 229.

18. PRO 31/3/142, fo. 12 (Barrillon to Louis); Bod. L., Carte MS 39, fo. 1 (Southwell to Ormonde).

19. HMC Ormonde MSS, NS iv. 292–3 (Wyche to Ormonde), 492–5 (Southwell to Ormonde).

20. Ibid. 494–5 (Southwell to Ormonde); Bod. L., Carte MS 232, fo. 30ᵛ (letter from Ellis); Chandaman, *English Public Revenue*, pp. 68, 241.

21. Kenyon, *Popish Plot*, pp. 156–66; Bod. L., Carte MS 243, fo. 356 (Clarendon to Ormonde); MS 39, fo. 1 (Southwell to Ormonde); Bod. L., Rawlinson MS A136, p. 106 (note by clerk upon Council papers); P/C 2/67, p. 1; SP 29/336,

p. 767 (Williamson's journal); HMC Ormonde MSS, NS iv. 497 (Southwell to Ormonde); PRO 31/3/142, fo. 24 (Barrillon to Louis); SP 29/411/16 (letter to Williamson).

22. Apart from Burnet and Barrillon, often quoted, see Evelyn, *Diary* (ed. De Beer), iv. 163.

23. HMC Savile–Foljambe MSS, pp. 127–8.

24. Ibid., Bod. L., Carte MS 221, fo. 130 (Arlington to Ormonde), MS 243, fo. 356 (Clarendon to Ormonde), and MS 70, fo. 481 (Ormonde to Southwell); PRO/31/3/142, fo. 34 (Barrillon to Louis); BL Add. MS 29577, fos. 179, 181 (letters to Hatton); BL Add. MS 18730, fo. 51ᵛ (Anglesey's diary); Bod. L., Carte MS 39, fo. 5 (Southwell to Ormonde); HMC Ormonde MSS, NS iv. 306–7 (Coventry to Ormonde), 308 (Howard to Ormonde), 316 (Molys to Ossory); SP 29/336, p. 811 (Williamson's journal); Bod. L., Carte MS 243, fo. 436 (letter from Thynne).

25. HMC Ormonde MSS, NS iv. 328 (Ossory to Ormonde); Josselin, *Diary* (Camden Soc., 9, 1908), pp. 175–6.

26. HMC Portland MSS, ii. 153 (Danby to Newcastle); *Hatton Correspondence*, p. 176 (Lyttleton to Hatton); SP 44/48, p. 89 (Monmouth to all officers); HMC Ormonde MSS, NS iv. 317 (Molys to Ormonde).

27. SP 29/366, p. 823.

28. Steele, *Proclamations*, vol. i, No. 3682.

29. HMC Lindsey MSS, p. 401 (the draft order); HMC Ormonde MSS, NS iv. 321 (Ossory to Ormonde).

30. BL Add. MS 18447, fo. 2 (James to Legge).

31. Though Kenyon, *Stuart England*, p. 229, concludes firmly (without more evidence) that it was a major blunder.

32. PRO/31/3/142, fo. 37–8 (Barrillon to Louis); BL Add. MS 28053, fo. 152 (Latimer to Danby).

33. SP 29/411/106 (Ranelagh to Conway).

34. HMC Ormonde MSS, iv. 356 (Locke to Ormonde).

35. HMC Finch MSS, ii. 46 (King to Finch), 48 (Daniel Finch to Sir John Finch).

36. BL Add. MS 28043, fo. 7 (Danby's notes); HMC Ormonde MSS, NS iv. 359 (Cooke to Ormonde).

37. See, as the latest example, Jones, *Charles II*, p. 141.

38. PRO/31/3/142, fo. 75 (to Louis).

39. BL Add. MS 28043, fo. 7 (Danby's 'diary'); HMC Ormonde MSS, NS iv. 259 (Cooke to Ormonde).

40. Ibid. iv. 370 (Cooke to Ormonde).

41. BL Add. MS 28043, fo. 7 (Danby's 'diary'); BL Add. MS 28049, fos. 12–20 (the notes), BL Add. MS 28040, fo. 10 (Danby's 'diary').

42. LJ xiii. 488–9, 527; Bod. L., Carte MS 54, fos. 616–17 (Dumbarton to Ormonde), MS 141, fo. 102 (Wilhelm to Ossory), and MS 146, fos. 177–80 (Ormonde to Coventry); *Letters of the Honourable Algernon Sidney* (1742), p. 25; Aydelotte, thesis, pp. 241–2; HMC Ormonde MSS, NS iv. 366 (Ossory

to Ormonde), v. 4 (Longford to Ormonde), 5 (Wyche to Ormonde).

43. *Hatton Correspondence*, p. 183 (Hatton to Hatton); *Savile Correspondence* (ed. W. D. Cooper, Camden Soc., 1858), pp. 76–7 (Halifax to Savile); BL Add. MS 15889, fo. 33 (Countess of Sunderland to Evelyn).

44. E. R. Turner, 'The Privy Council of 1679', *EHR* 30 (1915), pp. 251–66.

45. W. A. Aiken, 'The Admiralty in Conflict and Commission', in Aiken and B. D. Henning (eds.), *Conflict in Stuart England* (1960), pp. 205–6.

46. HMC Ormonde MS, NS v. 67 (Cooke to Ormonde).

47. Chandaman, *English Public Revenue*, pp. 243–8.

48. Bod. L., Carte MS 70, fo. 486 (Ormonde to Southwell); P/C 2/68, p. 51.

49. Aydelotte, thesis, p. 308; Egan, thesis, pp. 100–8; P/C 2/68, pp. 35, 47, 127, 182, 189; Bod. L., Carte MS 243, fo. 373 (Longford to Ormonde).

50. In the context of that week I find it impossible to accept the statement of Jones, *Charles II*, pp. 145–6, that the King was the sole author of the offer and made it confusing deliberately. But nor can I discover evidence for the assertion of Kenyon, *Sunderland*, p. 26, that Halifax devised it.

51. *Memoirs of Thomas, Earl of Ailesbury* (Roxburghe Club, 1890), i. 35.

52. The sources are cited in L. Glassey, *Politics and the Appointment of Justices of the Peace, 1675–1720* (Oxford, 1979), pp. 41–3. The anecdote is from Roger North, *Examen* (1740), pp. 77–8, a work which is generally inaccurate and suspect, though Dr Glassey takes it seriously. I doubt whether the purge would have been as wide-ranging as Dr Glassey thinks. Most benches were to be inspected wholly or partially by 'courtiers', and every recommendation had to be checked by Finch, the local bishop, the Lord-Lieutenant, custos rotulorum, *and* judges! (P/C 2/68, p. 47.)

53. Temple, *Works* (ed. 1754), i. 420–4, which disproves Jones, *Charles II*, p. 147, where it is asserted that the King took the decision alone.

54. The Venetian ambassador, quoted in Leopold von Ranke, *A History of England* (Oxford, 1875), iv. 84.

55. BL Add. MS 15643, fo. 8 (Committee register); Henry Sidney, *Diary of the Times of Charles the Second* (ed. R. W. Blencowe, 1843), i. 4–5, 10; Haley, *Shaftesbury*, pp. 531–3.

56. Sidney, *Diary*, i. 6; PRO/31/3/143, fo. 10 (Barrillon to Louis).

57. Sidney, *Diary*, i. 5.

58. SP 29/405/229 (newsletter); SP 29/29/407/105 (Mackaile to Adams); SP 57/4, p. 398 (warrant for Moray); Buckroyd, *Church and State*, p. 129; *RPCS* (1678–80), pp. 29–196.

59. SP 29/406/180 and 29/407/45, 77 (Mackaile to Adams).

60. CJ ix. 613–14; Temple, *Works*, i. 420; *Letters of Sidney*, p. 72.

61. See Buckroyd, *Church and State*, pp. 129–30, and Ian Cowan, *The Scottish Covenanters*, pp. 91–8.

62. *RPCS* (1678–80), pp. 210–39; Temple, *Works*, i. 426–8; Sidney, *Diary*, i. 5; HMC Ormonde MSS, NS iv. 523 (Southwell to Ormonde) and NS v. 133 (Longford to Ormonde), 135 (Bunnell to Watts); PRO/31/3/143, fos. 10–13

(Barrillon to Louis); BL Add. MS 28049, fo. 60 (Bath to Danby); P/C 268, pp. 101, 107.

63. SP 29/411/154 (Yard to Williamson); SP 57/5, p. 159 (Monmouth's instructions); *RPCS* (1678–80), pp. 247–52. This seems to be the origin of the story in Burnet, *History*, ii. 239, repeated in North, *Examen*, pp. 81–2, that Lauderdale had Monmouth's orders altered after he had left.

64. HMC Ormonde MSS, NS iv. 527–8 (Southwell to Ormonde) and v. 145 (Coventry to Ormonde).

65. Sidney, *Diary*, i. 11, 16; *Savile Correspondence*, p. 110 (Halifax to Savile).

66. Steele, *Proclamations*, vol. ii, Nos. 2466, 2470; HMC Ormonde MSS, NS iv. 529 (Southwell to Ormonde); *RPCS* (1678–80), pp. 280–304; HMC Hamilton MSS, Supplement, pp. 99 (Hamilton to Lawyers), 99–100 (Hamilton's Paper); Sidney, *Diary*, i. 11, 16, 35; Robert Wodrow, *The History of the Sufferings of the Church of Scotland* (Edinburgh, 1721), ii. 106–7; Burnet, *History*, ii. 235; SP 57/5, p. 214 (Burnet's warrant); *Letters of Sidney*, pp. 106–38; BL Add. MS 23244, fos. 20–7 (Mackenzie's paper). Together, these extend and elucidate the account in Buckroyd, *Church and State*, pp. 130–1.

67. Robin Clifton, *The Last Popular Rebellion* (1984), pp. 107–12, plus HMC Savile–Foljambe MSS, p. 125 (James to Wilhelm), and Sidney, *Diary*, i. 6.

68. Most of this story was first teased out by Kenyon, *Sunderland*, pp. 27–9. I have interleaved material from Sidney, *Diary*, i. 16, and PRO/31/3/143, fos. 24, 29 (Barrillon to Louis).

69. See Sidney, *Diary*, i. 17.

70. HMC Ormonde MSS, NS v. 144–5 (Ossory to Ormonde).

71. Ibid. v. 158 (the same). Jones, *Charles II*, pp. 148–9, far outruns the evidence, by stating that the King personally organized Wakeman's defence. Far more subtle and restrained is J. P. Kenyon, 'The Acquittal of Sir George Wakeman', *HJ* 14 (1971), pp. 693–708.

72. 'The King meddles in none' (Sunderland to Sidney, Sidney, *Diary*, i. 58–9).

73. Narcissus Luttrell, *A Brief Historical Relation of State Affairs* (Oxford, 1857), i. 18–20; SP 29/411/147 (Yard to Williamson); *Letters of Sidney*, p. 85; HMC Ormonde MSS, NS v. 108 (Cooke to Ormonde).

74. HMC Ormonde MSS, NS v. 75 (Cooke to Ormonde), 122 (letter to Boyle); *Letters to Sydney*, p. 131.

75. HMC Finch MSS, ii. 56 (Haxter to Finch); HMC Ormonde MSS, NS v. 179 (Armorer to Ormonde).

76. Chandaman, *English Public Revenue*, pp. 248–9; Sidney, *Diary*, i. 52–3 (Sidney to Essex).

77. PRO/31/3/143, fos. 25, 20.

78. Sidney, *Diary*, i. 87–8 (Sunderland to Sidney); HMC Ormonde MSS, NS iv. 535 (Southwell to Ormonde); Bod. L., Carte MS 228, fo. 121 (George to Thomas Wharton).

79. See Fraser, *Charles II*, p. 382, for a discussion of this point.

Chapter 14

As before, there will be no sources given to facts already familiar from the now standard works on the period, notably Kenyon, *Sunderland*, pp. 30–73; Jones, *First Whigs*, pp. 87–180, and *Charles II*, pp. 137–70, and Haley, *Shaftesbury*, pp. 545–637.

1. BL Add. MS 32680, fos. 114–15 (Mountstevens to Sidney); HMC Foljambe MSS, p. 137 (James to Wilhelm); Wood, *Life and Times*, ii. 462; HMC 7th Report, p. 474 (John Verney to Sir Richard Verney); Temple, *Works* (1754 edn.), i. 435–40; Bod. L., Carte MS 232, fo. 51 (Lonsford to Arran); Clarke (ed.), *Life of James II*, i. 564; Sidney, *Diary*, p. 176.
2. Kenyon, *Sunderland*, pp. 30–2, and *Popish Plot*, pp. 210–11. John Miller, *James II* (Hove, 1978), 99–100, also credits James with considerable strength of position and influence. And see Jones, *First Whigs*, p. 90.
3. K. Feiling and F. Needham (eds.), 'The Journals of Edmund Warcup', *EHR* 40 (1925), p. 243.
4. Clarke (ed.), *Life of James II*, p. 568.
5. Ibid., p. 569; SP 29/412/42 (letter from Yard); *Hatton Correspondence*, i. 195.
6. *RPCS* (1678–80), p. 316.
7. Clarke (ed.), *Life of James II*, i. 571; James Macpherson, *Original Papers* (1775), i. 95; Sidney, *Diary*, p. 161.
8. Bod. L., Carte MS 228, fo. 103 (Taylor to Wharton); *True Domestick Intelligence* (19 Sept. 1679).
9. PRO/31/3/143, fo. 66ᵛ.
10. HMC Ormonde MSS, NS iv. 537 (Southwell to Ormonde); SP 29/412/147 (newsletter); *Hatton Correspondence*, i. 197.
11. HMC Ormonde MSS, NS iv. 539 (Southwell to Ormonde).
12. Ibid., pp. 541–5; P/C 2/68, p. 229; BL Add. MS 29557, fo. 271 (Cholmeley to Hatton).
13. Wood, *Life and Times*, ii. 466; *Hatton Correspondence*, i. 198.
14. Sidney, *Diary*, i. 176–89; HMC Ormonde MSS, NS iv. 545, 557 (Southwell to Ormonde); HMC 7th Report, p. 476 (John Verney to Sir Richard Verney); *Hatton Correspondence*, p. 198; Temple, *Works*, i. 440–3; Bod. L., Carte MS 243, fo. 408 (Longford to Arran).
15. HMC Foljambe MSS, p. 139 (James to Wilhelm).
16. I prefer this to the view of Kenyon, *Popish Plot*, p. 210, that they were essentially James's men and promoted by him: as I have said (and shall say) I think his influence overrated at this point.
17. HMC Somerset MSS, p. 106 (Edward Seymour to Sir Edward Seymour); Luttrell, *Brief Historical Relation*, i. 27; Glassey, *Politics and the Appointment of Justices*, pp. 45–6.
18. Clarke (ed.), *Life of James II*, i. 583; PRO/31/3/143, fos. 97–100, and 144, fo. 94 (Barrillon's dispatches); P/C 2/68, pp. 247–327; Kenyon, *Sunderland*,

pp. 36–41; BL Add. MS 32680, fos. 175–6 (Lady Sunderland to Sidney); Sidney, *Diary*, pp. 199–200; HMC Lindsey MSS, p. 418 (ministers to Bertie).

19. HMC Ormonde MSS, NS iv. 557–8 (Southwell to Ormonde).
20. Ibid. iv. 536–7; Bod. L., Carte MS 232, fo. 60 (Longford to Ormonde).
21. Carte MS 232, fo. 55 (Longford to Ormonde).
22. See HMC Foljambe MSS, pp. 137, 139 (James to Wilhelm).
23. Dr Williams's L., Morrice MS 31P, pp. 241–2; *Mercurius Anglicus* (6–10 Dec. 1679); *Hatton Correspondence*, pp. 211–12; *CSPD* (1679–80), p. 307 (newsletter to Bowman); *True Domestick Intelligence* (12 Dec. 1679); *London Gazette* (8–11 Dec., 11–15 Dec. 1679); Steele, *Proclamations*, vol. i, Nos. 3702–3; BL Add. MS 18730, fo. 63^v (Anglesey's diary).
24. Haley, *Shaftesbury*, pp. 563–4.
25. HMC Le Fleming MSS, p. 165.
26. Sidney, *Diary*, p. 247; HMC Ormonde MSS, iv. 568 (Southwell to Ormonde).
27. *Lauderdale Papers*, iii. 180 (Mordinton to Lauderdale).
28. HMC Ormonde MSS, iv. 552 (Ormonde to Southwell); Sir John Lauder of Fountainhall, *Historical Observes* (Edinburgh, 1840).
29. Buckroyd, *Church and State*, pp. 132–3; HMC Ormonde MSS, NS v. 235 (Wharton to Ormonde); HMC Darmouth MSS, i. 41–2 (James to Legge); *Lauderdale Papers*, iii. 181–90 (letters between James and Lauderdale), 195 (Mackenzie to Lauderdale); Clarke (ed.), *Life of James II*, i. 580; Lauder, *Historical Observes*, p. 75; *RPCS* (1678–80), pp. 344–90; *True Domestick Intelligence* (9 Jan. 1680); Bod. L., Carte MS 243, fo. 402 (Longford to Arran); W. S. Singer (ed.), *The Correspondence of Henry Hyde, Earl of Clarendon* (1828), i. 82 (James to Hyde, misdated in edition); NLS MS 2512, fo. 220 (Burnet to Lauderdale).
30. BL Add. MS 32680, fo. 313 (Countess of Sunderland to Sidney); *Lauderdale Papers*, iii. 198 (James to Lauderdale); H. C. Foxwell (ed.), 'Some Unpublished Letters of Gilbert Burnet', *Camden Miscellany*, xi (1907), pp. 12–14, 19.
31. SP 57/6, pp. 45, 63, 80, 82, 210 (series of royal letters and warrants); 'Letters of Burnet', *Camden Miscellany*, xi. 19, 29, 37; Luttrell, *Brief Historical Relation*, i. 39; *Lauderdale Papers*, iii. 198 (James to Lauderdale), 210 (Murray to Lauderdale); *Life of Blair* (ed. M'Crie, 1848), pp. 570–2; *RPCS* (1678–80), pp. 432–72; Bod. L., Tanner MS 37, fos. 64, 196 (Scottish bishops to Sancroft), 120 (Burnet to Sancroft); NLS MS 2512, fo. 224 (Burnet to Lauderdale). I can find no evidence for the suggestion of Buckroyd, *Church and State*, p. 134, that much of this activity was aimed to discredit Monmouth. My impression of the state of Scottish dissent at this time is gained from ibid., pp. 134–5, and Cowan, *Scottish Covenanters*, pp. 105–7.
32. This is the account in Kenyon, *Sunderland*, pp. 41–7, given some different emphases from BL Add. MS 32680, fos. 251–2, 290 (Sunderland to Sidney); G. Groen Van Prinsterer, *Archives ou Correspondance Inédite de*

la Maison d'Orange-Nassau (Utrecht, 1861), v. 377–8, 380 (Temple to Wilhelm); C. Brinkmann, 'The Relations between England and Germany, 1660–1688', *EHR* 24 (1909), pp. 448–61; Sidney, *Diary*, i. 73; 'Letters of Burnet', *Camden Miscellany*, xi. 25; PRO 31/3/145, fos. 75, 87 (Barrillon's dispatches). Professor Kenyon portrays Charles as manipulated by Sunderland, while Professor Jones believes that Sunderland was manipulated by the King: *Charles II*, pp. 155–7. There is no evidence to support or refute either view. I prefer to believe that the logic of the situation acted upon both King and ministers, but that Charles, as usual, tried to protect his position from both sides.

33. HMC Ormonde MSS, NS iv. 578 (Southwell to Ormonde).
34. BL Althorp MS C4, Thynne to Halifax, 13 June 1680.
35. BL Add. MS 32680, fos. 296–7, 330 (Countess of Sunderland to Sidney).
36. 'Letters of Burnet', *Camden Miscellany*, xi. 28.
37. Luttrell, *Brief Historical Relation*, i. 43.
38. Allen, thesis, pp. 44–8.
39. Havighurst, *Law Quarterly Review*, 1950, p. 236.
40. Prinsterer (ed.), *Archives*, v. 393 (James to Wilhlem).
41. HMC Ormonde MSS, NS v. 318–19 (Gwyn to Ormonde).
42. The details are all in Aydelotte, thesis, pp. 106–19.
43. HMC Ormonde MSS, NS v. 280 (Gwyn to Ormonde).
44. 'Letters of Burnet', *Camden Miscellany*, xi. 16; Macpherson, *Original Papers*, i. 103 (Godolphin to Wilhelm); BL Add. MS 25124, fos. 229–31 (Coventry to King); Bod. L., Carte MS 39, fo. 127 (Reading to Arran); MS 243, fo. 456 (the same). This account is at variance with that in Haley, *Shaftesbury*, pp. 569–72.
45. HMC Ormonde MSS, v. 342–3 (Gwyn to Ormonde).
46. Ibid.; *CSPD* (1679–80), p. 596 (newsletter to Radcliffe); P/C 2169, p. 117.
47. Allen, thesis, pp. 41–3; SP 44/62, pp. 69–71 (Jenkins's letters).
48. Bod. L., Carte MS 243, fo. 506 (Longford to Arran).
49. Aydelotte, thesis, pp. 122–62, 243, 308–11; Egan, thesis, pp. 110–17; HMC Ormonde MSS, NS v. 425 (Sunderland to Ormonde), 431–9 (Longford to Ormonde); SP 44/62, p. 74 (Jenkins to Godolphin); Bod. L., Carte MS 219, fos. 168–210 (letters of Ormonde to Arran). It is remarkable how little knowledge even the best historians of Restoration England have possessed of the affairs of Ireland: see pp. 224–5 of Kenyon, *Popish Plot*, where the 'Irish Remonstrance' is misdated by ten years and Peter Talbot described as 'a man who enjoyed Charles II's personal regard'.
50. Reresby, *Memoirs*, p. 201.
51. SP 44/62, pp. 74–113 (Jenkins's letters); SP 29/414/104 (Godolphin to Jenkins), 109 (Anglesey to Mayor).
52. Kenyon, *Sunderland*, pp. 57–9, plus PRO/31/3/146, fo. 117 (Barrillon's dispatch); HMC Ormonde MSS, NS v. 459 (Gwyn to Ormonde); SP 57/6, p. 197 (Moray to Rothes).

53. Chandaman, *English Public Revenue*, pp. 69, 249–50; BL Add. MS 29657, fo. 271 (Cholmeley to Hatton); P/C 2/68, p. 343; Aiken, 'The Admiralty', in Aiken and Henning (eds.), *Conflict in Stuart England*, pp. 208–9; Bod. L., Carte MS 243, fo. 394 (Armorer to Arran).

54. Reresby, *Memoirs*, pp. 202–7; Sidney, *Diary*, p. 116.

55. Ibid., pp. 118–19.

56. PRO/31/3/147, fo. 33 (Barrillon's dispatch), where I take 'cabinet' to mean a piece of furniture and not a chamber, as some others have done.

57. Why does Professor Kenyon think that this famous aside, best known from Dalrymple, *Memoirs*, i. 290–1, referred to Sunderland? See his *Sunderland*, p. 66.

58. Reresby, *Memoirs*, p. 209.

59. PRO/31/3/147, fo. 68 (Barrillon's dispatch).

60. HMC Dartmouth MSS, i. 42–6.

61. Prinsterer (ed.), *Archives*, v. 451 (Jenkins to Wilhelm).

62. Dr Williams's L., Morrice MSS, MS 31P, p. 285 (list of votes); Ailesbury, *Memoirs* (Roxburghe Club, 1890), p. 50; HMC Ormonde MSS, v. 521 (Arran to Ormonde).

63. BL Add. MS 15643, fo. 46 (Committee for Intelligence); Clarke (ed.), *Life of James II*, i. 657–8; BL Add. MS 18730, fo. 80 (Anglesey's diary); HMC Kenyon MSS, p. 123 (newsletter).

64. Christie, *Life of Cooper*, vol. ii, app., pp. cxii–cxv (Locke to Stringer).

65. BL Add. MS 18730, fo. 80ᵛ (Anglesey's diary); HMC Ormonde MS, NS v. 555 (Gwyn to Ormonde). I cannot find the evidence for Miller's belief (*James II*, p. 103) that Hyde persuaded the King to prorogue and dissolve.

66. Temple, *Works* (1754 edn.), i. 460.

67. Singer (ed.), *Clarendon Correspondence*, i. 49 (James to Hyde); Leicestershire RO, Finch MSS, Box 56, Paper in hand of 2nd Earl of Nottingham headed 'for my children', fo. 8; Clarke (ed.), *Life of James II*, i. 659.

68. Most recently by Kenyon, *Sunderland*, p. 72; Haley, *Shaftesbury*, p. 622, and Jones, *Charles II*, pp. 166–7.

69. Ogg, *England In The Reign of Charles II*, ii. 599–601, accurately quotes Louis's dispatches in AAE CP (A). Barrillon's replies are in PRO/31/3/146, fos. 57–148, fo. 80. And see Clarke (ed.), *Life of James II*, i. 659.

70. HMC Ormonde MSS, NS v. 209 (Coventry to Ormonde).

71. *Hatton Correspondence*, i. 198 (Charles to Lord Hatton).

72. HMC 6th Report, p. 425 (Davies to Edwards).

73. Wood, *Life and Times*, ii. 524–9.

74. LJ xii. 745–6; *CSPD* (1680–1), p. 185 (newsletter to Pye); HMC Lindsey MSS, p. 424 (Latimer to Danby); BL Add. MS 32681, fos. 169–70 (Temple to Sidney); Dalrymple, *Memoirs*, i. 301 (Barrillon to Louis); Burnet, *History*, i. 281–2.

75. Jones, *Charles II*, pp. 168–9, represents the Fitzharris affair with admirable lucidity.

76. PRO/31/3/148, fos. 80–5 (Barrillon's dispatches). Chandaman, *English Public Revenue*, pp. 249–50, settled the financial question.

77. Christie, *Life of Cooper*, vol. ii, app., cxii–cxv (Locke to Stringer); HMC Beaufort MSS, pp. 83–4 (Marquis to Marchioness of Worcester).

78. Ailesbury, *Memoirs*, i. 56.

79. PRO/31/3/146, fo. 32 (Barrillon to Louis).

80. PRO/31/3/149, fos. 77–8.

81. Fraser, *Charles II*, pp. 368–70; Jones, *Charles II*, p. 139.

Chapter 15

Again, there will be no references to facts already familiar from standard histories such as Jones, *First Whigs*, pp. 181–208; Haley, *Shaftesbury*, pp. 639–701; and Ogg, *England in the Reign of Charles II*, ii. 620–56.

1. Reresby, *Memoirs*, p. 215; *Savile Correspondence*, p. 247; Burnet, *History*, i. 300; SP 44/62, p. 167 (Jenkins to Halifax).

2. Roger North, *Lives of the Norths* (ed. Augustus Jessopp, 1890), i. 302; Luttrell, *Brief Historical Relation*, i. 77.

3. Commenced by Gertrude Ann Jacobsen, *William Blathwayt* (New Haven, 1932), pp. 186–8, and taken to extraordinary lengths in Kenyon, *Sunderland*, p. 80.

4. North, *Lives*, i. 301; Burnet, *History*, i. 340; *Letters of Prideaux* (Camden Soc., 1875), p. 102; SP 29/415–16, *passim* (letters of Conway to Jenkins); BL Add. MS 35104 (Conway's letter-book); BL Add. MS 34339, fo. 83 (Dutch envoys' dispatch).

5. HMC Ormonde MSS, vi. 59 (letter from Ellis); Luttrell, *Brief Historical Relation*, i. 151, 161; Bod. L., Carte MS 222, fo. 288 (newsletter).

6. Bod. L., Carte MS 222, fo. 284 (newsletter); HMC Ormonde MSS, vi. 31 (Gwyn to Ormonde).

7. Glassey, *Politics and the Appointment of Justices*, pp. 52–5; Luttrell, *Brief Historical Relation*, i. 89; SP 44/62, pp. 140, 163 (Jenkins to Lord-Lieutenants); SP 29/416116 (Worcester to Jenkins); SP 44/68, p. 175 (Jenkins to Plymouth); HMC Beaufort MSS, p. 87 (Worcester to wife).

8. R. Beddard, 'The Commission for Ecclesiastical Promotions, 1681–1684', *HJ* 10 (1967), pp. 14–26. There is nothing in this essay or its sources to warrant the conclusions drawn in Jones, *Charles II*, p. 175.

9. SP 29/415/182 (Conway to Jenkins); SP 44/62, p. 173 (Jenkins to Bludworth); *The Answers Commanded By His Majesty* (1681).

10. SP 29/416/9 (Seymour to Jenkins).

11. PRO/31/3/149, fos. 54, 58 (Barrillon to Louis).

12. Ibid., fos. 60–1.

13. Reresby, *Memoirs*, p. 214; K. Feiling and F. R. D. Needham (eds.), 'The Jour-

nals of Edmund Warcup', *EHR* 11 (1925), p. 256; SP 29/416/47 (Warcup to Conway).

14. PRO/31/3/149, fo. 107ᵛ (Barrillon to Louis); 'Journals of Warcup', *EHR* 1925, p. 257.
15. Burnet, *History*, i. 300.
16. Listed in Smith, thesis, pp. 156–7.
17. Dr Williams's L., Morrice MSS, MS 31P, p. 321 (Roger Morrice's journal).
18. Carte, *Ormonde*, v. 164 (Ormonde to Arran).
19. Sidney, *Diary*, ii. 139 (Wilhelm to Jenkins); Prinsterer (ed.), *Archives*, v. 451 (reply); Dalrymple, *Memoirs*, i. 305–9 (Wilhelm's letters to Jenkins).
20. Bod. L., Carte MS 222, fo. 280 (newsletter); Sidney, *Diary*, pp. 200, 207, 220; BL Add. MS 32681, fo. 247 (Conway to Sidney); Prinsterer (ed.), *Archives*, v. 503–6 (Hyde to Wilhelm), 509–10 (James to Wilhelm); Dalrymple, *Memoirs*, ii. app., pp. 5 (Godolphin to Wilhelm), 9–10 (Sidney to Wilhelm).
21. *Hatton Correspondence*, ii. 4–5 (Lyttleton to Hatton).
22. PRO/31/3/149, fos. 32, 72–5 (Barrillon to Louis).
23. PRO/31/3/150, fos. 41–4, 55 (Barrillon to Louis); SP 44/62, pp. 309–12 (Jenkins to Conway); SP 29/417/13 (reply).
24. None of the existing literature does justice to English negotiations in this crisis: not H. C. Foxcroft, *The Life and Letters of Sir George Savile, First Marquis of Halifax* (1898), i. 318–44; Fraser, *Charles II*, pp. 429–30; Jones, *Charles II*, pp. 179–80; Ogg, *England in the Reign of Charles II*, ii. 621–3; nor Stephen G. Baxter, *William III* (1966), pp. 183–4. My account is based upon the original sources quoted in Foxcroft, plus Prinsterer (ed.), *Archives*, v. 525 (Conway to Wilhlem); PRO/31/3/150, fos. 63–141, and 151, fos. 4–98 (Barrillon's dispatches); BL Add. MS 35104, fos. 30–51 (Conway's letter-book); Sir Richard Bulstrode, *Memoirs and Reflections* (1721), p. 338 (Jenkins to Bulstrode); HMC Ormonde MSS, vi. 350 (Longford to Ormonde); SP 29/418/133, 149, 157 (Conway to Jenkins); SP 104/188 (Jenkins to Goodrick).
25. Baxter, *William III*, p. 184.
26. John B. Wolf, *Louis XIV* (1968), pp. 413–14.
27. Clarke (ed.), *Life of James II*, i. 674–726; PRO/31/3/150, fo. 5 (Barrillon to Louis); Dr Williams's L., Morrice MSS, MS 31P, p. 324 (Morrice's journal); HMC Dartmouth MSS, i. 67, 72 (James to Legge).
28. Clarke (ed.), *Life of James II*, i. 683, 694–5; HMC Ormonde MSS, vi. 113 (Williamson to Ormonde); SP 57/6, p. 374 (James's instructions); BL Add. MS 11252, fo. 8 (his secret instructions); Ailesbury, *Memoirs*, i. 62; NLS MS 597, fo. 279 (letter to Lord Register); NLS MS 2512, fo. 235 (Burnet to Lauderdale).
29. Miller, *James II*, pp. 108–9; HMC Hamilton MSS, pp. 164–5 (Perth to Hamilton); Burnet, *History*, i. 321–4; Prinsterer, *Archives*, v. 533, 538 (James to Wilhelm); Sir John Lauder, Lord Fountainhall, *Chronological*

Notes (Edinburgh, 1822), p. 21; HMC Ormonde MSS, vi. 351 (Longford to Ormonde); Clarke (ed.), *Life of James II*, 712; PRO/31/3/151, fos. 4, 55 (Barrillon to Louis); Dr Williams's L., Morrice MSS, MS 31P, pp. 324–5 (Morrice's journal); HMC Rutland MSS, ii. 63 (Bertie to Countess of Rutland).

30. Burnet, *History*, i. 325–8; Singer (ed.), *Clarendon Correspondence*, i. 69; *Letters to George, Earl of Aberdeen* (Spalding Club, 1851), pp. 9–26; Sir John Lauder of Fountainhall, *Historical Observes* (Bannatyne Club, 1840), pp. 68–9; Luttrell, *Brief Historical Relation*, i. 175; SP 57/7, pp. 117–25 (warrants for pensions).

31. HMC Hamilton MSS, p. 165 (Perth to Hamilton); *Letters to Aberdeen*, pp. 43–83; Lauder, *Chronological Notes*, p. 27; William Nelson Clarke (ed.), *A Collection of Letters* (Edinburgh, 1848), pp. 37, 39 (Burnet to Sancroft); Lauder, *Historical Observes*, pp. 73–9; RPCS (1681–2), pp. 543–4, 574; HMC Buccleuch and Queensberry (Drumlanrig), i. 173–4 (James to Queensberry), ii. 105–6 (Drummond to Queensberry); SP 57/7, p. 342, and 8, pp. 35/7 (warrants); PRO/31/3/153, fo. 29ᵛ (Barrillon to Louis); Bod. L., Carte MS 216, fo. 155 (Longford to Arran); Bod. L., MS Eng. Letters d. 72, fo. 6ᵛ (Wynne to Bulstrode).

32. Aydelotte, thesis, pp. 169–86, 311–59; Egan, thesis, pp. 118–32, 145–79; Maurice F. Bond (ed.), *The Diaries and Papers of Sir Edward Dering* (1976), pp. 120–8; Bod. L., Carte MS 70, fo. 559 (Ormonde to Arran); MS 69, fo. 75 (Southwell's notes); MS 219, fo. 345 (Ormonde to Arran).

33. Bod. L., Carte MS 70, fos. 559, 563 (Ormonde to Arran); MS 168, fo. 40 (Arran to Ormonde).

34. HMC Ormonde MSS, NS v. 503 (Cooke to Ormonde).

35. *Hatton Correspondence*, ii. 11–12 (Lyttleton to Hatton); HMC Frankland –Russell–Astley MSS, p. 48 (Fauconberg to Frankland); Luttrell, *Brief Historical Relation*, i. 73, 242, 295; Dr Williams's L., Morrice MSS, MS 31P, p. 411; BL Add. MS 49459, fo. 4 (Exchequer receipt).

36. Ailesbury, *Memoirs*, i. 86; Evelyn, *Diary* (ed. De Beer), iv. 268, 343; PRO/31/3/152, fo. 83 (Barrillon to Louis); Reresby, *Memoirs*, p. 217.

37. Reresby, *Memoirs*, p. 239; PRO/31/3/155, fo. 38ᵛ, and 156, fo. 50 (Barrillon to Louis); Bod. L., MS Eng. Letters d. 72, fo. 48 (Wynne to Bulstrode).

38. Most notably by Fraser, *Charles II*, pp. 410–11.

39. SP 29/423/127 (Gwyn to Conway); Reresby, *Memoirs*, p. 251.

40. Kenyon, *Sunderland*, pp. 81–6.

41. See the social visits in his diary, BL Add. MS 18730.

42. SP 29/418/153 (Conway to Jenkins).

43. Unfamiliar details have been added to this story from HMC Ormonde MSS, NS vi. 355 (Longford to Ormonde), and Bod. L., Carte MS 66, fo. 595 (Anglesey to King).

44. HMC Egmont MSS, iii. 120–1 (Barnette to Perceval); HMC 7th Report, p. 356 (Wynne to Preston); SP 44/68, p. 20 (Jenkins to Worcester); PRO/31/3/153, fo. 6ᵛ (Barrillon to Louis); Bod. L., Carte MS 70, fo. 559

(Ormonde to Arran); MS 216, fo. 137 (Longford to Arran); MS 222, fo. 288 (newsletter); MS 219, fo. 396 (Ormonde to Arran); *Hatton Correspondence*, ii. 97 (Lyttleton to Hatton).

45. Dalrymple, *Memoirs*, vol. ii, app., p. 53 (James to Wilhelm); Lauder, *Historical Observes*, p. 85; Dr Williams's L, Morrice MSS, MS31P, p. 349; North, *Lives*, i. 231, 318.

46. PRO/31/3/153, fo. 88, and 154, fos. 47, 53 (Barrillon to Louis); Carte, *Ormonde*, v. 165 (Ormonde to Southwell); Reresby, *Memoirs*, pp. 252–4; North, *Lives*, i. 237; Bod. L., Carte MS 70, fo. 558 (Ormonde to Arran); MS 216, fo. 393 (Reading to Arran); BL Add. MS 17017, fos. 127, 131 (Sunderland to Rochester); Bod. L., Carte MS 50, fo. 311 (Ormonde to Arran).

47. Thomas D'Urfey, *Wit and Mirth* (1719), i. 246–9.

48. Smith, thesis, pp. 157, 165–6; *Letters to Aberdeen*, pp. 32–3, 74–5; PRO/31/3/152, fo. 83 (Barrillon to Louis); Bod. L., Carte MS 216, fos. 86, 195 (Longford to Arran), 113 (Stewart to Arran); BL Add. MS 15643, fo. 51ᵛ (register of Committee for Intelligence); Viscount Dillon (ed.), 'Some familiar letters', *Archaeologia*, NS 8 (1902), p. 175 (James to Countess of Lichfield); SP 29/419/161 (Jenkins's notes); Bod. L., Carte MS 219, fos. 468–9 (Ormonde to Arran).

49. To Arran, Bod. L., Carte MS 70, fo. 558.

50. Jennifer Levin, *The Charter Controversy in the City of London, 1660–1688* (1969); Havighurst, *Law Quarterly Review*, 1950, pp. 244–5; Kenyon, *Sunderland*, p. 88; Fowler, thesis, pp. 28–9; Smith, thesis, pp. 307–28.

51. *Hatton Correspondence*, ii. 18 (Lyttleton to Hatton); North, *Lives*, i. 329.

52. I have added a few details to the familiar story, from Burnet, *History*, i. 364; *Letters to Aberdeen*, p. 131; Evelyn, *Diary* (ed. De Beer), iv. 328; PRO/31/3/155, fo. 50 (Barrillon to Louis); Bod. L., Carte MS 219, fo. 472 (Ormonde to Arran); *Hatton Correspondence*, ii. 24 (Lyttleton to Hatton). The latest considerations of the reality of the 'Rye House Plot' are Lois G. Schwoerer, *Lady Rachel Russell* (Baltimore, 1988), ch. 6, and Blair Worden, 'The Commonwealth Kidney of Algernon Sidney', *JBS* 24 (1985), pp. 1–40.

53. HMC Somerset MSS, p. 108 (newsletter).

54. PRO/31/3/152, fo. 32, and 153, fo. 6ᵛ (Barrillon to Louis); Edward Berwick (ed.), *The Rawdon Papers* (1819), p. 276 (Gwyn to Conway).

55. This is proved by SP 29/425/140 (Jenkins's notes).

56. To the familiar story I have added details from PRO/31/3/155, fos. 49, 71, and 156, fos. 63ᵛ, 79 (Barrillon to Louis); Bod. L., Carte MS 70, fo. 571 (Ormonde's notes).

57. PRO/31/3/155, fo. 56ᵛ (Barrillon to Louis).

58. Foxcroft, *Halifax*, i. 413.

59. Kenyon, *Sunderland*, p. 96; Browning, *Danby*, i. 347–54; Havighurst, *Law Quarterly Review*, 1950, pp. 248–9.

60. Cowan, *Scottish Covenanters*, pp. 107–21; William Nelson Clarke (ed.), *A Collection of Letters* (Edinburgh, 1848), pp. 44–5 (Burnet to Sancroft),

59–60 (Clarendon to Sancroft); HMC Buccleuch and Queensberry MSS, ii. 108.

61. Bod. L., Carte MS 50, fo. 287 (Ormonde to Boyle); MS 68, fo. 324 (Ormonde to Boyle); MS 219, fo. 488 (Ormonde to Arran); MS 168, fos, 152, 155, 161–2 (Arran to Ormonde).

62. Smith, thesis, pp. 254–75; Eveline Legh, Lady Newton, *Lyme Letters* (1925), p. 109; HMC Beaufort MSS, p. 87 (Marquis of Worcester to wife); HMC Le Fleming MSS, p. 184 (newsletter); Lauder, *Historical Observes*, p. 81; HMC Ormonde MSS, vi. 155 (Longford to Ormonde); SP 44/62, pp. 354, 358, 365, 370 (Jenkins to magistrates); SP 29/418/26 (Herbert to Jenkins), 138, 153 (Conway to Jenkins); SP 44/68, p. 277 (Jenkins to Mayor of Taunton); P/C 269, pp. 382, 386, 425. For local reactions, see Smith, thesis, as above; Andrew M. Coleby, *Central Government and the Localities* (Cambridge, 1987), pp. 196–204; Norrey, thesis, ch. 5.

63. Bod. L., Carte MS 219, fos. 402, 522–3 (Ormonde to Arran); MS 169, fo. 4 (reply); HMC Ormonde MSS, vii. 314–15 (Archbishop Marsh to Ormonde).

64. The accounts in Kenyon, *Sunderland*, p. 108, and Miller, *Popery and Politics*, pp. 194–5, do not seem to me to do justice to this debate. The fresh and detailed report by Barrillon in PRO/31/3/159, fos. 50, 56–7, seems far beter than the retrospective one in North, *Lives*, i. 309, which differs in important details. There is further information in PRO/31/3/160, fo. 25^v, and Macpherson, *Original Papers*, i. 142.

65. To which Kenyon, *Sunderland*, pp. 85–7, has added the refinement that he was talked into this by James and Sunderland.

66. Foxcroft, *Halifax*, i. 305–71; HMC 7th Report, p. 361 (Jenkins to Preston); HMC Downshire MSS, i. 16–17 (Jenkins to Preston); HMC Dartmouth MSS, i. 82 (Shovel's report).

67. BL Add. MS 34339, fos. 83–7, 102 (Dutch envoys' dispatches); PRO/31/3/152, fos. 1–2 (Barrillon to Louis).

68. PRO/31/3/153, fos. 30 (Barrillon to Louis); Singer (ed.), *Clarendon Correspondence*, i. 79 (Wilhelm to Hyde); Dalrymple, *Memoirs*, vol. ii, app., pp. 41–2 (Wilhelm to King), 46 (James to Wilhelm); HMC 7th Report, p. 357 (Jenkins to Preston).

69. PRO/31/3/155, fos. 36–7 (Barrillon to Louis); Baxter, *William III*, pp. 188–9; BL Add. MS 17017, fo. 134 (Sunderland to Rochester).

70. Ibid., fo. 135; PRO/31/3/154, fo. 46, and 155, fos. 14^v, 18^v, 92^v (Barrillon to Louis); Wood, *Life and Times*, iii. 67; HMC 3rd Report, p. 289 (letter from Clarges). Unhappily, the State Papers Danish for this period have vanished.

71. PRO/31/3/153, fo. 83, and 155, fos. 104–5 (Barrillon to Louis); BL Add. MS 17017, fo. 133 (Sunderland to Rochester).

72. Baxter, *William III*, pp. 189–91; Dalrymple, *Memoirs*, vol. ii, app., pp. 47–55 (James to Wilhelm); Prinsterer (ed.), *Archives*, 2nd ser., v. 582 (King to Wilhelm); PRO/31/3/155, fos. 105^v, 116; 159, fos. 4^v, 14–15; and

160, fo. 21 (Barrillon to Louis); Bod. L., Carte MS 217, fo. 11 (Bridgeman to Arran).

73. Baxter, *William III*, pp. 193–200; Kenyon, *Sunderland*, pp. 104–6; Bulstrode, *Memoirs*, pp. 376–91; PRO/31/3/155, fos. 31ᵛ, 83 (Barrillon to Louis).

74. Chandaman, *English Public Revenue*, pp. 34, 70–5, 102–5, 250–5.

75. Bond (ed.), *Diaries of Dering*, p. 140.

76. North, *Lives*, i. 329.

77. Evelyn, *Diary* (ed. De Beer), iv. 343; Bod. L., Carte MS 222, fo. 324 (newsletter); Christopher Clay, *Public Finance and Private Wealth* (Oxford, 1978), ch. vi.

78. Lady Newdigate-Newdegate, *Cavalier and Puritan* (1901), pp. 251–2 (Newdigate's diary).

79. *Sunderland*, pp. 97–107.

80. *Charles II*, pp. 418–20.

81. *Charles II*, pp. 170, 184–6.

82. *Sunderland*, p. 107. The playwright's story is from John Oldmixon, *The History of England during the Reigns of the Royal House of Stuart* (1730), p. 690.

83. HMC Buccleuch and Queensberry MSS (Drumlanrig), i. 168–87 (James to Queensberry), 277–9 (Hamilton to Queensberry).

84. Ibid. i. 207–11 (James to Queensberry), ii. 15–36 (Moray to Queensberry), 120–69 (Drummond to Queensberry); Lauder, *Chronological Notes*, pp. 37–8, and *Historical Observes*, pp. 131–8; HMC 7th Report, pp. 366 (Deanes to Preston), 378 (letter to Preston); HMC Ormonde MSS, ns vii. 272 (Perth to Ormonde); *The Gordon Letters* (Spalding Club Miscellany, iii, 1846), pp. 218–25 (James to Huntly); Dr Williams's L., Morrice MSS, MS 31P, pp. 437, 441; PRO/31/3/159, fo. 96 (Barrillon to Louis). I believe that Professor Kenyon confuses the Scottish and English 'secret committee'.

85. PRO/31/3/158, fo. 3 (Barrillon to Louis); HMC Ormonde MSS, ns vi. 233 (Arran to Ormonde); HMC 7th Report, pp. 366–75 (dispatches to Preston).

86. Evelyn, *Diary* (ed. De Beer), iv. 377; Bond (ed.), *Diaries of Dering*, pp. 149–50; J. P. Kenyon (ed.), *Halifax: Complete Works* (1969), p. 256.

87. PRO/31/3/154, fo. 53; 158, fos. 77ᵛ, 82ᵛ; and 159, fos. 5–50 (Barrillon to Louis); Reresby, *Memoirs*, pp. 254–5; Burnet, *History*, pp. 435–6; Singer (ed.), *Clarendon Correspondence*, pp. 82–3 (Sunderland to Rochester), 94–5 (Godolphin to Rochester); Lauder, *Historical Observes*, pp. 137–8; HMC 7th Report, p. 376 (Ball to Preston); Luttrell, *Brief Historical Relation*, i. 313; SP 104/16, Sunderland to Preston, 25 Aug. 1684; BL Add. MS 17017, fo. 136 (Sunderland to Rochester).

88. See the baffled remarks in Kenyon, *Stuart England*, p. 237; John Miller, 'The Crown and the Borough Charters in the reign of Charles II', *EHR* 100 (1985), pp. 75–6; Pickavance, thesis, pp. 129–30. The Lords' report is in the House of Lords RO, 'An Abstract of the Charters'.

89. SP 44/56, p. 22 (Sunderland to corporation); Reresby, *Memoirs*, p. 240.

90. Miller, *EHR* 1985, pp. 72–84, eked out slightly with SP 44/62, p. 288 (Jenkins to Bishop of Bristol) and *CSPD* (1682), p. 39 (newsletter to Squier).

91. Miller, *EHR* 1985, pp. 74, 76, 79–83; G. Forster, 'Government in Provincial England under the Later Stuarts', *TRHS* 5th ser., 33 (1983), pp. 45–6; Coleby, *Central Government and the Localities*, pp. 166–8; and especially Pickavance, thesis, *passim*; and Norrey, thesis, chs. 5–6.

92. North, *Lives*, i. 309; PRO/31/3/159, fo. 50 (Barrillon to Louis); HMC 9th Report, i. 200 (Jeffreys to corporation of Carlisle); Bod. L., Carte MS 50, fo. 344 (letter from Ormonde).

93. HMC Hastings MSS, ii. 392 (Conway to Rawdon).

94. HMC Ormonde MSS, vii. 92 (Ormonde to Arran); Bod. L., Carte MS 216, fo. 393 (Reading to Arran); Aydelotte, thesis, pp. 246–59.

95. Bod. L., Carte MS 220, fo. 66 (Ormonde to Arran); HMC Ormonde MSS, NS vii. 1, 234 (Mountjoy to Ormonde).

96. Ibid. v. 274 (Ossory to Ormonde); vi. 143 (Longford to Ormonde), 233 (Ormonde to Arran); Bod. L., Carte MS 168, fos. 138–41, 160–2 (Arran to Ormonde); MS 50, fo. 350 (letter from Ormonde); MS 69, fo. 76 (Southwell's notes); MS 218, fos. 340–1 (Ormonde to King); Luttrell, *Brief Historical Relation*, i. 314.

97. BL Add. MS 15643, fo. 52 (Committee for Intelligence).

98. Bod. L., Carte MS 69, fo. 76 (Southwell's notes); Dublin Central L., Gilbert Collection, MS 109 (Mountjoy's account); Carte, *Ormonde*, iv. 166–8 (letters of King, James, and Rochester to Ormonde); PRO/31/3/159, fo. 76 (Barrillon to Louis).

99. Burnet, *History*, i. 449; All Souls College L., Oxford, MS 317, fo. 15 (Trumbull's memoirs).

100. Bod. L., Carte MS 217, fo. 87 (Arran to Ormonde); HMC Ormonde MSS, NS vii. 314 (Rochester to Ormonde); H. C. Foxcroft, *A Supplement to Burnet's History* (Oxford, 1902), p. 135.

101. Bod. L., Carte MS 218, fos. 376 (MacCarthy to Ormonde), 382 (Clancarty to Ormonde); MS 168, fo. 316 (Ormonde to MacCarthy); PRO/31/3/160, fo. 7ᵛ (Barrillon to Louis).

102. What follows is based upon an amalgam of Samuel M. Janney, *The Life of William Penn* (New York, 1851), pp. 143–6; Joseph E. Illick, *William Penn the Politician* (Ithaca, 1965), pp. 11–69; David S. Lovejoy, *The Glorious Revolution in America* (New York, 1972), pp. 60–169; J. M. Sosin, *English America and the Restoration Monarchy of Charles II* (Lincoln, 1980), pp. 167–301; P. Haffenden, 'The Crown and the Colonial Charters, 1675–1688', *William and Mary Quarterly*, 3rd ser., 15 (1958), pp. 297–311, 452–66; Stephen Saunders Webb, *The Governors-General* (Chapel Hill, 1979), pp. 99–447.

103. PRO/31/3/159, fos. 94–5 (Barrillon to Louis).

104. Foxcroft, *Halifax*, i. 420–34; Kenyon, *Sunderland*, pp. 104–9; Browning, *Danby*, i. 361–3; Jones, *Charles II*, pp. 183–4; Bryant, *Charles II*, pp. 354–6; Ogg, *England in the Reign of Charles II*, pp. 654–6; Miller, *James II*, p. 188.

105. James Welwood, *Memoirs of the Most Material Transactions in England* (1700), p. 376.

106. BL Egerton MS 1527, fos. 17, 73.

107. Foxcroft, *Supplement to Burnet*, p. 133; HMC Buccleuch and Queensberry MSS, i. 212 (James to Queensberry).

108. PRO/31/3/159, fos. 95, 97, 102–3, and 160, fo. 9 (Barrillon to Louis); Dr Williams's L., Morrice MSS, MS 31P, p. 452 (Morrice's journal); Bod. L., Carte MS 217, fo. 89 (Arran to Ormonde); Browning, *Danby*, i. 363; All Souls College L., Oxford, MS 317, fo. 15 (Trumbull's memoirs).

109. PRO/31/3/152, fo. 35^v (Barrillon to Louis); HMC Buccleuch and Queensberry MSS, ii. 12–13 (Moray to Queensberry).

110. Reresby, *Memoirs*, p. 251; Ailesbury, *Memoirs*, i. 85; Bod. L., Carte MS 216, fo. 94 (Longford to Arran).

111. Fraser, *Charles II*, discusses the issue.

112. PRO/31/3/160, fos. 27–30 (Barrillon's dispatch); Royal Archives, SP1/14–15 (James's account); *Copies of Two papers Written by the late King Charles II* (1686); Burnet, *History*, i. 472; BL Add. Ms 34501, fo. 19 (James's narrative at Chaillot); J. G. Muddiman, 'The Death of Charles II', *The Month*, 160 (1932), pp. 523–5 (Gibbon's account); John Hudleston, *A Short and Plain Way to the Faith and Church* (1688).

113. All the known Protestant, and some of the Catholic, sources are listed in Raymond Crawfurd, *The Last Days of Charles II* (1909).

114. 'Last Moments of an English King', *Household Words*, 9 (1854), p. 279; PRO/31/3/160, fos. 27–30 (Barrillon to Louis); HMC Egmont MSS, ii. 147 (letter from Frazer); Welwood, *Memoirs*, p. 139; Evelyn, *Diary* (ed. De Beere), iv. 408–9; BL Add. MSS 19253, fo. 137^v (Chesterfield to Arran); Ailesbury, *Memoirs*, i. 90–1.

Conclusion

1. Ailesbury, *Memoirs*, i. 93.

2. Ibid.; Hore, *History of Newmarket*, p. 286; Evelyn, *Diary* (ed. De Beer), iii. 303–6, 387.

3. See Ailesbury, *Memoirs*, i. 95; Halifax, *Works*, p. 257; Foxcroft, *Supplement to Burnet*, p. 48.

4. Mapperton House, Sandwich MSS, Journal of the First Earl, ix. 44.

5. Ailesbury, *Memoirs*, i. 85.

6. *Savile Correspondence*, p. 196 (Jenkins to Savile).

7. Evelyn, *Diary* (ed. De Beer), iv. 266.

8. Ailesbury, *Memoirs*, i. 70.

9. Halifax, *Works*, p. 258.

10. Ailesbury, *Memoirs*, i. 93; Bryant (ed.), *Letters*, p. 122.

11. HMC Buccleuch and Queensberry MSS (Whitehall), i. 488, 497 (Montagu to Arlington); Evelyn, *Diary*, iii. 571.

12. Ailesbury, *Memoirs*, i. 95–6; Foxcroft, *Supplement to Burnet*, p. 49; Halifax, *Works*, p. 260.

13. Ailesbury, *Memoirs*, i. 93.

14. Bryant (ed.), *Letters*, p. 178.

15. Halifax, *Works*, p. 257.

16. John Oldmixon, *The History of England during the Reign of the Royal House of Stuart* (1730), p. 690.

17. See *Essex Papers*, i. 281.

18. HMC 7th Report, p. 464 (John Verney to Sir Ralph Verney).

19. SP 29/335/72 (to Arlington).

20. See Bryant (ed.), *Letters*, p. 183 (to Minette).

21. *Works*, p. 257.

22. Ibid., p. 262.

23. For a case of which, see Ailesbury, *Memoirs*, i. 95.

24. Henrietta Maria, *Letters*, pp. 350–7.

Index